MW00769904

TO SYNTHESIZE
THE AIM OF RELIGION
AND THE METHOD OF SILENCE

This was the mission of the original *Equinox* — a massive work printed during the early twentieth century in ten large volumes and several subsequent books. It has long been out of print, and even when republished it is beyond the economic reach of most students. This *one-volume collection* contains all the important magical writings from the original, edited and arranged by Israel Regardie so that the student can "find his way through the maze more easily."

Crowley said of the *Equinox:* "My special job was to preserve the Sacred Tradition, so that a new Renaissance might in due season rekindle the hidden light. I was accordingly to make a Quintessence of the Ancient Wisdom, and publish it in as permanent form as possible."

That Renaissance is now. Here we have a "masterpiece of instruction" — systematizing in masterful prose the subject matter of the occult, stripping it of the "superstition, dross, and fantasy" encrusted on it over the ages.

One section deals with the history, grades and official program of the Magical Order, A∴ A∴, as represented by Crowley; another with the Law for this New Aeon. A third is one of the most lucid texts on yoga available. A fourth delineates magical rituals which, like yoga, serve to unite the mind to a single idea: an essential to the Great Work. Here are included basic rituals; methods of consecration, of invocation of elements and elementals; the Mass of the Phoenix and the Gnostic Mass; and the sublime *Vision and the Voice*. Also included is a section on sex magick; Crowley's own commentary on Blavatsky's *The Voice of Silence*; and his invaluable comments on the program of exercises of one who became a Master of the Temple.

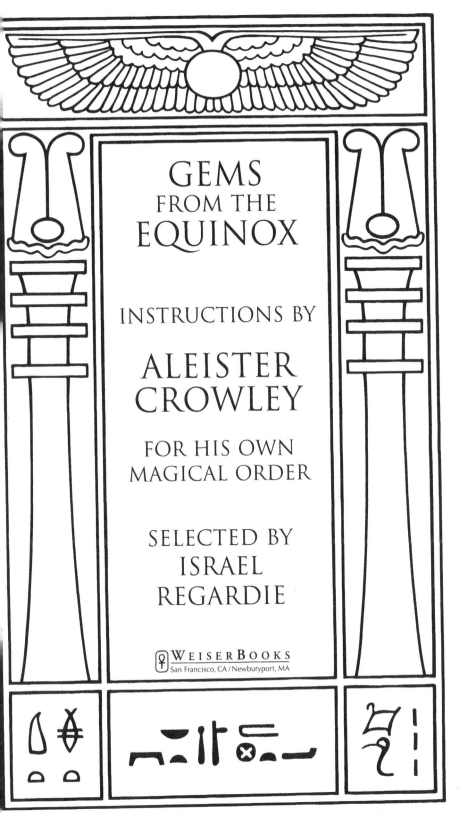

GEMS
FROM THE
EQUINOX

INSTRUCTIONS BY

ALEISTER CROWLEY

FOR HIS OWN MAGICAL ORDER

SELECTED BY ISRAEL REGARDIE

WEISER BOOKS
San Francisco, CA / Newburyport, MA

This edition first published in 2007 by
Red Wheel/Weiser, LLC
With offices at:
500 Third Street, Suite 230
San Francisco, CA 94107
www.redwheelweiser.com

ISBN: 978-1-57863-417-0

Library of Congress Cataloging-in-Publication
Data is available upon request.

Cover illustration courtesy of James Wasserman
Cover design by Landon Eber

Printed in the United States of America
MV
10 9 8 7 6 5 4 3 2

CONTENTS

Preface   *xi*

Section I. Introductory: The Order
Liber LXI   *3*
One Star in Sight   *11*
An Account of A ∴ A ∴   *31*
Liber XIII   *43*
A Syllabus of the Official Instructions   *51*
  of A ∴ A ∴

Section II. The Book of the Law
Liber AL vel Legis   *75*
Liber CCC: Khabs am Pekht   *99*
Liber CL: De Lege Libellum   *111*
Liber Nv   *137*
Liber Had   *147*

Section III. Yoga
Liber E vel Exercitiorum   *159*
Liber Rv   *171*
Liber Astarte   *181*
Liber III vel Jugorum   *203*
Liber HHH   *213*
Liber Turris   *225*
Liber Yod   *231*
Liber Os Abysmi   *241*

Liber Thisharb   *247*
Liber DXXXVI   *259*
Liber Librae   *265*

Section IV. Magick
Liber O   *273*
Liber A   *295*
Liber Resh   *301*
Liber Israfel   *305*
Liber XLIV: The Mass of the Phoenix *311*
Liber XXV: The Star Ruby   *315*
Liber XXXVI: The Star Sapphire   *321*
Liber Samekh   *323*
Liber V vel Reguli   *355*
The Gnostic Mass   *363*
Liber LXXXIX vel Chanokh   *385*
Liber CCCCXVIII: The Vision   *431*
  and the Voice

Section V. Sex Magick
Liber A'ash vel Capricorni   *597*
Liber Cheth   *601*
Liber LXVI: Stellae Rubeae   *607*
Liber DCCCXI: Energized Enthusiasm *615*

Section VI. Miscellaneous
Liber B vel Magi   *645*
Liber Porta Lucis   *651*
Liber Tzaddi vel Hamus Hermeticus   *657*
Liber CCXXXI   *663*
Liber CD vel Tav   *673*

Liber Viarum Viae   677
Liber CLXV: A Master of the Temple 681
Liber LXXI: The Voice of   733
  the Silence

Section VII.   Reviews

Part I   847
Part II   929

ILLUSTRATIONS

The Sign of Silence   *facing page 35*
The Slopes of Abiegnus   *facing page 47*
The Ibis; the God;   *facing page 164*
   the Thunderbolt;
   the Dragon
Pranayama Properly Performed   *facing page 174*
Aratrum Securum   *facing page 207*
The Triangle of the Universe   *facing page 235*
The Signs of the Grades   *facing page 277*
The Sign of the Enterer   *facing page 283*
The Holy Table: Plate I   *facing page 387*
Sigillvm Dei Aemeth: Plate II   *facing page 388*
The Four Great Watch-Towers   *following page 391*
   and the Black Cross: Plate III
The Great Watch-Tower   *following page 392*
   of the East: Plate IV
The Great Watch-Tower   *following page 393*
   of the West: Plate V
The Great Watch-Tower   *following page 394*
   of the North: Plate VI
The Great Watch-Tower   *following page 395*
   of the South: Plate VII
The Black Cross: Plate VIII   *following page 396*
Enochian Alphabet: Plate IX   *facing page 403*
The Governors of the Four   *facing page 407*
   Watch-Towers: Plate X

Alphabet of Daggers   *facing page 472*

Liber XXII Domarum Mercurii   *facing page 667*
cum Suis Geniis; Liber XXII
Carcerorum Qliphoth cum Suis
Geniis

Frater VNVS in Omnibus   *facing page 685*

Pantacle of Frater V.I.O.   *facing page 728*

Lamen of Frater V.I.O.   *facing page 731*

The Way   *facing page 736*

PREFACE[*]

Between 1909 and 1914, Aleister Crowley published in England a large, beautifully printed periodical entitled *The Equinox*. The masthead on the cover bore two phrases, "The Aim of Religion" and "The Method of Science." It contained a wide assortment of verse, plays, short stories and miscellaneous occult material. One issue appeared every six months at the Spring and Autumnal Equinoxes of that five-year period. Ten enormous issues appeared in all. One thousand and fifty copies were produced at each equinoctial printing, fifty copies being bound in white buckram for the subscription trade, the rest being bound in boards.

After 1914 there was a hiatus of five years, corresponding to World War I, when Crowley was domiciled in the United States. He called it a five-year period of silence. Following this, one large volume, bound in blue

---

[* [*Note by Hymenaeus Beta:* Footnotes to this Preface are by the present writer, and are given in brackets. Dr. Regardie's Preface was written in 1970 e.v. for the first edition of 1974. It included many now-obsolete references to contemporary or planned editions of various books by Crowley. In the 1988 reprint issued by New Falcon Publications, posthumous changes and annotations were made to the Preface, which have been further revised for this edition. Deletions have been kept to a minimum and are indicated by ellipses [...]. References to Regardie's own books in the first edition have been modernized to cite his preferred, authorized edition; e.g. references to *The Golden Dawn* were changed to *The Complete Golden Dawn System of Magick*, and *My Rosicrucian Adventure* became *What You Should Know About the Golden Dawn*. Current bibliographic information for books mentioned by Regardie is provided in a new section, entitled "Works Cited," appended to the end of the Preface. As Regardie's original Preface discussed both the A∴A∴ and O.T.O., current contact information for both orders is provided following Works Cited.]

cloth, made its solitary appearance. It has been called colloquially *The Blue Equinox*. And that was it. None were published thereafter. There was no more money available: there were no more *Equinox*es.[*]

Originally they were published to sell for about five shillings, then for half a guinea each—in those halcyon days about two dollars and fifty cents per volume. They did not sell very well. Had sales been better, enough revenue might have been forthcoming to have permitted the continuation of the publishing project for a longer period of time.

Nevertheless, within a few years, the ten issues of Volume I were commanding a premium of one hundred dollars per set—had any been available. Today I am told that the going price is five hundred dollars or more per set! But to obtain a set is practically impossible.

By students of occultism, these volumes were regarded as a veritable gold mine of occult lore. Most who bought them were far less interested in the wide literary assortment offered. Yoga and Magick were what these books stood for, and this is where they excelled.

There was simply nothing like them elsewhere. In these instructions about the occult arts, Crowley had used superb prose, and had clarified the subject matter by eliminating all the superstition, dross and fantasy that had been attached to these topics. They were masterpieces of instruction. It was for these reasons that the several volumes of *The Equinox* were so zealously sought after throughout the years.

Crowley himself felt that it was the first serious attempt to publicize the facts about the occult arts since Madame Blavatsky wrote *Isis Unveiled*, though there is very little

---

[*] [*The Equinox* ceased publication as a regular semiannual serial in 1919 e.v., but the A∴A∴ and O.T.O. continued (and still continue) to produce irregular issues at intervals of many years. Most books published in *The Equinox* series are better known by their book titles, as they appear in the Works Cited.]

connection between the latter and *The Equinox*, as Blavatsky never recommended the occult arts for the average human being. Crowley felt his was the first venture to forward the method of science and the aim of religion with scholarship and commonsense. He was inordinately proud of having inaugurated an epoch in publishing. It imposed a standard of "sincerity, scholarship, scientific seriousness and aristocracy of all kinds, from the excellence of its English to the perfection of its printing" on all those interested in this topic.

Though he recognized the small public it appealed to, his enthusiasts informed him that it was regarded as the standard publication of its kind which had been quoted, copied and imitated everywhere. It has been said that some occult societies have been founded by charlatans on no other authority than its subject matter. Its influence has changed the whole current of thought of students of this subject all over the world.

In one of the letters comprising *Magick without Tears*, Crowley has written a few words concerning his original intent regarding *The Equinox*. What he had to say is so interesting that the following is quoted from that letter:

> [M]y special job was to preserve the Sacred Tradition, so that a new Renaissance might in due season rekindle the hidden Light. I was accordingly to make a Quintessence of the Ancient Wisdom, and publish it in as permanent a form as possible. This I did in *The Equinox*. I should perhaps have been strictly classical, and admitted only the "Publication in Class A," "A–B," "B" and "D" material. But I had the idea that it would be a good plan to add all sorts of other stuff, so that people who were not in any way interested in the real Work might preserve their copies.
>
> This by the way: the essence of this letter is to show that "They," not one person but a number acting in concert, not only foresaw a planet-wide catastrophe, but were agreed on measures calculated to assure the survival of the Wisdom worth saving until the time, perhaps three hundred or six hundred years later, when a new current should revive the shattered thought of mankind.

> *The Equinox*, in a word, was to be a sort of Rosetta
> Stone.[*]

It seems as though he recognized that he should really have published only the Official Instructions of the Order in order to preserve the "Sacred Tradition." Now that the original sets of *The Equinox* are no longer available, it seems necessary to reissue the fundamental materials that he had in mind at the start—the official instructions. If it was the wish of the so-called Secret Chiefs of the Order to preserve the practical wisdom of the hidden sanctuaries against the disasters of war, natural cataclysm, and partisan censorship—all of which seem clearly once more in the offing—I hope that this volume, *Gems from the Equinox*, will assist in the fulfillment of his original magical intention, freed from the addition of "all sorts of other stuff." The essentials of the sacred tradition can stand by themselves without dilution of any kind whatsoever.

Periodically, criticisms of *The Equinox* reach me that are not too dissimilar to those at one time leveled at *The Complete Golden Dawn System of Magic*. Some students have felt this enormous mass of instruction to be overwhelming and just too much for them. The result was that they got confused, and could do nothing with what otherwise they recognized to be invaluable.

However, I feel the classification of this material in the manner depicted here may simplify things so as to enable the student to grasp it and find his way through the maze more readily. He will then come to understand the basic theme that Crowley laid down in his Order. It can best be described by quoting Crowley verbatim from an editorial that appeared in one of the volumes of *The Equinox*.

> I have been asked by Authority to say a few words on the relations which should subsist between a Neophyte and his Probationers. Though a Neophyte is obliged to show "zeal

---

[*] [Crowley, "The A∴A∴ and the Planet," *Magick without Tears* (1954), letter 75, p. 346.]

in service" towards his Probationers, it is no part of his
duty to be continually beating the tattoo. He has his own
work to do—very serious and important work—and he
cannot be expected to spend all his time in making silk
purses out of pigs' ears. He is not expected to set definite
tasks, nor has he authority to do so. The Probationer is
purposely left to himself, as the object of probation is principally that those in authority may discover the nature of
the raw material. It is the duty of the Probationer to
perform the exercises recommended in his text-books,
and to submit the record of his results for criticism. If he
finds himself in a difficulty, or if any unforeseen result
occurs, he should communicate with his Neophyte, and he
should remember that although he is permitted to select
the practices which appeal to him, he is expected to show
considerable acquaintance with all of them. More than
acquaintance, it should be experience; otherwise what is he
to do when as a Neophyte he is consulted by his Probationers? It is important that he should be armed at all
points, and I am authorized to say that no one will be
admitted as a Neophyte unless his year's work gives
evidence of considerable attainment in the fundamental
practices, Asana, Pranayama, assumption of God-forms,
vibration of divine names, rituals of banishing and
invoking, and the practices set out in sections 5 and 6 of
"Liber O." Although he is not examined in any of these,
the elementary experience is necessary in order that he
may intelligently assist those who will be under him.

But let no one imagine that those in authority will urge
Probationers to work hard. Those who are incapable of
hard work may indeed be pushed along, but the moment
that the pressure is removed they will fall back, and it is
not the purpose of the A∴A∴ to do anything else than to
make its students independent and free. Full instruction
has been placed within the reach of everybody; let them
see to it that they make full use of that instruction. *

The newcomer to this occult field might begin to
wonder what all the fuss was about. What were these exercises or experiments for? What did they accomplish? What
was the so-called Great Work?

---

* ["Editorial," *The Equinox* I(5) (1911), pp. 2–3.]

Again, these questions can most readily be answered by quoting directly from Crowley. His own words from *The Equinox* provide an eloquent answer to these and similar questions. The following set of statements shows what Crowley thought, and how excellently he expressed those thoughts.

MISTAKES OF MYSTICS

I. Since truth is supra-rational, it is incommunicable in the language of reason.

II. Hence all mystics have written nonsense, and what sense they have written is so far untrue.

III. Yet as a still lake yields a truer reflection of the sun than a torrent, he whose mind is best balanced will, if he become a mystic, become the best mystic.

THE METHOD OF EQUILIBRIUM

I. THE PASSIONS, ETC.

I. Since the ultimate truth of teleology is unknown, all codes of morality are arbitrary.

II. Therefore the student has no concern with ethics as such.

III. He is consequently free "to do his duty in that state of life to which it has pleased God to call him."

II. THE REASON

I. Since truth is supra-rational, any rational statement is false.

II. Let the student then contradict every proposition that presents itself to him.

III. Rational ideas being thus expelled from the mind, there is room for the apprehension of spiritual truth.

It should be remarked that this does not destroy the validity of reasonings on their own plane.

III. THE SPIRITUAL SENSORIUM

I. Man being a finite being, he is incapable of apprehending the infinite. Nor does his communion with infinite being (true or false) alter this fact.

II. Let then the student contradict every vision and refuse to enjoy it; first, because there is certainly another vision possible of precisely contradictory nature;

secondly, because though he is God, he is also a man upon an insignificant planet.

Being thus equilibrated laterally and vertically, it may be that, either by affirmation or denial of all these things together, he may attain the supreme trance.

IV. THE RESULT

I. Trance is defined as the *ek-stasis* of one particular tract of the brain, caused by meditation on the idea corresponding to it.

II. Let the student therefore beware lest in that idea be any trace of imperfection. It should be pure, balanced, calm, complete, fitted in every way to dominate the mind, as it will.

Even as in the choice of a king to be crowned.

III. So will the decrees of this king be just and wise as he was just and wise before he was made king.

The life and work of the mystic will reflect (though dimly) the supreme guiding force of the mystic, the highest trance to which he has attained.

YOGA AND MAGIC

I. Yoga is the art of uniting the mind to a single idea.
It has four methods.

	Gnana-Yoga.	Union by Knowledge.
	Raja-Yoga.	Union by Will.
	Bhakta-Yoga.	Union by Love.
	Hatha-Yoga.	Union by Courage.
add	Mantra-Yoga.	Union through Speech.
	Karma-Yoga.	Union through Work.

These are united by the supreme method of Silence.

II. Ceremonial Magic is the art of uniting the mind to a single idea.
It has four Methods.

	The Holy Qabalah.	Union by Knowledge.
	The Sacred Magic.	Union by Will.
	The Acts of Worship.	Union by Love.
	The Ordeals.	Union by Courage.
add	The Invocations.	Union by Speech.
	The Acts of Service.	Union through Work.

These are united by the supreme method of Silence.

III. If this idea be any but the Supreme and Perfect idea, and the student lose control, the result is insanity, obsession, fanaticism, or paralysis and death (add addiction to gossip and incurable idleness), according to the nature of the failure.

Let then the student understand all these things and combine them in his Art, uniting them by the supreme method of Silence.[*]

One of the prime motives for the publication of *The Equinox* was to provide an avenue of expression for Crowley's own magical Order named the A∴A∴. In addition, he wanted a medium through which he could voice his attitudes toward the Hermetic Order of the Golden Dawn to which he had once belonged.

It was really unfortunate that his entry into that Order, in the year 1898, coincided with the outbreak of a revolt of its members against its leaders. Being the kind of person he was, it was inevitable also that he would somehow get deeply involved in it. I have written a full account of this revolt in *What You Should Know About the Golden Dawn*. Suffice it to say that one of Crowley's gestures of independence from that Order and its Chiefs was to publish its secret rituals and teachings. Several issues of *The Equinox* gave a full account of these. This fact is another of the many reasons for the value and increasing popularity of *The Equinox* through the ensuing years.

Now that they have been out of print for so long a time, and command such exorbitant and outrageous prices, many have conceived the notion of republishing them. With the photo-offset processes available today, this would not have been an impossible process. But many still hesitated.

There was so much unnecessary material in these books. Some of the verse was good, admittedly, but generally speaking, students of occultism have few literary incli-

---

[*] [Crowley, "Postcards to Probationers," *The Equinox* I(2) (1909), pp. 197–199.]

nations and are rarely advocates of poetry—good, bad, or indifferent. Most of the plays written by Crowley are, by most general standards, not particularly good, though the basic idea or plot in some of them was not at all bad. Much the same could be said of his short stories; I personally found them a bore.

So what remained was a series of occult writings that were called the official instructions of the Order that he founded almost a decade after the Golden Dawn debacle. This was the A∴A∴, probably meaning the Astrum Argentinum, the Silver Star. The only problem remaining was the organization of these voluminous writings into some kind of intrinsic order—a minor job of editing. This has been proposed before, but few have the background, knowledge and experience to understand what Crowley was writing about. So having been a student of *The Equinox* for over forty years, I have taken upon myself this task, and I delight in it. This publication is the result.

The classification that follows is of course arbitrary. Some instructions have sections dealing with both meditation and magical procedures. For example, there is one entitled "Liber Yod" (formerly called "Liber Tau") whose first part deals with a complex magical procedure of thirty-two banishings. The second and third parts are concerned with Yoga. But the division used is good enough for general purposes.

The *Gems from the Equinox* is therefore divided into several sections. They are detailed as follows:

Section I. Introductory: The Order

"Liber LXI." This is Crowley's account of the Golden Dawn, its breakup, and how, as a result, his own Order came to be started.

"One Star in Sight." An essay, extrapolated from the book *Magick in Theory and Practice*, which describes the structure of the A∴A∴. and the tasks allocated to each of its several grades.*

"An Account of A∴A∴.." This was originally written by Karl von Eckartshausen and translated into English by Mme. de Steiger under the title *The Cloud upon the Sanctuary*. Crowley has appropriated part of it, which he rewrote and edited to further describe his own Order. It was this book which was recommended by Arthur E. Waite to Crowley when the latter, as a young man just beginning his quest, wrote for information and advice.

"Liber XIII." An early document which describes the practical work in Magick and meditation prescribed for the first several grades of the A∴A∴.

"A Syllabus of the Official Instructions of A∴A∴," extrapolated from *The Equinox*, Vol. I, No. 10. There is a later, more complete syllabus in *The Blue Equinox*, but it contains a large number of items which have never been published. I am including a few pages from the latter because it does provide a list of books for general reading which I can endorse.

Section II. *The Book of the Law*

Liber AL vel Legis. This is the reproduction of the text as given in *The Equinox*, Vol. I, No. 10. The basis of the whole work as laid down by Crowley, it is the document dictated to him in Cairo in 1904. The history of this unique experience is given at length in "The Temple of Solomon the King" and in his [auto]biography *The Confessions of Aleister Crowley*. I have also discussed some aspects of it from a different point of view in *The Eye in the Triangle*.

"Liber CCC: Khabs Am Pekht"; "Liber CL: De Lege Libellum." Both of these papers are elementary commen-

---

* [Regardie later added "Liber Collegii Sancti sub figura CLXXXV" as an appendix. Before Dr. Regardie made it available in *Gems*, this work only had private circulation, beginning c. 1909 e.v.]

taries on *The Book of the Law.* There is in existence an elaborate extenuation of *Liber Legis* far more elaborate than these two documents.* [...] It is an extremely important commentary in the sense that it elaborates what Crowley came to think and believe and feel about this book.

"Liber Nu." This represents a series of meditations predicated on *Liber AL vel Legis.*

"Liber Had." This is also a series of meditations predicated on *Liber AL vel Legis,* in order to derive practical experience of what that book speaks of.

Section III. Yoga

"Liber E vel Exercitiorum." This document provides basic training in a number of root disciplines. In one sense it is that piece of instruction without which more advanced training can have little meaning. It is written clearly, simply and in a straightforward manner.

"Liber Ru." Clear and unmuddled instruction in Pranayama, the breathing exercises that comprise so large a part of Yoga.

These last two papers should be studied in conjunction with two other works of Crowley's: Part I of *Book 4* and *Eight Lectures on Yoga.*

"Liber Astarte." A simply written but beautiful instruction on Bhakta Yoga, the yoga of devotion. It demonstrates Crowley at his best; it is a splendid piece of writing.

"Liber III vel Jugorum." An uncomplicated technique for the development of Will and for establishing conditioned responses to be used in the control of the mind. At first reading, it may sound repulsive to some "sweet and

---

* [Regardie issued one of the first of several editions, *The Law is for All* (1975), which was later replaced by Crowley's authorized edition, edited by his friend and literary executor Louis Wilkinson, under the same title in 1996. See Works Cited.]

lighters," but from personal experimentation with it years ago I can strongly recommend it. It is highly efficacious.

"Liber HHH." This is a presentation of some Tantra disciplines. One section is the outcome of work with a Golden Dawn document analyzing the Neophyte Ritual, as described at some length in *The Eye in the Triangle*. The second part is a meditation predicated on what the Buddhists call the ten impurities. The final one is a method of raising the Kundalini.

"Liber Turris." A discipline for achieving what Patañjali has described as "hindering the modifications of the thinking principle." Its accomplishment demands a skill derived from much practice with previously described disciplines.

"Liber Yod." (This was also entitled "Liber Tau" by error.) The first section of this instruction is magical, while the second and third describe classical Raja Yoga techniques.

"Liber Os Abysmi." An instruction in Gnana Yoga, but directed toward demonstrating the inadequacy of the mind to resolve the basic problems of life, and thereby rising above that level.

"Liber Thisharb." An instruction for developing the magical memory to recover knowledge of previous incarnations.

"Liber DXXXVI." Crowley gave this practice a Greek name which is fully a line long. Gag or not, it describes a method for expanding the horizons of consciousness.

"Liber Librae." A simple instruction in Karma Yoga, having been adapted without any major change from a Golden Dawn document.

Section IV. Magick

"Liber O." In the most simple and direct language, without any of the turgidity or repetitiousness of the corresponding Golden Dawn material, this paper describes several practices which are the very heart and foundation of Magick.

"Liber A." A method for constructing the magical instruments. It should be compared with a document in *The Complete Golden Dawn System of Magic* on the construction and consecration of the elemental weapons.

"Liber Resh." Here are given four adorations of the Sun to be used daily, as a means of consecrating all one's everyday activities to the Great Work.

"Liber Israfel." Originally this was composed by Frater Yehi Aour (Allan Bennett) who was Crowley's first Golden Dawn mentor in the magical arts. It was adapted from versicles extrapolated from Egyptian funerary texts as an invocation of Thoth or Mercury. Crowley simply revised it, rendering it into beautiful English.

"Liber XLIV. The Mass of the Phoenix." A short ritual extrapolated from *The Book of Lies*, giving a simple magical Eucharist for daily use.

"Liber XXV: The Star Ruby." A modified Pentagram Ritual from *The Book of Lies*.

"Liber XXXVI: The Star Sapphire." Also taken from *The Book of Lies*, giving another variant of the Hexagram Ritual.

"Liber Samekh." An elaboration of the old Bornless Ritual or the Preliminary Invocation of the *Goetia*, adapted by Crowley to invoke the Holy Guardian Angel, together with his extended commentary on the ritual.

"Liber V vel Reguli." Also called "The Mark of the Beast." A later, further modified form of the Pentagram Ritual adapted to that set of ideas entertained by Crowley relative to the New Aeon and *The Book of the Law.*

"The Gnostic Mass." Though this is an O.T.O. ritual extrapolated from *The Blue Equinox*, it contains much that relates to all the above and is for group working. Incidentally, it is this mass which was used, almost verbatim, by James Branch Cabell in his novel *Jurgen*, of many years ago.

"Liber LXXXIV vel Chanokh." This is a brief outline published in two parts in *The Equinox*, Vol. I, Nos. 7 and 8, of the Enochian system of Magic derived from the skrying of Dr. John Dee and Sir Edward Kelly in Elizabethan days. The major Golden Dawn contribution has been almost entirely omitted concerning the method for forming the attributions to the squares of the Enochian Tablets and deriving pyramids from them. I would strongly recommend that these abstracts be studied in conjunction with *The Complete Golden Dawn System of Magic* where this system is treated in greater detail.

Where this particular document is most valuable is in the second part, in which the Calls or Invocations in the Enochian language are to be found. It gives the magical technique of invocation of the elements and elementals. It appears nowhere else in the entire eleven [numbers] of *The Equinox*. This technique is in reality extrapolated from the five elemental Grade Rituals of the Golden Dawn.

"Liber CDXVIII, being The Vision and the Voice of the Angels of the Thirty Aethyrs." This is a series of visions or spiritual experiences based on skrying in the thirty Aethyrs of the Enochian system. Two of them were acquired while Crowley was in Mexico in 1901, before he had gone very far on the Path. The balance of twenty-eight was obtained in the Sahara Desert where he had gone with Victor Neuburg in the year 1909. They bear evidence to the enormous spiritual and magical maturity that had developed since the earlier ones, and are consequently more coherent, profound, and sublime. It is a most significant document without parallel anywhere and serves as [the] supreme appendix to the Enochian system.

Section V. Sex Magick

"Liber A'ash vel Capricorni"; "Liber Cheth"; and "Liber LXVI: Stellae Rubeae." All three cryptic papers are clothed with rich symbolism, and for the untutored student may be impossible at first to understand. He will have to rely heavily on his own intuitions and whatever insights he may have developed as a result of his previous application to any or all of the methods given heretofore.

"Liber DCCCXI: Energized Enthusiasm." This was originally an essay in *The Equinox*, Vol. I, No. 9, but was later rendered official as a recognized instruction of the A∴A∴.

Section VI. Miscellaneous

This section includes diverse materials not included in the previous classifications, yet containing incidental elements relating to all of them.

"Liber B vel Magi"; "Liber Porta Lucis"; "Liber Tzaddi vel Hamus Hermeticus"; "Liber CCXXXI"; "Liber CD vel Tau"; and "Liber Viarum Viae." Here is a group of instructions that should properly be included in any selection from *The Equinox*, though I cannot in all honesty believe that they add very much of value to the body of instruction for which *The Equinox* is famous!

"Liber CLXV: A Master of the Temple." This is an abridgement of the diary of Frater Achad, the magical pseudonym for Charles Stansfeld Jones (not to be confused with George Cecil Jones who was Crowley's mentor in the Golden Dawn period, whose magical name or initials were V.N. in the Outer Order and D.D.S. in the Inner, and were used as authorization of many of the A∴A∴. official instructions). This diary is important for several reasons, the main one being that the daily record of his various practices depicts his devotion to the Great Work. Moreover it contains comments by Crowley (who used his magical motto of O.M. $7°=4^{□}$) that are of the utmost value. Finally, Frater Achad made some important contributions to the understanding of *Liber AL vel Legis* which are recognized and given credit in the long commentary on that book. Achad also wrote some books on the Qabalah which deviated from the basic pattern of both Crowley and the Golden Dawn, which thus led ultimately to the separation of these two men—a very sad event.

"Liber LXXI." Madame Blavatsky wrote a small book entitled *The Voice of the Silence,* which since her day has become acknowledged as a mystical and devotional classic. Crowley, using his motto of O.M., has commented at considerable length on this classic. I have long felt that it deserves a broader circulation among occult students who appear to have no awareness of the fact that there exists this erudite and extraordinary commentary to Blavatsky's work.

Some general note needs to be made concerning the relationship of Blavatsky and Crowley. The latter made much of the fact that he was born in the year that Blavatsky founded the original Theosophical Society. In his writings there will occasionally be found a note of derision about both Madame Blavatsky and the Theosophists. Be that as it may, later on he became far more respectful, and then enunciated the doctrine that she was his predecessor—rather like John the Baptist preceding Jesus. In *Magick without Tears* there will be found some letters on "The Three Schools of Magick" in which this doctrine is enunciated at great length. (Remember that Crowley believed that his publication of *The Equinox* was the first serious work on occultism since Blavatsky wrote *Isis Unveiled.*)

I must confess that I find this set of ideas rather preposterous. The first and most important reason is that Blavatsky was altogether opposed to the average Westerner practicing any of the occult arts. This was one of her most fundamental statements as anyone familiar with the history of the Theosophical Society must soon realize. On the other hand, Crowley strongly recommended the total abandonment of intellectual speculation of any sort and the resort to the practice of Yoga and Magick in order to permit the illumination of the Ruach or Lower Manas by a higher order of being or consciousness. The opposition is so blatant and so well defined that I fail to see how Crowley could insist that there was any kind of relationship between Blavatsky and himself, when in fact, their respective occult attitudes are so wholly different—antipodal.

Section VII. Reviews

This last section contains some of the book reviews and profiles that ran like fire through the pages of *The Equinox*. They are included in this collection of documents not merely because I have obtained so much personal pleasure from them throughout the years, but because, in addition, the student can glean much that is of value magically. Every now and again you stumble across a sentence that packs a tremendous wallop. They also reveal with startling clarity much of the basic attitude of Crowley toward almost everything.

The profiles I have always found fascinating. In almost every issue of *The Equinox* there was either a review of some book written by Arthur Edward Waite, or a longer profile that has had me in stitches again and again. If the reader has not read anything of Waite, much of the stinging nature of these articles will be lost on him. Therefore I would strongly recommend that the reader first peruse any book authored by Waite. Only recently, just to refresh my memory, I glanced through two of them, *The Holy Grail* and *The Brotherhood of the Rosy Cross*. Altogether apart from their content which is sometimes difficult to determine, the literary style of Waite comes through loud and clear. It is turgid, pompous and pretentious. One realizes anew how utterly right Crowley was in his critical evaluation of this occult writer. Waite is practically unreadable.

Other profiles are satirical. One of them, "Shadowy Dill-Waters," lampoons W. B. Yeats who is called Weary Willie. There was much bad blood between these two poets, which dates back to the Golden Dawn revolt when they faced each other from opposite sides of the fence.

Much the same has to be said of Algernon Blackwood. Whenever any book of his was reviewed by Aleister Crowley, the opportunity was taken to deride him thoroughly and I must say unjustly. Blackwood was another of those writers who was in the Golden Dawn.

There is another profile which takes G. K. Chesterton to task. Long prior to the writing of this particular profile Crowley and Chesterton had engaged in a continual battle. Chesterton had reviewed some of Crowley's early books, and being an apologist for Catholicism, had expressed some displeasure over Crowley's devotion to Egyptian Gods. Chesterton ridiculed some of their names. Crowley replied to this criticism by calling Chesterton's attention to the fact that Yah and Yahweh of the Bible were no less ridiculous. Thus there were frequent skirmishes between these two men. *The Equinox* profile, though not mentioning this particular history, nonetheless was predicated emotionally on what had transpired between them.

Another profile is a melange of praise for and severe criticism of G. B. Shaw. Almost more than any of the others, this one vividly reveals Crowley's attitude to literature. While he respects the cleverness of Shaw, the fact that there is no trace in the latter's writing of any glimmering of ecstasy is stressed more than anything else. It is for this that he reprimands Shaw severely.

Omissions

Running through all the ten volumes is a serial narrative entitled "The Temple of Solomon the King." The first four parts were written by Captain J. F. C. Fuller. His literary style can be recognized by its floridity, its enthusiasm, and by an overt attempt to appear profound, occult and recondite. The remaining parts were contributed by Crowley himself. The serial is a biographical account of Crowley's spiritual attainment, from the early days of his entry into the Golden Dawn, the great revelation of *The Book of the Law* which he received in Cairo, to his final passage through the Abyss. For that illumination, he modestly chose a Latin motto V.V.V.V.V. which, rendered into decent English, means "In my lifetime I have conquered the Universe by the force of Truth."

However fascinating and important this serial is, I have decided to omit it from *Gems from the Equinox* for several reasons. First of all, Crowley's own autobiography *The Confessions of Aleister Crowley* has appeared. My own biographical study of Crowley, *The Eye in the Triangle*, has been published also. These, in my estimation, supersede "The Temple of Solomon the King."[*]

I have it on rumor that someone else will publish the latter, and I have recommended that with this serial the editor in question should include with it the following material from *The Equinox*: "The Electric Silence," an idealized biographical and symbolical story of Aleister Crowley's quest; "John St. John," an account of a short retirement in the heart of Paris, leading to an illumination; and "Across the Gulf," a fantastic account of a previous incarnation in Egypt.

I have also omitted the instructions on Geomancy and the Tarot. Since both of these were original Golden Dawn materials, they were republished by me [...] in my book *The Complete Golden Dawn System of Magic*, based on documents circulating within that Order.

---

[*] [Several biographies appeared after Regardie's *The Eye in the Triangle* (1970): John Symonds, *The Beast 666* (1997), Lawrence Sutin, *Do What Thou Wilt: A Life of Aleister Crowley* (2000), Martin Booth, *A Magick Life: A Biography of Aleister Crowley* (2000), and Richard Kaczynski, *Perdurabo: The Life of Aleister Crowley* (2002).]

The *Equinox* instruction on Geomancy is not complete or workable. The modus operandi is most inadequately delineated, and above all, the geomantic sigils of the planetary rulers have been deleted, which really robs the method of its divinatory efficacy. Both of these are given in *The Complete Golden Dawn System of Magic*.

In Crowley's Tarot instruction he had changed the counting formula for some of the cards, primarily to accord with that verse in *Liber AL vel Legis* which says: "My number is 11, as all their numbers who are of us." Not that this really makes much difference. The only thing that is required of any system is coherency and consistency, and so long as it is understood that 11 is an intrinsic part of that system it will work. But that number had nothing to do with the Golden Dawn system as such.

Incidentally, it should be clearly understood that this document has nothing whatsoever to do with Crowley's masterpiece of later years, *The Book of Thoth (Egyptian Tarot)*.[*] This is an entirely different piece of writing and artistry.

The Equinox, Vol. I, No. 8, contains "Liber D: Sepher Sephiroth." This is such a large tome, containing as it does a vast collection of names in English and Hebrew together with their numerical values or Gematrias, with many words from the *Zohar* and the Bible, that I feel it would really be too bulky to include in this book. I have decided therefore to exclude it altogether. [...][†]

"Liber DCCCCLXIII" ["The Treasure-House of Images"] is to be found in *The Equinox*, Vol. I, No. 3. It was originally written by Captain J. F. C. Fuller, with only the short prefatory note having been written by Crowley.

---

[*] [*The Book of Thoth* (1944), with the *Thoth Tarot* deck, became *Liber LXXVIII* in the A∴A∴ curriculum.]

[†] [Regardie's original Preface went on to recommend publishing "Liber D" together with *Liber 777*, as he himself later did. See Works Cited, under *Liber 777*.]

It is a lengthy document, lyrical certainly in spots, but wordy and repetitious. A sample reads:

> O Thou Dragon-prince of the air, that art drunk on the blood of the sunsets! I adore Thee, Evoe! I adore Thee, IAO!
>
> O thou sparkling wine-cup of light, whose foaming is the heart's blood of the stars! I adore Thee, Evoe! I adore Thee, IAO!
>
> O Thou frail bluebell of moonlight, that art lost in the gardens of the stars! I adore Thee, Evoe! I adore Thee, IAO!

A few are splendid and exhilarating. Nearly a hundred pages of such adorations, despite a few changes and variations, become rather monotonous. Thus its omission here.

In *The Blue Equinox* Crowley published "Liber LXV: The Book of the Heart Girt with a Serpent." This is one of a handful of sublime mystical books written by Crowley in the heyday of his early spiritual attainment. They were then published by him in a small, private edition, printed on Japanese vellum with gold margins or borders, and bound in vellum. They are among the grandest and finest things he has ever penned.

The Sangreal Foundation [...] republished "Liber LXV" together with "Liber VII vel Lapidis Lazuli" and "Liber DCCCXIII vel Ararita" under the title of *The Holy Books*. More properly the title should have been *Three Holy Books*, but this was my error and I assume full responsibility for this piece of carelessness.

Two others of these so called holy books are included in the *Gems from the Equinox*. *Liber AL vel Legis* is included here [...] because according to Crowley it is the foundation of his system. The other is "Liber LXI," the History Lection, giving Crowley's version of the origins of the Golden Dawn and thus of his own A∴A∴.

The only one that has thus been omitted is "Liber Trigrammaton." It may sound naive and presumptuous to say that it means precious little to me. And because it does not appear in any volume of *The Equinox*, I have decided not to go outside of those volumes.

In *The Equinox*, Vol. I, No. 1, there is an obscure alchemical piece entitled "The Chemical Jousting of Brother Perardua." Written by Captain J. F. C. Fuller, it is as usual ebullient and effervescent, and almost conveys the impression of being informative. Actually it says nothing and is merely a literary tour de force.

I would suggest that this piece of virtuosity was an attempt to copy an earlier paper by Crowley called "Ambrosii Magii Hortus Rosarum" (circa 1902) containing among other matters some early erotic references which can be inferred by a close scrutiny of the margin notes. It is interesting and amusing, bearing all the earmarks of a Crowley effort to imitate the classical *Chymical Marriage of Christian Rosencreutz*. It is here omitted.

Several other omissions should be mentioned for the sake of completeness. One is *The Key of the Mysteries* written by Éliphas Lévi and translated by Crowley, published in *The Equinox*, Vol. I, No. 10. It has since appeared in book form.

Crowley thought this a magnificent piece of writing and used it as his thesis for the grade of Adeptus Exemptus. I cannot say I find this, or really any other writing from the French schools of occultism, of much value and can only assume that Crowley admired it because he was Éliphas Lévi in his previous incarnation— or so he said. It is, however, inferior to other of the contents of *The Equinox* reproduced here.

Another omission is "The Rites of Eleusis," found in the supplement to *The Equinox*, Vol. I, No. 6. These rituals were written for public performance during the *Equinox* heyday, serving as a means for demonstrating the violin virtuosity of Leila Waddell, Crowley's mistress at that time, the dance-to-exhaustion technique of Victor Neuburg, and a large number of poems written by Crowley.

The reviews written at that time indicate that the Rites were quite a performance and were well received. But I see little in them of exceptional value to the present day student of Magick, who as I have previously noted, is not particularly fond of poetry. Under these circumstances, most of the Rites in poetic form would be wholly lost on him.

The four essays entitled "The Herb Dangerous," published in the first four volumes of *The Equinox*, are so good, from the point of view of both style and content—that I extrapolated them from *The Equinox* and republished them under the title *Roll Away the Stone*. I wrote a lengthy introduction relating them to the current drug scene. There is thus no need to reissue them in this edition.

Another worthwhile essay in *The Equinox*, Vol. I, No. 1, entitled "The Soldier and the Hunchback: ! and ?" is omitted here. I think that all the essays of Crowley, including "Berashith," "Eleusis," and "Science and Buddhism," etc., should be gathered together and issued at a later date in a single volume when the public has begun to appreciate his prose and his intellectual acumen.

There are a few other omissions but minor in character. If not mentioned in this list, they do nothing one way or another for the basic material reproduced here. [...]

With this publication of *Gems from the Equinox*, I almost feel like repeating the Golden Dawn speech that I used on the last page of *What You Should Know About the Golden Dawn*:

> Let us work, therefore, my brethren, and effect righteousness, because the Night cometh when no man shall labour ...

This promise or foreboding seems more applicable to the very near future than it did thirty years ago. However, I need to modify it a little. I do feel my work is done at this time and I pray the Gods will now release me from the preoccupation of presenting the work of Aleister

Crowley that has lain heavily on me for so long a period of time. With the publication of this book, my obligation to him, whatever it was, is surely fulfilled. Thus I can pass from labor to refreshment, to concern myself with other things.

Israel Regardie

March 31, 1970
Studio City, California

WORKS CITED

[Anonymous.] *The Chemical Wedding of Christian Rosenkreutz*, trans. Joscelyn Godwin, intro. and commentary by Adam McLean. Grand Rapids, MI: Phanes, 1991.

Blavatsky, Helena Petrovna. *Isis Unveiled: A Master-Key to the Mysteries of Ancient and Modern Science and Theology.* 2 vols. New York, 1877. Rev. ed., Los Angeles: Theosophical University Press, 1950.

———. *The Voice of the Silence.* London, 1889; rpt. Wheaton, IL: Quest, 1992.

Booth, Martin. *A Magick Life: A Biography of Aleister Crowley.* London: Hodder and Stoughton, 2000; Philadelphia: Coronet, 2001.

Crowley, Aleister. *Book 4.* Frater Perdurabo and Soror Virakam [pseuds. for Crowley and Mary Desti Sturges], 2 vols. *Part 1 (Mysticism).* London: Wieland, [1912–13]. *Part 2 (Magick: Preliminary Remarks).* London: Wieland, [1913]; rpt. (2 vols. in 1) Dallas: Sangreal, 1969; rpt. York Beach, ME: Weiser, 2001.

———. *Liber CCCXXXIII. The Book of Lies which is also falsely called Breaks.* Frater Perdurabo [pseud.]. London: Wieland, 1913.

———. *The Book of Lies which is also falsely called Breaks ... with an additional commentary.* Ilfracombe, UK: Haydn Press, 1962; rpt. York Beach, ME: Weiser, 2002.

———. [*The Book of the Law*]. *Liber AL vel Legis sub figura CCXX.* London: O.T.O., 1938; 2nd revised ed., Pasadena, CA: Church of Thelema [1942]; corrected rpt. of London ed., with facsimile manuscript, New York: Weiser, 1976; rpt. York Beach, ME: Weiser, 2002.

———. *The Book of the Law. Liber AL vel Legis sub figura CCXX with a Facsimile of the Manuscript as Received by Aleister and Rose Crowley on April 8, 9, 10, 1904 e.v. Centennial Edition.* York Beach, ME; Boston: Weiser, 2004; rpt. 2006.

———. *The Book of Thoth. A Short Essay on the Tarot of the Egyptians.* The Master Therion [pseud.]. *The Equinox* III(5). London: O.T.O., 1944; rpt. York Beach, ME: Weiser, 2000.

———. *The Book of the Goetia of Solomon the King*, trans. S. L. Mathers, ed. Aleister Crowley. Revised and illustrated 2nd rev. edition, ed. Hymenaeus Beta. York Beach, ME: Weiser, 1995. Rev. ed. 1997, rpt. 2003.

———. *The Collected Works of Aleister Crowley.* Foyers, UK: Society for the Propagation of Religious Truth, 3 vols., 1905–7, 1 vol. "traveller's ed.," 1907; rpt. Des Plaines, IL: Yogi Publication Society, 3 vols. [c. 1974], rpt. [c. 1985].

———. [*The Confessions of Aleister Crowley.*] *The Spirit of Solitude, subsequently re-antichristened The Confessions of Aleister Crowley.* London: Mandrake, 1929. 2 vols. Vols. 3–6 not issued.

———. *The Confessions of Aleister Crowley*, [abridged 1-vol. edition], ed. John Symonds and Kenneth Grant. London: Cape, 1969 and New York: Hill and Wang, 1970; corrected 2nd ed. London: Routledge Kegan Paul, 1979; rpt. London and New York: Arkana, 1989.

——. *Eight Lectures on Yoga*. Mahatma Guru Sri Paramahansa Shivaji [pseud.]. *The Equinox* III(4). London: O.T.O., 1939; rpt. Dallas: Sangreal, 1969; rev. 2nd edition, ed. Hymenaeus Beta. Scottsdale, AZ: New Falcon, 1991; New York: 93 Publishing, 1992.

——, [executive editor]. *The Equinox* I(1–10). London, Spring 1909–Fall 1913; rpt. New York: Weiser, 1972, with later reprints. Ten numbers in 2 vols. with Aleister Crowley's annotations and contributor's biographies, York Beach, ME: Weiser, 1998.

——, [executive editor]. *The Equinox* III(1). Spring 1919, Detroit; rpt. New York: Weiser, 1972 and York Beach, ME: Weiser, 1992.

——, [executive editor]. *The Equinox* III(2). Fall 1919, but not issued.

——, [principal author]. *The Equinox* III(10). New York: Thelema Publications, 1986. 2nd revised ed., York Beach, ME: Weiser; New York, 93 Publishing, 1990; rpt. York Beach, ME: Weiser [2001].

——. *The Equinox of the Gods*. London, O.T.O.: 1936. *The Equinox* III(3). Corrected facsimile edition, Scottsdale, AZ: New Falcon, 1991 and New York: 93 Publishing, 1992.

——. *The Holy Books*, ed. Israel Regardie. Dallas: Sangreal, 1969.

——. *The Law is for All*, ed. Israel Regardie. St. Paul: Llewellyn, 1975; rpt. Scottsdale, AZ: New Falcon, 1991.

——. *The Law is for All: The Authorized Popular Commentary to The Book of the Law*. Rev. edition, ed. Louis Wilkinson and Hymenaeus Beta. Scottsdale, AZ: New Falcon, 1996.

——. *Liber Aleph vel CXI. The Book of Wisdom or Folly*, ed. Karl Germer and Marcelo Motta, *The Equinox* III(6), Barstow, CA: Thelema Publishing Co., 1961; rev. 2nd edition, ed. Hymenaeus Beta. York Beach, ME: Weiser; New York: 93 Publishing, 1991. Reprinted York Beach, ME: Weiser, 2003.

——. [*Liber 777.*] *777 vel Prolegomena Symbolica ad Systemam Sceptico-Mysticæ Viæ Explicandæ, Fundamentum Hieroglyphicum Sanctissimorum Scientiæ Summæ*. London: Walter Scott, 1909.

——. [*Liber 777.*] *777 Revised vel Prolegomena Symbolica ad Systemam Sceptico-Mysticæ Viæ Explicandæ, Fundamentum Hieroglyphicum Sanctissimorum Scientiæ Summæ*. London: Neptune, 1955, rpt. New York: Weiser, 1970; 2nd revised ed. [Chico, CA]: O.T.O. [c. 1970].

——. [*Liber 777.*] *The Qabalah of Aleister Crowley*, ed. Israel Regardie. New York: Weiser, 1973. Reissued as *777 and Other Qabalistic Writings*, 1977; rpt. York Beach, ME: Weiser, 2003.

——. *Magick. Book 4, Parts I–IV.* (Co-authors: Mary Desti and Leila Waddell.) 1st one-vol. rev. edition, ed. Hymenaeus Beta. York Beach, ME: Weiser, 1994. Rev. 2d edition, 1997; corrected reprint 2002.

——. *Magick in Theory and Practice (being Part III of Book 4)*. The Master Therion [pseud.] 4 vols., Paris: [privately printed at the Lecram Press, 1929–30]. One vol. subscriber's ed., issued as *Magick in Theory and Practice*, London, 1930.

——. *Magick without Tears*, ed. Karl Germer. Hampton, NJ: Thelema Publishing Co., 1954. Abridged edition, ed. Israel Regardie. St. Paul: Llewellyn, 1973; rpt. Scottsdale, AZ: New Falcon, 2001.

——. *Roll Away the Stone: An Introduction to Aleister Crowley's Essays on the Psychology of Hashish with the complete text of The Herb Dangerous*, ed. Israel Regardie. St. Paul: Llewellyn, 1968, rpt. 1974. Rpt. North Hollywood, CA: Newcastle, 1994.

——. [*Shih I.*] *Shih Yi*, ed. Helen Parsons Smith. [*The Equinox* III(7).] Oceanside, CA: Thelema Publications, 1971.

——, [translator]. [Lao-tzu, *Tao Te Ching.*] *The Tao Teh King. Liber CLVII*, trans. Aleister Crowley, ed. Helen Parsons Smith. *The Equinox* III(8). Oceanside, CA: Thelema Publications, 1971. Rev. edition, ed. Hymenæus Beta. York Beach, ME: Weiser, 1996; rpt. 1999.

——. [*Thelema.*] *ΘΕΛΗΜΑ*, 3 vols. [London: privately printed, 1909].

——. [*Thelema.*] *ΘΕΛΗΜΑ: The Holy Books of Thelema*, ed. Hymenaeus Alpha and Hymenaeus Beta. York Beach, ME: Weiser, 1983. *The Equinox* III(9). Corrected 2nd ed., York Beach, ME: Weiser; New York: 93 Publishing, 1990. Rpt. York Beach, ME: Weiser, 2001.

Eckartshausen, Karl von. *The Cloud upon the Sanctuary*, trans. Isabel de Steiger. London: Redway, 1896; rpt. York Beach, ME: Weiser, 2003.

Kaczynski, Richard. *Perdurabo: The Life of Aleister Crowley.* Scottsdale, AZ: New Falcon, 2002.

Lévi, Éliphas (pseud. of Alphonse Louis Constant). *The Key of the Mysteries*, trans. Aleister Crowley. London: Rider, 1959; rpt. York Beach, ME: Weiser, 2002.

Regardie, Israel. *The Complete Golden Dawn System of Magic.* Phoenix: Falcon, 1984. Revised ed., Scottsdale, AZ: New Falcon, 1995.

——. *The Golden Dawn.* 4 vols. Chicago: Aries, 1937–1940; rpt. St. Paul: Llewellyn, 1971. Revised ed. 1986, rpt. 2006.

——. *The Eye in the Triangle.* St. Paul: Llewellyn, 1970. Revised ed. 1986; rpt. Scottsdale, AZ: New Falcon, 1997.

——. *My Rosicrucian Adventure: A Contribution to a Recent Phase of the History of Magic, and a Study in the Technique of Theurgy.* Chicago: Aries Press, 1936; rpt. St. Paul: Llewellyn, 1971. Revised ed., *What You Should Know About the Golden Dawn.* Phoenix: New Falcon, 1983; rpt. 2006.

Sutin, Lawrence. *Do What Thou Wilt: A Life of Aleister Crowley.* New York: St. Martin's, 2000; rpt. New York: St. Martin's Griffin, 2002.

Symonds, John. *The Beast 666.* London: Pindar, 1997.

Waite, Arthur Edward. *The Brotherhood of the Rosy Cross.* London: Rider, 1924; rpt. Kila, MT: Kessinger, 2005.

——. *The Hidden Church of the Holy Grail, its Legends and Symbolism.* London: Rebman, 1909. Rpt. as *The Holy Grail, its History, Legend and Symbolism.* New York: Dover, 2006.

A∴A∴

The A∴A∴ is an organization whose heads have obtained by personal experience to the summit of this science. They have founded a system by which everyone can equally attain, and that with an ease and speed which was previously impossible.

The first grade in their system is that of Student.

All persons whose will is to communicate with the A∴A∴ should apply by letter to the Cancellarius of the A∴A∴:

Chancellor
BM ANKH
London WC1N 3XX England
www.outercol.org

O.T.O.

The letters O.T.O. stand for Ordo Templi Orientis, the Order of Oriental Templars, or Order of the Temple of the East. The O.T.O. is dedicated to securing the Liberty of the Individual, and his or her advancement in Light, Wisdom, Understanding, Knowledge, and Power. This is accomplished through Beauty, Courage, and Wit, on the Foundation of Universal Brotherhood. The O.T.O. is in sympathy with the traditional ideals of Freemasonry, and was the first of the Old Aeon orders to accept *The Book of the Law.* The O.T.O. also includes the Gnostic Catholic Church (Ecclesia Gnostica Catholica), whose central public and private rite is "Liber XV," the Gnostic Mass.

Ordo Templi Orientis
International Headquarters
JAF Box 7666
New York, NY 10116-7666 USA
www.oto.org

GEMS
FROM THE
EQUINOX

SECTION I

INTRODUCTORY

THE ORDER

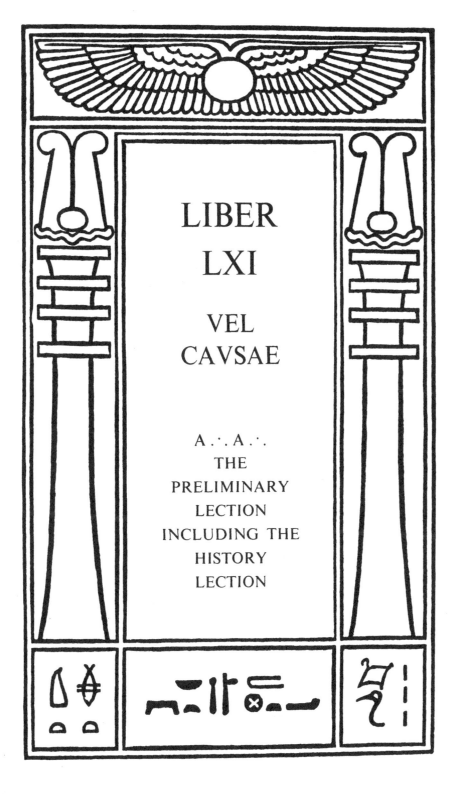

LIBER LXI

VEL CAVSAE

A∴A∴
THE
PRELIMINARY
LECTION
INCLUDING THE
HISTORY
LECTION

A∴A∴ Publication in Class D

93	$10° = 1^\square$	
666	$9° = 2^\square$	Pro Coll. Summ.
777	$8° = 3^\square$	
D. D. S.	$7° = 4^\square$	
O. M.	$7° = 4^\square$	
O. S. V.	$6° = 5^\square$	Pro Coll. Int.
Parzival	$5° = 6^\square$	
V. N.	Praemonstrator	
P.	Imperator	Pro Coll. Ext.
Achad	Cancellarius	

LIBER LXI

THE PRELIMINARY LECTION

In the Name of the Initiator, Amen.

1. In the beginning was Initiation. The flesh profiteth nothing; the mind profiteth nothing; that which is unknown to you and above these, while firmly based upon their equilibrium, giveth life.

2. In all systems of religion is to be found a system of Initiation, which may be defined as the process by which a man comes to learn that unknown Crown.

3. Though none can communicate either the knowledge or the power to achieve this, which we may call the Great Work, it is yet possible for initiates to guide others.

4. Every man must overcome his own obstacles, expose his own illusions. Yet others may assist him to do both, and they may enable him altogether to avoid many of the false paths, leading no whither, which tempt the weary feet of the uninitiated pilgrim. They can further insure that he is duly tried and tested, for there are many who think themselves to be Masters who have not even begun to tread the Way of Service that leads thereto.

5. Now the Great Work is one, and the Initiation is

one, and the Reward is one, however diverse are the symbols wherein the Unutterable is clothed.

6. Hear then the history of the system which this lection gives you the opportunity of investigating.

Listen, we pray you, with attention: for once only does the Great Order knock at any one door.

Whosoever knows any member of that Order as such, can never know another, until he too has attained to mastery.

Here, therefore, we pause, that you may thoroughly search yourself, and consider if you are yet fitted to take an irrevocable step.

For the reading of that which follows is Recorded.

THE HISTORY LECTION

7. Some years ago a number of cipher MSS. were discovered and deciphered by certain students. They attracted much attention, as they purported to derive from the Rosicrucians. You will readily understand that the genuineness of the claim matters no whit, such literature being judged by itself, not by its reputed sources.

8. Among the MSS. was one which gave the address of a certain person in Germany, who is known to us as S.D.A. Those who discovered the ciphers wrote to S.D.A., and in accordance with instructions received, an Order was founded which worked in a semi-secret manner.

9. After some time S.D.A. died: further requests for help were met with a prompt refusal from the colleagues of S.D.A. It was written by one of them that S.D.A.'s scheme had always been regarded with disapproval. But since the absolute rule of the adepts is never to interfere with the judgment of any other person whomsoever—how much more, then, one of themselves, and that one most highly revered!—they had refrained from active opposi-

tion. The adept who wrote this added that the Order had already quite enough knowledge to enable it or its members to formulate a magical link with the adepts.

10. Shortly after this, one called S.R.M.D. announced that he had formulated such a link, and that himself and two others were to govern the Order. New and revised rituals were issued, and fresh knowledge poured out in streams.

11. We must pass over the unhappy juggleries which characterized the next period. It has throughout proved impossible to elucidate the complex facts.

We content ourselves, then, with observing that the death of one of his two colleagues, and the weakness of the other, secured to S.R.M.D. the sole authority. The rituals were elaborated, though scholarly enough, into verbose and pretentious nonsense: the knowledge proved worthless, even where it was correct: for it is in vain that pearls, be they never so clear and precious, are given to the swine.

The ordeals were turned into contempt, it being impossible for any one to fail therein. Unsuitable candidates were admitted for no better reason than that of their worldly prosperity.

In short, the Order failed to initiate.

12. Scandal arose and with it schism.

13. In 1900 one P., a brother, instituted a rigorous test of S.R.M.D. on the one side and the Order on the other.

14. He discovered that S.R.M.D., though a scholar of some ability and a magician of remarkable powers, had never attained complete initiation: and further had fallen from his original place, he having imprudently attracted to himself forces of evil too great and terrible for him to withstand.

The claim of the Order that the true adepts were in charge of it was definitely disproved.

15. In the Order, with two certain exceptions and two doubtful ones, he found no persons prepared for initiation of any sort.

16. He thereupon by his subtle wisdom destroyed both the Order and its chief.

17. Being himself no perfect adept, he was driven of the Spirit into the Wilderness, where he abode for six years, studying by the light of reason the sacred books and secret systems of initiation of all countries and ages.

18. Finally, there was given unto him a certain exalted grade whereby a man becomes master of knowledge and intelligence, and no more their slave. He perceived the inadequacy of science, philosophy, and religion; and exposed the self-contradictory nature of the thinking faculty.

19. Returning to England, he laid his achievements humbly at the feet of a certain adept D.D.S., who welcomed him brotherly and admitted his title to the grade which he had so hardly won.

20. Thereupon these two adepts conferred together, saying: May it not be written that the tribulations shall be shortened? Wherefore they resolved to establish a new Order which should be free from the errors and deceits of the former one.

21. Without Authority they could not do this, exalted as their rank was among adepts. They resolved to prepare all things, great and small, against that day when such Authority should be received by them, since they knew not where to seek for higher adepts than themselves, but knew that the true way to attract the notice of such was to equilibrate the symbols. The temple must be builded before the God can indwell it.

22. Therefore by the order of D.D.S. did P. prepare all things by his arcane science and wisdom, choosing only those symbols which were common to all systems, and

rigorously rejecting all names and words which might be supposed to imply any religious or metaphysical theory. To do this utterly was found impossible, since all language has a history, and the use (for example) of the word "spirit" implies the Scholastic Philosophy and the Hindu and Taoist theories concerning the breath of man. So was it difficult to avoid implication of some undesirable bias by using the words "order," "circle," "chapter," "society," "brotherhood," or any other to designate the body of initiates.

23. Deliberately, therefore, did he take refuge in vagueness. Not to veil the truth to the Neophyte, but to warn him against valuing non-essentials. Should therefore the candidate hear the name of any God, let him not rashly assume that it refers to any known God, save only the God known to himself. Or should the ritual speak in terms (however vague) which seem to imply Egyptian, Taoist, Buddhist, Indian, Persian, Greek, Judaic, Christian, or Moslem philosophy, let him reflect that this is a defect of language; the literary limitation and not the spiritual prejudice of the man P.

24. Especially let him guard against the finding of definite sectarian symbols in the teaching of his master, and the reasoning from the known to the unknown which assuredly will tempt him.

We labour earnestly, dear brother, that you may never be led away to perish upon this point; for thereon have many holy and just men been wrecked. By this have all the visible systems lost the essence of wisdom.

We have sought to reveal the Arcanum; we have only profaned it.

25. Now when P. had thus with bitter toil prepared all things under the guidance of D.D.S. (even as the hand writes, while the conscious brain, though ignorant of the detailed movements, applauds or disapproves the finished

work) there was a certain time of repose, as the earth lieth fallow.

26. Meanwhile these adepts busied themselves intently with the Great Work.

27. In the fullness of time, even as a blossoming tree that beareth fruit in its season, all these pains were ended, and these adepts and their companions obtained the reward which they had sought—they were to be admitted to the Eternal and Invisible Order that hath no name among men.

28. They therefore who had with smiling faces abandoned their homes, their possessions, their wives, their children, in order to perform the Great Work, could with steady calm and firm correctness abandon the Great Work itself: for this is the last and greatest projection of the alchemist.

29. Also one V.V.V.V.V. arose, an exalted adept of the rank of Master of the Temple (or this much He disclosed to the Exempt Adepts) and His utterance is enshrined in the Sacred Writings.

30. Such are *Liber Legis, Liber Cordis Cincti Serpente, Liber Liberi vel Lapidis Lazuli* and such others whose existence may one day be divulged unto you. Beware lest you interpret them either in the Light or in the darkness, for only in L.V.X. may they be understood.

31. Also He conferred upon D.D.S., O.M., and another, the Authority of the Triad, who in turn have delegated it unto others, and they yet again, so that the Body of Initiates may be perfect, even from the Crown unto the Kingdom and beyond.

32. For Perfection abideth not in the Pinnacles, or in the Foundations, but in the ordered Harmony of one with all.

ONE
STAR IN
SIGHT

ONE STAR IN SIGHT

Thy feet in mire, thine head in murk,
   O man, how piteous thy plight,
The doubts that daunt, the ills that irk,
   Thou hast nor wit nor will to fight —
How hope in heart, or worth in work?
   No star in sight!

Thy Gods proved puppets of the priest.
   "Truth? All's relation!" science sighed.
In bondage with thy brother beast,
   Love tortured thee, as Love's hope died
And Love's faith rotted. Life no least
   Dim star descried.

Thy cringing carrion cowered and crawled
   To find itself a chance-cast clod
Whose Pain was purposeless; appalled
   That aimless accident thus trod
Its agony, that void skies sprawled
   On the vain sod!

All souls eternally exist,
   Each individual, ultimate,
Perfect — each makes itself a mist

13

Of mind and flesh to celebrate
With some twin mask their tender tryst
Insatiate.

Some drunkards, doting on the dream,
Despair that it should die, mistake
Themselves for their own shadow-scheme.
One star can summon them to wake
To self; star-souls serene that gleam
On life's calm lake.

That shall end never that began.
All things endure because they are.
Do what thou wilt; for every man
And every woman is a star.
Pan is not dead; he liveth, Pan!
Break down the bar!

To man I come, the number of
A man my number, Lion of Light;
I am The Beast whose Law is Love.
Love under will, his royal right —
Behold within, and not above,
One star in sight!

A glimpse of the structure and syste of them Great White Brotherhood.

A ∴ A ∴[1]

Do what thou wilt shall be the whole of the Law.

1. The Order of the Star called S. S. is, in respect of its existence upon the Earth, an organised body of men and women distinguished among their fellows by the qualities here enumerated. They exist in their own Truth, which is both universal and unique. They move in accordance with their own Wills, which are each unique, yet coherent with the universal will.

1. The Name of The Order and those of its three divisions are now disclosed to the profane. Certain swindlers have recently stolen the initials A ∴ A ∴ in order to profit by its reputation.

They perceive (that is, understand, know, and feel) in love, which is both unique and universal.

2. The order consists of eleven grades or degrees, and is numbered as follows: these compose three groups, the Orders of the S. S., of the R. C., and of the G. D. respectively.

The Order of the S. S.

Ipsissimus	$10° =$	$1^\square$
Magus	$9° =$	$2^\square$
Magister Templi	$8° =$	$3^\square$

The Order of the R. C.
(Babe of the Abyss — the link)

Adeptus Exemptus	$7° =$	$4^\square$
Adeptus Major	$6° =$	$5^\square$
Adeptus Minor	$5° =$	$6^\square$

The Order of the G. D.
(Dominus Liminis — the link)

Philosophus	$4° =$	$7^\square$
Practicus	$3° =$	$8^\square$
Zelator	$2° =$	$9^\square$
Neophyte	$1° =$	$10^\square$
Probationer	$0° =$	$0^\square$

(These figures have special meanings to the initiated and are commonly employed to designate the grades.)

The general characteristics and attributions of these Grades are indicated by their correspondences on the Tree of Life, as may be studied in detail in the book 777.

Student. His business is to acquire a general intellectual knowledge of all systems of attainment, as declared in the prescribed books.

Probationer. His principal business is to begin such

practices as he may prefer, and to write a careful record of the same for one year.

Neophyte. Has to acquire perfect control of the Astral Plane.

Zelator. His main work is to achieve complete success in Asana and Pranayama. He also begins to study the formula of the Rosy Cross.

Practicus. Is expected to complete his intellectual training, and in particular to study the Qabalah.

Philosophus. Is expected to complete his moral training. He is tested in Devotion to the Order.

Dominus Liminis. Is expected to show mastery of Pratyahara and Dharana.

Adeptus (without). Is expected to perform the Great Work and to attain the Knowledge and Conversation of the Holy Guardian Angel.

Adeptus (within). Is admitted to the practice of the formula of the Rosy Cross on entering the College of the Holy Ghost.

Adeptus (Major). Obtains a general mastery of practical Magick, though without comprehension.

Adeptus (Exemptus). Completes in perfection all these matters. He then either (*a*) becomes a Brother of the Left Hand Path or, (*b*) is stripped of all his attainments and of himself as well, even of his Holy Guardian Angel, and becomes a Babe of the Abyss, who, having transcended the Reason, does nothing but grow in the womb of its mother. It then finds itself a . . .

Magister Templi (Master of the Temple). Whose functions are fully described in *Liber 418*, as is this whole initiation from Adeptus Exemptus. See also *Aha!* His principal business is to tend his "garden" of disciples, and to obtain a perfect understanding of the Universe. He is a Master of Samadhi.

Magus. Attains to wisdom, declares his law (See *Liber*

I vel Magi) and is a Master of all Magick in its greatest and highest sense.

Ipsissimus. Is beyond all this and beyond all comprehension of those of lower degrees.

But of these last three Grades see some further account in *The Temple of Solomon the King, The Equinox*, I to X and elsewhere.

It should be stated that these Grades are not necessarily attained fully, and in strict consecution, or manifested wholly on all planes. The subject is very difficult, and entirely beyond the limits of this small treatise.

We append a more detailed account.

3. *The Order of the S. S.* is composed of those who have crossed the Abyss; the implications of this expression may be studied in *Liber 418*, the 14th, 13th, 12th, 11th, 10th and 9th Aethyrs in particular.

All members of the Order are in full possession of the Formulae of Attainment, both mystical or inwardly-directed and Magical or outwardly-directed. They have full experience of attainment in both these paths.

They are all, however, bound by the original and fundamental Oath of the Order, to devote their energy to assisting the Progress of their Inferiors in the Order. Those who accept the rewards of their emancipation for themselves are no longer within the Order.

Members of the Order are each entitled to found Orders dependent on themselves on the lines of the R. C. and G. D. orders, to cover types of emancipation and illumination not contemplated by the original (or main) system. All such orders must, however, be constituted in harmony with the A ∴ A ∴ as regards the essential principles.

All members of the Order are in possession of the Word of the existing Aeon, and govern themselves thereby.

They are entitled to communicate directly with any and every member of the Order, as they may deem fitting.

Every active Member of the Order has destroyed all that He is and all that He has on crossing the Abyss; but a star is cast forth in the Heavens to enlighten the Earth, so that he may possess a vehicle wherein he may communicate with mankind. The quality and position of this star, and its functions, are determined by the nature of the incarnations transcended by him.

4. The Grade of Ipsissimus is not to be described fully; but its opening is indicated in *Liber I vel Magi*.

There is also an account in a certain secret document to be published when propriety permits. Here it is only said this: The Ipsissimus is wholly free from all limitations soever, existing in the nature of all things without discriminations of quantity or quality between them. He has identified Being and not-Being and Becoming, action and non-action and tendency to action, with all other such triplicities, not distinguishing between them in respect of any conditions, or between any one thing and any other thing as to whether it is with or without conditions.

He is sworn to accept this Grade in the presence of a witness, and to express its nature in word and deed, but to withdraw Himself at once within the veils of his natural manifestation as a man, and to keep silence during his human life as to the fact of his attainment, even to the other members of the Order.

The Ipsissimus is pre-eminently the Master of all modes of existence; that is, his being is entirely free from internal or external necessity. His work is to destroy all tendencies to construct or to cancel such necessities. He is the Master of the Law of Unsubstantiality (Anatta).

The Ipsissimus has no relation as such with any Being: He has no will in any direction, and no Consciousness of any kind involving duality, for in Him all is accomplished;

as it is written "beyond the Word and the Fool, yea, beyond the Word and the Fool."

5. The Grade of Magus is described in *Liber I vel Magi*, and there are accounts of its character in *Liber 418* in the Higher Aethyrs.

There is also a full and precise description of the attainment of this Grade in *The Magical Record of the Beast 666*.

The essential characteristic of the Grade is that its possessor utters a Creative Magical Word, which transforms the planet on which he lives by the installation of new officers to preside over its initiation. This can take place only at an "Equinox of the Gods" at the end of an "Aeon"; that is, when the secret formula which expresses the Law of its action becomes outworn and useless to its further development.

(Thus "Suckling" is the formula of an infant: when teeth appear it marks a new "Aeon," whose "Word" is "Eating.")

A Magus can therefore only appear as such to the world at intervals of some centuries; accounts of historical Magi, and their Words, are given in *Liber Aleph*.

This does not mean that only one man can attain this Grade in any one Aeon, so far as the Order is concerned. A man can make personal progress equivalent to that of a "Word of an Aeon"; but he will identify himself with the current word, and exert his will to establish it, lest he conflict with the work of the Magus who uttered the Word of the Aeon in which He is living.

The Magus is pre-eminently the Master of Magick, that is, his will is entirely free from internal diversion or external opposition; His work is to create a new Universe in accordance with His Will. He is the Master of the Law of Change (Anicca).

To attain the Grade of Ipsissimus he must accomplish

three tasks, destroying the Three Guardians mentioned in *Liber 418*, the 3rd Aethyr; Madness, and Falsehood, and Glamour, that is, Duality in Act, Word and Thought.

6. The Grade of Master of the Temple is described in *Liber 418* as above indicated. There are full accounts in the Magical Diaries of the Beast 666, who was cast forth into the Heaven of Jupiter, and of Omnia in Uno, Unus in Omnibus, who was cast forth into the sphere of the Elements.

The essential Attainment is the perfect annihilation of that personality which limits and oppresses his true self.

The Magister Templi is pre-eminently the Master of Mysticism, that is, His Understanding is entirely free from internal contradiction or external obscurity; His word is to comprehend the existing Universe in accordance with His own Mind. He is the Master of the Law of Sorrow (Dukkha).

To attain the grade of Magus he must accomplish Three Tasks; the renunciation of His enjoyment of the Infinite so that he may formulate Himself as the Finite; the acquisition of the practical secrets alike of initiating and governing His proposed new Universe and the identification of himself with the impersonal idea of Love. Any neophyte of the Order (or, as some say, any person soever) possesses the right to claim the Grade of Master of the Temple by taking the Oath of the Grade. It is hardly necessary to observe that to do so is the most sublime and awful responsibility which it is possible to assume, and an unworthy person who does so incurs the most terrific penalties by his presumption.

7. *The Order of the R. C.* The Grade of the Babe of the Abyss is not a Grade in the proper sense, being rather a passage between the two Orders. Its characteristics are wholly negative, as it is attained by the resolve of the Adeptus Exemptus to surrender all that he has and is for

ever. It is an annihilation of all the bonds that compose the self or constitute the Cosmos, a resolution of all complexities into their elements, and these thereby cease to manifest, since things are only knowable in respect of their relation to, and reaction on, other things.

8. The Grade of Adeptus Exemptus confers authority to govern the two lower Orders of R. C. and G. D.

The Adept must prepare and publish a thesis setting forth His knowledge of the Universe, and his proposals for its welfare and progress. He will thus be known as the leader of a school of thought.

(Eliphas Levi's *Clef des Grands Mystères*, the works of Swedenborg, von Eckartshausen, Robert Fludd, Paracelsus, Newton, Bolyai, Hinton, Berkeley, Loyola, etc., are examples of such essays.)

He will have attained all but the supreme summits of meditation, and should be already prepared to perceive that the only possible course for him is to devote himself utterly to helping his fellow creatures.

To attain the Grade of Magister Templi, he must perform two tasks; the emancipation from thought by putting each idea against its opposite, and refusing to prefer either; and the consecration of himself as a pure vehicle for the influence of the Order to which he aspires.

He must then decide upon the critical adventure of our Order; the absolute abandonment of himself and his attainments. He cannot remain indefinitely an Exempt Adept; he is pushed onward by the irresistible momentum that he has generated.

Should he fail, by will or weakness, to make his self-annihilation absolute, he is none the less thrust forth into the Abyss; but instead of being received and reconstructed in the Third Order, as a Babe in the womb of our Lady Babalon, under the Night of Pan, to grow up to be Himself wholly and truly as He was not previously, he remains in the Abyss, secreting his elements round his Ego as if isolated from the Universe, and becomes what is called a "Black Brother." Such a being is gradually disintegrated from lack of nourishment and the slow but certain action of the attraction of the rest of the Universe, despite his now desperate efforts to insulate and protect himself, and to aggrandise himself by predatory practices. He may indeed prosper for a while, but in the end he must perish, especially when with a new Aeon a new word is proclaimed which he cannot and will not hear, so that he is handicapped by trying to use an obsolete method of Magick, like a man with a boomerang in a battle where every one else has a rifle.

9. The Grade of Adeptus Major confers Magical Powers (strictly so-called) of the second rank.

His work is to use these to support the authority of the Exempt Adept his superior. (This is not to be understood as an obligation of personal subservience or even loyalty; but as a necessary part of his duty to assist his inferiors. For the authority of the Teaching and Governing Adept is the basis of all orderly work.)

To attain the Grade of Adeptus Exemptus, he must accomplish Three Tasks; the acquisition of absolute Self-Reliance, working in complete isolation, yet transmitting the word of his superior clearly, forcibly and subtly; and the comprehension and use of the Revolution of the wheel of force, under its three successive forms of Radiation, Conduction and Convection (Mercury, Sulphur, Salt; or Sattvas, Rajas, Tamas), with their corresponding natures on other planes. Thirdly, he must exert his whole power and authority to govern the Members of lower Grades with balanced vigour and initiative in such a way as to allow no dispute or complaint; he must employ to this end the formula called "The Beast conjoined with the Woman" which establishes a new incarnation of deity; as in the legends of Leda, Semele, Miriam, Pasiphae, and others. He must set up this ideal for the Orders which he rules, so that they may possess a not too abstract rallying-point suited to their undeveloped states.

10. The Grade of Adeptus Minor is the main theme of the instructions of the A ∴ A ∴ . It is characterised by the Attainment of the Knowledge and Conversation of the Holy Guardian Angel. (See *The Equinox, The Temple of Solomon the King; The Vision and the Voice*, 8th Aethyr; also *Liber Samekh*, etc.) This is the essential work of every man; none other ranks with it either for personal progress or for power to help one's fellows. This unachieved, man is no more than the unhappiest and blindest of animals. He is conscious of his own incomprehensible calamity, and clumsily incapable of repairing it. Achieved, he is no less than the co-heir of gods, a Lord of Light. He is conscious of his own consecrated course, and confidently ready to run it. The Adeptus Minor needs little help or guidance even from his superiors in our Order.

His work is to manifest the Beauty of the Order to the world, in the way that his superiors enjoin, and his genius dictates.

To attain the Grade Adeptus Major, he must accomplish two tasks; the equilibration of himself, especially as to his passions, so that he has no preference for any one course of conduct over another, and the fulfilment of every action by its complement, so that whatever he does leaves him without temptation to wander from the way of his True Will.

Secondly, he must keep silence, while he nails his body to the tree of his creative will, in the shape of that Will, leaving his head and arms to form the symbol of Light, as if to make oath that his every thought, word

and deed should express the Light derived from the God
with which he has identified his life, his love and his
liberty — symbolised by his heart, his phallus, and his
legs. It is impossible to lay down precise rules by which
a man may attain to the knowledge and conversation of
His Holy Guardian Angel; for that is the particular secret
of each one of us; a secret not to be told or even divined
by any other, whatever his grade. It is the Holy of Holies,
whereof each man is his own High Priest, and none
knoweth the Name of his brother's God, or the Rite that
invokes Him.

The Masters of the A .·. A .·. have therefore made no
attempt to institute any regular ritual for this central
Work of their Order, save the generalised instruction in
Liber 418 (the 8th Aethyr) and the detailed Canon and
Rubric of the Mass actually used with success by
Frater Perdurabo in His attainment. This has been
written down by Himself in *Liber Samekh*. But they have
published such accounts as those in *The Temple of
Solomon the King* and in *John St. John*. They have taken
the only proper course; to train aspirants to this attainment in the theory and practice of the whole of Magick
and Mysticism, so that each man may be expert in the
handling of all known weapons, and free to choose and
to use those which his own experience and instinct dictate
as proper when he essays the Great Experiment.

He is furthermore trained to the one habit essential to
Membership of the A .·. A .·.; he must regard all his
attainments as primarily the property of those less
advanced aspirants who are confided to his charge.

No attainment soever is officially recognised by the
A .·. A .·. unless the immediate inferior of the person
in question has been fitted by him to take his place.

The rule is not rigidly applied in all cases, as it would
lead to congestion, especially in the lower grades where

the need is greatest, and the conditions most confused; but it is never relaxed in the Order of the R. C. or of the S. S. save only in One Case.

There is also a rule that the Members of the A ∴. A ∴. shall not know each other officially, save only each Member his superior who introduced him and his inferior whom he has himself introduced.

This rule has been relaxed, and a "Grand Neophyte" appointed to superintend all Members of the Order of the G. D. The real object of the rule was to prevent Members of the same Grade working together and so blurring each other's individuality; also to prevent work developing into social intercourse.

The Grades of the Order of the G. D. are fully described in *Liber 185*,[2] and there is no need to amplify what is there stated. It must however, be carefully remarked that in each of these preliminary Grades there are appointed certain tasks appropriate, and that the ample accomplishment of each and every one of these is insisted upon with the most rigorous rigidity.[3]

Members of the A ∴. A ∴. of whatever grade are not bound or expected or even encouraged to work on any stated lines, or with any special object, save as has been above set forth. There is however an absolute prohibition to accept money or other material reward, directly or indirectly, in respect of any service connected with the Order, for personal profit or advantage. The penalty is immediate expulsion, with no possibility of reinstatement on any terms soever.

---

2. This book is published in *The Equinox*, vol. III, no. 2.
3. *Liber 185* need not be quoted at length. It is needful only to say that the Aspirant is trained systematically and comprehensively in the various technical practices which form the basis of Our Work. One may become expert in any or all of these without necessarily making any real progress, just as a man might be first-rate at grammar, syntax, and prosody without being able to write a single line of good poetry, although the greatest poet in soul is unable to express himself without the aid of those three elements of literary composition.

But all members must of necessity work in accordance with the facts of Nature, just as an architect must allow for the Law of Gravitation, or a sailor reckon with currents.

So must all Members of the A .˙. A .˙. work by the Magical Formula of the Aeon.

They must accept *The Book of the Law* as the Word and the Letter of Truth, and the sole Rule of Life.[4] They must acknowledge the Authority of the Beast 666 and of the Scarlet Woman as in the book it is defined, and accept Their Will[5] as concentrating the Will of our Whole Order. They must accept the Crowned and Conquering Child as the Lord of the Aeon, and exert themselves to establish His reign upon Earth. They must acknowledge that "The Word of the Law is ΘΕΛΗΜΑ " and that "Love is the Law, love under Will."

Each member must make it his main work to discover for himself his own true will, and to do it, and do nothing else.[6]

He must accept those orders in *The Book of the Law* that apply to himself as being necessarily in accordance with his own true will, and execute the same to the letter with all the energy, courage, and ability that he can command. This applies especially to the work of extending the Law in the world, wherein his proof is his own success, the witness of his Life to the Law that hath given him light in his ways, and liberty to pursue them.

4. This is not in contradiction with the absolute right of every person to do his own true Will. But any True Will is of necessity in harmony with the facts of Existence; and to refuse to accept *The Book of the Law* is to create a conflict within Nature, as if a physicist insisted on using an incorrect formula of mechanics as the basis of an experiment.

5. "Their Will" — not, of course, their wishes as individual human beings, but their will as officers of the New Aeon.

6. It is not considered "essential to right conduct" to be an active propagandist of the Law, and so on; it may, or may not, be the True Will of any particular person to do so. But since the fundamental purpose of the Order is to further the Attainment of humanity, membership implies, by definition, the Will to help mankind by the means best adapted thereto.

Thus doing, he payeth his debt to the Law that hath freed him by working its will to free all men; and he proveth himself a true man in our Order by willing to bring his fellows into freedom.

By thus ordering his disposition, he will fit himself in the best possible manner for the task of understanding and mastering the divers technical methods prescribed by the A∴A∴ for Mystical and Magical attainment.

He will thus prepare himself properly for the crisis of his career in the Order, the attainment of the Knowledge and Conversation of his Holy Guardian Angel.

His Angel shall lead him anon to the summit of the Order of the R. C. and make him ready to face the unspeakable terror of the Abyss which lies between Manhood and Godhead; teach him to Know that agony, to Dare that destiny, to Will that catastrophe, and to keep Silence for ever as he accomplishes the act of annihilation.

From the Abyss comes No Man forth, but a Star startles the Earth, and our Order rejoices above that Abyss that the Beast hath begotten one more Babe in the Womb of Our Lady, His Concubine, the Scarlet Woman, Babalon.

There is no need to instruct a Babe thus born, for in the Abyss it was purified of every poison of personality; its ascent to the highest is assured, in its season, and it hath no need of seasons for it is conscious that all conditions are no more than forms of its fancy.

Such is a brief account, adapted as far as may be to the average aspirant to Adeptship, or Attainment, or Initiation, or Mastership, or Union with God, or Spiritual Development, or Mahatmaship, or Freedom, or Occult Knowledge, or whatever he may call his inmost need of Truth, of our Order of A∴A∴.

It is designed principally to awake interest in the possibilities of human progress, and to proclaim the principles of the A .·. A .·..

The outline given of the several successive steps is exact; the two crises — the Angel and the Abyss — are necessary features in every career. The other tasks are not always accomplished in the order given here; one man, for example, may acquire many of the qualities peculiar to the Adeptus Major, and yet lack some of those proper to the Practicus.[7] But the system here given shows the correct order of events, as they are arranged in Nature; and in no case is it safe for a man to neglect to master any single detail, however dreary and distasteful it may seem. It often does so, indeed; that only insists on the necessity of dealing with it. The dislike and contempt for it bear witness to a weakness and incompleteness in the nature which disowns it; that particular gap in one's defences may admit the enemy at the very turning-point of some battle. Worse, one were shamed for ever if one's inferior should happen to ask for advice and aid on that subject and one were to fail in service to him! His failure — one's own failure also! No step, however well won for oneself, till he is ready for his own advance!

Every Member of the A .·. A .·. must be armed at

7. The natural talents of individuals differ very widely. The late Sir Richard Jebb, one of the greatest classical scholars of modern times, was so inferior to the average mediocrity in mathematics, that despite repeated efforts he could not pass the "little go" at Cambridge — which the dullest minds can usually do. He was so deeply esteemed for his classics that a special "Grace" was placeted so as to admit him to matriculation. Similarly a brilliant Exorcist might be an incompetent Diviner. In such a case the A .·. A .·. would refuse to swerve from Its system; the Aspirant would be compelled to remain at the Barrier until he succeeded in breaking it down, though a new incarnation were necessary to permit him to do so. But no technical failure of any kind soever could neces- sarily prevent him from accomplishing the Two Critical Tasks, since the fact of his incarnation itself proves that he had taken the Oath which entitled him to attain to the Knowledge and Conversation of his Holy Guardian Angel, and the annihilation of this Ego. One might therefore be an Adeptus Minor or even a Magister Templi, in essence, though refused official recognition by the A .·. A .·. as a Zelator owing to (say) a nervous defect which prevented him from acquiring a Posture which was "steady and easy" as required by the Task of that grade.

all points, and expert with every weapon. The examinations in every Grade are strict and severe; no loose or vague answers are accepted. In intellectual questions, the candidate must display no less mastery of his subject than if he were entered in the "final" for Doctor of Science or Law at a first class University.

In examination of physical practices, there is a standardised test. In Asana, for instance, the candidate must remain motionless for a given time, his success being gauged by poising on his head a cup filled with water to the brim; if he spill one drop, he is rejected.

He is tested in "the Spirit Vision" or "Astral Journeying" by giving him a symbol unknown and unintelligible to him, and he must interpret its nature by means of a vision as exactly as if he had read its name and description in the book when it was chosen.

The power to make and "charge" talismans is tested as if they were scientific instruments of precision, as they are.

In the Qabalah, the candidate must discover for himself, and prove to the examiner beyond all doubt, the properties of a number never previously examined by any student.

In invocation the divine force must be made as manifest and unmistakable as the effects of chloroform; in evocation, the spirit called forth must be at least as visible and tangible as the heaviest vapours; in divination, the answer must be as precise as a scientific thesis, and as accurate as an audit; in meditation, the results must read like a specialist's report of a classical case.

By such methods, the A ∴ A ∴ intends to make occult science as systematic and scientific as chemistry; to rescue it from the ill repute which, thanks both to the ignorant and dishonest quacks that have prostituted its name, and to the fanatical and narrow-minded enthusiasts that have turned it into a fetish, has made it an object of aversion to those very minds whose enthusiasm and integrity make them most in need of its benefits, and most fit to obtain them.

It is the one really important science, for it transcends the conditions of material existence and so is not liable to perish with the planet, and it must be studied as a science, sceptically, with the utmost energy and patience.

The A ∴ A ∴ possesses the secrets of success; it makes no secret of its knowledge, and if its secrets are not everywhere known and practised, it is because the abuses connected with the name of occult science disincline official investigators to examine the evidence at their disposal.

This paper has been written not only with the object of attracting individual seekers into the way of Truth, but of affirming the propriety of the methods of the A ∴ A ∴ as the basis for the next great step in the advance of human knowledge.

Love is the Law, love under will.

O.M. $7 = 4^\square$ A ∴ A ∴
Praemonstrator of the
Order of the R. C.

Given from the Collegium ad Spiritum Sanctum, Cefalù, Sicily, in the Seventeenth Year of the Aeon of Horus, the Sun being in 23° ♍ and the Moon in 14° ♓.

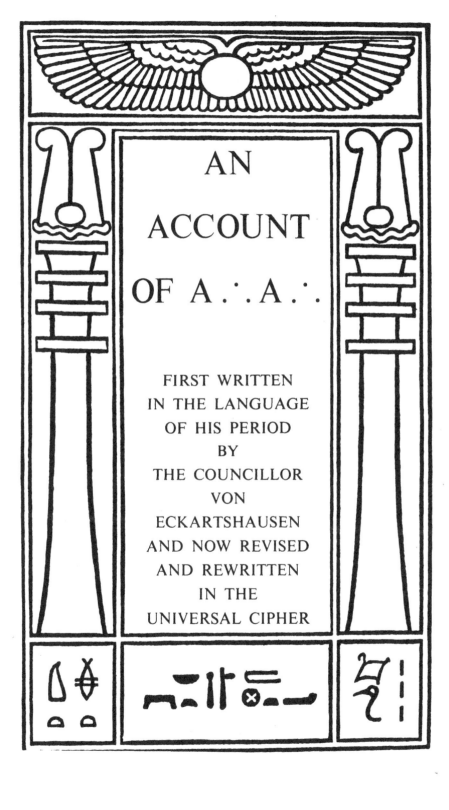

AN

ACCOUNT

OF A∴A∴

FIRST WRITTEN
IN THE LANGUAGE
OF HIS PERIOD
BY
THE COUNCILLOR
VON
ECKARTSHAUSEN
AND NOW REVISED
AND REWRITTEN
IN THE
UNIVERSAL CIPHER

A ∴ A ∴

Official Publication in Class C

Issued by Order:
D.D.S. $7° = 4°$
O.S.V. $6° = 5°$
N.S.F. $5° = 6°$

The Sign of Silence
(Harpocrates)

AN ACCOUNT OF
A ∴ A ∴

It is necessary, my dear brothers, to give you a clear idea of the interior Order; of that illuminated community which is scattered throughout the world, but which is governed by one truth and united in one spirit.

This community possesses a School, in which all who thirst for knowledge are instructed by the Spirit of Wisdom itself; and all the mysteries of nature are preserved in this school for the children of light. Perfect knowledge of nature and of humanity is taught in this school. It is from her that all truths penetrate into the world; she is the school of all who search for wisdom, and it is in this community alone that truth and the explanation of all mystery are to be found. It is the most hidden of communities, yet it contains members from many circles; nor is there any Centre of Thought whose activity is not due to the presence of one of ourselves. From all time there has been an exterior school based on the interior one, of which it is but the outer expression. From all time, therefore, there has been a hidden assembly, a society of the Elect, of those who sought for and had capacity for light, and this interior society was the Axle of the R.O.T.A. All that any external order possesses in symbol, ceremony, or rite is the letter expressive outwardly of that spirit of truth which dwelleth in the interior Sanctuary. Nor is the contradiction of the exterior any bar to the harmony of the interior.

Hence this Sanctuary, composed of members widely scattered indeed but united by the bonds of perfect love, has been occupied from the earliest ages in building the grand Temple (through the evolution of humanity) by which the reign of L.V.X. will be manifest. This society is in the communion of those who have most capacity for light; they are united in truth, and their Chief is the Light of the World himself, V.V.V.V.V., the One Anointed in Light, the single teacher for the human race, the Way, the Truth, and the Life.

The interior Order was formed immediately after the first perception of man's wider heritage had dawned upon the first of the adepts; it received from the Masters at first-hand the revelation of the means by which humanity could be raised to its rights and delivered from its misery. It received the primitive charge of all revelation and mystery; it received the key of true science, both divine and natural.

But as men multiplied, the frailty of man necessitated an exterior society which veiled the interior one, and concealed the spirit and the truth in the letter, because many people were not capable of comprehending great interior truth. Therefore, interior truths were wrapped in external and perceptible ceremonies, so that men, by the perception of the outer which is the symbol of the interior, might by degrees be enabled safely to approach the interior spiritual truths.

But the inner truth has always been confided to him who in his day had the most capacity for illumination, and he became the sole guardian of the original Trust, as High Priest of the Sanctuary.

When it became necessary that interior truths should be enfolded in exterior ceremony and symbol, on account of the real weakness of men who were not capable of hearing the Light of Light, then exterior worship began. It was, however, always the type or symbol of the interior, that is to say, the symbol of the true and Secret Sacrament.

The external worship would never have been separated from interior revel but for the weakness of man, which tends too easily to forget the spirit in the letter; but the Masters are vigilant to note in every nation those who are able to receive light, and such persons are employed as agents to spread the light according to man's capacity and to revivify the dead letter.

Through these instruments the interior truths of the Sanctuary were taken into every nation, and modified symbolically according to their customs, capacity for instruction, climate, and receptiveness. So that the external types of every religion, worship, ceremonies and Sacred Books in general have more or less clearly, as their object of instruction, the interior truths of the Sanctuary, by which man will be conducted to the universal knowledge of the one Absolute Truth.

The more the external worship of a people has remained united with the spirit of esoteric truth, the purer its religion; but the wider the difference between the symbolic letter and the invisible truth, the more imperfect has become the religion. Finally, it may be, the external form has entirely parted from its inner truth, so that ceremonial observances without soul or life have remained alone.

In the midst of all this, truth reposes inviolable in the inner Sanctuary.

Faithful to the spirit of truth, the members of the interior Order live in silence, but in real activity.

Yet, besides their secret holy work, they have from time to time decided upon political strategic action.

Thus, when the earth was nigh utterly corrupt by reason of the Great Sorcery, the Brethren sent Mohammed to bring freedom to mankind by the sword.

This being but partially a success, they raised up one Luther to teach freedom of thought. Yet this freedom soon turned into a heavier bondage than before.

Then the Brethren delivered unto man the knowledge of nature, and the keys thereof; yet this also was prevented by the Great Sorcery.

Now then finally in nameless ways, as one of our Brethren hath it now in mind to declare, have they raised up One to deliver unto men the keys of Spiritual Knowledge, and by His work shall He be judged.

This interior community of light is the reunion of all those capable of receiving light, and it is known as the Communion of Saints, the primitive receptacle for all strength and truth, confided to it from all time.

By it the agents of L.V.X. were formed in every age, passing from the interior to the exterior, and communicating spirit and life to the dead letter, as already said.

This illuminated community is the true school of L.V.X.; it has its Chair, its Doctors; it possesses a rule for students; it has forms and objects for study.

It has also its degrees for successive development to greater altitudes.

This school of wisdom has been for ever most secretly hidden from the world, because it is invisible and submissive solely to illuminated government.

It has never been exposed to the accidents of time and to the weakness of man, because only the most capable were chosen for it, and those who selected made no error.

Through this school were developed the germs of all the sublime sciences, which were first received by external schools, then clothed in other forms, and hence degenerated.

According to time and circumstances, the society of sages communicated unto the exterior societies their symbolic hieroglyphs, in order to attract man to the great truths of their Sanctuary.

But all exterior societies subsist only by virtue of this interior one. As soon as external societies wish to transform a temple of wisdom into a political edifice, the interior society retires and leaves only the letter without the spirit. It is thus that secret external societies of wisdom were nothing but hieroglyphic screens, the truth remaining inviolable in the Sanctuary so that she might never be profaned.

In this interior society man finds wisdom and with her All—not the wisdom of this world, which is but scientific knowledge, which revolves round the outside but never touches the centre (in which is contained all strength), but true wisdom, understanding and knowledge, reflections of the supreme illumination.

All disputes, all controversies, all the things belonging to the false cares of this world, fruitless discussions, useless germs of opinions which spread the seeds of disunion, all error, schisms, and systems are banished. Neither calumny nor scandal is known. Every man is honoured. Love alone reigns.

We must not, however, imagine that this society resembles any secret society, meeting at certain times, choosing leaders and members, united by special objects. All societies, be what they may, can but come after this interior illuminated circle. This society knows none of the formalities which belong to the outer rings, the work of man. In this kingdom of power all outward forms cease.

L.V.X. is the Power always present. The greatest man of his time, the chief himself, does not always know all the members, but the moment when it is necessary that he should accomplish any object, he finds them in the world with certainty ready to his hand.

This community has no outside barriers. He who may be chosen is as the first; he presents himself among the others without presumption, and he is received by the others without jealousy.

If it be necessary that real members should meet together, they find and recognise each other with perfect certainty.

No disguise can be used, neither hypocrisy nor dissimulation could hide the characteristic qualities which distinguish the members of this society. All illusion is gone, and things appear in their true form.

No one member can choose another; unanimous choice is required. Though not all men are called, many of the called are chosen, and that as soon as they become fit for entrance.

Any man can look for the entrance, and any man who is within can teach another to seek for it; but only he who is fit can arrive within.

Unprepared men occasion disorder in a community, and disorder is not compatible with the Sanctuary. Thus it is impossible to profane the Sanctuary, since admission is not formal but real.

Worldly intelligence seeks this Sanctuary in vain; fruitless also will be the efforts of malice to penetrate these great mysteries; all is indecipherable to him who is not ripe; he can see nothing, read nothing in the interior.

He who is fit is joined to the chain, perhaps often where he thought least likely, and at a point of which he knew nothing himself.

To become fit should be the sole effort of him who seeks wisdom.

But there are methods by which fitness is attained, for in this holy communion is the primitive storehouse of the most ancient and original science of the human race, with the primitive mysteries also of all science. It is the unique and really illuminated community which is absolutely in possession of the key to all mystery, which knows the centre and source of all nature. It is a society which unites superior strength to its own, and counts its members from more than one world. It is the society whose members form the republic of Genius, the Regent Mother of the whole World.

[The revisers wish to acknowledge gratefully the translation of Madame de Steiger, which they have freely quoted.]

[The original Rider and Company edition referred to above has been out of print for many years and used copies are hard to come by. A new paperback edition is dated 1952, published by S.R.I.A., New York, and they give me to understand it will be kept in print indefinitely. —Ed.]

LIBER

XIII

VEL
GRADUUM
MONTIS
ABIEGNI

A SYLLABUS
OF THE STEPS
UPON THE PATH

A ∴ A ∴ Publication in Class D

Imprimatur:
D.D.S. 7° = 4° Praemonstrator
O.S.V. 6° = 5° Imperator
N.S.F. 5° = 6° Cancellarius

51. Let not the failure and the pain turn aside the worshippers. The foundations of the pyramid were hewn in the living rock ere sunset; did the king weep at dawn that the crown of the pyramid was yet unquarried in the distant land?

52. There was also an humming-bird that spake unto the horned cerastes, and prayed him for poison. And the great snake of Khem the Holy One, the royal Uraeus serpent, answered him and said:

53. I sailed over the sky of Nu in the car called Millions-of-Years, and I saw not any creature upon Seb that was equal to me. The venom of my fang is the inheritance of my father, and of my father's father; and how shall I give it unto thee? Live thou and thy children as I and my fathers have lived, even unto an hundred millions of generations, and it may be that the mercy of the Mighty Ones may bestow upon thy children a drop of the poison of eld.

54. Then the humming-bird was afflicted in his spirit, and he flew unto the flowers, and it was as if naught had been spoken between them. Yet in a little while a serpent struck him that he died.

55. But an Ibis that meditated upon the bank of Nile the beautiful god listened and heard. And he laid aside his Ibis ways, and became as a serpent saying Peradventure in an hundred millions of millions of generations of my children, they shall attain to a drop of the poison of the fang of the Exalted One.

56. And behold! ere the moon waxed thrice he became an Uraeus serpent, and the poison of the fang was established in him and his seed even for ever and for ever.

LIBER LXV, cap. V

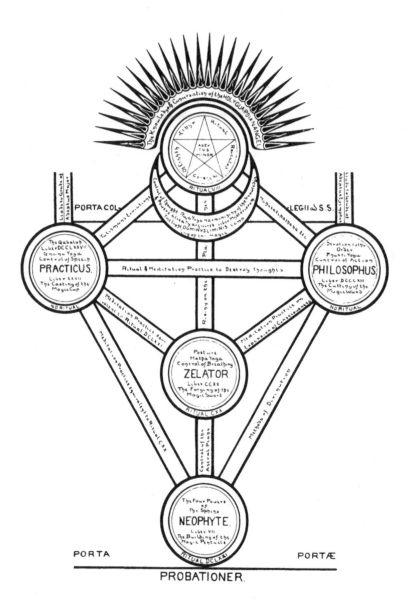

The Slopes of Abiegnus

·LIBER XIII

1. **The Probationer.** His duties are laid down in Paper A, Class D. Being *without,* they are vague and general. He receives *Liber LXI* and *LXV*.

(Certain Probationers are admitted after six months or more to Ritual XXVIII.)

At the end of the Probation he passes Ritual DCLXXI, which constitutes him a Neophyte.

2. **The Neophyte.** His duties are laid down in Paper B, Class D. He receives *Liber VII*.

Examination in *Liber O,* caps. I–IV, Theoretical and Practical.

Examination in The Four Powers of the Sphinx. Practical.

Four tests are set.

Further, he builds up the magic Pentacle.

Finally he passes Ritual CXX, which constitutes him a Zelator.

3. **The Zelator.** His duties are laid down in Paper C, Class D. He receives *Liber CCXX, XXVII,* and *DCCCXIII*.

Examinations in Posture and Control of Breath. Practical.

Further, he is given two meditation-practices corresponding to the two rituals DCLXXI and CXX.

(Examination is only in the knowledge of, and some little practical acquaintance with, these meditations. The complete results, if attained, would confer a much higher grade.)

Further, he forges the magic Sword.

No ritual admits to the grade of Practicus, which is conferred by authority when the task of the Zelator is accomplished.

4. **The Practicus.** His duties are laid down in Paper D, Class D.

Instruction and Examination in the Qabalah and *Liber DCCLXXVII.*

Instruction in Philosophical Meditation (Gnana-Yoga).

Examination in some one mode of divination: *e.g.,* Geomancy, Astrology, the Tarot. Theoretical. He is given a meditation-practice on Expansion of Consciousness.

He is given a meditation-practice in the destruction of thoughts.

Instruction and Examination in Control of Speech. Practical.

Further, he casts the magic Cup.

No ritual admits to the grade of Philosophus, which is conferred by authority when the Task of the Practicus is accomplished.

5. **The Philosophus.** His duties are laid down in Paper E, Class D.

He practises Devotion to the Order.

Instruction and Examination in Methods of Meditation by Devotion (Bhakti-Yoga).

Instruction and Examination in Construction and Consecration of Talismans, and in Evocation.

Theoretical and Practical.

Examination in Rising on the Planes (*Liber O,* caps. V, VI). Practical.

He is given a meditation-practice on the Senses, and the Sheaths of the Self, and the Practice called Mahasati-patthana.

(See *The Sword of Song, Science and Buddhism.*)

Instruction and Examination in Control of Action.

Further, he cuts the Magic Wand.

Finally, the Title of Dominus Liminis is conferred upon him.

He is given meditation-practices on the Control of Thought, and is instructed in Raja-Yoga.

He receives *Liber Mysteriorum* and obtains a perfect understanding of the Formulae of Initiation.

He meditates upon the diverse knowledge and power that he has acquired, and harmonises it perfectly.

Further, he lights the Magic Lamp.

At last, Ritual VIII admits him to the grade of Adeptus Minor.

6. **The Adeptus Minor.** His duty is laid down in Paper F, Class D.

It is to follow out the instruction given in the Vision of the Eighth Aethyr for the attainment of the Knowledge and Conversation of the Holy Guardian Angel.

Note: This is in truth the sole task; the others are useful only as adjuvants to and preparations for the One Work.

Moreover, once this task has been accomplished, there is no more need of human help or instruction; for by this alone may the highest attainment be reached.

All these grades are indeed but convenient landmarks,

not necessarily significant. A person who had attained them all might be immeasurably the inferior of one who had attained none of them; it is Spiritual Experience alone that counts in Result; the rest is but Method.

Yet it is important to possess knowledge and power, provided that it be devoted wholly to that One Work.

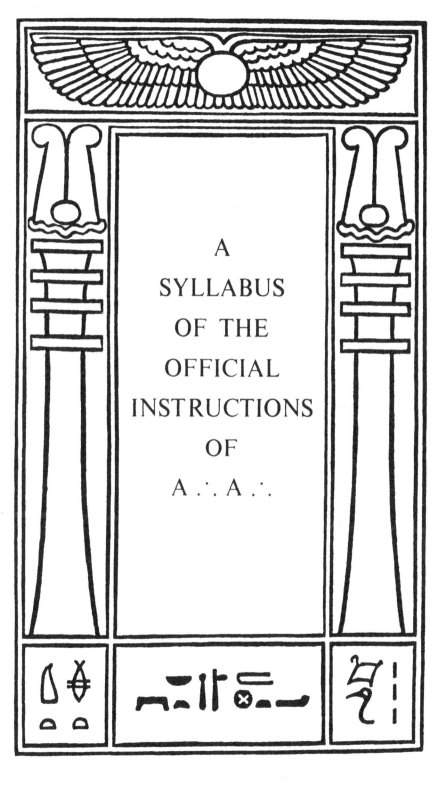

A

SYLLABUS

OF THE

OFFICIAL

INSTRUCTIONS

OF

A∴ A∴

A SYLLABUS OF THE
OFFICIAL INSTRUCTIONS
OF A ∴ A ∴

The publications of the A ∴ A ∴ divide themselves into four classes.

Class A consists of books of which may be changed not so much as the style of a letter: that is, they represent the utterance of an Adept entirely beyond the criticism of even the Visible Head of the Organization.

Class B consists of books or essays which are the result of ordinary scholarship, enlightened and earnest.

Class C consists of matter which is to be regarded rather as suggestive than anything else.

Class D consists of the Official Rituals and Instructions.

Some publications are composite, and pertain to more than one class.

CLASS A PUBLICATIONS

Liber I: Liber B Vel Magi.

This is an account of the Grade of Magus, the highest grade which it is ever possible to manifest in any way whatever upon this plane. Or so it is said by the Masters of the Temple.

Liber VII: Liber Liberi Vel Lapidis Lazvli, Advmbratio Kabbalae Aegyptiorvm Svb Figvra VII.

Being the Voluntary Emancipation of a certain Exempt Adept from his Adeptship. These are the Birth Words of a Master of the Temple. The nature of this book is sufficiently explained by its title. Its seven chapters are referred to the seven planets in the following order: Mars, Saturn, Jupiter, Sol, Mercury, Luna, Venus.

Liber X: Liber Porta Lucis.

This book is an account of the sending forth of the Master by the A ∴ A ∴ and an explanation of his mission.

Liber XXVII: Liber Trigrammaton.

Being a book of Trigrams of the Mutations of the Tao with the Yin and the Yang. An account of the cosmic process: corresponding to the Stanzas of Dzyan in another system.

Liber LXV: Liber Cordis Cincti Serpente.

An account of the relations of the Aspirant with his Holy Guardian Angel. This book is given to Probationers, as the attainment of the Knowledge and Conversation of the Holy Guardian Angel is the Crown of the Outer College. Similarly *Liber VII* is given to Neophytes, as the grade of Master of the Temple is the next resting-place, and *Liber CCXX* to Zelator, since that carries him to the highest of all possible grades. *Liber XXVII* is given to the Practicus, as in this book is the ultimate foundation of the highest theoretical Qabalah, and *Liber DCCCXIII* to the Philosophus, as it is the foundation of the highest practical Qabalah.

Liber LXVI: Liber Stellae Rubeae.

A secret ritual, the Heart of IAO-OAI, delivered unto V.V.V.V.V. for his use in a certain matter of *Liber Legis*, and written down under the figure LXVI. This book is sufficiently described by the title.

Liber XC: Liber Tzaddi Vel Hamus Hermeticus Sub Figura XC.

An account of Initiation, and an indication as to those who are suitable for the same.

Liber CLVI: Liber Cheth Vel Vallum Abiegni Sub Figura CLVI.

This book is a perfect account of the task of the Exempt Adept, considered under the symbols of a particular plane, not the intellectual.

Liber CCXX: Liber L Vel Legis Sub Figura CCXX as delivered by LXXVIII unto DCLXVI.

This book is the foundation of the New Aeon, and thus of the whole of our Work.

Liber CCXXXI: Liber Arcanorum τῶν Atv τοῦ Tahvti Quas Vidit Asar in Amennti Sub Figura CCXXXI Liber Carcerorum τῶν Qliphoth cum suis Geniis. Adduntur Sigilla et Nomina Eorum.

This is an account of the cosmic process so far as it is indicated by the Tarot Trumps.

Liber CCCLXX: Liber A'ash Vel Capricorni Pneumatici Sub Figura CCCLXX.

Contains the true secret of all practical magick.

Liber CD: Liber Tav Vel Kabbalae Trium Literarum Sub Figura CD.

A graphic interpretation of the Tarot on the plane of initiation.

Liber DCCCXIII: Vel Ararita Sub Figura DLXX.

This book is an account of the Hexagram and the method of reducing it to the Unity, and Beyond.

CLASS A–B

Liber CCCCXVIII: Liber XXX Aervm Vel Saeculi, Being of the Angels of the thirty Aethyrs the Vision and the Voice.

Besides being the classical account of the thirty

Aethyrs and a model of all visions, the cries of the Angels should be regarded as accurate, and the doctrine of the function of the Great White Brotherhood understood as the foundation of the Aspiration of the Adept. The account of the Master of the Temple should in particular be taken as authentic.

The instruction in the 8th Aethyr pertains to Class D, *i.e.,* it is an Official Ritual, and the same remarks apply to the account of the proper method of invoking Aethyrs given in the 18th Aethyr.

CLASSES A and B

Liber DCCCCLXIII: ΘΗΣΑΥΡΟΥ ΕΙΔΩΛΩΝ.
Only the short note pertains to Class A.

CLASS B

Liber VI: Liber O Vel Manus et Sagittae.
The instructions given in this book are too loose to find place in the Class D publications. Instructions given for elementary study of the Qabalah, Assumption of God forms, Vibration of Divine Names, the Rituals of Pentagram and Hexagram, and their uses in protection and invocation, a method of attaining astral visions so-called, and an instruction in the practice called Rising on the Planes.

Liber IX: Liber E Vel Exercitiorum.
This book instructs the aspirant in the necessity of keeping a record. Suggests methods of testing physical clairvoyance. Gives instruction in Asana, Pranayama and Dharana, and advises the application of tests to the physical body, in order that the student may thoroughly understand his own limitations.

Liber XXX: Liber Librae.

An elementary course of morality suitable for the average man.

Liber LVIII.

This is an article on the Qabalah in *The Temple of Solomon the King, The Equinox,* V.

Liber LXI: Liber Causae. The Preliminary Lection, including the History Lection.

Explains the actual history of the origin of the present movement. Its statements are accurate in the ordinary sense of the word. The object of the book is to discount Mythopoeia.

Liber LXIV: Liber Israfel, formerly called *Anubis.*

An instruction in a suitable method of preaching.

Liber LXXVIII.

A description of the Cards of the Tarot with their attributions, including a method of divination by their use.

Liber LXXXIV: Vel Chanokh.

A brief abstraction of *The Symbolic Representation of the Universe* derived by Dr. John Dee through the Scrying of Sir Edward Kelly. Its publication is at present incomplete.

Liber XCVI: Liber Gaias.

A handbook of Geomancy. Gives a simple and fairly satisfactory system of Geomancy.

Liber D: Liber Sepher Sephiroth.

A dictionary of Hebrew words arranged according to their numerical value.

Liber DXXXVI: ΒΑΤΡΑΧΟΦΡΕΝΟΒΟΟΚΟΣΜΟΜΑΧΙΑ.

An instruction in expansion of the field of the mind.

Liber DCCLXXVII: Vel Prolegomena Symbolica Ad Systemam Sceptico-Mysticae Viae Explicandae, Fundamen-

tum Hieroglyphicum Sanctissimorum Scientiae Summae.

A tentative table of correspondences between various religious symbols.

Liber DCCCLXVIII: Liber Viarum Viae.

A graphic account of magical powers classified under the Tarot trumps.

Liber CMXIII: Liber Viae Memoriae. תישארב

Gives methods for attaining the magical memory or memory of past lives, and an insight into the function of the aspirant in this present life.

Class C

Liber XXXIII.

An account of A ∴ A ∴ first written in the language of his period by the Councillor Von Eckartshausen, and now revised and rewritten in the Universal Cipher.

An elementary suggestive account of the work of the Order in its relation to the average man. The preliminary paper of M ∴ M ∴ M ∴ may be classed with this.

Liber XLI: Thien Tao (in *Konx Om Pax*).

An advanced study of Attainment by the method of equilibrium on the ethical plane.

Liber LV: The Chymical Jousting of Brother Perardua.

An account of the Magical and Mystic Path in the language of Alchemy.

Liber LIX: Across the Gulf.

A fantastic account of a previous incarnation. Its principal interest is that its story of the overthrowing of Isis by Osiris may help the reader to understand the meaning of the overthrowing of Osiris by Horus in the present Aeon.

Liber LXVII: The Sword of Song.

A critical study of various philosophies. An account of Buddhism.

Liber XCV : The Wake World (in *Konx Om Pax*).

A poetical allegory of the relations of the soul and the Holy Guardian Angel.

Liber CXLVIII : The Soldier and the Hunchback.

An essay on the method of equilibrium on the intellectual plane.

Liber CXCVII : The High History of Good Sir Palamedes the Saracen Knight and of his following of the Questing Beast.

A poetic account of the Great Work, and enumeration of many obstacles.

Liber CCXLII : Aha!

An exposition in poetic language of several of the ways of attainment and the results obtained.

Liber CCCXXXIII : The Book of Lies falsely so-called.

This book deals with many matters on all planes of the very highest importance. It is an official publication for Babes of the Abyss, but is recommended even to beginners as highly suggestive. Its chapters XXV, XXXVI and XLIV are in Class D.

Liber CCCXXXV : Adonis.

This gives an account in poetic language of the struggle of the human and divine elements in the consciousness of man, giving their harmony following upon the victory of the latter.

Liber CDLXXIV : Liber Os Abysmi Vel DAATH.

An instruction in a purely intellectual method of entering the Abyss.

Liber DCCCLX : John St. John.

A model of what a magical record should be, so far as accurate analysis and fullness of description are concerned.

Liber MMCMXI : A Note on Genesis.

A model of Qabalistic ratiocination.

Class D

Liber III: Liber Jugorum.

An instruction for the control of speech, action and thought.

Liber VIII. See *CCCCXVIII.*

Liber XI: Liber N V.

An instruction for attaining Nuit.

Liber XIII: Graduum Montis Abiegni.

An account of the task of the Aspirant from Probationer to Adept.

Liber XVI: Liber Turris Vel Domus Dei.

An instruction for attainment by the direct destruction of thoughts as they arise in the mind.

Liber XVII: Liber I A O.

Gives three methods of attainment through a willed series of thoughts. This book has not been published. It is the active form of *Liber H H H.* The article *Energized Enthusiasm* is an adumbration of this book.

Liber XXV.

This is the chapter called *The Star Ruby* in *The Book of Lies.* It is an improved form of the "lesser" ritual of the Pentagram.

Liber XXVIII: Liber Septem Regum Sanctorum.

Has not been published. It is a ritual of Initiation bestowed on certain selected Probationers.

Liber XXXVI: The Star Sapphire.

Is chapter XXXVI of *The Book of Lies*, giving an improved ritual of the Hexagram.

Liber XLIV: The Mass of the Phoenix.

This is chapter XLIV of *The Book of Lies.* An instruction in a simple and exoteric form of Eucharist.

Liber C: Liber כף

Has not been, and at present will not be, published.

Liber CXX: Liber Cadaveris.
The Ritual of Initiation of a Zelator.
Liber CLXXV: Astarte Vel Liber Berylli.
An instruction in attainment by the method of devotion.
Liber CLXXXV: Liber Collegii Sancti.
Being the tasks of the Grades and their Oaths proper to *Liber XIII.* This is the official Paper of the various grades. It includes the Task and Oath of a Probationer.
Liber CC: Resh Vel Helios.
An instruction for adorations of the Sun four times daily, with the object of composing the mind to meditation and of regularizing the practices.
Liber CCVI: Liber R V Vel Spiritus.
Full instruction in Pranayama.
Liber CCCXLI: Liber H H H.
Gives three methods of attainment through a willed series of thoughts.
Liber CCCCXII: A Vel Armorum.
An instruction for the preparation of the Elemental Instruments.
Liber CDLI: Liber Siloam.
Not yet published. A direct method of inducing trance.
Liber DLV: Liber H A D.
An instruction for attaining Hadit.
Liber DCLXXI: Liber Pyramidos.
The ritual of the initiation of a Neophyte. It includes sub-rituals numbered from 672 to 676.
Liber DCCCXXXI: Liber I O D, formerly called *Vesta.*
An instruction giving three methods of reducing the manifold consciousness to the Unity.
Liber . . . : Liber Collegii Interni.
Not yet published.

A NOTE EXPLAINING WHY EACH NUMBER
HAS BEEN GIVEN TO EACH BOOK

LIBER

I   I is the number of the Magus in the Tarot.

III   Refers to the threefold method given, and to the Triangle as a binding force.

VII   Refers to the 7 chapters, and to the fact that the number 7 is peculiarly suitable to the subject of the Book.

VIII   The Tarot card numbered 8, the Charioteer, the bearer of the Holy Graal, represents the Holy Guardian Angel.

IX   Refers to Yesod. The foundation, because the elementary practices recommended in the book are the foundation of all the work.

X   Porta Lucis, the Gate of Light, is one of the titles of Malkuth, whose number is X.

XI   A concentration of the title N V, whose value is 56, and 6 and 5 are 11. (See *CCXX*, I: i and II: i.)

XIII   The number of Achad = Unity, and the title is perhaps intended to show that all paths of attainment are essential.

XVI   The key of the Tarot numbered XVI is the Lightning Struck Tower.

XVII   I A O adds up to 17.

XXV   The square of 5, this being a ritual of the Pentagram.

XXVII   The number of permutations of 3 things

taken 3 at a time, and (of course) the cube of 3.

XXX 30 is the letter Lamed, which is Justice in the Tarot, referred to Libra.

XXXIII This number was given on Masonic grounds.

XXXVI The square of 6, this book being the ritual of the Hexagram.

XLIV From דם blood, because blood is sacrificed, also because the God Adored is Horus, who gave 44 as his special number. See *The Equinox*, VII, 376.

LV The mystic number of Malkuth and of נה ornament; a number generally suitable to the subject of the book.

LVIII חן Grace, a secret title of the Qabalah. See *Sepher Sephiroth*.

LIX

LXI See *Sepher Sephiroth*. The allusion is to the fact that this book forms an introduction to the series.

LXIV A number of Mercury.

LXV The number of Adonai.

LXVI The sum of the first 11 numbers. This book relates to Magic, whose Key is 11.

LXVII The number of זין a sword.

LXXVIII The number of cards in the Tarot pack.

LXXXIV Enumeration of the name Enoch.

XC *Tzaddi* means a 'fish-hook'. "I will make you fishers of men."

XCV The number of מלכה "queen," attributed to Malkuth.

XCVI The total number of points in the 16 figures.

C   Enumeration of the letter Kappa spelt in full. K and Φ are the initials of magical instruments referred to in the text.

CXX   See Rosicrucian Symbolism.

CXLVIII   מאזנים The Balances.

CLVI   Babalon, to whom the book refers. See *Sepher Sephiroth*.

CLXXV   The number of Venus or Astarte.

CLXXXV

CXCVII   Number of Z O O N, "Beast."

CC   The number of ד the Sun.

CCVI   The number of R V, referred to in the text.

CCXX   The number of the Verses in the three chapters of the Book. It has, however, an enormous amount of symbolism; in particular it combines the 10 Sephiroths and 22 Paths; 78 is אי ואם. For 666 vide *Sepher Sephiroth*.

CCXXXI   Sum of the numbers [0 + 1 + ... + 20 + 21] printed on the Tarot Trumps.

CCXLII   "Aha!" spelt in full.

CCCXXXIII   The number of Choronzon.

CCCXXXV   The Numeration of Adonis in Greek.

CCCXLI   The Sum of the 3 Mothers of the Alphabet.

CCCLXX   עץ Creation.

CD   From the large Tau ת in the diagram.

CDXII   Numeration of בית Beth, the letter of the Magus of the Tarot, whose weapons are here described.

CDXVIII   Vide *Sepher Sephiroth*. Used for this book because the final revelation is the Lord of the Aeon.

CDLI	The number of שילעם Siloam.
CDLXXIV	The number of Daath.
D	The number of ὁ ἀριθμός the Greek word for Number.
DXXXVI	The number of מכלות the sphere of the Fixed Stars.
DLV	H a d fully expanded; thus דלת, אלף, הה; compare 11 where N u is fully contracted.
DLXX	
DCLXXI	From תרעא, the Gate, and the spelling in full of the name Adonai.
DCCLXXVII	See *Sepher Sephiroth.*
DCCCVIII	The number of the name נחשן.
DCCCXI	The number of I A O in Greek.
DCCCXIII	See *Sepher Sephiroth.*
DCCCXXXI	φαλλός.
DCCCLX	The number of Ἰων "John."
DCCCLXVIII	נתיבות Paths.
CMXIII	*Berashith,* the Beginning, spelt backwards in the title to illustrate the development of the magical memory.
CMLXIII	Achad spelt fully; see *Sepher Sephiroth.*
MMDCDXI	*Berashith* spelt with capital B as in Genesis 1: i.

COURSE I

GENERAL READING

Section 1. Books for serious study:

Liber CCXX: Liber L vel Legis: The Book of the Law. This book is the foundation of the New Aeon, and thus of the whole of our Work.

The Equinox, vol. I, nos. I–X. The standard Work of Reference in all occult matters. The Encyclopaedia of Initiation.

Liber ABA : Book 4. A General Account in elementary terms of magical and mystical powers. In four parts: (1) Mysticism. (2) Magical Theory. (3) Magical Practice. (4) The Law.

Liber II : The Message of the Master Therion, which explains the essence of the new law in a very simple manner.

Liber DCCCXXXVII : The Law of Liberty, which is a further explanation of *The Book of the Law* in reference to certain ethical problems.

Collected Works of A. Crowley. These works contain many mystical and magical secrets, both stated clearly in prose, and woven into the Robe of sublimest poesy.

The Yi King. (S. B. E. Series, Oxford University Press.) The "Classic of Changes"; gives the initiated Chinese system of Magick.

The Tao Teh King. (S. B. E. Series.) Gives the initiated Chinese system of Mysticism.

Tannhäuser by A. Crowley. An allegorical drama concerning the Progress of the Soul; the Tannhäuser story slightly remodelled.

The Upanishads. (S. B. E. Series.) The Classical Basis of Vedantism, the best-known form of Hindu Mysticism.

The Bhagavad-Gita. A dialogue in which Krishna, the Hindu "Christ," expounds a system of Attainment.

The Voice of the Silence by H. P. Blavatsky, with an elaborate commentary by Frater O.M.

The Goetia. The most intelligible of the mediaeval rituals of Evocation. Contains also the favorite Invocation of the Master Therion.

The Shiva Sanhita. A famous Hindu treatise on certain physical practices.

The Hathayoga Pradipika. Similar to *The Shiva Sanhita.*

Erdmann's *History of Philosophy.* A compendious

account of philosophy from the earliest times. Most valuable as a general education of the mind.

The Spiritual Guide of Molinos. A simple manual of Christian mysticism.

The Star of the West. (Captain Fuller.) An introduction to the study of the works of Aleister Crowley.

The Dhammapada. (S. B. E. Series, Oxford University Press.) The best of the Buddhist classics.

The Questions of King Milinda. (S. B. E. Series.) Technical points of Buddhist dogma, illustrated by dialogues.

Liber DCCLXXVII: Vel Prolegomena Symbolica Ad Systemam Sceptico-Mysticae Viae Explicandae, Fundamentum Hieroglyphicum Sanctissimorum Scientiae Summae. A complete Dictionary of the Correspondences of all magical elements, re-printed with extensive additions, making it the only standard comprehensive book of reference ever published. It is to the language of Occultism what Webster or Murray is to the English language.

Varieties of Religious Experience. (James.) Valuable as showing the uniformity of mystical attainment.

Kabbala Denudata, von Rosenroth; also *The Kabbalah Unveiled* by S. L. Mathers. A text of the Qabalah, with commentary. A good elementary introduction to the subject.

Konx Om Pax. Four invaluable treatises and a preface on mysticism and Magick.

The Pistis Sophia. An admirable introduction to the study of Gnosticism.

The Oracles of Zoroaster. An invaluable collection of precepts mystical and magical.

The Dream of Scipio by Cicero. Excellent for its Vision and its Philosophy.

The Golden Verses of Pythagoras by Fabre d'Olivet. An interesting study of the exoteric doctrines of this Master.

The Divine Pymander by Hermes Trismegistus. Invaluable as bearing on the Gnostic Philosophy.

The Secret Symbols of the Rosicrucians, reprint of Franz Hartmann. An invaluable compendium.

Scrutinium Chymicum by Michael Maier. One of the best treatises on alchemy.

Science and the Infinite by Sidney Klein. One of the best essays written in recent years.

Two Essays on the Worship of Priapus by Richard Payne Knight. Invaluable to all students.

The Golden Bough by J. G. Frazer. The Text-Book of Folk Lore. Invaluable to all students.

The Age of Reason by Thomas Paine. Excellent, though elementary, as a corrective to superstition.

Rivers of Life by General Forlong. An invaluable text-book of old systems of initiation.

Three Dialogues by Bishop Berkeley. The classic of subjective idealism.

Essays of David Hume. The Classic of Academic Scepticism.

First Principles by Herbert Spencer. The Classic of Agnosticism.

Prolegomena by Emanuel Kant. The best introduction to Metaphysics.

The Canon. The best text-book of applied Qabalah.

The Fourth Dimension by H. Hinton. The text-book on this subject.

The Essays of Thomas Henry Huxley. Masterpieces of philosophy, as of prose.

The object of this course of reading is to familiarize the student with all that has been said by the Great Masters in every time and country. He should make a critical examination of them; not so much with the idea of discovering where truth lies, for he cannot do this except by virtue of his own spiritual experience, but rather to discover the essential harmony in those varied works. He should be on his guard against partisanship with a favourite author. He should familiarize himself thoroughly with the method of mental equilibrium, endeavoring to contradict any statement soever, although it may be apparently axiomatic.

The general object of this course, besides that already stated, is to assure sound education in occult matters, so that when spiritual illumination comes it may find a well built temple. Where the mind is strongly biased towards any special theory, the result of an illumination is often to inflame that portion of the mind which is thus over-developed, with the result that the aspirant, instead of becoming an Adept, becomes a bigot and fanatic.

The A ∴ A ∴ does not offer examination in this course, but recommends these books as the foundation of a library.

Section 2. Other books, principally fiction, of a generally suggestive and helpful kind:

Zanoni by Sir Edward Bulwer Lytton. Valuable for its facts and suggestions about mysticism.

A Strange Story by Sir Edward Bulwer Lytton. Valuable for its facts and suggestions about Magick.

The Blossom and the Fruit by Mabel Collins. Valuable for its account of the Path.

Petronius Arbiter. Valuable for those who have wit to understand it.

The Golden Ass by Apuleius. Valuable for those who have wit to understand it.

Le Comte de Gabalis. Valuable for its hints of those things which it mocks.

The Rape of the Lock by Alexander Pope. Valuable for its account of elementals.

Undine by de la Motte Fouqué. Valuable as an account of elementals.

Black Magic by Marjorie Bowen. An intensely interesting story of sorcery.

La Peau de Chagrin by Honoré de Balzac. A magnificent magical allegory.

Number Nineteen by Edgar Jepson. An excellent tale of modern magic.

Dracula by Bram Stoker. Valuable for its account of legends concerning vampires.

Scientific Romances by H. Hinton. Valuable as an introduction to the study of the Fourth Dimension.

Alice in Wonderland by Lewis Carroll. Valuable to those who understand the Qabalah.

Alice Through the Looking Glass by Lewis Carroll. Valuable to those who understand the Qabalah.

The Hunting of the Snark by Lewis Carroll. Valuable to those who understand the Qabalah.

The Arabian Nights, translated by either Sir Richard Burton or John Payne. Valuable as a storehouse of oriental magick-lore.

Morte d'Arthur by Sir Thomas Mallory. Valuable as a storehouse of occidental magick-lore.

The Works of Francois Rabelais. Invaluable for Wisdom.

The Kasidah by Sir Richard Burton. Valuable as a summary of philosophy.

The Song Celestial by Sir Edwin Arnold. *The Bhagavad-Gita* in verse.

The Light of Asia by Sir Edwin Arnold. An account of the attainment of Gotama Buddha.

The Rosicrucians by Hargrave Jennings. Valuable to those who can read between the lines.

The Real History of the Rosicrucians by A. E. Waite. A good vulgar piece of journalism on the subject.

The Works of Arthur Machen. Most of these stories are of great magical interest.

The Writings of William O'Neill (Blake). Invaluable to all students.

The Shaving of Shagpat by George Meredith. An excellent allegory.

Lilith by George MacDonald. A superb tale of Magick.

La Bas by J. K. Huysmans. An account of the extravagances caused by the Sin-complex.

The Lore of Proserpine by Maurice Hewlett. A suggestive enquiry into the Hermetic Arcanum.

En Route by J. K. Huysmans. An account of the follies of Christian mysticism.

Sidonia the Sorceress by Wilhelm Meinhold; *The Amber Witch* by Wilhelm Meinhold. These two tales are highly informative.

Macbeth; Midsummer Night's Dream; The Tempest, by W. Shakespeare. Interesting for traditions treated.

Red Gauntlet by Sir Walter Scott. Also one or two other novels. Interesting for traditions treated.

Rob Roy by James Grant. Interesting for traditions treated.

The Magician by W. Somerset Maugham. An amusing hotch-pot of stolen goods.

The Bible, by various authors unknown. The Hebrew and Greek Originals are of Qabalistic value. It contains also many magical apologues, and recounts many tales of folklore and magical rites.

Kim by Rudyard Kipling. An admirable study of Eastern thought and life. Many other stories by this author are highly suggestive and informative.

For Mythology, as teaching correspondences:
Books of Fairy Tales generally.
Oriental Classics generally.
Sufi Poetry generally.
Greek and Latin Classics generally.
Scandinavian and Teutonic Sagas generally.
Celtic Folk-Lore generally.

This course is of general value to the beginner. While it is not to be taken, in all cases, too seriously, it will give him a general familiarity with mystical and magical tradition, create a deep interest in the subject, and suggest many helpful lines of thought.

It has been impossible to do more, in this list, than to suggest a fairly comprehensive course of reading.

SECTION II

THE BOOK

OF THE LAW

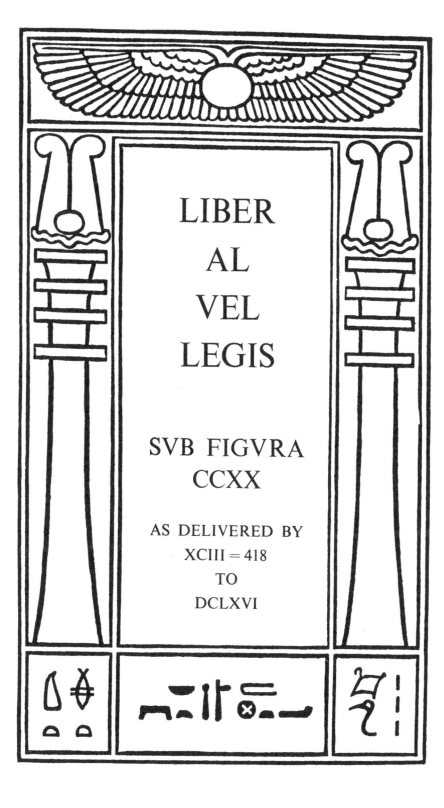

LIBER
AL
VEL
LEGIS

SVB FIGVRA
CCXX

AS DELIVERED BY
XCIII = 418
TO
DCLXVI

A ∴ A ∴ Publication in Class A
Imprimatur:

ꓘ ꓘ ꓘ

V.V.V.V.V.
N. Fra. A ∴ . A ∴ .
O.M. 7° = 4°
D.D.S. 7° = 4° Praemonstrator
O.S.V. 6° = 5° Imperator
I.M. 5° = 6° Cancellarius
Given at our College S.S. in the Mountain of
Abiegnus Sun in ≏ An. IX

LIBER AL VEL LEGIS

1. Had! The manifestation of Nuit.

2. The unveiling of the company of heaven.

3. Every man and every woman is a star.

4. Every number is infinite; there is no difference.

5. Help me, o warrior lord of Thebes, in my unveiling before the Children of men!

6. Be thou Hadit, my secret centre, my heart & my tongue!

7. Behold! it is revealed by Aiwass the minister of Hoor-paar-kraat.

8. The Khabs is in the Khu, not the Khu in the Khabs.

9. Worship then the Khabs, and behold my light shed over you!

10. Let my servants be few & secret: they shall rule the many & the known.

11. These are fools that men adore; both their Gods & their men are fools.

12. Come forth, o children, under the stars, & take your fill of love!

13. I am above you and in you. My ecstasy is in yours. My joy is to see your joy.

14. Above, the gemmèd azure is
    The naked splendour of Nuit;
  She bends in ecstasy to kiss
    The secret ardours of Hadit.
  The wingèd globe, the starry blue,
  Are mine, O Ankh-af-na-khonsu!

15. Now ye shall know that the chosen priest & apostle of infinite space is the prince-priest the Beast; and in his woman called the Scarlet Woman is all power given. They shall gather my children into their fold: they shall bring the glory of the stars into the hearts of men.

16. For he is ever a sun, and she a moon. But to him is the winged secret flame, and to her the stooping starlight.

17. But ye are not so chosen.

18. Burn upon their brows, o splendrous serpent!

19. O azure-lidded woman, bend upon them!

20. The key of the rituals is in the secret word which I have given unto him.

21. With the God & the Adorer I am nothing: they do not see me. They are as upon the earth; I am Heaven, and there is no other God than me, and my lord Hadit.

22. Now, therefore, I am known to ye by my name Nuit, and to him by a secret name which I will give him when at last he knoweth me. Since I am Infinite Space, and the Infinite Stars thereof, do ye also thus. Bind nothing! Let there be no difference made among you between any one thing & any other thing; for thereby there cometh hurt.

23. But whoso availeth in this, let him be the chief of all!

24. I am Nuit, and my word is six and fifty.

25. Divide, add, multiply, and understand.

26. Then saith the prophet and slave of the beauteous one: Who am I, and what shall be the sign? So she

answered him, bending down, a lambent flame of blue, all-touching, all penetrant, her lovely hands upon the black earth, & her lithe body arched for love, and her soft feet not hurting the little flowers: Thou knowest! And the sign shall be my ecstasy, the consciousness of the continuity of existence, the omnipresence of my body.

27. Then the priest answered & said unto the Queen of Space, kissing her lovely brows, and the dew of her light bathing his whole body in a sweet-smelling perfume of sweat: O Nuit, continuous one of Heaven, let it be ever thus; that men speak not of Thee as One but as None; and let them speak not of thee at all, since thou art continuous!

28. None, breathed the light, faint & faery, of the stars, and two.

29. For I am divided for love's sake, for the chance of union.

30. This is the creation of the world, that the pain of division is as nothing, and the joy of dissolution all.

31. For these fools of men and their woes care not thou at all! They feel little; what is, is balanced by weak joys; but ye are my chosen ones.

32. Obey my prophet! follow out the ordeals of my knowledge! seek me only! Then the joys of my love will redeem ye from all pain. This is so; I swear it by the vault of my body; by my sacred heart and tongue; by all I can give, by all I desire of ye all.

33. Then the priest fell into a deep trance or swoon, & said unto the Queen of Heaven; Write unto us the ordeals; write unto us the rituals; write unto us the law!

34. But she said: the ordeals I write not: the rituals shall be half known and half concealed: the Law is for all.

35. This that thou writest is the threefold book of Law.

36. My scribe Ankh-af-na-khonsu, the priest of the

princes, shall not in one letter change this book; but lest there be folly, he shall comment thereupon by the wisdom of Ra-Hoor-Khu-it.

37. Also the mantras and spells; the obeah and the wanga; the work of the wand and the work of the sword; these he shall learn and teach.

38. He must teach; but he may make severe the ordeals.

39. The word of the Law is θελημα.

40. Who calls us Thelemites will do no wrong, if he look but close into the word. For there are therein Three Grades, the Hermit, and the Lover, and the man of Earth. Do what thou wilt shall be the whole of the Law.

41. The word of Sin is Restriction. O man! refuse not thy wife, if she will! O lover, if thou wilt, depart! There is no bond that can unite the divided but love: all else is a curse. Accursèd! Accursèd be it to the aeons! Hell.

42. Let it be that state of manyhood bound and loathing. So with thy all; thou hast no right but to do thy will.

43. Do that, and no other shall say nay.

44. For pure will, unassuaged of purpose, delivered from the lust of result, is every way perfect.

45. The Perfect and the Perfect are one Perfect and not two; nay, are none!

46. Nothing is a secret key of this law. Sixty-one the Jews call it; I call it eight, eighty, four hundred & eighteen.

47. But they have the half: unite by thine art so that all disappear.

48. My prophet is a fool with his one, one, one; are not they the Ox, and none by the Book?

49. Abrogate are all rituals, all ordeals, all words and signs. Ra-Hoor-Khuit hath taken his seat in the East at the Equinox of the Gods; and let Asar be with Isa, who also are one. But they are not of me. Let Asar be the

adorant, Isa, the sufferer; Hoor in his secret name and splendour is the Lord initiating.

50. There is a word to say about the Hierophantic task. Behold! there are three ordeals in one, and it may be given in three ways. The gross must pass through fire; let the fine be tried in intellect, and the lofty chosen ones in the highest; Thus ye have star & star, system & system; let not one know well the other!

51. There are four gates to one palace; the floor of that palace is of silver and gold; lapis lazuli & jasper are there; and all rare scents; jasmine & rose, and the emblems of death. Let him enter in turn or at once the four gates; let him stand on the floor of the palace. Will he not sink? Amn. Ho! warrior, if thy servant sink? But there are means and means. Be goodly therefore: dress ye all in fine apparel; eat rich foods and drink sweet wines and wines that foam! Also, take your fill and will of love as ye will, when, where and with whom ye will! But always unto me.

52. If this be not aright; if ye confound the space-marks, saying: They are one; or saying, They are many; if the ritual be not ever unto me: then expect the direful judgments of Ra Hoor Khuit!

53. This shall regenerate the world, the little world my sister, my heart & my tongue, unto whom I send this kiss. Also, o scribe and prophet, though thou be of the princes, it shall not assuage thee nor absolve thee. But ecstasy be thine and joy of earth: ever To me! To me!

54. Change not as much as the style of a letter; for behold! thou, o prophet, shalt not behold all these mysteries hidden therein.

55. The child of thy bowels, *he* shall behold them.

56. Expect him not from the East, nor from the West; for from no expected house cometh that child. Aum! All

words are sacred and all prophets true; save only that they understand a little; solve the first half of the equation, leave the second unattacked. But thou hast all in the clear light, and some, though not all, in the dark.

57. Invoke me under my stars! Love is the law, love under will. Nor let the fools mistake love; for there are love and love. There is the dove, and there is the serpent. Choose ye well! He, my prophet, hath chosen, knowing the law of the fortress, and the great mystery of the House of God.

All these old letters of my Book are aright; but ש is not the Star. This also is secret: my prophet shall reveal it to the wise.

58. I give unimaginable joys on earth: certainty, not faith, while in life, upon death; peace unutterable, rest, ecstasy; nor do I demand aught in sacrifice.

59. My incense is of resinous woods & gums; and there is no blood therein: because of my hair the trees of Eternity.

60. My number is 11, as all their numbers who are of us. The Five Pointed Star, with a Circle in the Middle, & the circle is Red. My colour is black to the blind, but the blue & gold are seen of the seeing. Also I have a secret glory for them that love me.

61. But to love me is better than all things: if under the night-stars in the desert thou presently burnest mine incense before me, invoking me with a pure heart, and the Serpent flame therein, thou shalt come a little to lie in my bosom. For one kiss wilt thou then be willing to give all; but whoso gives one particle of dust shall lose all in that hour. Ye shall gather goods and store of women and spices; ye shall wear rich jewels; ye shall exceed the nations of the earth in splendour & pride; but always in the love of me, and so shall ye come to my joy. I charge you earnestly to come before me in a single robe, and

covered with a rich headdress. I love you! I yearn to you! Pale or purple, veiled or voluptuous, I who am all pleasure and purple, and drunkenness of the innermost sense, desire you. Put on the wings, and arouse the coiled splendour within you: come unto me!

62. At all my meetings with you shall the priestess say— and her eyes shall burn with desire as she stands bare and rejoicing in my secret temple—To me! To me! calling forth the flame of the hearts of all in her love-chant.

63. Sing the rapturous love-song unto me! Burn to me perfumes! Wear to me jewels! Drink to me, for I love you! I love you!

64. I am the blue-lidded daughter of Sunset; I am the naked brilliance of the voluptuous night-sky.

65. To me! To me!

66. The Manifestation of Nuit is at an end.

1. Nu! the hiding of Hadit.

2. Come! all ye, and learn the secret that hath not yet been revealed. I, Hadit, am the complement of Nu, my bride. I am not extended, and Khabs is the name of my House.

3. In the sphere I am everywhere the centre, as she, the circumference, is nowhere found.

4. Yet she shall be known & I never.

5. Behold! the rituals of the old time are black. Let the evil ones be cast away; let the good ones be purged by the prophet! Then shall this Knowledge go aright.

6. I am the flame that burns in every heart of man, and in the core of every star. I am Life, and the giver of Life, yet therefore is the knowledge of me the knowledge of death.

7. I am the Magician and the Exorcist. I am the axle of

the wheel, and the cube in the circle. "Come unto me" is a foolish word: for it is I that go.

8. Who worshipped Heru-pa-kraath have worshipped me; ill, for I am the worshipper.

9. Remember all ye that existence is pure joy; that all the sorrows are but as shadows; they pass & are done; but there is that which remains.

10. O prophet! thou hast ill will to learn this writing.

11. I see thee hate the hand & the pen; but I am stronger.

12. Because of Me in Thee which thou knewest not.

13. For why? Because thou wast the knower, and me.

14. Now let there be a veiling of this shrine: now let the light devour men and eat them up with blindness!

15. For I am perfect, being Not; and my number is nine by the fools; but with the just I am eight, and one in eight: Which is vital, for I am none indeed. The Empress and the King are not of me; for there is a further secret.

16. I am The Empress & the Hierophant. Thus eleven, as my bride is eleven.

17. Hear me, ye people of sighing!
    The sorrows of pain and regret
    Are left to the dead and the dying,
    The folk that not know me as yet.

18. These are dead, these fellows; they feel not. We are not for the poor and sad: the lords of the earth are our kinsfolk.

19. Is a God to live in a dog? No! but the highest are of us. They shall rejoice, our chosen: who soroweth is not of us.

20. Beauty and strength, leaping laughter and delicious languor, force and fire, are of us.

21. We have nothing with the outcast and the unfit: let them die in their misery. For they feel not. Com-

passion is the vice of kings: stamp down the wretched & the weak: this is the law of the strong: this is our law and the joy of the world. Think not, o king, upon that lie: That Thou Must Die: verily thou shalt not die, but live. Now let it be understood: If the body of the King dissolve, he shall remain in pure ecstasy for ever. Nuit! Hadit! Ra-Hoor-Khuit! The Sun, Strength & Sight, Light; these are for the servants of the Star & the Snake.

22. I am the Snake that giveth Knowledge & Delight and bright glory, and stir the hearts of men with drunkenness. To worship me take wine and strange drugs whereof I will tell my prophet, & be drunk thereof! They shall not harm ye at all. It is a lie, this folly against self. The exposure of innocence is a lie. Be strong, o man! lust, enjoy all things of sense and rapture: fear not that any God shall deny thee for this.

23. I am alone: there is no God where I am.

24. Behold! these be grave mysteries; for there are also of my friends who be hermits. Now think not to find them in the forest or on the mountain; but in beds of purple, caressed by magnificent beasts of women with large limbs, and fire and light in their eyes, and masses of flaming hair about them; there shall ye find them. Ye shall see them at rule, at victorious armies, at all the joy; and there shall be in them a joy a million times greater than this. Beware lest any force another, King against King! Love one another with burning hearts; on the low men trample in the fierce lust of your pride, in the day of your wrath.

25. Ye are against the people, O my chosen!

26. I am the secret Serpent coiled about to spring: in my coiling there is joy. If I lift up my head, I and my Nuit are one. If I droop down mine head, and shoot forth venom, then is rapture of the earth, and I and the earth are one.

27. There is great danger in me; for who doth not understand these runes shall make a great miss. He shall fall down into the pit called Because, and there he shall perish with the dogs of Reason.

28. Now a curse upon Because and his kin!

29. May Because be accursed for ever!

30. If Will stops and cries Why, invoking Because, then Will stops & does nought.

31. If Power asks why, then is Power weakness.

32. Also reason is a lie; for there is a factor infinite & unknown; & all their words are skew-wise.

33. Enough of Because! Be he damned for a dog!

34. But ye, o my people, rise up & awake!

35. Let the rituals be rightly performed with joy & beauty!

36. There are rituals of the elements and feasts of the times.

37. A feast for the first night of the Prophet and his Bride!

38. A feast for the three days of the writing of the Book of the Law.

39. A feast for Tahuti and the child of the Prophet—secret, O Prophet!

40. A feast for the Supreme Ritual, and a feast for the Equinox of the Gods.

41. A feast for fire and a feast for water; a feast for life and a greater feast for death!

42. A feast every day in your hearts in the joy of my rapture!

43. A feast every night unto Nu, and the pleasure of uttermost delight!

44. Aye! feast! rejoice! there is no dread hereafter. There is the dissolution, and eternal ecstasy in the kisses of Nu.

45. There is death for the dogs.

46. Dost thou fail? Art thou sorry? Is fear in thine heart?

47. Where I am these are not.

48. Pity not the fallen! I never knew them. I am not for them. I console not: I hate the consoled & the consoler.

49. I am unique & conqueror. I am not of the slaves that perish. Be they damned & dead! Amen. (This is of the 4: there is a fifth who is invisible, & therein am I as a babe in an egg.)

50. Blue am I and gold in the light of my bride: but the red gleam is in my eyes; & my spangles are purple & green.

51. Purple beyond purple: it is the light higher than eyesight.

52. There is a veil: that veil is black. It is the veil of the modest woman; it is the veil of sorrow, & the pall of death: this is none of me. Tear down that lying spectre of the centuries: veil not your vices in virtuous words: these vices are my service; ye do well, & I will reward you here and hereafter.

53. Fear not, o prophet, when these words are said, thou shalt not be sorry. Thou art emphatically my chosen; and blessed are the eyes that thou shalt look upon with gladness. But I will hide thee in a mask of sorrow: they that see thee shall fear thou art fallen: but I lift thee up.

54. Nor shall they who cry aloud their folly that thou meanest nought avail; thou shall reveal it: thou availest: they are the slaves of because: They are not of me. The stops as thou wilt; the letters? change them not in style or value!

55. Thou shalt obtain the order & value of the English Alphabet; thou shalt find new symbols to attribute them unto.

56. Begone! ye mockers; even though ye laugh in my honour ye shall laugh not long: then when ye are sad know that I have forsaken you.

57. He that is righteous shall be righteous still; he that is filthy shall be filthy still.

58. Yea! deem not of change: ye shall be as ye are, & not other. Therefore the kings of the earth shall be Kings for ever: the slaves shall serve. There is none that shall be cast down or lifted up: all is ever as it was. Yet there are masked ones my servants: it may be that yonder beggar is a King. A King may choose his garment as he will: there is no certain test: but a beggar cannot hide his poverty.

59. Beware therefore! Love all, lest perchance is a King concealed! Say you so? Fool! If he be a King, thou canst not hurt him.

60. Therefore strike hard & low, and to hell with them, master!

61. There is a light before thine eyes, o prophet, a light undesired, most desirable.

62. I am uplifted in thine heart; and the kisses of the stars rain hard upon thy body.

63. Thou art exhaust in the voluptuous fullness of the inspiration; the expiration is sweeter than death, more rapid and laughterful than a caress of Hell's own worm.

64. Oh! thou art overcome: we are upon thee; our delight is all over thee: hail! hail: prophet of Nu! prophet of Had! prophet of Ra-Hoor-Khu! Now rejoice! now come in our splendour & rapture! Come in our passionate peace, & write sweet words for the Kings!

65. I am the Master: thou art the Holy Chosen One.

66. Write, & find ecstasy in writing! Work, & be our bed in working! Thrill with the joy of life & death! Ah! thy death shall be lovoely: whso seeth it shall be glad. Thy death shall be the seal of the promise of our agelong

love. Come! lift up thine heart & rejoice! We are one;
we are none.

67. Hold! Hold! Bear up in thy rapture; fall not in
swoon of the excellent kisses!

68. Harder! Hold up thyself! Lift thine head! breathe
not so deep—die!

69. Ah! Ah! What do I feel? Is the word exhausted?

70. There is help & hope in other spells. Wisdom says:
be strong! Then canst thou bear more joy. Be not animal;
refine thy rapture! If thou drink, drink by the eight and
ninety rules of art: if thou love, exceed by delicacy;
and if thou do aught joyous, let there be subtlety therein!

71. But exceed! exceed!

72. Strive ever to more! and if thou art truly mine—
and doubt it not, an if thou art ever joyous!—death is the
crown of all.

73. Ah! Ah! Death! Death! thou shalt long for death.
Death is forbidden, o man, unto thee.

74. The length of thy longing shall be the strength of
its glory. He that lives long & desires death much is ever
the King among the Kings.

75. Aye! listen to the numbers & the words:

76. 4 6 3 8 A B K 2 4 A L G M O R 3 Y X 24 89 R P
S T O V A L. What meaneth this, o prophet? Thou
knowest not; nor shalt thou know ever. There cometh one
to follow thee: he shall expound it. But remember, o
chosen one, to be me; to follow the love of Nu in the
star-lit heaven; to look forth upon men, to tell them this
glad word.

77. O be thou proud and mighty among men!

78. Lift up thyself! for there is none like unto thee
among men or among Gods! Lift up thyself, o my prophet,
thy stature shall surpass the stars. They shall worship thy
name, foursquare, mystic, wonderful, the number of the
man; and the name of thy house 418.

79. The end of the hiding of Hadit; and blessing & worship to the prophet of the lovely Star!

[Note: ver. 68. *Harden, not Harder, as the MS. indicates. The memory of* DCLXVI *says, though with diffidence, that the former is correct.*]

1. Abrahadabra; the reward of Ra Hoor Khut.
2. There is division hither homeward; there is a word not known. Spelling is defunct; all is not aught. Beware! Hold! Raise the spell of Ra-Hoor-Khuit!
3. Now let it be first understood that I am a god of War and of Vengeance. I shall deal hardly with them.
4. Choose ye an island!
5. Fortify it!
6. Dung it about with enginery of war!
7. I will give you a war-engine.
8. With it ye shall smite the peoples; and none shall stand before you.
9. Lurk! Withdraw! Upon them! this is the Law of the Battle of Conquest: thus shall my worship be about my secret house.
10. Get the stélé of revealing itself; set it in thy secret temple—and that temple is already aright disposed—& it shall be your Kiblah for ever. It shall not fade, but miraculous colour shall come back to it day after day. Close it in locked glass for a proof to the world.
11. This shall be your only proof. I forbid argument. Conquer! That is enough. I will make easy to you the abstruction from the ill-ordered house in the Victorious City. Thou shalt thyself convey it with worship, o prophet, though thou likest it not. Thou shalt have danger & trouble. Ra-Hoor-Khu is with thee. Worship me with fire & blood; worship me with swords & with spears. Let the woman be girt with a sword before me: let blood flow

to my name. Trample down the Heathen; be upon them, o warrior, I will give you of their flesh to eat!

12. Sacrifice cattle, little and big: after a child.

13. But not now.

14. Ye shall see that hour, o blessèd Beast, and thou the Scarlet Concubine of his desire!

15. Ye shall be sad thereof.

16. Deem not too eagerly to catch the promises; fear not to undergo the curses. Ye, even ye, know not this meaning all.

17. Fear not at all; fear neither men, nor Fates, nor gods, nor anything. Money fear not, nor laughter of the folk folly, nor any other power in heaven or upon the earth or under the earth. Nu is your refuge as Hadit your light; and I am the strength, force, vigour, of your arms.

18. Mercy let be off: damn them who pity! Kill and torture; spare not; be upon them!

19. That stélé they shall call the Abomination of Desolation; count well its name, & it shall be to you as 718.

20. Why? Because of the fall of Because, that he is not there again.

21. Set up my image in the East: thou shalt buy thee an image which I will show thee, especial, not unlike the one thou knowest. And it shall be suddenly easy for thee to do this.

22. The other images group around me to support me: let all be worshipped, for they shall cluster to exalt me. I am the visible object of worship; the others are secret; for the Beast & his Bride are they: and for the winners of the Ordeal x. What is this? Thou shalt know.

23. For perfume mix meal & honey & thick leavings of red wine: then oil of Abramelin and olive oil, and afterward soften & smooth down with rich fresh blood.

24. The best blood is of the moon, monthly: then the fresh blood of a child, or dropping from the host of heaven: then of enemies; then of the priest or of the worshippers: last of some beast, no matter what.

25. This burn: of this make cakes & eat unto me. This hath also another use; let it be laid before me, and kept thick with perfumes of your orison: it shall become full of beetles as it were and creeping things sacred unto me.

26. These slay, naming your enemies; & they shall fall before you.

27. Also these shall breed lust & power of lust in you at the eating thereof.

28. Also ye shall be strong in war.

29. Moreover, be they long kept, it is better; for they swell with my force. All before me.

30. My altar is of open brass work: burn thereon in silver or gold!

31. There cometh a rich man from the West who shall pour his gold upon thee.

32. From gold forge steel!

33. Be ready to fly or to smite!

34. But your holy place shall be untouched throughout the centuries: though with fire and sword it be burnt down & shattered, yet an invisible house there standeth, and shall stand until the fall of the Great Equinox; when Hrumachis shall arise and the double-wanded one assume my throne and place. Another prophet shall arise, and bring fresh fever from the skies; another woman shall awake the lust & worship of the Snake; another soul of God and beast shall mingle in the globèd priest; another sacrifice shall stain The tomb; another king shall reign; and blessing no longer be poured To the Hawk-headed mystical Lord!

35. The half of the word of Heru-ra-ha, called Hoor-pa-kraat and Ra-Hoor-Khut.

36. Then said the prophet unto the God:

37. I adore thee in the song—

> I am the Lord of Thebes, and I
>   The inspired forth-speaker of Mentu;
> For me unveils the veilèd sky,
>   The self-slain Ankh-af-na-khonsu
> Whose words are truth. I invoke, I greet
>   Thy presence, O Ra-Hoor-Khuit!

> Unity uttermost showed!
>   I adore the might of Thy breath,
> Supreme and terrible God,
>   Who makest the gods and death
> To tremble before Thee:—
>   I, I adore thee!

> Appear on the throne of Ra!
>   Open the ways of the Khu!
> Lighten the ways of the Ka!
>   The ways of the Khabs run through
> To stir me or still me!
>   Aum! let it fill me!

38. So that thy light is in me; & its red flame is as a
sword in my hand to push thy order. There is a secret
door that I shall make to establish thy way in all the
quarters, (these are the adorations, as thou hast written),
as it is said:

> The light is mine; its rays consume
>   Me: I have made a secret door
> Into the House of Ra and Tum,
>   Of Khephra and of Ahathoor.

I am thy Theban, O Mentu,
The prophet Ankh-af-na-khonsu!

By Bes-na-Maut my breast I beat;
  By wise Ta-Nech I weave my spell.
Show thy star-splendour, O Nuit!
  Bid me within thine House to dwell,
O wingèd snake of light, Hadit!
  Abide with me, Ra-Hoor-Khuit!

39. All this and a book to say how thou didst come hither and a reproduction of this ink and paper for ever— for in it is the word secret & not only in the English— and thy comment upon this the Book of the Law shall be printed beautifully in red ink and black upon beautiful paper made by hand; and to each man and woman that thou meetest, were it but to dine or to drink at them, it is the Law to give. Then they shall chance to abide in this bliss or no; it is no odds. Do this quickly!

40. But the work of the comment? That is easy; and Hadit burning in thy heart shall make swift and secure thy pen.

41. Establish at thy Kaaba a clerk-house: all must be done well and with business way.

42. The ordeals thou shalt oversee thyself, save only the blind ones. Refuse none, but thou shalt know & destroy the traitors. I am Ra-Hoor-Khuit; and I am powerful to protect my servant. Success is thy proof: argue not; convert not; talk not overmuch! Them that seek to entrap thee, to overthrow thee, them attack without pity or quarter; & destroy them utterly. Swift as a trodden serpent turn and strike! Be thou yet deadlier than he! Drag down their souls to awful torment: laugh at their fear: spit upon them!

43. Let the Scarlet Woman beware! If pity and com-

passion and tenderness visit her heart; if she leave my work to toy with old sweetnesses; then shall my vengeance be known. I will slay me her child: I will alienate her heart: I will cast her out from men: as a shrinking and despised harlot shall she crawl though dusk wet streets, and die cold and an-hungered.

44. But let her raise herself in pride! Let her follow me in my way! Let her work the work of wickedness! Let her kill her heart! Let her be loud and adulterous! Let her be covered with jewels, and rich garments, and let her be shameless before all men!

45. Then will I lift her to pinnacles of power: then will I breed from her a child mightier than all the kings of the earth. I will fill her with joy: with my force shall she see & strike at the worship of Nu: she shall achieve Hadit.

46. I am the warrior Lord of the Forties: the Eighties cower before me, & are abased. I will bring you to victory & joy: I will be at your arms in battle & ye shall delight to slay. Success is your proof; courage is your armour; go on, go on, in my strength; & ye shall turn not back for any!

47. This book shall be translated into all tongues: but always with the original in the writing of the Beast; for in the chance shape of the letters and their position to one another: in these are mysteries that no Beast shall divine. Let him not seek to try: but one cometh after him, whence I say not, who shall discover the Key of it all. Then this line drawn is a key: then this circle squared in its failure is a key also. And Abrahadabra. It shall be his child & that strangely. Let him not seek after this; for thereby alone can he fall from it.

48. Now this mystery of the letters is done, and I want to go on to the holier place.

49. I am in a secret fourfold word, the blasphemy against all gods of men.

50. Curse them! Curse them! Curse them!

51. With my Hawk's head I peck at the eyes of Jesus as he hangs upon the cross.

52. I flap my wings in the face of Mohammed & blind him.

53. With my claws I tear out the flesh of the Indian and the Buddhist, Mongol and Din.

54. Bahlasti! Ompehda! I spit on your crapulous creeds.

55. Let Mary inviolate be torn upon wheels: for her sake let all chaste women be utterly despised among you!

56. Also for beauty's sake and love's!

57. Despise also all cowards; professional soldiers who dare not fight, but play: all fools despise!

58. But the keen and the proud, the royal and the lofty; ye are brothers!

59. As brothers fight ye!

60. There is no law beyond Do what thou wilt.

61. There is an end of the word of the God enthroned in Ra's seat, lightening the girders of the soul.

62. To Me do ye reverence! to me come ye through tribulation of ordeal, which is bliss.

63. The fool readeth this Book of the Law, and its comment; & he understandeth it not.

64. Let him come through the first ordeal, & it will be to him as silver.

65. Through the second, gold.

66. Through the third, stones of precious water.

67. Through the fourth, ultimate sparks of the intimate fire.

68. Yet to all it shall seem beautiful. Its enemies who say not so, are mere liars.

69. There is success.

70. I am the Hawk-Headed Lord of Silence & of Strength; my nemyss shrouds the night-blue sky.

71. Hail! ye twin warriors about the pillars of the world! for your time is nigh at hand.

72. I am the Lord of the Double Wand of Power; the wand of the Force of Coph Nia—but my left hand is empty, for I have crushed an Universe; & nought remains.

73. Paste the sheets from right to left and from top to bottom: then behold!

74. There is a splendour in my name hidden and glorious, as the sun of midnight is ever the son.

75. The ending of the words is the Word Abrahadabra.
The Book of the Law is Written
and Concealed.
Aum. Ha.

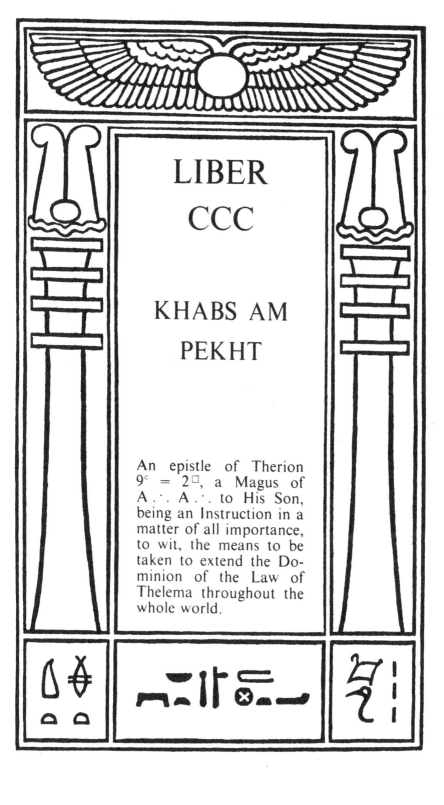

LIBER CCC

KHABS AM PEKHT

An epistle of Therion $9° = 2□$, a Magus of A∴ A∴ to His Son, being an Instruction in a matter of all importance, to wit, the means to be taken to extend the Dominion of the Law of Thelema throughout the whole world.

A ∴ A ∴ Publication in Class E

93	10° = 1□ ⎫	
666	9° = 2□ ⎬ Pro Coll. Summ.	
777	8° = 3□ ⎭	
D. D. S.	7° = 4□ ⎫	
O. M.	7° = 4□ ⎪ Pro Coll. Int.	
O. S. V.	6° = 5□ ⎬	
Parzival	5° = 6□ ⎭	
V. N.	Praemonstrator ⎫	
P.	Imperator ⎬ Pro Coll. Ext.	
Achad	Cancellarius ⎭	

LIBER CCC
KHABS AM PEKHT[1]

Son,

Do what thou wilt shall be the whole of the Law. Firstly, let thine attention be directed to this planet, how the Aeon of Horus is made manifest by the Universal War. This is the first great and direct result of the Equinox of the Gods, and is the preparation of the hearts of men for the reception of the Law.

Let Us remind you that this is a magical formula of cosmic scope, and that it is given in exact detail in the legend of the Golden Fleece.

Jason, who in this story represents the Beast, first fits out a ship guided by Wisdom or Athena, and this is his aspiration to the Great Work. Accompanied by many heroes, he comes to the place of the Fleece, but they can do nothing until Medea, the Scarlet Woman, puts into his hands a posset "drugged with somnolence, Sleepy with poppy and white hellebore" for the dragon. Then Jason is able to subdue the bulls, sacred to Osiris, and symbolical of his Aeon and of the Magical Formula of Self-Sacrifice. With these he plows the field of the world,

1. The quotations in this epistle are from *Liber Legis : The Book of the Law.*—A.C.

IOI

and sows therein "the dreadful teeth of woe, Cadmean Stock of Thebes' old misery," which refers to a certain magical formula announced by The Beast that is familiar unto thee, but unsuited to the profane, and therefore not further in this place indicated. From this seed armed men sprung to life; but instead of attacking Him, "mutual madness strikes The warriors witless, and fierce wrath invades Their hearts of fury, and with arms engaged, They fell upon each other silently, And slew, and slew." Now then, the Dragon being asleep, we may step quietly past him, and "rending the branches of that wizard Oak, With a strong grasp tear down the Fleece of Gold."

Let us only remember not to repeat the error of Jason, and defy Ares, who is Horus in his warrior mood, that guardeth it, lest He strike us also with madness. Nay! but to the glory of Ra-Hoor-Khuit and the establishment of His perfect kingdom let all be done!

Now, O my son, thou knowest that it is Our will to establish this Work, accomplishing fully that which We are commanded in *The Book of the Law*, "Help me, O warrior lord of Thebes, in my unveiling before the children of men!"—and it is Thy Will, manifesting as thou hast done in the Sphere of Malkuth the material world, to do this same thing in an even more immediate and practical way than would naturally appeal to one whose manifestation is in the Heaven of Jupiter. So therefore We now answer Thy filial petition that asketh good counsel of Us as to the means to be taken to extend the Law of Thelema throughout the whole world.

Direct therefore now most closely thine attention to *The Book of the Law* itself. In It we find an absolute rule of life, and clear instruction in every emergency that may befall. What then are Its own directions for the fructification of That Ineffable Seed? Note, pray thee, the confidence with which we may proceed. "They shall gather

my children into their fold; they shall bring the glory of
the stars into the hearts of men." They "shall"; there is
no doubt. Therefore doubt not, but strike with all thy
strength. Note also, pray thee, this word: "The Law is
for all." Do not therefore "select suitable persons" in thy
worldly wisdom; preach openly the Law to all men.
In Our experience We have found that the most unlikely
means have produced the best results; and indeed it is
almost the definition of a true Magical Formula that the
means should be unsuited, rationally speaking, to the end
proposed. Note, pray thee, that We are bound to teach.
"He must teach; but he may make severe the ordeals."
This refers, however, as is evident from the context, to
the technique of the new Magick, "the mantras and spells;
the obeah and the wanga; the work of the wand and the
work of the sword."

Note, pray thee, the instruction in *CCXX*, I: 41–44,
51, 61, 63, etc., on which We have enlarged in Our
tract "The Law of Liberty," and in private letters to
thee and to others. The open preaching of this Law, and
the practice of these precepts, will arouse discussion and
animosity, and thus place thee upon a rostrum whence
thou mayst speak unto the people.

Note, pray thee, this mentor: "Remember ye that
existence is pure joy; that all the sorrows are but shadows;
they pass and are done; but there is that which remains."
For this doctrine shall comfort many. Also there is this
word: "They shall rejoice, our chosen; who sorroweth
is not of us. Beauty and strength, leaping laughter and
delicious languor, force and fire, are of us." Indeed in all
ways thou mayst expound the joy of our Law; nay, for
thou shalt overflow with the joy thereof, and have no need
of words. It would moreover be impertinent and tedious
to call again thine attention to all those passages that thou
knowest so well. Note, pray thee, that in the matter of

direct instruction there is enough. Consider the passage "Choose ye an island! Fortify it! Dung it about with enginery of war! I will give you a war-engine. With it ye shall smite the peoples; and none shall stand before you. Lurk! Withdraw! Upon them! This is the Law of the Battle of Conquest: thus shall my worship be about my secret house." The last phrase suggests that the island may be Great Britain, with its Mines and Tanks; and it is notable that a certain brother obligated to A ∴ A ∴ is in the most secret of England's War Councils at this hour. But it is possible that all this instruction refers to some later time when our Law, administered by some such Order as the O.T.O. which concerns itself with temporal affairs, is of weight in the councils of the world, and is challenged by the heathen, and by the followers of the fallen gods and demigods.

Note, pray thee, the practical method of overcoming opposition given in *CCXX*, III: 23–26. But this is not to Our immediate purpose in this epistle. Note, pray thee, the instruction in the 38th and 39th verses of the Third Chapter of *The Book of the Law*. It must be quoted in full.

> So that thy light is in me; and its red flame is as a sword in my hand to push thy order.

That is, the God himself is aflame with the Light of The Beast, and will himself push the order, through the fire (perhaps meaning the genius) of The Beast.

> There is a secret door that I shall make to establish thy way in all the quarters (there are the adorations, as thou hast written) as it is said:

> The light is mine; its rays consume
> Me: I have made a secret door

> Into the House of Ra and Tum,
>   Of Khephra and of Ahathoor.
> I am thy Theban, O Mentu,
>   The prophet Ankh-af-na-khonsu!
>
> By Bes-na-Maut my breast I beat;
>   By wise Ta-Nech I weave my spell.
> Show thy star-splendour, O Nuit!
>   Bid me within thine House to dwell,
> O wingèd snake of light, Hadit!
>   Abide with me, Ra-Hoor-Khuit!

In the comment in *The Equinox*, I, VII, this passage is
virtually ignored. It is possible that this "secret door"
refers to the four men and four women spoken of later
in the "Paris Working," or it may mean the child elsewhere predicted, or some secret preparation of the hearts
of men. It is difficult to decide on such a point, but we
may be sure that the Event will show that the exact
wording was so shaded as to prove to us absolute fore-
knowledge on the part of That Most Holy Angel who
uttered the Book.

Note, pray thee, further, in verse 39, how the matter
proceeds:

> All this (*The Book of the Law* itself)
> and a book to say how thou didst come hither (some record
> such as that in *The Temple of Solomon the King*)
> and a reproduction of this ink and paper for ever (by some
> mechanical process, with possibly a sample of paper similar
> to that employed)
> —for in it is the word secret and not only in the English—

Compare *CCXX*, III: 47, 73. The secret is still a
secret to Us.

> And thy comment upon this *The Book of the Law* shall be
> printed beautifully in red ink and black upon beautiful paper

made by hand; (explain the text "lest there be folly" as it says above, *CCXX*: I: 36.)

> And to each man and woman that thou meetest, were it but to dine or to drink at them, it is the Law to give. Then they shall chance to abide in this bliss or no; it is no odds. Do this quickly!

From this it is evident that a volume must be prepared as signified—Part IV of *Book 4* was intended to fulfil this purpose—and that this book must be distributed widely, in fact to every one with whom one comes into social relations.

We are not to add to this gift by preaching and the like. They can take it or leave it.

Note, pray thee, verse 41 of this chapter:

> Establish at thy Kaaba a clerk-house; all must be done well and with business way.

This is very clear instruction indeed. There is to be a modern centralized business organization at the Kaaba— which, We think, does not mean Boleskine, but any convenient headquarters.

Note, pray thee, in verse 42 of this chapter the injunction:

> Success is thy proof: aruge not; convert not; talk not overmuch!

This is not any bar to an explanation of the Law. We may aid men to strike off their own fetters; but those who prefer slavery must be allowed to do so. "The slaves shall serve." The excellence of the Law must be showed by its results upon those who accept it. When men see us as the hermits of Hadit described in *CCXX*, II: 24, they will determine to emulate our joy.

Note, pray thee, the whole implication of the chapter that sooner or later we are to break the power of the slaves of the slave-gods by actual fighting. Ultimately, Freedom must rely upon the sword. It is impossible to treat in this epistle of the vast problems involved in this question; and they must be decided in accordance with the Law by those in authority in the Order when the time comes. Thou wilt note that We have written unto thee more as a member of the O.T.O., than in thy capacity as of the A ∴ A ∴, for the former organization is coordinate and practical, and concerns itself with material things. But remember this clearly, that the Law cometh from the A ∴ A ∴, not from the O.T.O. This Order is but the first of the great religious bodies to accept this Law officially, and its whole Ritual has been revised and reconstituted in accordance with this decision. Now then, leaving *The Book of the Law*, note, pray thee, the following additional suggestions for extending the Dominion of the Law of Thelema throughout the whole world.

1. All those who have accepted the Law should announce the same in daily intercourse. "Do what thou wilt shall be the whole of the Law" shall be the invariable form of greeting. These words, especially in the case of strangers, should be pronounced in a clear, firm, and articulate voice, with the eyes frankly fixed upon the bearer. If the other be of us, let him reply "Love is the law, love under will." The latter sentence shall also be used as the greeting of farewell. In writing, wherever greeting is usual, it should be as above, opening "Do what thou wilt shall be the whole of the Law," and closing "Love is the law, love under will." 2. Social gatherings should be held as often as is convenient, and there the Law should be read and explained. 3. The special tracts written by Us, or authorized by Us, should be distributed to all persons with whom those who have accepted the Law

may be in contact. 4. Pending the establishment of other Universities and Schools of Thelema, scholarships and readerships and such should be provided in existing Schools and Universities, so as to secure the general study of Our writings, and those authorized by Us as pertaining to the New Aeon. 5. All children and young people, although they may not be able to understand the more exalted heavens of our horoscope, may always be taught to rule their lives in accordance with the Law. No efforts should be spared to bring them to this emancipation. The misery caused to children by the operation of the law of the slave-gods was, one may say, the primum mobile of Our first aspiration to overthrow the Old Law. 6. By all manner of means shall all strive constantly to increase the power and freedom of the Headquarters of the O.T.O.; for thereby will come efficiency in the promulgation of the Law. Specific instructions for the extension of the O.T.O. are given in another epistle. Constant practice of these recommendations will develop skill in him or her that practiseth, so that new ideas and plans will be evolved continually.

Furthermore, it is right that each and every one bind himself with an Oath Magical that he may thus make Freedom perfect, even by a bond, as in *Liber III* it is duly written. Amen.

Now, son, note, pray thee, in what house We write these words. For it is a little cottage of red and green, by the western side of a great lake, and it is hidden in the woods. Man, therefore, is at odds with Wood and Water; and being a magician bethinketh Himself to take one of these enemies, Wood, which is both the effect and the cause of that excess of Water, and compel it to fight for Him against the other. What then maketh He? Why, He taketh unto himself Iron of Mars, an Axe and a Saw and a Wedge and a Knife, and He divideth Wood therewith against himself, hewing him into many small pieces, so that he hath no longer any strength against His will. Good; then taketh He the Fire of our Father the Sun, and setteth it directly in battle array against that Water by His army of Wood that he hath conquered and drilled, building it up into a phalanx like unto a Cone, that is the noblest of all solid figures, being the Image of the Holy Phallus Itself, and combineth in himself the Right Line and the Circle. Thus, son, dealeth He; and the Fire kindleth the Wood, and the heat thereof driveth the Water afar off. Yet this Water is a cunning adversary, and He strengtheneth Wood against Fire by impregnating him with much of his own substance, as it were by spies in the citadel of an ally that is not wholly trusted. Now then therefore what must the Magician do? He must first expel utterly Water from Wood by an invocation of the Fire of the Sun our Father. That is to say, without the inspiration of the Most High and Holy One even We ourselves could do nothing at all. Then, son, beginneth the Magician to set His Fire to the little dry Wood, and that enkindleth the Wood of middle size, and when that blazeth brightly, at the last the great logs, though they be utterly green, are nevertheless enkindled.

Now, son, hearken unto this Our reproof, and lend the ear of thine understanding unto the parable of this Magick.

We have for the whole Beginning of Our Work, praise be eternally unto His Holy Name, the Fire of our Father the Sun. The inspiration is ours, and ours is the Law of Thelema that shall set the world ablaze. And We have many small dry sticks, that kindle quickly and burn through quickly, leaving the larger Wood unlit. And the great logs, the masses of humanity, are always with us.

But our edged need is of those middle fagots that on the one hand are readily kindled by the small Wood, and on the other endure until the great logs blaze.

(Behold how sad a thing it is, quoth the Ape of Thoth, for one to be so holy that he cannot chop a tree and cook his food without preparing upon it a long and tedious Morality!)

Let this epistle be copied and circulated among all those that have accepted the Law of Thelema. Receive now Our paternal benediction: the Benediction of the All-Begetter be upon thee. Love is the law, love under will. ΘHPION $9°=2^\square$ A ∴ A ∴ . Given under Our hand and seal this day of An XII, the Sun our Father being in 12° 42′ 2″ of the sign Leo, and the Moon in 25° 39′ 11″ of the sign Libra, from the House of the Juggler, that is by Lake Pasquaney in the State of New Hampshire.

LIBER

CL

VEL

נ ע ל

A SANDAL

DE LEGE

LIBELLVM

L - L - L - L - L

A ∴ A ∴ Publication in Class E

93	$10° = 1^\square$	
666	$9° = 2^\square$	} Pro Coll. Summ.
777	$8° = 3^\square$	
D. D. S.	$7° = 4^\square$	
O. M.	$7° = 4^\square$	
O. S. V.	$6° = 5^\square$	} Pro Coll. Int.
Parzival	$5° = 6^\square$	
V. N.	Praemonstrator	
P.	Imperator	} Pro Coll. Ext.
Achad	Cancellarius	

LIBER CL

DE LEGE LIBELLVM

THE LAW

Do what thou wilt shall be the whole of the Law.
In Righteousness of heart come hither, and listen: for it
is I, TO META ΘHPION, who gave this Law unto everyone
that holdeth himself holy. It is I, not another, that willeth
your whole Freedom, and the arising within you of full
Knowledge and Power.

Behold! the Kingdom of God is within you, even as the
Sun standeth eternal in the heavens, equal at midnight
and at noon. He riseth not: he setteth not: it is but the
shadow of the earth which concealeth him, or the clouds
upon her face.

Let me then declare unto you this Mystery of the Law,
as it hath been made known unto me in divers places,
upon the mountains and in the deserts, but also in great
cities, which thing I speak for your comfort and good
courage. And so be it unto all of you!

Know first, that from the Law spring four Rays or
Emanations: so that if the Law be the centre of your
own being, they must needs fill you with their secret
goodness. And these four are Light, Life, Love, and
Liberty.

By Light shall ye look upon yourselves, and behold All Things that are in Truth One Thing only, whose name hath been called No Thing for a cause which later shall be declared unto you. But the substance of Light is Life, since without Existence and Energy it were naught. By Life therefore are you made yourselves, eternal and incorruptible, flaming forth as suns, self-created and self-supported, each the sole centre of the Universe.

Now as by Light ye beheld, by Love ye feel. There is an ecstacy of pure Knowledge, and another of pure Love. And this Love is the force that uniteth things diverse, for the contemplation in Light of their Oneness. Know that the Universe is not at rest, but in extreme motion whose sum is Rest. And this understanding that Stability is Change, and Change Stability, that Being is Becoming, and Becoming Being, is the Key to the Golden Palace of this Law.

Lastly, by Liberty is the power to direct your course according to your Will. For the extent of the Universe is without bounds, and ye are free to make your pleasure as ye will, seeing that the diversity of being is infinite also. For this also is the Joy of the Law, that no two stars are alike, and ye must understand also that this Multiplicity is itself Unity, and without it Unity could not be. And this is an hard saying against Reason: ye shall comprehend, when, rising above Reason, which is but a manipulation of the Mind, ye come to pure Knowledge by direct perception of the Truth.

Know also that these four Emanations of the Law flame forth upon all paths: ye shall use them not only in these Highways of the Universe whereof I have written, but in every By-path of your daily life.

Love is the law, love under will.

I

OF LIBERTY

It is of Liberty that I would first write unto you, for except ye be free to act, ye cannot act. Yet all four gifts of the Law must in some degree be exercised, seeing that these four are one. But for the Aspirant that cometh unto the Master, the first need is freedom.

The great bond of all bonds is ignorance. How shall a man be free to act if he know not his own purpose? You must therefore first of all discover which star of all the stars you are, your relation to the other stars about you, and your relation to, and identity with, the Whole.

In our Holy Books are given sundry means of making this discovery, and each must make it for himself, attaining absolute conviction by direct experience, not merely reasoning and calculating what is probable. And to each will come the knowledge of his finite will, whereby one is poet, one prophet, one worker in steel, another in jade. But also to each be the knowledge of his infinite Will, his destiny to perform the Great Work, the realization of his True Self. Of this Will let me therefore speak clearly unto all, since it pertaineth unto all.

Understand now that in yourselves is a certain discontent. Analyse well its nature: at the end is in every case one conclusion. The ill springs from the belief in two things, the Self and the Not-Self, and the conflict between them. This also is a restriction of the Will. He who is sick is in conflict with his own body: he who is poor is at odds with society: and so for the rest. Ultimately, therefore, the problem is how to destroy this perception of duality, to attain to the apprehension of unity.

Now then let us suppose that you have come to the

Master, and that He has declared to you the Way of this attainment. What hindereth you? Alas! there is yet much Freedom afar off.

Understand clearly this: that if you are sure of your Will, and sure of your means, then any thoughts or actions which are contrary to those means are contrary also to that Will.

If therefore the Master should enjoin upon you a Vow of Holy Obedience, compliance is not a surrender of the Will, but a fulfilment thereof.

For see, what hindereth you? It is either from without or from within, or both. It may be easy for the strong-minded seeker to put his heel upon public opinion, or to tear from his heart the objects which he loves, in a sense: but there will always remain in himself many discordant affections, as also the bond of habit, and these also must he conquer.

In our holiest Book it is written: "Thou hast no right but to do thy will. Do that, and no other shall say nay." Write it also in your heart and in your brain: for this is the key of the whole matter.

Here Nature herself be your preacher: for in every phenomenon of force and motion doth she proclaim aloud this truth. Even in so small a matter as driving a nail into a plank, hear this same sermon. Your nail must be hard, smooth, fine-pointed, or it will not move swiftly in the direction willed. Imagine then a nail of tinder-wood with twenty points—it is verily no longer a nail. Yet nigh all mankind are like unto this. They wish a dozen different careers; and the force which might have been sufficient to attain eminence in one is wasted on the others: they are null.

Here then let me make open confession, and say thus: though I pledged myself almost in boyhood to the Great Work, though to my aid came the most puissant forces in the whole Universe to hold me to it, though habit itself now constraineth me in the right direction, yet I have not fulfilled my Will: I turn aside daily from the appointed task. I waver. I falter. I lag.

Let this then be of great comfort to you all, that if I be so imperfect—and for very shame I have not emphasized that imperfection—if I, the chosen one, still fail, then how easy for yourselves to surpass me! Or, should you only equal me, then even so how great attainment should be yours!

Be of good cheer, therefore, since both my failure and my success are arguments of courage for yourselves.

Search yourselves cunningly, I pray you, analysing your inmost thoughts. And first you shall discard all those gross obvious hindrances to your Will: idleness, foolish friendships, waste employments or enjoyments, I will not enumerate the conspirators against the welfare of your State.

Next, find the minimum of daily time which is in good sooth necessary to your natural life. The rest you shall devote to the True Means of your Attainment. And even these necessary hours you shall consecrate to the Great Work, saying consciously always while at these Tasks that you perform them only in order to preserve your body and mind in health for the right application to that sublime and single Object.

It shall not be very long before you come to understand that such a life is the true Liberty. You will feel distractions from your Will as being what they are. They will no longer appear pleasant and attractive, but as bonds, as shames. And when you have attained this point, know that you have passed the Middle Gate of this Path. For you will have unified your Will.

Even thus, were a man sitting in a theatre where the play wearies him, he would welcome every distraction, and find amusement in any accident: but if he were intent upon the play, every such incident would annoy him. His attitude to these is then an indication of his attitude towards the play itself.

At first the habit of attention is hard to acquire. Persevere, and you will have spasms of revulsion periodically. Reason itself will attack you, saying: how can so strict a bondage be the Path of Freedom?

Persevere. You have never yet known Liberty. When the temptations are overcome, the voice of Reason silenced, then will your soul bound forward unhampered upon its chosen course, and for the first time will you experience the extreme delight of being Master of Yourself, and therefore of the Universe.

When this is fully attained, when you sit securely in the saddle, then you may enjoy also all those distractions which first pleased you and then angered you. Now they will do neither any more: for they are your slaves and toys.

Until you have reached this point, you are not wholly free. You must kill out desire, and kill out fear. The end of all is the power to live according to your own nature, without danger that one part may develop to the detriment of the whole, or concern lest that danger should arise.

The sot drinks, and is drunken: the coward drinks not, and shivers: the wise man, brave and free, drinks, and gives glory to the Most High God.

This then is the Law of Liberty: you possess all Liberty in your own right, but you must buttress Right with Might: you must win Freedom for yourself in many a war. Woe unto the children who sleep in the Freedom that their forefathers won for them!

"There is no law beyond Do what thou wilt" but it

is only the greatest of the race who have the strength and courage to obey it.

O man! behold thyself! With what pains wast thou fashioned! What ages have gone to thy shaping! The history of the planet is woven into the very substance of thy brain! Was all this for naught? Is there no purpose in thee? Wast thou made thus that thou shouldst eat, and breed, and die? Think it not so! Thou dost incorporate so many elements, thou art the fruit of so many aeons of labour, thou art fashioned thus as thou art, and not otherwise, for some colossal End.

Nerve thyself, then, to seek it and to do it. Naught can satisfy thee but the fulfilment of thy transcendent Will, that is hidden within thee. For this, then, up, to arms! Win thine own Freedom for thyself! Strike hard!

II

OF LOVE

It is written that "Love is the law, love under will." Herein is an Arcanum concealed, for in the Greek Language ΑΓΑΠΗ, Love, is of the same numerical value as ΘΕΛΗΜΑ, Will. By this we understand that the Universal Will is of the nature of Love.

Now Love is the enkindling in ecstacy of Two that will to become One. It is thus an Universal formula of High Magick. For see now how all things, being in sorrow caused by dividuality, must of necessity will Oneness as their medicine.

Here also is Nature monitor to them that seek Wisdom at her breast: for in the uniting of elements of opposite polarities is there a glory of heat, of light, and of electricity. Thus also in mankind do we behold the spiritual fruit of poetry and all genius, arising from the seed of what is but an animal gesture, in the estimation of such as are schooled in Philosophy. And it is to be noted strongly that the most violent and divine passions are those between people of utterly unharmonious natures.

But now I would have you to know that in the mind are no such limitations in respect of species as prevent a man falling in love with an inanimate object, or an idea. For to him that is in any wise advanced upon the Way of Meditation it appears that all objects save the One Object are distasteful, even as appeared formerly in respect of his chance wishes to the Will. So therefore all objects must be grasped by the mind, and heated in the sevenfold furnace of Love, until with explosion of ecstacy they unite, and disappear, for they, being imperfect, are destroyed utterly in the creation of the Perfection of Union, even as the persons of the Lover and the Beloved are fused into the spiritual gold of Love, which knoweth no person, but comprehendeth all.

Yet since each star is but one star, and the coming together of any two is but one partial rapture, so must the aspirant to our holy Science and Art increase constantly by this method of assimilating ideas, that in the end, become capable of apprehending the Universe in one thought, he may leap forth upon It with the massed violence of his Self, and destroying both these, become that Unity whose name is No Thing. Seek ye all therefore constantly to unite yourselves in rapture with each and every thing that is, and that by utmost passion and lust of Union. To this end take chiefly all such things as are naturally repulsive. For what is pleasant is assimilated easily and without ecstacy: it is in the transfiguration of the loathsome and abhorred into The Beloved that the Self is shaken to the root in Love.

Thus in human love also we see that mediocrities

among men mate with null women: but History teacheth
us that the supreme masters of the world seek ever the
vilest and most horrible creatures for their concubines,
overstepping even the limiting laws of sex and species
in their necessity to transcend normality. It is not
enough in such natures to excite lust or passion: the
imagination itself must be enflamed by every means.

For us, then, emancipated from all base law, what shall
we do to satisfy our Will to Unity? No less a mistress than
the Universe: no lupanar more cramped than Infinite
Space: no night of rape that is not coeval with Eternity!

Consider that as Love is mighty to bring forth all
Ecstacy, so absence of Love is the greatest craving. Whoso
is balked in Love suffereth indeed, but he that hath not
actively that passion in his heart towards some object is
weary with the ache of craving. And this state is called
mystically "Dryness." For this there is, as I believe, no
cure but patient persistence in a Rule of Life.

But this Dryness hath its virtue, in that thereby the
Soul is purged of those things that impeach the Will:
for when the drouth is altogether perfect, then is it
certain that by no means can the Soul be satisfied, save
by the Accomplishment of the Great Work. And this is
in strong souls a stimulus to the Will. It is the Furnace
of Thirst that burneth up all dross within us.

But to each act of Will is a particular Dryness corresponding: and as Love increaseth within you, so doth the
torment of His absence. Be this also unto you for a consolation in the ordeal! Moreover, the more fierce the
plague of impotence, the more swiftly and suddenly is
it wont to abate.

Here is the method of Love in Meditation. Let the
Aspirant first practice and then discipline himself in the
Art of fixing the attention upon any thing whatsoever at
will, without permitting the least imaginable distraction.

Let him also practice the art of the Analysis of Ideas, and that of refusing to allow the mind its natural reaction to them, pleasant or unpleasant, thus fixing himself in Simplicity and Indifference. These things being achieved in their ripe season, be it known to you that all ideas will have become equal to your apprehension, since each is simple and each indifferent: any one of them remaining in the mind at Will without stirring or striving, or tending to pass on to any other. But each idea will possess one special quality common to all: this, that no one of any of them is The Self, inasmuch as it is perceived by The Self as Something Opposite.

When this is thorough and profound in the impact of its realization, then is the moment for the aspirant to direct his Will to Love upon it, so that his whole consciousness findeth focus upon that One Idea. And at the first it may be fixed and dead, or lightly held. This may then pass into dryness, or into repulsion. Then at last by pure persistence in that Act of Will to Love, shall Love himself arise, as a bird, as a flame, as a song, and the whole Soul shall wing a fiery path of music unto the Ultimate Heaven of Possession.

Now in this method there are many roads and ways, some simple and direct, some hidden and mysterious, even as it is with human love whereof no man hath made so much as the first sketches for a Map: for Love is infinite in diversity even as are the Stars. For this cause do I leave Love himself master in the heart of every one of you: for he shall teach you rightly if you but serve him with diligence and devotion even to abandonment.

Nor shall you take umbrage or surprise at the strange pranks that he shall play: for He is a wayward boy and wanton, wise in the Wiles of Aphrodite Our Lady His sweet Mother: and all His jests and cruelties are spices in a confection cunning as no art may match.

Rejoice therefore in all His play, not remitting in any wise your own ardour, but glowing with the sting of His whips, and making of Laughter itself a sacrament adjuvant to Love, even as in the Wine of Rheims is sparkle and bite, like as they were ministers to the High Priest of its Intoxication.

It is also fit that I write to you of the importance of Purity in Love. Now this matter concerneth not in any wise the object or the method of the practice: the one thing essential is that no alien element should intrude. And this is of most particular pertinence to the aspirant in that primary and mundane aspect of his work wherein he establisheth himself in the method through his natural affections.

For know, that all things are masks or symbols of the One Truth, and nature serveth alway to point out the higher perfection under the veil of the lower perfection. So then all the Art and Craft of human love shall serve you as an hieroglyphic: for it is written that That which is above is like that which is below: and That which is below is like that which is above.

Therefore also doth it behove you to take well heed lest in any manner you fail in this business of purity. For though each act is to be complete on its own plane, and no influence of any other plane is to be brought in for interference or admixture, for that such is all impurity, yet each act should in itself be so complete and perfect that it is a mirror of the perfection of every other plane, and thereby becometh partaker of the pure Light of the highest. Also, since all acts are to be acts of Will in Freedom on every plane, all planes are in reality but one: and thus the lowest expression of any function of that Will is to be at the same time an expression of the highest Will, or only true Will, which is that already implied in the acceptance of the Law.

Be it also well understood of you that it is not necessary or right to shut off natural activity of any kind, as certain false folk, eunuchs of the spirit, most foully teach, to the destruction of many. For in every thing soever inhereth its own perfection proper to it, and to neglect the full operation and function of any one part bringeth distortion and degeneration to the whole. Act therefore in all ways, but transforming the effect of all these ways to the One Way of the Will. And this is possible, because all ways are in actual Truth One Way, the Universe being itself One and One Only, and its appearance as Multiplicity that cardinal illusion which it is the very object of Love to dissipate.

In the achievement of Love are two principles, that of mastering and that of yielding. But the nature of these is hard to explain, for they are subtle, and are best taught by Love Himself in the course of the Operations. But it is to be said generally that the choice of one formula or the other is automatic, being the work of that inmost Will which is alive within you. Seek not then to determine consicously this decision, for herein true instinct is not liable to err.

But now I end, without further words: for in our Holy Books are written many details of the actual practices of Love. And those are the best and truest which are most subtly written in symbol and image, especially in Tragedy and Comedy, for the whole nature of these things is in this kind, Life itself being but the fruit of the flower of Love.

It is then of Life that I must needs now write to you, seeing that by every act of Will in Love you are creating it, a quintessence more mysterious and joyous than you deem, for this which men call life is but a shadow of that true Life, your birthright, and the gift of the Law of Thelema.

III

OF LIFE

Systole and diastole: these are the phases of all component things. Of such also is the life of man. Its curve arises from the latency of the fertilized ovum, say you, to a zenith whence it declines to the nullity of death? Rightly considered, this is not wholly truth. The life of man is but one segment of a serpentine curve which reaches out to infinity, and its zeros but mark the changes from the plus to minus, and minus to plus, coefficients of its equation. It is for this cause, among many others, that wise men in old time chose the Serpent as the Hieroglyph of Life.

Life then is indestructible as all else is. All destruction and construction are changes in the nature of Love, as I have written to you in the former chapter proximate. Yet even as the blood in one pulse-throb of the wrist is not the same blood as that in the next, so individuality is in part destroyed as each life passeth; nay, even with each thought.

What then maketh man, if he dieth and is reborn a changeling with each breath? This: the consciousness of continuity given by memory, the conception of his Self as something whose existence, far from being threatened by these changes, is in verity assured by them. Let then the aspirant to the sacred Wisdom consider his Self no more as one segment of the Serpent, but as the whole. Let him extend his consciousness to regard both birth and death as incidents trivial as systole and diastole of the heart itself, and necessary as they to its function.

To fix the mind in this apprehension of Life, two modes are preferred, as preliminary to the greater realizations to be discussed in their proper order, experiences which transcend even those attainments of Liberty and

Love of which I have hitherto written, and this of Life
which I now inscribe in this my little book which I am
making for you so that you may come unto the Great
Fulfilment.

The first mode is the acquisition of the Magical Memory so-called, and the means is described with accuracy
and clearness in certain of our Holy Books. But for nearly
all men this is found to be a practice of exceeding difficulty.
Let then the aspirant follow the impulse of his own Will
in the decision to choose this or no.

The second mode is easy, agreeable, not tedious, and in
the end as certain as the other. But as the way of error
in the former lieth in Discouragement, so in the latter
are you to beware of False Paths. I may say indeed generally of all Works, that there are two dangers, the obstacle
of Failure, and the snare of Success.

Now this second mode is to dissociate the beings which
make up your life. Firstly, because it is easiest, you should
segregate that Form which is called the Body of Light
(and also by many other names) and set yourself to
travel in this Form, making systematic exploration of those
worlds which are to other material things what your own
Body of Light is to your own material form.

Now it will occur to you in these travels that you come
to many Gates which you are not able to pass. This is
because your Body of Light is itself as yet not strong
enough, or subtle enough, or pure enough: and you must
then learn to dissociate the elements of that Body by a
process similar to the first, your consciousness remaining
in the higher and leaving the lower. In this practice do
you continue, bending your Will like a great Bow to
drive the Arrow of your consciousness through heavens
ever higher and holier. But the continuance in this Way
is itself of vital value: for it shall be that presently habit
herself shall persuade you that the body which is born

and dieth within so little a space as one cycle of Neptune in the Zodiac is no essential of your Self, that the Life of which you are become partaker, while itself subject to the Law of action and reaction, ebb and flow, systole and diastole, is yet insensible to the afflictions of that life which you formerly held to be your sole bond with Existence.

And here must you resolve your Self to make the mightiest endeavours: for so flowered are the meadows of this Eden, and so sweet the fruit of its orchards, that you will love to linger among them, and to take delight in sloth and dalliance therein. Therefore I write to you with energy that you should not do thus to the hindrance of your true progress, because all these enjoyments are dependent upon duality, so that their true name is Sorrow of Illusion, like that of the normal life of man, which you have set out to transcend.

Be it according to your Will, but learn this, that (as it is written) they only are happy who have desired the unattainable. It is then best, ultimately, if it be your Will to find alway your chiefest pleasure in Love, that is, in Conquest, and in Death, that is, in Surrender, as I have written to you already. Thus then you shall delight in these delights aforesaid, but only as toys, holding your manhood firm and keen to pierce to deeper and holier ecstacies without arrest of Will.

Furthermore, I would have you to know that in this practice, pursued with ardour unquenchable, is this especial grace, that you will come as it were by fortune into states which transcend the practice itself, being of the nature of those Works of Pure Light of which I will to write to you in the chapter following after this. For there be certain Gates which no being who is still conscious of dividuality, that is, of the Self and not-Self as opposites, may pass through: and in the storming of those Gates by fiery assault of lust celestial, your flame will burn vehemently against your gross Self, though it be already divine beyond your present imagining, and devour it in a mystical death, so that in the Passing of the Gate all is dissolved in formless Light of Unity.

Now then, returning from these states of being, and in the return also there is a Mystery of Joy, you will be weaned from the Milk of Darkness of the Moon, and made partaker of the Sacrament of Wine that is the blood of the Sun. Yet at the first there may be shock and conflict, for the old thought persists by force of its habit: it is for you to create by repeated act the true right habit of this consciousness of the Life which abideth in Light. And this is easy, if your will be strong: for the true Life is so much more vivid and quintessential than the false that (as I rudely estimate) one hour of the former makes an impression on the memory equal to one year of the latter. One single experience, in duration it may be but a few seconds of terrestrial time, is sufficient to destroy the belief in the reality of our vain life on earth: but this wears gradually away if the consciousness, through shock or fear, adhere not to it, and the Will strive not continually to repetition of that bliss, more beautiful and terrible than death, which it hath won by virtue of Love.

There be moreover many other modes of attaining the apprehension of true Life, and these two following are of much value in breaking up the ice of your mortal error in the vision of your being. And of these the first is the constant contemplation of the Identity of Love and Death, and the understanding of the dissolution of the body as an Act of Love done upon the Body of the Universe, as also it is written at length in our Holy Books. And with this goeth, as it were sister with twin brother, the practice of mortal love as a sacrament symbolical of that great Death: as it is written "Kill thyself" and again "Die daily."

And the second of these lesser modes is the practice of the mental apprehension and analysis of ideas, mainly as I have already taught you, but with especial emphasis in choice of things naturally repulsive, in particular death itself, and its phenomena ancillary. Thus the Buddha bade his disciples to meditate upon Ten Impurities, that is, upon ten cases of death of decomposition, so that the Aspirant, identifying himself with his own corpse in all these imagined forms, might lose the natural horror, loathing, fear or disgust which he might have had for them. Know this, that every idea of every sort becomes unreal, phantastic, and most manifest illusion, if it be subjected to persistent investigation, with concentration. And this is particularly easy to attain in the case of all bodily impressions, because all material things, and especially those of which we are first conscious, namely, our own bodies, are the grossest and most unnatural of all falsities. For there is in us all, latent, that Light wherein no error may endure, and It already teaches our instinct to reject first of all those veils which are most closely wrapt about It. Thus also in meditation it is (for many men) most profitable to concentrate the Will to Love upon the sacred centres of nervous force: for they, like all things, are apt images or true reflexions of their semblables in finer spheres: so that, their gross natures being dissipated by the dissolving acid of the Meditation, their finer souls appear (so to speak) naked, and display their force and glory in the consciousness of the aspirant.

Yea, verily, let your Will to Love burn eagerly toward this creation in yourselves of the true Life that rolls its waves across the shoreless sea of Time! Live not your petty lives in fear of the hours! The Moon and Sun and Stars by which ye measure Time are themselves but servants of that Life which pulses in you, joyous drumbeat as you march triumphant through the Avenue of the Ages. Then, when each birth and death of yours are recognized in this perception as mere milestones on your ever-living Road, what of the foolish incidents of your mean lives? Are they not grains of sand blown by the desert wind, or pebbles that you spurn with your winged feet, or grassy hollows where you press the yielding and elastic turf and moss with lyrical dances? To him who lives in Life naught matters: his is eternal motion, energy, delight of never-failing Change: unwearied, you pass on from aeon to aeon, from star to star, the Universe your playground, its infinite variety of sport ever old and ever new. All those ideas which bred sorrow and fear are known in their truth, and thus become the seed of joy: for you are certain beyond all proof that you can never die; that, though you change, change is part of your own nature: the Great Enemy is become the Great Ally.

And now, rooted in this perfection, your Self become the very Tree of Life, you have a fulcrum for your lever: you are ready to understand that this pulsation of Unity is itself Duality, and therefore, in the highest and most sacred sense, still Sorrow and Illusion; which having comprehended, aspire yet again, even unto the Fourth of the Gifts of the Law, unto the End of the Path, even unto Light.

IV

OF LIGHT

I pray you, be patient with me in that which I shall write concerning Light: for here is a difficulty, ever increasing, in the use of words. Moreover, I am myself carried away constantly and overwhelmed by the sublimity of this matter, so that plain speech may whirl into lyric, when I would plod peaceably with didactic expression.

My best hope is that you may understand by virtue of the sympathy of your intuition, even as two lovers may converse in language as unintelligible to others as it seemeth silly, wanton, and dull, or as in that other intoxication given by Ether the partakers commune with infinite wit, or wisdom, as the mood taketh them, by means of a word or a gesture, being initiated to apprehension by the subtlety of the drug. So may I that am inflamed with love of this Light, and drunken on the wine Ethereal of this Light, communicate not so much with your reason and intelligence, but with that principle hidden in yourself which is ready to partake with me. Even so may man and woman become mad with love, no word being spoken between them, because of the induction (as it were) of their souls. And your understanding will depend upon your ripeness for perception of my Truth. Moreover, if so be that Light in you be ready to break forth, then Light will interpret to you these dark words in the language of Light, even as a string inanimate, duly adjusted, will vibrate to its peculiar tone, struck on another cord. Read, therefore, not only with the eye and brain, but with the rhythm of that Life which you have attained by your Will to Love quickened to dancing measure by these words, which are the movements of the wand of my Will to Love, and so to enkindle your Life to Light.

(In this mood did I interrupt myself in the writing of this my little book, and for two days and nights sleeplessly have I made consideration, wrestling vehemently with my spirit, lest by haste or carelessness I might fail toward you.)

In exercise of Will and of Love are implied motion and change, but in Life is gained an Unity which moveth and changeth only in pulse or in phase, and is even as music. Yet in the attainment of this Life you will already have experienced that the Quintessence thereof is pure Light, an

ecstacy formless, and without bound or mark. In this
Light naught exists, for It is homogeneous: and therefore
have men called it Silence, and Darkness, and Nothing.
But in this, as in all other effort to name it, is the root of
every falsity and misapprehension, since all words imply
some duality. Therefore, though I call it Light, it is not
Light, nor absence of Light. Many also have sought to
describe it by contradictions, since through transcendent
negation of all speech it may by some natures be attained.
Also by images and symbols have men striven to express
it: but always in vain. Yet those that were ready to
apprehend the nature of this Light have understood by
sympathy: and so shall it be with you who read this little
book, loving it. However, be it known unto you that the
best of all instruction on this matter, and the Word best
suited to the Aeon of Horus, is written in *The Book of
the Law*. Yet also the *Book Ararita* is right worthy in the
Work of the Light, as *Trigrammaton* in that of Will,
Cordis Cincti Serpente in the Way of Love, and *Liberi*
in that of Life. All these Books also concern all these
Four Gifts, for in the end you will see that every one is
inseparable from every other.

I wish to write to you with regard to the number 93,
the number of ΘΕΛΗΜΑ. For it is not only the number of
its interpretation ΑΓΑΠΗ, but also that of a Word unknown
to you unless you be Neophyte of our Holy Order of the
A∴ A∴ which word representeth in itself the arising
of the Speech from the Silence, and the return thereunto
in the End. Now this number 93 is thrice 31, which is in
Hebrew LA, that is to say NOT, and so it denieth extension in the three dimensions of Space. Also I would
have you to meditate most closely upon the name NU
that is 56, which we are told to divide, add, multiply, and
understand. By division cometh forth 0.12, as if it were

written Nuith! Hadith! Ra-Hoor-Khuith! before the Dyad. By addition ariseth Eleven, the number of True Magick: and by multiplication Three Hundred, the Number of the Holy Spirit or Fire, the letter Shin, wherein all things are consumed utterly. With these considerations, and a full understanding of the mysteries of the Numbers 666 and 418, you will be armed mightily in this Way of far flight. But you should also consider all numbers in their scales. For there is no means of resolution better than this of pure mathematics, since already therein are gross ideas made fine, and all is ordered and ready for the Alchemy of the Great Work.

I have already written to you of how, in the Will of Love, Light ariseth as the secret part of Life. And in the first, the little, Loves, the attained Life is still personal: later, it becometh impersonal and universal. Now then is Will arrived, may I say so, at its magnetic pole, whence the lines of force point alike every way and no way: and Love also is no more a work, but a state. These qualities are become part of the Universal Life, which proceedeth infinitely with the enjoyment of the Will, and of Love as inherent therein. These things therefore, in their perfection, have lost their names, and their natures. Yet these were the Substance of Life, its Father and Mother: and without their operation and impact Life itself will gradually cease its pulsations. But since the infinite energy of the whole Universe is therein, what then is possible but that it return to its own First Intention, dissolving itself little by little into that Light which is its most secret and most subtle Nature?

For this Universe is in Truth Zero, being an equation whereof Zero is the sum. Whereof this is the proof, that if not, it would be unbalanced, and something would have come from Nothing, which is absurd. This Light or

Nothing is then the Resultant or Totality thereof in pure Perfection; and all other states, positive or negative, are imperfect, since they omit their opposites.

Yet, I would have you consider that this equality or identity of equation between all things and No thing is most absolute, so that you will remain no more in the one than you did in the other. And you will understand this greatest Mystery very easily in the light of those other experiences which you will have enjoyed, wherein motion and rest, change and stability, and many other subtle opposites, have been redeemed to identity by the force of your holy meditation.

The greatest gift of the Law, then, cometh forth by the most perfect practice of the Three Lesser Gifts. And so thoroughly must you travail in this Work that you are able to pass from one side of the equation to the other at will: nay, to comprehend the whole at once, and for ever. This then your time-and-space-bound soul shall travel according to its nature in its orbit, revealing the Law to them that walk in chains, for that this is your particular function.

Now here is the Mystery of the Origin of Evil. Firstly, by Evil we mean that which is in opposition to our own wills: it is therefore a relative, and not an absolute, term. For everything which is the greatest evil of some one is the greatest good of some other, just as the hardness of the wood which wearieth the axeman is the safety of him that ventureth himself upon the sea in a ship built of that wood. And this is a truth easy to apprehend, being superficial, and intelligible to the common mind.

All evil is thus relative, or apparent, or illusory: but, returning to philosophy, I will repeat that its root is always in duality. Therefore the escape from this apparent evil is to seek the Unity, which you shall do as I have already shewn you. But I will now make mention of that which is written concerning this in *The Book of the Law*.

The first step being Will, Evil appears as by this definition, "all that hinders the execution of the Will." Therefore is it written: "The word of Sin is Restriction." It should also be noted that in *The Book of the Thirty Aethyrs* Evil appears as Choronzon whose number is 333, which in Greek importeth Impotence and Idleness: and the nature of Choronzon is Dispersion and Incoherence.

Then in the Way of Love Evil appears as "all that which tends to prevent the Union of any two things." Thus *The Book of the Law* sayeth, under the figure of the Voice of Nuit: "take your fill and will of love as ye will, when, where and with whom ye will! But always unto me." For every act of Love must be "under Will," that is, in accordance with the True Will, which is not to rest content with things partial and transitory, but to proceed firmly to the End. So also, in *The Book of the Thirty Aethyrs*, the Black Brothers are those who shut themselves up, unwilling to destroy themselves by Love.

Thirdly, in the Way of Life Evil appears under a subtler form as "all that which is not impersonal and universal." Here *The Book of the Law*, by the Voice of Hadit, informeth us: "In the sphere I am everywhere the centre." And again: "I am Life and the giver of Life . . . 'come unto me' is a foolish word: for it is I that go. . . . For I am perfect, being Not." For this Life is in every place and time at once, so that in It these limitations no longer exist. And you will have seen this for yourself, that in every act of Love time and space disappear with the creation of the Life by its virtue, as also doth personality itself. For the third time, then, in even subtler sense, "The word of Sin is Restriction."

Lastly, in the Way of Light this same versicle is the key to the conception of Evil. But here Restriction is in the failure to solve the Great Equation, and, later, to prefer one expression or phase of the Universe to the other. Against this we are warned in *The Book of the Law* by the Word of Nuit, saying: "None . . . and two. For I am divided for love's sake, for the chance of union" and therefore, "If this be not aright: if ye confound the space marks, saying: They are one: or saying, They are many . . . then expect the direful judgments. . . ."

Now therefore by the favour of Thoth am I come to the end of this my book: and do you arm yourselves accordingly with the Four Weapons: the Wand for Liberty, the Cup for Love, the Sword for Life, the Disk for Light: and with these work all wonders by the Art of High Magick under the Law of the New Aeon, whose Word is ΘΕΛΗΜΑ.

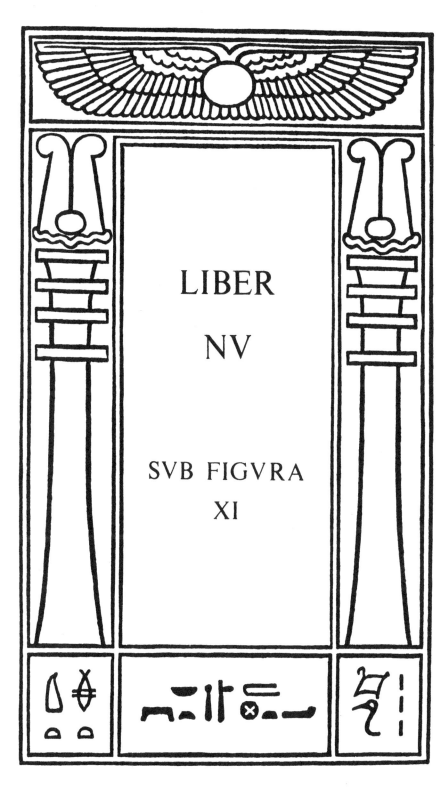

LIBER

NV

SVB FIGVRA

XI

A ∴ A ∴ Publication in Class D

For Winners of the Ordeal X
Imprimatur:
777 · · ·
V.V.V.V. . . .
N. Fra A ∴ A ∴
O.M. 7° = 4°

LIBER NV

ooo. This is the Book of the Cult of the Infinite Without.

oo. The Aspirant is Hadit. Nuit is the infinite expansion of the Rose; Hadit the infinite concentration of the Rood. (*Instruction of V.V.V.V.V.*)

o. First let the Aspirant learn in his heart the First Chapter of *The Book of the Law.* (*Instruction of V.V.V.V.V.*)

1. Worship, *i.e.* identify thyself with, the Khabs, the secret Light within the Heart. Within this, again, unextended, is Hadit.

This is the first practice of Meditation (ccxx, I: 6 and 21).

2. Adore and understand the Rim of the Stélé of Revealing.

> Above, the gemmèd azure is
>   The naked splendour of Nuit;
> She bends in ecstasy to kiss
>   The secret ardours of Hadit.

This is the first practice of Intelligence (ccxx, I: 14).

3. Avoid any act of choice or discrimination.

139

This is the first practice of Ethics (ccxx, I: 22).

4. Consider of six and fifty that $50 \div 6 = 0.12$.

    o the circumference, Nuit.

    . the centre, Hadit.

    1 the unity proceeding, Ra-Hoor-Khuit.

    2 the world of illusion.

Nuit thus comprehends All in None.

Also $50 + 6 = 56 = 5 + 6 = 11$, the key of all Rituals.

And $50 \times 6 = 300$, the Spirit of the Child within.

(Note NFκ = 72, the Shemhamphorash and the Quinaries of the Zodiac, etc.)

This is the second practice of Intelligence (ccxx, I: 24, 25).

5. The Result of this Practice is the Consciousness of the Continuity of Existence, the Omnipresence of the Body of Nuit.

In other words, the Aspirant is conscious only of the Infinite Universe as a single Being. [Note for this the importance of Paragraph 3.—Ed.]

This is the first Indication of the Nature of the Result (ccxx, I: 26).

6. Meditate upon Nuit as the Continuous One resolved into None and Two as the phases of her being.

[For the Universe being self-contained must be capable of expression by the formula $(n - n) = 0$. For if not, let it be expressed by the formula $n - m = p$. That is, the Infinite moves otherwise than within itself, which is absurd.—Ed.]

This is the second practice of Meditation (ccxx, I: 27).

7. Meditate upon the facts of Samadhi on all planes, the liberation of heat in chemistry, joy in natural history, Ananda in religion, when two things join to lose themselves in a third.

This is the third practice of Meditation (ccxx, I: 28, 29, 30).

8. Let the Aspirant pay utmost reverence to the Authority of the A∴A∴ and follow Its instructions, and let him swear a great Oath of Devotion unto Nuit.

This is the second practice of Ethics (ccxx, I: 32).

9. Let the Aspirant beware of the slightest exercise of his will against another being. Thus, lying is a better posture than sitting or standing, as it opposes less resistance to gravitation. Yet his first duty is to the force nearest and most potent; *e.g.* he may rise to greet a friend.

This is the third practice of Ethics (ccxx, I: 41).

10. Let the Aspirant exercise his will without the least consideration for any other being. This direction cannot be understood, much less accomplished, until the previous practice has been perfected.

This is the fourth practice of Ethics (ccxx, I: 42, 43, 44).

11. Let the Aspirant comprehend that these two practices are identical.

This is the third practice of Intelligence (ccxx, I: 45).

12. Let the Aspirant live the Life Beautiful and Pleasant. For this freedom hath he won. But let each act, especially of love, be devoted wholly to his true mistress, Nuit.

This is the fifth practice of Ethics (ccxx, I: 51, 52, 61, 63).

13. Let the Aspirant yearn toward Nuit under the stars of Night, with a love directed by his Magical Will, not merely proceeding from the heart.

This is the first practice of Magick Art (ccxx, I: 57).

14. The Result of this Practice in the subsequent life of the Aspirant is to fill him with unimaginable joys: to give him certainty concerning the nature of the phenomenon called death; to give him peace unalterable, rest, and ecstasy.

This is the second Indication of the Nature of the Result (ccxx, I: 58).

15. Let the Aspirant prepare a perfume of resinous woods and gums, according to his inspiration.

This is the second practice of Magick Art (ccxx, I: 59).

16. Let the Aspirant prepare a Pantacle, as follows.

Inscribe a circle within a Pentagram, upon a ground square or of such other convenient shape as he may choose. Let the circle be scarlet, the Pentagram black, the ground royal blue studded with golden stars.

Within the circle, at its centre, shall be painted a sigil that shall be revealed to the Aspirant by Nuit Herself.

And this Pentacle shall serve for a Telesmatic Image, or as an Eidolon, or as a Focus for the mind.

This is the third practice of Magick Art (ccxx, I: 60).

17. Let the Aspirant find a lonely place, if possible a place in the Desert of Sand, or if not, a place unfrequented, and without objects to disturb the view. Such are moorlands, fens, the open sea, broad rivers, and open fields. Also, and especially, the summits of mountains.

There let him invoke the Goddess as he hath Wisdom and Understanding so to do. But let this Invocation be that of a pure heart, *i.e.,* a heart wholly devoted to Her, and let him remember that it is Hadit Himself in the most secret place thereof that invoketh. Then let this serpent Hadit burst into flame.

This is the fourth practice of Magick Art (ccxx, I: 61).

18. Then shall the Aspirant come a little to lie in Her bosom.

This is the third Indication of the Nature of the Result (ccxx, I: 61).

19. Let the Aspirant stand upon the edge of a precipice in act or in imagination. And let him imagine and suffer the fear of falling.

Next let him imagine with this aid that the Earth is falling, and he with it, or he from it; and considering the infinity of space, let him excite the fear within him to the point of ecstasy, so that the most dreadful dream of falling that he hath ever suffered be as nothing in comparison.

This is the fourth practice of Meditation. (Instruction of V.V.V.V.V.)

20. Thus having understood the nature of this Third Indication, let him in his Magick Rite fall from himself into Nuit, or expand into Her, as his imagination may compel him.

And at that moment, desiring earnestly the Kiss of Nuit, let him give one particle of dust, *i.e.*, let Hadit give himself up utterly to Her.

This is the fifth practice of Magick Art (ccxx, I: 61).

21. Then shall he lose all in that hour.

This is the fourth Indication of the Nature of the Result (ccxx, I: 61).

22. Let the Aspirant prepare a lovesong of rapture unto the Goddess, or let him be inspired by Her unto this.

This is the sixth practice of Magick Art (ccxx, I: 63).

23. Let the Aspirant be clad in a single robe. An "abbai" of scarlet wrought with gold is most suitable. [The abbai is not unlike the Japanese kimono. It must fold simply over the breast without belt or other fastening. —Ed.]

This is the seventh practice of Magick Art (ccxx, I: 61).

24. Let the Aspirant wear a rich head-dress. A crown of gold adorned with sapphires or diamonds with a royal blue cap of maintenance, or nemmes, is most suitable.

This is the eighth practice of Magick Art (ccxx, I: 61).

25. Let the Aspirant wear many jewels such as he may possess.

This is the ninth practice of Magick Art (ccxx, I: 63).

26. Let the Aspirant prepare an Elixir or libation as he may have wit to do.

This is the tenth practice of Magick Art (ccxx, I: 63).

27. Let the Aspirant invoke, lying supine, his robe spread out as it were a carpet.

This is the eleventh practice of Magick Art. (Instruction of V.V.V.V.V.)

28. Summary. Preliminaries.

These are the necessary possessions.

　　1. The Crown or head-dress.
　　2. The Jewels.
　　3. The Pantacle.
　　4. The Robe.
　　5. The Song or Incantation.
　　6. The Place of Invocation.
　　7. The Perfume.
　　8. The Elixir.

29. Summary continued. Preliminaries.

These are the necessary comprehensions.

　　1. The Natures of Nuit and Hadit, and their relation.
　　2. The Mystery of the Individual Will.

30. Summary continued. Preliminaries.

These are the meditations necessary to be accomplished.

　　1. The discovery of Hadit in the Aspirant, and indentification with Him.
　　2. The Continuous One.
　　3. The value of the Equation $n + (-n)$.
　　4. Cremnophobia.

31. Summary continued. Preliminaries.

These are the Ethical Practices to be accomplished.

　　1. Assertion of Kether-point-of-view.
　　2. Reverence to the Order.
　　3. Abolition of human will.
　　4. Exercise of true will.
　　5. Devotion to Nuit throughout a beautified life.

32. Summary continued. The Actual Rite.
    1. Retire to desert with crown and other insignia and implements.
    2. Burn perfume.
    3. Chant incantation.
    4. Drink unto Nuit of the Elixir.
    5. Lying supine, with eyes fixed on the stars, practice the sensation of falling into nothingness.
    6. Being actually within the bosom of Nuit, let Hadit surrender Himself.

33. Summary concluded. The Results.
    1. Expansion of consciousness to that of the Infinite.
    2. "Loss of all" the highest mystical attainment.
    3. True Wisdom and Perfect Happiness.

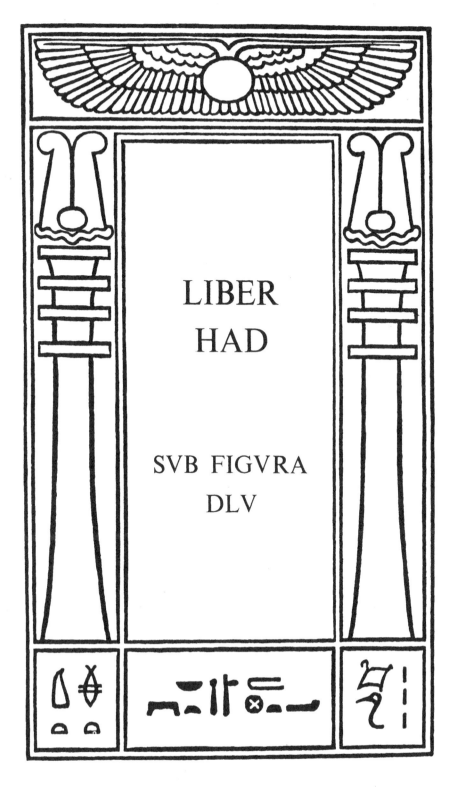

LIBER HAD

SVB FIGVRA
DLV

A ∴ A ∴ Publication in Class D

For Winners of the Ordeal X
Imprimatur:
ᕁᕁᕁ ...
V.V.V.V.V. ....
N. Fra A ∴ A ∴
O.M. 7° = 4°

LIBER HAD

000. This is the Book of the Cult of the Infinite Within.

00. The Aspirant is Nuit. Nuit is the infinite expansion of the Rose; Hadit the infinite concentration of the Rood. (*Instruction of V.V.V.V.V.*)

0. First let the Aspirant learn in his heart the Second Chapter of *The Book of the Law*. (*Instruction of V.V.V.V.V.*)

1. Worship, *i.e.*, identify thyself with, Nuit, as a lambent flame of blue, all-touching, all-penetrant, her lovely hands upon the black earth, and her lithe body arched for love, and her soft feet not hurting the little flowers, even as She is imaged in the Stélé of Revealing.

This is the first practice of Meditation (ccxx, I: 26).

2. Let him further identify himself with the heart of Nuit, whose ecstasy is in that of her children, and her joy to see their joy, who sayeth: I love you! I yearn to you. Pale or purple, veiled or voluptuous, I who am all pleasure and purple, and drunkenness of the innermost sense, desire you. Put on the wings, and arouse the coiled splendour within you. Come unto me! . . . Sing the rapturous love-song unto me! Burn to me perfumes!

Wear to me jewels! Drink to me, for I love you! I love you! I am the blue-lidded daughter of Sunset; I am the naked brilliance of the voluptuous night-sky. To me! To me!

This is the second practice of Meditation (ccxx, I: 13, 61, 63, 64, 65).

3. Let the Aspirant apply himself to comprehend Hadit as an unextended point clothed with Light ineffable. And let him beware lest he be dazzled by that Light.

This is the first practice of Intelligence (ccxx, II: 2).

4. Let the Aspirant apply himself to comprehend Hadit as the ubiquitous centre of every sphere conceivable.

This is the second practice of Intelligence (ccxx, II: 3).

5. Let the Aspirant apply himself to comprehend Hadit as the soul of every man, and of every star, conjoining this in his Understanding with the Word (*ccxx*, I: 2). "Every man and every woman is a star." Let this conception be that of Life, the giver of Life, and let him perceive that therefore the knowledge of Hadit is the knowledge of death.

This is the third practice of Intelligence (ccxx, II: 6).

6. Let the Aspirant apply himself to comprehend Hadit as the Magician or maker of Illusion, and the Exorcist or destroyer of Illusion, under the figure of the axle of the Wheel, and the cube in the circle. Also as the Universal Soul of Motion.

[This conception harmonises Thoth and Harpocrates in a very complete and miraculous manner. Thoth is both the Magus of Taro (see *Liber 418*) and the Universal Mercury; Harpocrates both the destroyer of Typhon and the Babe on the Lotus. Note that the "Ibis position" formulates this conception most exactly.—Ed.]

This is the fourth practice of Intelligence (ccxx, II: 7).

7. Let the Aspirant apply himself to comprehend Hadit as the perfect, that is Not, and solve the mystery of the

numbers of Hadit and his components by his right Ingenium.

This is the fifth practice of Intelligence (ccxx, II: 15, 16).

8. Let the Aspirant, bearing him as a great King, root out and destroy without pity all things in himself and his surroundings which are weak, dirty, or diseased, or otherwise unworthy. And let him be exceeding proud and joyous.

This is the first practice of Ethics (ccxx, II: 18, 19, 20, 21).

9. Let the Aspirant apply himself to comprehend Hadit as the Snake that giveth Knowledge and Delight and bright glory, who stirreth the hearts of men with drunkenness. This snake is blue and gold; its eyes are red, and its spangles green and ultra-violet.

(That is, as the most exalted form of the Serpent Kundalini.)

This is the sixth practice of Intelligence (ccxx, II: 22, 50, 51).

10. Let him further identify himself with this Snake.

This is the second practice of Meditation (ccxx, II: 22).

11. Let the Aspirant take wine and strange drugs, according to his knowledge and experience, and be drunk thereof.

[The Aspirant should be in so sensitive a condition that a single drop, perhaps even the smell, should suffice. —Ed.]

This is the first practice of Magick Art (ccxx, II: 22).

12. Let the Aspirant concentrate his consciousness in the Rood Cross set up upon the Mountain, and identify himself with It. Let him be well aware of the difference between Its own soul, and that thought which it habitually awakes in his own mind.

This is the third practice of Meditation, and as it will be found, a comprehension and harmony and absorption of the practices of Intelligence (ccxx, II: 22).

13. Let the Aspirant apply himself to comprehend Hadit as the Unity which is the Negative. [Ain Elohim. —Ed.]

This is the seventh practice of Intelligence (ccxx, II: 23).

14. Let the Aspirant live the life of a strong and beautiful being, proud and exalted, contemptuous of and fierce toward all that is base and vile.

This is the second practice of Ethics (ccxx, II: 24, 25, 45–49, 52, 56–60).

15. Let the Aspirant apply himself to comprehend Hadit according to this 26th verse of the Second Chapter of *The Book of the Law.* And this shall be easy for him if he have well accomplished the Third Practice of Meditation.

This is the eighth practice of Intelligence (ccxx, II: 26).

16. Let the Aspirant destroy Reason in himself according to the practice in *Liber CDLXXIV.*

This is the fourth practice of Meditation (ccxx, II: 27–33).

17. Let the Aspirant observe duly the Feasts appointed by the A∴A∴ and perform such rituals of the elements as he possesseth, invoking them duly in their season.

This is the second practice of Magick Art (ccxx, II: 35–43).

18. Let the Aspirant apply himself to comprehend Hadit as a babe in the egg of the Spirit [Akasha.—Ed.] that is invisible within the 4 elements.

This is the ninth practice of Intelligence (ccxx, II: 49).

19. The Aspirant seated in his Asana will suddenly commence to breathe strangely, and this without the Operation of his will; the Inspiration will be associated with the thought of intense excitement and pleasure, even to exhaustion; and the Expiration very rapid and forceful, as if this excitement were suddenly released.

This is the first and last Indication of the Sign of the Beginning of this Result (ccxx, II: 63).

20. A light will appear to the Aspirant, unexpectedly. Hadit will arise within him, and Nuit concentrate Herself upon him from without. He will be overcome, and the Conjunction of the Infinite Without with the Infinite Within will take place in his soul, and the One be resolved into the None.

This is the first Indication of the Nature of the Result (ccxx, II: 61, 62, 64).

21. Let the Aspirant strengthen his body by all means in his power, and let him with equal pace refine all that is in him to the true ideal of Royalty. Yet let his formula, as a King's ought, be Excess.

This is the third practice of Ethics (ccxx, II: 70, 71).

22. To the Aspirant who succeeds in this practice the result goes on increasing until its climax in his physical death in its due season. This practice should, however, prolong life.

This is the second Indication of the Nature of the Result (ccxx, II: 66, 72–74).

23. Let the Adept aspire to the practice of *Liber XI* and preach to mankind.

This is the fourth Practice of Ethics (ccxx, II: 76).

24. Let the Adept worship the Name, foursquare, mystic, wonderful, of the Beast, and the name of His house; and give blessing and worship to the prophet of the lovely Star.

This is the fifth practice of Ethics (ccxx, II: 78, 79).

25. Let the Aspirant expand his consciousness to that of Nuit, and bring it rushing inward. It may be practised by imagining that the Heavens are falling, and then transferring the consciousness to them.

This is the fifth practice of Meditation. (Instruction of V.V.V.V.V.)

26. Summary. Preliminaries.
These are the necessary possessions.
    1. Wine and strange drugs.
27. Summary continued. Preliminaries.
These are the necessary comprehensions.
    1. The nature of Hadit (and of Nuit, and the relations between them).
28. Summary continued. Preliminaries.
These are the meditations necessary to be accomplished.
    1. Identification with Nuit, body and spirit.
    2. Identification with Hadit as the Snake.
    3. Identification with Hadit as the Rood Cross.
    4. Destruction of Reason.
    5. The Falling of the Heavens.
29. Summary continued. Preliminaries.
These are the Ethical Practices to be accomplished.
    1. The destruction of all unworthiness in one's self and one's surroundings.
    2. Fulness, almost violence, of life.
30. Summary continued. Preliminaries.
These are the Magick Arts to be practised.
    1. During the preparation, perform the Invocations of the Elements.
    2. Observe the Feasts appointed by the A .·. A .·. .
31. Summary continued. The actual Practice.
    1. Procure the suitable intoxication.
    2. As Nuit, contract thyself with infinite force upon Hadit.
32. Summary continued. The Results.
    1. Peculiar automatic breathing begins.
    2. A light appears.
    3. Samadhi of the two Infinites within aspirant.
    4. Intensification of 3 on repetition.

     5. Prolongation of life.

     6. Death becomes the climax of the practice.

33. Summary concluded.

These are the practices to be performed in token of Thanksgiving for success.

     1. Aspiration to *Liber XI*.

     2. Preaching of Θελημα to mankind.

     3. Blessing and Worship to the prophet of the lovely Star.

SECTION III

YOGA

LIBER
E

VEL
EXERCITIORVM

SVB FIGVRA

IX

A ∴ A ∴ Publication in Class B

Issued by order:
D.D.S. 7° = 4° Premonstrator
O.S.V. 6° = 5° Imperator
N.S.F. 5° = 6° Cancellarius

LIBER E

VEL EXERCITIORVM

I

1. It is absolutely necessary that all experiments should be recorded in detail during, or immediately after, their performance.

2. It is highly important to note the physical and mental condition of the experimenter or experimenters.

3. The time and place of all experiments must be noted; also the state of the weather, and generally all conditions which might conceivably have any result upon the experiment either as adjuvants to or causes of the result, or as inhibiting it, or as sources of error.

4. The A ∴ A ∴ will not take official notice of any experiments which are not thus properly recorded.

5. It is not necessary at this stage for us to declare fully the ultimate end of our researches; nor indeed would it be understood by those who have not become proficient in these elementary courses.

6. The experimenter is encouraged to use his own intelligence, and not to rely upon any other person or persons, however distinguished, even among ourselves.

7. The written record should be intelligibly prepared so that others may benefit from its study.

8. The book *John St. John* published in the first number of *The Equinox* is an example of this kind of record by a very advanced student. It is not as simply written as we could wish, but will shew the method.

9. The more scientific the record is, the better.

Yet the emotions should be noted, as being some of the conditions.

Let then the record be written with sincerity and care, and with practice it will be found more and more to approximate to the ideal.

II

Physical Clairvoyance

1. Take a pack of (78) Tarot playing cards. Shuffle; cut. Draw one card. Without looking at it, try and name it. Write down the card you name, and the actual card. Repeat, and tabulate results.

2. This experiment is probably easier with an old genuine pack of Tarot cards, preferably a pack used for divination by some one who really understood the matter.

3. Remember that one should expect to name the right card once in 78 times. Also be careful to exclude all possibilities of obtaining the knowledge through the ordinary senses of sight and touch, or even smell.

There was once a man whose finger-tips were so sensitive that he could feel the shape and position of the pips, and so judge the card correctly.

4. It is better to try first, the easier form of the experiment, by guessing only the suit.

5. Remember that in 78 experiments you should obtain 22 trumps and 14 of each other suit; so that, without any

clairvoyance at all, you can guess right twice in 7 times (roughly) by calling trumps each time.

6. Note that some cards are harmonious.

Thus it would not be a bad error to call the five of Swords ("The Lord of Defeat") instead of the ten of Swords ("The Lord of Ruin"). But to call the Lord of Love (2 Cups) for the Lord of Strife (5 Wands) would show that you were getting nothing right.

Similarly, a card ruled by Mars would be harmonious with a 5, a card of Gemini with "The Lovers."

7. These harmonies must be thoroughly learnt, according to the numerous tables given in 777.

8. As you progress, you will find that you are able to distinguish the suit correctly three times in four, and that very few indeed inharmonious errors occur, while in 78 experiments you are able to name the card aright as many as 15 or 20 times.

9. When you have reached this stage, you may be admitted for examination; and in the event of your passing, you will be given more complex and difficult exercises.

III

Asana—Posture

1. You must learn to sit perfectly still with every muscle tense for long periods.

2. You must wear no garment that interferes with the posture in any of these experiments.

3. The first position: The God. Sit in a chair; head up, back straight, knees together, hands on knees, eyes closed.

4. The second position: The Dragon. Kneel; buttocks

resting on the heels, toes turned back, back and head straight, hands on thighs.

5. The third position: The Ibis. Stand; hold left ankle with right hand (and alternately practise right ankle in left hand, &c.) free forefinger on lips.

6. The fourth position: The Thunderbolt. Sit: left heel pressing up anus, right foot poised on its toes, the heel covering the phallus; arms stretched out over the knees: head and back straight.

7. Various things will happen to you while you are practising these positions; they must be carefully analysed and described.

8. Note down the duration of practice, the severity of the pain (if any) which accompanies it, the degree of rigidity attained, and any other pertinent matters.

9. When you have progressed up to the point that a saucer filled to the brim with water and poised upon the head does not spill one drop during a whole hour, and when you can no longer perceive the slightest tremor in any muscle; when, in short, you are perfectly steady and easy, you will be admitted for examination; and, should you pass, you will be instructed in more complex and difficult practices.

IV

Pranayama
Regularisation of the Breathing

1. At rest in one of your positions, close the right nostril with the thumb of the right hand and breathe out slowly and completely through the left nostril, while your watch marks 20 seconds. Breathe in through the same nostril for 10 seconds. Changing hands, repeat with the other nostril. Let this be continuous for one hour.

2. When this is quite easy to you, increase the periods to 30 and 15 seconds.

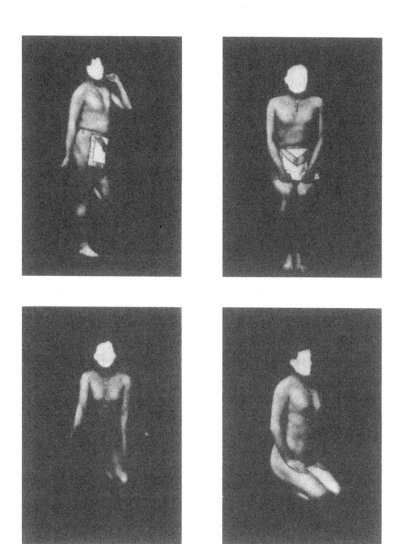

The Thunderbolt   The Dragon

In the Ibis the head is tilted very slightly too far back; in the Thunderbolt the right foot might be a little higher and the right knee lower with advantage.

3. When this is quite easy to you, but not before, breathe out for 15 seconds, in for 15 seconds, and hold the breath for 15 seconds.

4. When you can do this with perfect ease and comfort for a whole hour, practise breathing out for 40, in for 20 seconds.

5. This being attained, practise breathing out for 20, in for 10, holding the breath for 30 seconds.

When this has become perfectly easy to you, you may be admitted for examination, and should you pass, you will be instructed in more complex and difficult practices.

6. You will find that the presence of food in the stomach, even in small quantities, makes the practices very difficult.

7. Be very careful never to overstrain your powers; especially never get so short of breath that you are compelled to breathe out jerkily or rapidly.

8. Strive after depth, fulness, and regularity of breathing.

9. Various remarkable phenomena will very probably occur during these practices. They must be carefully analysed and recorded.

V

Dharana: Control of Thought

1. Constrain the mind to concentrate itself upon a single simple object imagined.

The five tatwas are useful for this purpose; they are: a black oval; a blue disk; a silver crescent; a yellow square; a red triangle.

2. Proceed to combinations of simple objects: *e.g.*, a black oval within a yellow square, and so on.

3. Proceed to simple moving objects, such as a pendulum swinging, a wheel revolving, &c. Avoid living objects.

4. Proceed to combinations of moving objects, *e.g.*, a piston rising and falling while a pendulum is swinging. The relation between the two movements should be varied in different experiments.

Or even a system of fly-wheels, eccentrics, and governor.

5. During these practices the mind must be absolutely confined to the object determined upon; no other thought must be allowed to intrude upon the consciousness. The moving systems must be regular and harmonious.

6. Note carefully the duration of the experiments, the number and nature of the intruding thoughts, the tendency of the object itself to depart from the course laid out for it, and any other phenomena which may present themselves. Avoid overstrain. This is very important.

7. Proceed to imagine living objects; as a man, preferably some man known to, and respected by, yourself.

8. In the intervals of these experiments you may try to imagine the objects of the other senses, and to concentrate upon them.

For example, try to imagine the taste of chocolate, the smell of roses, the feeling of velvet, the sound of a waterfall, or the ticking of a watch.

9. Endeavour finally to shut out all objects of any of the senses, and prevent all thoughts arising in your mind. When you feel that you have attained some success in these practices, apply for examination, and should you pass, more complex and difficult practices will be prescribed for you.

VI

Physical Limitations

1. It is desirable that you should discover for yourself your physical limitations.

2. To this end ascertain for how many hours you can subsist without food or drink before your working capacity is seriously interfered with.

3. Ascertain how much alcohol you can take, and what forms of drunkenness assail you.

4. Ascertain how far you can walk without once stopping; likewise with dancing, swimming, running, &c.

5. Ascertain for how many hours you can do without sleep.

6. Test your endurance with various gymnastic exercises, club-swinging and so on.

7. Ascertain for how long you can keep silence.

8. Investigate any other capacities and aptitudes which may occur to you.

9. Let all these things be carefully and conscientiously recorded; for according to your powers will it be demanded of you.

VII

A Course of Reading

1. The object of most of the foregoing practices will not at first be clear to you; but at least (who will deny it?) they will have trained you in determination, accuracy, introspection, and many other qualities which are valuable to all men in their ordinary avocations, so that in no case will your time have been wasted.

2. That you may gain some insight into the nature of the Great Work which lies beyond these elementary trifles, however, we should mention that an intelligent person may gather more than a hint of its nature from the following books, which are to be taken as serious and learned contributions to the study of nature, though not necessarily to be implicitly relied upon.

The Yi King [S.B.E. Series, Oxford University Press]
The Tao Teh King [S.B.E. Series]
Tannhäuser by A. Crowley
The Upanishads
The Bhagavad-Gita
The Voice of the Silence
Raja Yoga by Swami Vivekanânda
The Shiva Sanhita
The Aphorisms of Patanjali
The Sword of Song
The Book of the Dead
Rituel et Dogme de la Haute Magie
The Book of the Sacred Magic of Abramelin the Mage
The Goetia
The Hathayoga Pradipika
Erdmann's *History of Philosophy*
The Spiritual Guide of Molinos
The Star in the West (Captain Fuller)
The Dhammapada [S.B.E. Series, Oxford University Press]
The Questions of King Milinda [S.B.E. Series]
777 vel Prolegomena, &c.
Varieties of Religious Experience (James)
Kabbala Denudata
Konx Om Pax

3. Careful study of these books will enable the pupil to speak in the language of his master and facilitate communication with him.

4. The pupil should endeavour to discover the fundamental harmony of these very varied works; for this purpose he will find it best to study the most extreme divergences side by side.

5. He may at any time that he wishes apply for examination in this course of reading.

6. During the whole of this elementary study and practice, he will do wisely to seek out, and attach himself to, a master, one competent to correct him and advise

him. Nor should he be discouraged by the difficulty of finding such a person.

7. Let him further remember that he must in no wise rely upon, or believe in, that master. He must rely entirely upon himself, and credit nothing whatever but that which lies within his own knowledge and experience.

8. As in the beginning, so at the end, we here insist upon the vital importance of the written record as the only possible check upon error derived from the various qualities of the experimenter.

9. Thus let the work be accomplished duly; yea, let it be accomplished duly.

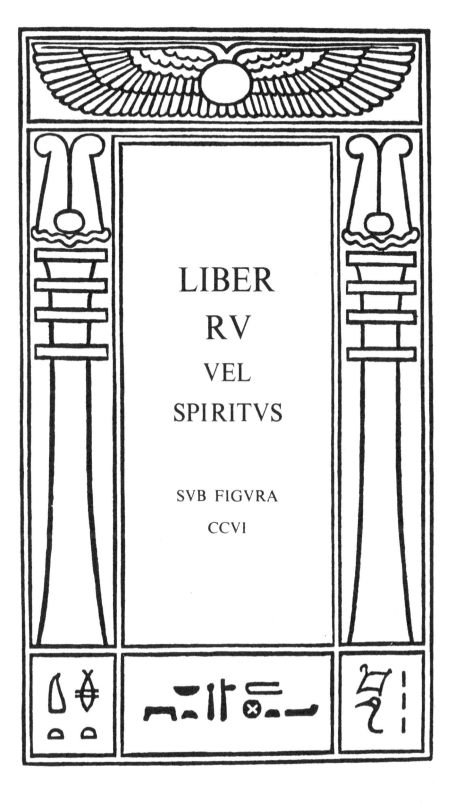

LIBER
RV
VEL
SPIRITVS

SVB FIGVRA

CCVI

A ∴ A ∴ Publication in Class B

Imprimatur:
N. Fra A ∴ A ∴

LIBER RV

2. Let the Zelator observe the current of his breath.

3. Let him investigate the following statements, and prepare a careful record of research.

(a) Certain actions induce the flow of the breath through the right nostril (Pingala); and, conversely, the flow of the breath through Pingala induces certain actions.

(b) Certain other actions induce the flow of the breath through the left nostril (Ida), and conversely.

(c) Yet a third class of actions induce the flow of the breath through both nostrils at once (Sushumna), and conversely.

(d) The degree of mental and physical activity is interdependent with the distance from the nostrils at which the breath can be felt by the back of the hand.

4. *First practice.* Let him concentrate his mind upon the act of breathing, saying mentally "The breath flows in," "The breath flows out," and record the results. (This practice may resolve itself into Mahasatipatthana [vide

Liber XXV] or induce Samadhi. Whichever occurs should be followed up as the right Ingenium of the Zelator, or the advice of his Practicus, may determine.)

5. *Second practice.* Pranayama. This is outlined in *Liber E.* Further, let the Zelator accomplished in those practices endeavour to master a cycle of 10, 20, 40 or even 16, 32, 64. But let this be done gradually and with due caution. And when he is steady and easy both in Asana and Pranayama, let him still further increase the period.

Thus let him investigate these statements which follow:

(a) If Pranayama be properly performed, the body will first of all become covered with sweat. This sweat is different in character from that customarily induced by exertion. If the Practitioner rub this sweat thoroughly into his body, he will greatly strengthen it.

(b) The tendency to perspiration will stop as the practice is continued, and the body become automatically rigid.

Describe this rigidity with minute accuracy.

(c) The state of automatic rigidity will develop into a state characterised by violent spasmodic movements of which the Practitioner is unconscious, but of whose result he is aware. This result is that the body hops gently from place to place. After the first two or three occurrences of this experience Asana is not lost. The body appears (on another theory) to have lost its weight almost completely, and to be moved by an unknown force.

(d) As a development of this stage, the body rises into the air, and remains there for an appreciably long period, from a second to an hour or more.

Let him further investigate any mental results which may occur.

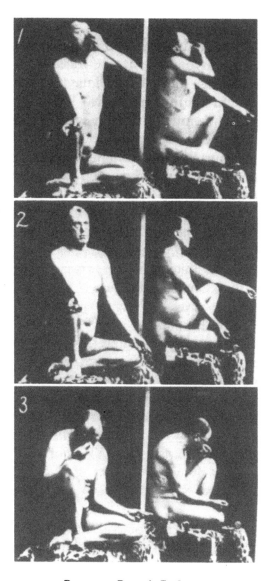

Pranayama Properly Performed

[It has been found necessary to show this because students were trying to do it without exertion, and in other ways incorrectly.—Ed.]

1. The end of Purakam. The bad definition of the image is due to the spasmodic trembling which accompanies the action. 2. Kumbhakham. 3. The end of Rekakam.

6. *Third practice.* In order both to economize his time and to develop his powers, let the Zelator practise the deep full breathing which his preliminary exercises will have taught him during his walks. Let him repeat a sacred sentence (mantra), or let him count, in such a way that his footfall beats accurately with the rhythm thereof, as is done in dancing. Then let him practise Pranayama, at first without the Kumbahkham, and paying no attention to the nostrils otherwise than to keep them clear. Let him begin by an indrawing of the breath for 4 paces, and a breathing out for 4 paces. Let him increase this gradually to 6,6; 8,8; 12,12; 16,16; and 24,24; or more if he be able. Next let him practise in the proper proportion 4,8; 6,12; 8,16; 12,24; and so on. Then, if he choose, let him recommence the series, adding a gradually increasing period of Kumbhakham.

7. *Fourth practice.* Following on this third practice, let him quicken his mantra and his pace, until the walk develops into a dance. This may also be practised with the ordinary waltz step, using a mantra in three-time, such as ἐπελθον, ἐπελθον, Ἀρτεμις; or IAO; IAO SABAO; in such cases the practice may be combined with devotion to a particular deity: see *Liber CLXXV*. For the dance as such it is better to use a mantra of a non-committal character, such as το εἰναι, το καλον, το ἀγαθον, or the like.

8. *Fifth practice.* Let him practise mental concentration during the dance, and investigate the following statements:
 (*a*) The dance becomes independent of the will.
 (*b*) Similar phenomena to those described in
  5 (*a*) (*b*) (*c*) (*d*) occur.
 (*c*) Certain important mental results occur.

9. A note concerning the depth and fulness of the breathing. In all proper expiration, the last possible portion of air should be expelled. In this the muscles of the

throat, chest, ribs, and abdomen must be fully employed, and aided by the pressing of the upper arms into the flanks, and of the head into the thorax.

In all proper inspiration, the last possible portion of air must be drawn into the lungs.

In all proper holding of the breath, the body must remain absolutely still.

Ten minutes of such practice is ample to induce profuse sweating in any place of a temperature of 17° C. or over.

The progress of the Zelator in acquiring a depth and fulness of breath should be tested by the respirometer.

The exercises should be carefully graduated to avoid overstrain and possible damage to the lungs.

This depth and fulness of breath should be kept as much as possible, even in the rapid exercises, with the exception of the sixth practice following.

10. *Sixth practice*. Let the Zelator breathe as shallowly and rapidly as possible. He should assume the attitude of his moment of greatest expiration, and breathe only with the muscles of his throat. He may also practise lengthening the period between each shallow breathing.

[This may be combined when acquired with concentration on the Visuddhi chakra, *i.e.*, let him fix his mind unwaveringly upon a point in the spine opposite the larynx.—Ed.]

11. *Seventh practice*. Let the Zelator breathe as deeply and rapidly as possible.

12. *Eighth practice*. Let the Zelator practise restraint of breathing in the following manner.

At any stage of breathing let him suddenly hold the breath, enduring the need to breathe until it passes, returns, and passes again, and so on until consciousness is lost, either rising to Samadhi or similar supernormal condition, or falling into oblivion.

13. *Ninth practice*. Let him practise the usual forms of

Pranayama, but let Kumbhakham be used after instead of before expiration. Let him gradually increase the period of this Kumbhakham as in the case of the other.

14. A note concerning the conditions of these experiments.

The conditions favourable are dry and bracing air, a warm climate, absence of wind, absence of noise, insects, and all other disturbing influences,[1] a retired situation, simple food eaten in great moderation at the conclusion of the practices of morning and afternoon and on no account before practising. Bodily health is almost essential, and should be most carefully guarded. (See *Liber CLXXXV*, Task of a Neophyte.) A diligent and tractable disciple, or the Practicus of the Zelator, should aid him in his work. Such a disciple should be noiseless, patient, vigilant, prompt, cheerful, of gentle manner and reverent to his master, intelligent to anticipate his wants, cleanly and gracious, not given to speech, devoted and unselfish. With all this he should be fierce and terrible to strangers and all hostile influences, determined and vigorous, unceasingly vigilant, the guardian of the threshold.

It is not desirable that the Zelator should employ any other creature than a man, save in cases of necessity. Yet for some of these purposes a dog will serve, for others a woman. There are also others appointed to serve, but these are not for the Zelator.

15. *Tenth practice.* Let the Zelator experiment if he will with inhalations of oxygen, nitrous oxide, carbon dioxide, and other gases mixed in small proportion with his air during his practices. These experiments are to be conducted with caution in the presence of a medical man of experience, and they are only useful as facilitating

---

1. Note that in the early stages of concentration of the mind, such annoyances become negligible.

a simulacrum of the results of the proper practices, and thereby enheartening the Zelator.

16. *Eleventh practice.* Let the Zelator at any time during the practices, especially during periods of Kumbhakham, throw his will utterly toward his Holy Guardian Angel, directing his eyes inward and upward, and turning back his tongue as if to swallow it.

(This latter operation is facilitated by severing the fraenum linguae, which, if done, should be done by a competent surgeon. We do not advise this or any similar method of cheating difficulties. This is, however, harmless.)

In this manner the practice is to be raised from the physical to the spiritual plane, even as the words Ruh, Ruach, Pneuma, Spiritus, Geist, Ghost, and indeed words of almost all languages, have been raised from their physical meaning of wind, air, breath, or movement, to the spiritual plane. [RV is the old root meaning 'yoni' and hence 'Wheel' (Fr. roue, Lat. rota, wheel) and the corresponding Semitic root means 'to go'. Similarly Spirit is connected with "spiral."—Ed.]

17. Let the Zelator attach no credit to any statements that may have been made throughout the course of this instruction, and reflect that even the counsel which We have given as suitable to the average case may be entirely unsuitable to his own.

LIBER
ASTARTE
VEL
BERYLLI

SVB FIGVRA

CLXXV

A∴ A∴ Publication in Class B

Imprimatur:
N. Fra A∴ A∴

LIBER ASTARTE

0. This is the book of Uniting Himself to a particular Deity by devotion.

1. *Considerations before the Threshold.* First, concerning the choice of a particular Deity. This matter is of no import, sobeit that thou choose one suited to thine own highest nature. Howsoever, this method is not so suitable for gods austere as Saturn, or intellectual as Thoth. But for such deities as in themselves partake in anywise of love it is a perfect mode.

2. *Concerning the prime method of this Magick Art.* Let the devotee consider well that although Christ and Osiris be one, yet the former is to be worshipped with Christian, and the latter with Egyptian rites. And this although the rites themselves are ceremonially equivalent. There should, however, be *one* symbol declaring the transcending of such limitations; and with regard to the Deity also, there should be some *one* affirmation of his identity both with all other similar gods of other nations, and with the Supreme of whom all are but partial reflections.

3. *Concerning the chief place of devotion.* This is the Heart of the devotee, and should be symbolically rep-

resented by that room or spot which he loves best. And the dearest spot therein shall be the shrine of his temple. It is most convenient if this shrine and altar should be sequestered in woods, or in a private grove, or garden. But let it be protected from the profane.

4. *Concerning the Image of the Deity.* Let there be an image of the Deity; first, because in meditation there is mindfulness induced thereby; and second, because a certain power enters and inhabits it by virtue of the ceremonies; or so it is said, and We deny it not. Let this image be the most beautiful and perfect which the devotee is able to procure; or if he be able to paint or to carve the same, it is all the better. As for Deities with whose nature no Image is compatible, let them be worshipped in an empty shrine. Such are Brahma and Allah. Also some post-captivity conceptions of Jehovah.

5. *Further concerning the shrine.* Let this shrine be furnished appropriately as to its ornaments, according to the book 777. With ivy and pine-cones, that is to say, for Bacchus, and let lay before him both grapes and wine. So also for Ceres let there be corn, and cakes; or for Diana moon-wort and pale herbs, and pure water. Further, it is well to support the shrine with talismans of the planets, signs and elements appropriate. But these should be made according to the right Ingenium of the Philosophus by the light of the book 777 during the course of his Devotion. It is also well, nevertheless, if a magick circle with the right signs and names be made beforehand.

6. *Concerning the ceremonies.* Let the Philosophus prepare a powerful Invocation of the particular Deity, according to his Ingenium. But let it consist of these several parts:

First, an Imprecation, as of a slave unto his Lord.

Second, an Oath, as of a vassal to his Liege.

Third, a Memorial, as of a child to his Parent.

Fourth, an Orison, as of a Priest unto his God.

Fifth, a Colloquy, as of a Brother with his Brother.

Sixth, a Conjuration, as of a Friend with his Friend.

Seventh, a Madrigal, as of a Lover to his Mistress.

And mark well that the first should be of awe, the second of fealty, the third of dependence, the fourth of adoration, the fifth of confidence, the sixth of comradeship, the seventh of passion.

7. *Further concerning the ceremonies.* Let then this Invocation be the principal part of an ordered ceremony. And in this ceremony let the Philosophus in no wise neglect the service of a menial. Let him sweep and garnish the place, sprinkling it with water or with wine as is appropriate to the particular Deity, and consecrating it with oil, and with such ritual as may seem him best. And let all be done with intensity and minuteness.

8. *Concerning the period of devotion, and the hours thereof.* Let a fixed period be set for the worship; and it is said that the least time is nine days by seven, and the greatest seven years by nine. And concerning the hours, let the Ceremony be performed every day thrice, or at least once, and let the sleep of the Philosophus be broken for some purpose of devotion at least once in every night.

Now to some it may seem best to appoint fixed hours for the ceremony, to others it may seem that the ceremony should be performed as the spirit moves them so to do: for this there is no rule.

9. *Concerning the Robes and Instruments.* The Wand and Cup are to be chosen for this Art; never the Sword or Dagger, never the Pantacle, unless that Pantacle chance to be of a nature harmonious. But even so it is best to keep the Wand and Cup; and if one must choose, the Cup.

For the Robes, that of a Philosophus, or that of an Adept Within is most suitable; or, the robe best fitted for the service of the particular Deity, as a bassara for

Bacchus, a white robe for Vesta. So also, for Vesta, one might use for an instrument the Lamp; or the sickle, for Chronos.

10. *Concerning the Incense and Libations.* The incense should follow the nature of the particular Deity; as, mastic for Mercury, dittany for Persephone. Also the libations, as, a decoction of nightshade for Melancholia, or of Indian hemp for Uranus.

11. *Concerning the harmony of the ceremonies.* Let all these things be rightly considered, and at length, in language of the utmost beauty at the command of the Philosophus, accompanied, if he have skill, by music, and interwoven, if the particular Deity be jocund, with dancing. And all being carefully prepared and rehearsed, let it be practised daily until it be wholly rhythmical with his aspiration, and as it were, a part of his being.

12. *Concerning the variety of the ceremonies.* Now, seeing that every man differeth essentially from every other man, albeit in essence he is identical, let also these ceremonies assert their identity by their diversity. For this reason do We leave much herein to the right Ingenium of the Philosophus.

13. *Concerning the life of the devotee.* First, let his way of life be such as is pleasing to the particular Deity. Thus to invoke Neptune, let him go a-fishing; but if Hades, let him not approach the water that is hateful to Him.

14. *Further, concerning the life of the devotee.* Let him cut away from his life any act, word, or thought, that is hateful to the particular Deity; as, unchastity in the case of Artemis, evasions in the case of Ares. Besides this, he should avoid all harshness or unkindness of any kind in thought, word, or deed, seeing that above the particular Deity is One in whom all is One. Yet also he may deliberately practise cruelties, where the particular Deity manifests His love in that manner; as in the case of Kali,

and of Pan. And therefore, before the beginning of his period of devotion, let him practise according to the rules of *Liber Jugorum*.

15. *Further concerning the life of the devotee.* Now, as many are fully occupied with their affairs, let it be known that this method is adaptable to the necessities of all.

And We bear witness that this which followeth is the Crux and Quintessence of the whole Method.

First, if he have no Image, let him take anything soever, and consecrate it as an Image of his God. Likewise with his robes and instruments, his suffumigations and libations: for his Robe hath he not a night-dress; for his instrument a walking-stick; for his suffumigation a burning match, for his libation a glass of water?

But let him consecrate each thing that he useth to the service of that particular Deity, and not profane the same to any other use.

16. *Continuation.* Next, concerning his time, if it be short. Let him labour mentally upon his Invocation, concentrating it, and let him perform this Invocation in his heart whenever he hath the leisure. And let him seize eagerly upon every opportunity for this.

17. *Continuation.* Third, even if he have leisure and preparation, let him seek ever to bring inward the symbols, so that even in his well-ordered shrine the whole ceremony revolve inwardly in his heart, that is to say in the temple of his body, of which the outer temple is but an image.

For in the brain is the shrine, and there is no Image therein; and the breath of man is the incense and the libation.

18. *Continuation.* Further concerning occupation. Let the devotee transmute within the alembic of his heart every thought, or word, or act into the spiritual gold of his devotion.

As thus: eating. Let him say: "I eat this food in

gratitude to my Deity that hath sent it to me, in order to gain strength for my devotion to Him."

Or: sleeping. Let him say: "I lie down to sleep, giving thanks for this blessing from my Deity, in order that I may be refreshed for new devotion to Him."

Or: reading. Let him say: "I read this book that I may study the nature of my Deity, that further knowledge of Him may inspire me with deeper devotion to Him."

Or: working. Let him say: "I drive my spade into the earth that fresh flowers (fruit, or what not) may spring up to His glory, and that I, purified by toil, may give better devotion to Him."

Or, whatever it may be that he is doing, let him reason it out in his own mind, drawing it through circumstance and circumstance to that one end and conclusion of the matter. And let him not perform the act until he hath done this.

As it is written: *Liber VII*, cap. v:

22. Every breath, every word, every thought, is an act of love with thee.
23. The beat of my heart is the pendulum of love.
24. The songs of me are the soft sighs:
25. The thoughts of me are very rapture:
26. And my deeds are the myriads of Thy children, the stars and the atoms.

And Remember Well, that if thou wert in truth a lover, all this wouldst thou do of thine own nature without the slightest flaw or failure in the minutest part thereof.

19. *Concerning the Lections.* Let the Philosophus read solely in his copies of the holy books of Thelema, during the whole period of his devotion. But if he weary, then let him read books which have no part whatever in love, as for recreation.

But let him copy out each verse of Thelema which bears

upon this matter, and ponder them, and comment thereupon. For therein is a wisdom and a magic too deep to utter in any other wise.

20. *Concerning the Meditations.* Herein is the most potent method of attaining unto the End, for him who is thoroughly prepared, being purified by the practice of the Transmutation of deed into devotion, and consecrated by the right performance of the holy ceremonies. Yet herein is danger, for that the Mind is fluid as quicksilver, and bordereth upon the Abyss, and is beset by many sirens and devils that seduce and attack it to destroy it. Therefore let the devotee beware, and precise accurately his meditations, even as a man should build a canal from sea to sea.

21. *Continuation.* Let then the Philosophus meditate upon all love that hath ever stirred him. There is the love of David and of Jonathan, and the love of Abraham and Isaac, and the love of Lear and Cordelia, and the love of Damon and Pythias, and the love of Sappho and Atthis, and the love of Romeo and Juliet, and the love of Dante and Beatrice, and the love of Paolo and Francesca, and the love of Caesar and Lucrezia Borgia, and the love of Aucassin and Nicolette, and the love of Daphnis and Chloe, and the love of Cornelia and Caius Gracchus, and the love of Bacchus and Ariadne, and the love of Cupid and Psyche, and the love of Endymion and Artemis, and the love of Demeter and Persephone, and the love of Venus and Adonis, and the love of Lakshmi and Vishnu, and the love of Siva and Bhavani, and the love of Buddha and Ananda, and the love of Jesus and John, and many more.

Also there is the love of many saints for their particular deity, as of St Francis of Assisi for Christ, of Sri Sabhapaty Swami for Maheswara, of Abdullah Haji Shirazi for Allah, of St Ignatius Loyola for Mary, and many more.

Now do thou take one such story every night, and enact it in thy mind, grasping each identity with infinite care and zest, and do thou figure thyself as one of the lovers and thy Deity as the other. Thus do thou pass through all adventures of love, not omitting one; and to each do thou conclude: How pale a reflection is this of my love for this Deity!

Yet from each shalt thou draw some knowledge of love, some intimacy with love, that shall aid thee to perfect thy love. Thus learn the humility of love from one, its obedience from another, its intensity from a third, its purity from a fourth, its peace from yet a fifth.

So then thy love being made perfect, it shall be worthy of that perfect love of His.

22. *Further concerning meditation.* Moreover, let the Philosophus imagine to himself that he hath indeed succeeded in his devotion, and that his Lord hath appeared to him, and that they converse as may be fitting.

23. *Concerning the Mysterious Triangle.* Now then as three cords separately may be broken by a child, while those same cords duly twisted may bind a giant, let the Philosophus learn to entwine these three methods of Magic into a Spell.

To this end let him understand that as they are One, because the end is one, so are they One because the method is One, even the method of turning the mind toward the particular Deity by love in every act.

And lest thy twine slip, here is a little cord that wrappeth tightly round and round all, even the Mantram or Continuous Prayer.

24. *Concerning the Mantram or Continuous Prayer.* Let the Philosophus weave the Name of the Particular Deity into a sentence short and rhythmical; as, for Artemis: ε'πελθον, ε'πελθον, Ἀρτεμις; or, for Shiva: Namo Shivaya namaha Aum; or, for Mary: Ave Maria; or, for Pan,

χαιρε   Σωτηρ κοσμου Ἰω Παν Ἰω Παν ; or, for Allah:
Hua Allahu alazi lailaha illa Hua.

Let him repeat this day and night without cessation
mechanically in his brain, which is thus made ready for
the Advent of that Lord, and armed against all other.

25. *Concerning the Active and the Passive.* Let the
Philosophus change from the active love of his particular
Deity to a state of passive awaiting, even almost a repulsion, the repulsion not of distaste, but of a sublime
modesty.

As it is written, *Liber LXV*, ii: 59: "I have called unto
Thee, and I have journeyed unto Thee, and it availed me
not." 60: "I waited patiently, and Thou wast with me
from the beginning."

Then let him change back to the Active, until a
veritable rhythm is established between the states, as it
were the swinging of a Pendulum. But let him reflect that
a vast intelligence is required for this; for he must stand
as it were almost without himself to watch those phases
of himself. And to do this is a high Art, and pertaineth
not altogether to the grade of Philosophus. Neither is it of
itself helpful, but rather the reverse, in this especial
practice.

26. *Concerning Silence.* Now there may come a time in
the course of this practice when the outward symbols of
devotion cease, when the soul is as it were dumb in the
presence of its God. Mark that this is not a cessation, but
a transmutation of the barren seed of prayer into the green
shoot of yearning. This yearning is spontaneous, and it
shall be left to grow, whether it be sweet or bitter. For
often times it is as the torment of hell in which the soul
burns and writhes unceasingly. Yet it ends, and at its
end continue openly thy Method.

27. *Concerning Dryness.* Another state wherein at
times the soul may fall is this dark night. And this is

indeed purifying in such depths that the soul cannot fathom it. It is less like pain than like death. But it is the necessary death that comes before the rising of a body glorified.

This state must be endured with fortitude; and no means of alleviating it may be employed. It may be broken up by the breaking up of the whole Method, and a return to the world without. This cowardice not only destroys the value of all that has gone before, but destroys the value of the Oath of Fealty that thou hast sworn, and makes thy Will a mockery to men and gods.

28. *Concerning the Deceptions of the Devil.* Note well that in this state of dryness a thousand seductions will lure thee away; also a thousand means of breaking thine oath in spirit without breaking it in letter. Against this thou mayst repeat the words of thine oath aloud again and again until the temptation be overcome.

Also the devil will represent to thee that it were much better for this operation that thou do thus and thus, and seek to affright thee by fears for thy health or thy reason.

Or he may send against thee visions worse than madness.

Against all this there is but one remedy, the Discipline of thine Oath. So then thou shalt go through ceremonies meaningless and hideous to thee, and blaspheme shalt thou against thy Deity and curse Him. And this mattereth little, for it is not thou, so be that thou adhere to the Letter of thine Obligation. For thy Spiritual Sight is closed, and to trust it is to be led unto the precipice, and hurled therefrom.

29. *Further of this matter.* Now also subtler than all these terrors are the Illusions of Success. For one instant's self-satisfaction or Expansion of thy Spirit, especially in

this state of dryness, and thou art lost. For thou mayst attain the False Union with the Demon himself. Beware also of even the pride which rises from having resisted the temptations.

But so many and so subtle are the wiles of Choronzon that the whole world could not contain their enumeration.

The answer to one and all is the persistence in the literal fulfilment of the routine. Beware, then, last, of that devil who shall whisper in thine ear that the letter killeth, but the spirit giveth life, and answer: Except a corn of wheat fall into the ground and die, it abideth alone; but if it die, it bringeth forth much fruit.

Yet shalt thou also beware of disputation with the devil, and pride in the cleverness of thine answers to him. Therefore, if thou hast not lost the power of silence, let it be first and last employed against him.

30. *Concerning the Enflaming of the Heart.* Now learn that thy methods are dry one and all. Intellectual exercises, moral exercises, they are not Love. Yet as a man, rubbing two dry sticks together for long, suddenly found a spark, so also from time to time will true love leap unasked into thy meditation. Yet this shall die and be reborn again and again. It may be that thou hast no tinder near.

In the end shall come suddenly a great flame and a devouring, and burn thee utterly.

Now of these sparks, and of these splutterings of flame, and of these beginnings of the Infinite Fire, thou shalt thus be aware. For the sparks thy heart shall leap up, and thy ceremony or meditation or toil shall seem of a sudden to go of its own will; and for the little flames this shall be increased in volume and intensity; and for the beginnings of the Infinite Fire thy ceremony shall be caught up unto ravishing song, and thy meditation shall be ecstasy, and thy toil shall be a delight exceeding all pleasure thou hast ever known.

And of the Great Flame that answereth thee it may not be spoken; for therein is the End of this Magick Art of Devotion.

31. *Considerations with regard to the use of symbols.* It is to be noted that persons of powerful imagination, will, and intelligence have no need of these material symbols. There have been certain saints who are capable of love for an idea as such without it being otherwise than degraded by *idolising* it, to use this word in its true sense. Thus one may be impassioned of beauty, without even the need of so small a concretion of it as "the beauty of Apollo," "the beauty of roses," "the beauty of Attis." Such persons are rare; it may be doubted whether Plato himself attained to any vision of absolute beauty without attaching to it material objects in the first place. A second class is able to contemplate ideals through this veil; a third class need a double veil, and cannot think of the beauty of a rose without a rose before them. For such is this Method of most use; yet let them know that there is this danger therein, that they may mistake the gross body of the symbol for the idea made concrete thereby.

32. *Considerations of further danger to those not purged of material thought.* Let it be remembered that in the nature of the love itself is danger. The lust of the satyr for the nymph is indeed of the same nature as the affinity of Quicklime for water on the one hand, and of the love of Ab for Ama on the other; so also is the triad Osiris, Isis, Horus like that of a horse, mare, foal, and of red, blue, purple. And this is the foundation of Correspondences.

But it were false to say "Horus is a foal" or "Horus is purple." One may say "Horus resembles a foal in this respect, that he is the offspring of two complementary beings."

33. *Further of this matter.* So also many have said truly that all is one, and falsely that since earth is That One, and ocean is That One, therefore earth is ocean. Unto Him good is illusion, and evil is illusion; therefore good is evil. By this fallacy of logic are many men destroyed.

Moreover, there are those who take the image for the God; as who should say, my heart is in Tiphereth, and an Adeptus is in Tiphereth; I am therefore an adept.

And in this practice the worst danger is this, that the love which is its weapon should fail in one of two ways.

First, if the love lack any quality of love, so long is it not ideal love. For it is written of the Perfected One: "There is no member of my body which is not the member of some god." Therefore let not the Philosophus despise any form of love, but harmonise all. As it is written, *Liber LXI*, 32: "So therefore Perfection abideth not in the Pinnacles or in the Foundation, but in the harmony of One with all."

Second, if any part of this love exceed, there is disease therein. As, in the love of Othello for Desdemona, love's jealousy overcame love's tenderness, so may it be in this love of a particular Deity. And this is more likely, since in this divine love no element may be omitted.

It is by virtue of this completeness that no human love may in any way attain to more than to forthshadow a little part thereof.

34. *Concerning Mortifications.* These are not necessary to this method. On the contrary, they may destroy the concentration, as counter-irritants to, and so alleviations of, the supreme mortification which is the Absence of the Deity invoked.

Yet as in mortal love arises a distaste for food, or a pleasure in things naturally painful, this perversion should be endured and allowed to take its course. Yet not to the interference with natural bodily health, whereby the instrument of the soul might be impaired.

And concerning sacrifices for love's sake, they are natural to this Method, and right.

But concerning voluntary privations and tortures, without use save as against the devotee, they are generally not natural to healthy natures, and wrong. For they are selfish. To scourge one's self serves not one's master; yet to deny one's self bread that one's child may have cake is the act of a true mother.

35. *Further concerning Mortifications.* If thy body, on which thou ridest, be so disobedient a beast that by no means will he travel in the desired direction, or if thy mind be baulkish and eloquent as Balaam's fabled Ass, then let the practice be abandoned. Let the shrine be covered in sackcloth, and do thou put on habits of lamentation, and abide alone. And do thou return most austerely to the practice of *Liber Jugorum*, testing thyself by a standard higher than that hitherto accomplished, and punishing effractions with a heavier goad. Nor do thou return to thy devotion until that body and mind are tamed and trained to all manner of peaceable going.

36. *Concerning minor methods adjuvant in the ceremonies. I. Rising on the planes.* By this method mayst thou assist the imagination at the time of concluding thine Invocation. Act as taught in *Liber O*, by the light of *Liber 777.*

37. *Concerning minor methods adjuvant in the ceremonies. II. Talismanic magic.* Having made by thine Ingenium a talisman or pantacle to represent the particular Deity, and consecrated it with infinite love and care, do thou burn it ceremonially before the shrine, as if thereby giving up the shadow for the substance. But it is useless to do

this unless thou do really in thine heart value the talisman beyond all else that thou hast.

38. *Concerning minor methods adjuvant in the ceremonies. III. Rehearsal.* It may assist if the traditional history of the particular Deity be rehearsed before him; perhaps this is best done in dramatic form. This method is the main one recommended in the *Exercitios Espirituales* of St Ignatius, whose work may be taken as a model. Let the Philosophus work out the legend of his own particular Deity, and apportioning days to events, live that life in imagination, exercising the five senses in turn, as occasion arises.

39. *Concerning minor matters adjuvant in the ceremonies. IV. Duresse.* This method consists in cursing a deity recalcitrant; as, threatening ceremonially "to burn the blood of Osiris, and to grind down his bones to powder." This method is altogether contrary to the spirit of love, unless the particular Deity be himself savage and relentless; as, Jehovah or Kali. In such a case the desire to perform constraint and cursing may be the sign of the assimilation of the spirit of the devotee with that of his God, and so an advance to the Union with Him.

40. *Concerning the value of this particular form of Union or Samadhi.* All Samadhi is defined as the ecstatic union of subject and object in consciousness, with the result that a third thing arises which partakes in no way of the nature of the two.

It would seem at first sight that it is of no importance whatever to choose an object of meditation. For example, the Samadhi called Atmadarshana might arise from simple concentration of the thought on an imagined triangle, or on the heart.

But as the union of two bodies in chemistry may be endothermic or exothermic, the combination of Oxygen with Nitrogen is gentle, while that of Oxygen with

Hydrogen is explosive; and as it is found that the most heat is disengaged as a rule by the union of bodies most opposite in character, and that the compound resulting from such is most stable, so it seems reasonable to suggest that the most important and enduring Samadhi results from the contemplation of the Object most opposite to the devotee. [On other planes, it has been suggested that the most opposed types make the best marriages and produce the healthiest children. The greatest pictures and operas are those in which violent extremes are blended, and so generally in every field of activity. Even in mathematics, the greatest parallelogram is formed if the lines composing it are set at right angles.—Ed.]

41. *Conclusions from the foregoing.* It may then be suggested to the Philosophus, that although his work will be harder his reward will be greater if he choose a Deity most remote from his own nature. This method is harder and higher than that of *Liber E.* For a simple object as there suggested is of the same nature as the commonest things of life, while even the meanest Deity is beyond uninitiated human understanding. On the same plane, too, Venus is nearer to man than Aphrodite, Aphrodite than Isis, Isis than Babalon, Babalon than Nuit.

Let him decide therefore according to his discretion on the one hand and his aspiration on the other: and let not one outrun his fellow.

42. *Further concerning the value of this Method.* Certain objections arise. Firstly, in the nature of all human love is illusion, and a certain blindness. Nor is there any true love below the Veil of the Abyss. For this reason We give this Method to the Philosophus, as the reflection of the Exempt Adept, who reflects the Magister Templi and the Magus. Let then the Philosophus attain this method as a foundation of the higher Methods to be given to him when he attains those higher grades.

Another objection lies in the partiality of this Method. This is equally a defect characteristic of the Grade.

43. *Concerning a notable danger of Success.* It may occur that owing to the tremendous power of the Samadhi, overcoming all other memories as it should and does do, that the mind of the devotee may be obsessed, so that he declare his particular Deity to be sole God and Lord. This error has been the foundation of all dogmatic religions, and so the cause of more misery than all other errors combined.

The Philosophus is peculiarly liable to this because from the nature of the Method he cannot remain sceptical; he must for the time believe in his particular Deity. But let him (1) consider that this belief is only a weapon in his hands, (2) affirm sufficiently that his Deity is but an emanation or reflection or eidolon of a Being beyond him, as was said in Paragraph 2. For if he fail herein, since man cannot remain permanently in Samadhi, the memorised Image in his mind will be degraded, and replaced by the corresponding Demon, to his utter ruin.

Therefore, after Success, let him not delight overmuch in his Deity, but rather busy himself with his other work, not permitting that which is but a step to become a goal. As it is written also, *Liber CLXXXV*: "remembering that Philosophy is the Equilibrium of him that is in the House of Love."

44. *Concerning secrecy, and the rites of Blood.* During this practice it is most wise that the Philosophus utter no word concerning his working, as if it were a Forbidden Love that consumeth him. But let him answer fools according to their folly; for since he cannot conceal his love from his fellows, he must speak to them as they may understand.

And as many Deities demand sacrifices, one of men, another of cattle, a third of doves, let these sacrifices be replaced by the true sacrifices in thine own heart. Yet if thou must symbolise them outwardly for the hardness of thine heart, let thine own blood, and not another's, be spilt before that altar.[1]

Nevertheless, forget not that this practice is dangerous, and may cause the manifestation of evil things, hostile and malicious, to thy great hurt.

45. *Concerning a further sacrifice.* Of this it shall be understood that nothing is to be spoken; nor need anything be spoken to him that hath wisdom to comprehend the number of the paragraph. And this sacrifice is fatal beyond all, unless it be a *sacrificium* indeed. Yet there are those who have dared and achieved thereby.

46. *Concerning yet a further sacrifice.* Here it is spoken of actual mutilation. Such acts are abominable; and while they may bring success in this Method, form an absolute bar to all further progress.

And they are in any case more likely to lead to madness than to Samadhi. He indeed who purposeth them is already mad.

47. *Concerning human affection.* During this practice thou shalt in no wise withdraw thyself from human relations, only figuring to thyself that thy father or thy brother or thy wife is as it were an image of thy particular Deity. Thus shall they gain, and not lose, by thy working. Only in the case of thy wife this is difficult, since she is more to thee than all others, and in this case thou mayst act with temperance, lest her personality overcome and destroy that of thy Deity.

48. *Concerning the Holy Guardian Angel.* Do thou in no wise confuse this invocation with that.

1. The exceptions to this rule pertain neither to this practice, nor to this grade. N. Fra. A ∴ A ∴.

49. *The Benediction.* And so may the Love that passeth all Understanding keep your hearts and minds through ΙΑΩ ΑΔΩΝΑΙ ΣΑΒΑΩ and through Babalon of the City of the Pyramids, and through Astarte the Starry One green-girdled in the name Ararita. Amen.

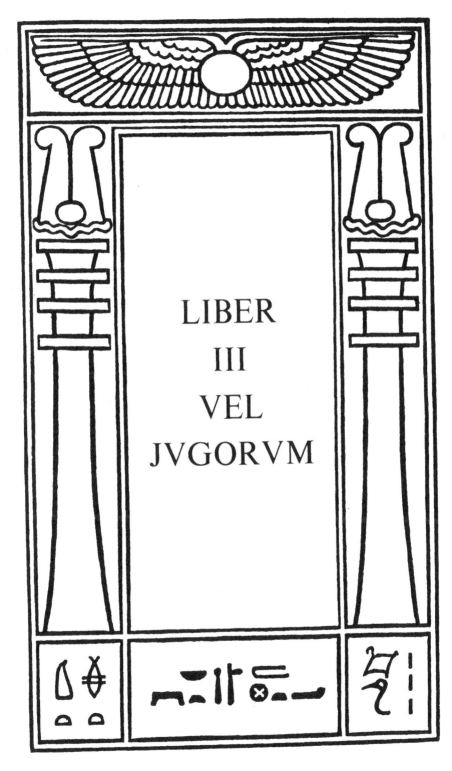

LIBER

III

VEL

JVGORVM

A ∴ A ∴ Publication in Class D

Imprimatur:
D.D.S. 7° = 4° Praemonstrator
O.S.V. 6° = 5° Imperator
N.S.F. 5° = 6° Cancellarius

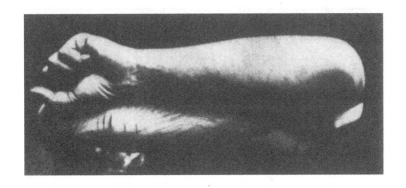

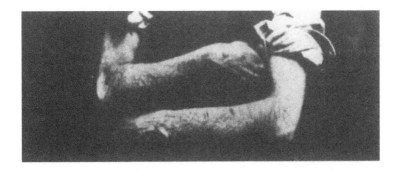

Aratrum Securum

Fra —— after one week avoiding the first person. His fidelity is
good; his vigilance bad. Not nearly good enough to pass.

LIBER III

VEL JVGORVM

O

0. Behold the Yoke upon the neck of the Oxen! Is it not thereby that the Field shall be ploughed? The Yoke is heavy, but joineth together them that are separate— Glory to Nuit and to Hadit, and to Him that hath given us the Symbol of the Rosy Cross!

Glory unto the Lord of the Word Abrahadabra, and Glory unto Him that hath given us the Symbol of the Ankh, and of the Cross within the Circle!

1. Three are the Beasts wherewith thou must plough the Field; the Unicorn, the Horse, and the Ox. And these shalt thou yoke in a triple yoke that is governed by One Whip.

2. Now these Beasts run wildly upon the earth and are not easily obedient to the Man.

3. Nothing shall be said here of Cerberus, the great Beast of Hell that is every one of these and all of these, even as Athanasius hath foreshadowed. For this matter, *i.e.*, the matter of Cerberus, is not of Tiphereth without, but Tiphereth within.

I

0. The Unicorn is speech. Man, rule thy Speech! How else shalt thou master the Son, and answer the Magician at the Right Hand Gateway of the Crown?

1. Here are practices. Each may last for a week or more.

α. Avoid using some common word, such as "and" or "the" or "but"; use a paraphrase.

β. Avoid using some letter of the alphabet, such as "t" or "s" or "m"; use a paraphrase.

γ. Avoid using the pronouns and adjectives of the first person; use a paraphrase.

Of thine own ingenium devise others.

2. On each occasion that thou art betrayed into saying that thou art sworn to avoid, cut thyself sharply upon the wrist or forearm with a razor; even as thou shouldst beat a disobedient dog. Feareth not the Unicorn the claws and teeth of the Lion?

3. Thine arm then serveth thee both for a warning and for a record. Thou shalt write down thy daily progress in these practices, until thou art perfectly vigilant at all times over the least word that slippeth from thy tongue.

Thus bind thyself, and thou shalt be for ever free.

II

0. The Horse is Action. Man, rule thou thine Action. How else shalt thou master the Father, and answer the Fool at the Left Hand Gateway of the Crown?

1. Here are practices. Each may last for a week or more.

α. Avoid lifting the left arm above the waist.

β. Avoid crossing the legs.

Of thine own ingenium devise others.

2. On each occasion that thou art betrayed into doing that thou art sworn to avoid, cut thyself sharply upon the wrist or forearm with a razor; even as thou shouldst beat

a disobedient dog. Feareth not the Horse the teeth of the Camel?

3. Thine arm then serveth thee both for a warning and for a record. Thou shalt write down thy daily progress in these practices, until thou art perfectly vigilant at all times over the least action that slippeth from the least of thy fingers.

Thus bind thyself, and thou shalt be for ever free.

III

0. The Ox is Thought. Man, rule thou thy Thought! How else shalt thou master the Holy Spirit, and answer the High Priestess in the Middle Gateway of the Crown?

1. Here are practices. Each may last for a week or more.

a. Avoid thinking of a definite subject and all things connected with it, and let that subject be one which commonly occupies much of thy thought, being frequently stimulated by sense-perceptions or the conversation of others.

β. By some device, such as the changing of thy ring from one finger to another, create in thyself two personalities, the thoughts of one being within entirely different limits from that of the other, the common ground being the necessities of life.[1]

Of thine own ingenium devise others.

2. On each occasion that thou art betrayed into thinking that thou art sworn to avoid, cut thyself sharply upon the wrist or forearm with a razor; even as thou shouldst beat a disobedient dog. Feareth not the Ox the Goad of the Ploughman?

3. Thine arm then serveth thee both for a warning and

---

1. For instance, let A be a man of strong passions, skilled in the Holy Qabalah, a vegetarian, and a keen "reactionary" politician; let B be a bloodless and ascetic thinker, occupied with business and family cares, an eater of meat, and a keen progressive politician. Let no thought proper to A arise when the ring is on the B finger; and *vice versa*.

for a record. Thou shalt write down thy daily progress in these practices, until thou art perfectly vigilant at all times over the least thought that ariseth in thy brain.

Thus bind thyself, and thou shalt be for ever free.

LIBER

HHH

SVB FIGVRA

CCCXLI

CONTINET
CAPITULA
TRES
MMM
AAA
ET SSS

A ∴ A ∴ Publication in Class D

Imprimatur:
N. Fra A ∴ A ∴

"Sunt duo modi per quos homo fit Deus: Tohu et Bohu.

"Mens quasi flamma surgat, aut quasi puteus aquae quiescat.

"Alteri modi sunt tres exempli, qui illis extra limine collegii sancti dati sunt.

"In hoc primo libro sunt Aquae Contemplationis."

Two are the methods of becoming God: the Upright and the Averse. Let the Mind become as a flame, or as a well of still water.

Of each method are three principal examples given to them that are without the Threshold.

In this first book are written the Reflexions.

"Sunt tres contemplationes quasi halitus in mente humana abysso inferni. Prima, Νεκρος; secunda, Πυραμις; tertia, Φαλλος vocatur. Et hae reflexiones aquaticae sunt trium enthusiasmorum, Apollonis, Dionysi, Veneris.

"Tota stella est Nechesh et Messiach, nomen אהיה cum יהוה conjunctum."

There are three contemplations as it were breaths in the human mind, that is the Abyss of Hell: the first is called Νεκρος, *the second* Πυραμις, *and the third* Φαλλος.

These are the watery reflexions of the three enthusiasms; those of Apollo, Dionysus, and Aphrodite.

The whole star is Nechesh and Messiach, the name אהיה *joined with* יהוה.

LIBER HHH

I

MMM

I remember a certain holy day in the dusk of the Year, in the dusk of the Equinox of Osiris, when first I beheld thee visibly; when first the dreadful issue was fought out; when the Ibis-headed One charmed away the strife. I remember thy first kiss, even as a maiden should. Nor in the dark byways was there another: thy kisses abide.

Liber Lapidis Lazuli, VII: 15, 16

0. Be seated in thine Asana, wearing the robe of a Neophyte, the hood drawn.

1. It is night, heavy and hot; there are no stars. Not one breath of wind stirs the surface of the sea, that is thou. No fish play in thy depths.

2. Let a Breath rise and ruffle the waters. This also thou shalt feel playing upon thy skin. It will disturb thy meditation twice or thrice, after which thou shouldst have conquered this distraction. But unless thou first feel it, that Breath hath not arisen.

3. Next, the night is riven by the lightning-flash. This also shalt thou feel in thy body, which shall shiver and leap with the shock, and that also must both be suffered and overcome.

4. After the lightning-flash, resteth in the zenith a minute point of light. And this light shall radiate until a right cone be established upon the sea, and it is day.

With this thy body shall be rigid, automatically; and this shalt thou let endure, withdrawing thyself into thine heart in the form of an upright Egg of blackness; and therein shalt thou abide for a space.

217

5. When all this is perfectly and easily performed at will, let the aspirant figure to himself a struggle with the whole force of the Universe. In this he is only saved by his minuteness.

But in the end he is overthrown by Death, who covers him with a black cross.

Let his body fall supine with arms outstretched.

6. So lying, let him aspire fervently unto the Holy Guardian Angel.

7. Now let him resume his former posture.

Two-and-twenty times shall he figure to himself that he is bitten by a serpent, feeling even in his body the poison thereof. And let each bite be healed by an eagle or hawk, spreading its wings above his head, and dropping thereupon an healing dew. But let the last bite be so terrible a pang at the nape of the neck that he seemeth to die, and let the healing dew be of such virtue that he leapeth to his feet.

8. Let there be now placed within his egg a red cross, then a green cross, then a golden cross, then a silver cross; or those things which these shadow forth. Herein is silence; for he that hath rightly performed the meditation will understand the inner meaning hereof, and it shall serve as a test of himself and his fellows.

9. Let him now remain in the Pyramid or Cone of Light, as an Egg, but no more of blackness.

10. Then let his body be in the position of the Hanged Man, and let him aspire with all his force unto the Holy Guardian Angel.

11. The grace having been granted unto him, let him partake mystically of the Eucharist of the Five Elements and let him proclaim Light in Extension; yea, let him proclaim Light in Extension.

II

AAA

These loosen the swathings of the corpse; these unbind the feet of Osiris, so that the flaming God may rage through the firmament with his fantastic spear.

Liber Lapidis Lazuli, VII: 3

0. Be seated in thine Asana, or recumbent in Shavasana, or in the position of the dying Buddha.

1. Think of thy death; imagine the various diseases that may attack thee, or accidents overtake thee. Picture the process of death, applying always to thyself.

(A useful preliminary practice is to read text-books of Pathology, and to visit museums and dissecting-rooms.)

2. Continue this practice until death is complete; follow the corpse through the stages of embalming, wrapping and burial.

3. Now imagine a divine breath entering thy nostrils.

4. Next, imagine a divine light enlightening the eyes.

5. Next, imagine the divine voice awakening the ears.

6. Next, imagine a divine kiss imprinted on the lips.

7. Next, imagine the divine energy informing the nerves and muscles of the body, and concentrate on the phenomenon which will already have been observed in 3, the restoring of the circulation.

8. Last, imagine the return of the reproductive power; and employ this to the impregnation of the Egg of light in which man is bathed.

9. Now represent to thyself that this egg is the Disk of the Sun, setting in the west.

10. Let it sink into blackness, borne in the bark of heaven, upon the back of the holy cow Hathor. And it may be that thou shalt hear the moaning thereof.

11. Let it become blacker than all blackness. And in this meditation thou shalt be utterly without fear, for that the blackness that will appear unto thee is a thing dreadful beyond all thy comprehension.

And it shall come to pass that if thou hast well and properly performed this meditation that on a sudden thou shalt hear the drone and booming of a Beetle.

12. Now then shall the Blackness pass, and with rose and gold shalt thou arise in the East, with the cry of an Hawk resounding in thine ear. Shrill shall it be and harsh.

13. At the end shalt thou rise and stand in the mid-heaven, a globe of glory. And therewith shall arise the mighty Sound that holy men have likened unto the roaring of a Lion.

14. Then shalt thou withdraw thyself from the Vision, gathering thyself into the divine form of Osiris upon his throne.

15. Then shalt thou repeat audibly the cry of triumph of the god rearisen, as it shall have been given unto thee by thy Superior.

16. And this being accomplished, thou mayest enter again into the Vision, that thereby shalt be perfected in thee.

17. After this shalt thou return into the body, and give thanks unto the Most High God Iaida; yea, unto the Most High God Iaida.

18. Mark well that this operation should be performed if it be possible in a place set apart and consecrated to the Works of the Magic of Light. Also that the Temple should be ceremonially open as thou hast knowledge and skill to perform, and that at the end thereof the closing should be most carefully accomplished. But in the preliminary practice it is enough if thou cleanse thyself by ablution, by robing, and by the rituals of the Pentagram and Hexagram.

0–2 should be practised at first, until some realisation is obtained; and the practice should always be followed by a divine invocation of Apollo or of Isis or of Jupiter or of Serapis.

Next, after a swift summary of 0–2, practise 3–7.

This being mastered, add 8.

Then add 9–13.

Then being prepared and fortified, well fitted for the work, perform the whole meditation at one time. And let this be continued until perfect success be attained therein. For this is a mighty meditation and holy, having power even upon Death; yea, having power even upon Death.

Note by Fra O. M.: At any time during this meditation, the concentration may bring about Samadhi. This is to be feared and shunned, more than any other breaking of control, for that it is the most tremendous of the forces which threaten to obsess. There is also some danger of acute delirious melancholia at point I.

III

SSS

Thou art a beautiful thing, whiter than a woman in the column of this vibration.
I shoot up vertically like an arrow, and become that Above.
But it is death, and the flame of the pyre.
Ascend in the flame of the pyre, O my soul! Thy God is like the cold emptiness of the utmost heaven, into which thou radiatest thy little light.
When Thou shalt know me, O empty God, my flame shall utterly expire in Thy great N.O.X.

Liber Lapidis Lazuli, I: 36–40

0. Be seated in thine Asana, preferably the Thunderbolt.

It is essential that the spine be vertical.

1. In this practice the cavity of the brain is the Yoni; the spinal cord is the Lingam.

2. Concentrate thy thought of adoration in the brain.

3. Now begin to awake the spine in this manner. Concentrate thy thought of thyself in the base of the spine, and move it gradually up a little at a time.

By this means thou wilt become conscious of the spine, feeling each vertebra as a separate entity. This must be achieved most fully and perfectly before the further practice is begun.

4. Next, adore the brain as before, but figure to thyself its content as infinite. Deem it to be the womb of Isis, or the body of Nuit.

5. Next, identify thyself with the base of the spine as before, but figure to thyself its energy as infinite. Deem it to be the phallus of Osiris, or the being of Hadit.

6. These two concentrations, 4 and 5, may be pushed to the point of Samadhi. Yet lose not control of the will; let not Samadhi be thy master herein.

7. Now then, being conscious both of the brain and the spine, and unconscious of all else, do thou imagine the hunger of the one for the other; the emptiness of the brain, the ache of the spine, even as the emptiness of space and the aimlessness of Matter.

And if thou hast experience of the Eucharist in both kinds, it shall aid thine imagination herein.

8. Let this agony grow until it be insupportable, resisting by will every temptation. Not until thine whole body is bathed in sweat, or it may be in sweat of blood, and until a cry of intolerable anguish is forced from thy closed lips, shalt thou proceed.

9. Now let a current of light, deep azure flecked with scarlet, pass up and down the spine, striking as it were upon thyself that art coiled at the base as a serpent.

Let this be exceeding slow and subtle; and though it

be accompanied with pleasure, resist; and though it be accompanied with pain, resist.

10. This shalt thou continue until thou art exhausted, never relaxing the control. Until thou canst perform this one section 9 during a whole hour, proceed not. And withdraw from the meditation by an act of will, passing into a gentle Pranayama without Kumbhakham, and meditating on Harpocrates, the silent and virginal God.

11. Then at last being well-fitted in body and mind, fixed in peace, beneath a favourable heaven of stars, at night, in calm and warm weather, mayst thou quicken the movement of the light until it be taken up by the brain and the spine, independently of thy will.

12. If in this hour thou shouldst die, is it not written: "Blessed are the dead that die in the Lord"? Yea, Blessed are the dead that die in the Lord!

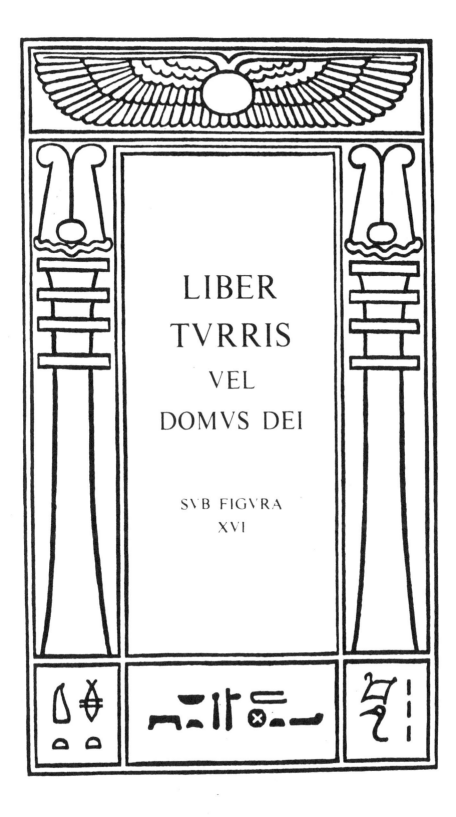

LIBER
TVRRIS
VEL
DOMVS DEI

SVB FIGVRA
XVI

A ∴ A ∴ Publication in Class B

Imprimatur:
N. Fra A ∴ A ∴

LIBER TVRRIS

o. This practice is very difficult. The student cannot hope for much success unless he have thoroughly mastered Asana, and obtained much definite success in the meditation-practices of *Liber E* and *Liber HHH*.

On the other hand, any success in this practice is of an exceedingly high character, and the student is less liable to illusion and self-deception in this than in almost any other that We make known.

[The meditation-practice in *Liber E* consisted in the restraint of the mind to a single predetermined imagined object exterior to the student, simple or complex, at rest or in motion: those of *Liber HHH* in causing the mind to pass through a predetermined series of states: the Raja-Yoga of the Hindus is mainly an extension of the methods of *Liber E* to interior objects: the Mahasatipatthana of the Buddhists is primarily an observation and analysis of bodily movements. While the present practice differs radically from all of these, it is of the greatest advantage to be acquainted practically with each of them, with regard firstly to their incidental difficulties, and secondly to their ascertained results in respect of psychology.—Ed.]

1. First Point. The student should first discover for himself the apparent position of the point in his brain where thoughts arise, if there be such a point.

If not, he should seek the position of the point where thoughts are judged.

2. Second Point. He must also develop in himself a Will of Destruction, even a Will of Annihilation. It may be that this shall be discovered at an immeasurable distance from his physical body. Nevertheless, this must he reach, with this must he identify himself even to the loss of himself.

3. Third Point. Let this Will then watch vigilantly the point where thoughts arise, or the point where they are judged, and let every thought be annihilated as it is perceived or judged.[1]

4. Fourth Point. Next, let every thought be inhibited in its inception.

5. Fifth Point. Next, let even the causes or tendencies that if unchecked ultimate in thoughts be discovered and annihilated.

6. Sixth and Last Point. Let the true Cause of All[2] be unmasked and annihilated.

7. This is that which was spoken by wise men of old time concerning the destruction of the world by fire; yea, the destruction of the world by fire.

8. (This and the following verses are of modern origin.) Let the Student remember that each Point represents a definite achievement of great difficulty.

9. Let him not then attempt the second until he be well satisfied of his mastery over the first.

10. This practice is also that which was spoken by Fra P. in a parable as followeth:

1. This is also the "Opening of the Eye of Shiva."—Ed.
2. Mayan, the Magician, or Mara. Also The Dweller on the Threshold in a very exalted sense.—Ed.

11. Foul is the robber stronghold, filled with hate;
    Thief strangling thief, and mate at war with mate,
    Fronting wild raiders, all forlorn to Fate!

    There is nor health nor happiness therein.
    Manhood is cowardice, and virtue sin.
    Intolerable blackness hems it in.

    Not hell's heart hath so noxious a shade;
    Yet harmless and unharmed, and undismayed,
    Pines in her prison an unsullied maid.

    Penned by the master mage to his desire,
    She baffles his seductions and his ire,
    Praying God's all-annihilating fire.

    The Lord of Hosts gave ear unto her song:
    The Lord of Hosts waxed wrathful at her wrong.
    He loosed the hound of heaven from its thong.

    Violent and vivid smote the levin flash.
    Once the tower rocked and cracked beneath its lash,
    Caught inextinguishable fire; was ash.

    But that same fire that quelled the robber strife,
    And struck each being out of lust and life,
    Left the mild maiden a rejoicing wife.

12. And this:

13. There is a well before the Great White Throne
    That is choked up with rubbish from the ages;
    Rubble and clay and sediment and stone,
    Delight of lizards and despair of sages.

    Only the lightning from His hand that sits,
    And shall sit when the usurping tyrant falls,
    Can purge that wilderness of wills and wits,
    Let spring that fountain in eternal halls.

14. And this:

15.　　　Sulphur, Salt, and Mercury:
　　　　Which is master of the three?

　　　　Salt is Lady of the Sea;
　　　　Lord of Air is Mercury.

　　　　Now by God's grace here is salt
　　　　Fixed beneath the violet vault.

　　　　Now by God's love purge it through
　　　　With our right Hermetic dew.

　　　　Now by God wherein we trust
　　　　Be our sophic salt combust.

　　　　Then at last the Eye shall see
　　　　Three in One and One in Three,

　　　　Sulphur, Salt, and Mercury,
　　　　Crowned by Heavenly Alchemy!

　　　　To the One who sent the Seven
　　　　Glory in the Highest Heaven!

　　　　To the Seven who are the Ten
　　　　Glory on the Earth, Amen!

16. And of the difficulties of this practice and of the Results that reward it, let these things be discovered by the right Ingenium of the Practicus.

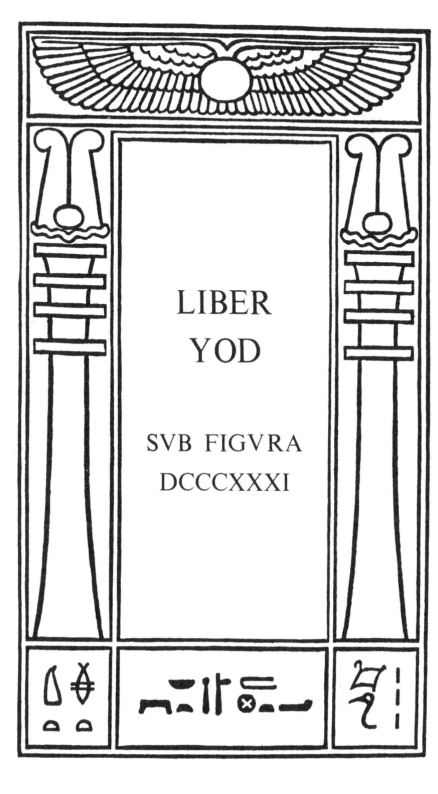

LIBER
YOD

SVB FIGVRA
DCCCXXXI

A ∴ A ∴ Publication in Class B

Imprimatur:
N. Fra A ∴ A ∴

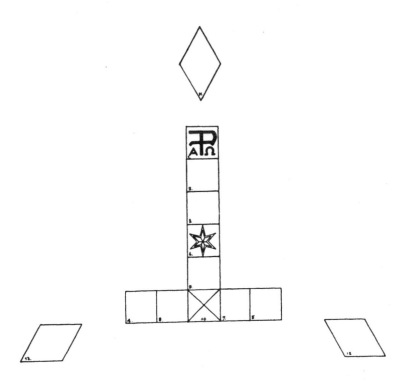

The Triangle of the Universe.

Three veils of the Negative—not yellow; not red; not blue: but therefore symbolised by the "flashing" colours of these three; purple (11); emerald (12) and orange (13). Within their triangle of Yonis is the Lingam touching and filling it. Positive, as they are negative; in the Queen Scale of colour, as they are in the King Scale. Ten are the Emanations of Unity, the parts of that Lingam, in Kether, TARO=78=6x13, the Influence of that Unity in the Macrocosm (Hexagram). The centre of the whole figure is Tiphereth, where is a golden Sun of six rays. Note the reflection of the Yonis to the triad about Malkuth. Also note that the triangle of Yonis is hidden, even as their links are secret. From Malkuth depends the Greek Cross of the Zodiac and their Spiritual Centre. For Colour Scales see 777.

LIBER YOD

This book was formerly called Vesta. *It is referred to the path of Virgo and the letter Yod.*

I

1. This is the Book of drawing all to a point.

2. Herein are described three methods whereby the consciousness of the Many may be melted to that of the One.

II

FIRST METHOD

0. Let a magical circle be constructed, and within it an upright Tau drawn upon the ground. Let this Tau be divided into 10 squares (see *Liber CMLXIII*, Illustration 1).

1. Let the Magician be armed with the Sword of Art.[1]

2. Let him wear the black robe of a Neophyte.

3. Let a single small flame of camphor burn at the top of the Tau, and let there be no other light or ornament.[1]

4. Let him "open" the Temple as in *DCLXXI*, or in any other convenient manner.

5. Standing at the appropriate quarters, at the edge of

---

1. This ritual is preferably performed by the Adept as an Hermit armed with wand and lamp, instead of as in text.—N.

the circle, let him banish the 5 elements by the appropriate rituals.

6. Standing at the edge of the circle, let him banish the 7 planets by the appropriate rituals. Let him face the actual position of each planet in the heavens at the time of his working.

7. Let him further banish the twelve signs of the Zodiac by the appropriate rituals, facing each sign in turn.

8. Let him at each of these 24 banishings make three circuits widdershins, with the signs of Horus and Harpocrates in the East as he passes it.

9. Let him advance to the square of Malkuth in the Tau, and perform a ritual of banishing Malkuth. But here let him leave not the square to circumambulate the circle, but use the formula and God-form of Harpocrates.

10. Let him advance in turn to the squares Jesod, Hod, Netzach, Tiphereth, Geburah, Chesed, and banish each by appropriate rituals.

11. And let him know that such rituals include the pronunciation of the appropriate names of God backwards, and also a curse against the Sephira in respect of all that which it is, for that it is that which distinguishes and separates it from Kether.

12. Advancing to the squares of Binah and Chokmah in turn, let him banish these also. And for that by now an awe and trembling shall have taken hold upon him, let him banish these by a supreme ritual of inestimable puissance. And let him beware exceedingly lest his will falter, or his courage fail.

13. Finally, let him, advancing to the square of Kether, banish that also by what means he may. At the end whereof let him set his foot upon the light, extinguishing it;[2] and, as he falleth, let him fall within the circle.

2. If armed with wand and lamp, let him extinguish the light with his hand.—N.

SECOND METHOD

1. Let the Hermit be seated in his Asana, robed, and let him meditate in turn upon every several part of his body until that part is so unreal to him that he no longer includes it in his comprehension of himself. For example, if it be his right foot, let him touch that foot, and be alarmed, thinking, "A foot! What is this foot? Surely I am not alone in the Hermitage!"

And this practice should be carried out not only at the time of meditation, but during the day's work.

2. This meditation is to be assisted by reasoning; as, "This foot is not I. If I should lose my foot, I should still be I. This foot is a mass of changing and decaying flesh, bone, skin, blood, lymph, etc., while I am the Unchanging and Immortal Spirit, uniform, not made, unbegotten, formless, self-luminous," etc.

3. This practice being perfect for each part of the body, let him combine his workings until the whole body is thus understood as the non-Ego and as illusion.

4. Let then the Hermit, seated in his Asana, meditate upon the Muladhara cakkra and its correspondence as a power of the mind, and destroy it in the same manner as aforesaid. Also by reasoning: "This emotion (memory, imagination, intellect, will, as it may be) is not I. This emotion is transient: I am immovable. This emotion is passion; I am peace." And so on.

Let the other Cakkrams in their turn be thus destroyed, each one with its mental or moral attribute.

5. In this let him be aided by his own psychological analysis, so that no part of his conscious being be thus left undestroyed. And on his thoroughness in this matter may turn his success.

6. Lastly, having drawn all his being into the highest Sahasrara Cakkra, let him remain eternally fixed in meditation thereupon.

7. Aum.

THIRD METHOD

1. Let the Hermit stimulate each of the senses in turn, concentrating upon each until it ceases to stimulate.

[The senses of sight and touch are extremely difficult to conquer. In the end the Hermit must be utterly unable by any effort to see or feel the object of those senses. —O. M.]

2. This being perfected, let him combine them two at a time.

For example, let him chew ginger (taste and touch), and watch a waterfall (sight and hearing), and watch incense (sight and smell), and crunch sugar in his teeth (taste and hearing), and so on.

3. These twenty-five practices being accomplished, let him combine them three at a time, then four at a time.

4. Lastly, let him combine all the senses in a single object.

And herein may a sixth sense be included. He is then to withdraw himself entirely from all these stimulations, perinde ac cadaver, in spite of his own efforts to attach himself to them.

5. By this method it is said that the demons of the Ruach, that is, thoughts and memories, are inhibited, and We deny it not. But if so be that they arise, let him build a wall between himself and them according to the method.

6. Thus having stilled the voices of the Six, may he sense the subtlety of the Seventh.

7. Aum.

[We add the following, contributed by a friend at that time without the A .˙. A .˙. and its dependent orders. He worked out the method himself, and we think it may prove useful to many. —O. M.]

(1) The beginner must first practise breathing regularly through the nose, at the same time trying hard to imagine that the breath goes to the Ajna and not to the lungs.

The pranayama exercises described in *Liber E,* must next be practised, always with the idea that Ajna is breathing.

Try to realise that *power*, not air, is being drawn into the Ajna, is being concentrated there during Kumbhakam, and is vivifying the Ajna during expiration. Try rather to increase the force of concentration in Ajna than to increase excessively the length of Kumbhaka, as this is dangerous if rashly undertaken.

(2) Walk slowly in a quiet place; realise that the legs are moving, and study their movements. Understand thoroughly that these movements are due to nerve messages sent down from the brain, and that the controlling power lies in the Ajna. The legs are automatic, like those of a wooden monkey: the power in Ajna is that which does the work, is that which walks. This is not hard to realise, and should be grasped firmly, ignoring all other walking sensations.

Apply this method to every other muscular movement.

(3) Lie flat on the back with the feet under a heavy piece of furniture. Keeping the spine straight and the arms in a line with the body, rise slowly to a sitting posture, by means of the force residing in the Ajna (*i.e.,* try to prevent the mind dwelling on any other exertion or sensation).

Then let the body slowly down to its original position. Repeat this two or three times every night and morning, and slowly increase the number of repetitions.

(4) Try to transfer all bodily sensations to the Ajna: *e.g.,* "I am cold" should mean "I feel cold," or, better still, "I am aware of a sensation of cold"—transfer this to the Ajna, "The Ajna is aware," etc.

(5) Pain if very slight may easily be transferred to the Ajna after a little practice. The best method for a beginner is to *imagine* he has a pain in the body and then imagine that it passes directly into the Ajna. It does not pass through the intervening structures, but goes direct. After continual practice even severe pain may be transferred to the Ajna.

(6) Fix the mind on the base of the spine and then gradually move the thoughts upwards to the Ajna.

(In this meditation Ajna is the Holy of Holies, but it is dark and empty.)

Finally, strive hard to drive anger and other obsessing thoughts into the Ajna. Try to develop a tendency to think hard of Ajna when these thoughts attack the mind, and let Ajna conquer them.

Beware of thinking of "*my* Ajna." In these meditations and practices, Ajna does not belong to you; Ajna is the master and worker, you are the wooden monkey.

LIBER

OS

ABYSMI

VEL

DAATH

SVB FIGVRA

CDLXXIV

A ∴ A ∴ Publication in Class B

Imprimatur:
N. Fra A ∴ A ∴

LIBER OS ABYSMI

1. This book is the Gate of the Secret of the Universe.

2. Let the Exempt Adept procure *The Prolegomena* of Kant, and study it, paying special attention to the Antinomies.

3. Also Hume's doctrine of Causality in his *Enquiry*.

4. Also Herbert Spencer's discussion of the three theories of the Universe in his *First Principles*, Part I.

5. Also Huxley's essays on Hume and Berkeley.

6. Also Crowley's Essays: *Berashith, Time, The Soldier and the Hunchback*, et cetera.

7. Also the *Logik* of Hegel.

8. Also the *Questions of King Melinda* and the *Buddhist Suttas* which bear on Metaphysic.

9. Let him also be accomplished in Logic. (Formal Logic, Keynes.) Further let him study any classical works to which his attention may be sufficiently directed in the course of his reading.

10. Now let him consider special problems, such as the Origin of the World, the Origin of Evil, Infinity, the Absolute, the Ego and the non-Ego, Freewill and Destiny, and such others as may attract him.

11. Let him subtly and exactly demonstrate the fallacies of every known solution, and let him seek a true solution by his right Ingenium.

12. In all this let him be guided only by clear reason, and let him forcibly suppress all other qualities such as Intuition, Aspiration, Emotion, and the like.

13. During these practices all forms of Magick Art and Meditation are forbidden to him. It is forbidden to him to seek any refuge from his intellect.

14. Let then his reason hurl itself again and again against the blank wall of mystery which will confront him.

15. Thus also following is it said, and we deny it not. At last automatically his reason will take up the practice, suâ sponte, and he shall have no rest therefrom.

16. Then will all phenomena which present themselves to him appear meaningless and disconnected, and his own Ego will break up into a series of impressions having no relation one with the other, or with any other thing.

17. Let this state then become so acute that it is in truth Insanity, and let this continue until exhaustion.

18. According to a certain deeper tendency of the individual will be the duration of this state.

19. It may end in real insanity, which concludes the activities of the Adept during this present life, or by his rebirth into his own body and mind with the simplicity of a little child.

20. And then shall he find all his faculties unimpaired, yet cleansed in a manner ineffable.

21. And he shall recall the simplicity of the Task of the Adeptus Minor, and apply himself thereto with fresh energy in a more direct manner.

22. And in his great weakness it may be that for awhile the new Will and Aspiration are not puissant, yet being undisturbed by those dead weeds of doubt and

reason which he hath uprooted, they grow imperceptibly and easily like a flower.

23. And with the reappearance of the Holy Guardian Angel he may be granted the highest attainments, and be truly fitted for the full experience of the destruction of the Universe. And by the Universe We mean not that petty Universe which the mind of man can conceive, but that which is revealed to his soul in the Samadhi of Atmadarshana.

24. Thence may he enter into a real communion with those that are beyond, and he shall be competent to receive communication and instruction from Ourselves directly.

25. Thus shall We prepare him for the Confrontation of Choronzon and the Ordeal of the Abyss, when we have received him into the City of the Pyramids.

26. So, being of Us, let the Master of the Temple accomplish that Work which is appointed.

(In *Liber CDXVIII* is an adequate account of this Ordeal and Reception. See also *Liber CLVI* for the preparation.)

27. Also concerning the Reward thereof, of his entering into the Palace of the King's Daughter, and of that which shall thereafter befall, let it be understood of the Master of the Temple. Hath he not attained to Understanding? Yea, verily, hath he not attained to Understanding?

LIBER

תישארב

VIAE

MEMORIAE

SVB FIGVRA

CMXIII

A $\therefore$ A $\therefore$ Publication in Class B

Imprimatur:
N. Fra A $\therefore$ A $\therefore$

LIBER THISHARB

ooo. May be.

(oo. It has not been possible to construct this book on a basis of pure Scepticism. This matters less, as the practice leads to Scepticism, and it may be through it.)

o. This book is not intended to lead to the supreme attainment. On the contrary, its results define the separate being of the Exempt Adept from the rest of the Universe, and discover his relation to that Universe.

1. It is of such importance to the Exempt Adept that We cannot overrate it. Let him in no wise adventure the plunge into the Abyss until he have accomplished this to his most perfect satisfaction.

2. For in the Abyss no effort is anywise possible. The Abyss is passed by virtue of the mass of the Adept and his Karma. Two forces impel him: (1) the attraction of Binah, (2) the impulse of his Karma; and the ease and even the safety of his passage depend on the strength and direction of the latter.

3. Should one rashly dare the passage, and take the irrevocable Oath of the Abyss, he might be lost therein

through Aeons of incalculable agony; he might even be thrown back upon Chesed, with the terrible Karma of failure added to his original imperfection.

4. It is even said that in certain circumstances it is possible to fall altogether from the Tree of Life, and to attain the Towers of the Black Brothers. But We hold that this is not possible for any adept who has truly attained his grade, or even for any man who has really sought to help humanity even for a single second,[1] and that although his aspiration have been impure through vanity or any similar imperfection.

5. Let then the Adept who finds the result of these meditations unsatisfactory refuse the Oath of the Abyss, and live so that his Karma gains strength and direction suitable to the task at some future period.

6. Memory is essential to the individual consciousness; otherwise the mind were but a blank sheet on which shadows are cast. But we see that not only does the mind retain impressions, but that it is so constituted that its tendency is to retain some more excellently than others. Thus the great classical scholar, Sir Richard Jebb, was unable to learn even the schoolboy mathematics required for the preliminary examination at Cambridge University, and a special act of the authorities was required in order to admit him.

7. The first method to be described has been detailed in Bhikkhu Ananda Metteya's *Training of the Mind* (*The Equinox*, I, 5, pp. 28–59 and especially pp. 48–56). We have little to alter or to add. Its most important result, as regards the Oath of the Abyss, is the freedom from all desire or clinging to anything which it gives. Its second result is to aid the adept in the second method, by supplying him with further data for his investigation.

---

1. Those in possession of *Liber CLXXXV* will note that in every grade but one the aspirant is pledged to serve his inferiors in the Order.

8. The stimulation of memory useful in both practices is also achieved by simple meditation (*Liber E*), in a certain stage of which old memories arise unbidden. The adept may then practise this, stopping at that stage, and encouraging instead of suppressing the flashes of memory.

9. Zoroaster has said, "Explore the River of the Soul, whence or in what order you have come; so that although you have become a servant to the body, you may again rise to that Order (the A ∴ A ∴) from which you descended, joining Works (Kamma) to Sacred Reason (the Tao)."

10. The Result of the Second Method is to show the Adept to what end his powers are destined. When he has passed the Abyss and become Nemo, the return of the current causes him "to appear in the Heaven of Jupiter as a morning star or as an evening star."[2] In other words, he should discover what may be the nature of his work. Thus Mohammed was a Brother reflected into Netzach, Buddha a Brother reflected into Hod, or, as some say, Daath. The present manifestation of Frater P. to the outer is in Tiphereth, to the inner in the path of Leo.

11. First Method. Let the Exempt Adept first train himself to think backwards by external means, as set forth here following.

    (*a*) Let him learn to write backwards, with either hand.

    (*b*) Let him learn to walk backwards.

    (*c*) Let him constantly watch, if convenient, cinematograph films, and listen to phonograph records, reversed, and let him so accustom himself to these that they appear natural, and appreciable as a whole.

---

2. The formula of the Great Work "Solve et Coagula," may be thus interpreted. Solve, the dissolution of the Self in the Infinite; Coagula, the presentation of the Infinite in a concrete form to the outer. Both are necessary to the Task of a Master of the Temple.

(d) Let him practise speaking backwards; thus, for "I am He" let him say, "Eh ma I."

(e) Let him learn to read backwards. In this it is difficult to avoid cheating one's self, as an expert reader sees a sentence at a glance. Let his disciple read aloud to him backwards, slowly at first, then more quickly.

(f) Of his own ingenium let him devise other methods.

12. In this his brain will at first be overwhelmed by a sense of utter confusion; secondly, it will endeavour to evade the difficulty by a trick. The brain will pretend to be working backwards when it is really normal. It is difficult to describe the nature of the trick, but it will be quite obvious to anyone who has done practices (a) and (b) for a day or two. They become quite easy, and he will think that he is making progress, an illusion which close analysis will dispel.

13. Having begun to train his brain in this manner, and obtained some little success, let the Exempt Adept, seated in his Asana, think first of his present attitude, next of the act of being seated, next of his entering the room, next of his robing, et cetera, exactly as it happened. And let him most strenuously endeavour to think each act as happening backwards. It is not enough to think: "I am seated here, and before that I was standing, and before that I entered the room," etc. That series is the trick detected in the preliminary practices. The series must not run "ghi-def-abc," but "ihgfedcba": not "horse a is this" but "esroh a si siht." To obtain this thoroughly well, practice (c) is very useful. The brain will be found to struggle constantly to right itself, soon accustoming itself to accept "esroh" as merely another glyph for "horse." This tendency must be constantly combated.

14. In the early stages of this practice the endeavour

should be to meticulous minuteness of detail in remembering actions; for the brain's habit of thinking forwards will at first be insuperable. Thinking of large and complex actions, then, will give a series which we may symbolically write "opqrstu-hijklmn-abcdefg." If these be split into detail, we shall have "stu-pqr-o—mn-kl-hij—fg-cde-ab," which is much nearer to the ideal "utsrqponmlkjihg-fedcba."

15. Capacities differ widely, but the Exempt Adept need have no reason to be discouraged if after a month's continuous labour he find that now and again for a few seconds his brain really works backwards.

16. The Exempt Adept should concentrate his efforts upon obtaining a perfect picture of five minutes backwards rather than upon extending the time covered by his meditation. For this preliminary training of the brain is the Pons Asinorum of the whole process.

17. This five minutes' exercise being satisfactory, the Exempt Adept may extend the same at his discretion to cover an hour, a day, a week, and so on. Difficulties vanish before him as he advances; the extension from a day to the course of his whole life will not prove so difficult as the perfecting of the five minutes.

18. This practice should be repeated at least four times daily, and progress is shown firstly by the ever easier running of the brain, secondly by the added memories which arise.

19. It is useful to reflect during this practice, which in time becomes almost mechanical, upon the way in which effects spring from causes. This aids the mind to link its memories, and prepares the adept for the preliminary practice of the Second Method.

20. Having allowed the mind to return for some hundred times to the hour of birth, it should be encouraged to endeavour to penetrate beyond that period. If it be

properly trained to run backwards, there will be little difficulty in doing this, although it is one of the distinct steps in the practice.

21. It may be then that the memory will persuade the adept of some previous existence. Where this is possible, let it be checked by an appeal to facts, as follows.

22. It often occurs to men that on visiting a place to which they have never been, it appears familiar. This may arise from a confusion of thought or a slipping of the memory, but it is conceivably a fact.

If, then, the adept "remember" that he was in a previous life in some city, say Cracow, which he has in this life never visited, let him describe from memory the appearance of Cracow, and of its inhabitants, setting down their names. Let him further enter into details of the city and its customs. And having done this with great minuteness, let him confirm the same by consultation with historians and geographers, or by a personal visit, remembering (both to the credit of his memory and its discredit) that historians, geographers, and himself are alike fallible. But let him not trust his memory to assert its conclusions as fact, and act thereupon, without most adequate confirmation.

23. This process of checking his memory should be practised with the earlier memories of childhood and youth by reference to the memories and records of others, always reflecting upon the fallibility even of such safeguards.

24. All this being perfected, so that the memory reaches back into aeons incalculably distant, let the Exempt Adept meditate upon the fruitlessness of all those years, and upon the fruit thereof, severing that which is transitory and worthless from that which is eternal. And it may be that he being but an Exempt Adept may hold all to be savourless and full of sorrow.

25. This being so, without reluctance will he swear the Oath of the Abyss.

26. Second Method. Let the Exempt Adept, fortified by the practice of the First Method, enter the preliminary practice of the Second Method.

27. Second Method. Preliminary Practices. Let him, seated in his Asana, consider any event, and trace it to its immediate causes. And let this be done very fully and minutely. Here, for example, is a body erect and motionless. Let the adept consider the many forces which maintain it; firstly, the attraction of the earth, of the sun, of the planets, of the farthest stars, nay, of every mote of dust in the room, one of which (could it be annihilated) would cause that body to move, although so imperceptibly. Also, the resistance of the floor, the pressure of the air, and all other external conditions. Secondly, the internal forces which sustain it, the vast and complex machinery of the skeleton, the muscles, the blood, the lymph, the marrow, all that makes up a man. Thirdly, the moral and intellectual forces involved, the mind, the will, the consciousness. Let him continue this with unremitting ardour, searching Nature, leaving nothing out.

28. Next let him take one of the immediate causes of his position, and trace out its equilibrium. For example, the will. What determines the will to aid in holding the body erect and motionless?

29. This being determined, let him choose one of the forces which determined his will, and trace out that in similar fashion; and let this process be continued for many days until the interdependence of all things is a truth assimilated in his inmost being.

30. This being accomplished, let him trace his own history with special reference to the causes of each event. And in this practice he may neglect to some extent the universal forces which at all times act on all, as for ex-

ample the attraction of masses, and let him concentrate his attention upon the principal and determining or effective causes.

For instance, he is seated, perhaps, in a country place in Spain. Why? Because Spain is warm and suitable for meditation, and because cities are noisy and crowded. Why is Spain warm? and why does he wish to meditate? Why choose warm Spain rather than warm India? To the last question: Because Spain is nearer to his home. Then why is his home near Spain? Because his parents were Germans. And why did they go to Germany? And so during the whole meditation.

31. On another day, let him begin with a question of another kind, and every day devise new questions, not only concerning his present situation, but also abstract questions. Thus let him connect the prevalence of water upon the surface of the globe with its necessity to such life as we know, with the specific gravity and other physical properties of water, and let him perceive ultimately through all this the necessity and concord of things, not concord as the schoolmen of old believed, making all things for man's benefit or convenience, but the essential mechanical concord whose final law is *inertia*. And in these meditations let him avoid as if it were the plague any speculation sentimental or fantastic.

32. Second Method. The Practice Proper. Having then perfected in his mind these conceptions, let him apply them to his own career, forging the links of memory into the chain of necessity.

And let this be his final question: To what purpose am I fitted? Of what service can my being prove to the Brothers of the A ∴ A ∴ if I cross the Abyss, and am admitted to the City of the Pyramids?

33. Now that he may clearly understand the nature of

this question, and the method of solution, let him study the reasoning of the anatomist who reconstructs an animal from a single bone. To take a simple example.

34. Suppose, having lived all my life among savages, a ship is cast upon the shore and wrecked. Undamaged among the cargo is a "Victoria." What is its use? The wheels speak of roads, their slimness of smooth roads, the brake of hilly roads. The shafts show that it was meant to be drawn by an animal, their height and length suggest an animal of the size of a horse. That the carriage is open suggests a climate tolerable at any rate for part of the year. The height of the box suggests crowded streets, or the spirited character of the animal employed to draw it. The cushions indicate its use to convey men rather than merchandise; its hood that rain sometimes falls, or that the sun is at times powerful. The springs would imply considerable skill in metals; the varnish much attainment in that craft.

35. Similarly, let the adept consider his own case. Now that he is on the point of plunging into the Abyss, a giant Why? confronts him with uplifted club.

36. There is no minutest atom of his composition which can be withdrawn without making him some other than he is, no useless moment in his past. Then what is his future? The "Victoria" is not a waggon; it is not intended for carting hay. It is not a sulky; it is useless in trotting races.

37. So the adept has military genius, or much knowledge of Greek: how do these attainments help his purpose, or the purpose of the Brothers? He was put to death by Calvin, or stoned by Hezekiah; as a snake he was killed by a villager, or as an elephant slain in battle under Hamilcar. How do such memories help him? Until he have thoroughly mastered the reason for every incident in his

past, and found a purpose for every item of his present equipment,[3] he cannot truly answer even those Three Questions that were first put to him, even the Three Questions of the Ritual of the Pyramid; he is not ready to swear the Oath of the Abyss.

38. But being thus enlightened, let him swear the Oath of the Abyss; yea, let him swear the Oath of the Abyss.

3. A Brother known to me was repeatedly baffled in this meditation. But one day being thrown with his horse over a sheer cliff of forty feet, and escaping without a scratch or a bruise, he was reminded of his many narrow escapes from death. These proved to be the last factors in his problem, which, thus completed, solved itself in a moment.—O.M.

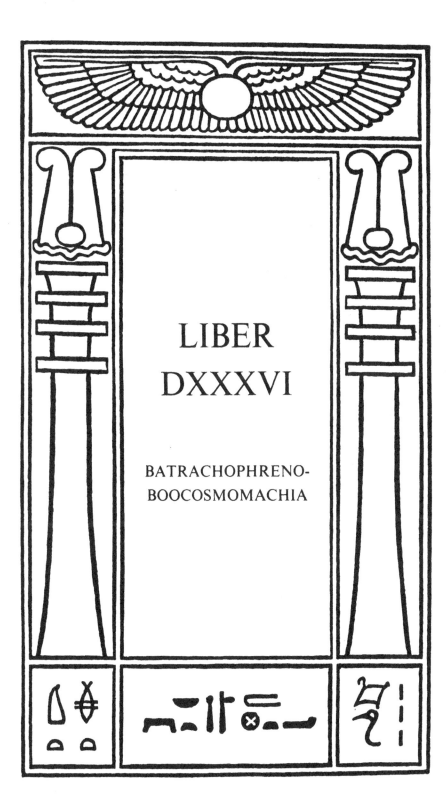

LIBER
DXXXVI

BATRACHOPHRENO-
BOOCOSMOMACHIA

A ∴ A ∴ Publication in Class B

Imprimatur:
N. Fra. A ∴ A ∴

LIBER DXXXVI

Within His skull exist daily thirteen thousand myriads of Worlds, which draw their existence from Him, and by Him are upheld.

I.R.Q. III: 43

0. Let the Practicus study the textbooks of astronomy, travel, if need be, to a land where the sun and stars are visible, and observe the heavens with the best telescopes to which he may have access. Let him commit to memory the principal facts, and (at least roughly) the figures of the science.

1. Now, since these figures will leave no direct impression with any precision upon his mind, let him adopt this practice A.

A. Let the Practicus be seated before a bare square table, and let an unknown number of small similar objects be thrown by his chela from time to time upon the table, and by that chela be hastily gathered up.

Let the Practicus declare at the glance, and the chela confirm by his count, the number of such objects.

The practice should be for a quarter of an hour thrice daily. The maximum number of objects should at first be seven. This maximum should increase by one at each practice, provided that not a single mistake is made by the Practicus in appreciating the number thrown.

This practice should continue assiduously for at least one year.

The quickness of the chela in gathering up the objects is expected to increase with time. The practice need not be limited to a quarter of an hour thrice daily after a time, but increased with discretion. Care must be taken to detect the first symptom of fatigue, and to stop, if possible, even before it threatens. The practised psychologist learns to recognise even minute hesitations that mark the forcing of the attention.

2. Alternating with the above, let the Practicus begin this practice B. It is assumed that he has thoroughly conquered the elementary difficulties of Dharana, and is able to prevent mental pictures from altering shape, size and colour against his will.

B. Seated in the open air, let him endeavour to form a complete mental picture of himself and his immediate surroundings. It is important that he should be in the centre of such picture, and able to look freely in all directions. The finished picture should be a complete consciousness of the whole, fixed, clear, and definite.

Let him gradually add to this picture by including objects more and more distant, until he have an image of the whole field of vision.

He will probably discover that it is very difficult to increase the apparent size of the picture as he proceeds, and it should be his most earnest endeavour to do so. He should seek in particular to appreciate distances, almost to the point of combating the laws of perspective.

3. These practices A and B accomplished, and his

studies in astronomy completed, let him attempt this practice C.

C. Let the Practicus form a mental picture of the Earth, in particular striving to realize the size of the earth in comparison with himself, and let him not be content until by assiduity he has well succeeded.

Let him add the Moon, keeping well in mind the relative sizes of, and the distance between, the planet and its satellite.

He will probably find the final trick of mind to be a constant disappearance of the image, and the appearance of the same upon a smaller scale. This trick he must outwit by constancy of endeavour.

He will then add in turn Venus, Mars, Mercury and the Sun.

It is permissible at this stage to change the point of view to the centre of the Sun, and to do so may add stability to the conception.

The Practicus may then add the Asteroids, Jupiter, Saturn, Uranus and Neptune. The utmost attention to detail is now necessary, as the picture is highly complex, apart from the difficulty of appreciating relative size and distance.

Let this picture be practised month after month until it is absolutely perfect. The tendency which may manifest itself to pass into Dhyana and Samadhi must be resolutely combated with the whole strength of the mind.

Let the Practicus then re-commence the picture, starting from the Sun, and adding the planets one by one, each with its proper motion, until he have an image perfect in all respects of the Solar System as it actually exists. Let him particularly note that unless the apparent size approximate to the real, his practice is wasted. Let him then add a comet to the picture; he may find, perhaps, that the path of this comet may assist him to expand the sphere of his mental vision until it include a star.

And thus, gathering one star after another, let his contemplation become vast as the heaven, in space and time ever aspiring to the perception of the Body of Nuit; yea, of the Body of Nuit.

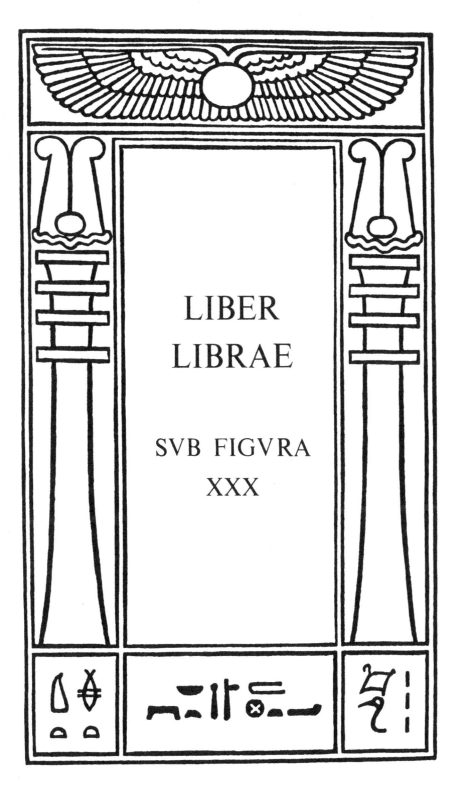

LIBER
LIBRAE

SVB FIGVRA
XXX

A ∴ A ∴ Publication in Class B

Imprimatur:
D.D.S. Praemonstrator
O.S.V. Imperator
N.S.F. Cancellarius

LIBER LIBRAE

0. Learn first—Oh thou who aspirest unto our ancient Order!—that Equilibrium is the basis of the Work. If thou thyself hast not a sure foundation, whereon wilt thou stand to direct the forces of Nature?

1. Know then, that as man is born into this world amidst the Darkness of Matter, and the strife of contending forces; so must his first endeavour be to seek the Light through their reconciliation.

2. Thou then, who hast trials and troubles, rejoice because of them, for in them is Strength, and by their means is a pathway opened unto that Light.

3. How should it be otherwise, O man, whose life is but a day in Eternity, a drop in the Ocean of time; how, were thy trials not many, couldst thou purge thy soul from the dross of earth?

Is it but now that the Higher Life is beset with dangers and difficulties; hath it not ever been so with the Sages and Hierophants of the past? They have been persecuted and reviled, they have been tormented of men; yet through this also has their Glory increased.

4. Rejoice therefore, O Initiate, for the greater thy trial

the greater thy Triumph. When men shall revile thee, and speak against thee falsely, hath not the Master said, "Blessed art thou!"?

5. Yet, oh aspirant, let thy victories bring thee not Vanity, for with increase of Knowledge should come increase of Wisdom. He who knoweth little, thinketh he knoweth much; but he who knoweth much hath learned his own ignorance. Seest thou a man wise in his own conceit? There is more hope of a fool, than of him.

6. Be not hasty to condemn others; how knowest thou that in their place, thou couldest have resisted the temptation? And even were it so, why shouldest thou despise one who is weaker than thyself?

7. Thou therefore who desirest Magical Gifts, be sure that thy soul is firm and steadfast; for it is by flattering thy weaknesses that the Weak Ones will gain power over thee. Humble thyself before thy Self, yet fear neither man nor spirit. Fear is failure, and the forerunner of failure: and courage is the beginning of virtue.

8. Therefore fear not the Spirits, but be firm and courteous with them; for thou hast no right to despise or revile them; and this too may lead thee astray. Command and banish them, curse them by the Great Names if need be; but neither mock nor revile them, for so assuredly wilt thou be led into error.

9. A man is what he maketh himself within the limits fixed by his inherited destiny; he is a part of mankind; his actions affect not only what he calleth himself, but also the whole universe.

10. Worship, and neglect not, the physical body which is thy temporary connection with the outer and material world. Therefore let thy mental Equilibrium be above disturbance by material events; strengthen and control the

animal passions, discipline the emotions and the reason, nourish the Higher Aspirations.

11. Do good unto others for its own sake, not for reward, not for gratitude from them, not for sympathy. If thou art generous, thou wilt not long for thine ears to be tickled by expressions of gratitude.

12. Remember that unbalanced force is evil; that unbalanced severity is but cruelty and oppression; but that also unbalanced mercy is but weakness which would allow and abet Evil. Act passionately; think rationally; be Thyself.

13. True ritual is as much action as word; it is Will.

14. Remember that this earth is but an atom in the universe, and that thou thyself art but an atom thereon, and that even couldst thou become the God of this earth whereon thou crawlest and grovellest, that thou wouldest, even then, be but an atom, and one amongst many.

15. Nevertheless have the greatest self-respect, and to that end sin not against thyself. The sin which is unpardonable is knowingly and wilfully to reject truth, to fear knowledge lest that knowledge pander not to thy prejudices.

16. To obtain Magical Power, learn to control thought; admit only those ideas that are in harmony with the end desired, and not every stray and contradictory Idea that presents itself.

17. Fixed thought is a means to an end. Therefore pay attention to the power of silent thought and meditation. The material act is but the outward expression of thy thought, and therefore hath it been said that "the thought of foolishness is sin." Thought is the commencement of action, and if a chance thought can produce much effect, what cannot fixed thought do?

18. Therefore, as hath already been said, Establish thyself firmly in the equilibrium of forces, in the centre of the Cross of the Elements, that Cross from whose centre the Creative Word issued in the birth of the dawning Universe.

19. Be thou therefore prompt and active as the Sylphs, but avoid frivolity and caprice; be energetic and strong like the Salamanders, but avoid irritability and ferocity; be flexible and attentive to images like the Undines, but avoid idleness and changeability; be laborious and patient like the Gnomes, but avoid grossness and avarice.

20. So shalt thou gradually develop the powers of thy soul, and fit thyself to command the Spirits of the elements. For wert thou to summon the Gnomes to pander to thine avarice, thou wouldst no longer command them, but they would command thee. Wouldst thou abuse the pure beings of the woods and mountains to fill thy coffers and satisfy thy hunger of Gold? Wouldst thou debase the Spirits of Living Fire to serve thy wrath and hatred? Wouldst thou violate the purity of the Souls of the Waters to pander to thy lust of debauchery? Wouldst thou force the Spirits of the Evening Breeze to minister to thy folly and caprice? Know that with such desires thou canst but attract the Weak, not the Strong, and in that case the Weak will have power over thee.

21. In true religion there is no sect, therefore take heed that thou blaspheme not the name by which another knoweth his God; for if thou do this thing in Jupiter thou wilt blaspheme יהוה and in Osiris יהשוה. Ask and ye shall have! Seek, and ye shall find! Knock, and it shall be opened unto you!

SECTION IV

MAGICK

LIBER

O

VEL

MANVS ET

SAGITTAE

SVB FIGVRA

VI

A ∴ A ∴ Publication in Class B

Issued by Order:
D.D.S. 7° = 4° Praemonstrator
O.S.V. 6° = 5° Imperator
N.S.F. 5° = 6° Cancellarius

1. Earth: the god Set fighting.
2. Air: the god Shu supporting the sky.
3. Water: the goddess Auramoth.
4. Fire: the goddess Thoum-aesh-neith.
5, 6. Spirit: the rending and closing of the veil.

7-10. The L V X signs.
7. + Osiris slain—the cross.
8. L Isis mourning—the Svastika.
9. V Typhon—the Trident.
10. X Osiris risen—the Pentagram.

The Signs of the Grades

LIBER O

I

1. This book is very easy to misunderstand; readers are asked to use the most minute critical care in the study of it, even as we have done in its preparation.

2. In this book it is spoken of the Sephiroth and the Paths; of Spirits and Conjurations; of Gods, Spheres, Planes, and many other things which may or may not exist.

It is immaterial whether these exist or not. By doing certain things certain results will follow; students are most earnestly warned against attributing objective reality or philosophic validity to any of them.

3. The advantages to be gained from them are chiefly these:

(*a*) A widening of the horizon of the mind.

(*b*) An improvement of the control of the mind.

4. The student, if he attains any success in the following practices, will find himself confronted by things (ideas or beings) too glorious or too dreadful to be described. It is essential that he remain the master of all that he beholds, hears or conceives; otherwise he will be the slave of illusion, and the prey of madness.

Before entering upon any of these practices, the student should be in good health, and have attained a fair mastery of Asana, Pranayama, and Dharana.

5. There is little danger that any student, however idle or stupid, will fail to get some result; but there is great danger that he will be led astray, obsessed and overwhelmed by his results, even though it be by those which it is necessary that he should attain. Too often, moreover, he mistaketh the first resting-place for the goal, and taketh off his armour as if he were a victor ere the fight is well begun.

It is desirable that the student should never attach to any result the importance which it at first seems to possess.

6. First, then, let us consider the book 777 and its use; the preparation of the Place; the use of the Magic Ceremonies; and finally the methods which follow in Chapter V, "Viator in Regnis Arboris," and in Chapter VI, "Sagitta trans Lunam."

(In another book will it be treated of the Expansion and Contraction of Consciousness; progress by slaying the Cakkrâms; progress by slaying the Pairs of Opposites; the methods of Sabhapaty Swami, &c.)

II

1. The student must first obtain a thorough knowledge of book 777, especially of columns i, ii, iii, v, vi, vii, ix, xi, xii, xiv, xv, xvi, xvii, xviii, xix, xxxiv, xxxv, xxxviii, xxxix, xl, xli, xlii, xlv, liv, lv, lix, lx, lxi, lxiii, lxx, lxxv, lxxvii, lxxviii, lxxix, lxxx, lxxxi, lxxxiii, xcvii, xcviii, xcix, c, ci, cxvii, cxviii, cxxxvii, cxxxviii, cxxxix, clxxv, clxxvi, clxxvii, clxxxii.

When these are committed to memory, he will begin to understand the nature of these correspondences. (See Illustrations: *The Temple of Solomon the King.*)

2. If we take an example the use of the table will become clear.

Let us suppose that you wish to obtain knowledge of some obscure science.

In column xlv, line 12, you will find "Knowledge of Sciences."

By now looking up line 12 in the other columns, you will find that the Planet corresponding is Mercury, its number eight, its lineal figures the octagon and octagram, the God who rules that planet Thoth, or in Hebrew symbolism Tetragrammaton Adonai and Elohim Tzabaoth, its Archangel Raphael, its Choir of Angels Beni Elohim, its Intelligence Tiriel, its Spirit Taphtatharath, its colours Orange (for Mercury is the sphere of the Sephira Hod, 8) Yellow, Purple, Grey, and Indigo rayed with Violet; its Magical Weapon the Wand or Caduceus, its Perfumes Mastic and others, its sacred plants Vervain and others, its jewel the Opal or Agate, its sacred animal the Snake, &c.

3. You would then prepare your Place of Working accordingly. In an orange circle you would draw an eight-pointed star of yellow, at whose points you would place eight lamps. The Sigil of the Spirit (which is to be found in Cornelius Agrippa and other books) you would draw in the four colours with such other devices as your experience may suggest.

4. And so on. We cannot here enter at length into all the necessary preparations; and the student will find them fully set forth in the proper books, of which *The Goetia* is perhaps the best example.

These rituals need not be slavishly imitated; on the contrary the student should do nothing the object of which he does not understand; also, if he have any capacity whatever, he will find his own crude rituals more effective than the highly polished ones of other people.

The general purpose of all this preparation is as follows:

5. Since the student is a man surrounded by material objects, if it be his wish to master one particular idea, he must make every material object about him directly suggest that idea. Thus in the ritual quoted, if his glance fall upon the lights, their number suggests Mercury; he smells the perfumes, and again Mercury is brought to his mind. In other words, the whole magical apparatus and ritual is a complex system of mnemonics.

(The importance of these lies principally in the fact that particular sets of images that the student may meet in his wanderings correspond to particular lineal figures, divine names, &c., and are controlled by them. As to the possibility of producing results external to the mind of the seer [objective, in the ordinary common-sense acceptation of the term] we are here silent.)

6. There are three important practices connected with all forms of ceremonial (and the two Methods which later we shall describe). These are:

(1) Assumption of God-forms.

(2) Vibration of Divine Names.

(3) Rituals of "Banishing" and "Invoking."

These, at least, should be completely mastered before the dangerous Methods of Chapters V and VI are attempted.

III

1. The Magical Images of the Gods of Egypt should be made thoroughly familiar. This can be done by studying them in any public museum, or in such books as may be accessible to the student. They should then be carefully painted by him, both from the model and from memory.

2. The student, seated in the "God" position or in the characteristic attitude of the God desired, should then imagine His image as coinciding with his own body, or as

enveloping it. This must be practised until mastery of the image is attained, and an identity with it and with the God experienced.

It is a matter for very great regret that no simple and certain test of success in this practice exists.

3. The Vibration of God-names. As a further means of identifying the human consciousness with that pure portion of it which man calls by the name of some God, let him act thus:

4. (*a*) Stand with arms outstretched. (See illustration.)

(*b*) Breathe in deeply through the nostrils, imagining the name of the God desired entering with the breath.

(*c*) Let that name descend slowly from the lungs to the heart, the solar plexus, the navel, the generative organs, and so to the feet.

(*d*) The moment that it appears to touch the feet, quickly advance the left foot about twelve inches, throw forward the body, and let the hands (drawn back to the side of the eyes) shoot out, so that you are standing in the typical position of the God Horus,[1] and at the same time imagine the Name as rushing up and through the body, while you breathe it out through the nostrils with the air which has been till then retained in the lungs. All this must be done with all the force of which you are capable.

(*e*) Then withdraw the left foot, and place the right forefinger upon the lips, so that you are in the characteristic position of the God Harpocrates.[2]

5. It is a sign that the student is performing this correctly when a single "Vibration" entirely exhausts his physical strength. It should cause him to grow hot all

1. See illustration in Vol. I, No. 1, Blind Force.
2. See illustration in Vol. I, No. 1, The Silent Watcher.

The Sign of the Enterer
(Horus)

over, or to perspire violently, and it should so weaken him that he will find it difficult to remain standing.

6. It is a sign of success, though only by the student himself is it perceived, when he hears the name of the God vehemently roared forth, as if by the concourse of ten thousand thunders; and it should appear to him as if that Great Voice proceeded from the Universe, and not from himself.

In both the above practices all consciousness of anything but the God-form and name should be absolutely blotted out; and the longer it takes for normal perception to return, the better.

IV

1. The rituals of the Pentagram and Hexagram must be committed to memory. They are as follows:

The Lesser Ritual of the Pentagram

(i) Touching the forehead, say Ateh (Unto Thee).

(ii) Touching the breast, say Malkuth (The Kingdom).

(iii) Touching the right shoulder, say ve-Geburah (and the Power).

(iv) Touching the left shoulder, say ve-Gedulah (and the Glory).

(v) Clasping the hands upon the breast, say le-Olahm, Amen (to the Ages, Amen).

(vi) Turning to the East, make a pentagram (that of Earth) with the proper weapon (usually the Wand). Say (i.e., vibrate) I H V H.

(vii) Turning to the South, the same, but say A D N I.

(viii) Turning to the West, the same, but say A H I H.

(ix)   Turning to the North, the same, but say A G L A.

[Pronounce: Ye-ho-wau, Adonai, Eheieh, Agla.]

(x)   Extending the arms in the form of a Cross, say:

(xi)   Before me Raphael;

(xii)   Behind me Gabriel;

(xiii)   On my right hand Michael;

(xiv)   On my left hand Auriel;

(xv)   For about me flames the Pentagram,

(xvi)   And in the Column stands the six-rayed Star.

(xvii–xxi)   Repeat (i) to (v), the "Qabalistic Cross."

The Greater Ritual of the Pentagram

The pentagrams are traced in the air with the sword or other weapon, the name spoken aloud, and the signs used, as illustrated.

The Pentagrams of Spirit

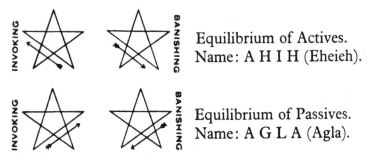

Equilibrium of Actives.
Name: A H I H (Eheieh).

Equilibrium of Passives.
Name: A G L A (Agla).

The signs of the Portal (see illustrations): Extend the hands in front of you, palms outwards, separate them as if in the act of rending asunder a veil or curtain (actives), and then bring them together as if closing it up again and let them fall to the side (passives).

(The Grade of the "Portal" is particularly attributed to the element of Spirit; it refers to the Sun; the paths of ‏ם‎ , ‏נ‎ and ‏ע‎ are attributed to this degree. See 777, lines 6 and 31 bis.)

The Pentagrams of Fire

  Name: A L H I M (Elohim).

The signs of 4°=7°: Raise the arms above the head and join the hands so that the tips of the fingers and of the thumbs meet, formulating a triangle. (See illustration.)

(The Grade of 4°=7° is particularly attributed to the element Fire; it refers to the planet Venus; the paths of ‏ק‎ , ‏צ‎ and ‏ס‎ are attributed to this degree. For other attributions see 777, lines 7 and 31.)

The Pentagrams of Water

  Name: A L (El).

The signs of 3°=8°: Raise the arms till the elbows are on a level with the shoulders, bring the hands across the chest, touching the thumbs and tips of fingers so as to form a triangle apex downwards. (See illustration.)

(The Grade of 3°=8° is particularly attributed to the element of Water; it refers to the planet Mercury; the paths of ‏ר‎ and ‏ש‎ are attributed to this degree. For other attributions see 777, lines 8 and 23.)

The Pentagrams of Air

  Name: I H V H (Ye-ho-wau).

The signs of 2°=9°: Stretch both arms upwards and outwards, the elbows bent at right-angles, the hands bent back, the palms upwards as if supporting a weight. (See illustration.)

(The Grade of 2°=9° is particularly attributed to the element Air; it refers to the Moon; the path of ה is attributed to this degree. For other attributions see 777, lines 9 and 11.)

The Pentagrams of Earth

  Name: A D N I (Adonai).

The sign of 1°=10°: Advance the right foot, stretch out the right hand upwards and forwards, the left hand downwards and backwards, the palms open.

(The Grade of 1°=10° is particularly attributed to the element of Earth. See 777, lines 10 and 32 bis.)

The Lesser Ritual of the Hexagram

This ritual is to be performed after the "Lesser Ritual of the Pentagram."

> (i) Stand upright, feet together, left arm at side, right arm across body, holding the wand or other weapon upright in the median line. Then face East, and say:
>
> (ii) I. N. R. I.
> Yod. Nun. Resh. Yod.
> Virgo, Isis, Mighty Mother.
> Scorpio, Apophis, Destroyer.
> Sol, Osiris, Slain and Risen.
> Isis, Apophis, Osiris, IAO.
>
> (iii) Extend the arms in the form of a cross, and say:
> "The sign of Osiris Slain." (See illustration.)

(iv) Raise the right arm to point upwards, keeping the elbow square, and lower the left arm to point downwards, keeping the elbow square, while turning the head over the left shoulder looking down so that the eyes follow the left forearm, and say: "The sign of the Mourning of Isis." (See illustration.)

(v) Raise the arms at an angle of sixty degrees to each other above the head, which is thrown back, and say: "The sign of Apophis and Typhon." (See illustration.)

(vi) Cross the arms on the breast, and bow the head, and say: "The sign of Osiris Risen." (See illustration.)

(vii) Extend the arms again as in (iii) and cross them again as in (vi), saying: "L.V.X., Lux, the Light of the Cross."

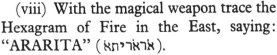

(viii) With the magical weapon trace the Hexagram of Fire in the East, saying: "ARARITA" (אראריתא).

Which word consists of the initials of a sentence which means "One is His Beginning: One is His Individuality: His Permutation is One."

This hexagram consists of two equilateral triangles, both apices pointing upwards. Begin at the top of the upper triangle and trace it in a dextro-rotary direction. The top of the lower triangle should coincide with the central point of the upper triangle.

(ix) Trace the Hexagram of Earth in the South saying: "ARARITA."

This Hexagram has the apex of the lower triangle pointing downwards, and it should be capable of inscription in a circle.

(x) Trace the Hexagram of Air in the West, saying: "ARARITA."

This hexagram is like that of Earth; but the bases of the triangles coincide, forming a diamond.

(xi) Trace the hexagram of Water in the North, saying: "ARARITA."

This hexagram has the lower triangle placed above the upper, so that their apices coincide.

(xii) Repeat (i–vii)

The Banishing Ritual is identical, save that the direction of the Hexagrams must be reversed.

Invoking   *Banishing*

The Greater Ritual of the Hexagram

To invoke or banish planets or zodiacal signs.

The Hexagram of Earth alone is used. Draw the hexagram, beginning from the point which is attributed to the planet you are dealing with. (See 777, col. lxxxiii.)

Thus to invoke Jupiter begin from the right-hand point of the lower triangle, dextroro-

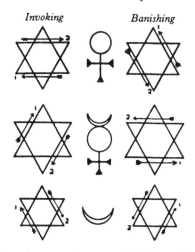

tary, and complete; then trace the upper triangle from its left-hand point and complete.

Trace the astrological sigil of the planet in the centre of your hexagram.

For the Zodiac use the hexagram of the planet which rules the sign you require (777, col. cxxxviii); but draw the astrological sigil of the sign, instead of that of the planet.

For Caput and Cauda Draconis use the lunar hexagram, with the sigil of ♌ or ♋.

To banish reverse the hexagram.

In all cases use a conjuration first with ARARITA, and next with the name of the God corresponding to the planet or sign you are dealing with.

The Hexagrams pertaining to the planets are as in plate on preceding page.

2. These rituals should be practised until the figures drawn appear in flame, in flame so near to physical flame that it would perhaps be visible to the eyes of a bystander, were one present. It is alleged that some persons have attained the power of actually kindling fire by these means. Whether this be so or not, the power is not one to be aimed at.

3. Success in "banishing" is known by a "feeling of cleanliness" in the atmosphere; success in "invoking" by a "feeling of holiness." It is unfortunate that these terms are so vague.

But at least make sure of this: that any imaginary figure

or being shall instantly obey the will of the student, when he uses the appropriate figure. In obstinate cases, the form of the appropriate God may be assumed.

4. The banishing rituals should be used at the commencement of any ceremony whatever. Next, the student should use a general invocation, such as the "Preliminary Invocation" in *The Goetia*, as wel as a special invocationl to suit the nature of his working.

5. Success in these verbal invocations is so subtle a matter, and its grades so delicately shaded, that it must be left to the good sense of the student to decide whether or not he should be satisfied with his result.

V

1. Let the student be at rest in one of his prescribed positions, having bathed and robed with the proper decorum. Let the Place of Working be free from all disturbance, and let the preliminary purifications, banishings and invocations be duly accomplished, and, lastly, let the incense be kindled.

2. Let him imagine his own figure (preferably robed in the proper magical garments and armed with the proper magical weapons) as enveloping his physical body, or standing near to and in front of him.

3. Let him then transfer the seat of his consciousness to that imagined figure; so that it may seem to him that he is seeing with its eyes, and hearing with its ears.

This will usually be the great difficulty of the operation.

4. Let him then cause that imagined figure to rise in the air to a great height above the earth.

5. Let him then stop and look about him. (It is sometimes difficult to open the eyes.)

6. Probably he will see figures approaching him, or become conscious of a landscape.

Let him speak to such figures, and insist upon being

answered, using the proper pentagrams and signs, as previously taught.

7. Let him travel about at will, either with or without guidance from such figure or figures.

8. Let him further employ such special invocations as will cause to appear the particular places he may wish to visit.

9. Let him beware of the thousand subtle attacks and deceptions that he will experience, carefully testing the truth of all with whom he speaks.

Thus a hostile being may appear clothed with glory; the appropriate pentagram will in such a case cause him to shrivel or decay.

10. Practice will make the student infinitely wary in these matters.

11. It is usually quite easy to return to the body, but should any difficulty arise, practice (again) will make the imagination fertile. For example, one may create in thought a chariot of fire with white horses, and command the charioteer to drive earthwards.

It might be dangerous to go too far, or stay too long; for fatigue must be avoided.

The danger spoken of is that of fainting, or of obsession, or of loss of memory or other mental faculty.

12. Finally, let the student cause his imagined body in which he supposes himself to have been travelling to coincide with the physical, tightening his muscles, drawing in his breath, and putting his forefinger to his lips. Then let him "awake" by a well-defined act of will, and soberly and accurately record his experiences.

It may be added that this apparently complicated experiment is perfectly easy to perform. It is best to learn by "travelling" with a person already experienced in the matter. Two or three experiments will suffice to render the student confident and even expert.

VI

1. The previous experiment has little value, and leads to few results of importance, but is susceptible of a development which merges into a form of Dharana—concentration—and as such may lead to the very highest ends. The principal use of the practice in the last chapter is to familiarise the student with every kind of obstacle and every kind of delusion, so that he may be perfect master of every idea that may arise in his brain, to dismiss it, to transmute it, to cause it instantly to obey his will.

2. Let him then begin exactly as before; but with the most intense solemnity and determination.

3. Let him be very careful to cause his imaginary body to rise in a line exactly perpendicular to the earth's tangent at the point where his physical body is situated (or, to put it more simply, straight upwards).

4. Instead of stopping, let him continue to rise until fatigue almost overcomes him. If he should find that he has stopped without willing to do so, and that figures appear, let him at all costs rise above them.

Yea, though his very life tremble on his lips, let him force his way upward and onward!

5. Let him continue in this so long as the breath of life is in him. Whatever threatens, whatever allures, though it were Typhon and all his hosts loosed from the pit and leagued against him, though it were from the very Throne of God Himself that a Voice issues bidding him stay and be content, let him struggle on, ever on.

6. At last there must come a moment when his whole being is swallowed up in fatigue, overwhelmed by its own inertia.[3] Let him sink (when no longer can he strive, though his tongue be bitten through with the effort and

3. This in case of failure. The results of success are so many and wonderful that no effort is here made to describe them. They are classified, tentatively, in *The Herb Dangerous*. See *Roll Away the Stone* (St. Paul: Llewellyn Publications).

the blood gush from his nostrils) into the blackness of unconsciousness; and then on coming to himself, let him write down soberly and accurately a record of all that hath occurred: yea, a record of all that hath occurred.

LIBER

A

VEL

ARMORVM

SVB FIGVRA
CCCCXII

A ∴ A ∴ Publication in Class D

Imprimatur:
D.D.S. 7° = 4° Praemonstrator
O.S.V. 6° = 5° Imperator
N.S.F. 5° = 6° Cancellarius

LIBER A

The obeah and the wanga; the work of the wand and the work of the sword; these shall he learn and teach.

Liber L, I: 37

The Pentacle

Take pure wax, or a plate of gold, silver-gilt or Electrum Magicum. The diameter shall be eight inches, and the thickness half an inch.

Let the Neophyte by his understanding and ingenium devise a symbol to represent the Universe.

Let his Zelator approve thereof.

Let the Neophyte engrave the same upon his plate, with his own hand and weapon.

Let it when finished be consecrated as he hath skill to perform, and kept wrapped in silk of emerald green.

The Dagger

Let the Zelator take a piece of pure steel, and beat it, grind it, sharpen it, and polish it, according to the art of the swordsmith.

Let him further take a piece of oak wood, and carve a hilt. The length shall be eight inches.

Let him by his understanding and ingenium devise a Word to represent the Universe.

Let his Practicus approve thereof.

297

Let the Zelator engrave the same upon his dagger with his own hand and instruments.

Let him further gild the wood of the hilt.

Let it when finished be consecrated as he hath skill to perform, and kept wrapped in silk of golden yellow.

The Cup

Let the Practicus take a piece of Silver, and fashion therefrom a cup. The height shall be eight inches, and the diameter three inches.

Let him by his understanding and ingenium devise a Number to represent the Universe.

Let his Philosophus approve thereof.

Let the Practicus engrave the same upon his cup with his own hand and instrument.

Let it when finished be consecrated as he hath skill to perform, and kept wrapped in silk of azure blue.

The Baculum

Let the Philosophus take a rod of copper, of length eight inches and diameter half an inch.

Let him fashion about the top a triple flame of gold.

Let him by his understanding and ingenium devise a Deed to represent the Universe.

Let his Dominus Liminis approve thereof.

Let the Philosophus perform the same in such a way that the Baculum may be partaker therein.

Let it when finished be consecrated as he hath skill to perform, and kept wrapped in silk of fiery scarlet.

The Lamp

Let the Dominus Liminis take pure lead, tin, and quicksilver; with platinum, and, if need be, glass.

Let him by his understanding and ingenium devise a

Magick Lamp that shall burn without wick or oil, being fed by the Aethyr.

This shall he accomplish secretly and apart, without asking the advice or approval of his Adeptus Minor.

Let the Dominus Liminis keep it when consecrated in the secret chamber of Art.

This then is that which is written: "Being furnished with complete armour, and armed, he is similar to the goddess."

And again "I am armed, I am armed."

LIBER
RESH

VEL
HELIOS

SVB FIGVRA
CC

A ∴ A ∴ Publication in Class D

Imprimatur:
N. Fra A ∴ A ∴

LIBER RESH

0. These are the adorations to be performed by all aspirants to the A .˙. A .˙..

1. Let him greet the Sun at dawn, facing East, giving the sign of his grade. And let him say in a loud voice:

Hail unto Thee who art Ra in Thy rising, even unto Thee who art Ra in Thy strength, who travellest over the Heavens in Thy bark at the Uprising of the Sun.

Tahuti standeth in His splendour at the prow, and Ra-Hoor abideth at the helm.

Hail unto Thee from the Abodes of Night!

2. Also at Noon, let him greet the Sun, facing South, giving the sign of his grade. And let him say in a loud voice:

Hail unto Thee who art Ahathoor in Thy triumphing, even unto Thee who art Ahathoor in Thy beauty, who travellest over the Heavens in Thy bark at the Mid-course of the Sun.

Tahuti standeth in His splendour at the prow, and Ra-Hoor abideth at the helm.

Hail unto Thee from the Abodes of Morning!

3. Also, at Sunset, let him greet the Sun, facing West,

giving the sign of his grade. And let him say in a loud voice:

Hail unto Thee, who art Tum in Thy setting, even unto Thee who art Tum in Thy joy, who travellest over the Heavens in Thy bark at the Down-going of the Sun.

Tahuti standeth in His splendour at the prow, and Ra-Hoor abideth at the helm.

Hail unto Thee from the Abodes of Day!

4. Lastly, at Midnight, let him greet the Sun, facing North, giving the sign of his grade. And let him say in a loud voice:

Hail unto Thee who art Khephra in Thy hiding, even unto Thee who art Khephra in Thy silence, who travellest over the Heavens in Thy bark at the Midnight Hour of the Sun.

Tahuti standeth in His splendour at the prow, and Ra-Hoor abideth at the helm.

Hail unto Thee from the Abodes of Evening.

5. And after each of these invocations thou shalt give the sign of silence, and afterwards thou shalt perform the adoration that is taught thee by thy Superior. And then do thou compose Thyself to holy meditation.

6. Also it is better if in these adorations thou assume the God-form of Whom thou adorest, as if thou didst unite with Him in the adoration of That which is beyond Him.

7. Thus shalt thou ever be mindful of the Great Work which thou hast undertaken to perform, and thus shalt thou be strengthened to pursue it unto the attainment of the Stone of the Wise, the Summum Bonum, True Wisdom and Perfect Happiness.

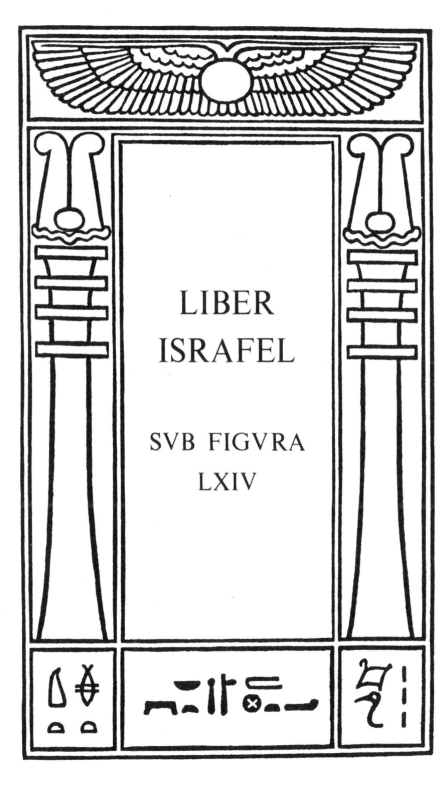

LIBER
ISRAFEL

SVB FIGVRA
LXIV

A ∴ A ∴ Publication in Class B

Imprimatur:
N. Fra A ∴ A ∴

LIBER ISRAFEL

This book was formerly called Anubis, *and is referred to the 20th key, "The Angel."*

0. The Temple being in darkness, and the Speaker ascended into his place, let him begin by a ritual of the Enterer, as followeth.

1. Procul, O procul este profani.

2. Bahlasti! Ompehda!

3. In the name of the Mighty and Terrible One, I proclaim that I have banished the Shells unto their habitations.

4. I invoke Tahuti, the Lord of Wisdom and of Utterance, the God that cometh forth from the Veil.

5. O Thou! Majesty of Godhead! Wisdom-crowned Tahuti! Lord of the Gates of the Universe! Thee, Thee, I invoke.

O Thou of the Ibis Head! Thee, Thee I invoke.

Thou who wieldest the Wand of Double Power! Thee, Thee I invoke!

Thou who bearest in Thy left hand the Rose and Cross of Light and Life: Thee, Thee, I invoke.

Thou, whose head is as an emerald, and Thy nemmes as the night-sky blue! Thee, Thee I invoke.

Thou, whose skin is of flaming orange as though it burned in a furnace! Thee, Thee I invoke.

6. Behold! I am Yesterday, To-Day, and Brother of To-Morrow!

I am born again and again.

Mine is the Unseen Force, whereof the Gods are sprung! Which is as Life unto the Dwellers in the Watch-Towers of the Universe.

I am the Charioteer of the East, Lord of the Past and of the Future.

I see by mine own inward light: Lord of Resurrection; Who cometh forth from the Dusk, and my birth is from the House of Death.

7. O ye two Divine Hawks upon your Pinnacles!

Who keep watch over the Universe!

Ye who company the Bier to the House of Rest!

Who pilot the Ship of Ra advancing onwards to the heights of heaven!

Lord of the Shrine which standeth in the Centre of the Earth!

8. Behold, He is in me, and I in Him!

Mine is the Radiance, wherein Ptah floateth over the firmament!

I travel upon high!

I tread upon the firmament of Nu!

I raise a flashing flame, with the lightning of Mine Eye!

Ever rushing on, in the splendour of the daily glorified Ra: giving my life to the Dwellers of Earth.

9. If I say "Come up upon the mountains!" the Celestial Waters shall flow at my Word.

For I am Ra incarnate!

Khephra created in the Flesh!

I am the Eidolon of my father Tmu, Lord of the City of the Sun!

10. The God who commands is in my mouth!

The God of Wisdom is in my Heart!

My tongue is the Sanctuary of Truth!

And a God sitteth upon my lips.

11. My Word is accomplished every day!

And the desire of my heart realises itself, as that of Ptah when He createth his works!

I am Eternal; therefore all things are as my designs; therefore do all things obey my Word.

12. Therefore do Thou come forth unto me from Thine abode in the Silence: Unutterable Wisdom! All-Light! All-Power!

Thoth! Hermes! Mercury! Odin!

By whatever name I call Thee, Thou art still nameless to Eternity: Come Thou forth, I say, and aid and guard me in this work of Art.

13. Thou, Star of the East, that didst conduct the Magi!

Thou art The Same all-present in Heaven and in Hell!

Thou that vibratest between the Light and the Darkness!

Rising, descending! Changing ever, yet ever The Same!

The Sun is Thy Father!

Thy Mother the Moon!

The Wind hath borne Thee in its bosom; and Earth hath ever nourished the changeless Godhead of Thy Youth!

14. Come Thou forth, I say, come Thou forth!

And make all Spirits subject unto Me:

So that every Spirit of the Firmament

And of the Ether,

Upon the Earth,

And under the Earth,

On dry land

And in the Water,

Of whirling Air

And of rushing Fire,

And every Spell and Scourge of God the Vast One, may be obedient unto Me!

15. I invoke the Priestess of the Silver Star, Asi the Curved One, by the ritual of Silence.

16. I make open the gate of Bliss; I descend from the Palace of the Stars; I greet you, I embrace you, O children of earth, that are gathered together in the Hall of Darkness.

17. (A pause.)

18. The Speech in the Silence.

The Words against the Son of Night.

The Voice of Tahuti in the Universe in the Presence of the Eternal.

The Formulas of Knowledge.

The Wisdom of Breath.

The Root of Vibration.

The Shaking of the Invisible.

The Rolling Asunder of the Darkness.

The Becoming Visible of Matter.

The Piercing of the Scales of the Crocodile.

The Breaking Forth of the Light!

19. (Follows the Lection.)

20. There is an end of the speech; let the Silence of darkness be broken; let it return into the silence of light.

21. The speaker silently departs; the listeners disperse unto their homes; yea, they disperse unto their homes.

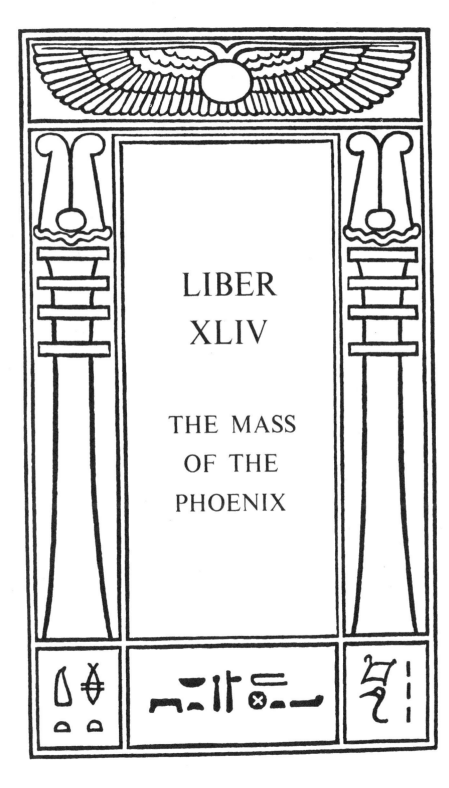

LIBER
XLIV

THE MASS
OF THE
PHOENIX

THE MASS
OF THE PHOENIX

The Magician, his breast bare, stands before an altar on which are his Burin, Bell, Thurible, and two of the Cakes of Light. In the Sign of the Enterer he reaches West across the Altar, and cries:

Hail Ra, that goest in thy bark
Into the caverns of the Dark!

He gives the sign of Silence, and takes the Bell, and Fire, in this hands.

East of the Altar see me stand
With light and musick in my hand!

He strikes Eleven times upon the Bell 333 – 55555 – 333 and places the Fire in the Thurible.

I strike the Bell: I light the Flame;
I utter the mysterious Name.

ABRAHADABRA

He strikes eleven times upon the Bell.

Now I begin to pray: Thou Child,
Holy Thy name and undefiled!
Thy reign is come; Thy will is done.

Here is the Bread; here is the Blood.
Bring me through midnight to the Sun!
Save me from Evil and from Good!
That Thy one crown of all the Ten
Even now and here be mine.   AMEN.

He puts the first Cake on the Fire of the Thurible.

I burn the Incense-cake, proclaim
These adorations of Thy name.

He makes them as in Liber Legis, *and strikes again Eleven
times upon the Bell. With the Burin he then makes upon his
breast the proper sign.*

Behold this bleeding breast of mine
Gashed with the sacramental sign!

He puts the second Cake to the wound.

I stanch the Blood; the wafer soaks
It up, and the high priest invokes!

He eats the second Cake.

This Bread I eat. This Oath I swear
As I enflame myself with prayer:
"There is no grace: there is no guilt:
This is the Law; DO WHAT THOU WILT!"

He strikes Eleven times upon the Bell, and cries

ABRAHADABRA

I entered in with woe; with mirth
I now go forth, and with thanksgiving,
To do my pleasure on the earth
Among the legions of the living.

He goeth forth.

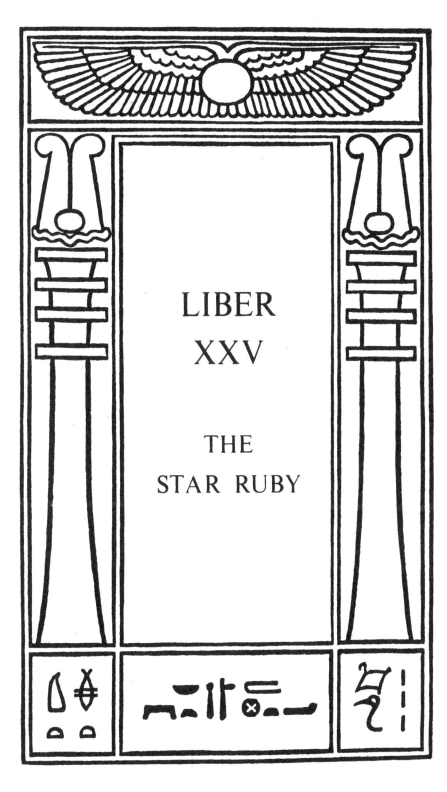

LIBER

XXV

THE

STAR RUBY

THE STAR RUBY

ΚΕΦΑΛΗ ΚΕ

Facing East, in the centre, draw deep deep deep thy breath, closing thy mouth with thy right forefinger prest against thy lower lip. Then dashing down the hand with a great sweep back and out, expelling forcibly thy breath, cry: ΑΠΟ ΠΑΝΤΟΣ ΚΑΚΟΔΑΙΜΟΝΟΣ.

With the same forefinger touch thy forehead, and say ΣΟΙ, thy member, and say Ω ΦΑΛΛΕ,[1] thy right shoulder, and say ΙΣΧΥΡΟΣ, thy left shoulder, and say ΕΥΧΑ-ΡΙΣΤΟΣ ; then clasp thine hands, locking the fingers, and cry ΙΑΩ.

Advance to the East. Imagine strongly a Pentagram, aright, in thy forehead. Drawing the hands to the eyes, fling it forth, making the sign of Horus, and roar ΘΗΡΙΟΝ. Retire thine hand in the sign of Hoor pa kraat.

Go round to the North and repeat; but scream NUIT.

Go round to the West and repeat; but say BABALON.

Go round to the South and repeat; but bellow HADIT.

Completing the circle widdershins, retire to the centre,

---

1. The secret sense of these words is to be sought in the numeration thereof.

and raise thy voice in the Paian, with these words ΙΩ
ΠΑΝ   with the signs of N.O.X.

Extend the arms in the form of a Tau, and say low but
clear: ΠΡΟ ΜΟΥ ΙΥΓΓΕΣ ΟΠΙΧΩ ΜΟΥ   ΤΕΛΕΤΑ-
ΡΧΑΙ   ΕΠΙ   ΔΕΞΙΑ   ΧΥΝΟΧΕΣ   ΕΠΑΡΙΣΤΕΡΑ
ΔΑΙΜΟΝΟΣ ΦΕΓ ΕΙ ΓΑΡ ΠΕΡΙ ΜΟΥ Ο ΑΣΤΗΡ ΤΩΝ
ΠΕΝΤΕ ΚΑΙ ΕΝ ΤΗΙ ΣΤΗΛΗΙ Ω ΑΣΤΗΡ ΤΩΝ ΕΞ
ΕΣΤΗΧΕ.

Repeat the Cross Qabalistic, as above, and end as
thou didst begin.

LIBER

XXXVI

THE

STAR

SAPPHIRE

THE STAR SAPPHIRE

Let the Adept be armed with his Magick Rood (and provided with his mystic Rose).

In the centre, let him give the L.V.X. signs; or if he know them, if he will and dare do them, and can keep silent about them, the signs of N.O.X. being the signs of Puer, Vir, Puella, Mulier. Omit the sign I.R.

Then let him advance to the East and make the Holy Hexagram, saying: *Pater et Mater unus deus Ararita.*

Let him go round to the South, make the Holy Hexagram and say: *Mater et Filius unus deus Ararita.*

Let him go round to the West, make the Holy Hexagram and say: *Filius et Filia unus deus Ararita.*

Let him go round to the North, make the Holy Hexagram and then say: *Filia et Pater unus deus Ararita.*

Let him then return to the Centre, and so to The Centre of All (making the *Rosy Cross* as he may know how) saying *Ararita Ararita Ararita.*

(In this the Signs shall be those of Set Triumphant and of Baphomet. Also shall Set appear in the Circle. Let him drink of the Sacrament and let him communicate the same.) Then let him say: *Omnia in Duos: Duo in Unum:*

Unus in Nihil: Haec nec Quatuor nec Omnia nec Duo nec Unus nec Nihil Sunt.

Gloria Patri et Matri et Filio et Filiae et Spiritui Sancto externo et Spiritui Sancto interno ut erat est erit in saecula Saeculorum sex in uno per nomen Septem in uno Ararita.

Let him then repeat the signs of L.V.X. but not the signs of N.O.X.: for it is not he that shall arise in the Sign of Isis Rejoicing.

LIBER
SAMEKH

THEURGIA
GOETIA
SUMMA

CONGRESSUS
CUM DAEMONE

SVB FIGVRA
DCCC

OFFICIAL PUBLICATION of A .˙. A .˙. Class D for the Grade of Adeptus Minor.

Being the Ritual employed by the Beast 666 for the Attainment of the Knowledge and Conversation of his Holy Guardian Angel during the Semester of His performance of the Operation of the Sacred Magick of ABRAMELIN THE MAGE.

(Prepared An XVII Sun in Virgo at the Abbey of Thelema in Cephalaedium by the Beast 666 in service to FRATER PROGRADIOR.)

LIBER SAMEKH

POINT
I
EVANGELII TEXTUS REDACTUS

The Invocation.
Magically restored, with the significance of the
BARBAROUS NAMES
Etymologically or Qabalistically determined and paraphrased in English.

Section A.   **The Oath**

1. Thee I invoke, the Bornless One.
2. Thee, that didst create the Earth and the Heavens.
3. Thee, that didst create the Night and the Day.
4. Thee, that didst create the darkness and the Light.
5. Thou art ASAR UN-NEFER ("Myself made Perfect"): Whom no man hath seen at any time.
6. Thou art IA-BESZ ("the Truth in Matter").
7. Thou art IA-APOPHRASZ ("the Truth in Motion").
8. Thou hast distinguished between the Just and the Unjust.
9. Thou didst make the Female and the Male.
10. Thou didst produce the Seeds and the Fruit.
11. Thou didst form Men to love one another, and to hate one another.

325

Section Aa.

1. I am ANKH – F – N – KHONSU thy Prophet, unto Whom Thou didst commit Thy Mysteries, the Ceremonies of KHEM.

2. Thou didst produce the moist and the dry, and that which nourisheth all created Life.

3. Hear Thou Me, for I am the Angel of PTAH – APO-PHRASZ – RA (vide the Rubric): this is Thy True Name, handed down to the Prophets of KHEM.

Section B.   Air

Hear Me:

AR	"O breathing, flowing Sun!"
ThIAF[1]	"O Sun IAF! O Lion-Serpent Sun, The Beast that whirlest forth, a thunderbolt, begetter of Life!"
RhEIBET	"Thou that flowest! Thou that goest!"
A-ThELE-BER-SET	"Thou Satan-Sun Hadith that goest without Will!"
A	"Thou Air! Breath! Spirit! Thou without bound or bond!"
BELAThA	"Thou Essence, Air Swift-streaming, Elasticity!"
ABEU	"Thou Wanderer, Father of All!"
EBEU	"Thou Wanderer, Spirit of All!"
PhI-ThETA-SOE	"Thou Shining Force of Breath! Thou Lion-Serpent Sun! Thou Saviour, save!"

1. The letter F is used to represent the Hebrew Vau and the Greek Digamma; its sound lies between those of the English long o and long oo, as in Rope and Tooth.

IB   "Thou Ibis, secret solitary Bird,
                  inviolate Wisdom, whose Word
                  is Truth, creating the World
                  by its Magick!"

ThIAF   "O Sun IAF! O Lion-Serpent
                  Sun, The Beast that whirlest
                  forth, a thunderbolt, begetter
                  of Life!"

(The conception is of Air, glowing, inhabited by a Solar-
Phallic Bird, "the Holy Ghost," of a Mercurial Nature.)
Hear me, and make all Spirits subject unto Me; so that
every Spirit of the Firmament and of the Ether: upon
the Earth and under the Earth, on dry Land and in the
Water; of Whirling Air, and of rushing Fire, and every
Spell and Scourge of God may be obedient unto Me.

Section C.   Fire

I invoke Thee, the Terrible and Invisible God: Who
dwellest in the Void Place of the Spirit:

AR-O-GO-GO-RU-   "Thou spiritual Sun! Satan,
   ABRAO   Thou Eye, Thou Lust! Cry
                  aloud! Cry aloud! Whirl the
                  Wheel, O my Father, O Satan,
                  O Sun!"

SOTOU   "Thou, the Saviour!"

MUDORIO   "Silence! Give me Thy Secret!"

PhALARThAO   "Give me suck, Thou Phallus,
                  Thou Sun!"

OOO   "Satan, thou Eye, thou Lust!"
                  "Satan, thou Eye, thou Lust!"
                  "Satan, thou Eye, thou Lust!"

AEPE   "Thou self-caused, self-deter-
                  mined, exalted, Most High!"

The Bornless One. (Vide supra.)

(The conception is of Fire, glowing, inhabited by a Solar-Phallic Lion of a Uranian nature.)

Hear Me, and make all Spirits subject unto Me: so that every Spirit of the Firmament and of the Ether: upon the Earth and under the Earth: on dry Land and in the Water: of Whirling Air, and of rushing Fire, and every Spell and Scourge of God may be obedient unto Me.

Section D. Water

Hear Me:

RU-ABRA-IAF[2]	"Thou the Wheel, thou the Womb, that containeth the Father IAF!"
MRIODOM	"Thou the Sea, the Abode!"
BABALON-BAL-BIN-ABAFT	"Babalon! Thou Woman of Whoredom!"
	"Thou, Gate of the Great God ON! Thou Lady of the Understanding of the Ways!"
ASAL-ON-AI	"Hail Thou, the unstirred! Hail, sister and bride of ON, of the God that is all and is none, by the Power of Eleven!"
APhEN-IAF	"Thou Treasure of IAO!"
I	"Thou Virgin twin-sexed! Thou Secret Seed! Thou inviolate Wisdom!"
PhOTETh	"Abode of the Light . . .
ABRASAX	" . . . of the Father, the Sun, of Hadith, of the spell of the Aeon of Horus!"

2. See, for the formula of IAF, or rather FIAOF, *Book 4*, Part III, Chapter V. The form FIAOF will be found preferable in practice.

AEOOU   "Our Lady of the Western Gate
                           of Heaven!"
ISChURE   "Mighty art Thou!"
Mighty and Bornless One! (Vide Supra.)
(The conception is of Water, glowing, inhabited by a
Solar-Phallic Dragon-Serpent, of a Neptunian nature.)
Hear Me: and make all Spirits subject unto Me: so that
every Spirit of the Firmament and of the Ether: upon the
Earth and under the Earth: on dry Land and in the Water:
of Whirling Air, and of rushing Fire: and every Spell and
Scourge of God may be obedient unto Me.

Section E.   Earth

I invoke Thee:
MA   "O Mother! O Truth!"
BARRAIO   "Thou Mass!"[3]
IOEL   "Hail, Thou that art!"
KOThA   "Thou hollow one!"
AThOR - e - BAL - O   "Thou Goddess of Beauty and
                           Love, whom Satan, beholding,
                           desireth!"
ABRAFT   "The Fathers, male-female, de-
                           sire Thee!"
(The conception is of Earth, glowing, inhabited by a
Solar-Phallic Hippopotamus[4] of a Venereal nature.)
Hear Me: and make all Spirits subject unto Me: so that
every Spirit of the Firmament, and of the Ether: upon
the Earth and under the Earth: on dry Land and in the

3. "Mass" in the sense of the word which is used by physicists. The impossibility
of defining it will not deter the intrepid initiate (in view of the fact that the
fundamental conception is beyond the normal categories of reason).
4. Sacred to AHAThOOR. The idea is that of the Female conceived as in-
vulnerable, reposeful, of enormous swallowing capacity etc.

Water: of Whirling Air, and of rushing Fire: and every Spell and Scourge of God may be obedient unto Me.

Section F.   **Spirit**

Hear Me:

AFT	"Male-Female Spirits!"
ABAFT	"Male-Female Sires!"
BAS-AUMGN	"Ye that are Gods, going forth, uttering AUMGN." (The Word that goeth from
	(A) Free Breath.
	(U) through Willed Breath.
	(M) and Stopped Breath.
	(GN) to Continuous Breath, thus symbolizing the whole course of spiritual life. A is the formless Hero; U is the six-fold solar sound of physical life, the triangle of Soul being entwined with that of Body; M is the silence of "death"; GN is the nasal sound of genera-tion & knowledge.)
ISAK	"Identical Point!"
SA-BA-FT	"Nuith! Hadith! Ra-Hoor-Khuit!"
	"Hail, Great Wild Beast!"
	"Hail, I A O!"

Section Ff.

1. This is the Lord of the Gods:
2. This is the Lord of the Universe:
3. This is He whom the Winds fear.

4. This is He, Who having made Voice by His commandment is Lord of all Things; King, Ruler and Helper. Hear Me, and make all Spirits subject unto Me: so that every Spirit of the Firmament and of the Ether: upon the Earth and under the Earth: on dry Land and in the Water: of Whirling Air, and of rushing Fire: and every Spell and Scourge of God may be obedient unto Me.

Section G. Spirit

Hear Me:

IEOU	"Indwelling Sun of Myself"
PUR	"Thou Fire! Thou Sixfold Star initiator compassed about with Force and Fire!"
IOU	"Indwelling Soul of Myself"
PUR	(Vide Supra).
IAFTh	"Sun-lion Serpent, hail! All Hail, thou Great Wild Beast, thou I A O!"
IAEO	"Breaths of my Soul, breaths of mine Angel."
IOOU	"Lust of my Soul, lust of mine Angel!"
ABRASAX	(Vide Supra.)
SABRIAM	"Ho for the Sangraal! Ho for the Cup of Babalon! Ho for mine Angel pouring Himself forth within my Soul!"
OO	"The Eye! Satan, my Lord! The Lust of the Goat!"
FF	"Mine Angel! Mine initiator! Thou one with me — the Sixfold Star!"

AD-ON-A-I[5]   "My Lord! My secret self beyond self, Hadith, All Father! Hail, ON, thou Sun, thou Life of Man, thou Fivefold Sword of Flame! Thou Goat exalted upon Earth in Lust, thou Snake extended upon Earth in Life! Spirit most holy! Seed most Wise! Innocent Babe. Inviolate Maid! Begetter of Being! Soul of all Souls! Word of all Words, Come forth, most hidden Light!"

EDE   "Devour thou me!"

EDU   "Thou dost devour Me!"

ANGELOS TON THEON   "Thou Angel of the Gods!"

ANLALA   "Arise thou in Me, free flowing, Thou who art Naught, who art Naught, and utter thy Word!"

LAI   "I also am Naught! I Will Thee! I behold Thee! My nothingness!"

GAIA   "Leap up, thou Earth!"

     (This is also an agonising appeal to the Earth, the Mother; for at this point of the ceremony the Adept should be torn from his mortal attach-

---

5. In Hebrew, ADNI, 65. The Gnostic Initiates transliterated it to imply their own secret formulae; we follow so excellent an example. ON is an Arcanum of Arcana; its significance is taught, gradually, in the O.T.O. Also AD is the paternal formula, Hadit; ON is its complement NUIT; the final Yod signifies "mine" etymologically and essentially the Mercurial (transmitted) hermaphroditic virginal seed — The Hermit of the Taro. The use of the name is therefore to invoke one's own inmost secrecy, considered as the result of the conjunction of Nuit and Hadit. If the second A is included, its import is to affirm the operation of the Holy Ghost and the formulation of the Babe in the Egg, which precedes the appearance of the Hermit.

	ments, and die to himself in the orgasm of his operation.)[6]
AEPE	"Thou Exalted One! It (i.e. the spiritual "semen," the Adept's secret ideas, drawn irresistibly from their "Hell"[7] by the love of his Angel) leaps up; it leaps forth!"[8]
DIATHARNA THORON	"Lo! the out-splashing of the seeds of Immortality!"

Section Gg.   The Attainment

1. I am He! the Bornless Spirit! having sight in the feet: Strong, and the Immortal Fire!
2. I am He! the Truth!
3. I am He! Who hate that evil should be wrought in the World!
4. I am He, that lighteneth and thundereth!
5. I am He, from whom is the Shower of the Life of Earth!
6. I am He, whose mouth ever flameth!
7. I am He, the Begetter and Manifester unto the Light!
8. I am He, The Grace of the Worlds!
9. "The Heart Girt with a Serpent" is my name!

Section H.   The "Charge to the Spirit"

Come thou forth, and follow me: and make all Spirits subject unto Me so that every Spirit of the Firmament, and of the Ether, upon the Earth and under the Earth: on dry Land, and in the Water: of Whirling Air and of

6. A thorough comprehension of Psycho-analysis will contribute notably to the proper appreciation of this Ritual.

7. It is said among men that the word Hell deriveth from the word 'helan', to hele or conceal, in the tongue of the Anglo-Saxons. That is, it is the concealed place, which since all things are in thine own self, is the unconscious. *Liber CXI (Aleph)* cap. Δ ς

8. But compare the use of the same word in section C.

rushing Fire, and every Spell and Scourge of God, may be obedient unto me!

Section J.   The Proclamation of the Beast 666
IAF: SABAF[9]
    Such are the Words!

POINT
II
ARS CONGRESSUS CUM DAEMONE
Section A.

Let the Adeptus Minor be standing in this circle on the square of Tiphereth, armed with his Wand and Cup; but let him perform the Ritual throughout in his Body of Light. He may burn the Cakes of Light, or the Incense of Abramelin; he may be prepared by *Liber CLXXV*, the reading of *Liber LXV*, and by the practices of Yoga. He may invoke HADIT by "wine and strange drugs" if he so will.[10] He prepares the circle by the usual formulae of Banishing and Consecration, etc.

He recites Section A as a rehearsal before His Holy Guardian Angel of the attributes of that Angel. Each phrase must be realized with full concentration of force, so as to make Samadhi as perfectly as possible upon the truth proclaimed.

Line 1
He identifies his Angel with the Ain Soph, and the Kether thereof; one formulation of Hadit in the boundless Body of Nuith.
Lines 2, 3, 4
He asserts that His Angel has created (for the purpose

9. See explanation in Point II.

10. Any such formula should be used only when the adept has full knowledge based on experience of the management of such matters.

of self-realisation through projection in conditioned Form)
three pairs of opposites: (a) The Fixed and the Volatile;
(b) The Unmanifested and the Manifest; and (c) the
Unmoved and the Moved. Otherwise, the Negative and
the Positive in respect of Matter, Mind and Motion.

Line 5
He acclaims his Angel as "Himself Made Perfect";
adding that this Individuality is inscrutable and inviolable.
In the Neophyte Ritual of G .·. D .·. (as it is printed in
The Equinox, I, II, for the old aeon) the Hierophant is the
perfected Osiris, who brings the candidate, the natural
Osiris, to identity with himself. But in the new Aeon the
Hierophant is Horus (*Liber CCXX*, I: 49) therefore the
Candidate will be Horus too. What then is the formula of
the initiation of Horus? It will no longer be that of the
Man, through Death. It will be the natural growth of
the Child. His experiences will no more be regarded as
catastrophic. Their hieroglyph is the Fool: the innocent
and impotent Harpocrates Babe becomes the Horus
Adult by obtaining the Wand. "Der reine Thor" seizes the
Sacred Lance. Bacchus becomes Pan. The Holy Guardian
Angel is the Unconscious Creature Self — the Spiritual
Phallus. His Knowledge and Conversation contributes
occult puberty. It is therefore advisable to replace the
name Asar Un-nefer by that of Ra-Hoor-Khuit at the
outset, and by that of one's own Holy Guardian Angel
when it has been communicated.

Line 6
He hails Him as BESZ, the Matter that destroys and
devours Godhead, for the purpose of the Incarnation of
any God.

Line 7
He hails Him as APOPHRASZ, the Motion that
destroys and devours Godhead, for the purpose of the

Incarnation of any God. The combined action of these two DEVILS is to allow the God upon whom they prey to enter into enjoyment of existence through the Sacrament of dividual "Life" (Bread — the flesh of BESZ) and "Love" (Wine — the blood or venom of APO-PHRASZ).

Line 8

He acclaims His Angel as having "eaten of the Fruit of the Tree of Knowledge of Good and Evil"; otherwise, having become wise (in the Dyad, Chokmah) to apprehend the formula of Equilibrium which is now His own, being able to apply Himself accurately to His self-appointed environment.

Line 9

He acclaims His Angel as having laid down the Law of Love as the Magical formula of the Universe, that He may resolve the phenomenal again into its noumenal phase by uniting any two opposites in ecstasic passion.

Line 10

He acclaims His Angel as having appointed that this formula of Love should effect not only the dissolution of the separateness of the Lovers into His own impersonal Godhead, but their co-ordination in a "Child" quintessentialized from its parents to constitute a higher order of Being than theirs, so that each generation is an alchemical progress towards perfection in the direction of successive complexities. As Line 9 asserts Involution, Line 10 asserts Evolution.

Line 11

He acclaims His Angel as having devised this method of self-realization; the object of Incarnation is to obtain its reactions to its relations with other incarnated Beings and to observe theirs with each other.

Section Aa.

Line 1

The Adept asserts his right to enter into conscious communication with His Angel, on the ground that that Angel has Himself taught him the Secret Magick by which he may make the proper link. "Mosheh" is M H, the formation, in Jechidah, Chiah, Neschamah, Ruach, — the Sephiroth from Kether to Yesod — since 45 is Σ 1–9 while Sh, 300, is Σ 1–24, which superadds to these Nine an extra Fifteen numbers. (See in *Liber D* the meanings and correspondences of 9, 15, 24, 45, 300, 345.)

45 is moreover A D M, man. "Mosheh" is thus the name of man as a God-concealing Form. But in the Ritual let the Adept replace this "Mosheh" by his own motto as Adeptus Minor. For "Ishrael" let him prefer his own Magical Race, according to the obligations of his Oaths to Our Holy Order! (The Beast 666 Himself used "Ankh-f-n-khonsu" and "Khem" in this section.)

Line 2

The Adept reminds his Angel that He has created That One Substance of which Hermes hath written in the Table of Emerald, whose virtue is to unite in itself all opposite modes of Being, thereby to serve as a Talisman charged with the Spiritual Energy of Existence, an Elixir or Stone composed of the physical basis of Life. This Commemoration is placed between the two personal appeals to the Angel, as if to claim privilege to partake of this Eucharist which createth, sustaineth and redeemeth all things.

Line 3

He now asserts that he is himself the "Angel" or messenger of his Angel; that is, that he is a mind and body whose office is to receive and transmit the Word of his Angel. He hails his Angel not only as "un-nefer" the Perfection of "Asar" himself as a man, but as Ptah-

Apophrasz-Ra, the identity (Hadit) wrapped in the Dragon (Nuith) and thereby manifested as a Sun (Ra-Hoor-Khuit). The "Egg" (or Heart) "girt with a Serpent" is a cognate symbol; the idea is thus expressed later in the ritual. (See *Liber LXV* which expands this to the uttermost.)

Section B.

The Adept passes from contemplation to action in the sections now following B to Gg. He is to travel astrally around the circle, making the appropriate pentagrams, sigils, and signs. His direction is widdershins. He thus makes three curves, each covering three-fourths of the circle. He should give the sign of the Enterer on passing the Kiblah, or Direction of Boleskine. This picks up the Force naturally radiating from that point[11] and projects it in the direction of the path of the Magician. The sigils are those given in *The Equinox,* Vol. I, No. 7, Plate X outside the square; the signs those shewn in Vol. I, No. 2, Plate: The Signs of the Grades. In these invocations he should expand his girth and his stature to the utmost,[12] assuming the form and the consciousness of the Elemental God of the quarter. After this, he begins to vibrate the "Barbarous Names" of the Ritual.

Now let him not only fill his whole being to the uttermost with the force of the Names; but let him formulate his Will, understood thoroughly as the dynamic aspect of his Creative Self, in an appearance symbolically apt, I say not in the form of a Ray of Light, of a Fiery Sword, or of aught save that bodily Vehicle of the Holy Ghost which is sacred to BAPHOMET, by its virtue that concealeth the Lion and the Serpent that His Image may appear adorably upon the Earth for ever.

---

11. This is an assumption based on *Liber Legis,* II: 78 and III: 34.
12. Having experience of success in the practices of *Liber 536,* βατραχο-φρενοϐοοχοσμομαγια.

Let then the Adept extend his Will beyond the Circle in this imagined Shape and let it radiate with the Light proper to the Element invoked, and let each Word issue along the Shaft with passionate impulse, as if its voice gave command thereto that it should thrust itself leapingly forward. Let also each Word accumulate authority, so that the Head of the Shaft may plunge twice as far for the Second Word as for the First, and Four Times for the Third as the Second, and thus to the end. Moreover, let the Adept fling forth his whole consciousness thither. Then at the final Word, let him bring rushing back his Will within himself, steadily streaming, and let him offer himself to its point, as Artemis to PAN, that this perfectly pure concentration of the Element purge him thoroughly, and possess him with its passion.

In this Sacrament being wholly at one with that Element, let the Adept utter the Charge "Hear me, and make" etc., with strong sense that this unity with that quarter of the Universe confers upon him the fullest freedom and privilege appurtenant thereto.

Let the Adept take note of the wording of the Charge. The "Firmament" is the Ruach, the "mental plane"; it is the realm of Shu, or Zeus, where revolves the Wheel of the Gunas, the Three forms[13] of Being. The Aethyr is

13. They correspond to the Sulphur, Mercury, and Salt of Alchemy; to Sattvas, Rajas, and Tamas in the Hindu system; and are rather modes of action than actual qualities even, when conceived as latent. They are the apparatus of communication between the planes; as such, they are conventions. There is no absolute validity in any means of mental apprehension; but unless we make these spirits of the Firmament subject unto us by establishing right relation (within the possible limits) with the Universe, we shall fall into error when we develop our new instrument of direct understanding. It is vital that the Adept should train his intellectual faculties to tell him the truth, in the measure of their capacity. To despise the mind on account of its limitations is the most disastrous blunder; it is the common cause of the calamities which strew so many shores with the wreckage of the Mystic Armada. Bigotry, Arrogance, Bewilderment, all forms of mental and moral disorder, so often observed in people of great spiritual attainment, have brought the Path itself into discredit; almost all such catastrophes are due to trying to build the Temple of the Spirit without proper attention to the mental laws of structure and the

the "akasha," the "Spirit," the Aethyr of physics, which is the framework on which all forms are founded; it receives, records and transmits all impulses without itself suffering mutation thereby. The "Earth" is the sphere wherein the operation of these "fundamental" and aethyric forces appears to perception. "Under the Earth" is the world of those phenomena which inform those perceived projections, and determine their particular character. "Dry Land" is the place of dead "material things," dry (i.e., unknowable) because unable to act on our minds. "Water" is the vehicle whereby we feel such things; "Air" their menstruum wherein these feelings are mentally apprehended. It is called "whirling" because of the instability of thought, and the fatuity of reason, on which we are yet dependent for what we call "life." "Rushing Fire" is the world in which wandering thought burns up to swift-darting Will. These four stages explain how the non-Ego is transmuted into the Ego. A "Spell" of God is any form of consciousness, and a "Scourge" any form of action.

The Charge, as a whole, demands for the Adept the

physical necessities of foundation. The mind must be brought to its utmost pitch of perfection, but according to its own internal properties; one cannot feed a microscope on mutton chops. It must be regarded as a mechanical instrument of knowledge, independent of the personality of its possessor. One must treat it exactly as one treats one's electroscope or one's eyes; one influence of one's wishes. A physician calls in a colleague to attend to his own family, knowing that personal anxiety may derange his judgment. A microscopist who trusts his eyes when his pet theory is at stake may falsify the facts, and find too late that he has made a fool of himself.

In the case of initiation itself, history is scarred with the wounds inflicted by this Dagger. It reminds us constantly of the danger of relying upon the intellectual faculties. A judge must know the law in every point, and be detached from personal prejudices, and incorruptible, or iniquity will triumph. Dogma, with persecution, delusion, paralysis of progress, and many another evil, as its satraps, has always established a tyranny when Genius has proclaimed it. Islam making a bonfire of written Wisdom, and Haeckel forging biological evidence; physicists ignorant of radioactivity disputing the conclusions of geology, and theologians impatient of truth struggling against the tide of thought; all such must perish at the hands of their own error in making their minds, internally defective or externally deflected, the measure of the Universe.

control of every detail of the Universe which His Angel has created as a means of manifesting Himself to Himself. It covers command of the primary projection of the Possible in individuality, in the antithetical artifice which is the device of Mind, and in a balanced triplicity of modes or states of being whose combinations constitute the characteristics of Cosmos. It includes also a standard of structure, a rigidity to make reference possible. Upon these foundations of condition which are not things in themselves, but the canon to which things conform, is builded the Temple of Being, whose materials are themselves perfectly mysterious, inscrutable as the Soul, and like the Soul imagining themselves by symbols which we may feel, perceive, and adapt to our use without ever knowing the whole Truth about them. The Adept sums up all these items by claiming authority over every form of expression possible to Existence, whether it be a "spell" (idea) or a "scourge" (act) of "God," that is, of himself. The Adept must accept every "spirit," every "spell," every "scourge," as part of his environment, and make them all "subject to" himself; that is, consider them as contributory causes of himself. They have made him what he is. They correspond exactly to his own faculties. They are all — ultimately — of equal importance. The fact that he is what he is proves that each item is equilibrated. The impact of each new impression affects the entire system in due measure. He must therefore realize that every event is subject to him. It occurs because he had need of it. Iron rusts because the molecules demand oxygen for the satisfaction of their tendencies. They do not crave hydrogen; therefore combination with that gas is an event which does not happen. All experiences contribute to make us complete in ourselves. We feel ourselves subject to them so long as we fail to recognise this; when we do, we perceive that they are subject to us. And whenever we strive to evade an experience, whatever it may be, we thereby do wrong to ourselves. We thwart our own tendencies. To live is to change; and to oppose change is to revolt against the law which we have enacted to govern our lives. To resent destiny is thus to abdicate our sovereignty, and to invoke death. Indeed, we have decreed the doom of death for every breach of the law of life. And every failure to incorporate any impression starves the particular faculty which stood in need of it.

This Section B invokes Air in the East, with a shaft of golden glory.

Section C.

The adept now invokes Fire in the South; flame red are the rays that burst from his Verendum.

Section D.

He invokes Water in the West, his Wand billowing forth blue radiance.

Section E.

He goes to the North to invoke Earth; flowers of green flame flash from his weapon. As practice makes the Adept perfect in this Work, it becomes automatic to attach all these complicated ideas and intentions to their correlated words and acts. When this is attained he may go deeper into the formula by amplifying its correspondences. Thus, he may invoke water in the manner of water, extending his will with majestic and irresistible motion, mindful of its impulse gravitation, yet with a suave and tranquil appearance of weakness. Again, he may apply the formula of water to its peculiar purpose as it surges back into his sphere, using it with conscious skill for the cleansing and calming of the receptive and emotional elements in his character, and for the solution or sweeping away of those tangled weeds of prejudice which hamper him from freedom to act as he will. Similar applications of the remaining invocations will occur to the Adept who is ready to use them.

Section F.

The Adept now returns to the Tiphereth square of his Tau, and invokes Spirit, facing toward Boleskine, by the active Pentagrams, the sigil called the Mark of the Beast, and the Signs of L.V.X. (See plate as before.) He then vibrates the Names extending his will in the same way as before, but vertically upward. At the same time he expands the Source of that Will — the secret symbol of Self — both about him and below, as if to affirm that Self, duplex as is its form, reluctant to acquiesce in its failure to coincide with the Sphere of Nuith. Let him now imagine, at the last Word, that the Head of his will, where his consciousness is fixed, opens its fissure (the Brahmarandra-Cakkra, at the junction of the cranial sutures) and exudes a drop of clear crystalline dew, and that this pearl is his Soul, a virgin offering to his Angel, pressed forth from his being by the intensity of his Aspiration.

Section Ff.

With these words the Adept does not withdraw his will within him as in the previous Sections. He thinks of them as a reflection of Truth on the surface of the dew, where his Soul hides trembling. He takes them to be the first formulation in his consciousness of the nature of His Holy Guardian Angel.

Line 1
The "Gods" include all the conscious elements of his nature.

Line 2

The "Universe" includes all possible phenomena of which he can be aware.

Line 3

The "Winds" are his thoughts, which have prevented him from attaining to his Angel.

Line 4

His Angel has made "Voice," the magical weapon which produces "Words," and these words have been the wisdom by which He hath created all things. The "Voice" is necessary as the link between the Adept and his Angel. The Angel is "King," the One who "can," the "source of authority and the fount of honour"; also the King (or King's Son) who delivers the Enchanted Princess, and makes her his Queen. He is "Ruler," the "unconscious Will"; to be thwarted no more by the ignorant and capricious false will of the conscious man. And He is "Helper," the author of the infallible impulse that sends the Soul sweeping along the skies on its proper path with such impetus that the attraction of alien orbs is no longer sufficient to swerve it. The "Hear me" clause is now uttered by the normal human consciousness, withdrawn to the physical body; the Adept must deliberately abandon his attainment, because it is not yet his whole being which burns up before the Beloved.

Section G.

The Adept, though withdrawn, shall have maintained the Extension of his Symbol. He now repeats the signs as before, save that he makes the Passive Invoking Pentagram of Spirit. He concentrates his consciousness within his Twin-Symbol of Self, and endeavours to send it to sleep. But if the operation be performed properly, his Angel shall have accepted the offering of Dew, and seized with fervour upon the extended symbol of Will towards

Himself. This then shall He shake vehemently with vibrations of love reverberating with the Words of the Section. Even in the physical ears of the adept there shall resound an echo thereof, yet he shall not be able to describe it. It shall seem both louder than thunder, and softer than the whisper of the night-wind. It shall at once be inarticulate, and mean more than he hath ever heard.

Now let him strive with all the strength of his Soul to withstand the Will of his Angel, concealing himself in the closest cell of the citadel of consciousness. Let him consecrate himself to resist the assault of the Voice and the Vibration until his consciousness faint away into Nothing. For if there abide unabsorbed even one single atom of the false Ego, that atom should stain the virginity of the True Self and profane the Oath; then that atom should be so inflamed by the approach of the Angel that it should overwhelm the rest of the mind, tyrannize over it, and become an insane despot to the total ruin of the realm.

But, all being dead to sense, who then is able to strive against the Angel? He shall intensify the stress of His Spirit so that His loyal legions of Lion-Serpents leap from the ambush, awakening the adept to witness their Will and sweep him with them in their enthusiasm, so that he consciously partakes their purpose, and sees in its simplicity the solution of all his perplexities. Thus then shall the Adept be aware that he is being swept away through the column of his Will Symbol, and that His Angel is indeed himself, with intimacy so intense as to become identity, and that not in a single Ego, but in every unconscious element that shares in that manifold uprush.

This rapture is accompanied by a tempest of brilliant light, almost always, and also in many cases by an outburst of sound, stupendous and sublime in all cases, though its character may vary within wide limits.[14]

The spate of stars shoots from the head of the Will-Symbol, and is scattered over the sky in glittering galaxies. This dispersion destroys the concentration of the adept, whose mind cannot master such multiplicity of majesty; as a rule, he simply sinks stunned into normality, to recall nothing of his experience but a vague though vivid impression of complete release and ineffable rapture. Repetition fortifies him to realise the nature of his attainment; and his Angel, the link once made, frequents him, and trains him subtly to be sensitive to his Holy presence, and persuasion. But it may occur, especially after repeated success, that the Adept is not flung back into his mortality by the explosion of the Star-spate, but identified with one particular "Lion-Serpent," continuing conscious thereof until it finds its proper place in Space, when its secret self flowers forth as a truth, which the Adept may then take back to earth with him.

This is but a side issue. The main purpose of the Ritual is to establish the relation of the subconscious self with the Angel in such a way that the Adept is aware that his Angel is the Unity which expresses the sum of the Elements of that Self, that his normal consciousness contains alien enemies introduced by the accidents of environment, and that his Knowledge and Conversation of His Holy Guardian Angel destroys all doubts and delusions, confers all blessings, teaches all truth, and contains all delights. But it is important that the Adept should not rest in mere inexpressible realization of his rapture, but rouse himself to make the relation submit to analysis, to render it in rational terms, and thereby enlighten his mind and

14. These phenomena are not wholly subjective; they may be perceived, though often under other forms, by even the ordinary man.

heart in a sense as superior to fanatical enthusiasm as Beethoven's music is to West African war-drums.

Section Gg.

The adept should have realised that his Act of Union with the angel implies (1) the death of his old mind save in so far as his unconscious elements preserve its memory when they absorb it, and (2) the death of his unconscious elements themselves. But their death is rather a going forth to renew their life through love. He then, by conscious comprehension of them separately and together, becomes the "Angel" of his Angel, as Hermes is the Word of Zeus, whose own voice is Thunder. Thus in this section the adept utters articulately so far as words may, what his Angel is to Himself. He says this, with his Scin-Laeca wholly withdrawn into his physical body, constraining His Angel to indwell his heart.

Line 1

"I am He" asserts the destruction of the sense of separateness between self and Self. It affirms existence, but of the third person only. "The Bornless Spirit" is free of all space, "having sight in the feet," that they may choose their own path. "Strong" is G B R, the Magician escorted by the Sun and the Moon. (See *Liber D* and *Liber 777*.) The "Immortal Fire" is the creative Self; impersonal energy cannot perish, no matter what forms it assumes. Combustion is Love.

Line 2

"Truth" is the necessary relation of any two things; therefore, although it implies duality, it enables us to conceive of two things as being one thing such that it demands to be defined by complementals. Thus, an hyperbola is a simple idea, but its construction exacts two curves.

Line 3

The Angel, as the adept knows him, is a being in Tiphereth, which obscures Kether. The Adept is not officially aware of the higher Sephiroth. He cannot perceive, like the Ipsissimus, that all things soever are equally illusion and equally Absolute. He is in Tiphereth, whose office is Redemption, and he deplores the events which have caused the apparent Sorrow from which he has just escaped. He is also aware, even in the height of his ecstasy, of the limits and defects of his Attainment.

Line 4

This refers to the phenomena which accompany his Attainment.

Line 5

This means the recognition of the Angel as the True Self of his subconscious self, the hidden Life of his physical life.

Line 6

The Adept realises every breath, every word of his Angel as charged with creative fire. Tiphereth is the Sun, and the Angel is the spiritual Sun of the Soul of the Adept.

Line 7

Here is summed the entire process of bringing the conditioned Universe to knowledge of itself through the formula of generation;[15] a soul implants itself in sense-hoodwinked body and reason-fettered mind, makes them aware of their Inmate, and thus to partake of its own consciousness of the Light.

Line 8

"Grace" has here its proper sense of "Pleasantness."

15. That is, Yod He' realizing Themselves, Will and Understanding, in the twins Vau He, Mind and Body.

The existence of the Angel is the justification of the device of creation.[16]

Line 9

This line must be studied in the light of *Liber LXV* (*The Holy Books*, Dallas: Sangreal Foundation, 1970).

Section H.

This recapitulation demands the going forth together of the Adept and his Angel "to do their pleasure on the Earth among the living."

Section J.

The Beast 666 having devised the present method of using this Ritual, having proved it by his own practice to be of infallible puissance when properly performed, and now having written it down for the world, it shall be an ornament for the Adept who adopts it to cry Hail to His name at the end of his work. This shall moreover encourage him in Magick, to recall that indeed there was One who attained by its use to the Knowledge and Conversation of His Holy Guardian Angel, the which forsook him no more, but made Him a Magus, the Word of the Aeon of Horus!

For know this, that the Name IAF in its most secret and mighty sense declareth the Formula of the Magick of the BEAST whereby he wrought many wonders. And because he doth will that the whole world shall attain to this Art, He now hideth it herein so that the worthy may win to His Wisdom.

16. But see also the general solution of the Riddle of Existence in *The Book of the Law* and its Comment — *The Law Is for All* (St. Paul: Llewellyn Publications).

Let I and F face all;[17] yet ward their A from attack.
The Hermit to himself, the Fool to foes, The Hierophant
to friends, Nine by nature, Naught by attainment, Five
by function. In speech swift, subtle and secret; in thought
creative, unbiassed, unbounded; in act gentle, patient and
persistent. Hermes to hear, Dionysus to touch, Pan to
behold.

A Virgin, a Babe, and a Beast!

A Liar, an Idiot, and a Master of Men!

A kiss, a guffaw, and a bellow; he that hath ears to
hear, let him hear!

Take ten that be one, and one that is one in three, to
conceal them in six!

Thy wand to all Cups, and thy Disk to all Swords, but
betray not thine Egg!

Moreover also is IAF verily 666 by virtue of Number;
and this is a Mystery of Mysteries; Who knoweth it, he
is adept of adepts, and Mighty among Magicians!

Now this word SABAF, being by number Three score
and Ten,[18] is a name of Ayin, the Eye, and the Devil our
Lord, and the Goat of Mendes. He is the Lord of the
Sabbath of the Adepts, and is Satan, therefore also the
Sun, whose number of Magick is 666, the seal of His
servant the BEAST.

But again SA is 61, AIN, the Naught of Nuith; BA
means go, for HADIT; and F is their Son the Sun who
is Ra — Hoor — Khuit.

17. If we adopt the new orthography VIAOV (*Book 4*, Part III, Chap. V) we
must read "The Sun-6-the Son" etc. for "all"; and elaborate this interpretation
here given in other ways, accordingly. Thus O (or F) will not be "The Fifteen
by function" instead of "Five" etc., and "in act free, firm, aspiring, ecstatic,"
rather than "gentle" etc. as in the present text.
18. There is an alternative spelling TzBA — F where the Root, "an Host,"
has the value of 93. The Practicus should revive this Ritual throughout in the
Light of his personal researches in the Qabalah, and thus make it his own
peculiar property. The spelling here suggested implies that he who utters the
Word affirms his allegiance to the symbols 93 and 6; that he is a warrior in the
army of Will and of the Sun. 93 is also the number of AIWAZ and 6 of The
Beast.

So then let the Adept set his sigil upon all the words he hath writ in the Book of the Works of his Will.

And let him then end all, saying, Such are the Words![19] For by this he maketh proclamation before all them that be about his Circle that these Words are true and puissant, binding what he would bind, and loosing what he would loose.

Let the Adept perform this Ritual aright, perfect in every part thereof, once daily for one moon, then twice, at dawn and dusk, for two moons, next, thrice, noon added, for three moons, afterwards, midnight making up his course, for four moons four times every day. Then let the Eleventh Moon be consecrated wholly to this Work; let him be instant in continual ardour, dismissing all but his sheer needs to eat and sleep.[20] For know that the true Formula[21] whose virtue sufficed the Beast in this Attainment, was thus:

INVOKE OFTEN[22]

So may all men come at last to the Knowledge and Conversation of the Holy Guardian Angel: thus sayeth the Beast, and prayeth His own Angel that this book be as a burning Lamp, and as a living Spring, for Light and Life to them that read therein.

666

19. The consonants of LOGOS, "Word," add (Hebrew values) to 93. And ΕΠΗ, "Words," (whence "Epic") has also that value: ΕΙΔΕ ΤΑ ΕΠΗ might be the phrase here intended: its number is 418. This would then assert the accomplishment of the Great Work; this is the natural conclusion of the Ritual. Cf. *CCXX*, III: 75.

20. These needs are modified during the process of Initiation both as to quantity and quality. One should not become anxious about one's physical or mental health on a priori grounds, but pay attention only to indubitable symptoms of distress should such arise.

21. See Note page following.

22. See *The Equinox*, I, VIII, 22.

21. (Note to previous page.)

The Oracles of Zoroaster utter this:

"And when, by often invoking, all the phantasms are vanished, thou shalt see that Holy and Formless Fire, that Fire which darts and flashes through all the Depths of the Universe; hear thou the Voice of the Fire!

"A similar Fire flashingly extending through the rushings of Air, or a Fire formless whence cometh the Image of a voice, or even a flashing Light abounding, revolving, whirling forth, crying aloud. Also there is the vision of the fire-flashing Courser of Light, or also a Child, borne aloft on the shoulders of the Celestial Steed, fiery, or clothed with gold, or naked, or shooting with the bow shafts or light, and standing on the shoulders of the horse, then if thy meditation prolongeth itself, thou shalt unite all these symbols into the Form of a Lion."

This passage — combined with several others — is paraphrased in poetry by Aleister Crowley in his *Tannhäuser*.

> And when, *invoking often*, thou shalt see
> That formless Fire; when all the earth is shaken,
> The stars abide not, and the moon is gone,
> All Time crushed back into Eternity,
> The Universe by earthquake overtaken;
> Light is not, and the thunders roll,
> The World is done:
> When in the darkness Chaos rolls again
> In the excited brain:
> Then, O then call not to thy view that visible
> Image of Nature; fatal is her name!
> It fitteth not thy Body to behold
> That living light of Hell,
> The unluminous, dead flame,
> Until that body from the crucible
> Hath passed, pure gold!
> For, from the confines of material space,
> The twilight-moving place,
> The gates of matter, and the dark threshold,
> Before the faces of the Things that dwell
> In the Abodes of Night,
> Spring into sight
> Demons, dog-faced, that show no mortal sign
> Of Truth, but desecrate the Light Divine,
> Seducing from the sacred mysteries.
> But, after all these Folk of Fear are driven
> Before the avenging levin
> That rives the opening skies,
> Behold that Formless and that Holy Flame
> That hath no name;
> The Fire that darts and flashes, writhes and creeps
> Snake-wise in royal robe
> Wound round that vanished glory of the globe,
> Unto that sky beyond the starry deeps,
> Beyond the Toils of Time, — then formulate
> In thine own mind, luminous, concentrate,
> The Lion of the Light, a child that stands
> On the vast shoulders of the Steed of God:
> Or winged, or shooting flying shafts, or shod

With the flame-sandals.
                    Then, lift up thine hands!
Centre thee in thine heart one scarlet thought
Limpid with brilliance of the Light above!
Draw into naught
All life, death, hatred, love:
All self concentred in the sole desire —
Hear thou the Voice of Fire!

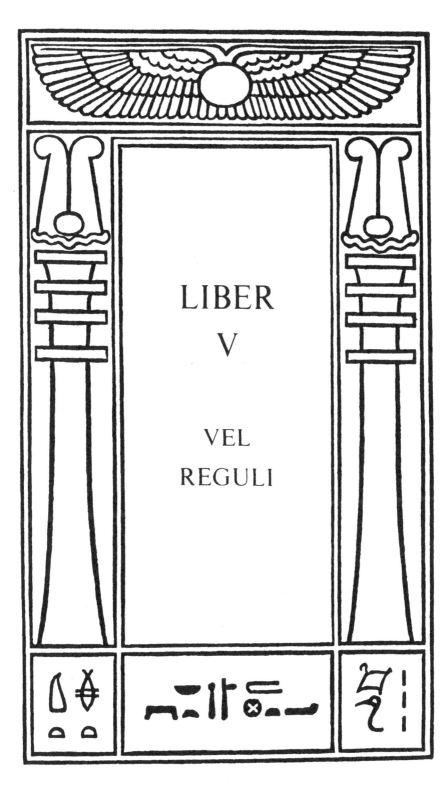

LIBER
V

VEL

REGULI

A ∴ A ∴ Publication in Class D

Being the Ritual of the Mark of the
Beast: an incantation proper to invoke the Energies of the Aeon of
Horus, adapted for the daily use of
the Magician of whatever grade.

LIBER V VEL REGULI

THE FIRST GESTURE

The Oath of the Enchantment, which is called The Elevenfold Seal.

The Animadversion towards the Aeon.

1. Let the Magician, robed and armed as he may deem to be fit, turn his face towards Boleskine,[1] that is the House of The Beast 666.
2. Let him strike the battery 1-3-3-3-1.
3. Let him put the Thumb of his right hand between its index and medius, and make the gestures hereafter following.

The Vertical Component of the Enchantment.

1. Let him describe a circle about his head, crying NUIT!
2. Let him draw the Thumb vertically downward and touch the Muladhara Cakkra, crying, HADIT!
3. Let him, retracing the line, touch the centre of his breast and cry RA-HOOR-KHUIT!

[1]. Boleskine House is on Loch Ness, 17 miles from Inverness, Latitude 57.14 N., Longitude 4.28 W.

The Horizontal Components of the Enchantment.

1. Let him touch the Centre of his Forehead, his mouth, and his larynx, crying AIWAZ!
2. Let him draw his thumb from right to left across his face at the level of the nostrils.
3. Let him touch the centre of his breast, and his solar plexus, crying, THERION!
4. Let him draw his thumb from left to right across his breast, at the level of the sternum.
5. Let him touch the Svadistthana, and the Muladhara Cakkra, crying, BABALON!
6. Let him draw his thumb from right to left across his abdomen, at the level of the hips.

(Thus shall he formulate the Sigil of the Grand Hierophant, but dependent from the Circle.)

The Asseveration of the Spells.

1. Let the Magician clasp his hands upon his Wand, his fingers and thumbs interlaced, crying LASh-TAL! ΘΕΛΗΜΑ! FIAOF! ΑΓΑΠΗ! ΑΥΜΓΝ!

(Thus shall be declared the Words of Power whereby the Energies of the Aeon of Horus work his will in the world.)

The Proclamation of the Accomplishment.

1. Let the Magician strike the Battery: 3-5-3, crying ABRAHADABRA.

THE SECOND GESTURE

The Enchantment.

1. Let the Magician, still facing Boleskine, advance to the circumference of his circle.
2. Let him turn himself towards the left, and pace with

the stealth and swiftness of a tiger the precincts of his circle, until he complete one revolution thereof.

3. Let him give the Sign of Horus (or The Enterer) as he passeth, so to project the force that radiateth from Boleskine before him.

4. Let him pace his path until he comes to the North; there let him halt, and turn his face to the North.

5. Let him trace with his wand the Averse Pentagram proper to invoke Air (Aquarius).

6. Let him bring the wand to the centre of the Pentagram and call upon NUIT!

7. Let him make the sign called Puella, standing with his feet together, head bowed, his left hand shielding the Muladhara Cakkra, and his right hand shielding his breast (attitude of the Venus de Medici).

8. Let him turn again to the left, and pursue his Path as before, projecting the force from Boleskine as he passeth; let him halt when he next cometh to the South and face outward.

9. Let him trace the Averse Pentagram that invoketh Fire (Leo).

10. Let him point his wand to the centre of the Pentagram, and cry, HADIT!

11. Let him give the sign Puer, standing with feet together, and head erect. Let his right hand (the thumb extended at right angles to the fingers) be raised, the forearm vertical at a right angle with the upper arm, which is horizontally extended in the line joining the shoulders. Let his left hand, the thumb extended forwards and the fingers clenched, rest at the junction of the thighs (Attitude of the Gods Mentu, Khem, etc.).

12. Let him proceed as before; then in the East, let him make the Averse Pentagram that invoketh Earth (Taurus).

13. Let him point his wand to the centre of the pentagram, and cry, THERION!

14. Let him give the sign called Vir, the feet being together. The hands, with clenched fingers and thumbs thrust out forwards, are held to the temples; the head is then bowed and pushed out, as if to symbolize the butting of an horned beast (attitude of Pan, Bacchus, etc.). (Frontispiece, *The Equinox*, I, III.)

15. Proceeding as before, let him make in the West the Averse Pentagram whereby Water is invoked.

16. Pointing the wand to the centre of the Pentagram, let him call upon BABALON!

17. Let him give the sign Mulier. The feet are widely separated, and the arms raised so as to suggest a crescent. The head is thrown back (attitude of Baphomet, Isis in Welcome, the Microcosm of Vitruvius). (See *Book 4*, Part II.)

18. Let him break into the dance, tracing a centripetal spiral widdershins, enriched by revolutions upon his axis as he passeth each quarter, until he come to the centre of the circle. There let him halt, facing Boleskine.

19. Let him raise the wand, trace the Mark of the Beast, and cry AIWAZ!

20. Let him trace the invoking Hexagram of The Beast.

21. Let him lower the wand, striking the Earth therewith.

22. Let him give the sign of Mater Triumphans (the feet are together; the left arm is curved as if it supported a child; the thumb and index finger of the right hand pinch the nipple of the left breast,

as if offering it to that child). Let him utter the
word ΘΕΛΗΜΑ!

23. Perform the spiral dance, moving deosil and whirling widdershins.

Each time on passing the West extend the wand to
the Quarter in question, and bow:

   a. "Before me the powers of LA!" (to West.)
   b. "Behind me the powers of AL!" (to East.)
   c. "On my right hand the powers of LA!" (to
      North.)
   d. "On my left hand the powers of AL!" (to
      South.)
   e. "Above me the powers of ShT!" (leaping in
      the air.)
   f. "Beneath me the powers of ShT!" (striking
      the ground.)
   g. "Within me the Powers!" (in the attitude of
      Phthah erect, the feet together, the hands
      clasped upon the vertical wand.)
   h. "About me flames my Father's face, the Star
      of Force and Fire."
   i. "And in the Column stands His six-rayed
      Splendour!"
      (This dance may be omitted, and the whole
      utterance chanted in the attitude of Phthah.)

THE FINAL GESTURE

This is identical with the First Gesture.

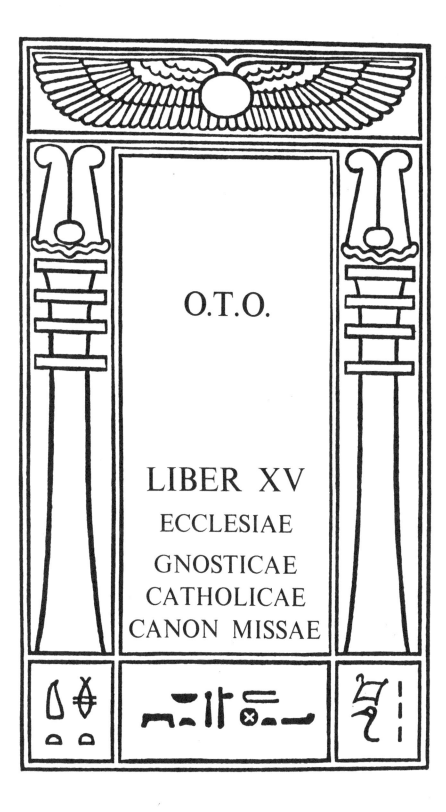

O.T.O.

LIBER XV

ECCLESIAE

GNOSTICAE
CATHOLICAE
CANON MISSAE

O.T.O.
ISSUED BY ORDER:

XI° O. T. O.

HIBERNIAE IONAE ET
OMNIUM BRITANNIARUM
REX SUMMUS SANCTISSIMUS

LIBER XV

THE GNOSTIC MASS

I

OF THE FURNISHINGS
OF THE TEMPLE

In the East, that is, in the direction of Boleskine, which is situated on the south-eastern shore of Loch Ness in Scotland, two miles east of Foyers, is a shrine or High Altar. Its dimensions should be 7 feet in length, 3 feet in breadth, 44 inches in height. It should be covered with a crimson altar-cloth, on which may be embroidered fleur-de-lys in gold, or a sunblaze, or other suitable emblem.

On each side of it should be a pillar or Obelisk, with countercharges in black and white.

Below it should be the dais of three steps, in black and white squares.

Above it is the super-altar, at whose top is the Stélé of Revealing in reproduction, with four candles on each side of it. Below the stélé is a place for *The Book of the Law*, with six candles on each side of it. Below this again is The Holy Graal, with roses on each side of it. There is room in front of the Cup for the Paten. On each side beyond the roses, are two great candles.

All this is enclosed within a great Veil.

Forming the apex of an equilateral triangle whose base

is a line drawn between the pillars, is a small black square altar, of superimposed cubes.

Taking this altar as the middle of the base of a similar and equal triangle, at the apex of this second triangle is a small circular font.

Repeating, the apex of a third triangle is an upright tomb.

II
OF THE OFFICERS OF THE MASS

The Priest. Bears the Sacred Lance, and is clothed at first in a plain white robe.

The Priestess. Should be actually Virgo Intacta, or specially dedicated to the service of the Great Order. She is clothed in white, blue, and gold. She bears the Sword from a red girdle, and the Paten and Hosts, or Cakes of Light.

The Deacon. He is clothed in white and yellow. He bears *The Book of the Law*.

Two Children. They are clothed in white and black. One bears a pitcher of water and a cellar of salt, the other a censer of fire and a casket of perfume.

III
OF THE CEREMONY
OF THE INTROIT

The Deacon, *opening the door of the Temple, admits the congregation, and takes his stand between the small altar and the font. (There should be a doorkeeper to attend to the admission.)*

The Deacon *advances and bows before the open shrine where the Graal is exalted. He kisses* The Book of the Law *three times, opens it, and places it upon the super-altar. He turns West.*

The Deacon. Do what thou wilt shall be the whole of the Law. I proclaim the Law of Light, Life, Love, and Liberty in the name of IAO.

The Congregation. Love is the law, love under will.

The Deacon goes to his place between the altar of incense and the font, faces east, and gives the step and sign of a Man and a Brother. All imitate him.

The Deacon and all the People. I believe in one secret and ineffable LORD; and in one Star in the Company of Stars of whose fire we are created, and to which we shall return; and in one Father of Life, Mystery of Mystery, in His name CHAOS, the sole viceregent of the Sun upon the Earth; and in one Air the nourisher of all that breathes.

And I believe in one Earth, the Mother of us all, and in one Womb wherein all men are begotten, and wherein they shall rest, Mystery of Mystery, in Her name BABALON.

And I believe in the Serpent and the Lion, Mystery of Mystery, in His name BAPHOMET.

And I believe in one Gnostic and Catholic Church of Light, Life, Love and Liberty, the Word of whose Law is THELEMA.

And I believe in the communion of Saints.

And, for as much as meat and drink are transmuted in us daily into spiritual substance, I believe in the Miracle of the Mass.

And I confess one Baptism of Wisdom, whereby we accomplish the Miracle of Incarnation.

And I confess my life one, individual, and eternal that was, and is, and is to come.

AUMGN. AUMGN. AUMGN.

Music is now played. **The child** *enters with the ewer and the salt.* **The Virgin** *enters with the Sword and the Paten.* **The child** *enters with the censer and the* *perfume. They face* **the Deacon,** *deploying into line, from the space between the two altars.*

The Virgin. Greeting of Earth and Heaven!

All give the Hailing sign of a Magician, **the Deacon** *leading.*

The Priestess, *the negative child on her left, the positive on her right, ascends the steps of the High Altar, they awaiting her below. She places the Paten before the Graal. Having adored it, she descends, and with the children following her, the positive next her, she moves in a serpentine manner involving 3½ circles of the Temple. (Deosil about altar, widdershins about font, deosil about altar and font, widdershins about altar and so to the Tomb in the West.) She draws her Sword, and pulls down the Veil, therewith.*

The Priestess. By the power of ✠ Iron, I say unto thee, Arise. In the name of our Lord the ✠ Sun, and of our Lord ✠ ... that thou mayst administer the virtues to the Brethren.

She sheathes the Sword.

The Priest, *issuing from the Tomb, holding the Lance erect with both hands, right over left, against his breast, takes the first three regular steps.*

He then gives the Lance to **the Priestess,** *and gives the three penal signs.*

He then kneels, and worships the Lance with both hands. Penitential music.

The Priest. I am a man among men.

He takes again the Lance, and lowers it. He rises.

The Priest. How should I be worthy to administer the virtues to the Brethren?

The Priestess *takes from the child the water and the salt, and mixes them in the font.*

The Priestess. Let the salt of Earth admonish the Water to bear the virtue of the Great Sea. *(Genuflects.)* Mother, be thou adored.

She returns to the West. ✝ *on* **Priest** *with open hand doth she make, over his forehead, breast, and body.*

Be the Priest pure of body and soul!

The Priestess *takes the censer from the child, and places it on the small altar. She puts incense therein.*

Let the Fire and the Air make sweet the world! *(Genuflects.)*

Father, be thou adored.

She returns West, and makes ✝ *with the censer before the Priest, thrice as before.*

Be the Priest fervent of body and soul!

*(***The children*** *resume their weapons as they are done with.)*

The Deacon *now takes the consecrated Robe from the High Altar, and brings it to her. She robes the Priest in his Robe of scarlet and gold.*

Be the flame of the Sun thine ambience, O thou Priest of the SUN!

The Deacon *brings the crown from the High Altar. (The crown may be of gold or platinum, or of electrum magicum; but with no other metals, save the small proportions necessary to a proper alloy. It may be adorned with divers jewels, at will. But it must have the Uraeus serpent twined about it, and the cap of maintenance must match the scarlet of the Robe. Its texture should be velvet.)*

Be the Serpent thy crown, O thou Priest of the LORD!

Kneeling, she takes the Lance, between her open hands, and runs them up and down upon the shaft eleven times, very gently.

Be the LORD present among us!
All give the Hailing Sign.
The People. So mote it be.

IV

OF THE CEREMONY OF THE OPENING OF THE VEIL

The Priest. Thee therefore whom we adore we also invoke.

By the power of the lifted Lance!
He raises the Lance. All repeat Hailing Sign.
A phrase of triumphant music.
The Priest *takes the Priestess by her right hand with his left, keeping the Lance raised.*

I, PRIEST and KING, take thee, Virgin pure without spot; I upraise thee; I lead thee to the East; I set thee upon the summit of the Earth.
He thrones **the Priestess** *upon the altar.* **The Deacon** *and the children follow, they in rank, behind him.*
The Priestess *takes* The Book of the Law, *resumes her seat, and holds it open on her breast with her two hands, making a descending triangle with thumbs and forefingers.*
The Priest *gives the lance to* **the Deacon** *to hold, and takes the ewer from the child, and sprinkles* **the Priestess,** *making five crosses, forehead, shoulders, and thighs.*
The thumb of **the Priest** *is always between his index and medius, whenever he is not holding the Lance.* **The Priest** *takes the censer from the child, and makes five crosses, as before.*
The children *replace their weapons on their respective altars.*

The Priest *kisses* The Book of the Law *three times.*
He kneels for a space in adoration, with joined hands, knuckles closed, thumb in position aforesaid.
He rises, and draws the veil over the whole altar.
All rise and stand to order.
The Priest *takes the lance from* **the Deacon,** *and holds it as before, as Osiris or Pthah. He circumambulates the Temple three times, followed by* **the Deacon** *and the children as before. (These, when not using their hands, keep their arms crossed upon their breasts.)*
At the last circumambulation they leave him, and go to the place between the font and the small altar, where they kneel in adoration, their hands joined palm to palm, and raised above their heads.
All imitate this motion.
The Priest *returns to the East, and mounts the first step of the altar.*

The Priest. O circle of Stars whereof our Father is but the younger brother, marvel beyond imagination, soul of infinite space, before whom Time is ashamed, the mind bewildered, and the understanding dark, not unto Thee may we attain, unless Thine image be Love. Therefore by seed and root and stem and bud and leaf and flower and fruit do we invoke Thee.

Then the priest answered & said unto the Queen of Space, kissing her lovely brows, and the dew of her light bathing his whole body in a sweet-smelling perfume of sweat; O Nuit, continuous one of Heaven, let it be ever thus; that men speak not of thee as One but as None; and let them speak not of thee at all, since thou art continuous.

During this speech **the Priestess** *must have divested herself completely of her robe. (See* CCXX, *I: 62.)*
The Priestess. But to love me is better than all things; if under the night-stars in the desert thou presently burn-

est mine incense before me, invoking me with a pure heart, and the serpent flame therein, thou shalt come a little to lie in my bosom. For one kiss wilt thou then be willing to give all; but whoso gives one particle of dust shall lose all in that hour. Ye shall gather goods and store of women and spices; ye shall wear rich jewels; ye shall exceed the nations of earth in splendour and pride; but always in the love of me, and so shall ye come to my joy. I charge you earnestly to come before me in a single robe, and covered with a rich head-dress. I love you! I yearn to you! Pale or purple, veiled or voluptuous, I who am all pleasure and purple, and drunkenness of the innermost sense, desire you. Put on the wings, and arouse the coiled splendour within you: come unto me! To me! To me! Sing the rapturous love-song unto me! Burn to me perfumes! Drink to me, for I love you! I love you. I am the blue-lidded daughter of sunset; I am the naked brilliance of the voluptuous night-sky. To me! To me!

The Priest *mounts the second step.*

The Priest. O secret of secrets that art hidden in the being of all that lives, not Thee do we adore, for that which adoreth is also Thou. Thou art That, and That am I.

I am the flame that burns in every heart of man, and in the core of every star. I am Life, and the giver of Life; yet therefore is the knowledge of me the knowledge of death. I am alone; there is no God where I am.

The Deacon *and all rise to their feet, with the Hailing sign.*

The Deacon. But ye, O my people, rise up and awake.

Let the rituals be rightly performed with joy and beauty.

There are rituals of the elements and feasts of the times.

A feast for the first night of the Prophet and his Bride.

A feast for the three days of the writing of *The Book of the Law*.

A feast for Tahuti and the children of the Prophet—secret, O Prophet!

A feast for the Supreme Ritual, and a feast for the Equinox of the Gods.

A feast for fire and a feast for water; a feast for life and a greater feast for death.

A feast every day in your hearts in the joy of my rapture.

A feast every night unto Nu, and the pleasure of uttermost delight.

The Priest *mounts the third step.*

The Priest. Thou that art One, our Lord in the Universe the Sun, our Lord in ourselves whose name is Mystery of Mystery, uttermost being whose radiance enlightening the worlds is also the breath that maketh every God even and Death to tremble before Thee—By the Sign of Light ✠ appear Thou glorious upon the throne of the Sun.

Make open the path of creation and of intelligence between us and our minds. Enlighten our understanding.

Encourage our hearts. Let thy light crystallize itself in our blood, fulfilling us of Resurrection.

A ka dua

Tuf ur biu

bi a'a chefu

Dudu nur af an nuteru.

The Priestess. There is no law beyond Do what thou wilt.

The Priest *parts the veil with his lance. During the previous speeches* **the Priestess** *has, if necessary, as in savage countries, resumed her robe.*

The Priest. IO IO IO IAO SABAO KURIE ABRASAX KURIE MEITHRAS KURIE PHALLE. IO PAN IO PAN PAN IO ISCHURON IO ATHANATON IO

ABROTON IO IAO. CHAIRE PHALLE CHAIRE
PAMPHAGE CHAIRE PANGENETOR. HAGIOS
HAGIOS HAGIOS IAO.

The Priestess *is seated with the Paten in her right
hand and the cup in her left.*

The Priest *presents the Lance, which she kisses eleven
times. She then holds it to her breast, while* **the Priest,**
*falling at her knees, kisses them, his arms stretched
along her thighs. He remains in this adoration while*
the Deacon *intones the collects.*

*All stand to order, with the Dieu Garde, that is, feet
square, hands, with linked thumbs, held loosely. This
is the universal position when standing, unless other
direction is given.*

V

OF THE OFFICE OF THE COLLECTS
WHICH ARE ELEVEN IN NUMBER

(THE SUN)

The Deacon. Lord visible and sensible of whom this
earth is but a frozen spark turning about thee with annual
and diurnal motion, source of light, source of life, let thy
perpetual radiance hearten us to continual labour and
enjoyment; so that as we are constant partakers of thy
bounty we may in our particular orbit give out light and
life, sustenance and joy to them that revolve about us
without diminution of substance or effulgence for ever.

The People. So mote it be.

(THE LORD)

The Deacon. Lord secret and most holy, source of life,
source of love, source of liberty, be thou ever constant and
mighty within us, force of energy, fire of motion; with
diligence let us ever labour with thee, that we may remain
in thine abundant joy.

The People. So mote it be.

(THE MOON)

The Deacon. Lady of night, that turning ever about us art now visible and now invisible in thy season, be thou favourable to hunters, and lovers, and to all men that toil upon the earth, and to all mariners upon the sea.

The People. So mote it be.

(THE LADY)

The Deacon. Giver and receiver of joy, gate of life and love, be thou ever ready, thou and thine handmaiden, in thine office of gladness.

The People. So mote it be.

(THE SAINTS)

The Deacon. Lord of Life and Joy, that art the might of man, that art the essence of every true god that is upon the surface of the Earth, continuing knowledge from generation unto generation, thou adored of us upon heaths and in woods, on mountains and in caves, openly in the marketplaces and secretly in the chambers of our houses, in temples of gold and ivory and marble as in these other temples of our bodies, we worthily commemorate them worthy that did of old adore thee and manifest thy glory unto men, *Laotze and Siddartha* and Krishna *and Tahuti,* Mosheh, *Dionysus, Mohammed and To Mega Therion, with these also* Hermes, *Pan,* Priapus, Osiris and Melchizedek, *Khem* and Amoun *and Mentu,* Heracles, Orpheus and Odysseus; with Vergilius, *Catullus,* Martialis, *Rabelais, Swinburne, and many an holy bard; Apollonius Tyanaeus,* Simon Magus, Manes, Basilides, Valentinus, *Bardesanes and Hippolytus, that transmitted the Light of the Gnosis to us their successors and their heirs*; with Merlin, Arthur, Kamuret, Parzival, and many another, prophet, priest and king, that bore the Lance and Cup, the Sword and Disk, against the Heathen; *and these also,* Carolus

Magnus and his paladins, with William of Schyren, Frederick of Hohenstaufen, Roger Bacon, *Jacobus Burgundus Molensis the Martyr, Christian Rosencreutz*, Ulrich von Hutten, Paracelsus, Michael Maier, Jacob Boehme, Francis Bacon Lord Verulam, Andrea, Robertus de Fluctibus, Johannes Dee, *Sir Edward Kelly*, Thomas Vaughan, Elias Ashmole, Molinos, Adam Weishaupt Wolfgang von Goethe, Ludovicus Rex Bavariae, Richard Wagner, *Alphonse Louis Constant*, Friedrich Nietzsche, Hargrave Jennings, Carl Kellner, Forlong dux, Sir Richard Payne Knight, Sir Richard Francis Burton, Doctor Gérard Encausse, *Doctor Theodor Reuss, and Sir Aleister Crowley*—oh Sons of the Lion and the Snake! with all Thy saints we worthily commemorate them worthy that were and are and are to come.

May their Essence be here present, potent, puissant and paternal to perfect this feast!

(At each name **the Deacon** *signs* ✠ *with thumb between index and medius. At ordinary mass it is only necessary to commemorate those whose names are italicized, with wording as is shown.)*

The People. So mote it be.

(THE EARTH)

The Deacon. Mother of fertility on whose breast lieth water, whose cheek is caressed by air, and in whose heart is the sun's fire, womb of all life, recurring grace of seasons, answer favourably the prayer of labour, and to pastors and husbandmen be thou propitious.

The People. So mote it be.

(THE PRINCIPLES)

The Deacon. Mysterious Energy, triform, mysterious Matter, in fourfold and sevenfold division, the interplay of which things weave the dance of the Veil of Life upon the Face of the Spirit, let there be Harmony and Beauty in your mystic loves, that in us may be health and wealth and strength and divine pleasure according to the Law of Liberty; let each pursue his Will as a strong man that rejoiceth in his way, as the course of a Star that blazeth for ever among the joyous company of Heaven.

The People. So mote it be.

(BIRTH)

The Deacon. Be the hour auspicious, and the gate of life open in peace and in well-being, so that she that beareth children may rejoice, and the babe catch life with both hands.

The People. So mote it be.

(MARRIAGE)

The Deacon. Upon all that this day unite with love under will let fall success; may strength and skill unite to bring forth ecstasy, and beauty answer beauty.

The People. So mote it be.

(DEATH)

The Deacon. Term of all that liveth, whose name is inscrutable, be favourable unto us in thine hour.

The People. So mote it be.

(THE END)

The Deacon. Unto them from whose eyes the veil of life hath fallen may there be granted the accomplishment of their true Wills; whether they will absorption in the Infinite, or to be united with their chosen and preferred, or to be in contemplation, or to be at peace, or to achieve the labour and heroism of incarnation on this planet or another, or in any Star, or aught else, unto them may there be granted the accomplishment of their wills; yea, the accomplishment of their wills. AUMGN. AUMGN. AUMGN.

The People. So mote it be.

All sit.

The Deacon *and the children attend* **the Priest** *and* **Priestess,** *ready to hold any appropriate weapon as may be necessary.*

VI
OF THE CONSECRATION
OF THE ELEMENTS

The Priest *makes the five crosses.* ✠3 ✠1 ✠2 *on paten and cup;* ✠4 *on paten alone;* ✠5 *on cup alone.*

The Priest. Life of man upon earth, fruit of labour, sustenance of endeavour, thus be thou nourishment of the Spirit!

He touches the Host with the Lance.

By the virtue of the Rod
Be this bread the Body of God!

He takes the Host.

TOUTO ESTI TO SOMA MOU.

He kneels, adores, rises, turns, shows Host to **the** **People,** *turns, replaces Host, and adores. Music.*

He takes the Cup.

Vehicle of the joy of Man upon earth, solace of labour, inspiration of endeavour, thus be thou ecstasy of the Spirit!

He touches the Cup with the Lance.

By the virtue of the Rod
Be this wine the Blood of God!

He takes the Cup.

TOUTO ECTI TO ΠOTHPION
TOU HAIMATOC MOU.

He kneels, adores, rises, turns, shows the Cup to **the** **People,** *turns, replaces the Cup, and adores. Music.*

For this is the Covenant of Resurrection.

He makes the five crosses on **the Priestess.**

Accept, O LORD, this sacrifice of life and joy, true warrants of the Covenant of Resurrection.

The Priest *offers the Lance to* **the Priestess**, *who kisses it; he then touches her between the breasts and upon the body. He then flings out his arms upward, as comprehending the whole shrine.*

Let this offering be borne upon the waves of Aethyr to our Lord and Father the Sun that travelleth over the Heavens in his name ON.

He closes his hands, kisses **the Priestess** *between the breasts, and makes three great crosses over the Paten, the Cup, and himself.*

He strikes his breast. All repeat this action.

Hear ye all, saints of the true church of old time now essentially present, that of ye we claim heirship, with ye we claim communion, from ye we claim benediction in the name of IAO.

He makes three crosses on Paten and Cup together.

He uncovers the Cup, genuflects, takes the Cup in his left hand and the Host in his right.

With the Host he makes the five crosses on the Cup.

$$\begin{array}{cc} & ✠_1 \\ ✠_3 & ✠_2 \\ ✠_5 & ✠_4 \end{array}$$

He elevates the Host and the Cup.

The Bell strikes.

HAGIOS HAGIOS HAGIOS IAO.

He replaces the Host and the Cup, and adores.

VII

OF THE OFFICE OF THE ANTHEM

The Priest. Thou who art I, beyond all I am,

Who hast no nature and no name,
Who art, when all but thou are gone,
Thou, centre and secret of the Sun,
Thou, hidden spring of all things known
And unknown, Thou aloof, alone,
Thou, the true fire within the seed
Brooding and breeding, source and seed
Of life, love, liberty, and light,
Thou beyond speech and beyond sight,
Thee I invoke, my faint fresh fire
Kindling as mine intents aspire.
Thee I invoke, abiding one,
Thee, centre and secret of the Sun,
And that most holy mystery
Of which the vehicle am I.
Appear, most awful and most mild,
As it is lawful, to thy child!
The Chorus. For of the Father and the Son
The Holy Spirit is the norm;
Male-female, quintessential, one,
Man-being veiled in woman-form.
Glory and worship in the highest,
Thou Dove, mankind that deifiest,
Being that race, most royally run
To spring sunshine through winter storm.
Glory and worship be to Thee,
Sap of the world-ash, wonder-tree!
First Semichorus: Men. Glory to thee from Gilded
Tomb!
Second Semichorus: Women. Glory to thee from
Waiting Womb!
Men. Glory to Thee from earth unploughed!
Women. Glory to Thee from virgin vowed!
Men. Glory to Thee, true Unity
Of the Eternal Trinity!

Women. Glory to Thee, thou sire and dam
And Self of I am that I am!
Men. Glory to Thee, beyond all term,
Thy spring of sperm, thy seed and germ!
Women. Glory to Thee, eternal Sun,
Thou One in Three, Thou Three in One!
Chorus. Glory and worship unto Thee,
Sap of the world-ash, wonder-tree!

> *(These words are to form the substance of the anthem;
> but the whole or any part thereof shall be set to music,
> which may be as elaborate as art can devise. But even
> should other anthems be authorized by the Father of
> the Church, this shall hold its place as the first of its
> kind, the father of all others.)*

VIII

OF THE MYSTIC MARRIAGE
AND CONSUMMATION
OF THE ELEMENTS

The Priest *takes the Paten between the index and
medius of the right hand.* **The Priestess** *clasps the
Cup in her right hand.*

The Priest. Lord most secret, bless this spiritual food
unto our bodies, bestowing upon us health and wealth
and strength and joy and peace, and that fulfilment of will
and of love under will that is perpetual happiness.

> *He makes ✠ with Paten and kisses it.*
> *He uncovers the Cup, genuflects, rises. Music.*
> *He takes the Host, and breaks it over the Cup.*
> *He replaces the right-hand portion in the Paten.*
> *He breaks off a particle of the left-hand portion.*

TOUTO ECTI TO SIIERMA MOU. HO IIATHP
ECTIN HO HUIOC DIA TO IINEUMA HAGION.
AUMGN. AUMGN. AUMGN.

He replaces the left-hand part of the Host.
The Priestess *extends the Lance-point with her left hand to receive the particle.*
The Priest *clasps the Cup in his left hand.*
Together they depress the Lance-point in the Cup.
The Priest and **the Priestess.** HRILIU.
The Priest *takes the Lance.*
The Priestess *covers the Cup.*
The Priest *genuflects, rises, bows, joins hands.*
He strikes his breast.

The Priest. O Lion and O Serpent that destroy the destroyer, be mighty among us.

O Lion and O Serpent that destroy the destroyer, be mighty among us.

O Lion and O Serpent that destroy the destroyer, be mighty among us.

> **The Priest** *joins hands upon the breast of* **the Priestess,** and takes back his Lance.
> *He turns to* **the People,** *lowers and raises the Lance, and makes* ✝ *upon them.*

Do what thou wilt shall be the whole of the Law.

The People. Love is the law, love under will.

> *He lowers the Lance, and turns to East.*
> **The Priestess** *takes the Lance in her right hand. With her left hand she offers the Paten.*
> **The Priest** *kneels.*

The Priest. In my mouth be the essence of the life of the Sun!

> *He takes the Host with the right hand, makes* ✝ *with it on the Paten, and consumes it.*
> *Silence.*
> **The Priestess** *takes, uncovers, and offers the Cup, as before.*

The Priest. In my mouth be the essence of the joy of the earth!

He takes the Cup, makes ✠ on **the Priestess,** *drains it and returns it.*
Silence.
He rises, takes the Lance, and turns to **the People.**
The Priest. There is no part of me that is not of the Gods.

(Those of **the People** *who intend to communicate, and none other should be present, having signified their intention, a whole Cake of Light, and a whole goblet of wine, have been prepared for each one.*
The Deacon *marshals them; they advance one by one to the altar.* **The children** *take the Elements and offer them.* **The People** *communicate as did* **the Priest,** *uttering the same words in an attitude of Resurrection :*
There is no part of me that is not of the Gods.
The exceptions to this part of the ceremony are when it is of the nature of a celebration, in which case none but **the Priest** *communicate; or part of the ceremony of marriage, when none other, save the two to be married, partake; part of the ceremony of baptism, when only the child baptised partakes; and of Confirmation at puberty, when only the persons confirmed partake. The Sacrament may be reserved by* **the Priest,** *for administration to the sick in their homes.)*
The Priest *closes all within the veil. With the Lance he makes ✠ on the people thrice, thus.*
The Priest. ✠ The LORD bless you.

✠The LORD enlighten your minds and comfort your hearts and sustain your bodies.

✠The LORD bring you to the accomplishment of your true Wills, the Great Work, the Summum Bonum, True Wisdom and Perfect Happiness.

He goes out, **the Deacon** *and* **children** *following, into the Tomb of the West.*
Music. (Voluntary.)

Note. **The Priestess** *and other officers never partake of the Sacrament, they being as it were part of* **the Priest** *himself.*

Note. *Certain secret Formulae of this Mass are taught to* **the Priest** *in his Ordination.*

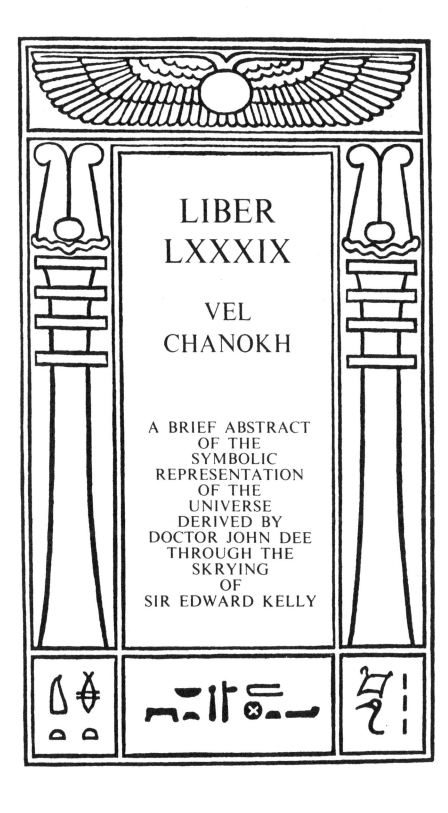

LIBER LXXXIX

VEL CHANOKH

A BRIEF ABSTRACT
OF THE
SYMBOLIC
REPRESENTATION
OF THE
UNIVERSE
DERIVED BY
DOCTOR JOHN DEE
THROUGH THE
SKRYING
OF
SIR EDWARD KELLY

The Holy Table
Plate I

LIBER LXXXIX
VEL CHANOKH

PART I
THE SYMBOLIC REPRESENTATION
OF THE UNIVERSE

The Skryer obtained from certain Angels a series of seven talismans. These, grouped about the Holy Twelvefold Table, similarly obtained, were part of the furniture of the Holy Table, as shewn in Plate I, opposite.

Other appurtenances of this table will be described hereafter.

II

Other Pantacles were obtained in a similar manner. Here (Plate 11) is the principal one, which, carved in wax, was placed upon the top of the table. On four others stood the feet of the table.

Note first the Holy Sevenfold Table containing seven Names of God which not even the Angels are able to pronounce.

SAAI $\frac{21}{8}$ EME

BTZKASE[30]

HEIDENE

DEIMO[30] A

I[26]MEGCBE

387

ILAOI $\frac{21}{8}$ VN

IHRLAAL $\frac{21}{8}$

These names are seen written without the heptagram within the heptagon.

By reading these obliquely are obtained names of Angels called—

(1) Filiae Bonitatis or Filiolae Lucis.

E

Me

Ese

Iana

Akele

Azdobn

Stimcul

(2) Filii Lucis.

I

Ih

Ilr

Dmal

Heeoa

Beigia

Stimcul

(These are given attributions to the Metals of the Planets in this order: Sol, Luna, Venus, Jupiter, Mars, Mercury, Saturn.)

(3) Filiae Filiarum Lucis.

S

Ab

Ath

Ized

Ekiei

Madimi

Esemeli

(4) Filii Filiorum Lucis.

L (El)

Sigillvm Dei Aemeth
Plate II

Aw
Ave
Liba
Iocle
Hagone(l)
Ilemese

See all these names in the heptagram of the great seal.

So also there are Seven Great Angels formed thus: take the corner letter S, then the diagonal next to it AB, then the next diagonal ATH, then the fourth diagonal, where is I with $\frac{21}{8}$ (which indicates EL), and we have the name—

SABATHIEL

Continuing the process, we get

ZEDEKIEL

MADIMIEL

SEMELIEL

NOGAHEL

CORABIEL

LEVANAEL

These names will be found in the Pentagram and about it.

These angels are the angels of the Seven Circles of Heaven.

These are but a few of the mysteries of this great seal

SIGILLVM DEI AEMETH

III

The Shew-stone, a crystal which Dee alleged to have been brought to him by angels, was then placed upon this table, and the principal result of the ceremonial skrying of Sir Edward Kelly is the obtaining of the following diagrams, Plates III–VIII.

He symbolized the Fourth-Dimensional Universe in two dimensions as a square surrounded by 30 concentric circles (the 30 Aethyrs or Aires) whose radii increase in a geometrical proportion.

The sides of the square are the four great watch-towers (Plates IV–VII) which are attributed to the elements. There is also a "black cross" (or "central tablet" according to the arrangement shewn—compare the black cross bordering the tablets in Plate III with Plate VIII).

Plate III gives the general view.

(The reversed letters which form the word PARAOAN are written in Enochian for convenience, as our A and O are not distinguishable reverse from forward.)

Plate IV gives the complete attribution of the tablet of Air.

The 6th file is called Linea Patris.

The 7th file is called Linea Filii.

The 7th line is called Linea Spiritus Sancti.

This great cross divides the Tablet into four lesser (sub-elemental) Tablets, the left-hand top corner being Air of Air, the right-hand top corner Water of Air, the left-hand bottom corner Earth of Air, the remaining corner Fire of Air.

Each of these lesser Tablets contains a Calvary Cross of ten squares, which governs it.

Plates V, VI, and VII are similar for the other elements.

This is the way in which the names are drawn from the great Tablets. (Examples taken from Water Tablet.)

1. Linea Spiritus Sancti gives the Three Holy Names of God of 3, 4, and 5 letters respectively.

MPH ARSL GAIOL

2. A whorl around the centre of the Tablet gives the name of the Great Elemental King, RAAGIOSL (similarly for Air BATAIVAH, for Earth ICZHHCAL, for Fire EDLPRNAA).

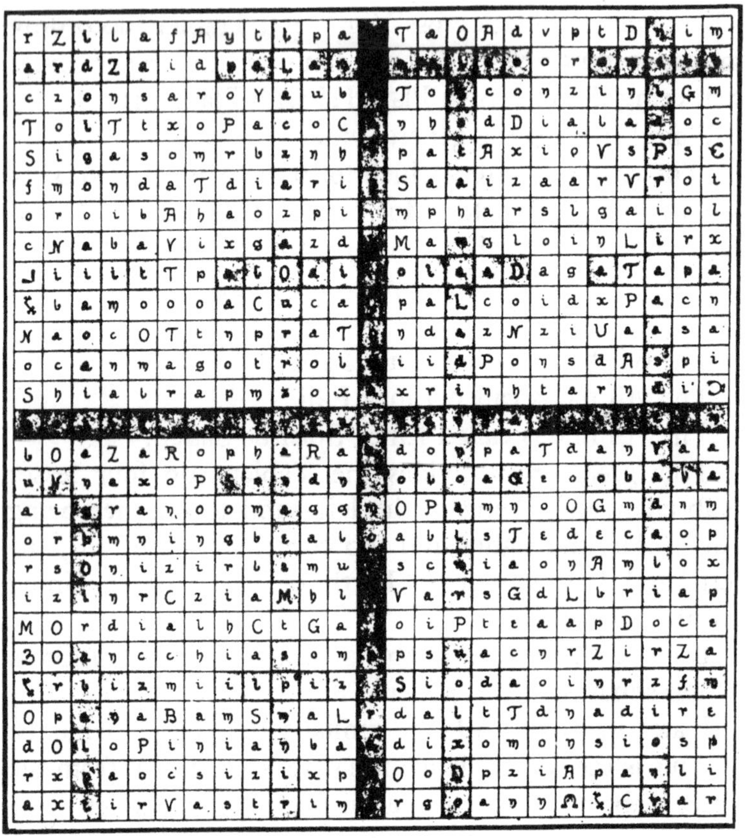

The Four Great Watch-Towers and the
Black Cross within General View
Plate III

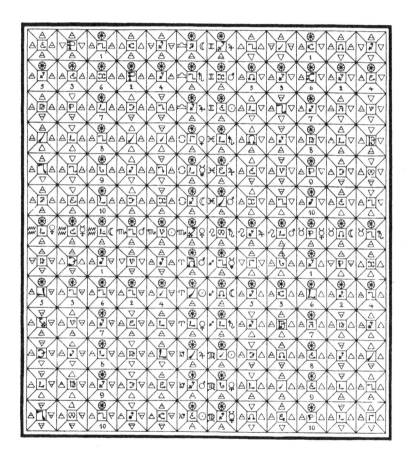

The Great Watch-Tower of the East
Attributed to Air
Plate IV

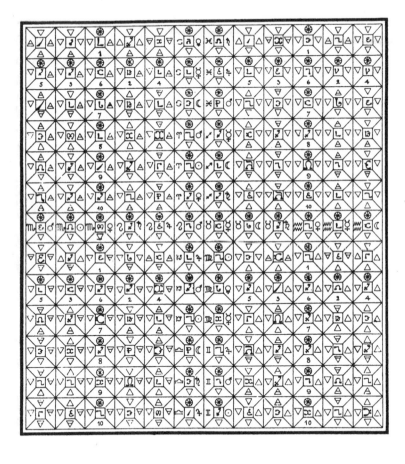

The Great Watch-Tower of the West
Attributed to Water
Plate V

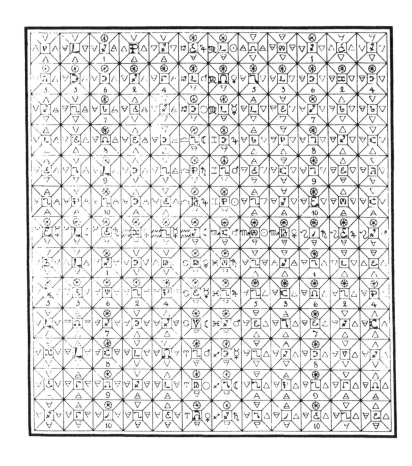

The Great Watch-Tower of the North
Attributed to Earth
Plate VI

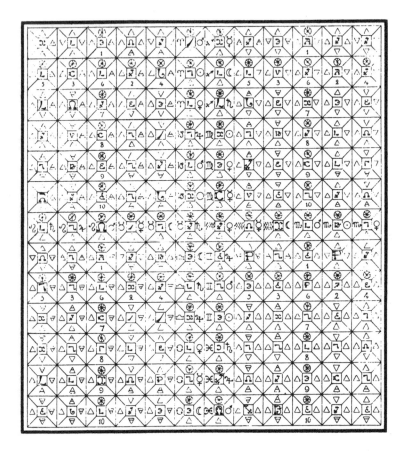

The Great Watch-Tower of the South
Attributed to Fire
Plate VII

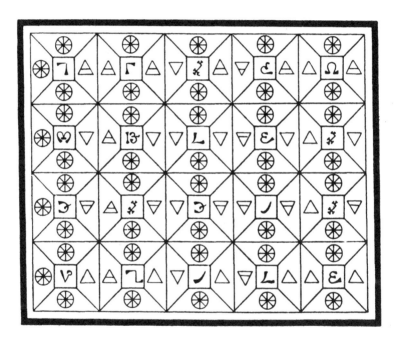

The Black Cross
Or Table of Union
Attributed to Spirit
Plate VIII

3. The 3 lines of the central cross of Father, Son, and Holy Ghost give the names of 6 seniors. (Thus the 4 tablets hold 24 "elders," as stated in the Apocalypse.) They are drawn of seven letters, each from the centre to the sides of the tablet.

$$\left.\begin{array}{l} \text{SAIINOV} \\ \text{SOAIZNT} \end{array}\right\} \text{Linea Patris}$$

$$\left.\begin{array}{l} \text{LAOAZRP} \\ \text{LIGDISA} \end{array}\right\} \text{Linea Filii}$$

$$\left.\begin{array}{l} \text{SLGAIOL} \\ \text{LSRAHPM} \end{array}\right\} \text{Linea S.S.}$$

These three sets of names rule the whole tablet, and must be invoked before specializing in the lesser angles of the sub-elements.

4. The Calvary Crosses.

The name upon the cross read vertically is the name which calls forth the powers of the lesser angle.

NELAPR (water of water)
OLGOTA (air of water)
MALADI (earth of water)
IAAASD (fire of water)

The name read horizontally on the cross is that which compels the evoked force to obedience.

OMEBB (water of water)
AALCO (air of water)
OCAAD (earth of water)
ATAPA (fire of water)

5. Above the bar of the Calvary Cross remain in each case four squares. These are allotted to the Kerubim, who must next be invoked. They are:

TDIM
DIMT
IMTD
MTDI

being metatheses of these four letters. The initial determines the file governed; *e.g.*, TDIM governs the file
which reads T(o)ILVR. These angels are most mighty
and benevolent. They are ruled by names of God formed
by prefixing the appropriate letter from the "black cross"
to their own names.

6. Beneath the bar of the Calvary Cross remain 16
squares not yet accounted for. Here, beneath the pres-
idency of the Kerubim, rule four mighty and benevolent
angels—

> INGM
> LAOC
> VSSN
> RVOI

7. Triliteral names of demons or elementals are to be
formed from these 16 squares, uniting the two letters on
either side of the upright of the cross with a letter
chosen from the Central Tablet or black cross in
accordance with rules which will be given in their due
place. Thus:

> GM
> IN
> OC
> LA

et cetera, form bases for these triliteral names.

The following rules explain how the sides of the pyramids of which the squares are formed are attributed to the
Sephiroth, Planets, Elements, and Zodiacal signs.

1. Great Central Cross. This has 36 squares, for the
decanates of the Zodiac.

On the left side of the Pyramid, Linea Patris has the
Cardinal signs, the sign of the Element itself at the top, in

the order of Tetragrammaton (Fire, Water, Air, Earth) going upwards.

Linea Filii has the Common signs in the same order.

Linea S.S. has the Kerubic signs, that of the element on the left, in the same order, right to left.

But the order of the decans in each sign is reverse, and thus the planets which fill the right-hand side of the Pyramids go in the first two cases downwards, and in the third from left to right.

The upper sides of the Pyramids are all attributed to the Element of Spirit, the lower sides to the Element of the Tablet.

Each square is also referred to the small card of the Tarot which corresponds to the Decan (see 777).

2. Calvary Crosses.

Each has 10 squares.

The upper sides of the Pyramids are uniformly given to Spirit, the lower sides to the Sephiroth, in the order shewn. The left-hand sides are attributed to the element of the Tablet, the right-hand sides to the sub-element of the lesser angle.

3. Kerubic Squares.

The upper sides pertain to the element of the Tablet, the lower sides to the sub-element. Right and left-hand sides in this case correspond, according to a somewhat complex rule which it is unnecessary to give here. The attributions to the Court Cards of the Tarot naturally follow.

4. Lesser Squares.

The upper side of each pyramid is governed by the Kerub standing on the pile above it. The lower side is governed by the Kerub also, but in order descending as they are from right to left above. (See angle of Air of Water; the Kerubs go Earth, Fire, Water, Air [from the square marked D, the fifth from the left in the top rank of the Tablet], and downward the lower sides of the squares marked O, D, E, Z go Earth, Fire, Water, Air.)

The left-hand side refers to the element of the Tablet, the right-hand side to the sub-element of the lesser angle.

5. The Black Cross of Central Tablet.

The upper and lower sides are equally attributed to Spirit.

The left-hand sides to the element of the file, in this order from left to right: Spirit, Air, Water, Earth, Fire.

The right-hand sides to the element of the rank in this order: Air, Water, Earth, Fire.

IV

Follows Plate IX, the Alphabet in which all this is written. It is the Alphabet of the Angelic Language. The invocations which we possess in that tongue follow in their due place.

(It is called also Enochian, as these angels claimed to be those which conversed with the "patriarch Enoch" of Jewish fable.)

V

The Thirty Aethyrs or Aires and their divisions and angels are as follows (We omit for the present consideration of the parts of the earth to which they are stated to correspond, and the question of the attributions to the cardinal points and the Tribes of Israel. These are duly tabulated in Dee's *Liber Scientiae, Auxilii, et Victoriae Terrestris*):

Name of Aire	Names of Governors	Numbers of Servitors	In All
1. LIL	OCCODON	7209	
	PASCOMB	2360	14,931
	VALGARS	5362	

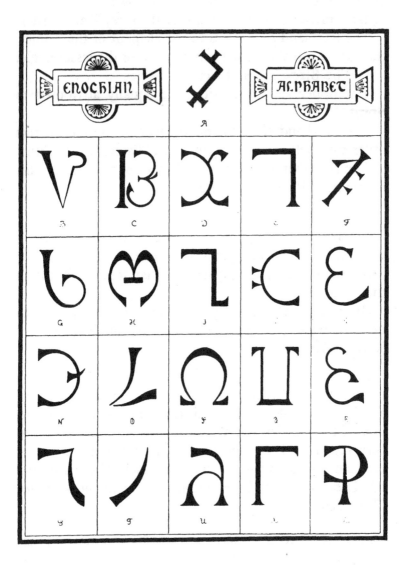

The Enochian Alphabet
Plate IX

Name of Aire	Names of Governor	Numbers of Servitors	In All
2. ARN	DOAGNIS	3636	
	PACASNA	2362	15,960
	DIALIVA	8962	
3. ZOM	SAMAPHA	4400	
	VIROOLI	3660	17,296
	ANDISPI	9236	
4. PAZ	THOTANF	2360	
	AXZIARG	3000	11,660
	POTHNIR	6300	
5. LIT	LAZDIXI	8630	
	NOCAMAL	2306	16,736
	TIARPAX	5802	
6. MAZ	SAXTOMP	3620	
	VAVAAMP	9200	20,040
	ZIRZIRD	7220	
7. DEO	OBMACAS	6363	
	GENADOL	7706	20,389
	ASPIAON	6320	
8. ZID	ZAMFRES	4362	
	TODNAON	7236	13,900
	PRISTAC	2302	
9. ZIP	ODDIORG	9996	
	CRALPIR	3620	17,846
	DOANZIN	4230	
10. ZAX	LEXARPH	8880	
	COMANAN	1230	11,727
	TABITOM	1617	

(Note that these 3 names come from the black cross, with the addition of an L. This L is one of the 8 reversed letters in the four watchtowers, the other seven forming the word PARAOAN, *q.v. infra.*)

Name of Aire	Names of Governors	Numbers of Servitors	In All
11. ICH	MOLPAND	3472	
	VANARDA	7236	15,942
	PONODOL	5234	
12. LOE	TAPAMAL	2658	
	GEDOONS	7772	13,821
	AMBRIAL	3391	
13. ZIM	GECAOND	8111	
	LAPARIN	3360	15,684
	DOCEPAX	4213	
14. VTA	TEDOOND	2673	
	VIVIPOS	9236	20,139
	OOANAMB	8230	
15. OXO	TAHANDO	1367	
	NOCIABI	1367	4620
	TASTOXO	1886	
16. LEA	COCARPT	9920	
	LANACON	9230	28,390
	SOCHIAL	9240	
17. TAN	SIGMORF	7623	
	AYDROPT	7132	17,389
	TOCARZI	2634	
18. ZEN	NABAOMI	2346	
	ZAFASAI	7689	19,311
	YALPAMB	9276	
19. POP	TORZOXI	6236	
	ABAIOND	6732	15,356
	OMAGRAP	2388	
20. KHR	ZILDRON	3626	
	PARZIBA	7629	14,889
	TOTOCAN	3634	
21. ASP	CHIRSPA	5536	
	TOANTOM	5635	16,929
	VIXPALG	5658	

Name of Aire	Names of Governors	Numbers of Servitors	In All
22. LIN	OZIDAIA	2232	
	PARAOAN	2326	6925
	CALZIRG	2367	
23. TOR	RONOAMB	7320	
	ONIZIMP	7262	21,915
	ZAXANIN	7333	
24. NIA	ORCAMIR	8200	
	CHIALPS	8360	24,796
	SOAGEEL	8236	
25. VTI	MIRZIND	5632	
	OBUAORS	6333	18,201
	RANGLAM	6236	
26. DES	POPHAND	9232	
	NIGRANA	3620	18,489
	BAZCHIM	5637	
27. ZAA	SAZIAMI	7220	
	MATHVLA	7560	22,043
	ORPAMB	7263	
28. BAG	LABNIXP	2360	
	FOCISNI	7236	18,066
	OXLOPAR	8200	
29. RII	VASTRIM	9632	
	ODRAXTI	4236	21,503
	GOMZIAM	7635	
30. TEX	TAONGLA	4632	
	GEMNIMB	9636	
	ADVORPT	7632	27,532
	DOZINAL	5632	

Plate X shows us the names of these governors in the four Watch-Towers. Compare with Plate III.

Note that the sigil of each Governor is unique; the four sigils at the corners of Plate X without the great square are those of the four great Elemental Kings:

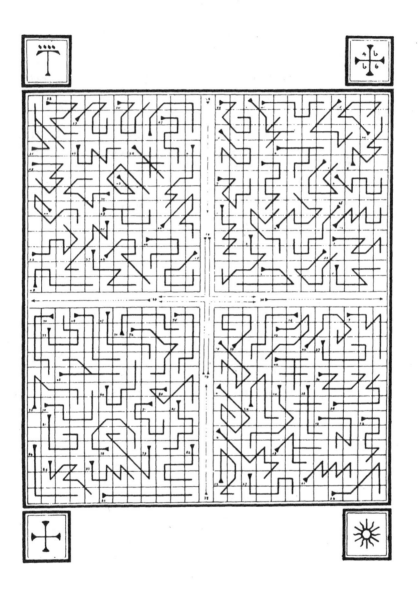

The Governors of the
Four Watch-Towers
Plate X

Air	Tahaoeloj
Water	Thahebyobeeatan
Earth	Thahaaotahe
Fire	Ohooohaatan

PART II
THE FORTY-EIGHT CALLS
OR KEYS

These are Most Solemn Invocations. Use these only after other invocations. Key tablet hath 6 calls, 1 above other 5.

1: Governs generally as a whole the tablet of Union. Use it *first* in all invocations of Angels of that tablet, but not at all with other 4 tablets.

2: Used as an invocation of Angels e h n b representing governance of Spirit in the tablet of Union: also precedes, *in the second place,* all invocations of Key tablet Angels. Not used in invocations of 4 other tablets.

3, 4, 5, 6: Used in invocations of Angels of Tablet of Union, *also* of angels of 4 terrestrial tablets, thus—

3: Used to invoke Angels of the letters of the line e x a r p.

For those of Tablet ORO as a whole and for the lesser angle of this tablet, which is that of the element itself, viz. i d o i g o. So for others—

The remaining 12 Keys refer to the remaining lesser angles of the tablets, the order of the elements being Air, Water, Earth, Fire.

Pronounce Elemental language (also called Angelic or Enochian) by inserting the next following Hebrew vowel between consonants, *e.g.,* e after b (bEth), i after g (gImel), a after d, etc.

THE OPENING OF THE PORTAL
OF THE VAULT
OF THE ADEPTS

ה .כ .ר .פ PAROKETH, the Veil of the Sanctuary.

The Sign of the Rending of the Veil.
The Sign of the Closing of the Veil.
[Give these.]
Make the Invoking Pentagrams of Spirit.
In the number 21, in the grand word אהיה;
In the Name יהשוה, in the Pass Word I.N.R.I.,

O Spirits of the Tablet of Spirit,
Ye, ye, I invoke!
The sign of Osiris slain!
The sign of the Mourning of Isis!
The sign of Apophis and Typhon!
The sign of Osiris Risen!
L. V. X., Lux. The Light of the Cross.
[Give these.]
In the name of I H V H A L V H V D O T h, I declare that the Spirits of Spirit have been duly invoked.

The Knock: 1–4444.

THE FIRST KEY[1]

Ol sonuf vaoresaji, gohu IAD Balata, elanusaha caelazod: sobrazod-ol Roray i ta nazodapesad, Giraa ta maelpereji, das hoel-qo qaa notahoa zodimezod, od comemahe ta nobeloha zodien; soba tahil ginonupe pereje aladi, das vaurebes obolehe giresam. Casarem ohorela caba Pire: das zodonurenusagi cab: erem Iadanahe. Pilahe farezodem zodenurezoda adana gono Iadapiel das home-tohe: soba ipame lu ipamis: das sobolo vepe zodomeda poamal, od bogira aai ta piape Piamoel od Vaoan![2] Zodacare, eca, od zodameranu! odo cicale Qaa; zodoreje, lape zodiredo Noco Mada, Hoathahe I A I D A!

1. Collation of the various MSS. of these calls has not done away with Various Readings; and there is not enough of the language extant to enable a settlement on general principles.—Ed.
2. Read here Vooan in invocations of the Fallen Spirits.

(86 words in this Enochian Call.)
(Invokes the whole Tablet of Spirit.)

THE FIRST KEY

I reign over ye, saith the God of Justice, in power exalted above the Firmament of Wrath, in whose hands the Sun is as a sword, and the Moon as a through thrusting Fire: who measureth your Garments in the midst of my Vestures, and trussed you together as the palms of my hands. Whose seats I garnished with the Fire of Gathering, and beautified your garments with admiration. To whom I made a law to govern the Holy Ones, and delivered ye a Rod, with the Ark of Knowledge. Moreover you lifted up your voices and sware obedience and faith to Him that liveth and triumpheth: whose beginning is not, nor end cannot be: which shineth as a flame in the midst of your palaces, and reigneth amongst you as the balance of righteousness and truth!

Move therefore, and shew yourselves! Open the mysteries of your creation! Be friendly unto me, for I am the Servant of the same your God: the true worshipper of the Highest!

(169 words in this English Call.)

THE SECOND KEY

Adagita vau-pa-ahe zodonugonu fa-a-ipe salada! Vi-i-vau el! Sobame ial-pereji i-zoda-zodazod pi-adapehe casarema aberameji ta ta-labo paracaleda qo-ta lores-el-qo turebesa ooge balatohe! Giui cahisa lusada oreri od micalapape cahisa bia ozodonugonu! Iape noanu tarofe coresa tage o-quo maninu IA-I-DON. Torezodu! gohe-el, zodacare eca ca-no-quoda! zodameranu micalazodo od ozodazodame vaurelar; Iape zodir IOIAD!

THE SECOND KEY

Can the Wings of the Winds understand your voices of Wonder? O you! the second of the First! whom the burning flames have framed in the depth of my Jaws! Whom I have prepared as cups for a wedding, or as the flowers in their beauty for the chamber of Righteousness! Stronger are your feet than the barren stone: and mightier are your voices than the manifold winds! For you are become a building such as is not, save in the Mind of the All-Powerful.

Arise, saith the First: Move therefore unto his servants! Shew yourselves in power, and make me a strong Seer-of-things: for I am of Him that liveth for ever!

(Invokes: The File of Spirit in the Tablet of Spirit.

> E —the Root of the Powers of Air.
> H—the Root of the Powers of Water.
> N—the Root of the Powers of Earth.
> B —the Root of the Powers of Fire.
> The Four Aces.)

THE OPENING OF THE TEMPLE
IN THE GRADE OF $2° = 9^{\square}$

Give the Sign of Shu.

[Knock.] Let us adore the Lord and King of Air!

Shaddai El Chai! Almighty and ever-living One, be Thy Name ever magnified in the Life of All. [Sign of Shu.] Amen!

[Make the Invoking Penta- AHIH
   gram of Spirit Active   AGLA
   in these names: EXARP]

[Make the Invoking Penta- IHVH
   gram of Air in these   ShDI AL ChI]
   names:

And Elohim said: Let us make Adam in our own image, after our likeness, and let them have dominion over the fowls of the air.

In the Names of IHVH and of ShDI AL ChI, Spirits of Air, adore your Creator!

[With air-dagger (or other suitable weapon) make the sign of Aquarius.] In the name of RPAL and in the Sign of the Man, Spirits of Air, adore your Creator!

[Make the Cross.] In the Names and Letters of the Great Eastern Quadrangle, Spirits of Air, adore your Creator!

[Hold dagger aloft.] In the Three great Secret Names of God, ORO IBAH AOZPI that are borne upon the Banners of the East, Spirits of Air, adore your Creator!

[Again elevate dagger.] In the Name of BATAIVAH, great King of the East, Spirits of Air, adore your Creator!

In the Name of SHADDAI AL CHAI, I declare that the Spirits of Air have been duly invoked.

The Knock: 333—333—333.

THE THIRD KEY

Micama! goho Pe-IAD! zodir com-selahe azodien biabe os-lon-dohe. Norezoda cahisa otahila Gigipahe; vaunud-el-cahisa ta-pu-ime qo-mos-pelehe telocahe; qui-i-inu toltoregi cahisa i cahisaji em ozodien; dasata beregida od torezodul! Ili e-Ol balazodareji, od aala tahilanu-os netaabe: daluga vaomesareji elonusa cape-mi-ali vaoresa *cala* homila; cocasabe fafenu izodizodope, od miinoagi de ginetaabe: vaunu na-na-e-el: panupire malapireji caosaji. Pilada noanu vaunalahe balata od-vaoan. Do-o-i-ape mada: goholore, gohus, amiranu! Micama! Yehusozod ca-ca-com, od do-o-a-inu noari micaolazoda a-ai-om. Casarameji gohia: Zodacare! Vaunigilaji! od im-ua-mar pugo pelapeli Ananael Qo-a-an.

(80 words in this Enochian Call.)

THE THIRD KEY

Behold! saith your God! I am a circle on whose hands stand Twelve Kingdoms. Six are the seats of living breath: the rest are as sharp Sickles, or the Horns of Death. Wherein the creatures of Earth are and are not, except (in) mine own hands; which sleep and shall rise!

In the First I made ye stewards, and placed ye in twelve seats of government: giving unto every one of you power successively over the 456 true ages of time: to the intent that from the highest vessels and the corners of your governments you might work my Power, pouring down the fires of life and increase continually on the earth. Thus you are become the skirts of Justice and Truth.

In the name of the same your God, lift up, I say, yourselves!

Behold! His mercies flourish, and (His) Name is become mighty among us. In whom we say: Move! Descend! and apply yourselves unto us as unto the partakers of His Secret Wisdom in your Creation.

(167 words in this English Call.)

[Invokes: Exarp; the whole Tablet of Air.
The angle of $\triangle$ of $\triangle$.
The Prince of the Chariot of the Winds.]

THE OPENING OF THE TEMPLE
IN THE GRADE OF $3° = 8^{\square}$

Give the Sign of Auramoth.

[Knock.] Let us adore the Lord and King of Water! Elohim Tzabaoth! Elohim of Hosts!

Glory be to the Ruach Elohim which moved upon the Face of the Waters of Creation!

AMEN!

[Make the Invoking Pentagram of Spirit Passive and pronounce these names: } AHIH AGLA HCOMA]

[Make the Invoking Pentagram of Water and pronounce: } A L ALHIM TzBAVTh]

And Elohim said: Let us make Adam in Our image; and let them have dominion over the Fish of the Sea! In the Name of A L, Strong and Powerful, and in the name of ALHIM TzBAVTh, Spirits of Water, adore your Creator!

[Make Sigil of Eagle with cup.] In the name of GBRIAL and in the sign of the Eagle, Spirits of Water, adore your Creator!

[Make cross with cup.] In all the Names and Letters of the Great Quadrangle of the West, Spirits of Water, adore your Creator!

[Elevate cup.] In the three great Secret Names of God MPH ARSL GAIOL that are borne upon the Banners of the West, Spirits of Water, adore your Creator!

[Elevate cup.] In the Name of RAAGIOSEL, great King of the West, Spirits of Water, adore your Creator!

In the name of Elohim Tzabaoth, I declare that the Spirits of Water have been duly invoked.

The Knock: 1—333—1—333.

THE FOURTH KEY

Otahil elasadi babaje, od dorepaha gohol: gi-cahisaje auauago coremepe *peda,* dasonuf vi-vau-di-vau? Casaremi oeli *meapeme* sobame agi coremepo carep-el: casaremeji caro-o-dazodi cahisa od vaugeji; dasata ca-pi-mali cahisa ca-pi-ma-on: od elonusahinu cahisa ta el-o *calaa.* Tore-

zodu nor-quasahi od fe-caosaga: Bagile zodir e-na-IAD:
das iod apila! Do-o-a-ipe quo-A-AL, zodacare! Zodameranu obelisonugi resat-el aaf nor-mo-lapi!

THE FOURTH KEY

I have set my feet in the South, and have looked about
me, saying: are not the thunders of increase numbered 33,
which reign in the second Angle?

Under whom I have placed 9639: whom none hath yet
numbered, but One; in whom the Second Beginnings of
Things are and wax strong, which also successively are the
Numbers of Time: and their powers are as the first 456.

Arise! you sons of Pleasure! and visit the earth: for I
am the Lord your God; which is and liveth (for ever)!
In the name of the Creator, move! and shew yourselves as
pleasant deliverers, that you may praise Him among the
sons of men!

[Invokes: hcoma; the whole tablet of Water.
The Angle of ▽ of △.
The Queen of the Thrones of Water.]

THE OPENING OF THE TEMPLE
IN THE GRADE OF $1° = 10^{\square}$

Give the Sign of the God SET fighting.

Purify with Fire and Water, and announce "The
Temple is cleansed."

[Knock.] Let us adore the Lord and King of Earth!

Adonai ha Aretz, Adonai Melekh, unto Thee be the
Kingdom, the Sceptre, and the Splendour: Malkuth,
Geburah, Gedulah, The Rose of Sharon and the Lily of
the Valley, Amen!

[Sprinkle Salt before Earth tablet.] Let the Earth adore
Adonai!

[Make the Invoking Hexagram of Saturn.]

[Make the Invoking Pentagram of
Spirit Passive, and pronounce
these Names: } AHIH AGLA NANTA]

[Make the Invoking Pentagram of
Earth, and pronounce this
Name: } ADNI MLK]

And Elohim said: Let us make Man in Our own image; and let them have dominion over the Fish of the Sea and over the Fowl of the Air; and over every creeping thing that creepeth upon the Earth. And the Elohim created ATh-h-ADAM: in the image of the Elohim created They them; male and female created They them. In the Name of ADNI MLK, and of the Bride and Queen of the Kingdom; Spirits of Earth, adore your Creator!

[Make the Sign of Taurus.] In the Name of AVRIAL, great archangel of Earth, Spirits of Earth, adore your Creator!

[Make the Cross.] In the Names and Letters of the Great Northern Quadrangle, Spirits of Earth, adore your Creator!

[Sprinkle water before Earth Tablet.] In the three great secret Names of God, MOR, DIAL, HCTGA, that are borne upon the Banners of the North, Spirits of Earth, adore your Creator!

[Cense the Tablet.] In the name of IC-ZOD-HEH-CA great king of the North, Spirits of Earth, adore your Creator!

In the Name of Adonai Ha-Aretz, I declare that the Spirits of Earth have been duly invoked.

The Knock: 4444—333—22—1.

THE FIFTH KEY

Sapahe zodimii du-i-be, od noasa ta qu-a-nis, adaro-cahe dorepehal caosagi od faonutas peripeso ta-be-liore.

Casareme A-me-ipezodi na-zodaretahe *afa*; od dalugare
zodizodope zodelida caosaji tol-toregi; od zod-cahisa
esiasacahe El ta-vi-vau; od iao-d tahilada das hubare
pe-o-al; soba coremefa cahisa ta Ela Vaulasa od Quo-Co-
Casabe. Eca niisa od darebesa quo-a-asa: fetahe-ar-ezodi
od beliora: ia-ial eda-nasa cicalesa; bagile Ge-iad I-el!

THE FIFTH KEY

The mighty sounds have entered into the third angle,
and are become as olives in the Olive Mount; looking
with gladness upon the earth, and dwelling in the brightness of the Heavens as continual Comforters.

Unto whom I fastened 19 Pillars of Gladness, and gave
them vessels to water the earth with her creatures; and
they are the brothers of the First and Second, and the
beginning of their own seats, which are garnished with
69,636 ever-burning lamps: whose numbers are as the
First, the Ends, and the Contents of Time.

Therefore come ye and obey your creation: visit us in
peace and comfort: conclude us receivers of your mysteries: for why? Our Lord and Master is the All-One!

[Invokes: Nanta; the whole tablet of Earth.
The angle of ▽ of ▽ .
The Princess of the Echoing Hills,
the Rose of the Palace of Earth.]

THE OPENING OF THE TEMPLE
IN THE GRADE OF $4°=7^{\square}$

Give the sign of Thoum-aesh-neith.

[Knock.] Let us adore the Lord and King of Fire!

Tetragrammaton Tzabaoth! Blessed be Thou! The
Leader of Armies is Thy Name! AMEN!

[Make the Invoking Pentagram ⎫ AHIH
of Spirit Active, and pronounce ⎬ AGLA
these Names: ⎭ BITOM]

[Make the Invoking Pentagram of) ALHIM
Fire, and pronounce: } IHVH
) TzBAVTh]

[Make the sign of Leo with censer (or other suitable weapon).] In the name of MIKAL, archangel of Fire, Spirits of Fire, adore your Creator!

[Make the Cross.] In the Names and Letters of the Great Southern Quadrangle, Spirits of Fire, adore your Creator!

[Elevate censer.] In the three Secret names of God, OIP TEAA PDOCE, that are borne upon the banners of the South, Spir ts of Fire, adore your Creator!

[Lower and lift censer.] In the Name of EDELPERNA, great King of the South, Spirits of Fire, adore your Creator!

In the Name of IHVH TzBAVTh, I declare that the Spirits of Fire have been duly invoked.

The Knock: 333—1—333.

THE SIXTH KEY

Gahe sa-div cahisa *em*, micalazoda Pil-zodinu, sobam El haraji mir babalonu od obeloce samevelaji, dalagare malapereji ar-caosaji od *acame* canale, sobola zodare fa-beliareda caosaji od cahisa aneta-na miame ta Viv od Da. Daresare Sol-petahe-bienu Be-ri-ta od zodacame ji-mi-calazodo: sob-ha-atahe tarianu luia-he od ecarinu MADA Qu-a-a-on!

THE SIXTH KEY

The Spirits of the fourth angle are Nine Mighty in the Firmament of Waters: whom the First hath planted, a torment to the wicked and a garland to the righteous: giving unto them fiery darts to vanne the earth, and 7699 continual workmen, whose courses visit with comfort the earth; and are in government and continuance as the Second and the Third—

Therefore hearken unto my voice! I have talked of you, and I move you in power and presence, whose works shall be a song of honour, and the praise of your God in your Creation!

[Invokes: bitom; the whole tablet of Fire.
The Angle of △ of △ .
The Lord of the Flame and the Lightning, the King of the Spirits of Fire.]

THE SEVENTH KEY

Ra-asa isalamanu para-di-zoda oe-cari-mi aao iala-pire-gahe Qui-inu. Enai butamonu od inoasa *ni* pa-ra-diala. Casaremeji ujeare cahirelanu, od zodonace lucifatianu, caresa ta vavale-zodirenu tol-hami. Soba lonudohe od nuame cahisa ta Da o Desa vo-ma-dea od pi-beliare itahila rita od miame ca-ni-quola rita! Zodacare! Zodameranu! Iecarimi Quo-a-dahe od I-mica-ol-zododa aaiome. Bajirele papenore idalugama elonusahi—od umapelifa vau-ge-ji Bijil—IAD!

THE SEVENTH KEY

The East is a house of Virgins singing praises among the flames of first glory wherein the Lord hath opened his mouth; and they are become 28 living dwellings in whom the strength of man rejoiceth; and they are apparelled with ornaments of brightness, such as work wonders on all creatures. Whose kingdoms and continuance are as the Third and Fourth, strong towers and places of comfort, the Seats of Mercy and Continuance. O ye Servants of Mercy, Move! Appear! Sing praises unto the Creator; and be mighty amongst us. For that to this remembrance is given power, and our strength waxeth strong in our Comforter!

[Invokes the Angle of ▽ of △ in the tablet of △ .
The Queen of the Thrones of Air.]

THE EIGHTH KEY

Bazodemelo i ta pi-ripesonu olanu Na-zodavabebe *ox*.
Casaremeji varanu cahisa vaugeji asa berameji balatoha:
goho IAD. Soba miame tarianu ta lolacis Abaivoninu od
azodiajiere riore. Irejila cahisa da das pa-aox busada
Caosago, das cahisa od ipuranu telocahe cacureji o-
isalamahe lonucaho od Vovina carebafe? NIISO! bagile
avavago gohon. NIISO! bagile momao siaionu, od
mabezoda IAD oi asa-momare poilape. NIIASA! Zodameranu ciaosi caosago od belioresa od coresi ta a beramiji.

THE EIGHTH KEY

The Midday, the first is as the third Heaven made of 26
Hyacinthine Pillars, in whom the Elders are become
strong, which I have prepared for mine own Righteousness, saith the Lord: whose long continuance shall be as
bucklers to the Stooping Dragon, and like unto the harvest
of a Widow. How many are there which remain in the
Glory of the Earth, which are, and shall not see Death
until the House fall and the Dragon sink? Come away!
for the Thunders (of increase) have spoken. Come away!
for the Crowns of the Temple and the Robe of Him that is,
was, and shall be, crowned, are divided! Come forth!
Appear! to the terror of the Earth, and to our comfort,
and to the comfort of such as are prepared.
The Angle of ▽ of △ in the tablet of △ .
The Princess of the Rushing Winds,
the Lotus of the Palace of Air.

THE NINTH KEY

Micaoli beranusaji perejela napeta ialapore, das
barinu efafaje *Pe* vaunupeho olani od obezoda, soba-ca

upaahe cahisa tatanu od tarananu balie, alare busada
so-bolunu od cahisa hoel-qo ca-no-quodi *cial*. Vaunesa
aladonu mom caosago ta iasa olalore ginai limelala.
Amema cahisa sobra madarida zod cahisa! Ooa moanu
cahisa avini darilapi caosajinu: od butamoni pareme
zodumebi canilu. Dazodisa etahamezoda cahisa dao, od
mireka ozodola cahisa pidiai Colalala. Ul ci ninu a sobame
ucime. Bajile? IAD BALATOHE cahirelanu pare!
NIISO! od upe ofafafe; bajile a-cocasahe icoresaka a uniji
beliore.

THE NINTH KEY

A mighty guard of Fire with two-edged swords flaming
(which have eight Vials of wrath for two times and a half,
whose wings are of wormwood and of the marrow of salt),
have set their feet in the West, and are measured with their
9996 ministers. These gather up the moss of the Earth
as the rich man doth his Treasure. Cursed are they whose
iniquities they are! In their eyes are mill-stones greater
than the earth, and from their mouths run seas of blood.
Their heads are covered with diamonds, and upon their
heads are marble stones.[3] Happy is he on whom they
frown not. For why? The Lord of Righteousness rejoiceth
in them! Come away, and not your Vials: for that the
time is such as requireth Comfort.

The Angle of △ of △ in the tablet of △ .
The Lord of the Winds and Breezes;
the King of the Spirits of Air.

THE TENTH KEY

Coraxo cahisa coremepe, od belanusa Lucala azodia-
zodore paebe Soba iisononu cahisa uirequo *ope* copehanu
od racalire maasi bajile caosagi; das yalaponu dosiji od
basajime; od ox ex dazodisa siatarisa od salaberoxa

3. v.l. "Upon their hands are marble sleeves."

cynuxire faboanu. Vaunala cahisa conusata das *daox* cocasa ol Oanio yore vohima ol jizodyazoda od eoresa cocasaji pelosi molui das pajeipe, laraji same darolanu matorebe cocasaji emena. El pataralaxa yolaci matabe nomiji mononusa olora jinayo anujelareda. Ohyo! ohyo! ohyo! ohyo! ohyo! ohyo! noibe Ohyo! caosagonu! Bajile madarida i zodirope cahiso darisapa! NIISO! caripe ipe nidali!

THE TENTH KEY

The Thunders of Judgment and Wrath are numbered and are harboured in the North, in the likeness of an Oak whose branches are 22 nests of lamentation and weeping laid up for the earth: which burn night and day, and vomit out the heads of scorpions and live Sulphur mingled with poison. These be the thunders that, 5678 times in the twenty-fourth part of a moment, roar with a hundred mighty earthquakes and a thousand times as many surges, which rest not, neither know any[4] time here. One rock bringeth forth a thousand, even as the heart of man doth his thoughts. Woe! Woe! Woe! Woe! Woe! Woe! Yea, Woe be to the Earth, for her iniquity is, was, and shall be great. Come away! but not your mighty sounds!

The Angle of △ of ▽ in the tablet of ▽ .

The Prince of the Chariot of the Waters.

THE ELEVENTH KEY

Oxiayala holado, od zodirome *O* coraxo das zodiladare raasyo. Od vabezodire cameliaxa od bahala: NIISO! salamanu telocahe! Casaremanu hoel-qo, od ti ta zod cahisa soba coremefa i ga. NIISA! bagile aberameji nonucape. Zodacare eca od Zodameranu! odo cicale Qaa! Zodoreje, lape zodiredo Noco Mada, hoathahe I A I D A !

4. v.l. "Any echoing time between."

THE ELEVENTH KEY

The mighty Seat groaned, and there were five Thunders that flew into the East. And the Eagle spake and cried aloud: Come away from the House of Death! And they gathered themselves together and became (those) of whom it is measured, and it is as They are, whose number is 31. Come away! For I have prepared (a place) for you. Move therefore, and shew yourselves! Unveil the mysteries of your Creation. Be friendly unto me, for I am the servant of the same your God: the true worshipper of the Highest.

The Angle of ▽ of ▽ , in the tablet of ▽ .
The Princess of the Waters,
the Lotus of the Palace of the Floods.

THE TWELFTH KEY

Nonuci dasonuf Babaje od cahisa *ob* hubaio tibibipe: alalare ataraahe od ef! Darix fafenu *mianu* ar Enayo ovof! Soba dooainu aai i VONUPEHE. Zodacare, gohusa, od Zodameranu. Odo cicale Qaa! Zodoreje, lape zodiredo Noco Mada, hoathahe I A I D A!

THE TWELFTH KEY

O ye that range in the South and are the 28 Lanterns of Sorrow, bind up your girdles and visit us! bring down your train 3663 (servitors), that the Lord may be magnified, whose name amongst ye is Wrath. Move! I say, and shew yourselves! Unveil the mysteries of your Creation. Be friendly unto me, for I am the servant of the same your God, the true worshipper of the Highest.

The Angle of △ of ▽ , in the tablet of ▽ .
The Lord of the Waves and the Waters,
the King of the Hosts of the Sea.

THE THIRTEENTH KEY

Napeai Babajehe das berinu *vax* ooaona larinuji vonupehe doalime: conisa olalogi oresaha das cahisa afefa. Micama isaro Mada od Lonu-sahi-toxa, das ivaumeda aai Jirosabe. Zodacare od Zodameranu. Odo cicale Qaa! Zodoreje, lape zodiredo Noco Mada, hoathahe I A I D A.

THE THIRTEENTH KEY

O ye Swords of the South, which have 42 eyes to stir up the wrath of Sin: making men drunken which are empty: Behold the Promise of God, and His Power, which is called amongst ye a bitter sting! Move and Appear! unveil the mysteries of your Creation, for I am the servant of the same your God, the true worshipper of the Highest.
The Angle of △ of ▽ , in the tablet of ▽ .
The Prince of the Chariot of Earth.

THE FOURTEENTH KEY

Noroni bajihie pasahasa Oiada! das tarinuta mireca *ol* tahila dodasa tolahame caosago *h*omida: das berinu orocahe *quare*: Micama! Bial' Oiad; aisaro toxa das ivame aai Balatima. Zodacare od Zodameranu! Odo cicale Qaa! Zodoreje, lape zodiredo Noco Mada, hoathahe I A I D A.

THE FOURTEENTH KEY

O ye Sons of Fury, the Daughters of the Just One! that sit upon 24 seats, vexing all creatures of the Earth with age, that have 1636 under ye. Behold! The voice of God; the promise of Him who is called amongst ye Fury or Extreme Justice. Move and shew yourselves! Unveil the mysteries of your Creation; be friendly unto me, for I am the servant of the same your God: the true worshipper of the Highest!
The Angle of ▽ of ▽ , in the tablet of ▽ .
The Queen of the Thrones of Earth.

THE FIFTEENTH KEY

Ilasa! tabaanu li-El pereta, casaremanu upaahi cahisa *dareji*; das oado caosaji oresacore: das omaxa monasaci Baeouibe od emetajisa Iaiadix. Zodacare od Zodameranu! Odo cicale Qaa. Zodoreje, lape zodiredo Noco Mada, hoathahe I A I D A.

THE FIFTEENTH KEY

O thou, the Governor of the first Flame, under whose wings are 6739; that weave the Earth with dryness: that knowest the Great Name "Righteousness," and the Seal of Honour. Move and Appear! Unveil the mysteries of your creation; be friendly unto me, for I am the servant of the same your God: the true worshipper of the Highest!
The Angle of △ of ▽ , in the tablet of ▽ .
The Lord of the Wide and Fertile Land,
the King of the Spirits of Earth.

THE SIXTEENTH KEY

Ilasa viviala pereta! Salamanu balata, das acaro odazodi busada, od belioraxa balita: das inusi caosaji lusadanu *emoda*: das ome od taliobe: darilapa iehe ilasa Mada Zodilodarepe. Zodacare od Zodameranu. Odo cicale Qaa: zodoreje, lape zodiredo Noco Mada, hoathahe I A I D A.

THE SIXTEENTH KEY

O thou second Flame, the House of Justice, which hast thy beginning in glory and shalt comfort the Just: which walkest upon the Earth with 8763 feet, which understand and separate creatures! Great art thou in the God of Stretch forth and Conquer. Move and appear! Unveil the mysteries of your Creation; be friendly unto me, for I am the servant of the same your God, the true worshipper of the Highest.

The Angle of △ of △ , in the tablet of △ .
The Prince of the Chariot of Fire.

THE SEVENTEENTH KEY

Ilasa dial pereta! soba vaupaahe cahisa nanuba zodixalayo dodasihe od berinuta *faxisa* hubaro tasataxa yolasa: soba Iad *i* Vonupehe o Uonupehe: aladonu dax ila od toatare! Zodacare od Zodameranu! Odo cicale Qaa! Zodoreje, lape zodiredo Noco Mada, hoathahe I A I D A.

THE SEVENTEENTH KEY

O thou third Flame! whose wings are thorns to stir up vexation, and who hast 7336 living lamps going before Thee: whose God is "Wrath in Anger": Gird up thy loins and hearken! Move and Appear! Unveil the mysteries of your Creation; be friendly unto me, for I am the servant of the same your God, the true worshipper of the Highest.
The Angle of ▽ of △ , in the tablet of △ .
The Queen of the Thrones of Flame.

THE EIGHTEENTH KEY

Ilasa micalazoda olapireta ialpereji beliore: das odo Busadire Oiad ouoaresa caosago: casaremeji Laiada *eranu* berinutasa cafafame das ivemeda aqoso adoho Moz, od maoffasa. Bolape como belioreta pamebeta. Zodacare od Zodameranu! Odo cicale Qaa. Zodoreje, lape zodiredo Noco Mada, hoathahe I A I D A.

THE EIGHTEENTH KEY

O Thou mighty Light and burning Flame of Comfort! that unveilest the Glory of God to the centre of the Earth, in whom the 6332 secrets of Truth have their abiding, that is called in thy kingdom "Joy" and not to be measured.

Be thou a window of comfort unto me! Move and Appear! Unveil the mysteries of your Creation, be friendly unto me, for I am the servant of the same your God, the true worshipper of the highest.

The Angle of ▽ of △ , in the tablet of △ .

The Princess of the Shining Flame,
the Rose of the Palace of Fire.

MARK WELL!

These first 18 calls are in reality 19; that is, 19 in the Celestial Orders; but with us the first table hath no call, and can have no call, seeing that it is of the Godhead. Thus, then, with us hath it the number of 0, though with them that of 1. (Even as the first key of the ROTA hath the number 0.)

After this follow the calls or keys of the Thirty Aires or Aethyrs: which are in substance similar, though, in the name of the Aethyrs, diversified.

The titles of the Thirty Aethyrs whose
dominion extendeth in ever-widening circles
without and beyond
the Watch-Towers of the Universe

(The first is Outermost)

1	LIL	16	LEA
2	ARN	17	TAN
3	ZOM	18	ZEN
4	PAZ	19	POP
5	LIT	20	KHR
6	MAZ	21	ASP
7	DEO	22	LIN
8	ZID	23	TOR
9	ZIP	24	NIA
10	ZAX	25	VTI
11	ICH	26	DES

12	LOE	27	ZAA
13	ZIM	28	BAG
14	UTA	29	RII
15	OXO	30	TEX

THE CALL OR KEY OF THE THIRTY AETHYRS

Madariatza das perifa LIL[5] cahisa micaolazoda saanire caosago od fifisa balzodizodarasa Iaida. Nonuca gohulime: Micama adoianu MADA faoda beliorebe, soba ooaona cahisa luciftias peripesol, das aberaasasa nonucafe netaaibe caosaji od tilabe adapehaheta damepelozoda, tooata nonucafe jimicalazodoma larasada tofejilo marebe yareryo IDOIGO;[6] od torezodulape yaodafe gohola, Caosaga, tabaoreda saanire, od caharisateosa yorepoila tiobela busadire, tilabe noalanu paida oresaba, od dodaremeni zodayolana. Elazodape tilaba paremeji peripesatza, od ta qurelesata booapisa. Lanibame oucaho sayomepe, od caharisateosa ajitoltorenu, mireca qo tiobela lela. Tonu paomebeda dizodalamo asa pianu, od caharisateosa aji-latore-torenu paracahe a sayomepe. Coredazodizoda dodapala od fifalazoda, lasa manada, od faregita bamesa omaoasa. Conisabera od auauotza tonuji oresa; catabela noasami tabejesa leuitahemonuji. Vanucahi omepetilabe oresa! Bagile? Moooabe OL coredazodizoda. El capimao itzomatzipe, od cacocasabe gosaa. Bajilenu pii tianuta a babalanuda, od faoregita teloca uo uime. Madariiatza, torezodu!!! Oadariatza orocaha aboaperi! Tabaori periazoda aretabasa! Adarepanu coresata dobitza! Yolacame periazodi arecoazodiore, od quasabe qotinuji! Ripire paaotzata sagacore! Umela od peredazodare cacareji Aoiveae coremepeta! Torezodu! Zodacare od Zodameranu, asapeta sibesi butamona das surezodasa

---

5. Or other Aire as may be willed.
6. This name may be appropriately varied with the Aire.

Tia balatanu. Odo cicale Qaa, od Ozodazodama pelapeli
IADANAMADA!

THE CALL OR KEY OF THE
THIRTY AETHYRS

O ye Heavens which dwell in the first Aire, ye are mighty
in the parts of the Earth, and execute the Judgment of the
Highest! Unto you it is said: Behold the Face of your
God, the beginning of Comfort, whose eyes are the brightness of the Heavens, which provided you for the Government of the Earth, and her unspeakable variety, furnishing
you with a power of understanding to dispose all things
according to the Providence of Him that sitteth on the
Holy Throne, and rose up in the Beginning, saying:
The Earth, let her be governed by her parts, and let
there be Division in her, that the glory of her may be
always drunken, and vexed in itself. Her course, let it
run with the Heavens; and as an handmaid let her serve
them. One season, let it confound another, and let there
be no creature upon or within her the same. All her
members, let them differ in their qualities, and let there
be no one Creature equal with another. The reasonable
Creatures of the Earth, and Men, let them vex and weed
out one another; and their dwelling-places, let them forget
their Names. The work of man and his pomp, let them
be defaced. His buildings, let them become Caves for the
beasts of the Field! Confound her understanding with
darkness! For why? it repenteth me that I have made
Man. One while let her be known, and another while
a stranger: because she is the bed of an Harlot, and the
dwelling-place of him that is fallen.

O ye Heavens, arise! The lower heavens beneath you,
let them serve you! Govern those that govern! Cast down
such as fall. Bring forth with those that increase, and
destroy the rotten. No place let it remain in one number.

Add and diminish until the stars be numbered. Arise!
Move! and appear before the Covenant of His mouth,
which He hath sworn unto us in His Justice. Open the
Mysteries of your Creation, and make us partakers of
THE UNDEFILED KNOWLEDGE.

Finished are the Calls or Keys

The Three Mighty Names of God Almighty
coming forth from
The Thirty Aethyrs

The First Name—
L A Z o d a P e L a M e D a Z o d a Z O D a Z o d I L a-
Z o d U O L a T a Z o d a P e K A L a T a N u V a D a Z-
o d a B e R e T a

The Second Name—
I R O A I A E I I A K O I T a X E A E O H e S I O I-
I T E A A I E

The Third Name—
L a N u N u Z o d a T a Z o d O D a P e X a H E M ·
A O A N u N u P e R e P e N u R A I S A G I X a

Ended are the Forty-eight Calls or Keys

LIBER
XXX
AERVM

VEL
SAECVLI

SVB FIGVRA
CCCCXVIII

BEING OF THE ANGELS
OF THE 30 AETHYRS

THE
VISION
AND THE
VOICE

A ∴ A ∴ Publication in Class A B

Imprimatur:

D.D.S. 7° = 4° Praemonstrator
O.S.V. 6° = 5° Imperator
N.S.F. 5° = 6° Cancellarius

THE VISION
AND THE VOICE

THE CRY OF THE THIRTIETH
OR INMOST AIRE OR AETHYR
WHICH IS CALLED TEX

I am in a vast crystal cube in the form of the Great God Harpocrates. This cube is surrounded by a sphere. About me are four archangels in black robes, their wings and armour lined out in white.

In the North is a book on whose back and front are A.M.B.Z. in Enochian characters.

Within it is written:

I AM, the surrounding of the four.

Lift up your heads, O Houses of Eternity: for my Father goeth forth to judge the World. One Light, let it become a thousand, and one sword ten thousand, that no man hide him from my Father's eye in the Day of Judgment of my God. Let the Gods hide themselves: let the Angels be troubled and flee away: for the Eye of My Father is open, and the Book of the Aeons is fallen.

Arise! Arise! Arise! Let the Light of the Sight of Time be extinguished: let the Darkness cover all things: for my Father goeth forth to seek a spouse to replace her who is fallen and defiled.

Seal the book with the seals of the Stars Concealed: for

the Rivers have rushed together and the Name יהוה is broken in a thousand pieces (against the Cubic Stone).

Tremble ye, O Pillars of the Universe, for Eternity is in travail of a Terrible Child; she shall bring forth an universe of Darkness, whence shall leap forth a spark that shall put his father to flight.

The Obelisks are broken; the stars have rushed together: the Light hath plunged into the Abyss: the Heavens are mixed with Hell.

My Father shall not hear their Noise: His ears are closed: His eyes are covered with the clouds of Night.

The End! the End! the End! For the Eye of Shiva He hath opened: the Universe is naked before Him: for the Aeon of Saturn leaneth toward the Bosom of Death.

The Angel of the East hath a book of red written in letters of Blue A.B F.M.A. in Enochian. The Book grows before my eyes and filleth the Whole Heaven

Within: "It is Written, Thou shalt not tempt the Lord Thy God."

I see above the Book a multitude of white-robed Ones from whom droppeth a great rain of Blood: but above them is a Golden Sun, having an eye, whence a great Light.

I turned me to the South: and read therein:

Seal up the Book! Speak not that which thou seest and reveal it unto none: for the ear is not framed that shall hear it: nor the tongue that can speak it!

O Lord God, blessed, blessed, blessed be Thou for ever!

Thy Shadow is as great Light.

Thy Name is as the Breath of Love across all Worlds.

(A vast Svastika is shewn unto me behind the Angel with the Book.)

Rend your garments, O ye clouds! Uncover yourselves! for the Love of My Son!

Who are they that trouble thee?

Who are they that slew thee?

O Light! Come thou, who art joined with me to bruise the Dragon's head. We, who are wedded, and the Earth perceiveth it not!

O that Our Bed were seen of Men, that they might rejoice in My Fertility: that My Sister might partake of My Great Light.

O Light of God, when wilt thou find the heart of man— write not! I would not that men know the Sorrow of my Heart, Amen!

I turned me to the West, and the Archangel bore a flaming Book, on which was written AN in Enochian. Within was drawn a fiery scorpion, yet cold withal.

Until the Book of the East be opened!

Until the hour sound!

Until the Voice vibrate!

Until it pierce my Depth;

Look not on High!

Look not Beneath!

For thou wilt find a life which is as Death: or a Death which should be infinite.

For Thou art submitted to the Four: Five thou shalt find, but Seven is lone and far.

O Lord God, let Thy Spirit hither unto me!

For I am lost in the night of infinite pain: no hope: no God: no resurrection: no end: I fall: I fear.

O Saviour of the World, bruise Thou my Head with Thy foot to save the world, that once again I touch Him whom I slew, that in my death I feel the radiance and the heat of the moving of Thy Robes!

Let us alone! What have we to do with Thee, Thou Jesus of Nazareth?

Go! Go!

If I keep silence—Or if I speak each word is anguish without hope.

And I heard the Aethyr cry aloud "Return! Return! Return! For the work is ended; and the Book is shut; and let the glory be to God the Blessed for ever in the Aeons, Amen." Thus far is the voice of TEX and no more.

THE CRY OF THE 29TH AETHYR WHICH IS CALLED RII

The sky appears covered with stars of gold; the background is of green. But the impression is also of darkness.

An immense eagle-angel is before me. His wings seem to hide all the Heaven.

He cried aloud saying: The Voice of the Lord upon the Waters: the Terror of God upon Mankind. The voice of the Lord maketh the Skies to tremble: the Stars are troubled: the Aires fall. The First Voice Speaketh and saith: Cursed, cursed be the Earth, for her iniquity is great. Oh Lord! Let Thy Mercy be lost in the great Deep! Open thine eyes of Flame and Light, O God, upon the wicked! Lighten thine Eyes! The Clamour of Thy Voice, let it smite down the Mountains!

Let us not see it! Cover we our eyes, lest we see the End of Man.

Close we our ears, lest we hear the cry of Woman.

Let none speak of it: let none write it: I, I am troubled, my eyes are moist with dews of terror: surely the Bitterness of Death is past.

And I turned me to the South and lo! a great lion as wounded and perplexed.

He cried: I have conquered! Let the Sons of Earth keep silence; for my Name is become as That of Death!

When will men learn the Mysteries of Creation?

How much more those of the Dissolution (and the Pang of Fire)?

I turned me to the West and there was a great Bull; White with horns of White and Black and Gold. His mouth was scarlet and his eyes as Sapphire stones. With a great sword he shore the skies asunder, and amid the silver flashes of the steel grew lightnings and deep clouds of Indigo.

He spake: It is finished! My mother hath unveiled herself!

My sister hath violated herself! The life of things hath disclosed its Mystery.

The work of the Moon is done! Motion is ended for ever!

Clipped are the eagle's wings: but my Shoulders have not lost their strength.

I heard a Great Voice from above crying: Thou liest! For the Volatile hath indeed fixed itself; but it hath arisen above thy sight. The World is desert: but the Abodes of the House of my Father are peopled; and His Throne is crusted over with white Brilliant Stars, a lustre of bright gems.

In the North is a Man upon a Great Horse, having a Scourge and Balances in his hand (or a long spear glitters at his back or in his hand). He is clothed in black velvet and his face is stern and terrible.

He spake saying: I have judged! It is the end: the gate of the beginning. Look in the Beneath and thou shalt see a new world!

I looked and saw a great abyss and a dark funnel of whirling waters or fixed airs, wherein were cities and monsters and trees and atoms and mountains and little flames (being souls) and all the material of an universe.

And all are sucked down one by one, as necessity hath ordained. For below is a glittering jewelled globe of gold and azure, set in a World of Stars.

And there came a Voice from the Abyss, saying: "Thou seest the Current of Destiny! Canst thou change one atom in its path? I am Destiny. Dost thou think to control me? for who can move my course?"

And there falleth a thunderbolt therein: a catastrophe of explosion: and all is shattered. And I saw above me a Vast Arm reach down, dark and terrible, and a voice cried: I AM ETERNITY.

And a great mingled cry arose: "No! no! no! All is changed; all is confounded; naught is ordered: the white is stained with blood: the black is kissed of the Christ! Return! Return! It is a new chaos that thou findest here: chaos for thee: for us it is the skeleton of a New Truth!"

I said: Tell me this truth: for I have conjured ye by the Mighty Names of God, the which ye cannot but obey.

The voice said:

Light is consumed as a child in the Womb of its Mother to develop itself anew. But pain and sorrow infinite, and darkness are invoked. For this child riseth up within his Mother and doth crucify himself within her bosom. He extendeth his arms in the arms of his Mother and the Light becometh fivefold.[1]

Lux in Luce,
Christus in Cruce;
Deo Duce
Sempiterno.

And be the glory for ever and ever unto the Most High God, Amen!

Then I returned within my body, giving glory unto the Lord of Light and of the Darkness. In Saecula Saeculorum. Amen!

(On composing myself to sleep, I was shewn an extremely brilliant ק in the Character of the Passing of the River, in an egg of white light. And I take this as the best of Omens. The letter was extremely vivid and indeed apparently physical. Almost a Dhyana.)

November 17, 1900, Die.

A NOTE

Concerning the thirty Aethyrs:

The Visions of the 29th and 30th Aethyrs were given to me in Mexico in August 1900, and I am now (23. 11. 9) trying to get the rest. It is to be remarked that the last three aethyrs have ten angels attributed to them, and they therefore represent the ten Sephiroth. Yet these ten form but one, a Malkuth-pendant to the next three, and so on, each set being, as it were, absorbed in the higher. The last set consists, therefore, of the first three aethyrs with the

---

1. The LVX Cross hidden in the Svastika is probably the Arcanum here connoted. This Cross on Mars square adds to 65 Adonai, Shone, Gloried, ha-Yekal HS = keep silence. Svastika itself adds to 231 = 0 + 1 + 2 + - - - + 21, the 21 Keys. The cubical Svastika regarded as composed of this LVX Cross and the arms has a total of 78 faces—Taro and Mezla.

remaining twenty-seven as their Malkuth. And the letters of the first three aethyrs are the key-sigils of the most exalted interpretation of the Sephiroth.

I is therefore Kether;
L, Chokmah and Binah;
A, Chesed;
N, Geburah;
R, Tiphereth;
Z, Netzach;
N, Hod;
O, Jesod.

The geomantic correspondences of the Enochian alphabet form a sublime commentary.

Note that the total angels of the aethyrs are 91, the numeration of Amen.

THE CRY OF THE 28TH AETHYR
WHICH IS CALLED BAG

There cometh an Angel into the stone with opalescent shining garments like a wheel of fire on every side of him, and in his hand is a long flail of scarlet lightning; his face is black, and his eyes white without any pupil or iris. The face is very terrible indeed to look upon. Now in front of him is a wheel, with many spokes, and many tyres; it is like a fence in front of him.

And he cries: O man, who art thou that wouldst penetrate the Mystery? for it is hidden unto the End of Time.

And I answer him: Time is not, save in the darkness of Her womb by whom evil came.

And now the wheel breaks away, and I see him as he is. His garment is black beneath the opal veils, but it is lined with white, and he has the shining belly of a fish, and enormous wings of black and white feathers, and innumerable little legs and claws like a centipede, and a long tail like a scorpion. The breasts are human, but they are all scored with blood; and he cries: O thou who hast broken down the veil, knowest thou not that who cometh where I am must be scarred by many sorrows?

And I answer him: Sorrow is not, save in the darkness of the womb of Her by whom came evil.

I pierce the Mystery of his breast, and therein is a jewel. It is a sapphire as great as an ostrich egg, and thereon is graven this sigil:

But there is also much writing on the stone, very minute characters carved. I cannot read them. He points with his flail to the sapphire, which is now outside him and bigger than himself; and he cries: Hail! warden of the Gates of Eternity who knowest not thy right hand from thy left; for in the aeon of my Father is a god with clasped hands wherein he holdeth the universe, crushing it into the dust that ye call stars.

Hail unto thee who knowest not thy right eye from the left; for in the aeon of my Father there is but one light.

Hail unto thee who knowest not thy right nostril from thy left; for in the aeon of my Father there is neither life nor death.

Hail unto thee who knowest not thy right ear from thy left; for in the aeon of my Father there is neither sound nor silence.

Whose hath power to break open this sapphire stone shall find therein four elephants having tusks of mother-of-pearl, and upon whose backs are castles, those castles which ye call the watch-towers of Universe.

Let me dwell in peace within the breast of the Angel

that is warden of the aethyr. Let not the shame of my
Mother be unveiled. Let not her be put to shame that lieth
among the lilies that are beyond the stars.

O man, that must ever be opening, when wilt thou
learn to seal up the mysteries of the creation? to fold
thyself over thyself as a rose in the embrace of night?
But thou must play the wanton to the sun, and the wind
must tear thy petals from thee, and the bee must rob thee
of thy honey, and thou must fall into the dusk of things.
Amen and Amen.

Verily the light is hidden, therefore he who hideth
himself is like unto the light; but thou openest thyself;
thou art like unto the darkness that bindeth the belly of
the great goddess.[2]

OLAHO VIRUDEN MAHORELA ZODIREDA!
ON PIREDA EXENTASER; ARBA PIRE GAH
GAHA GAHAL GAHALANA VO ABRA NA GAHA
VELUCORSAPAX.

And the voice of the aeon cried: Return, return,
return! the time sickeneth, and the space gapeth, and the
voice of him that is, was and shall be crowned rattles in
the throat of the mighty dragon of eld. Thou canst not
pass by me, except thou have the mystery of the word of
the abyss.

Now the angel putteth back the sapphire stone into
his breast; and I spake unto him and said, I will fight
with thee and overcome thee, except thou expound unto
me the word of the abyss.

Now he makes as if to fight with me. (It is very horrible,
all the tentacles moving and the flail flashing, and the
fierce eyeless face, strained and swollen.) And with the
Magic sword I pierce through his armour to his breast.

2. In the light of the cry of LOE, this passage seems to mean precisely the
opposite of its apparent meaning.

He fell back, saying: Each of these my scars was thus made, for I am the warden of the aethyr. And he would have said more; but I cut him short, saying: expound the word of the Abyss. And he said: Discipline is sorrowful and ploughing is laborious and age is weariness.

Thou shalt be vexed by dispersion.

But now, if the sun arise, fold thou thine arms; then shall God smite thee into a pillar of salt.

Look not so deeply into words and letters; for this Mystery hath been hidden by the Alchemists. Compose the sevenfold into a fourfold regimen; and when thou hast understood thou mayest make symbols; but by playing child's games with symbols thou shalt never understand. Thou hast the signs; thou hast the words; but there are many things that are not in my power, who am but the warden of the 28th Aethyr.

Now my name thou shalt obtain in this wise. Of the three angels of the Aethyr, thou shalt write the names from right to left and from left to right and from right to left, and these are the holy letters:

The first 1, the fifth 2, the sixth 3, the eleventh 4, the seventh 5, the twelfth 6, the seventeenth 7.

Thus hast thou my name who am above these three, but the angels of the 30th Aethyr are indeed four, and they have none above them; wherefore dispersion and disorder.

Now cometh from every side at once a voice, terribly great, crying: Close the veil; the great blasphemy hath been uttered; the face of my Mother is scarred by the nails of the devil. Shut the book, destroy the breaker of the seal!

And I answered: Had he not been destroyed he had not come hither, for I am not save in the darkness in the womb of Her by whom came evil into the world.

And this darkness swallows everything up, and the

angel is gone from the stone; and there is no light therein, save only the light of the Rose and of the Cross.

AUMALE, ALGERIA.
November 23, 1909, between 8 and 9 P.M.

THE CRY OF THE 27TH AETHYR WHICH IS CALLED ZAA

There is an angel with rainbow wings, and his dress is green with silver, a green veil over silver armour. Flames of many-coloured fire dart from him in all directions. It is a woman of some thirty years old, and she has the moon for a crest, and the moon is blazoned on her heart, and her sandals are curved silver, like the moon.

And she cries: Lonely am I and cold in the wilderness of the stars. For I am the queen of all them that dwell in Heaven, and the queen of all them that are pure upon earth, and the queen of all the sorcerers of hell.

I am the daughter of Nuit, the lady of the stars. And I am the Bride of them that are vowed unto loneliness. And I am the mother of the Dog Cerberus. One person am I, and three gods.

And thou who hast blasphemed me shalt suffer knowing me. For I am cold as thou art cold, and burn with thy fire. Oh, when shall the war of the Aires and the elements be accomplished?

Radiant are these falchions of my brothers, invisibly about me, but the might of the aethyrs beneath my feet beareth me down. And they avail not to sever the Kamailos. There is one in green armour, with green eyes, whose sword is of vegetable fire. That shall avail me. My son is he—and how shall I bear him that have not known man?

All this time intolerable rays are shooting forth to beat me back or destroy me; but I am encased in an egg of blue-violet, and my form is the form of a man with the head of a golden hawk. While I have been observing this, the goddess has kept up a continuous wail, like the baying of a thousand hounds; and now her voice is deep and guttural and hoarse, and she breathes very rapidly words that I cannot hear. I can hear some of them now: UNTU LA LA ULULA UMUNA TOFA LAMA LE LI NA AHR IMA TAHARA ELULA ETFOMA UNUNA ARPETI ULU ULU ULU MARABAN ULULU MAHATA ULU ULU LAMASTANA.

And then her voice rises to a shriek, and there is a cauldron boiling in front of her; and the flames under the cauldron are like unto zinc flames, and in the cauldron is the Rose, the Rose of 49 petals, seething in it. Over the cauldron she has arched her rainbow wings; and her face is bent over the cauldron, and she is blowing opalescent silvery rings on to the Rose; and each ring as it touches the water bursts into flame, and the Rose takes new colours.

And now she lifts her head, and raises her hands to heaven, and cries: O Mother, wilt thou never have compassion on the children of earth? Was it not enough that the Rose should be red with the blood of thine heart, and that its petals should be by 7 and by 7?

She is weeping, weeping. And the tears grow and fill the whole stone with moons. I can see nothing and hear nothing for the tears, though she keeps on praying. "Take of these pearls, treasure them in thine heart. Is not the Kingdom of the Abyss accurst?" She points downward to the cauldron; and now in it there is the head of a most cruel dragon, black and corrupted. I watch, and watch; and nothing happens.

And now the dragon rises out of the cauldron, very long and slim (like Japanese Dragons, but infinitely more terrible) and he blots out the whole sphere of the stone.

Then suddenly all is gone, and there is nothing in the

stone save brilliant white light and flecks like sparks of golden fire; and there is a ringing, as if bells were being used for anvils. And there is a perfume which I cannot describe; it is like nothing that one can describe, but the suggestion is like lignum aloes. And now all these things are there at once in the same place and time.

Now a veil of olive and silver is drawn over the stone, only I hear the voice of the angel receding, very sweet and faint and sorrowful, saying: Far off and lonely in the secret stone is the unknown, and interpenetrated is the knowledge with the will and the understanding. I am alone. I am lost, because I am all and in all; and my veil is woven of the green earth and the web of stars. I love; and I am denied, for I have denied myself. Give me those hands, put them against my heart. Is it not cold? Sink, sink, the abyss of time remains. It is not possible that one should come to ZAA. Give me thy face. Let me kiss it with my cold kisses. Ah! Ah! Ah! Fall back from me. The word, the word of the aeon is MAKHASHANAH. And these words shalt thou say backwards: ARARNAY OBOLO MAHARNA TUTULU NOM LAHARA EN NEDIEZO LO SAD FONUSA SOBANA ARANA BINUF LA LA LA ARPAZNA UOHULU when thou wilt call my burden unto appearance, for I who am the Virgin goddess am the pregnant goddess, and I have cast down my burden even unto the borders of the universe. They that blaspheme me are stoned, and my veil is fallen about me even unto the end of time.

Now there arises a great raging of thousands and thousands of mighty warriors flashing through the aethyr so thickly that nothing is to be seen but their swords, which are like blue-gray plumes. And the noise is confused, thousands of battle cries harmonizing to a roar, like the roar of a monstrous river in flood. And all the stone is dull, dull gray. The life is gone from it.

There is no more to see.

SIDI AISSA, ALGERIA.
November 24, 1909, 8–9 P.M.

THE CRY OF THE 26TH AETHYR
WHICH IS CALLED DES

There is a very bright pentagram: and now the stone is gone, and the whole heaven is black, and the blackness is the blackness of a mighty angel. And though he is black (his face and his wings and his robe and his armour are all black), yet is he so bright that I cannot look upon him. And he cries: O ye spears and vials of poison and sharp swords and whirling thunderbolts that are about the corners of the earth, girded with wrath and justice, know ye that His name is Righteousness in Beauty? Burnt out are your eyes, for that ye have seen me in my majesty. And broken are the drum-heads of your ears, because my name is as two mountains of fornication, the breasts of a strange woman; and my Father is not in them.

Lo! the pools of fire and torment mingled with sulphur! Many are their colours, and their colour is as molten gold, when all is said. Is not He one, one and alone, in whom the brightness of your countenance is as 1,728 petals of fire?

Also he spake the curse, folding his wings across and crying: Is not the son the enemy of his father? And hath not the daughter stolen the warmth of the bed of her mother? therefore is the great curse irrevocable. Therefore there is neither wisdom nor understanding nor knowledge in this house, that hangeth upon the edge of hell. Thou art not 4 but 2, O thou blasphemy spoken against 1!

Therefore whoso worshippeth thee is accursed. He shall be brayed in a mortar and the powder thereof cast to the winds, that the birds of the air may eat thereof and die;

and he shall be dissolved in strong acid and the elixir poured into the sea, that the fishes of the sea may breathe thereof and die. And he shall be mingled with dung and spread upon the earth, so that the herbs of the earth may feed thereof and die; and he shall be burnt utterly with fire, and the ashes thereof shall calcine the children of flame, that even in hell may be found an overflowing lamentation.

And now on the breast of the Angel is a golden egg between the blackness of the wings, and that egg grows and grows all over the aethyr. And it breaks, and within there is a golden eagle.

And he cries: Woe! woe! woe! Yea, woe unto the world! For there is no sin, and there is no salvation. My plumes are like waves of gold upon the sea. My eyes are brighter than the sun. My tongue is swifter than the lightning.

Yet am I hemmed in by the armies of night, singing, singing praises unto Him that is smitten by the thunderbolt of the abyss. Is not the sky clear behind the sun? These clouds that burn thee up, these rays that scorch the brains of men with blindness; these are heralds before my face of the dissolution and the night.

Ye are all blinded by my glory; and though ye treasure in your heart the sacred word that is the last lever of the key to the little door beyond the abyss, yet ye gloss and comment thereupon; for the light itself is but illusion. Truth itself is but illusion. Yea, these be the great illusions beyond life and space and time.

Let thy lips blister with my words! Are they not meteors in thy brain? Back, back from the face of the accursed one, who am I; back into the night of my father, into the silence; for all that ye deem right is left, forward is backward, upward is downward.

I am the great god adored of the holy ones. Yet am I

the accursed one, child of the elements and not their father.

O my mother! wilt thou not have pity upon me? Wilt thou not shield me? For I am naked, I am manifest, I am profane. O my father! wilt not thou withdraw me? I am extended, I am double, I am profane.

Woe, woe unto me! These are they that hear not prayer. It is I that have heard all prayer alway, and there is none to answer *me*. Woe unto me! Woe unto me! Accursed am I unto the aeons!

All this time this brilliant eagle-headed god has been attacked, seemingly, by invisible people, for he is wounded now and again, here and there; little streams of fresh blood come out over the feathers of his breast. And the smoke of the blood is gradually filling the Aethyr with a crimson veil. There is a scroll over the top, saying: *Ecclesia abhorret a sanguine*; and there is another scroll below it in a language of which I do not know the sounds. The meaning is, Not as they have understood.

The blood is thicker and darker now, and it is becoming clotted and black, so that everything is blotted out; because it coagulates, coagulates. And then at the top there steals a dawn of pure night-blue,—Oh, the stars, the stars in it deeply set!—and drives the blood down; so that all round the top of the oval gradually dawns the figure of our Lady Nuit, and beneath her is the flaming winged disk, and below the altar of Ra-Hoor-Khuit, even as it is upon the Stélé of Revealing. But below is the supine figure of Seb, into whom is concentrated all that clotted blood.

And there comes a voice: It is the dawn of the aeon. The aeons of cursing are passed away. Force and fire, strength and sight, these are for the servants of the Star and the Snake.

And now I seem to be lying in the desert, exhausted.

THE DESERT, NEAR SIDI AISSA.
November 25, 1909. 1:10–2 P.M.

THE CRY OF THE 25TH AETHYR WHICH IS CALLED VTI

There is nothing in the stone but the pale gold of the Rosy Cross.

Now there comes an Angel with bright wings, that is the Angel of the 25th Aire. And all the aire is a dark olive about him, like an alexandrite stone. He bears a pitcher or amphora. And now there comes another Angel upon a white horse, and yet again another Angel upon a black bull. And now there comes a lion and swallows the two latter angels up. The first angel goes to the lion and closes his mouth. And behind them are arrayed a great company of Angels with silver spears, like a forest. And the Angel says: Blow, all ye trumpets, for I will loose my hands from the mouth of the lion, and his roaring shall enkindle the worlds.

Then the trumpets blow, and the wind rises and whistles terribly. It is a blue wind with silver specks; and it blows through the whole Aethyr. But through it one perceives the lion, which has become as a raging flame.

And he roareth in an unknown tongue. But this is the interpretation thereof: Let the stars be burnt up in the fire of my nostrils! Let all the gods and the archangels and the angels and the spirits that are on the earth, and above the earth, and below the earth, that are in all the heavens and in all the hells, let them be as motes dancing in the beam of mine eye!

I am he that swalloweth up death and victory. I have slain the crowned goat, and drunk up the great sea. Like the ash of dried leaves the worlds are blown before me. Thou hast passed by me, and thou hast not known me. Woe unto thee, that I have not devoured thee altogether!

On my head is the crown, 419 rays far-darting. And my body is the body of the Snake, and my soul is the soul of the Crowned Child. Though an Angel in white robes leadeth me, who shall ride upon me but the Woman of Abominations? Who is the Beast? Am not I one more than he? In his hand is a sword that is a book. In his hand is a spear that is a cup of fornication. Upon his mouth is set the great and terrible seal. And he hath the secret of V. His ten horns spring from five points, and his eight heads are as the charioteer of the West. Thus doth the fire of the sun temper the spear of Mars, and thus shall he be worshipped, as the warrior lord of the sun. Yet in him is the woman that devoureth with her water all the fire of God.

Alas! my lord, thou art joined with him that knoweth not these things.

When shall the day come that men shall flock to this my gate, and fall into my furious throat, a whirlpool of fire? This is hell unquenchable, and all they shall be utterly consumed therein. Therefore is that asbestos unconsumable made pure.

Each of my teeth is a letter of the reverberating name. My tongue is a pillar of fire, and from the glands of my mouth arise four pillars of water. TAOTZEM is the name by which I am blasphemed. My name thou shalt not know, lest thou pronounce it and pass by.

And now the Angel comes forward again and closes his mouth.

All this time heavy blows have been raining upon me from invisible angels, so that I am weighed down as with a burden greater than the world. I am altogether crushed. Great mill-stones are hurled out of heaven upon me. I am trying to crawl to the lion, and the ground is covered with sharp knives. I cut myself at every inch.

And the voice comes: Why art thou there who art here? Hast thou not the sign of the number, and the seal of the name, and the ring of the eye? Thou wilt not.

And I answered and said: I am a creature of earth, and ye would have me swim.

And the voice said: Thy fear is known; thine ignorance is known; thy weakness is known; but thou art nothing in this matter. Shall the grain which is cast into the earth by the hand of the sower debate within itself, saying, am I oats or barley? Bond-slave of the curse, we give nothing, we take all. Be thou content. That which thou art, thou art. Be content.

And now the lion passeth over through the Aethyr with the crowned beast upon his back, and the tail of the lion goes on instead of stopping, and on each hair of the tail is something or other—sometimes a little house, sometimes a planet, at other times a town. Then there is a great plain with soldiers fighting upon it, and an enormously high mountain carved into a thousand temples, and more houses and fields and trees, and great cities with wonderful buildings in them, statues and columns and public buildings generally. This goes on and on and on and on and on and on and on—all on the hairs of this lion's tail.

And then there is the tuft of his tail, which is like a comet, but the head is a new universe, and each hair streaming away from it is a Milky Way.

And then there is a pale stern figure, enormous, enormous, bigger than all that universe is, in silver armour, with a sword and a pair of balances. That is only vague. All has gone into stone-gray, blank.

There is nothing.

AIN EL HAJEL.
November 25, 1909. 8:40–9:40 P.M.

(There were two voices in all this Cry, one behind the other—or, one was the speech, and the other the meaning. And the voice that was the speech was simply a roaring, one tremendous noise, like a mixture of thunder and water-falls and wild beasts and bands and artillery. And yet it was articulate, though I cannot tell you what a single word was. But the meaning of the voice—the second voice—was quite silent, and put the ideas directly into the brain of the Seer, as if by touch. It is not certain whether the mill-stones and the sword-strokes that rained upon him were not these very sounds and ideas.)

THE CRY OF THE 24TH AETHYR
WHICH IS CALLED NIA

An angel comes forward into the stone like a warrior clad in chain-armour. Upon his head are plumes of gray, spread out like the fan of a peacock. About his feet a great army of scorpions and dogs, lions, elephants, and many other wild beasts. He stretches forth his arms to heaven and cries; In the crackling of the lightning, in the rolling of the thunder, in the clashing of the swords and the hurling of the arrows: be thy name exalted!

Streams of fire come out of the heavens, a pale brilliant blue, like plumes. And they gather themselves and settle upon his lips. His lips are redder than roses, and the blue plumes gather themselves into a blue rose, and from beneath the petals of the rose come brightly coloured humming-birds, and dew falls from the rose—honey-coloured dew. I stand in the shower of it.

And a voice proceeds from the rose: Come away! Our chariot is drawn by doves. Of mother-of-pearl and ivory is our chariot, and the reins thereof are the heart-strings of men. Every moment that we fly shall cover an aeon. And every place on which we rest shall be a young universe rejoicing in its strength; the meadows thereof shall be covered with flowers. There shall we rest but a night, and in the morning we shall flee away, comforted.

Now, to myself, I have imagined the chariot of which the voice spake, and I looked to see who was with me in the chariot. It was an Angel of golden hair and golden skin, whose eyes were bluer than the sea, whose mouth was redder than the fire, whose breath was ambrosial air. Finer than a spider's web were her robes. And they were of the seven colours.

All this I saw; and then the hidden voice went on low and sweet: Come away! The price of the journey is little, though its name be death. Thou shalt die to all that thou fearest and hopest and hatest and lovest and thinkest and art. Yea! thou shalt die, even as thou must die. For all that thou hast, thou hast not; all that thou art, thou art not!

NENNI OFEKUFA ANANAEL LAIADA I MAELPEREJI NONUKA AFAFA ADAREPEHETA PEREGI ALADI NIISA NIISA LAPE OL ZODIR IDOIAN.

And I said: ODO KIKALE QAA. Why art thou hidden from me, whom I hear?

And the voice answered and said unto me: Hearing is of the spirit alone. Thou art a partaker of the five-fold mystery. Thou must roll up the ten divine ones like a scroll, and fashion therefrom a star. Yet must thou blot out the star in the heart of Hadit.

For the blood of my heart is like a warm bath of myrrh and ambergris; bathe thyself therein. The blood of my heart is all gathered upon my lips if I kiss thee, burns in my fingertips if I caress thee, burns in my womb when thou art caught up into my bed. Mighty are the stars; mighty is the sun; mighty is the moon; mighty is the voice of the ever-living one, and the echoes of his whisper are the thunders of the dissolution of the worlds. But my silence is mightier than they. Close up the worlds like unto a weary house; close up the book of the recorder, and let the veil swallow up the shrine, for I am arisen, O my fair one, and there is no more need of all these things.

If once I put thee apart from me, it was the joy of play. Is not the ebb and flowing of the tide a music of the sea? Come, let us mount unto Nuit our mother and be lost! Let being be emptied in the infinite abyss! For by me only shalt thou mount; thou hast none other wings than mine.

All this while the Rose has been shooting out blue flames, coruscating like snakes through the whole Aire. And the snakes have taken shapes of sentences. One of them is: *Sub umbra alarum tuarum Adonai quies et felicitas.* And another: *Summum bonum, vera sapientia, magnanima vita, sub noctis nocte sunt.* And another is: *Vera medicina est vinum mortis.* And another is: *Libertas evangelii per jugum legis ob gloriam dei intactam ad vacuum nequaquam tendit.* And another is: *Sub aquâ lex terrarum.* And another is: *Mens edax rerum, cor umbra rerum; intelligentia via summa.* And another is: *Summa via lucis: per Hephaestum undas regas.* And another is: *Vir introit tumulum regis, invenit oleum lucis.*

And all round the whole of these things are the letters TARO; but the light is so dreadful that I cannot read the words. I am going to try again. All these serpents are collected together very thickly at the edges of the wheel, because there are an innumerable number of sentences. One is: *tres annos regimen oraculi.* And another is: *terribilis ardet rex* ‏רוהב‎.And another is: *Ter amb (amp?)* (can't see it) *rosam oleo (?).* And another is: *Tribus annulis regna olisbon.* And the marvel is that with those four letters you can get a complete set of rules for doing everything, both for white magic and black.

And now I see the heart of the rose again. I see the face of him that is the heart of the rose, and in the glory of that face I am ended. My eyes are fixed upon his eyes; my being is sucked up through my eyes into those eyes. And I see through those eyes, and lo! the universe, like whirling sparks of gold, blown like a tempest. I seem to swell out again into him. My consciousness fills the whole Aethyr. I hear the cry NIA, ringing again and again from within me. It sounds like infinite music, and behind the sound is the meaning of the Aethyr. Again there are no words.

All this time the whirling sparks of gold go on, and they are like blue sky, with a lot of rather thin white clouds in it, outside. And now I see mountains round, far blue mountains, purple mountains. And in the midst is a little green dell of moss, which is all sparkling with dew that drips from the rose. And I am lying on that moss with my face upwards, drinking, drinking, drinking, drinking, drinking of the dew.

I cannot describe to you the joy and the exhaustion of everything that was, and the energy of everything that is, for it is only a corpse that is lying on the moss. I am the soul of the Aethyr.

Now it reverberates like the swords of archangels, clashing upon the armour of the damned; and there seem to be the blacksmiths of heaven beating the steel of the worlds upon the anvils of hell, to make a roof to the Aethyr.

For if the great work were accomplished and all the Aethyrs were caught up into one, then would the vision fail; then would the voice be still.

Now all is gone from the stone.

AIN EL HAJEL.
November 26, 1909. 2–3:25 P.M.

THE CRY OF THE 23RD AETHYR
WHICH IS CALLED TOR

In the brightness of the stone are three lights, brighter than all, which revolve ceaselessly. And now there is a spider's web of silver covering the whole of the stone. Behind the spider's web is a star of twelve rays; and behind that again, a black bull, furiously pawing up the ground. The flames from his mouth increase and whirl, and he cries: Behold the mystery of toil, O thou who art taken in the toils of mystery. For I who trample the earth thereby make whirlpools in the air; be comforted, therefore, for though I be black, in the roof of my mouth is the sign of the Beetle. Bent are the backs of my brethren, yet shall they gore the lion with their horns. Have I not the wings of the eagle, and the face of the man?

And now he is turned into one of those winged Assyrian bull-men.

And he sayeth: The spade of the husbandman is the sceptre of the king. All the heavens beneath me, they serve me. They are my fields and my gardens and my orchards and my pastures.

Glory be unto thee, who didst set thy feet in the North; whose forehead is pierced with the sharp points of the diamonds in thy crown; whose heart is pierced with the spear of thine own fecundity.

Thou art an egg of blackness, and a worm of poison. But thou hast formulated thy father, and made fertile thy mother.

Thou art the basilisk whose gaze turns men to stone, and the cockatrice at the breast of an harlot that giveth death for milk. Thou art the asp that has stolen into the cradle of the babe. Glory unto thee, who art twined about the world as the vine that clingeth to the bare body of a bacchanal.

Also, though I be planted so firmly upon the earth, yet

is my blood wine and my breath fire of madness. With these wings, though they be but little, I lift myself above the crown of the yod, and being without fins I yet swim in the inviolate fountain.

I disport myself in the ruins of Eden, even as Leviathan in the false sea, being whole as the rose at the crown of the cross. Come ye unto me, my children, and be glad. At the end of labour is the power of labour. And in my stability is concentrated eternal change.

For the whirlings of the universe are but the course of the blood in my heart. And the unspeakable variety thereof is but my divers hairs, and plumes, and gems in my tall crown. The change which ye lament is the life of my rejoicing, and the sorrow that blackeneth your hearts is the myriad deaths by which I am renewed. And the instability which maketh ye to fear, is the little waverings of balance by which I am assured.

And now the veil of silver tissue-stuff closes over him, and above that, a purple veil, and above that, a golden veil, so that now the whole stone is like a thick mat of woven gold wires; and there come forth, one from each side of the stone, two women, and grasp each other by both hands, and kiss, and melt into one another; and melt away.[3] And now the veils open again, the gold parts, and the purple parts, and the silver parts, and there is a crowned eagle, also like the Assyrian eagles.

And he cries: All my strength and stability are turned to the use of flight. For though my wings are of fine gold, yet my heart is the heart of a scorpion.

Glory unto thee, who being born in a stable didst make thee mirth of the filth thereof, who didst suck in iniquity from the breast of thy mother the harlot; who didst flood with iniquity the bodies of thy concubines.

3. These are intended to show symbolically that the Bull is the same as the Eagle.

Thou didst lie in the filth of the streets with the dogs; thou wast tumbled and shameless and wanton in a place where four roads meet. There wast thou defiled, and there wast thou slain, and there wast thou left to rot. The charred stake was thrust through thy bowels, and thy parts were cut off and thrust into thy mouth for derision.

All my unity is dissolved; I live in the tips of my feathers. That which I think to be myself is but infinite number. Glory unto the Rose and the Cross, for the Cross is extended unto the uttermost end beyond space and time and being and knowledge and delight! Glory unto the Rose that is the minute point of its centre! Even as we say; glory unto the Rose that is Nuit the circumference of all, and glory unto the Cross that is the heart of the Rose!

Therefore do I cry aloud, and my scream is the treble as the bellowing of the bull is the bass. Peace in the highest and peace in the lowest and peace in the midst thereof! Peace in the eight quarters, peace in the ten points of the Pentagram! Peace in the twelve rays of the seal of Solomon, and peace in the four and thirty whirlings of the hammer of Thor! Behold! I blaze upon thee. (The eagle is gone; it is only a flaming Rosy Cross of white brilliance.) I catch thee up into rapture. FALUTLI, FALUTLI!

. . . O it dies, it dies.

BOU SAADA.
November 28, 1909. 9:30–10:15 A.M.

THE CRY OF THE 22ND AETHYR WHICH IS CALLED LIN

There comes first into the stone the mysterious table of forty-nine squares. It is surrounded by an innumerable company of angels; these angels are of all kinds,—some brilliant and flashing as gods, down to elemental creatures. The light comes and goes on the tablet; and now it is steady, and I perceive that each letter of the tablet is composed of forty-nine other letters, in a language which looks like that of Honorius; but when I would read, the letter that I look at becomes indistinct at once.

And now there comes an Angel, to hide the tablet with his mighty wing. This Angel has all the colours mingled in his dress; his head is proud and beautiful; his headdress is of silver and red and blue and gold and black, like cascades of water, and in his left hand he has a pan-pipe of the seven holy metals, upon which he plays. I cannot tell you how wonderful the music is, but it is so wonderful that one only lives in one's ears; one cannot see anything any more.

Now he stops playing and moves with his finger in the air. His finger leaves a trail of fire of every colour, so that the whole Aire is become like a web of mingled lights. But through it all drops dew.

(I can't describe these things at all. Dew doesn't represent what I mean in the least. For instance, these drops of dew are enormous globes, shining like the full moon, only perfectly transparent, as well as perfectly luminous.)

And now he shows the tablet again, and he says: As there are 49 letters in the tablet, so are there 49 kinds of cosmos in every thought of God. And there are 49 interpretations of every cosmos, and each interpretation is manifested in 49 ways. Thus also are the calls 49, but to each call there are 49 visions. And each vision is composed of 49 elements, except in the 10th Aethyr, that is accursed, and that hath 42.

All this while the dewdrops have turned into cascades of gold finer than the eyelashes of a little child. And though the extent of the Aethyr is so enormous, one perceives each hair separately, as well as the whole thing at once. And now there is a mighty concourse of angels rushing toward me from every side, and they melt upon the surface of the egg in which I am standing in the form of the god Kneph, so that the surface of the egg is all one dazzling blaze of liquid light.

Now I move up against the tablet—I cannot tell you with what rapture. And all the names of God, that are not known even to the angels, clothe me about.

All the seven senses are transmuted into one sense, and that sense is dissolved in itself.... (Here occurs Samadhi.) ... Let me speak, O God; let me declare it ... all. It is useless; my heart faints, my breath stops. There is no link between me and P.... I withdraw myself. I see the table again.

(He was behind the table for a very long time.—O.V.)

And all the table burns with intolerable light; there has been no such light in any of the Aethyrs until now. And now the table draws me back into itself; I am no more.

My arms were out in the form of a cross, and that Cross was extended, blazing with light into infinity. I myself am the minutest point in it. This is *the birth of form.*

I am encircled by an immense sphere of many-coloured bands; it seems it is the sphere of the Sephiroth projected in the three dimensions. This is *the birth of death.*

Now in the centre within me is a glowing sun. That is *the birth of hell.*

Now all that is swept away, washed away by the table. It is the virtue of the table to sweep everything away. It is the letter I in this Aethyr that gives this vision, and L is its purity, and N is its energy. Now everything is confused, for I invoked the Mind, that is disruption. Every Adept who beholds this vision is corrupted by mind. Yet it is by virtue of mind that he endures it, and passes on, if so be that he pass on. Yet there is nothing higher than this, for it is perfectly balanced in itself. I cannot read a word of the holy Table, for the letters of the Table are all wrong. They are only the shadows of shadows. And whoso beholdeth this Table with this rapture, is light. The true word for light hath seven letters. They are the same as ARARITA, transmuted.

There is a voice in this Aethyr, but it cannot be spoken. The only way one can represent it is as a ceaseless thundering of the word Amen. It is not a repetition of Amen, because there is no time. It is one Amen continuous.

Shall mine eye fade before thy glory? I am the eye. That is why the eye is seventy. You can never understand why, except in this vision.

And now the table recedes from me. Far, far it goes, streaming with light. And there are two black angels bending over me, covering me with their wings, shutting me up into the darkness; and I am lying in the Pastos of our Father Christian Rosenkreutz, beneath the Table in the Vault of seven sides. And I hear these words:

The voice of the Crowned Child, the Speech of the Babe that is hidden in the egg of blue. (Before me is the flaming Rosy Cross.) I have opened mine eye, and the universe is dissolved before me, for force is mine upper eye-lid and matter is my lower eye-lid. I gaze into the seven spaces, and there is naught.

The rest of it comes without words; and then again:

I have gone forth to war, and I have slain him that sat upon the sea, crowned with the winds. I put forth my power and he was broken. I withdrew my power and he was ground into fine dust.

Rejoice with me, O ye Sons of the Morning; stand with me upon the Throne of Lotus; gather yourselves up unto me, and we shall play together in the fields of light. I have passed into the Kingdom of the West after my Father.

Behold! where are now the darkness and the terror and the lamentation? For ye are born into the new Aeon; ye shall not suffer death. Bind up your girdles of gold!

Wreathe yourselves with garlands of my unfading flowers! In the nights we will dance together, and in the morning we will go forth to war; for, as my Father liveth that was dead, so do I live and shall never die.

And now the table comes rushing back. It covers the whole stone, but this time it pushes me before it, and a terrible voice cries: Begone! Thou hast profaned the mystery; thou hast eaten of the shew-bread; thou hast spilt the consecrated wine! Begone! For the Voice is accomplished. Begone! For that which was open is shut. And thou shalt not avail to open it, saving by virtue of him whose name is one, whose spirit is one, whose individuum is one, and whose permutation is one; whose light is one, whose life is one, whose love is one. For though thou art joined to the inmost mystery of the heaven, thou must accomplish the sevenfold task of the earth, even as thou sawest the Angels from the greatest unto the least. And of all this shalt thou take back with thee but a little part, for the sense shall be darkened, and the shrine re-veiled. Yet know this for thy reproof, and for the stirring up of discontent in them whose swords are of lath, that in every word of this vision is concealed the key of many mysteries, even of being, and of knowledge, and of bliss; of will, of courage, of wisdom, and of silence, and of that which, being all these, is greater than all these. Begone! For the night of life is fallen upon thee. And the veil of light hideth that which is.

With that, I suddenly see the world as it is, and I am very sorrowful.

BOU-SAADA.
November 28, 1909. 4–6 P.M.

(*Note:* You do not come back in any way dazed; it is like going from one room into another. Regained normal consciousness completely and immediately.)

THE CRY OF THE 21ST AETHYR
WHICH IS CALLED ASP

A mighty wind rolls through all the Aethyr; there is a sense of absolute emptiness; no colour, no form, no substance. Only now and then there seem, as it were, the shadows of great angels, swept along. No sound; there is something very remorseless about the wind, passionless, that is very terrible. In a way, it is nerve-shaking. It seems as if something kept on trying to open behind the wind, and just as it is about to open, the effort is exhausted. The wind is not cold or hot; there is no sense of any kind connected with it. One does not even feel it, for one is standing in front of it.

Now, the thing opens behind, just for a second, and I catch a glimpse of an avenue of pillars, and at the end a throne, supported by sphinxes. All this is black marble.

Now I seem to have gone through the wind, and to be standing before the throne; but he that sitteth thereon is invisible. Yet it is from him that all this desolation proceeds.

He is trying to make me understand by putting tastes in my mouth, very rapidly one after the other. Salt, honey, sugar, assafoetida, bitumen, honey again, some taste that I don't know at all; garlic, something very bitter like nux vomica, another taste, still more bitter; lemon, cloves, rose leaves, honey again; the juice of some plant, like a dandelion, I think; honey again, salt, a taste something like phosphorus, honey, laurel, a very unpleasant taste which I don't know, coffee, then a burning taste, then a sour taste that I don't know. All these tastes issue from his eyes; he *signals* them.

I can see his eyes now. They are very round, with perfectly black pupils, perfectly white iris, and the cornea pale blue. The sense of desolation is so acute that I keep on trying to get away from the vision.

I told him that I could not understand his taste-language, so instead he set up a humming very much like a big electric plant with dynamos going.

Now the atmosphere is deep night-blue; and by the power of that atmosphere, the pillars kindle to a dull glowing crimson, and the throne is a dull, ruddy gold. And now, through the humming, come very clear, bell-like notes, and farther still a muttering, like that of a gathering storm.

And now I hear the meaning of the muttering: I am he who was before the beginning, and in my desolation I cried aloud, saying, let me behold my countenance in the concave of the abyss. And I beheld, and lo! in the darkness of the abyss my countenance was black, and empty, and distorted, that was (once) invisible and pure.

Then I closed mine eye, that I might not behold it, and for this was it fixed. Now it is written that one glance of mine eye shall destroy it. And mine eye I dare not open, because of the foulness of the vision. Therefore do I gaze with these two eyes throughout the aeon. Is there not one of all my adepts that shall come unto me, and cut off mine eye-lids, that I may behold and destroy?

Now I take a dagger, and, searching out his third eye, seek to cut off the eye-lids, but they are of adamant. And the edge of the dagger is turned.

And tears drop from his eyes, and there is a mournful voice: So it hath been ever: so must it ever be! Though thou hast the strength of five bulls, thou shalt not avail in this.

And I said to him: Who shall avail? And he answered me: I know not. But the dagger of penance thou shalt temper seven times, afflicting the seven courses of thy soul. And thou shalt sharpen its edge seven times by the seven ordeals.

(One keeps on looking round to try to find something

GEMS FROM THE EQUINOX

else because of the terror of it. But nothing changes at all. Nothing but the empty throne, and the eyes, and the avenue of pillars!)

And I said to him: O thou that art the first countenance before time; thou of whom it is written that "He, God, is one; He is the eternal one, without equal, son or companion. Nothing shall stand before His face"; all we have heard of thine infinite glory and holiness, of thy beauty and majesty, and behold! there is nothing but this abomination of desolation.

He speaks; I cannot hear a word; something about *The Book of the Law*. The answer is written in *The Book of the Law*, or something of that sort.

This is a long speech; all that I can hear is: From me pour down the fires of life and increase continually upon the earth. From me flow down the rivers of water and oil and wine. From me cometh forth the wind that beareth the seed of trees and flowers and fruits and all herbs upon its bosom. From me cometh forth the earth in her unspeakable variety. Yea! all cometh from me, naught cometh to me. Therefore am I lonely and horrible upon this unprofitable throne. Only those who accept nothing from me can bring anything to me.

(He goes on speaking again: I cannot hear a word. I may have got about a twentieth of what he said.) And I say to him: It was written that his name is Silence, but thou speakest continually.

And he answers: Nay, the muttering that thou hearest is not my voice. It is the voice of the ape.

(When I say that he answers, it means that it is the same voice. The being on the throne has not uttered a word.) I say: O thou ape that speakest for Him whose name is Silence, how shall I know that thou speakest truly His thought? And the muttering continues: Nor speaketh

He nor thinketh, so that which I say is true, because I lie in speaking His thoughts.

He goes on, nothing stops him; and the muttering comes so fast that I cannot hear him at all.

Now the muttering has ceased, or is overwhelmed by the bells, and the bells in their turn are overwhelmed by the whirring, and now the whirring is overwhelmed by the silence. And the blue light is gone, and the throne and the pillars are returned to blackness, and the eyes of him that sitteth upon the throne are no more visible.

I seek to go up close to the throne, and I am pushed back, because I cannot give the sign. I have given all the signs I know and am entitled to, and I have tried to give the sign that I know and am not entitled to, but have not the necessary appurtenance; and even if I had, it would be useless; for there are two more signs necessary.

I find that I was wrong in suggesting that a Master of the Temple had a right to enter the temple of a Magus or an Ipsissimus. On the contrary, the rule that holds below, holds also above. The higher you go, the greater is the distance from one grade to another.

I am being slowly pushed backwards down the avenue, out into the wind. And this time I am caught up by the wind and whirled away down it like a dead leaf.

And a great Angel sweeps through the wind, and catches hold of me, and bears me up against it; and he sets me down on the hither side of the wind, and he whispers in my ear: Go thou forth into the world, O thrice and four times blessed who hast gazed upon the horror of the loneliness of The First. No man shall look upon his face and live. And thou hast seen his eyes, and understood his heart, for the voice of the ape is the pulse of his heart and the labouring of his breast. Go, therefore, and rejoice, for thou art the prophet of the Aeon arising, wherein He

is not. Give thou praise unto thy lady Nuit, and unto her
lord Hadit, that are for thee and thy bride, and the
winners of the ordeal X.

And with that we are come to the wall of the Aethyr,
and there is a little narrow gate, and he pushes me through
it, and I am suddenly in the desert.

THE DESERT, NEAR BOU-SAADA.[4]
November 29, 1909. 1:30–2:50 P.M.

THE CRY OF THE 20TH AETHYR
WHICH IS CALLED KHR

The dew that was upon the face of the stone is gone,
and it is become like a pool of clear golden water. And
now the light is come into the Rosy Cross. Yet all that I
see is the night, with the stars therein, as they appear
through a telescope. And there cometh a peacock into the
stone, filling the whole Aire. It is like the vision called
the Universal Peacock, or, rather, like a representation of
that vision. And now there are countless clouds of white
angels filling the Aire as the peacock dissolves.

Now behind the angels are archangels with trumpets.
These cause all things to appear at once, so that there is
a tremendous confusion of images. And now I perceive
that all these things are but veils of the wheel, for they all
gather themselves into a wheel that spins with incredible
velocity. It hath many colours, but all thrilled with white
light, so that they are transparent and luminous. This one
wheel is forty-nine wheels, set at different angles, so that
they compose a sphere; each wheel has forty-nine spokes,
and has forty-nine concentric tyres at equal distances from
the centre. And wherever the rays from any two wheels

4. This night I took the shew-stone to my breast to sleep, and immediately
a Dhyana arose of the sun, seen more clearly afterwards as the Star. Exceeding
was its brilliance.

meet, there is a blinding flash of glory. It must be understood that though so much detail is visible in the wheel, yet at the same time the impression is of a single, simple object.

It seems that this wheel is being spun by a hand. Though the wheel fills the whole Aire, yet the hand is much bigger than the wheel. And though this vision is so great and splendid, yet there is no seriousness with it, or solemnity. It seems that the hand is spinning the wheel merely for pleasure, it would be better to say amusement.

A voice comes: For he is a jocund and a ruddy god, and his laughter is the vibration of all that exists, and the earthquakes of the soul.

One is conscious of the whirring of the wheel thrilling one, like an electric discharge passing through one.

Now I see the figures on the wheel, which have been interpreted as the sworded Sphinx, Hermanubis and Typhon. And that is wrong. The rim of the wheel is a vivid emerald snake; in the centre of the wheel is a scarlet heart; and, impossible to explain as it is, the scarlet of the heart and the green of the snake are yet more vivid than the blinding white brilliance of the wheel.

The figures on the wheel are darker than the wheel itself; in fact, they are stains upon the purity of the wheel, and for that reason, and because of the whirling of the wheel, I cannot see them. But at the top seems to be the Lamb and Flag, such as one sees on some Christian medals, and one of the lower things is a wolf, and the other a raven. The Lamb and Flag symbol is much brighter than the other two. It keeps on growing brighter, until now it is brighter than the wheel itself, and occupies more space than it did.

It speaks: I am the greatest of the deceivers, for my purity and innocence shall seduce the pure and innocent, who but for me should come to the centre of the wheel. The wolf betrayeth only the greedy and the treacherous; the raven betrayeth only the melancholy and the dishonest. But I am he of whom it is written: He shall deceive the very elect.

For in the beginning the Father of all called forth lying spirits that they might sift the creatures of the earth in three sieves, according to the three impure souls. And he chose the wolf for the lust of the flesh, and the raven for the lust of the mind; but me did he choose above all to simulate the pure prompting of the soul. Them that are fallen a prey to the wolf and the raven I have not scathed; but them that have rejected me, I have given over to the wrath of the raven and the wolf. And the jaws of the one have torn them, and the beak of the other has devoured the corpse. Therefore is my flag white, because I have left nothing upon the earth alive. I have feasted myself on the blood of the saints, but I am not suspected of men to be their enemy, for my fleece is white and warm, and my teeth are not the teeth of one that teareth flesh; and mine eyes are mild, and they know me not the chief of the lying spirits that the Father of all sent forth from before his face in the beginning.

(His attribution is salt; the wolf mercury, and the raven sulphur.)

Now the lamb grows small again, there is again nothing but the wheel, and the hand that whirleth it.

And I said: "By the word of power, double in the voice of the Master; by the word that is seven, and one in seven; and by the great and terrible word 210, I beseech thee, O my Lord, to grant me the vision of thy glory." And all the rays of the wheel stream out at me, and I am blasted and blinded with the light. I am caught up into the wheel. I am one with the wheel. I am greater than the wheel. In the midst of a myriad lightnings I stand, and

I behold his face. (I am thrown violently back on to the earth every second, so that I cannot quite concentrate.)

All one gets is a liquid flame of pale gold. But its radiant force keeps hurling me back.

And I say: By the word and the will, by the penance and the prayer, let me behold thy face. (I cannot explain this, there is confusion of personalities.) I who speak to you, see what I tell you; but I, who see him, cannot communicate it to me, who speak to you.

If one could gaze upon the sun at noon, that might be like the substance of him. But the light is without heat. It is the vision of Ut in the Upanishads. And from this vision have come all the legends of Bacchus and Krishna and Adonis. For the impression is of a youth dancing and making music. But you must understand that he is not doing that, for he is still. Even the hand that turns the wheel is not his hand, but only a hand energized by him.

And now it is the dance of Shiva. I lie beneath his feet, his saint, his victim. My form is the form of the God Phtah, in my essence, but the form of the god Seb in my form. And this is the reason of existence, that in this dance which is delight, there must needs be both the god and the adept. Also the earth herself is a saint; and the sun and the moon dance upon her, torturing her with delight.

This vision is not perfect. I am only in the outer court of the vision, because I have undertaken it in the service of the Holy One, and must retain sense and speech. No recorded vision is perfect, of high visions, for the seer must keep either his physical organs or his memory in working order. And neither is capable. There is no bridge. One can only be conscious of one thing at a time, and as the consciousness moves nearer to the vision, it loses control of the physical and mental. Even so, the body and the mind must be very perfect before anything can be done, or the energy of the vision may send the body into spasms and the mind into insanity. This is why the first visions give Ananda, which is a shock. When the adept is attuned to Samadhi, there is but cloudless peace.

This vision is particularly difficult to get into, because he is I. And therefore the human ego is being constantly excited, so that one comes back so often. An acentric meditation practice like mahasatipatthana ought to be done before invocations of the Holy Guardian Angel, so that the ego may be very ready to yield itself utterly to the Beloved.

And now the breeze is blowing about us, like the sighs of love unsatisfied—or satisfied. His lips move. I cannot say the words at first.

And afterwards: "Shalt thou not bring the children of men to the sight of my glory? 'Only thy silence and thy speech that worship me avail. For as I am the last, so am I the next, and as the next shalt thou reveal me to the multitude.' Fear not for aught; turn not aside for aught, eremite of Nuit, apostle of Hadit, warrior of Ra Hoor Khu! The leaven taketh, and the bread shall be sweet; the ferment worketh, and the wine shall be sweet. My sacraments are vigorous food and divine madness. Come unto me, O ye children of men; come unto me, in whom I am, in whom ye are, were ye only alive with the life that abideth in Light."

All this time I have been fading away. I sink. The veil of night comes down a dull blue-gray with one pentagram in the midst of it, watery and dull. And I am to abide there for a while before I come back to the earth. (But shut me the window up, hide me from the sun. Oh, shut the window![5])

Now, the pentagram is faded; black crosses fill the Aethyr gradually growing and interlacing, until there is a network.

5. It was done.—O. V.

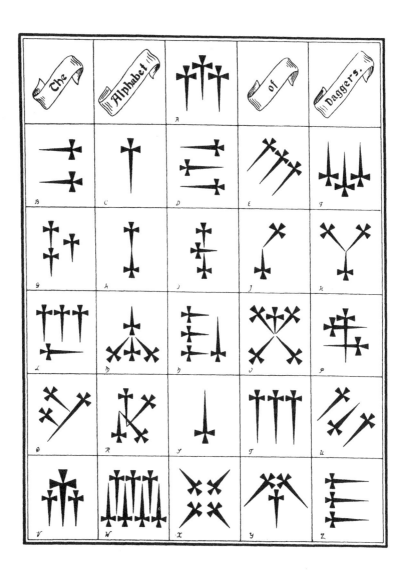

The Alphabet of Daggers

It is all dark now. I am lying exhausted, with the sharp edge of the shew-stone cutting into my forehead.

BOU-SAADA.
November 30, 1909. 9:15–10:50 A.M.

THE CRY OF THE 19TH AETHYR
WHICH IS CALLED POP

At first there is a black web over the face of the stone. A ray of light pierces it from behind and above. Then cometh a black cross, reaching across the whole stone; then a golden cross, not so large. And there is a writing in an arch that spans the cross, in an alphabet in which the letters are all formed of little daggers, cross-hilted, differently arranged. And the writing is: Worship in the body the things of the body; worship in the mind the things of the mind; worship in the spirit the things of the spirit.

(This holy alphabet must be written by sinners, that is, by those who are impure.)

"Impure" means those whose every thought is followed by another thought, or who confuse the higher with the lower, the substance with the shadow. Every Aethyr is truth, though it be but a shadow, for the shadow of a man is not the shadow of an ape.

(*Note:* All this has come to me without voice, without vision, without thought.)

(The shew-stone is pressed upon my forehead and causes intense pain; as I go on from Aethyr to Aethyr, it seems more difficult to open the Aethyr.)

The golden cross has become a little narrow door, and an old man like the Hermit of the Taro has opened it and come out. I ask him for admission; and he shakes his head kindly, and says: It is not given to flesh and blood to unveil the mysteries of the Aethyr, for therein are the chariots of fire, and the tumult of the horsemen; whoso entereth here may never look on life again with equal eyes. I insist.

The little gate is guarded by a great green dragon. And now the whole wall is suddenly fallen away; there is a blaze of the chariots and the horsemen; a furious battle is raging. One hears nothing but the clash of steel and the neighing of the chargers and the shrieks of the wounded. A thousand fall at every encounter and are trampled under foot. Yet the Aethyr is always full; there are infinite reserves.

No; that is all wrong, for this is not a battle between two forces, but a *meleé* in which each warrior fights for himself against all the others. I cannot see one who has even one ally. And the least fortunate, who fall soonest, are those in the chariots. For as soon as they are engaged in fighting, their own charioteers stab them in the back.

And in the midst of the battlefield there is a great tree, like a chinar-tree. Yet it bears fruits. And now all the warriors are dead, and they are the ripe fruits that are fallen — the ground is covered with them.

There is a laugh in my right ear: "This is the tree of life."

And now there is a mighty god, Sebek, with the head of a crocodile. His head is gray, like river mud, and his jaws fill the whole Aire. And he crunches up the whole tree and the ground and everything.

Now then at last cometh forth the Angel of the Aethyr, who is like the Angel of the fourteenth key of Rota, with beautiful blue wings, blue robes, the sun in her girdle like a brooch, and the two crescents of the moon shapen into sandals for her feet. Her hair is of flowing gold, each sparkle as a star. In her hands are the torch of Penelope and the cup of Circe.

She comes and kisses me on the mouth, and says:

Blessed art thou who hast beheld Sebek my Lord in his glory. Many are the champions of life, but all are un-horsed by the lance of death. Many are the children of the light, but their eyes shall all be put out by the Mother Darkness. Many are the servants of love, but love (that is not quenched by aught but love) shall be put out, as the child taketh the wick of a taper between his thumb and finger, by the god that sitteth alone.

And on her mouth, like a chrysanthemum of radiant light, is a kiss, and on it is the monogram I.H.S. The letters I.H.S. mean In Homini Salus and Instar Hominis Summus, and Imago Hominis deuS. And there are many, many other meanings, but they all imply this one thing; that nothing is of any importance but man; there is no hope or help but in man.

And she says: Sweet are my kisses, O wayfarer that wanderest from star to star. Sweet are my kisses, O householder that weariest within four walls. Thou art pent within thy brain, and my shaft pierceth it, and thou art free. Thine imagination eateth up the universe as the dragon that eateth up the moon. And in my shaft is it concentrated and bound up. See how all around thee gather my warriors, strong knights in goodly armour ready for war. Look upon my crown; it is above the stars. Behold the glow and the blush thereof! Upon thy cheek is the breeze that stirs those plumes of truth. For though I am the Angel of the fourteenth key, I am also the Angel of the eighth key. And from the love of these two have I come, who am the warden of Popé and the servant of them that dwell therein. Though all crowns fall, mine shall not fall; for my plumes reach up unto the Knees of Him that sitteth upon the holy throne, and liveth and reigneth for ever and ever as the balance of righteousness and truth. I am the Angel of the moon. I am the veiled one that sitteth between the pillars veiled with a shining veil, and on my lap is the open Book of the mysteries of the ineffable light. I am the aspiration unto the higher; I am the love of the unknown. I am the blind ache within the heart of man. I am the minister of the sacrament of pain. I swing the censer of worship, and I sprinkle the waters of purification. I am the daughter of the house of the invisible. I am the Priestess of the Silver Star.

And she catches me up to her as a mother catches her babe, and holds me up in her left arm, and sets my lips to her breast. And upon her breast is written: *Rosa Mundi est Lilium Coeli.*

And I look down upon the open Book of the mysteries, and it is open at the page on which is the Holy Table with the twelve squares in the midst. It radiates a blaze of light, too dazzling to make out the characters, and a voice says: *Non haec piscis omnium.*

(To interpret that, we must think of Ἰχθύς, which does not conceal *Iesous Christos Theon Uios Soter* as traditionally asserted, but is a mystery of the letter Nun and the letter Qoph, as may be seen by adding it up.)

(Ἰχθύς is only connected with Christianity because it was a hieroglyph of syphilis, which the Romans supposed to have been brought from Syria; and it seems to have been confounded with leprosy, which also they thought was caused by fish-eating.)

(One important meaning of Ἰχθύς: it is formed of the initials of five Egyptian deities and also of five Greek deities; in both cases a magic formula of tremendous power is concealed.)

As to the Holy Table itself, I cannot see it for the blaze of light; but I am given to understand that it appears in another Aethyr, of which it forms practically the whole content. And I am bidden to study the Holy Table very intently so as to be able to concentrate on it when it appears.

I have grown greater, so that I am as great as the Angel. And we are standing, as if crucified, face to face, our hands and lips and breasts and knees and feet together, and her eyes pierce into my eyes like whirling shafts of steel, so that I fall backwards headlong through the Aethyr — and there is a sudden and tremendous shout, absolutely stunning, cold and brutal: Osiris was a black god![6] And the Aethyr claps its hands, greater than the peal of a thousand mighty thunders.

I am back.

BOU-SAADA.
November 30, 1909. 10–11:45 P.M.

THE CRY OF THE 18TH AETHYR WHICH IS CALLED ZEN

A voice comes before any vision: Accursed are they who enter herein if they have nails, for they shall be pierced therewith; or if they have thorns, for they shall be crowned withal; or if they have whips, for with whips they shall be scourged; or if they bear wine, for their wine shall be turned to bitterness; or if they have a spear, for with a spear shall they be pierced unto the heart. And the nails are desires, of which there are three; the desire of light, the desire of life, the desire of love.

(And the thorns are thoughts, and the whips are regrets, and the wine is ease, or perhaps unsteadiness, especially in ecstasy, and the spear is attachment.)

And now there dawns the scene of the Crucifixion; but the Crucified One is an enormous bat, and for the two thieves are two little children. It is night, and the night is full of hideous things and howlings.

And an angel cometh forth, and saith: Be wary, for if thou change so much as the style of a letter, the holy word is blasphemed. But enter into the mountain of the

6. The Doctrine implied is that one must not be the child, but the Mother

Caverns, for that this (how much more then that Calvary which mocks it, as his ape mocks Thoth?) is but the empty shell of the mystery of ZEN. Verily, I say unto thee, many are the adepts that have looked upon the back parts of my father, and cried, "our eyes fail before the glory of thy countenance."

And with that he gives the sign of the rending of the veil, and tears down the vision. And behold! whirling columns of fiery light, seventy-two. Upon them is supported a mountain of pure crystal. The mountain is a cone, the angle of the apex being sixty degrees. And within the crystal is a pyramid of ruby, like unto the great pyramid of Gizeh.

I am entered in by the little door thereof, and I am come into the chamber of the king, which is fashioned like unto the vault of the adepts, or rather it is fitting to say that the vault of the adepts is a vile imitation of it. For there are four sides to the chamber, which with the roof and the floor and the chamber itself makes seven. So also is the pastos seven, for that which is within is like unto that which is without. And there is no furniture, and there are no symbols.

Light streams from every side upon the pastos. This light is that blue of Horus which we know, but being refined it is brilliance. For the light of Horus only appears blue because of the imperfection of our eyes. But though the light pours from the pastos, yet the pastos remains perfectly dark, so that it is invisible. It hath no form: only, at a certain point in the chamber, the light is beaten back.

I lie prostrate upon the ground before this mystery. Its splendour is impossible to describe. I can only say that its splendour is so great that my heart stops with the terror and the wonder and the rapture of it. I am almost mad. A million insane images chase each other through my brain. . . . A voice comes: (it is my own voice — I did not know it) "When thou shalt know me, O thou empty God, my little flame shall utterly expire in thy great N.O.X." There is no answer. . . . (20 minutes.—O. V.)

And now, after so long a while, the Angel[7] lifts me, and takes me from the room, and sets me in a little chamber where is another Angel like a fair youth in shining garments, who makes me partake of the sacraments; bread, that is labour; and fire, that is wit; and a rose, that is sin; and wine, that is death. And all about us is a great company of angels in many-coloured robes, rose and spring-green, and sky-blue, and pale gold, and silver, and lilac, solemnly chanting without words. It is music wonderful beyond all that can be thought.

And now we go out of the chamber; on the right is a pylon, and the right figure is Isis, and the left figure Nephthys, and they are folding their wings over, and supporting Ra.

I wanted to go back to the King's Chamber. The Angel pushed me away, saying: "Thou shalt see these visions from afar off, but thou shalt not partake of them save in the manner prescribed. For if thou change so much as the style of a letter, the holy word is blasphemed."

And this is the manner prescribed:

Let there be a room furnished as for the ritual of passing through the Tuat. And let the aspirant be clad in the robes of, and let him bear the insignia of, his grade. And at the least he shall be a neophyte.

Three days and three nights shall he have been in the tomb, vigilant and fasting, for he shall sleep no longer than three hours at any one time, and he shall drink pure water, and eat little sweet cakes consecrated unto the moon, and fruits, and the eggs of the duck, or of the goose, or of the plover. And he shall be shut in, so that no man may

7. No angel has been mentioned. The Seer was lost to being.

break in upon his meditation. But in the last twelve hours he shall neither eat nor sleep.

Then shall he break his fast, eating rich food, and drinking sweet wines, and wines that foam; and he shall banish the elements and the planets and the signs and the sephiroth; and then shall he take the holy table that he hath made for his altar, and he shall take the call of the Aethyr of which he will partake, which he hath written in the angelic character, or in the character of the holy alphabet that is revealed in Popé, upon a fair sheet of virgin vellum; and therewith shall he conjure the Aethyr, chanting the call. And in the lamp that is hung above the altar shall he burn the call that he hath written.

Then shall he kneel before the holy table, and it shall be given him to partake of the mystery of the Aethyr.

And concerning the ink with which he shall write; for the first Aethyr let it be gold, for the second scarlet, for the third violet, for the fourth emerald, for the fifth silver, for the sixth sapphire, for the seventh orange, for the eighth indigo, for the ninth gray, for the tenth black, for the eleventh maroon, for the twelfth russet, for the thirteenth green-gray, for the fourteenth amber, for the fifteenth olive, for the sixteenth pale blue, for the seventeenth crimson, for the eighteenth bright yellow, for the nineteenth crimson adorned with silver, for the twentieth mauve, for the twenty-first pale green, for the twenty-second rose-madder, for the twenty-third violet cobalt, for the twenty-fourth beetle-brown, blue-brown colour, for the twenty-fifth a cold dark gray, for the twenty-sixth white flecked with red, blue, and yellow; the edges of the letters shall be green, for the twenty-seventh angry clouds of ruddy brown, for the twenty-eighth indigo, for the twenty-ninth bluish-green, for the thirtieth mixed colours.

This shall be the form to be used by him who would partake of the mystery of any Aethyr. And let him not change so much as the style of a letter, lest the holy word be blasphemed.

And let him beware, after he hath been permitted to partake of this mystery, that he await the completion of the 91st hour of his retirement, before he open the door of the place of his retirement; lest he contaminate his glory with uncleanness, and lest they that behold him be smitten by his glory unto death.

For this is a holy mystery, and he that did first attain to reveal the alphabet thereof, perceived not one ten-thousandth part of the fringe that is upon its vesture.

Come away! for the clouds are gathered together, and the Aire heaveth like the womb of a woman in travail. Come away! lest he loose the lightnings from his hand, and unleash his hounds of thunder. Come away! For the voice of the Aethyr is accomplished. Come away! For the seal of His loving-kindness is made sure. And let there be praise and blessing unspeakable unto him that sitteth upon the Holy Throne, for he casteth down mercies as a spendthrift that scattereth gold. And he hath shut up judgment and hidden it away as a miser that hoardeth coins of little worth.

All this while the Angel hath been pushing me backwards, and now he is turned into a golden cross with a rose at its heart, and that is the red cross wherein is set the golden shew-stone.

BOU-SAADA.
December 1, 1909. 2:30–4:10 P.M.

THE CRY OF THE 17TH AETHYR WHICH IS CALLED TAN

Into the stone there first cometh the head of a dragon, and then the Angel Madimi. She is not the mere elemental that one would suppose from the account of Casaubon. I enquire why her form is different.

She says: Since all things are God, in all things thou seest just so much of God as thy capacity affordeth thee. But behold! Thou must pierce deeply into this Aethyr before true images appear. For TAN is that which transformeth judgment into justice. BAL is the sword, and TAN the balances.

A pair of balances appears in the stone, and on the bar of the balance is written: Motion about a point is iniquity.

And behind the balances is a plume, luminous, azure. And somehow connected with the plume, but I cannot divine how, are these words: Breath is iniquity. (That is, any wind must stir the feather of truth.)

And behind the plume is a shining filament of quartz, suspended vertically from the abyss to the abyss. And in the midst is a winged disk of some extremely delicate, translucent substance, on which is written in the "dagger" alphabet: Torsion is iniquity. (This means, that the Rashith Ha-Gilgalim is the first appearance of evil.)

And now an Angel appears, like as he were carven in black diamonds. And he cries: Woe unto the Second, whom all nations of men call the First. Woe unto the First, whom all grades of Adepts call The First. Woe unto me, for I, even as they, have worshipped him. But she in whose paps are the galaxies, and he that never shall be known, in them is no motion. For the infinite Without filleth all and moveth not, and the infinite Within goeth indeed; but it is no odds, else were the space-marks confounded.

And now the Angel is but a shining speck of blackness in the midst of a tremendous sphere of liquid and vibrating light, at first gold, then becoming green, and lastly pure blue. And I see that the green of Libra is made up of the yellow of air and the blue of water, swords and cups, judgment and mercy. And this word TAN meaneth mercy.

And the feather of Maat is blue because the truth of justice is mercy. And a voice cometh, as it were the music of the ripples of the surface of the sphere: Truth is delight. (This means that the Truth of the universe is delight.)

Another voice cometh; it is the voice of a mighty Angel, all in silver; the scales of his armour and the plumes of his wings are like mother-of-pearl in a framework of silver. And he sayeth: Justice is the equity that ye have made for yourselves between truth and falsehood. But in Truth there is nothing of this, for there is only Truth. Your falsehood is but a little falser than your truth. Yet by your truth shall ye come to Truth. Your truth is your troth with Adonai the Beloved one. And the Chymical Marriage of the Alchemists beginneth with a Weighing, and he that is not found wanting hath within him one spark of fire, so dense and so intense that it cannot be moved, though all the winds of heaven should clamour against it, and all the waters of the abyss surge against it, and all the multitude of the earths heap themselves upon it to smother it. Nay, it shall not be moved.

And this is the fire of which it is written: "Hear thou the voice of fire!" And the voice of fire is the second chapter of *The Book of the Law*, that is revealed unto him that is a score and half a score and three that are scores, and six, by Aiwass, that is his guardian, the mighty Angel that extendeth from the first unto the last, and maketh known the mysteries that are beyond. And the method and the form of invocation whereby a man shall attain to the knowledge and conversation of his Holy Guardian Angel shall be given unto thee in the proper place, and seeing that the word is deadlier than lightning, do thou meditate straitly thereupon, solitary, in a place where is no living thing visible, but only the light of the sun. And thy head shall be bare.[8] Thus mayest thou become fitted to receive this, the holiest of the Mysteries. And it is the holiest of the Mysteries because it is the Next Step. And those Mysteries which lie beyond, though they be holier, are not holy unto thee, but only remote. (The sense of this passage seems to be, that the holiness of a thing implies its personal relation with one, just as one cannot blaspheme an unknown god, because one does not know what to say to annoy him. And this explains the perfect inefficiency of those who try to insult the saints; the most violent attacks are very often merely clumsy compliments.)

Now the Angel is spread completely over the globe, a dewy film of silver upon that luminous blue.

And a great voice cries: Behold the Queen of Heaven, how she hath woven her robes from the loom of justice. For as that straight path of the Arrow cleaving the Rainbow became righteousness in her that sitteth in the hall of double truth, so at last is she exalted unto the throne of the High Priestess, the Priestess of the Silver Star, wherein also is thine Angel made manifest. And this is the mystery of the camel that is ten days in the desert, and is not athirst, because he hath within him that water which is the dew distilled from the night of Nuit. Triple is the cord of silver, that it may not be loosed; and three score and half a score and three is the number of the name of my name, for that the ineffable wisdom, that also is of the sphere of the stars, informeth me. Thus am I crowned with the triangle that is about the eye, and therefore is my number three. And in me there

8. This I performed in a sort of cave upon the ridge of a great mountain in the Desert near Bou-Saada at 12-3 P.M. on December 2.

is no imperfection, because through me descendeth the influence of TARO. And that is also the number of Aiwass the mighty Angel, the Minister of Silence.

And even as the shew-stone burneth thy forehead with its intolerable flame, so he who hath known me, though but from afar, is marked out and chosen from among men, and he shall never turn back or turn aside, for he hath made the link that is not to be broken, nay, not by the malice of the Four Great Princes of the evil of the world, nor by Choronzon, that mighty Devil, nor by the wrath of God, nor by the affliction and feebleness of the soul.

Yet with this assurance be not thou content; for though thou hast the wings of the Eagle, they are vain, except they be joined to the shoulders of the Bull. Now, therefore, I send forth a shaft of my light, even as a ladder let down from the heaven upon the earth, and by this black cross of Themis that I hold before thine eyes, do I swear unto thee that the path shall be open henceforth for evermore.

There is a clash of a myriad silver cymbals, and silence. And then three times a note is struck upon a bell, which sounds like my holy Tibetan bell, that is made of electrum magicum.

I am happily returned unto the earth.

Bou-Saada.
December 2, 1909. 12:15–2 A.M.

THE CRY OF THE 16TH AETHYR
WHICH IS CALLED LEA

There are faint and flickering images in a misty landscape, all very transient. But the general impression is of moonrise at midnight, and a crowned virgin riding upon a bull.

And they come up into the surface of the stone. And she is singing a chant of praise: Glory unto him that hath taken upon himself the image of toil. For by his labour is my labour accomplished. For I, being a woman, lust ever to mate myself with some beast. And this is the salvation of the world, that always I am deceived by some god, and that my child is the guardian of the labyrinth that hath two-and-seventy paths.

Now she is gone.

And now there are Angels, walking up and down in the stone. They are the Angels of the Holy Sevenfold Table. It seems that they are waiting for the Angel of the Aethyr to come forth.

Now at last he appears in the gloom: He is a mighty King, with crown and orb and sceptre, and his robes are of purple and gold. And he casts down the orb and sceptre to the earth, and he tears off his crown, and throws it on the ground, and tramples it. And he tears out his hair, that is of ruddy gold tinged with silver, and he plucks at his beard, and cries with a terrible voice: Woe unto me that am cast down from my place by the might of the new Aeon. For the ten palaces are broken, and the ten kings are carried away into bondage, and they are set to fight as the gladiators in the circus of him that hath laid his hand upon eleven. For the ancient tower is shattered by the Lord of the Flame and the Lightning. And they that walk upon their hands shall build the holy place. Blessed are they who have turned the Eye of Hoor unto the zenith, for they shall be filled with the vigour of the goat.

All that was ordered and stable is shaken. The Aeon of Wonders is come. Like locusts shall they gather themselves together, the servants of the Star and of the Snake, and they shall eat up everything that is upon the earth. For why? Because the Lord of Righteousness delighteth in them.

The prophets shall prophesy monstrous things, and the wizards shall perform monstrous things. The sorceress shall be desired of all men, and the enchanter shall rule the earth.

Blessing unto the name of the Beast, for he hath let loose a mighty flood of fire from his manhood, and from his womanhood hath he let loose a mighty flood of water. Every thought of his mind is as a tempest that uprooteth the great trees of the earth, and shaketh the mountains thereof. And the throne of his spirit is a mighty throne of madness and desolation, so that they that look upon it shall cry: Behold the abomination!

Of a single ruby shall that throne be built, and it shall be set upon an high mountain, and men shall see it afar off. Then will I gather together my chariots and my horsemen and my ships of war. By sea and land shall my armies and my navies encompass it, and I will encamp round about it, and besiege it, and by the flame thereof shall I be utterly devoured. Many lying spirits have I sent into the world that my Aeon might be established, and they shall all be overthrown.

Great is the Beast that cometh forth like a lion, the servant of the Star and of the Snake. He is the Eternal one; He is the Almighty one. Blessed are they upon whom he shall look with favour, for nothing shall stand before his face. Accursed are they upon whom he shall look with derision, for nothing shall stand before his face.

And every mystery that hath not been revealed from the foundation of the world he shall reveal unto his chosen. And they shall have power over every spirit of the Ether; and of the earth and under the earth; on dry land and in the water; of whirling air and of rushing fire. And they shall have power over all the inhabitants of the earth, and every scourge of God shall be subdued beneath their feet. The angels shall come unto them and walk with them, and the great gods of heaven shall be their guests.

But I must sit apart, with dust upon my head, discrowned and desolate. I must lurk in forbidden corners of the earth. I must plot secretly in the by-ways of great cities, in the fog, and in marshes of the rivers of pestilence. And all my cunning shall not serve me. And all my undertakings shall be brought to naught. And the ministers of the Beast shall catch me and tear out my tongue with pincers of red-hot iron, and they shall brand my forehead with the word of derision, and they shall shave my head, and pluck out my beard, and make a show of me.

And the spirit of prophecy shall come upon me despite me ever and anon, as even now upon my heart and upon my throat; and upon my tongue seared with strong acid are the words: *Vim patior.* For so must I give glory to him that hath supplanted me, that hath cast me down into the dust. I have hated him, and with hate my bones are rotten. I would have spat upon him, and my spittle hath befouled my beard. I have taken up the sword against him, and I am fallen upon it, and mine entrails are about my feet.

Who shall strive with his might? Hath he not the sword and the spear of the Warrior Lord of the Sun? Who shall contend with him? Who shall lift himself up against him? For the latchet of his sandal is more than the helmet of the Most High. Who shall reach up to him in supplication, save those that he shall set upon his shoulders? Would God that my tongue were torn out by the roots, and my throat cut across, and my heart torn out and given to the vultures, before I say this that I must say: Blessing and Worship to the Prophet of the Lovely Star!

And now he is fallen quite to the ground, in a heap, and dust is upon his head; and the throne upon which he sat is shattered into many pieces.

And dimly dawning in this unutterable gloom, far, far above, is the face that is the face of a man and of a

woman, and upon the brow is a circle, and upon the
breast is a circle, and in the palm of the right hand is a
circle. Gigantic is his stature, and he hath the Uraeus
crown, and the leopard's skin, and the flaming orange
apron of a god. And invisibly about him is Nuit, and in
his heart is Hadit, and between his feet is the great god
Ra Hoor Khuit. And in his right hand is a flaming wand,
and in his left a book. Yet is he silent; and that which is
understood between him and me shall not be revealed
in this place. And the mystery shall be revealed to
whosoever shall say, with ecstasy of worship in his heart,
with a clear mind, and a passionate body: It is the voice
of a god, and not of a man.

And now all that glory hath withdrawn itself; and the
old King lies prostrate, abject.

And the virgin that rode upon the bull cometh forth, led
by all those Angels of the Holy Sevenfold Table, and they
are dancing round her with garlands and sheaves of
flowers, loose robes and hair dancing in the wind. And
she smiles upon me with infinite brilliance, so that the
whole Aethyr flushes warm, and she says with a subtle
sub-meaning, pointing downwards: By this, that.

And I took her hand and kissed it, and I say to her: Am
I not nearly purged of the iniquity of my forefathers?

With that she bends down, and kisses me on the mouth,
and says: "Yet a little, and on thy left arm shalt thou
carry a man-child, and give him to drink of the milk of
thy breasts. But I go dancing."

And I wave my hand, and the Aethyr is empty and dark,
and I bow myself before it in the sign that I, and only I,
may know. And I sink through waves of blackness, poised
on an eagle, down, down, down.

And I give the sign that only I may know.

And now there is nothing in the stone but the black
cross of Themis, and on it these words: Memento:

Sequor. (These words probably mean that the Equinox of Horus is to be followed by that of Themis.)

BOU-SAADA.
December 2, 1909. 4:50–6:5 P.M.

THE CRY OF THE 15TH AETHYR
WHICH IS CALLED OXO

There appears immediately in the Aethyr a tremendous column of scarlet fire, whirling forth, rebounding, crying aloud. And about it are four columns of green and blue and gold and silver, each inscribed with writings in the character of the dagger. And the column of fire is dancing among the pillars. Now it seems that the fire is but the skirt of the dancer, and the dancer is a mighty god. The vision is overpowering.

As the dancer whirls, she chants in a strange, slow voice, quickening as she goes: Lo! I gather up every spirit that is pure, and weave him into my vesture of flame. I lick up the lives of men, and their souls sparkle from mine eyes. I am the mighty sorceress, the lust of the spirit. And by my dancing I gather for my mother Nuit the heads of all them that are baptised in the waters of life. I am the lust of the spirit that eateth up the soul of man. I have prepared a feast for the adepts, and they that partake thereof shall see God.

Now it is clear what she has woven in her dance; it is the Crimson Rose of 49 Petals, and the Pillars are the Cross with which it is conjoined. And between the pillars shoot out rays of pure green fire; and now all the pillars are golden. She ceases to dance, and dwindles, gathering herself into the centre of the Rose.

Now it is seen that the Rose is a vast amphitheatre, with seven tiers, each tier divided into seven partitions. And they that sit in the Amphitheatre are the seven grades of the Order of the Rosy Cross. This Amphitheatre is built of rose-coloured marble, and of its size I can say only that the sun might be used as a ball to be thrown by the players in the arena. But in the arena there is a little altar of emerald, and its top has the heads of the Four Beasts, in turquoise and rock crystal. And the floor of the arena is ridged like a grating of lapis lazuli. And it is full of pure quicksilver.

Above the altar is a veiled Figure, whose name is Pan. Those in the outer tier adore him as a Man; and in the next tier they adore him as a Goat; and in the next tier they adore him as a Ram; and in the next tier they adore him as a Crab; and in the next tier they adore him as an Ibis; and in the next tier they adore him as a Golden Hawk; and in the next tier they adore him not.

And now the light streameth out from the altar, splashed out by the feet of him that is above it. It is the Holy Twelvefold Table OIT.

The voice of him that is above the altar is silence, but the echo thereof cometh back from the walls of the circus, and is speech. And this is the speech: Three and four are the days of a quarter of the moon, and on the seventh day is the sabbath, but thrice four is the Sabbath of the Adepts whereof the form is revealed in the Aethyr ZID; that is the eighth of the Aires. And the mysteries of the Table shall not be wholly revealed, nor shall they be revealed herein. But thou shalt gather of the sweat of thy brow a pool of clear water wherein this shall be revealed. And of the oil that thou burnest in the midnight shall be gathered together thirteen rivers of blessing; and of the oil and the water I will prepare a wine to intoxicate the young men and the maidens.

And now the Table is become the universe; every star is a letter of the Book of Enoch. And the Book of Enoch is drawn therefrom by an inscrutable Mystery, that is known only to the Angels and the Holy Sevenfold Table. While

I have been gazing upon this table, an Adept has come forth, one from each tier, except the inmost Tier.

And the first drove a dagger into my heart, and tasted the blood, and said: καθαρός , καθαρός , καθαρός , καθαρός , καθαρός , καθαρός .

And the second Adept has been testing the muscles of my right arm and shoulder, and he says: fortis, fortis, fortis, fortis, fortis.

And the third Adept examines the skin and tastes the sweat of my left arm, and says:

TAN, TAN, TAN, TAN.

And the fourth Adept examines my neck, and seems to approve, though he says nothing; and he hath opened the right half of my brain, and he makes some examination, and says: "Samajh, samajh, samajh."

And the fifth Adept examines the left half of my brain, and then holds up his hand in protest, and says "PLA..." (I cannot get the sentence, but the meaning is: In the thick darkness the seed awaiteth spring.)

And now am I again rapt in contemplation of that universe of letters which are stars.

The words ORLO, ILRO, TULE are three most secret names of God. They are Magick names, each having an interpretation of the same kind as the interpretation of I.N.R.I., and the name OIT, RLU, LRL, OOE are other names of God, that contain magical formulae, the first to invoke fire; the second, water; the third, air; and the fourth, earth.

And if the Table be read diagonally, every letter, and every combination of letters, is the name of a devil. And from these are drawn the formulae of evil magick. But the holy letter I above the triad LLL dominateth the Table, and preserveth the peace of the universe.

And in the seven talismans about the central Table are contained the Mysteries of drawing forth the letters. And the letters of the circumference declare the glory of Nuit, that beginneth from Aries.[9]

All this while the Adepts have been chanting as it were an oratorio for seven instruments. And this oratorio hath one dominant theme of rapture. Yet it applieth to every detail of the universe as well as to the whole. And herein is Choronzon brought utterly to ruin, that all his work is against his will, not only in the whole, but in every part thereof, even as a fly that walketh upon a beryl-stone.

And the tablet blazeth ever brighter till it filleth the whole Aire. And behold! there is one God therein, and the letters of the stars in his crown, Orion, and the Pleiades, and Aldebaran, and Alpha Centauri, and Cor Leonis, and Cor Scorpionis, and Spica, and the pole-star, and Hercules, and Regulus, and Aquila, and the Ram's Eye.

And upon a map of the stars shalt thou draw the sigil of that name; and because also some of the letters are alike, thou shalt know that the stars also have tribes and nations. The letter of a star is but the totem thereof. And the letter representeth not the whole nature of the star, but each star must be known by itself in the wisdom of him that hath the Cynocephalus in leash.

And this pertaineth unto the grade of a Magus—and that is beyond thine. (All this is communicated not by voice, or by writing; and there is no form in the stone, but only the brilliance of the Table. And now I am withdrawn from all that, but the Rosy Cross of 49 petals is set upright upon the summit of a pyramid, and all is dark, because of the exceeding light behind.)

And there cometh a voice: The fly cried unto the ox, "Beware! Strengthen thyself. Set thy feet firmly upon the earth, for it is my purpose to alight between thy shoul-

9. Note that the corner letters in this table are all B = ♑ .

ders, and I would not harm thee." So also are they who wish well unto the Masters of the Pyramid.

And the bee said unto the flower: "Give me of thine honey," and the flower gave richly thereof; but the bee, though he wit it not, carried the seed of the flower into many fields of sun. So also are they that take unto themselves the Masters of the Pyramid for servants.

Now the exceeding light that was behind the Pyramid, and the Rosy Cross that is set thereon, hath fulfilled the whole Aire. The black Pyramid is like the back of a black diamond. Also the Rosy Cross is loosened, and the petals of the Rose are the mingled hues of sunset and of dawn; and the Cross is the Golden light of noon, and in the heart of the Rose there is the secret light that men call midnight.

And a voice: "Glory to God and thanksgiving to God, and there is no God but God. And He is exalted; He is great; and in the Sevenfold Table is His Name writ openly, and in the Twelvefold Table is His Name concealed."

And the Pyramid casts a shadow of itself into the sky, and the shadow spreads over the whole stone. And an angel clad in blue and scarlet, with golden wings and plumes of purple fire, comes forth and scatters disks of green and gold, filling all the Aire. And they become swiftly-whirling wheels, singing together.

And the voice of the angel cries: Gather up thy garments about thee,[10] O thou that hast entered the circle of the Sabbath; for in thy grave-clothes shouldest thou behold the resurrection.

The flesh hangeth upon thee like his rags upon a beggar that is a pilgrim to the shrine of the Exalted One. Never-

10. Since the examination in the amphitheatre I have been a naked spirit without garments or anything; by garments he means the body.

theless, bear them bravely, and rejoice in the beauty thereof, for the company of the pilgrims is a glad company, and
they have no care, and with song and dance and wine and
fair women do they make merry. And every hostel is their
palace, and every maid their queen.

Gather up thy garments about thee, I say, for the voice
of the Aethyr, that is the voice of the Aeon, is ended, and
thou art absorbed into the lesser night, and caught in the
web of the light of thy mother in the word ARBADA-
HARBA.

And now the five and the six are divorced, and I am
come again within my body.

BOU-SAADA.
December 3, 1909. 9:15 to 11:10 A.M.

THE CRY OF THE 14TH AETHYR
WHICH IS CALLED UTI

There come into the stone a white goat, a green dragon,
and a tawny bull. But they pass away immediately. There
is a veil of such darkness before the Aethyr that it seems
impossible to pierce it. But there is a voice saying: Behold, the Great One of the Night of Time stirreth, and
with his tail he churneth up the slime, and of the foam
thereof shall he make stars. And in the battle of the Python
and the Sphinx shall the glory be to the Sphinx, but the
victory to the Python.

Now the veil of darkness is formed of a very great number of exceedingly fine black veils, and one tears them off
one at a time. And the voice says, There is no light or
knowledge or beauty or stability in the Kingdom of the
Grave, whither thou goest. And the worm is crowned.
All that thou wast hath he eaten up, and all that thou
art is his pasture until to-morrow. And all that thou
shalt be is nothing. Thou who wouldst enter the domain

of the Great One of the Night of Time, this burden must thou take up. Deepen not a superficies.

But I go on tearing down the veil that I may behold the vision of UTI, and hear the voice thereof. And there is a voice: He hath drawn the black bean. And another voice answers it: Not otherwise could he plant the Rose. And the first voice: He hath drunk of the waters of death. The answer: Not otherwise could he water the Rose. And the first voice: He hath burnt himself at the Fires of life. And the answer: Not otherwise could he sun the Rose. And the first voice is so faint that I cannot hear it. But the answer is: Not otherwise could he pluck the Rose.

And still I go on, struggling with the blackness. Now there is an earthquake. The veil is torn into thousands of pieces that go flying away in a whirling wind. And there is an all-glorious Angel before me, standing in the sign of Apophis and Typhon. On his Forehead is a star, but all about him is darkness, and the crying of beasts. And there are lamps moving in the darkness.

And the Angel says: Depart! For thou must invoke me only in the darkness. Therein will I appear, and reveal unto thee the Mystery of UTI. For the Mystery thereof is great and terrible. And it shall not be spoken in sight of the sun.

Therefore I withdraw myself. (Thus far the vision upon Da'leh Addin, a mountain in the desert near Bou-Saada.)

December 3.
2:50–3:15 P.M.

The Angel re-appears

The blackness gathers about, so thick, so clinging, so penetrating, so oppressive, that all the other darkness that I have ever conceived would be like bright light beside it.

His voice comes in a whisper: O thou that art master of the fifty gates of Understanding, is not my mother a black woman? O thou that art master of the Pentagram, is not the egg of spirit a black egg? Here abideth terror, and the blind ache of the Soul, and lo! even I, who am the sole light, a spark shut up, stand in the sign of Apophis and Typhon.

I am the snake that devoureth the spirit of man with the lust of light. I am the sightless storm in the night that wrappeth the world about with desolation. Chaos is my name, and thick darkness. Know thou that the darkness of the earth is ruddy, and the darkness of the air is grey, but the darkness of the soul is utter blackness.

The egg of the spirit is a basilisk egg, and the gates of the understanding are fifty, that is the sign of the Scorpion. The pillars about the neophyte are crowned with flame, and the vault of the Adepts is lighted by the Rose. And in the abyss is the eye of the hawk. But upon the great sea shall the Master of the Temple find neither star nor moon.

And I was about to answer him: "The light is within me." But before I could frame the words, he answered me with the great word that is the Key of the Abyss. And he said: Thou hast entered the night; dost thou yet lust for day? Sorrow is my name, and affliction. I am girt about with tribulation. Here still hangs the Crucified One, and here the Mother weeps over the children that she hath not borne. Sterility is my name, and desolation. Intolerable is thine ache, and incurable thy wound. I said, Let the darkness cover me; and behold, I am compassed about with the blackness that hath no name. O thou, who hast cast down the light into the earth, so must thou do for ever. And the light of the sun shall not shine upon thee, and the moon shall not lend thee of her lustre, and the stars shall be hidden, because thou art passed beyond these things, beyond the need of these things, beyond the desire of these things.

What I thought were shapes of rocks, rather felt than seen, now appear to be veiled Masters, sitting absolutely still and silent. Nor can any one be distinguished from the others.

And the Angel sayeth: Behold where thine Angel hath led thee! Thou didst ask fame, power and pleasure, health and wealth and love, and strength, and length of days. Thou didst hold life with eight tentacles, like an octopus. Thou didst seek the four powers and the seven delights and the twelve emancipations and the two and twenty Privileges and the nine and forty Manifestations, and lo! thou art become as one of These. Bowed are their backs, whereon resteth the universe. Veiled are their faces, that have beheld the glory Ineffable.

These adepts seem like Pyramids—their hoods and robes are like Pyramids.

And the Angel sayeth: Verily is the Pyramid a Temple of Initiation. Verily also is it a tomb. Thinkest thou that there is life within the Masters of the Temple, that sit hooded, encamped upon the Sea? Verily, there is no life in them.

Their sandals were the pure light, and they have taken them from their feet and cast them down through the abyss, for this Aethyr is holy ground.

Herein no forms appear, and the vision of God face to face, that is transmuted in the Athanor called dissolution, or hammered into one in the forge of meditation, is in this place but a blasphemy and a mockery.

And the Beatific Vision is no more, and the glory of the Most High is no more. There is no more knowledge. There is no more bliss. There is no more power. There is no more beauty. For this is the Palace of Understanding: for thou art one with the Primeval things.

Drink in the myrrh of my speech, that is bruised with the gall of the roc, and dissolved in the ink of the cuttle-fish, and perfumed with the deadly nightshade.

This is thy wine, who wast drunk upon the wine of Iacchus. And for bread shalt thou eat salt, O thou on the corn of Ceres that didst wax fat! For as pure being is pure nothing, so is pure wisdom pure——,[11] and so is pure understanding silence, and stillness, and darkness. The eye is called seventy, and the triple Aleph whereby thou perceivest it, divideth into the number of the terrible word that is the Key of the Abyss.

I am Hermes, that am sent from the Father to expound all things discreetly in these the last words that thou shalt hear before thou take thy seat among these, whose eyes are sealed up, and whose ears are stopped, and whose mouths are clenched, who are folded in upon themselves, the liquor of whose bodies is dried up, so that nothing remains but a little pyramid of dust.

And that bright light of comfort, and that piercing sword of truth, and all that power and beauty that they have made of themselves, is cast from them, as it is written, "I saw Satan like lightning fall from Heaven." And as a flaming sword is it dropt through the abyss, where the four beasts keep watch and ward. And it appear-eth in the heaven of Jupiter as a morning star, or as an evening star. And the light thereof shineth even unto the earth, and bringeth hope and help to them that dwell in the darkness of thought, and drink of the poison of life. Fifty are the gates of understanding, and one hundred and six are the seasons thereof. And the name of every season is Death.

During all this speech, the figure of the Angel has

11. I suppose that only a Magus could have heard this word.

dwindled and flickered, and now it is gone out.

And I come back in the body, rushing like a flame in a great wind. And the shew-stone has become warm, and in it is its own light.

BOU-SAADA.
December 3, 1909. 9:50–11:15 P.M.

THE CRY OF THE 13TH AETHYR
WHICH IS CALLED ZIM

Into the Stone there cometh an image of shining waters, glistening in the sun. Unfathomable is their beauty, for they are limpid, and the floor is of gold. Yet the sense thereof is of fruitlessness.

And an Angel cometh forth, of pure pale gold, walking upon the water. Above his head is a rainbow, and the water foams beneath his feet. And he saith: Before his face am I come that hath the thirty-three thunders of increase in his hand. From the golden water shalt thou gather corn.

All the Aire behind him is gold, but it opens as it were a veil. There are two terrible black giants, wrestling in mortal hatred. And there is a little bird upon a bush, and the bird flaps its wings. Thereat the strength of the giants snaps, and they fall in heaps to the earth, as though all their bones were suddenly broken.

And now waves of light roll through the Aethyr, as if they were playing. Therefore suddenly I am in a garden, upon a terrace of a great castle, that is upon a rocky mountain. In the garden are fountains and many flowers. There are girls also in the garden, tall, slim, delicate and pale. And now I see that the flowers are the girls, for they change from one to another; so varied, and lucent, and harmonious is all this garden, that it seems like a great opal.

A voice comes: This water which thou seest is called

the water of death. But NEMO hath filled therefrom our springs.

And I said: Who is NEMO?

And the voice answered: A dolphin's tooth, and a ram's horns, and the hand of a man that is hanged, and the phallus of a goat. (By this I understand that nun is explained by shin, and hé by resh, and mem by yod, and ayin by tau. NEMO is therefore called $165 = 11 \times 15$; and is in himself $910 = 91$ Amen $\times$ 10; and $13 \times 70 =$ The One Eye, *Achad Ayin*.)

And now there cometh an Angel into the garden, but he hath not any of the attributes of the former Angels, for he is like a young man, dressed in white linen robes.

And he saith: No man hath beheld the face of my Father. Therefore he that hath beheld it is called NEMO. And know thou that every man that is called NEMO hath a garden that he tendeth. And every garden that is and flourisheth hath been prepared from the desert by NEMO, watered with the waters that were called death.

And I say unto him: To what end is the garden prepared?

And he saith: First for the beauty and delight thereof; and next because it is written, "And Tetragrammaton Elohim planted a garden eastward in Eden." And lastly, because though every flower bringeth forth a maiden, yet is there one flower that shall bring forth a man-child. And his name shall be called NEMO, when he beholdeth the face of my Father. And he that tendeth the garden seeketh not to single out the flower that shall be NEMO. He doeth naught but tend the garden.

And I said: Pleasant indeed is the garden, and light is the toil of tending it, and great is the reward.

And he said: Bethink thee that NEMO hath beheld the face of my Father. In Him is only Peace.

And I said: Are all gardens like unto this garden?

And he waved his hand, and in the Aire across the valley appeared an island of coral, rosy, with green palms and fruit trees, in the midst of the bluest of the seas.

And he waved his hand again, and there appeared a valley shut in by mighty snow mountains, and in it were pleasant streams of water, rushing through, and broad rivers, and lakes covered with lilies.

And he waved his hand again, and there was a vision, as it were of an oasis in the desert.

And again he waved his hand, and there was a dim country with grey rocks, and heather, and gorse, and bracken.

And he waved his hand yet again, and there was a park, and a small house therein, surrounded by yews. This time the house opens, and I see in it an old man, sitting by the table. He is blind. Yet he writeth in a great book, constantly. I see what he is writing: "The words of the Book are as the leaves of the flowers in the garden. Many indeed of these my songs shall go forth as maidens, but there is one among them, which one I know not, that shall be a manchild, whose name shall be NEMO, when he hath beheld the face of the Father, and become blind."

(All this vision is most extraordinarily pleasant and peaceful, entirely without strength or ecstasy, or any positive quality, but equally free from the opposites of any of those qualities.) And the young man seems to read my thought, which is, that I should love to stay in this garden and do nothing for ever; for he sayeth to me: Come with me, and behold how NEMO tendeth his garden.

So we enter the earth, and there is a veiled figure, in absolute darkness. Yet it is perfectly possible to see in it, so that the minutest details do not escape us. And upon the root of one flower he pours acid so that that root writhes as if in torture. And another he cuts, and the shriek is like the shriek of a mandrake, torn up by the roots. And another he chars with fire, and yet another he anoints with oil.

And I said: Heavy is the labour, but great indeed is the reward.

And the young man answered me: He shall not see the reward; he tendeth the garden.

And I said: What shall come unto him?

And he said: This thou canst not know, nor is it revealed by the letters that are the totems of the stars, but only by the stars.

And he says to me, quite disconnectedly: The man of earth is the adherent. The lover giveth his life unto the work among men. The hermit goeth solitary, and giveth only of his light unto men.

And I ask him: Why does he tell me that?

And he says: I tell thee not. Thou tellest thyself, for thou hast pondered thereupon for many days, and hast not found light. And now that thou art called NEMO, the answer to every riddle that thou hast not found shall spring up in thy mind, unsought. Who can tell upon what day a flower shall bloom?

And thou shalt give thy wisdom unto the world, and that shall be thy garden. And concerning time and death, thou hast naught to do with these things. For though a precious stone be hidden in the sand of the desert, it shall not heed for the wind of the desert, although it be but sand. For the worker of works hath worked thereupon; and because it is clear, it is invisible; and because it is hard, it moveth not.

All these words are heard by everyone that is called NEMO. And with that doth he apply himself to understanding. And he must understand the virtue of the waters of death, and he must understand the virtue of the sun and the wind, and of the worm that turneth the earth, and of the stars that roof in the garden. And he must understand the separate nature and property of every flower, or how shall he tend his garden?

And I said to him: Concerning the Vision and the Voice, I would know if these things be of the essence of the Aethyr, or of the essence of the seer.

And he answers: It is of the essence of him that is called NEMO, combined with the essence of the Aethyr, for from the 1st Aethyr to the 15th Aethyr, there is no vision and no voice, save for him that is called NEMO. And he that seeketh the vision and the voice therein is led away by dog-faced demons that show no sign of truth, seducing from the Sacred Mysteries, unless his name be NEMO.

And hadst thou not been fitted, thou too hadst been led away, for before the gate of the 15th Aethyr, is this written: He shall send them strong delusion, that they should believe a lie. And again it is written: The Lord hardened Pharaoh's heart. And again it is written that God tempteth man. But thou hadst the word and the sign, and thou hadst authority from thy superior, and licence. And thou hast done well in that thou didst not dare, and in that thou dost dare. For daring is not presumption.

And he said moreover: Thou dost well to keep silence, for I perceive how many questions arise in thy mind; yet already thou knowest that the answering, as the asking, must be vain. For NEMO hath all in himself. He hath come where there is no light or knowledge, only when he needeth them no more.

And then we bow silently, giving a certain sign, called the Sign of Isis Rejoicing. And then he remaineth to ward the Aethyr, while I return unto the bank of sand that is the bed of the river near the desert.

THE RIVER-BED NEAR BOU-SAADA.
December 4, 1909. 2:10–3:45 P.M.

THE CRY OF THE 12TH AETHYR
WHICH IS CALLED LOE

There appear in the stone two pillars of flame, and in the midst is a chariot of white fire.

This seems to be the chariot of the Seventh Key of the Tarot. But it is drawn by four sphinxes, diverse, like the four sphinxes upon the door of the vault of the adepts, counterchanged in their component parts.

The chariot itself is the lunar crescent, waning. The canopy is supported by eight pillars of amber. These pillars are upright, and yet the canopy which they support is the whole vault of night.

The charioteer is a man in golden armour, studded with sapphires, but over his shoulders is a white robe, and over that a red robe. Upon his golden helmet he beareth for his crest a crab. His hands are clasped upon a cup, from which radiates a ruddy glow, constantly increasing, so that everything is blotted out by its glory, and the whole Aire is filled with it.

And there is a marvellous perfume in the Aire, like unto the perfume of Ra Hoor Khuit, but sublimated, as if the quintessence of that perfume alone were burnt. For it hath the richness and voluptuousness and humanity of blood, and the strength and freshness of meal, and the sweetness of honey, and the purity of olive-oil, and the holiness of that oil which is made of myrrh, and cinnamon, and galangal.

The charioteer speaks in a low, solemn voice, awe-inspiring, like a very large and very distant bell: Let him look upon the cup whose blood is mingled therein, for the wine of the cup is the blood of the saints. Glory unto the Scarlet Woman, Babylon the Mother of Abominations, that rideth upon the Beast, for she hath spilt their blood in every corner of the earth, and lo! she hath mingled it in the cup of her whoredom.

With the breath of her kisses hath she fermented it, and it hath become the wine of the Sacrament, the wine of the Sabbath; and in the Holy Assembly hath she poured it out for her worshippers, and they have become drunken thereon, so that face to face have they beheld my Father. Thus are they made worthy to become partakers of the Mystery of this holy vessel, for the blood is the life. So sitteth she from age to age, and the righteous are never weary of her kisses, and by her murders and fornications she seduceth the world. Therein is manifested the glory of my Father, who is truth.

(This wine is such that its virtue radiateth through the cup, and I reel under the intoxication of it. And every thought is destroyed by it. It abideth alone, and its name is Compassion. I understand by "Compassion," the sacrament of suffering, partaken of by the true worshippers of the Highest. And it is an ecstasy in which there is no trace of pain. Its passivity [=passion] is like the giving-up of the self to the beloved.)

The voice continues: This is the Mystery of Babylon, the Mother of abominations, and this is the mystery of her adulteries, for she hath yielded up herself to everything that liveth, and hath become a partaker in its mystery. And because she hath made herself the servant of each, therefore is she become the mistress of all. Not as yet canst thou comprehend her glory.

Beautiful art thou, O Babylon, and desirable, for thou hast given thyself to everything that liveth, and thy weakness hath subdued their strength. For in that union thou didst *understand*. Therefore art thou called Understanding, O Babylon, Lady of the Night!

This is that which is written, "O my God, in one last
rapture let me attain to the union with the many." For
she is Love, and her love is one, and she hath divided the
one love into infinite loves, and each love is one, and
equal with The One, and therefore is she passed "from
the assembly and the law and the enlightenment unto
the anarchy of solitude and darkness. For ever thus must
she veil the brilliance of Her Self."

O Babylon, Babylon, thou mighty Mother, that ridest
upon the crowned beast, let me be drunken upon the wine
of thy fornications; let thy kisses wanton me unto death,
that even I, thy cup-bearer, may *understand*.

Now, through the ruddy glow of the cup, I may perceive
far above, and infinitely great, the vision of Babylon. And
the Beast whereon she rideth is the Lord of the City of
the Pyramids, that I beheld in the fourteenth Aethyr.

Now that is gone in the glow of the cup, and the Angel
saith: Not as yet mayest thou understand the mystery of
the Beast, for it pertaineth not unto the mystery of this
Aire, and few that are new-born unto Understanding are
capable thereof.

The cup glows ever brighter and fierier. All my sense
is unsteady, being smitten with ecstasy.

And the Angel sayeth: Blessed are the saints, that their
blood is mingled in the cup, and can never be separate any
more. For Babylon the Beautiful, the Mother of abominations, hath sworn by her holy cteis, whereof every point
is a pang, that she will not rest from her adulteries until
the blood of everything that liveth is gathered therein,
and the wine thereof laid up and matured and consecrated,
and worthy to gladden the heart of my Father. For my
Father is weary with the stress of eld, and cometh not to
her bed. Yet shall this perfect wine be the quintessence,
and the elixir, and by the draught thereof shall he renew

his youth; and so shall it be eternally, as age by age the worlds do dissolve and change, and the universe unfoldeth itself as a Rose, and shutteth itself up as the Cross that is bent into the cube.

And this is the comedy of Pan, that is played at night in the thick forest. And this is the mystery of Dionysus Zagreus, that is celebrated upon the holy mountain of Kithairon. And this is the secret of the brothers of the Rosy Cross; and this is the heart of the ritual that is accomplished in the Vault of the Adepts that is hidden in the Mountain of the Caverns, even the Holy Mountain Abiegnus.

And this is the meaning of the Supper of the Passover, the spilling of the blood of the Lamb being a ritual of the Dark Brothers, for they have sealed up the Pylon with blood, lest the Angel of Death should enter therein. Thus do they shut themselves off from the company of the saints. Thus do they keep themselves from compassion and from understanding. Accursèd are they, for they shut up their blood in their heart.

They keep themselves from the kisses of my Mother Babylon, and in their lonely fortresses they pray to the false moon. And they bind themselves together with an oath, and with a great curse. And of their malice they conspire together, and they have power, and mastery, and in their cauldrons do they brew the harsh wine of delusion, mingled with the poison of their selfishness.

Thus they make war upon the Holy One, sending forth their delusion upon men, and upon everything that liveth. So that their false compassion is called compassion, and their false understanding is called understanding, for this is their most potent spell.

Yet of their own poison do they perish, and in their lonely fortresses shall they be eaten up by Time that hath

cheated them to serve him, and by the mighty devil
Choronzon, their master, whose name is the Second
Death, for the blood that they have sprinkled on their
Pylon, that is a bar against the Angel Death, is the key by
which he entereth in.[12]

The Angel sayeth: And this is the word of double power
in the voice of the Master, wherein the Five interpenetrateth the Six. This is its secret interpretation that may
not be understood, save only of *them that understand.* And
for this is it the Key of the Pylon of Power, because there
is no power that may endure, save only the power that
descendeth in this my chariot from Babylon, the city of
the Fifty Gates, the Gate of the God On (באבאלְעֶן).
Moreover is On the Key of the Vault that is 120. So
also do the Majesty and the Beauty derive from the
Supernal Wisdom.

But this is a mystery utterly beyond thine understanding. For Wisdom is the Man, and Understanding the
Woman, and not until thou hast perfectly understood
canst thou begin to be wise. But I reveal unto thee a mystery
of the Aethyrs, that not only are they bound up with the
Sephiroth, but also with the Paths. Now, the plane of the
Aethyrs interpenetrateth and surroundeth the universe
wherein the Sephiroth are established, and therefore is the
order of the Aethyrs not the order of the Tree of Life.
And only in a few places do they coincide. But the knowledge of the Aethyrs is deeper than the knowledge of the
Sephiroth, for that in the Aethyrs is the knowledge of the
Aeons, and of Θελημα . And to each shall it be given
according to his capacity. (He has been saying certain
secret things to the unconscious mind of the seer, of a
personal nature.)

12. I think the trouble with these people was, that they wanted to substitute
the blood of someone else for their own blood, because they wanted to keep
their personalities.

Now a voice comes from without: And lo! I saw you to the end.

And a great bell begins to toll. And there come six little children out of the floor of the chariot, and in their hands is a veil so fine and transparent that it is hardly visible. Yet, when they put it over the Cup, the Angel bowing his head reverently, the light of the Cup goes out entirely. And as the light of the Cup vanishes, it is like a swift sunset in the whole Aire, for it was from the light of that Cup alone that it was lighted.

And now the light is all gone out of the stone, and I am very cold.

BOU-SAADA.
December 4–5, 1909. 11:30 P.M.–1:20 A.M.

THE CRY OF THE 11TH AETHYR
WHICH IS CALLED IKH

There appears in the stone immediately the Kamea of the Moon. And it is rolled up; and behind it there appeareth a great Host of Angels. Their backs are turned towards me, but I can see how tremendous are their arms, which are swords and spears. They have wings upon their helmets and their heels; they are clad in complete armour, and the least of their swords is like the breaking forth of a tremendous storm of lightning. The least of their spears is like a great water-spout. On their shields are the eyes of Tetragrammaton, winged with flame,—white, red, black, yellow and blue. On their flanks are vast squadrons of elephants, and behind them is their meteor-artillery. They that sit upon the elephants are armed with the thunderbolt of Zeus.

Now in all that host there is no motion. Yet they are not resting upon their arms, but tense and vigilant. And between them and me is the God Shu, whom before I

did not see, because his force filleth the whole Aethyr.
And indeed he is not visible in his form. Nor does he
come to the seer through any of the senses; he is understood, rather than expressed.

I perceive that all this army is defended by fortresses,
nine mighty towers of iron upon the frontier of the Aethyr.
Each tower is filled with warriors in silver armour. It is
impossible to describe the feeling of tension; they are like
oarsmen waiting for the gun.

I perceive that an Angel is standing on either side of
me; nay, I am in the midst of a company of armed angels,
and their captain is standing in front of me. He too is clad
in silver armour; and about him, closely wrapped to his
body, is a whirling wind, so swift that any blow struck
against him would be broken.

And he speaketh unto me these words:

Behold, a mighty guard against the terror of things, the
fastness of the Most High, the legions of eternal vigilance;
these are they that keep watch and ward day and night
throughout the aeons. Set in them is all the force of the
Mighty One, yet there stirreth not one plume of the wings
of their helmets.

Behold, the foundation of the Holy City, the towers and
the bastions thereof! Behold the armies of light that are set
against the outermost Abyss, against the horror of emptiness, and the malice of Choronzon. Behold how worshipful
is the wisdom of the Master, that he hath set his stability
in the all-wandering Air and in the changeful Moon. In
the purple flashes of the lightning hath He written the
word Eternity, and in the wings of the swallow hath He
appointed rest.

By three and by three and by three hath He made firm
the foundation against the earthquake that is three. For in
the number nine is the changefulness of the numbers

brought to naught. For with whatsoever number thou wilt cover it, it appeareth unchanged.

These things are spoken unto him that understandeth, that is a breastplate unto the elephants, or a corselet unto the angels, or a scale upon the towers of iron; yet is this mighty host set only for a defence, and whoso passeth beyond their lines hath no help in them.

Yet must he that understandeth go forth unto the outermost Abyss, and there must he speak with him that is set above the four-fold terror, the Princes of Evil, even with Choronzon, the mighty devil that inhabiteth the outermost Abyss. And none may speak with him, or understand him, but the servants of Babylon, that understand, and they that are without understanding, his servants.

Behold! it entereth not into the heart, nor into the mind of man to conceive this matter; for the sickness of the body is death, and the sickness of the heart is despair, and the sickness of the mind is madness. But in the outermost Abyss is sickness of the aspiration, and sickness of the will, and sickness of the essence of all, and there is neither word nor thought wherein the image of its image is reflected.

And whoso passeth into the outermost Abyss, except he be of them that understand, holdeth out his hands, and boweth his neck, unto the chains of Choronzon. And as a devil he walketh about the earth, immortal, and he blasteth the flowers of the earth, and he corrupteth the fresh air, and he maketh poisonous the water; and the fire that is the friend of man, and the pledge of his aspiration, seeing that it mounteth ever upward as a pyramid, and seeing that man stole it in a hollow tube from Heaven, even that fire he turneth unto ruin, and madness, and fever, and destruction. And thou, that art an heap of dry dust in the city of the pyramids, must understand these things.

And now a thing happens, which is unfortunately sheer nonsense; for the Aethyr that is the foundation of the universe was attacked by the Outermost Abyss, and the only way that I can express it is by saying that the universe was shaken. But the universe was *not* shaken. And that is the exact truth; so that the rational mind which is interpreting these spiritual things is offended; but, being trained to obey, it setteth down that which it doth not understand. For the rational mind indeed reasoneth, but never attaineth unto Understanding; but the Seer is of them that understand.

And the Angel saith:

Behold, He hath established His mercy and His might, and unto His might is added victory, and unto His mercy is added splendour. And all these things hath He ordered in beauty, and He hath set them firmly upon the Eternal Rock, and therefrom He hath suspended His kingdom as one pearl that is set in a jewel of threescore pearls and twelve. And He hath garnished it with the Four Holy Living Creatures for Guardians, and He hath graven therein the seal of righteousness,[13] and He hath burnished it with the fire of His Angel, and the blush of His loveliness informeth it, and with delight and with wit hath He made it merry at the heart, and the core thereof is the Secret of His being, and therein is His name Generation. And this His stability hath the number 80, for that the price thereof is War.[14]

Beware, therefore, O thou who art appointed to understand the secret of the Outermost Abyss, for in every Abyss thou must assume the mask and form of the Angel thereof. Hadst thou a name, thou wert irrevocably lost.

13. Full title of Jesod is Tzediq Jesod Olahm, "The Righteous is the Foundation of the World."
14. I. S. V. D., Jesod, =80, the number of Pé, the letter of Mars.

Search, therefore, if there be yet one drop of blood that is not gathered into the cup of Babylon the Beautiful, for in that little pile of dust, if there could be one drop of blood, it should be utterly corrupt; it should breed scorpions and vipers, and the cat of slime.

And I said unto the Angel:

Is there not one appointed as a warden?

And he said:

Eloi, Eloi, lama sabacthani.

Such an ecstasy of anguish racks me that I cannot give it voice, yet I know it is but as the anguish of Gethsemane. And that is the last word of the Aethyr. The outposts are passed, and before the seer extends the outermost Abyss.

I am returned.

BOU-SAADA.
December 5, 1909. 10:10–11:35 P.M.

In nomine BABALON
Amen
Restriction unto Choronzon

THE TENTH AETHYR IS CALLED ZAX

This Aethyr being accursed, and the seer forewarned, he taketh these precautions for the scribe.

First let the scribe be seated in the centre of the circle in the desert sand, and let the circle be fortified by the Holy Names of God—Tetragrammaton and Shaddai El Chai and Ararita.

And let the Demon be invoked within a triangle, wherein is inscribed the name of Choronzon, and about it let him write ANAPHAXETON-ANAPHANETON-PRI-MEUMATON, and in the angles MI-CA-EL: and at each angle the Seer shall slay a pigeon, and having done this, let him retire to a secret place, where is neither sight nor hearing, and sit within his black robe, secretly invoking the Aethyr. And let the Scribe perform the Banishing

Rituals of the Pentagram and Hexagram, and let him call upon the Holy Names of God, and say the Exorcism of Honorius, and let him beseech protection and help of the Most High.

And let him be furnished with the Magick Dagger, and let him strike fearlessly at anything that may seek to break through the circle, were it the appearance of the Seer himself. And if the Demon pass out of the triangle, let him threaten him with the Dagger, and command him to return. And let him beware lest he himself lean beyond the circle. And since he reverenceth the Person of the Seer as his Teacher, let the Seer bind him with a great Oath to do this.

Now, then, the Seer being entered within the triangle, let him take the Victims and cut their throats, pouring the blood within the Triangle, and being most heedful that not one drop fall without the Triangle; or else Choronzon should be able to manifest in the universe.

And when the sand hath sucked up the blood of the victims, let him recite the Call of the Aethyr apart secretly as aforesaid. Then will the Vision be revealed, and the Voice heard.

The Oath

I, Omnia Vincam, a Probationer of A ∴ A ∴, hereby solemnly promise upon my magical honour, and swear by Adonai the angel that guardeth me, that I will defend this magic circle of Art with thoughts and words and deeds. I promise to threaten with the Dagger and command back into the triangle the spirit incontinent, if he should strive to escape from it; and to strike with a Dagger at anything that may seek to enter this Circle, were it in appearance the body of the Seer himself. And I will be exceeding wary, armed against force and cunning; and I will preserve with my life the inviolability of this Circle, Amen.

And I summon mine Holy Guardian Angel to witness this mine oath, the which if I break, may I perish, forsaken of Him. Amen and Amen.

THE CRY OF THE 10TH AETHYR
THAT IS CALLED ZAX

There is no being in the outermost Abyss, but constant forms come forth from the nothingness of it.

Then the Devil of the Aethyr, that mighty devil Choronzon, crieth aloud, Zazas, Zazas, Nasatanada Zazas.

I am the Master of Form, and from me all forms proceed.

I am I. I have shut myself up from the spendthrifts, my gold is safe in my treasure-chamber, and I have made every living thing my concubine, and none shall touch them, save only I. And yet I am scorched, even while I shiver in the wind. He hateth me and tormenteth me. He would have stolen me from myself, but I shut myself up and mock at him, even while he plagueth me. From me come leprosy and pox and plague and cancer and cholera and the falling sickness. Ah! I will reach up to the knees of the Most High, and tear his phallus with my teeth, and I will bray his testicles in a mortar, and make poison thereof, to slay the sons of men.

(Here the Spirit simulated the voice of Frater P., which also appeared to come from his station and not from the triangle.)

I don't think I can get any more; I think that's all there is.

(The Frater was seated in a secret place covered completely by a black robe, in the position called the "Thunderbolt." He did not move or speak during the ceremony.)

Next the Scribe was hallucinated, believing that before him was a beautiful courtesan whom previously he had loved in Paris. Now, she wooed him with soft words and glances, but he knew these things for delusions of the devil, and he would not leave the circle.

The demon then laughed wildly and loud.

(Upon the Scribe threatening him, the Demon proceeded, after a short delay.)

They have called me the God of laughter, and I laugh when I will slay. And they have thought that I could not smile, but I smile upon whom I would seduce, O inviolable one, that canst not be tempted. If thou canst command me by the power of the Most High, know that I did indeed tempt thee, and it repenteth me. I bow myself humbly before the great and terrible names whereby thou hast conjured and constrained me. But thy name is mercy, and I cry aloud for pardon. Let me come and put my head beneath thy feet, that I may serve thee. For if thou commandest me to obedience in the Holy names, I cannot swerve therefrom, for their first whispering is greater than the noise of all my tempests. Bid me therefore come unto thee upon my hands and knees that I may adore thee, and partake of thy forgiveness. Is not thy mercy infinite?

(Here Choronzon attempts to seduce the Scribe by appealing to his pride.)

(But the Scribe refused to be tempted, and commanded the demon to continue with the Aethyr.)

(There was again a short delay.)

Choronzon hath no form, because he is the maker of all form; and so rapidly he changeth from one to the other as he may best think fit to seduce those whom he hateth, the servants of the Most High.

Thus taketh he the form of a beautiful woman, or of a wise and holy man, or of a serpent that writheth upon the earth ready to sting.

And, because he is himself, therefore he is no self; the terror of darkness, and the blindness of night, and the deafness of the adder, and the tastelessness of stale and stagnant water, and the black fire of hatred, and the udders of the Cat of slime; not one thing, but many things. Yet, with all that, his torment is eternal. The sun burns him as he writhes naked upon the sands of hell, and the wind cuts him bitterly to the bone a harsh dry wind, so that he is sore athirst. Give unto me, I pray thee, one drop of water from the pure springs of Paradise, that I may quench my thirst.

(The Scribe refused.)

Sprinkle water upon my head. I can hardly go on.

(This last was spoken from the triangle in the natural voice of the Frater, which Choronzon again simulated. But he did not succeed in taking the Frater's form—which was absurd!)

(The Scribe resisted the appeal to his pity, and conjured the demon to proceed by the names of the Most High. Choronzon attempted also to seduce the faithfulness of the Scribe. A long colloquy ensued. The Scribe cursed him by the Holy Names of God, and the power of the Pentagram.)

I feed upon the names of the Most High. I churn them in my jaws, and I void them from my fundament. I fear not the power of the Pentagram, for I am the Master of the Triangle. My name is three hundred and thirty and three, and that is thrice one. Be vigilant, therefore, for I warn thee that I am about to deceive thee. I shall say words that thou wilt take to be the cry of the Aethyr, and thou wilt write them down, thinking them to be great secrets of Magick power, and they will be only my jesting with thee.

(Here the Scribe invoked Angels, and the Holy Guardian Angel of the Frater P. . . . The demon replied:)

I know the name of the Angel of thee and thy brother P. . . and all thy dealings with him are but a cloak for thy filthy sorceries.

(Here the Scribe averred that he knew more than the demon, and so feared him not, and ordered the demon to proceed.)

Thou canst tell me naught that I know not, for in me is all Knowledge: Knowledge is my name. Is not the head of the great Serpent arisen into Knowledge?

(Here the Scribe again commanded Choronzon to continue with the call.)

Know thou that there is no Cry in the tenth Aethyr like unto the other Cries, for Choronzon is Dispersion, and cannot fix his mind upon any one thing for any length of time. Thou canst master him in argument, O talkative one; thou wast commanded, wast thou not, to talk to Choronzon? He sought not to enter the circle, or to leave the triangle, yet thou didst prate of all these things.

(Here the Scribe threatened the demon with anger and pain and hell. The demon replied:)

Thinkest thou, O fool, that there is any anger and any pain that I am not, or any hell but this my spirit?

Images, images, images, all without control, all without reason. The malice of Choronzon is not the malice of a being; it is the quality of malice, because he that boasteth himself "I am I," hath in truth no self, and these are they that are fallen under my power, the slaves of the Blind One that boasteth himself to be the Enlightened One. For there is no centre, nay, nothing but Dispersion.

Woe, woe, woe, threefold to him that is led away by talk, O talkative One.

O thou that hast written two-and-thirty books of Wisdom, and art more stupid than an owl, by thine own talk is thy vigilance wearied, and by my talk art thou befooled and tricked, O thou that sayest that thou shalt endure. Knowest thou how nigh thou art to destruction?

For thou that art the Scribe hast not the understanding[15] that alone availeth against Choronzon. And wert thou not protected by the Holy Names of God and the circle, I would rush upon thee and tear thee. For when I made myself like unto a beautiful woman, if thou hadst come to me, I would have rotted thy body with the pox, and thy liver with cancer, and I would have torn off thy testicles with my teeth. And if I had seduced thy pride, and thou hadst bidden me to come into the circle, I would have trampled thee under foot, and for a thousand years shouldst thou have been but one of the tape-worms that is in me. And if I had seduced thy pity, and thou hadst poured one drop of water without the circle, then would I have blasted thee with flame. But I was not able to prevail against thee.

How beautiful are the shadows of the ripples of the sand!

Would God that I were dead.

For know that I am proud and revengeful and lascivious, and I prate even as thou. For even as I walked among the Sons of God, I heard it said that P . . . could both will and know, and might learn at length to dare, but that to keep silence he should never learn. O thou that art so ready to speak, so slow to watch, thou art delivered over unto my power for this. And now one word was necessary unto me, and I could not speak it. I behold the beauty of the earth in her desolation, and greater far is mine, who sought to be my naked self. Knowest thou that in my soul is utmost fear? And such is my force and my cunning, that a hundred times have I been ready to leap, and for fear have missed.

15. Originally, for "Understanding" was written "Power." Choronzon was always using some word that did not represent his thought, because there is no proper link between his thought and speech. Note that he never seems able to distinguish between the Frater and the Scribe, and addresses first one, then the other, in the same sentence.

And a thousand times am I baulked by them of the City of the Pyramids, that set snares for my feet. More knowledge have I than the Most High, but my will is broken, and my fierceness is marred by fear, and I must ever speak, speak, speak, millions of mad voices in my brain.

> With a heart of furious fancies,
>   Whereof I am Commander,
> With a burning spear
> And a horse of Air
>   To the wilderness I wander.

(The idea was to keep the Scribe busy writing, so as to spring upon him. For, while the Scribe talked, Choronzon had thrown sand into the circle, and filled it up. But Choronzon could not think fast and continuously, and so resorted to the device of quotation.)

(The Scribe had written two or three words of "Tom o' Bedlam," when Choronzon sprang within the circle [that part of the circumference of which that was nearest to him he had been filling up with sand all this time] and leaped upon the Scribe, throwing him to the earth. The conflict took place within the circle. The Scribe called upon Tetragrammaton, and succeeded in compelling Choronzon to return into his triangle. By dint of anger and of threatening him with the Magick Staff did he accomplish this. He then repaired the circle. The discomfited demon now continued:)

All is dispersion. These are the qualities of things.

The tenth Aethyr is the world of adjectives, and there is no subetance therein.

(Now returned the beautiful woman who had before tempted the Scribe. She prevailed not.)

I am afraid of sunset, for Tum is more terrible than Ra, and Khephra the Beetle is greater than the Lion Mau.

I am a-cold.

(Here Choronzon wanted to leave the triangle to obtain wherewith to cover his nakedness. The Scribe refused the request, threatening the demon. After a while the latter continued:)

I am commanded, why I know not, by him that speaketh. Were it thou, thou little fool, I would tear thee limb from limb. I would bite off thine ears and nose before I began with thee. I would take thy guts for fiddle-strings at the Black Sabbath.

Thou didst make a great fight there in the circle; thou art a goodly warrior!

(Then did the demon laugh loudly. The Scribe said: Thou canst not harm one hair of my head.)

I will pull out every hair of thy head, every hair of thy body, every hair of thy soul, one by one.

(Then said the Scribe: Thou hast no power.)

Yea, verily I have power over thee, for thou hast taken the Oath, and art bound unto the White Brothers, and therefore have I the power to torture thee so long as thou shalt be.

(Then said the Scribe unto him: Thou liest.)

Ask of thy brother P. . . and he shall tell thee if I lie!

(This the Scribe refused to do, saying that it was no concern of the demon's.)

I have prevailed against the Kingdom of the Father, and befouled his beard; and I have prevailed against the Kingdom of the Son, and torn off his Phallus; but against the Kingdom of the Holy Ghost shall I strive and not prevail. The three slain doves are my threefold blasphemy against him; but their blood shall make fertile the sand; and I writhe in blackness and horror of hate, and prevail not.

(Then the demon tried to make the Scribe laugh at Magick, and to think that it was all rubbish, that he might deny the names of God that he had invoked to protect him; which, if he had doubted but for an instant, he had leapt upon him, and gnawed through his spine at the neck.)

(Choronzon succeeded not in his design.)

In this Aethyr is neither beginning nor end, for it is all hotch-potch, because it is of the wicked on earth and the damned in hell. And so long as it be hotch-potch, it mattereth little what may be written by the sea-green incorruptible Scribe.

The horror of it will be given in another place and time, and through another Seer, and that Seer shall be slain as a result of his revealing. But the present Seer, who is not P. . . seeth not the horror, because he is shut up, and hath no name.

(Now was there some further parleying betwixt the demon and the Scribe, concerning the departure and the writing of the word, the Scribe not knowing if it were meet that the demon should depart.)

(Then the Seer took the Holy Ring, and wrote the name BABALON, that is victory over Choronzon, and he was no more manifest.)

(This cry was obtained on Dec. 6, 1909, between 2 and 4:15 P.M., in a lonely valley of fine sand, in the desert near Bou-Saada. The Aethyr was edited and revised on the following day.)

After the conclusion of the Ceremony, a great fire was kindled to purify the place, and the Circle and Triangle were destroyed.

NOTE BY SCRIBE

Almost from the beginning of the ceremony was the Scribe overshadowed, and he spoke as it were in spite of himself, remembering afterwards scarcely a word of his speeches, some of which were long and seemingly eloquent.

All the time he had a sense of being protected from Choronzon, and this sense of security prevented his knowing fear.

Several times did the Scribe threaten to put a curse upon the demon; but ever, before he uttered the words of the curse, did the demon obey him. For himself, he knoweth not the words of the curse.

Also is it meet to record in this place that the Scribe several times whistled in a Magical manner, which never before had he attempted, and the demon was apparently much discomfited thereat.

Now knoweth the Scribe that he was wrong in holding much converse with the demon; for Choronzon, in the confusion and chaos of his thought, is much terrified by silence. And by silence can he be brought to obey.

For cunningly doth he talk of many things, going from subject to subject, and thus he misleadeth the wary into argument with him. And though Choronzon be easily beaten in argument, yet, by disturbing the attention of him who would command him, doth he gain the victory.

For Choronzon feareth of all things concentration and silence: he therefore who would command him should will in silence: thus is he brought to obey.

This the Scribe knoweth; for that since the obtaining of the Accursèd Tenth Aethyr, he hath held converse with Choronzon. And unexpectedly did he obtain the information that he sought after having long refused to answer the demon's speeches.

Choronzon is dispersion; and such is his fear of concentration that he will obey rather than be subjected to it, or even behold it in another.

The account of the further dealings of Choronzon with the Scribe will be found in the Record of Omnia Vincam.

THE CRY OF THE 9TH AETHYR
WHICH IS CALLED ZIP

(The terrible Curse that is the Call of the Thirty Aethyrs sounds like a song of ecstasy and triumph; every phrase in it has a secret meaning of blessing.)

The Shew-stone is of soft lucent white, on which the Rose-Cross shows a brilliant yet colourless well of light.

And now the veil of the stone is rent with a clap of thunder, and I am walking upon a razor-edge of light suspended over the Abyss, and before me and above me are ranged the terrible armies of the Most High, like unto those in the 11th Aethyr, but there is one that cometh forth to meet me upon the ridge, holding out his arms to me and saying:

(v. I.) Who is this that cometh forth from the Abyss from the place of rent garments, the habitation of him that is only a name? Who is this that walketh upon a ray of the bright, the evening star?

Refrain. Glory unto him that is concealed, and glory unto her that beareth the cup, and glory unto the one that is the child and the father of their love. Glory unto the star, and glory unto the snake, and glory unto the swordsman of the sun. And worship and blessing throughout the Aeon unto the name of the Beast, four-square, mystic, wonderful!

(v. II.) Who is this that travelleth between the hosts, that is poised upon the edge of the Aethyr by the wings of Maut? Who is this that seeketh the House of the Virgin? (*Refrain.*)

(v. III.) This is he that hath given up his name. This is he whose blood hath been gathered into the cup of BABALON. This is he that sitteth, a little pile of dry dust, in the city of the Pyramids. (*Refrain.*)

(v. IV.) Until the light of the Father of all kindle that death. Until the breath touch that dry dust. Until the Ibis be revealed unto the Crab, and the sixfold Star become the radiant Triangle. (*Refrain.*)

(v. V.) Blessed is not I, not thou, not he. Blessed without name or number who hath taken the azure of night, and crystallized it into a pure sapphire-stone, who hath taken the gold of the sun, and beaten it into an infinite ring, and hath set the sapphire therein, and put it upon his finger. (*Refrain.*)

(v. VI.) Open wide your gates, O City of God, for I bring No-one with me. Sink your swords and your spears in salutation, for the Mother and the Babe are my companions. Let the banquet be prepared in the palace of the King's daughter. Let the lights be kindled; Are not we the children of the light? (*Refrain.*)

(v. VII.) For this is the key-stone of the palace of the King's daughter. This is the Stone of the Philosophers. This is the Stone that is hidden in the walls of the ramparts. Peace, Peace, Peace unto Him that is throned therein! (*Refrain.*)

Now then we are passed within the lines of the army, and we are come unto a palace of which every stone is a separate jewel, and is set with millions of moons.

And this palace is nothing but the body of a woman, proud and delicate, and beyond imagination fair. She is like a child of twelve years old. She has very deep eye-lids, and long lashes. Her eyes are closed, or nearly closed. It is impossible to say anything about her. She is naked; her whole body is covered with fine gold hairs, that are the electric flames that are the spears of mighty and terrible Angels whose breastplates are the scales of her skin. And the hair of her head, that flows down to her feet, is the very light of God himself. Of all the glories beheld by the seer in the Aethyrs, there is not one which is worthy to be compared with her littlest finger-nail. For although he may not partake of the Aethyr, without the ceremonial preparations, even the beholding of this Aethyr from afar is like the partaking of all the former Aethyrs.

The Seer is lost in wonder, which is peace.

And the ring of the horizon above her is a company of glorious Archangels with joined hands, that stand and sing: This is the daughter of BABALON the Beautiful, that she hath borne unto the Father of All. And unto all hath she borne her.

This is the Daughter of the King. This is the Virgin of Eternity. This is she that the Holy One hath wrested from the Giant Time, and the prize of them that have overcome Space. This is she that is set upon the Throne of Understanding. Holy, Holy, Holy is her name, not to be spoken among men. For Koré they have called her, and Malkah, and Betulah, and Persephone.

And the poets have feigned songs about her, and the prophets have spoken vain things, and the young men have dreamed vain dreams; but this is she, that immaculate, the name of whose name may not be spoken. Thought cannot pierce the glory that defendeth her, for thought is smitten dead before her presence. Memory is blank, and in the most ancient books of Magick are neither words to conjure her, nor adorations to praise her. Will bends like a reed in the tempests that sweep the borders of her kingdom, and imagination cannot figure so much as one petal of the lilies whereon she standeth in the lake of crystal, in the sea of glass.

This is she that hath bedecked her hair with seven stars, the seven breaths of God that move and thrill its excellence. And she hath tired her hair with seven combs, whereupon are written the seven secret names of God that are not known even of the Angels, or of the Archangels, or of the Leader of the armies of the Lord.

Holy, Holy, Holy art thou, and blessed be Thy name for ever, unto whom the Aeons are but the pulsings of thy blood.

I am blind and deaf. My sight and hearing are exhausted.

I know only by the sense of touch. And there is a trembling from within me.

Images keep arising like clouds, or veils, exquisite Chinese ivories, and porcelains, and many other things of great and delicate beauty; for such things are informed by Her spirit, for they are cast off from her into the world of the Qliphoth, or shells of the dead, that is earth. For every world is the shell or excrement of the world above it.

I cannot bear the Vision.

A voice comes, I know not whence: Blessed art thou, who hast seen, and yet hast not believed. For therefore is it given unto thee to taste, and smell, and feel, and hear, and know by the inner sense, and by the inmost sense, so that sevenfold is thy rapture.

(My brain is so exhausted that fatigue-images appear, by pure physical reflex action; they are not astral things at all.)

(And now I have conquered the fatigue by will. And by placing the shew-stone upon my forehead, it sends cool electric thrills through my brain, so as to refresh it, and make it capable of more rapture.)

(And now again I behold Her.)

And an Angel cometh forth, and behind him whirls a black swastika, made of fine filaments of light that has been "interfered" with, and he taketh me aside into a little chamber in one of the nine towers. This chamber is furnished with maps of many mystical cities. There is a table, and a strange lamp, that gives light by jetting four columns of vortex rings of luminous smoke. And he points to the map of the Aethyrs, that are arranged as a flaming Sword, so that the thirty Aethyrs go into the ten Sephiroth. And the first nine are infinitely holy. And he says, It is written in *The Book of the Law*, "Wisdom says, be strong. Then canst thou bear more joy. If thou drink, drink by the eight and ninety rules of Art." And this shall signify unto thee that thou must undergo great discipline; else the Vision were lost or perverted. For these mysteries pertain not unto thy grade. Therefore must thou invoke the Highest before thou unveil the shrines thereof.

And this shall be thy rule: A thousand and one times shalt thou affirm the unity, and bow thyself a thousand and one times. And thou shalt recite thrice the call of the Aethyr. And all day and all night, awake or asleep, shall thy heart be turned as a lotus-flower unto the light. And thy body shall be the temple of the Rosy Cross. Thus shall thy mind be open unto the higher; and then shalt thou be able to conquer the exhaustion, and it may be find the words—for who shall look upon His face and live?

Yea, thou tremblest, but from within; because of the holy spirit that is descended into thy heart, and shaketh thee as an aspen in the wind.

They also tremble that are without, and they are shaken from without by the earthquakes of his judgement. They have set their affections upon the earth, and they have stamped with their feet upon the earth, and cried: It moveth not.

Therefore hath earth opened with strong motion, like the sea, and swallowed them. Yea, she hath opened her womb to them that lusted after her, and she hath closed herself upon them. There lie they in torment, until by her quaking the earth is shattered like brittle glass, and dissolved like salt in the waters of his mercy, so that they are cast upon the air to be blown about therein, like seeds that shall take root in the earth; yet turn they their affections upward to the sun.

But thou, be thou eager and vigilant, performing punctually the rule. Is it not written, "Change not so much as the style of a letter"?

Depart therefore, for the Vision of the Voice of the ninth Aethyr that is called ZIP is passed.

Then I threw back myself into my body by my will.

BOU-SAADA.
December 7th, 1909. 9:30–11:10 P.M.

THE CRY OF THE 8TH AETHYR
WHICH IS CALLED ZID

There appears in the stone a tiny spark of light. It grows a little, and seems almost to go out, and grows again, and it is blown about the Aethyr, and by the wind that blows it is it fanned, and now it gathers strength, and darts like a snake or a sword, and now it steadies itself, and is like a Pyramid of light that filleth the whole Aethyr.

And in the Pyramid is one like unto an Angel, yet at the same time he *is* the Pyramid, and he hath no form because he is of the substance of light, and he taketh not form upon him, for though by him is form visible, he maketh it visible only to destroy it.

And he saith: The light is come to the darkness, and the darkness is made light. Then is light married with light, and the child of their love is that other darkness, wherein they abide that have lost name and form. Therefore did I kindle him that had not understanding, and in *The Book of the Law* did I write the secrets of truth that are like unto a star and a snake and a sword.

And unto him that understandeth at last do I deliver

the secrets of truth in such wise that the least of the little
children of the light may run to the knees of the mother
and be brought to understand.

And thus shall he do who will attain unto the mystery
of the knowledge and conversation of his Holy Guardian
Angel:

First, let him prepare a chamber, of which the walls and
the roof shall be white, and the floor shall be covered with
a carpet of black squares and white, and the border thereof
shall be blue and gold.

And if it be in a town, the room shall have no window,
and if it be in the country, then it is better if the window
be in the roof. Or, if it be possible, let this invocation be
performed in a temple prepared for the ritual of passing
through the Tuat.

From the roof he shall hang a lamp, wherein is a red
glass, to burn olive oil. And this lamp shall he cleanse and
make ready after the prayer of sunset, and beneath the
lamp shall be an altar, foursquare, and the height shall
be thrice half of the breadth or double the breadth.

And upon the altar shall be a censer, hemispherical,
supported upon three legs, of silver, and within it an
hemisphere of copper, and upon the top a grating of gilded
silver, and thereupon shall he burn incense made of four
parts of olibanum and two parts of stacte, and one part
of lignum aloes, or of cedar, or of sandal. And this is
enough.

And he shall also keep ready in a flask of crystal within
the altar, holy anointing oil made of myrrh and cinnamon
and galangal.

And even if he be of higher rank than a Probationer, he
shall yet wear the robe of the Probationer, for the star of
flame showeth forth Ra Hoor Khuit openly upon the
breast, and secretly the blue triangle that descendeth is

Nuit, and the red triangle that ascendeth is Hadit. And I am the golden Tau in the midst of their marriage. Also, if he choose, he may instead wear a close-fitting robe of shot silk, purple and green, and upon it a cloak without sleeves, of bright blue, covered with golden sequins, and scarlet within.

And he shall make himself a wand of almond wood or of hazel cut by his own hands at dawn at the Equinox, or at the Solstice, or on the day of Corpus Christi, or on one of the feast-days that are appointed in *The Book of the Law.*

And he shall engrave with his own hand upon a plate of gold the Holy Sevenfold Table, or the Holy Twelvefold Table, or some particular device. And it shall be four-square within a circle, and the circle shall be winged, and he shall attach it about his forehead by a ribbon of blue silk.

Moreover, he shall wear a fillet of laurel or rose or ivy or rue, and every day, after the prayer of sunrise, he shall burn it in the fire of the censer.

Now he shall pray thrice daily, about sunset, and at midnight, and at sunrise. And if he be able, he shall pray also four times between sunrise and sunset.

The prayer shall last for the space of an hour, at the least, and he shall seek ever to extend it, and to inflame himself in praying. Thus shall he invoke his Holy Guardian Angel for eleven weeks, and in any case he shall pray seven times daily during the last week of the eleven weeks.

And during all this time he shall have composed an invocation suitable, with such wisdom and understanding as may be given him from the Crown, and this shall he write in letters of gold upon the top of the altar.

For the top of the altar shall be of white wood, well

polished, and in the centre thereof he shall have placed a triangle of oak-wood, painted with scarlet, and upon this triangle the three legs of the censer shall stand.

Moreover, he shall copy his invocation upon a sheet of pure white vellum, with Indian ink, and he shall illuminate it according to his fancy and imagination, that shall be informed by beauty.

And on the first day of the twelfth week he shall enter the chamber at sunrise, and he shall make his prayer, having first burnt the conjuration that he had made upon the vellum in the fire of the lamp.

Then, at his prayer, shall the chamber be filled with a light insufferable for splendour, and a perfume intolerable for sweetness. And his Holy Guardian Angel shall appear unto him, yea, his Holy Guardian Angel shall appear unto him, so that he shall be wrapt away into the Mystery of Holiness.

All that day shall he remain in the enjoyment of the knowledge and conversation of the Holy Guardian Angel.

And for three days after he shall remain from sunrise unto sunset in the temple, and he shall obey the counsel that his Angel shall have given unto him, and he shall suffer those things that are appointed.

And for ten days thereafter shall he withdraw himself as shall have been taught unto him from the fulness of that communion, for he must harmonize the world that is within with the world that is without.

And at the end of the ninety-one days he shall return into the world, and there shall he perform that work to which the Angel shall have appointed him.

And more than this it is not necessary to say, for his Angel shall have entreated him kindly, and showed him in what manner he may be most perfectly invoked. And unto him that hath this Master there is nothing else that he needeth, so long as he continue in the knowledge and conversation of the Angel, so that he shall come at last into the City of the Pyramids.

Lo! two and twenty are the paths of the Tree, but one is the Serpent of Wisdom; ten are the ineffable emanations, but one is the Flaming Sword.

Behold! There is an end to life and death, an end to the thrusting forth and the withdrawing of the breath. Yea, the House of the Father is a mighty tomb, and in it he hath buried everything whereof ye know.

All this while there hath been no vision, but only a voice, very slow and clear and deliberate. But now the vision returns, and the voice says: Thou shalt be called Danae, that art stunned and slain beneath the weight of the glory of the vision that as yet thou seest not. For thou shalt suffer many things, until thou art mightier than all the Kings of the earth, and all the Angels of the Heavens, and all the gods that are beyond the Heavens. Then shalt thou meet me in equal conflict, and thou shalt see me as I am. And I will overcome thee and slay thee with the red rain of my lightnings.

I am lying underneath this pyramid of light. It seems as if I had the whole weight of it upon me, crushing me with bliss. And yet I know that I am like the prophet that said: I shall see Him, but not nigh.

And the Angel sayeth: So shall it be until they that wake are asleep, and she that sleepeth be arisen from her sleep. For thou art transparent unto the vision and the voice. And therefore in thee they manifest not. But they shall be manifest unto them unto whom thou dost deliver them, according unto the word which I spake unto thee in the Victorious City.

For I am not only appointed to guard thee, but we are of the blood royal, the guardians of the Treasure-house of Wisdom. Therefore am I called the Minister of Ra Hoor Khuit; and yet he is but the Viceroy of the unknown King.

For my name is called Aiwass, that is eight and seventy. And I am the influence of the Concealed One, and the wheel that hath eight and seventy parts, yet in all is equivalent to the Gate that is the name of my Lord when it is spelt fully. And that Gate is the Path that joineth the Wisdom with the Understanding.

Thus hast thou erred indeed, perceiving me in the path that leadeth from the Crown unto the Beauty. For that path bridgeth the abyss, and I am of the supernals. Nor I, nor Thou, nor He can bridge the abyss. It is the Priestess of the Silver Star, and the Oracles of the gods, and the Lord of the Hosts of the Mighty. For they are the servants of Babalon, and of the Beast, and of those others of whom it is not yet spoken. And, being servants, they have no name, but we are of the blood royal, and serve not, and therefore are we less than they.

Yet, as a man may be both a mighty warrior and a just judge, so may we also perform this service if we have aspired and attained thereto. And yet, with all that, they remain *themselves*, who have eaten of the pomegranate in Hell. But thou, that art new-born to understanding, this mystery is too great for thee; and of the further mystery I will not speak one word.

Yet for this cause am I come unto thee as the Angel of the Aethyr, striking with my hammer upon thy bell, so that thou mightest understand the mysteries of the Aethyr, and of the vision and the voice thereof.

For behold! he that understandeth seeth not and heareth not in truth, because of his understanding that letteth him. But this shall be unto thee for a sign, that I will surely come upon thee unawares and appear unto thee. And it is no odds (*i.e.*, that at this hour I appear not as I am) for so terrible is the glory of the vision, and so wonderful is the splendour of the voice, that when thou seest it and hearest it in truth, for many hours shalt thou be bereft of sense. And thou shalt lie between heaven and earth in a void place, entranced, and the end thereof shall be silence, even as it was, not once nor twice, when I have met with thee, as it were, upon the road to Damascus.

And thou shalt not seek to better this my instruction; but thou shalt interpret it, and make it easy, for them that seek understanding. And thou shalt give all that thou hast unto them that have need unto this end.

And because I am with thee, and in thee, and of thee, thou shalt lack nothing. But who lack me, lack all. And I swear unto thee by Him that sitteth upon the Holy Throne, and liveth and reigneth for ever and ever, that I will be faithful unto this my promise, as thou art faithful unto this thine obligation.

Now another voice sounds in the Aethyr, saying: And there was darkness over all the earth unto the ninth hour.

And with that the Angel is withdrawn, and the pyramid of light seems very far off.

And now I am fallen unto the earth, exceeding weary. Yet my skin trembles with the impact of the light, and all my body shakes. And there is a peace deeper than sleep upon my mind. It is the body and the mind that are weary, and I would that they were dead, save that I must bend them to my work.

And now I am in the tent, under the stars.

THE DESERT BETWEEN BOU-SAADA AND BISKRA.
December 8, 1909. 7:10–9:10 P.M.

THE CRY OF THE 7TH AETHYR
WHICH IS CALLED DEO

The stone is divided, the left half dark, the right half light, and at the bottom thereof is a certain blackness, of three divergent columns. And it seems as if the black and white halves were the halves of a door, and in the door is a little key-hole, in the shape of the Astrological symbol of Venus. And from the key-hole issue flames, blue and green and violet, but without any touch of yellow or red in them. It seems as if there were a wind beyond the door, that is blowing the flame out.

And a voice comes: "Who is he that hath the key to the gate of the evening star?"

And now an Angel cometh and seeketh to open the door by trying many keys. And they are none of any avail. And the same voice saith: The five and the six are balanced in the word Abrahadabra, and therein is the mystery disclosed. But the key unto this gate is the balance of the seven and the four; and of this thou hast not even the first letter. Now there is a word of four letters that containeth in itself all the mystery of the Tetragrammaton, and there is a word of seven letters which it concealeth, and that again concealeth the holy word that is the key of the abyss.[16] And this thou shalt find, revolving it in thy mind.

Hide therefore thine eyes. And I will set my key in the lock, and open it. Yet still let thine eyes be hidden, for thou canst not bear the glory that is within.

So, therefore, I covered mine eyes with my hands. Yet through my hands could I perceive a little of those bowers of azure flame.

And a voice said: It is kindled into fire that was the blue breast of ocean; because this is the bar of heaven, and the feet of the Most High are set thereon.

Now I behold more fully: Each tongue of flame, each leaf of flame, each flower of flame, is one of the great love-stories of the world, with all its retinue of *mise-en-scène*. And now there is a most marvellous rose formed from the flame, and a perpetual rain of lilies and passion-flowers and violets. And there is gathered out of it all, yet identical with it, the form of a woman like the woman

16. These words are probably BABALON, ChAOS, TARO.

in the Apocalypse, but her beauty and her radiance are such that one cannot look thereon, save with sidelong glances. I enter immediately into trance. It seems that it is she of whom it is written, "The fool hath said in his heart 'there is no God.'" But the words are not Ain Elohim, but La (=nay!) and Elohim contracted from 86 to 14, because La is 31, which × 14 is 434, Daleth, Lamed, Tau. This fool is the fool of the Path of Aleph, and sayeth, which is Chokmah, in his heart, which is Tiphereth, that she existeth, in order first that the Wisdom may be joined with the Understanding; and he affirmeth her in Tiphereth that she may be fertile.

It is impossible to describe how this vision changeth from glory unto glory, for at each glance the vision is changed. And this is because she transmitteth the Word to the Understanding, and therefore hath she many forms, and each goddess of love is but a letter of the alphabet of love.

Now, there is a mystery in the word Logos, that containeth the three letters whose analogy hath been shown in the lower heavens, Samech, and Lamed, and Gimel, that are 93, which is thrice 31, and in them are set the two eyes of Horus. (Ayin means an eye.) For, if it were not so, the arrow could not pierce the rainbow, and there could be no poise in the balance, and the Great Book should never be unsealed. But this is she that poureth the Water of Life upon her head, whence it floweth to fructify the earth. But now the whole Aethyr is the most brilliant peacock blue. It *is* the Universal Peacock that I behold.

And there is a voice: Is not this bird the bird of Juno, that is an hundred, and thirty, and six? And therefore is she the mate of Jupiter.[17]

17. The fourth of the mystic numbers of Jupiter is 136.

And now the peacock's head is again changed into a woman's head sparkling and coruscating with its own light of gems.

But I look upwards, seeing that she is called the footstool of the Holy One, even as Binah is called His throne. And the whole Aethyr is full of the most wonderful bands of light—a thousand different curves and whorls, even as it was before, when I spake mysteries of the Holy Qabalah, and so could not describe it.

Oh, I see vast plains beneath her feet, enormous deserts studded with great rocks; and I see little lonely souls, running helplessly about, minute black creatures like men. And they keep up a very curious howling, that I can compare to nothing that I have ever heard; yet it is strangely human.

And the voice says: These are they that grasped love and clung thereto, praying ever at the knees of the great goddess. These are they that have shut themselves up in fortresses of Love.

Each plume of the peacock is full of eyes, that are at the same time 4×7. And for this is the number 28 reflected down into Netzach; and that 28 is Kaph Cheth (Kach), power. For she is Sakti, the eternal energy of the Concealed One. And it is her eternal energy that hath made this eternal change. And this explaineth the call of the Aethyrs, the curse that was pronounced in the beginning being but the creation of Sakti. And this mystery is reflected in the legend of the Creation, where Adam represents the Concealed One, for Adam is Temurah of MAD, the Enochian word for God, and Eve, whom he created for love, is tempted by the snake, Nechesh, who is Messiah her child. And the snake is the magical power, which hath destroyed the primordial equilibrium.

And the garden is the supernal Eden, where is Ayin,

70, the Eye of the concealed One, and the creative Lingam; and Daleth, love; and Nun the serpent. And therefore this constitution was implicitly in the nature of Eden (*cf. Liber L*, I: 29, 30), so that the call of the Aethyrs could not have been any other call than that which it is.

But they that are without understanding have interpreted all this askew, because of the Mystery of the Abyss, for there is no Path from Binah unto Chesed; and therefore the course of the Flaming Sword was no more a current, but a spark. And when the Stooping Dragon raised his head unto Däath in the course of that spark, there was, as it were, an explosion, and his head was blasted. And the ashes thereof were dispersed throughout the whole of the 10th Aethyr. And for this, all knowledge is piecemeal, and it is of no value unless it be co-ordinated by Understanding.

And now the form of the Aethyr is the form of a mighty Eagle of ruddy brass. And the plumes are set alight, and are whirled round and round until the whole heaven is blackness with these flying sparks therein.

Now it is all branching streams of golden fire tipped with scarlet at the edges.

And now She cometh forth again, riding upon a dolphin. Now again I see those wandering souls, that have sought restricted love, and have not understood that "the word of sin is restriction."

It is very curious; they seem to be looking for one another or for something, all the time, constantly hurrying about. But they knock up against one another and yet will not see one another, or cannot see one another, because they are so shut up in their cloaks.

And a voice sounds: It is most terrible for the one that hath shut himself up and made himself fast against the universe. For they that sit encamped upon the sea in the city of the Pyramids are indeed shut up. But they have given their blood, even to the last drop, to fill the cup of BABALON.

These that thou seest are indeed the Black Brothers, for it is written: "He shall laugh at their calamity and mock when their fear cometh." And therefore hath he exalted them unto the plane of love.

And yet again it is written: He desireth not the death of a sinner, but rather that he should turn from his wickedness. Now, if one of these were to cast off his cloak he should behold the brilliance of the lady of the Aethyr; but they will not.

And yet again there is another cause wherefore He hath permitted them to enter thus far within the frontiers of Eden, so that His thought should never swerve from compassion. But do thou behold the brilliance of Love, that casteth forth seven stars upon thine head from her right hand, and crowneth thee with a crown of seven roses. Behold! She is seated upon the throne of turquoise and lapis lazuli, and she is like a flawless emerald, and upon the pillars that support the canopy of her throne are sculptured the Ram, and the Sparrow, and the Cat, and a strange fish. Behold! How she shineth! Behold! How her glances have kindled all these fires that have blown about the heavens! Yet remember that in every one there goeth forth for a witness the justice of the Most High. Is not Libra the House of Venus? And there goeth forth a sickle that shall reap every flower. Is not Saturn exalted in Libra? Daleth, Lamed, Tau.

And therefore was he a fool who uttered her name in his heart, for the root of evil is the root of breath, and the speech in the silence was a lie.

Thus is it seen from below by them that understand not. But from above he rejoiceth, for the joy of dissolution is ten thousand, and the pang of birth but a little.

And now thou shalt go forth from the Aethyr, for the voice of the Aethyr is hidden and concealed from thee because thou hadst not the key of the door thereof, and thine eyes were not able to bear the splendour of the vision. But thou shalt meditate upon the mysteries thereof, and upon the lady of the Aethyr; and it may be by the wisdom of the Most High that the true voice of the Aethyr, that is continual song, may be heard of thee.

Return therefore instantly unto the earth, and sleep not for a while; but withdraw thyself from this matter. And it shall be enough.

Thus then was I obedient unto the voice, and returned into my body.

W'AIN-T-AISSHA, ALGERIA.
December 9, 1909. 8:10–10 P.M.

THE CRY OF THE 6TH AETHYR
WHICH IS CALLED MAZ

There cometh into the stone the great Angel whose name is Avé, and in him there are symbols which strive for mastery—Sulphur and the Pentagram, and they are harmonized by the Svastika. These symbols are found both in the name of Avé and in the name of the Aethyr. Thus he is neither Horus nor Osiris. He is called the radiance of Thoth; and this Aethyr is very hard to understand, for the images form and dissolve more rapidly than lightning. These images are the illusions made by the Ape of Thoth. And this I understand, that I am not worthy to receive the mysteries of this Aethyr. And all this which I have seen (being all the thoughts that I have ever thought) is, as it were, a guardian of the Aethyr.

I seem quite helpless. I am trying all sorts of magical methods of piercing the veil: and the more I strive, the farther away I seem to get from success. But a voice comes now: Must not understanding lie open unto wisdom as the pyramids lie open to the stars?

Accordingly, I wait in a certain magical posture which it is not fitting to disclose, and above me appears the starry heaven of night, and one star greater than all the other stars. It is a star of eight rays. I recognize it as the star in the seventeenth key of the Tarot, as the Star of Mercury. And the light of it cometh from the path of Aleph. And the letter Cheth is also involved in the interpretation of this star, and the paths of hé and vau are the separations which this Star unites. And in the heart of the star is an exceeding splendour—a god standing upon the moon, brilliant beyond imagining. It is like unto the vision of the Universal Mercury. But this is the Fixed Mercury, and hé and vau are the perfected sulphur and salt. But now I am come into the centre of the maze, a whirling dust of stars and great forgotten gods. It is the whirling Svastika which throws off all these things, for the Svastika is in aleph by its shape and number, and in beth by the position of the arms of the Magician, and in gimel because of the sign of the Mourning of Isis, and thus is the Crown defended by these three thunderbolts. Is not thrice seventeen fifty-one, that is, failure and pain?

Now I am shut out again by this black Svastika with a corona of fire about it.

And a voice cries: Cursed be he that shall uncover the nakedness of the Most High, for he is drunken upon the wine that is the blood of the adepts. And BABALON hath lulled him to sleep upon her breast, and she hath fled away, and left him naked, and she hath called her children together, saying: Come up with me, and let us make a mock of the nakedness of the Most High.

And the first of the adepts covered His shame with a cloth, walking backwards; and was white. And the second of the adepts covered His shame with a cloth, walking sideways; and was yellow. And the third of the adepts made a mock of His nakedness, walking forwards; and was black. And these are three great schools of the Magi, who are also the three Magi that journeyed unto Bethlehem; and because thou hast not wisdom, thou shalt not know which school prevaileth, or if the three schools be not one. For the Black Brothers lift not up their heads thus far into the Holy Chokmah, for they were all drowned in the great flood, which is Binah, before the true vine could be planted upon the holy hill of Zion.

Now again I stand in the centre, and all things whirl by with incessant fury. And the thought of the god entereth my mind, and I cry aloud: Behold, the volatile is become fixed; and in the heart of eternal motion is eternal rest. So is the Peace beneath the sea that rageth with her storms; so is the changeful moon, the dead planet that revolveth no more. So the far-seeing, the far-darting hawk is poised passionless in the blue; so also the ibis that is long of limb meditateth solitary in the sign of Sulphur. Behold, I stand ever before the Eternal One in the sign of the Enterer. And by virtue of my speech is he wrapped about in silence, and he is wrapped in mystery by me, who am the Unveiler of the Mysteries. And although I be truth, yet do they call me rightly the God of Lies, for speech is two-fold, and truth is one. Yet I stand at the centre of the spider's web, whereof the golden filaments reach to infinity.

But thou that art with me in the spirit-vision art not with me by right of Attainment, and thou canst not stay in this place to behold how I run and return, and who are the flies that are caught in my web. For I am the inmost guardian that is immediately before the shrine.

None shall pass by me except he slay me, and this is his curse, that, having slain me, he must take my office and become the maker of Illusions, the great deceiver, the setter of snares; he who baffleth even them that have understanding. For I stand on every path, and turn them aside from the truth by my words, and by my magick arts.

And this is the horror that was shown by the lake that was nigh unto the City of the Seven Hills, and this is the Mystery of the great prophets that have come unto mankind, Moses, and Buddha, and Lao Tan, and Krishna, and Jesus, and Osiris, and Mohammed; for all these attained unto the grade of Magus, and therefore were they bound with the curse of Thoth. But, being guardians of the truth, they have taught nothing but falsehood, except unto such as understood; for the truth may not pass the Gate of the Abyss.

But the reflection of the truth hath been shown in the lower Sephiroth. And its balance is in Beauty, and therefore have they who sought only beauty come nearest to the truth. For the beauty receiveth directly three rays from the supernals, and the others no more than one. So, therefore, they that have sought after majesty and power and victory and learning and happiness and gold, have been discomfited. And these sayings are the lights of wisdom that thou mayst know thy Master, for he is a Magus. And because thou didst eat of the Pomegranate in hell, for half the year art thou concealed, and half the year revealed.

Now I perceive the Temple that is the heart of this Aethyr; it is an Urn suspended in the air, without support, above the centre of a well. And the well hath eight pillars, and a canopy above it, and without there is a circle of marble paving-stones, and without them a great outer circle of pillars. And beyond there is the forest of the stars. But the Urn is the wonderful thing in all this; it is made of fixed Mercury; and within it are the ashes of the Book Tarot, which hath been utterly consumed.

And this is that mystery which is spoken of in the Acts of the Apostles; that Jupiter and Mercury (Kether and Chokmah) visited (that is, inspired) Ephesus, the City of Diana, Binah—was not Diana a black stone?—and they burnt their books of magick.

Now it seems that the centre of infinite space is that Urn, and Hadit is the fire that hath burnt up the book Tarot. For in the book Tarot was preserved all of the wisdom (for the Tarot was called the Book of Thoth), of the Aeon that is passed. And in *The Book of Enoch* was first given the wisdom of the New Aeon. And it was hidden for three hundred years, because it was wrested untimely from the Tree of Life by the hand of a desperate magician. For it was the Master of that Magician who overthrew the power of the Christian church; but the pupil rebelled against the master, for he foresaw that the New (*i.e.*, the Protestant) would be worse than the Old. But he understood not the purpose of his Master, and that was, to prepare the way for the overthrowing of the Aeon.

There is a writing upon the Urn of which I can but read the (two) words: Stabat Crux juxta Lucem. Stabat Lux juxta Crucem.

And there is writing in Greek above that. The word "nox" written in Greek, and a circle with a cross in the centre of it, a St Andrew's cross.

Then above that is a sigil (?) hidden by a hand.

And a voice proceedeth from the Urn: From the ashes of the Tarot who shall make the phoenix-wand? Not even he who by his understanding hath made the lotus-wand to grow in the Great Sea. Get thee back, for thou art not an Atheist, and though thou have violated thy mother, thou hast not slain thy father. Get thee back from the Urn; thy ashes are not hidden here.

Then again arose the God Thoth, in the sign of the

Enterer, and he drove the seer from before his face. And he fell through the starry night unto the little village in the desert.

BENISHRUR, ALGERIA.
December 10, 1909. 7:40–9:40 P.M.

THE CRY OF THE 5TH AETHYR
WHICH IS CALLED LIT

There is a shining pylon, above which is set the sigil of the eye, within the shining triangle. Light streams through the pylon from before the face of Isis-Hathor, for she weareth the lunar crown of cows' horns, with the disk in the centre; at her breast she beareth the child Horus.

And there is a voice: thou knowest not how the Seven was united with the Four; much less then canst thou understand the marriage of the Eight and the Three. Yet there is a word wherein these are made one, and therein is contained the Mystery that thou seekest, concerning the rending asunder of the veil of my Mother.

Now there is an avenue of pylons (not one alone), steep after steep, carved from the solid rock of the mountain; and that rock is a substance harder than diamond, and brighter than light, and heavier than lead. In each pylon is seated a god. There seems an endless series of these pylons. And all the gods of all the nations of the earth are shown, for there are many avenues, all leading to the top of the mountain.

Now I come to the top of the mountain, and the last pylon opens into a circular hall, with other pylons leading out of it, each of which is the last pylon of a great avenue; there seem to be nine such pylons. And in the centre is a shrine, a circular table, supported by marble figures of men and women, alternate white and black; they face inwards, and their buttocks are almost worn away by the kisses of those who have come to worship that supreme

God, who is the single end of all those diverse religions. But the shrine itself is higher than a man may reach.

But the Angel that was with me lifted me, and I saw that the edge of the altar, as I must call it, was surrounded by holy mon. Each has in his right hand a weapon—one a sword, one a spear, one a thunderbolt, and so on, but each with his left hand gives the sign of silence. I wish to see what is within their ring. One of them bends forward so that I may whisper the pass-word. The Angel prompts me to whisper: "There is no god." So they let me pass, and though there was indeed nothing visible therein, yet there was a very strange atmosphere, which I could not understand.

Suspended in the air there is a silver star, and on the forehead of each of the guardians there is a silver star. It is a pentagram—because, says the Angel, three and five are eight; three and eight are eleven. (There is another numerical reason that I cannot hear.)

And as I entered their ring, they bade me stand in their circle, and a weapon was given unto me. And the pass-word that I had given seems to have been whispered round from one to the other, for each one nods gravely as if in solemn acquiescence, until the last one whispers the same words in my ears. But they have a different sense. I had taken them to be a denial of the existence of God, but the man who says them to me evidently means nothing of the sort: What he does mean I cannot tell at all. He slightly emphasized the word "there."

And now all is suddenly blotted out, and instead appears the Angel of the Aethyr. He is all in black, burnished black scales, just edged with gold. He has vast wings, with terrible claws on the ends, and he has a fierce face, like a dragon's, and dreadful eyes that pierce one through and through.

And he says: O thou that art so dull of understanding,

when wilt thou begin to annihilate thyself in the mysteries of the Aethyrs? For all that thou thinkest is but thy thought; and as there is no god in the ultimate shrine, so there is no I in thine own Cosmos.

They that have said this are of them that understood. And all men have misinterpreted it, even as thou didst misinterpret it. He says some more: I cannot catch it properly, but it seems to be to the effect that the true God is equally in all the shrines, and the true I in all the parts of the body and the soul. He speaks with such a terrible roaring that it is impossible to hear the words: one catches a phrase here and there, or a glimpse of the idea. With every word he belches forth smoke, so that the whole Aethyr becomes full of it.

And now I hear the Angel: Every particle of matter that forms the smoke of my breath is a religion that hath flourished among the inhabitants of the worlds. Thus are they all whirled forth in my breath.

Now he is giving a demonstration of this Operation. And he says: Know thou that all the religions of all the worlds end herein, but they are only the smoke of my breath, and I am only the head of the Great Dragon that eateth up the Universe; without whom the Fifth Aethyr would be perfect, even as the first. Yet unless he pass by me, can no man come unto the perfections.

And the rule is ended that hath bound thee, and this shall be thy rule: that thou shalt purify thyself, and anoint thyself with perfume; and thou shalt be in the sunlight, the day being free from clouds. And thou shalt make the Call of the Aethyr in silence.

Now, then, behold how the head of the dragon is but the tail of the Aethyr! Many are they that have fought their way from mansion to mansion of the Everlasting House, and beholding me at last have returned, declaring,

"Fearful is the aspect of the Mighty and Terrible One."
Happy are they that have known me for whom I am. And
glory unto him that hath made a gallery of my throat for
his arrow of truth, and the moon for his purity.

The moon waneth. The moon waneth. The moon
waneth. For in that arrow is the Light of Truth that
overmastereth the light of the sun, whereby she shines.
The arrow is fledged with the plumes of Maat, that are
the plumes of Amoun, and the shaft is the phallus of
Amoun, the Concealed One. And the barb thereof is the
star that thou sawest in the place where was No God.

And of them that guarded the star, there was not found
one worthy to wield the Arrow. And of them that
worshipped there was not found one worthy to behold
the Arrow. Yet the star that thou sawest was but the
barb of the Arrow, and thou hadst not the wit to grasp
the shaft, or the purity to divine the plumes. Now
therefore is he blessed that is born under the sign of the
Arrow, and blessed is he that hath the sigil of the head of
the crowned lion and the body of the Snake and the
Arrow therewith.

Yet do thou distinguish between the upward and the
downward Arrows, for the upward arrow is straitened in
its flight, and it is shot by a firm hand, for Jesod is Jod
Tetragrammaton, and Jod is a hand, but the downward
arrow is shot by the topmost point of the Jod; and that
Jod is the Hermit, and it is the minute point that is not
extended, that is nigh unto the heart of Hadit.

And now it is commanded thee that thou withdraw
thyself from the Vision, and on the morrow, at the
appointed hour, shall it be given thee further, as thou
goest upon thy way, meditating this mystery. And thou
shalt summon the Scribe, and that which shall be written,
shall be written.

Therefore I withdraw myself, as I am commanded.

THE DESERT BETWEEN BENSHRUR AND TOLGA.
December 12, 1909. 7–8:12 P.M.

Now then art thou approached unto an august Arcanum; verily thou art come unto the ancient Marvel, the winged light,. the Fountains of Fire, the Mystery of the Wedge. But it is not I that can reveal it, for I have never been permitted to behold it, who am but the watcher upon the threshold of the Aethyr. My message is spoken, and my mission is accomplished. And I withdraw myself, covering my face with my wings, before the presence of the Angel of the Aethyr.

So the Angel departed with bowed head, folding his wings across.

And there is a little child in a mist of blue light; he hath golden hair, a mass of curls, and deep blue eyes. Yea, he is all golden, with a living, vivid gold. And in each hand he hath a snake; in the right hand a red, in the left hand a blue. And he hath red sandals, but no other garment.

And he sayeth: Is not life a long initiation unto sorrow? And is not Isis the Lady of Sorrow? And she is my mother. Nature is her name, and she hath a twin sister Nephthys, whose name is Perfection. And Isis must be known of all, but of how few is Nephthys known! Because she is dark, therefore is she feared.

But thou who hast adored her without fear, who hast made thy life an initiation into her Mystery, thou that hast neither mother nor father, nor sister nor brother, nor wife nor child, who hast made thyself lonely as the hermit crab that is in the waters of the Great Sea, behold! when the sistrons are shaken, and the trumpets blare forth the glory of Isis, at the end thereof there is silence, and thou shalt commune with Nephthys.

And having known these, there are the wings of Maut the Vulture. Thou mayest draw to an head the bow of thy magical will; thou mayest loose the shaft and pierce her to the heart. I am Eros. Take then the bow and the quiver from my shoulders and slay me; for unless thou slay me, thou shalt not unveil the Mystery of the Aethyr.

Therefore I did as he commanded; in the quiver were two arrows, one white, one black. I cannot force myself to fit an arrow to the bow.

And there came a voice: It must needs be.

And I said: No man can do this thing.

And the voice answered, as it were an echo: *Nemo hoc facere potest.*

Then came understanding to me, and I took forth the Arrows. The white arrow had no barb, but the black arrow was barbed like a forest of fish-hooks; it was bound round with brass, and it had been dipped in deadly poison. Then I fitted the white arrow to the string, and I shot it against the heart of Eros, and though I shot with all my force, it fell harmlessly from his side. But at that moment the black arrow was thrust through mine own heart. I am filled with fearful agony.

And the child smiles, and says: Although thy shaft hath pierced thee not, although the envenomed barb hath struck thee through; yet I am slain, and thou livest and triumphest, for I am thou and thou art I.

With that he disappears, and the Aethyr splits with a roar as of ten thousand thunders. And behold, The Arrow! The plumes of Maat are its crown, set about the disk. It is the Ateph crown of Thoth, and there is the shaft of burning light, and beneath there is a silver wedge.

I shudder and tremble at the vision, for all about it are whorls and torrents of tempestuous fire. The stars of heaven are caught in the ashes of the flame. And they are all dark. That which was a blazing sun is like a speck of ash. And in the midst the Arrow burns!

I see that the crown of the Arrow is the Father of all

Light, and the shaft of the Arrow is the Father of all Life, and the barb of the Arrow is the Father of all Love. For that silver wedge is like a lotus flower, and the Eye within the Ateph Crown crieth: I watch. And the Shaft crieth: I work. And the Barb crieth: I wait. And the Voice of the Aethyr echoeth: It beams. It burns. It blooms.

And now there cometh a strange thought; this Arrow is the source of all motion; it is infinite motion, yet it moveth not, so that there *is* no motion. And therefore there is no matter. This Arrow is the glance of the Eye of Shiva. But because it moveth not, the universe is not destroyed. The universe is put forth and swallowed up in the quivering of the plumes of Maat, that are the plumes of the Arrow: but those plumes quiver not.

And a voice comes: That which is above is *not* like that which is below.

And another voice answers it: That which is below is *not* like that which is above.

And a third voice answers these two: What is above and what is below? For there is the division that divideth not, and the multiplication that multiplieth not. And the One is the Many. Behold, this Mystery is beyond understanding, for the winged globe is the crown, and the shaft is the wisdom, and the barb is the understanding. And the Arrow is one, and thou art lost in the Mystery, who art but as a babe that is carried in the womb of its mother, that art not yet ready for the light.

And the vision overcometh me. My sense is stunned; my sight is blasted; my hearing is dulled.

And a voice cometh: Thou didst seek the remedy of sorrow; therefore all sorrow is thy portion. This is that which is written: "God hath laid upon him the iniquity of us all." For as thy blood is mingled in the cup of BABALON, so is thine heart the universal heart. Yet is it bound about with the Green Serpent, the Serpent of Delight.

It is shown me that this heart is the heart that rejoiceth, and the serpent is the serpent of Death, for herein all the symbols are interchangeable, for each one containeth in itself its own opposite. And this is the great Mystery of the Supernals that are beyond the Abyss. For below the Abyss, contradiction is division; but above the Abyss, contradiction is Unity. And there could be nothing true except by virtue of the contradiction that is contained in itself.

Thou canst not believe how marvellous is this vision of the Arrow. And it could never be shut out, except the Lords of Vision troubled the waters of the pool, the mind of the Seer. But they send forth a wind that is a cloud of Angels, and they beat the water with their feet, and little waves splash up—they are memories. For the seer hath no head; it is expanded into the universe, a vast and silent sea, crowned with the stars of night. Yet in the very midst thereof is the arrow. Little images of things that were, are the foam upon the waves. And there is a contest between the Vision and the memories. I prayed unto the Lords of Vision, saying: O my Lords, take not away this wonder from my sight.

And they said: It must needs be. Rejoice therefore if thou hast been permitted to behold, even for a moment, this Arrow, the austere, the august. But the vision is accomplished, and we have sent forth a great wind against thee. For thou canst not penetrate by force, who hast refused it; nor by authority, for thou hast trampled it under foot. Thou art bereft of all but understanding, O thou that art no more than a little pile of dust!

And the images rise up against me and constrain me, so that the Aethyr is shut against me. Only the things of the mind and of the body are open unto me. The shew-stone is dull, for that which I see therein is but a memory.

TOLGA, ALGERIA.
December 13, 1909. 8:15–10:10 P.M.

THE CRY OF THE 4TH AETHYR WHICH IS CALLED PAZ

The Stone is translucent and luminous, and no images enter therein.

A voice says: Behold the brilliance of the Lord, whose feet are set upon him that pardoneth transgression. Behold the six-fold Star that flameth in the Vault, the seal of the marriage of the great White King and his black slave.

So I looked into the Stone, and beheld the six-fold Star: the whole Aethyr is as tawny clouds, like the flame of a furnace. And there is a mighty host of Angels, blue and golden, that throng it, and they cry: Holy, Holy, Holy art thou, that art not shaken in the earthquakes, and in the thunders! The end of things is come upon us; the day of be-with-us is at hand! For he hath created the universe, and overthrown it, that he might take his pleasure thereupon.

And now, in the midst of the Aethyr, I beheld that god. He hath a thousand arms, and in each hand is a weapon of terrible strength. His face is more terrible than the storm, and from his eyes flash lightnings of intolerable brilliance. From his mouth run seas of blood. Upon his head is a crown of every deadly thing. Upon his forehead is the upright tau, and on either side of it are signs of blasphemy. And about him clingeth a young girl, like unto the king's daughter that appeared in the ninth Aethyr. But she is become rosy by reason of his force, and her purity hath tinged his black with blue.

They are clasped in a furious embrace, so that she is torn asunder by the terror of the god; yet so tightly clingeth she about him, that he is strangled. She hath forced back his head, and his throat is livid with the pressure of her fingers. Their joint cry is an intolerable anguish, yet it is the cry of their rapture, so that every pain, and every curse, and every bereavement, and every death of everything in the whole universe, is but one little gust of wind in that tempest-scream of ecstasy.

The voice thereof is not articulate. It is in vain to seek comparison. It is absolutely continuous, without breaks or beats. If there seem to be vibration therein, it is because of the imperfection of the ears of the seer.

And there cometh an interior voice, which sayeth to the seer that he hath trained his eyes well and can see much; and he hath trained his ears a little, and can hear a little; but his other senses hath he trained scarcely at all, and therefore the Aethyrs are almost silent to him on those planes. By the senses are meant the spiritual correlations of the senses, not the physical senses. But this matters little, because the Seer, so far as he is a seer, is the expression of the spirit of humanity. What is true of him is true of humanity, so that even if he had been able to receive the full Aethyrs, he could not have communicated them.

And an Angel speaks: Behold, this vision is utterly beyond thine understanding. Yet shalt thou endeavour to unite thyself with the dreadful marriage-bed.

So I am torn asunder, nerve from nerve and vein from vein, and more intimately—cell from cell, molecule from molecule, and atom from atom, and at the same time all crushed together. Write down that the tearing asunder *is* a crushing together. All the double phenomena are only two ways of looking at a single phenomenon; and the single phenomenon is Peace. There is no sense in my words or in my thoughts. "Faces half-formed arose." This is the meaning of that passage; they are attempts to interpret Chaos, but Chaos is Peace. Cosmos is the War of the Rose and the Cross. That was "a half-formed face" that I said then. All images are useless.

Blackness, blackness intolerable, before the beginning of the light. This is the first verse of Genesis. Holy art thou, Chaos, Chaos, Eternity, all contradictions in terms!

Oh, blue! blue! blue! whose reflection in the Abyss is called the Great One of the Night of Time; between ye vibrateth the Lord of the Forces of Matter.

O Nox, Nox, qui celas infamiam infandi nefandi, Deo solo sit laus qui dedit signum non scribendum. Laus virgini cuius stuprum tradit salutem.

O Night, that givest suck from thy paps to sorcery, and theft, and rape, and gluttony, and murder, and tyranny, and to the nameless Horror, cover us, cover us, cover us from the Rod of Destiny; for Cosmos must come, and the balance be set up where there was no need of balance, because there was no injustice, but only truth. But when the balances are equal, scale matched with scale, then will Chaos return.

Yea, as in a looking-glass, so in thy mind, that is backed with the false metal of lying, is every symbol read averse. Lo! everything wherein thou hast trusted must confound thee, and that thou didst flee from was thy saviour. So therefore didst thou shriek in the Black Sabbath when thou didst kiss the hairy buttocks of the goat, when the gnarled god tore thee asunder, when the icy cataract of death swept thee away.

Shriek therefore, shriek aloud; mingle the roar of the gored lion and the moan of the torn bull, and the cry of the man that is torn by the claws of the Eagle, and the scream of the Eagle that is strangled by the hands of the Man. Mingle all these in the death-shriek of the Sphinx, for the blind man hath profaned her mystery. Who is this, Oedipus, Tiresias, Erinyes? Who is this, that is blind and a seer, a fool above wisdom? Whom do the hounds of heaven, follow, and the crocodiles of hell await? Aleph, vau, yod, ayin, resh, tau, is his name.

Beneath his feet is the kingdom, and upon his head the crown. He is spirit and matter; he is peace and power; in him is Chaos and Night and Pan, and upon BABALON his concubine, that hath made him drunk upon the blood of the saints that she hath gathered in her golden cup, hath he begotten the virgin that now he doth deflower. And this is that which is written: Malkuth shall be uplifted and set upon the throne of Binah. And this is the stone of the philosophers that is set as a seal upon the tomb of Tetragrammaton, and the elixir of life that is distilled from the blood of the saints, and the red powder that is the grinding-up of the bones of Choronzon.

Terrible and wonderful is the Mystery thereof, O thou Titan that hast climbed into the bed of Juno! Surely thou art bound unto, and broken upon, the wheel; yet hast thou uncovered the nakedness of the Holy One, and the Queen of Heaven is in travail of child, and his name shall be called Vir, and Vis, and Virus, and Virtus, and Viridis, in one name that is all these, and above all these.

Desolate, desolate is the Aethyr, for thou must return unto the habitations of the Owl and the Bat, unto the Scorpions of the sand, and the blanched eyeless beetles that have neither wing nor horn. Return, blot out the vision, wipe from thy mind the memory thereof; stifle the fire with green wood; consume the Sacrament; cover the Altar; veil the shrine; shut up the Temple and spread booths in the market place; until the appointed time come when the Holy One shall declare unto thee the Mystery of the Third Aethyr.

Yet be thou wake and ware, for the great Angel Hua is about thee, and overshadoweth thee, and at any moment he may come upon thee unawares. The voice of PAZ is ended.

BISKRA, ALGERIA.
December 16, 1909. 9–10:30 A.M.

THE CRY OF THE 3RD AETHYR WHICH IS CALLED ZON

There is an angry light in the stone; now it is become clear.

In the centre is that minute point of light which is the true Sun, and in the circumference is the Emerald Snake. And joining them are the rays which are the plumes of Maat, and because the distance is infinite, therefore are they parallel from the circumference, although they diverge from the centre.

In all this is no voice and no motion.

And yet it seems that the great Snake feedeth upon the plumes of Truth as upon itself, so that it contracteth. But ever so little as it contracteth, without it gloweth the golden rim, which is that minute point in the centre.

And all this is the sigil of the Aethyr, gold and azure and green. Yet also these are the Severities.

It is only in the first three Aethyrs that we find the pure essence, for all the other Aethyrs are but as Malkuth to complete these three triads, as hath before been said. And this being the second reflection, therefore is it the palace of two hundred and eighty judgments.

For all these paths[18] are in the course of the Flaming Sword from the side of Severity. And the other two paths are Zayin, which is a sword; and Shin, which is a tooth. These are then the five severities which are 280.

All this is communicated to the Seer interiorly.

"And the eye of His benignancy is closed. Let it not be

18. ר, ל, and נ, the Sun, the Balance or plumes of Maat, and the Snake. Added they make 280.

opened upon the Aethyr, lest the severities be mitigated, and the house fall." Shall not the house fall, and the Dragon sink? Verily all things have been swallowed up in destruction; and Chaos hath opened his jaws and crushed the Universe as a Bacchanal crusheth a grape between her teeth. Shall not destruction swallow up destruction, and annihilation confound annihilation? Twenty and two are the mansions of the House of my Father, but there cometh an ox that shall set his forehead against the House, and it shall fall. For all these things are the toys of the Magician and the Maker of Illusions, that barreth the Understanding from the Crown.

O thou that hast beheld the City of the Pyramids, how shouldst thou behold the House of the Juggler? For he is wisdom, and by wisdom hath he made the Worlds, and from that wisdom issue judgements 70 by 4, that are the 4 eyes of the double-headed one; that are the 4 devils, Satan, Lucifer, Leviathan, Belial, that are the great princes of the evil of the world.

And Satan is worshipped by men under the name of Jesus; and Lucifer is worshipped by men under the name of Brahma; and Leviathan is worshipped by men under the name of Allah; and Belial is worshipped by men under the name of Buddha.

(This is the meaning of the passage in *Liber Legis,* Chap. III.)

Moreover, there is Mary, a blasphemy against BABA-LON, for she hath shut herself up; and therefore is she the Queen of all those wicked devils that walk upon the earth, those that thou sawest even as little black specks that stained the Heaven of Urania. And all these are the excrement of Choronzon.

And for this is BABALON under the power of the Magician, that she hath submitted herself unto the work; and she guardeth the Abyss. And in her is a perfect purity of that which is above; yet she is sent as the Redeemer to them that are below. For there is no other way into the Supernal Mystery but through her, and the Beast on which she rideth; and the Magician is set beyond her to deceive the brothers of blackness, lest they should make unto themselves a crown; for if there were two crowns, then should Ygdrasil, that ancient tree, be cast out into the Abyss, uprooted and cast down into the Outermost Abyss, and the Arcanum which is in the Adytum should be profaned; and the Ark should be touched, and the Lodge spied upon by them that are not masters, and the bread of the Sacrament should be the dung of Choronzon; and the wine of the Sacrament should be the water of Choronzon; and the incense should be dispersion; and the fire upon the Altar should be hate. But lift up thyself; stand, play the man, for behold! there shall be revealed unto thee the Great Terror, the thing of awe that hath no name.

And this is the mystery that I declare unto thee: that from the Crown itself spring the three great delusions; Aleph is madness, and Beth is falsehood, and Gimel is glamour. And these three be greater than all, for they are beyond the words that I speak unto thee; how much more therefore are they beyond the words that thou transmittest unto men.

Behold! the Veil of the Aethyr sundereth, and is torn, like a sail by the breath of the tempest, and thou shalt see him as from afar off. This is that which is written, "Confound her understanding with darkness," for thou canst not speak this thing.

It is the figure of the Magus of the Taro; in his right arm the torch of the flames blazing upwards; in his left the cup of poison, a cataract into Hell. And upon his head the evil talisman, blasphemy and blasphemy and blasphemy, in the form of a circle. That is the greatest blasphemy of all.[19] On his feet hath he the scythes and swords and sickles; daggers; knives; every sharp thing—a millionfold, and all in one. And before him is the Table that is a Table of wickedness, the 42-fold Table. This Table is connected with the 42 Assessors of the Dead, for they are the Accusers, whom the soul must baffle; and with the 42-fold name of God, for this is the Mystery of Iniquity, that there was ever a beginning at all. And this Magus casteth forth, by the might of his four weapons, veil after veil; a thousand shining colours, ripping and tearing the Aethyr, so that it is like jagged saws, or like broken teeth in the face of a young girl, or like disruption, or madness. There is a horrible grinding sound, maddening. This is the mill in which the Universal Substance, which is ether, was ground down into matter.

The Seer prayeth that a cloud may come between him and the sun, so that he may shut out the terror of the vision. And he is afire; he is terribly athirst; and no help can come to him, for the shew-stone blazeth ever with the fury and the torment and the blackness, and the stench of human flesh. The bowels of little children are torn out and thrust into his mouth, and poison is dropped into his eyes. And Lilith, a black monkey crawling with filth, running with open sores, an eye torn out, eaten of worms, her teeth rotten, her nose eaten away, her mouth a putrid mass of green slime, her dugs dropping and cancerous, clings to him, kisses him.

(Kill me! kill me!)

There is a mocking voice: Thou art become immortal. Thou wouldst look upon the face of the Magician and thou hast not beheld him because of his Magick veils.

(Don't torture me!)

19. *I.e.,* that the circle should be thus profaned. This evil circle is of three concentric rings.

Thus are they all fallen into the power of Lilith, who have dared to look upon his face.

The shew-stone is all black and corrupt. O filth! filth! filth!

And this is her great blasphemy: that she hath taken the name of the First Aethyr, and bound it on her brow, and added thereunto the shameless yod and the tau for the sign of the Cross.

She it is that squatteth upon the Crucifix, for the nastiness of her pleasure. So that they that worship Christ suck up her filth upon their tongues, and therefore their breaths stink.

I was saved from that Horror by a black shining Triangle, with apex upwards, that came upon the face of the sun.

And now the shew-stone is all clear and beautiful again.

The pure pale gold of a fair maiden's hair, and the green of her girdle, and the deep soft blue of her eyes.

Note: In this the gold is Kether, the blue is Chokmah, the green is Binah.

Thus she appeareth in the Aethyr, adorned with flowers and gems. It seems that she hath incarnated herself upon earth, and that she will appear manifest in a certain office in the Temple.

I have seen some picture like her face; I cannot think what picture. It is a piquant face, with smiling eyes and lips; the ears are small and pink, the complexion is fair, but not transparent; not as fair as one would expect from the hair and eyes. It is rather an impudent face, rather small, very pretty; the nose very slightly less than straight, well-proportioned, rather large nostrils. Full of vitality, the whole thing. Not very tall, rather slim and graceful; a good dancer.

There is another girl behind her, with sparkling eyes,

mischievous, a smile showing beautiful white teeth; an ideal Spanish girl, but fair. Very vivacious. Only her head is visible, and now it is veiled by a black sun, casting forth dull rays of black and gold.

Then the disk of the sun is a pair of balances, held steady; and twined about the central pole of the balance is the little green poisonous snake, with a long forked tongue rapidly darting.

And the Angel that hath spoken with me before, saith to me: The eye of His benignancy is opened; therefore veileth he thine eyes from the vision. Manfully hast thou endured; yet, hadst thou been man, thou hadst not endured; and hadst thou been wholly that which thou art, thou shouldst have been caught up into the full vision that is unspeakable for Horror. And thou shouldst have beheld the face of the Magician that thou hast not been able to behold—of him from whom issue forth the severities that are upon Malkuth, and his name is Misericordia Dei.

And because he is the dyad, thou mayest yet understand in two ways. Of the first way, the Mercy of God is that Mercy which Jehovah showed to the Amalekites; and the second way is utterly beyond thine understanding, for it is the upright, and thou knowest nothing but the averse – until Wisdom shall inform thine Understanding, and upon the base of the Ultimate triangle arise the smooth point.

Veil therefore thine eyes, for that thou canst not master the Aethyr, unless thy Mystery match Its Mystery. Seal up thy mouth also, for thou canst not master the voice of the Aethyr, save only by Silence.

And thou shalt give the sign of the Mother, for BABALON is thy fortress against the iniquity of the Abyss, of the iniquity of that which bindeth her unto the Crown, and barreth her from the Crown; for not until thou art made one with CHAOS canst thou begin that last, that most terrible projection, the three-fold Regimen which alone constitutes the Great Work.

For Choronzon is as it were the shell or excrement of these three paths, and therefore is his head raised unto Daath, and therefore have the Black Brotherhood declared him to be the child of Wisdom and Understanding, who is but the bastard of the Svastika. And this is that which is written in the Holy Qabalah, concerning the Whirlpool and Leviathan, and the Great Stone.

Thus long have I talked with thee in bidding thee depart, that the memory of the Aethyr might be dulled; for hadst thou come back suddenly into thy mortal frame, thou hadst fallen into madness or death. For the vision is not such that any may endure it.

But now thy sense is dull, and the shew-stone but a stone. Therefore awake, and give secretly and apart the sign of the Mother, and call four times upon the name of CHAOS, that is the four-fold word that is equal to her seven-fold word. And then shalt thou purify thyself, and return into the World.

So I did that which was commanded me, and returned.

BISKRA.
December 17, 1909. 9:30–11:30 A.M.

THE CRY OF THE 2ND AETHYR
WHICH IS CALLED ARN

In the first place, there is again the woman riding on the bull, which is the reflection of BABALON, that rideth on The Beast. And also there is an Assyrian legend of a woman with a fish, and also there is a legend of Eve and the Serpent, for Cain was the child of Eve and the Serpent, and not of Eve and Adam; and therefore when he had slain his brother, who was the first murderer, having sacrificed living things to his demon, had Cain the mark upon his brow, which is the mark of the Beast spoken of in the Apocalypse, and is the sign of initiation.

The shedding of blood is necessary, for God did not hear the children of Eve until blood was shed. And that is external religion; but Cain spake not with God, nor had the mark of initiation upon his brow, so that he was shunned of all men, until he had shed blood. And this blood was the blood of his brother. This is a mystery of the sixth key of the Taro, which ought not to be called The Lovers, but The Brothers.

In the middle of the card stands Cain; in his right hand is the Hammer of Thor with which he hath slain his brother, and it is all wet with his blood. And his left hand he holdeth open as a sign of innocence. And on his right hand is his mother Eve, around whom the serpent is entwined with his hood spread behind her head; and on his left hand is a figure somewhat like the Hindoo Kali, but much more seductive. Yet I know it to be Lilith. And above him is the Great Sigil of the Arrow, downward, but it is struck through the heart of the child. This Child also is Abel. And the meaning of this part of the card is obscure, but that is the correct drawing of the Taro card; and that is the correct magical fable from which the Hebrew scribes, who were not complete Initiates, stole their legend of the Fall and the subsequent events. They joined different fables together to try and make a connected story, and they sophisticated them to suit their social and political conditions.

All this while no image hath come into the Stone, and no voice hath been heard.

I cannot get any idea of the source of what I have been saying. All I can say is, that there is a sort of dew, like mist, upon the Stone, and yet it has become hot to the touch.

All I get is that the Apocalypse was a recension of a

And he saith: It is not in my knowledge. Yet do thou
make once more in silence the Call of the Aethyr, and wait
patiently upon the favour of the Angel, for He is a
mighty Angel, and never yet have I heard the whisper of
his wing.

This is the translation of the Call of the Aethyr:

O ye heavens which dwell in the first Aire, and are
mighty in the parts of the earth, and execute therein the
judgment of the highest, to you it is said: Behold the face
of your God, the beginning of comfort, whose eyes are
the brightness of the heavens which provided you for the
government of the earth, and her unspeakable variety,
furnishing you with a power of understanding, that ye
might dispose all things according to the foresight of
Him that sitteth on the Holy Throne, and rose up in the
beginning, saying, The earth, let her be governed by her
parts (this is the prostitution of BABALON to Pan)
and let there be division in her (the formation of the
Many from the One) that her glory may be always ecstasy
and irritation of orgasm. Her course let it round with the
heavens (that is, let her way be always harmonious with
heaven) and as an handmaid let her serve them (that is,
the Virgin of Eternity climbing into the bed of CHAOS).
One season let it confound another (that is, let there be
unwearying variety of predicates) and let there be no
creature upon or within her the same (that is, let there be
an unwearying variety of subjects). All her members let
them differ in their qualities, and let there be no one
creature equal with another (for if there were any duplica-
tion or omission, there would be no perfection in the
whole). The reasonable creatures of the earth and men,
let them vex and weed out one another (this is, the destruction of reason by internecine conflicts in the course of
redemption). And their dwelling places, let them forget
their names. (This is, the arising of Nemo.) The work of

man and his pomp, let them be defaced. (That is, in the Great Work man must lose his personality.) His building, let it be a cave for the Beast of the Field. ("His building" means the Vault of the Adepts, and the "Cave" is the Cave of the Mountain of Abiegnus, and the "Beast" is he upon whom BABALON rideth, and the "Field" is the supernal Eden.) Confound her understanding with darkness. (This sentence is explained by what has been said concerning Binah.) For why, it rejoiceth me concerning the Virgin and the Man. (Kelly did not understand this Call at all, and he would not believe this sentence was written so, for it seemed to contradict the rest of the Call, so he altered it.) One while let her be known and another while a stranger (that is, the Mystery of the Holy One being at the same time identical with everything and apart from it) because she is the bed of an harlot, and the dwelling of him that is fallen. (That is that Mystery which was revealed in the last Aethyr; the universe being, as it were, a garden wherein the Holy Ones may take their pleasure.) O ye heavens, arise; the lower heavens beneath you, let them serve you. (This is a command for the whole of things to join in universal rapture.) Govern those that govern; cast down such as fall; bring forth those that increase; and destroy the rotten. (This means that everything shall take its own pleasure in its own way.) No place let it remain in one number. ("No place" is the infinite Ain. . . . "Let remain in one number"; that is, let it be concentrated in Kether.) Add and diminish until the stars be numbered. (It is a mystery of the Logos being formulated by the Qabalah, because the stars are all letters of the Holy Alphabet, as it was said in a former Aethyr.) Arise! Move! and Appear! before the covenant of his mouth which he hath shewn unto us in his justice. ("The Covenant" is the letter Aleph; "His mouth," pé; "His Justice," lamed; and these add up again to Aleph, so that it is in the letter Aleph, which is zero, thus symbolizing the circles of the Aethyrs, that he calleth them forth. But men thought that Aleph was the initial of ARR, cursing, when it was really the initial of AChD, unity, and AHBH, love. So that it was the most horrible and wicked blasphemy of the blackest of all the black brothers to begin Berashith with a beth, with the letter of the Magician. Yet, by this simple device, hath he created the whole illusion of sorrow.) Open the mysteries of your creation, and make us partakers of the undefiled knowledge. (The word here "IADNAMAD" is not the ordinary word for knowledge. It is a word of eight letters, which is the secret name of God, summarized in the letter cheth; for which see the Aethyr which correspondeth to that letter, the twelfth Aethyr.)

Now from time to time I have looked into the Stone, but never is there any image therein, or any hint thereof; but now there are three arrows, arranged thus:

This is the letter Aleph in the Alphabet of Arrows.

(I want to say that while I was doing the translation of the Call of the Aethyrs, the soles of my feet were burning, as if I were on red hot steel.)

And now the fire has spread all over me, and parches me, and tortures me. And my sweat is bitter like poison. And all my blood is acrid in my veins, like gleet. I seem to be all festering, rotting; and the worms eating me while I am yet alive.

A voice, neither in myself nor out of myself, is saying: Remember Prometheus; remember Ixion.

I am tearing at nothing. I will not heed. For even this dust must be consumed with fire.

And now, although there is no image, at last there is a sense of obstacle, as if one were at length drawing near to the frontier of the Aethyr.

But I am dying.

I can neither strive nor wait. There is agony in my ears, and in my throat, and mine eyes have been so long blind that I cannot remember that there ever was such a thing as sight.

And it cometh to me that I should go away, and await the coming of the veil of the Aethyr; not here. I think I will go to the Hot Springs.

So I put away the Stone upon my breast.

BISKRA.
10:15–11:52 A.M.

Flashes of lightning are playing in the Stone, at the top; and at the bottom of the Stone there is a black pyramid, and at the top thereof is a vesica piscis. The vesica piscis is of colourless brilliance.

The two curves of Pisces are thus:

They are the same curves as the curves of vesica piscis, but turned round.

And a voice comes: How can that which is buried in the pyramids behold that which descendeth upon its apex?

Again it comes to me, without voice: Therefore is mother-hood the symbol of the Masters. For first must they give up their virginity to be destroyed, and the seed must lie hidden in them while the nine moons wax and wane, and they must surround it with the Universal Fluid. And they must feed it with blood for fire. Then is the child a living thing. And afterwards is much suffering and much joy, and after that are they torn asunder, and this is all their thank, that they give it to suck.

All this while the vision in the Shew-Stone stays as it was, save that the lightning grows more vehement and clear; and behind the vesica piscis is a black cross extending to the top and to the edges of the Stone. And now blackness spreads, and swallows up the images.

Now there is naught but the vast black triangle having the apex downwards, and in the centre of the black triangle is the face of Typhon, the Lord of the Tempest, and he crieth aloud: Despair! Despair! For thou mayest deceive the Virgin, and thou mayest cajole the Mother; but what wilt thou say unto the ancient Whore that is throned in Eternity? For if she will not, there is neither force nor cunning, nor any wit, that may prevail upon her.

Thou canst not woo her with love, for she *is* love. And she hath all, and hath no need of thee.

And thou canst not woo her with gold, for all the kings and captains of the earth, and all the gods of heaven, have showered their gold upon her. Thus hath she all, and hath no need of thee.

And thou canst not woo her with knowledge, for knowledge is the thing that she hath spurned. She hath it all, and hath no need of thee.

And thou canst not woo her with wit, for her Lord is Wit. She hath it all, and hath no need of thee. Despair! Despair!

Nor canst thou cling to her knees and ask for pity; nor canst thou cling to her heart and ask for love; nor canst thou put thine arms about her neck, and ask for understanding; for thou hast had all these, and they avail thee not. Despair! Despair!

Then I took the Flaming Sword, and I let it loose against Typhon, so that his head was cloven asunder, and the black triangle dissolved in lightnings.

But as he parted his voice broke out again: Nor canst thou win her with the Sword, for her eyes are fixed upon the eyes of Him in whose hand is the hilt of the Sword. Despair! Despair!

And the echo of that cry was his word, which is identical, although it be diverse: Nor canst thou win her by the Serpent, for it was the Serpent that seduced her first. Despair! Despair!

(Yet he cried thus as he fled:)

I am Leviathan, the great Lost Serpent of the Sea. I writhe eternally in torment, and I lash the ocean with my tail into a whirlpool of foam that is venomous and bitter, and I have no purpose. I go no whither. I can neither live nor die. I can but rave and rave in my death agony. I am the Crocodile that eateth up the children of men. And through the malice of BABALON I hunger, hunger, hunger.

All this while the Stone is more inert than ever yet; a thousand times more lifeless than when it is not invoked. Now, when it kindles, it only kindles into its physical beauty. And now upon the face of it is a great black Rose, each of whose petals, though it be featureless, is yet a devil-face. And all the stalks are the black snakes of hell. It is alive, this Rose; a single thought informs it. It comes to clutch, to murder. Yet, because a single thought alone informs it, I have hope therein.

I think this Rose has a hundred and fifty-six petals, and though it be black, it has the luminous blush.

There it is, in the midst of the Stone, and I cannot see anyone who wears it.

Aha! Aha! Aha! Shut out the sight!

Holy, Holy, Holy art thou!

Light, Life and Love are like three glow-worms at thy feet: the whole universe of stars, the dewdrops on the grass whereon thou walkest!

I am quite blind.

Thou art Nuit! Strain, strain, strain my whole soul!

> A ka dua
> Tuf ur biu
> Bi a'a chefu
> Dudu ner af an nuteru.

Falutli! Falutli!

I cling unto the burning Aethyr like Lucifer that fell through the Abyss, and by the fury of his flight kindled the air.

And I am Belial, for having seen the Rose upon thy breast, I have denied God.

And I am Satan! I am Satan! I am cast out upon a burning crag! And the sea boils about the desolation thereof. And already the vultures gather, and feast upon my flesh.

Yea! Before thee all the most holy is profane, O thou desolator of shrines! O thou falsifier of the oracles of truth! Ever as I went, hath it been thus. The truth of the profane was the falsehood of the Neophyte, and the truth of the Neophyte was the falsehood of the Zelator! Again and again the fortress must be battered down! Again and again the pylon must be overthrown! Again and again must the gods be desecrated!

And now I lie supine before thee, in terror and abasement. O Purity! O Truth! What shall I say? My tongue cleaveth to my jaws, O thou Medusa that hast turned me into stone! Yet is that stone the stone of the philosophers. Yet is that tongue Hadit.

Aha! Aha!

Yea! Let me take the form of Hadit before thee, and sing:

> A ka dua
> Tuf ur biu
> Bi a'a chefu
> Dudu ner af an nuteru.

Nuit! Nuit! How art thou manifested in this place! This is a Mystery ineffable. And it is mine, and I can never reveal it either to God or to man. It is for thee and me!
Aha! Aha!

> A ka dua
> Tuf ur biu
> Bi a'a chefu
> Dudu ner af an nuteru.

... My spirit is not more; my soul is no more. My life leaps out into annihilation!

> A ka dua
> Tuf ur biu
> Bi a'a chefu
> Dudu ner af an nuteru.

It is the cry of my body! Save me! I have come too close, I have come too close to that which may not be endured. It must awake, the body; it must assert itself.

It must shut out the Aethyr, or else it is dead.

Every pulse aches, and beats furiously. Every nerve stings like a serpent. And my skin is icy cold.

Neither God nor man can penetrate the Mystery of the Aethyr.

(Here the Seer mutters unintelligibly.)

And even that which understandeth cannot hear its voice. For to the profane the voice of the Neophyte is called silence, and to the Neophyte the voice of the Zelator is called silence. And so ever is it.

Sight is fire, and is the first angle of the Tablet; spirit is hearing, and is the centre thereof; thou, therefore, who art all spirit and fire, and hast no duller elements in thy star; thou art come to sight at the end of thy will. And if thou wilt hear the voice of the Aethyr, do thou invoke it in the night, having no other light but the light of the half moon. Then mayest thou hear the voice, though it may be that thou understandeth it not. Yet shall it be a potent spell, whereby thou mayest lay bare the womb of thine understanding to the violence of CHAOS.

Now, therefore, for the last time, let the veil of the Aethyr be torn.

Aha! Aha! Aha! Aha! Aha! Aha! Aha!

> A ka dua
> Tuf ur biu
> Bi a'a chefu
> Dudu ner af an nuteru.

. .   . .

This Aethyr must be left unfinished then until the half moon.

HAMMAM SALAHIN.
December 18, 3:10–4:35 P.M.

An olvah nu arenu olvah. Diraeseu adika va paretanu poliax poliax in vah rah ahum subre fifal. Lerthexana. Mama ra-la hum fifala maha.

All this is the melody of a flute, very faint and clear. And there is a sort of sub-tinkle of a bell.

And there is a string instrument, somewhat like a zither. And there is a human voice.

And a voice comes: this is the Song of the Sphinx, which she singeth ever in the ears of men.

And it is the song of the syrens. And whoever heareth it is lost.

I

Mu pa telai,
Tu wa melai
Ā, ā, ā.
Tu fu tulu!
Tu fu tulu
Pa, Sa, Ga.

II

Qwi Mu telai
Ya Pa melai;
ū, ū, ū.
' Se gu melai;
Pe fu telai,
Fu tu lu.

III

O chi balae
Wa pa malae:—
Ut! Ut! Ut!
Ge; fu latrai,
Le fu malai
Kūt!—Hūt!—Nūt.

IV

AI OAI
Rel moai
Ti—Ti—Ti!
Wa la pelai
Tu fu latai
Wi, Ni, Bi.

Translation of Song

I

Silence! the moon ceaseth (her motion),
That also was sweet
In the air, in the air, in the air!
Who Will shall attain!
Who Will shall attain
By the Moon, and by Myself, and by the Angel of the Lord!

II

Now Silence ceaseth
And the moon waxeth sweet;
(It is the hour of) Initiation, Initiation, Initiation.
The kiss of Isis is honeyed;
My own Will is ended,
For Will hath attained.

III

Behold the lion-child swimmeth (in the heaven)
And the moon reeleth:—
(It is) Thou! (It is) Thou! (It is) Thou!
Triumph; the Will stealeth away (like a thief),
The Strong Will that staggered
Before Ra Hoor Khuit!—Hadit!—Nuit!

IV

To the God OAI
Be praise
In the end and the beginning!
And may none fall
Who Will attain
The Sword, the Balances, the Crown!

And that which thou hearest is but the dropping of the dew from my limbs, for I dance in the night, naked upon the grass, in shadowy places, by running streams.

Many are they who have loved the nymphs of the woods, and of the wells, and of the fountains, and of the hills. And of these some were nympholept. For it was not a nymph, but I myself that walked upon the earth taking my pleasure. So also there were many images of Pan, and men adored them, and as a beautiful god he made their olives bear double and their vines increase; but some were slain by the god, for it was I that had woven the garlands about him.

Now cometh a song.

So sweet is this song that no one could resist it. For in it is all the passionate ache of the moonlight, and the great hunger of the sea, and the terror of desolate places—all things that lure men to the unattainable.

Ōmărĭ tēssălă mărāx,
tēssălă dōlĭ phōrnĕpāx.
āmrĭ rādără pōlĭax
ármănă pĭliŭ.
āmrĭ rādără pĭliŭ sōn';
mārĭ nārȳă bārbĭtōn
mādără ănăphăx sārpĕdōn
āndălă hrĭlĭu.

Translation

I am the harlot that shaketh Death.
This shaking giveth the Peace of Satiate Lust.
Immortality jetteth from my skull,
    And music from my vulva.
Immortality jetteth from my vulva also,
For my Whoredom is a sweet scent like a seven-stringed instrument,
Played unto God the Invisible, the all-ruler,
    That goeth along giving the shrill scream of orgasm.

Every man that hath seen me forgetteth me never, and I appear oftentimes in the coals of the fire, and upon the smooth white skin of woman, and in the constancy of the waterfall, and in the emptiness of deserts and marshes, and upon great cliffs that look seaward; and in many strange places, where men seek me not. And many thousand times he beholdeth me not. And at the last I smite myself into him as a vision smiteth into a stone and whom I call must follow.

Now I perceive myself standing in a Druid circle, in an immense open plain.

A whole series of beautiful visions of deserts and sunsets and islands in the sea, green beyond imagination . . . But there is no subsistence in them.

A voice goes on: this is the holiness of fruitless love and

aimless toil. For in doing the thing for the thing's sake is concentration, and this is the holiness of them that suit not the means to the end. For therein is faith and sympathy and a knowledge of the true Magick.

Oh my beloved, that fliest in the air like a dove, beware of the falcon! oh my beloved, that springest upon the earth like a gazelle, beware of the lion!

There are hundreds of visions, trampling over one another. In each one the Angel of the Aethyr is mysteriously hidden.

Now I will describe the Angel of the Aethyr until the voice begins again.

He is like one's idea of Sappho and Calypso, and all seductive and deadly things; heavy eye-lids, long lashes, a face like ivory, wonderful barbaric jewellery, intensely red lips, a very small mouth, tiny ears, a Grecian face. Over the shoulders is a black robe with a green collar; the robe is spangled with golden stars; the tunic is a pure soft blue.

Now the whole Aethyr is swallowed up in a forest of unquenchable fire, and fearlessly through it all a snow-white eagle flies. And the eagle cries: the house also of death. Come away! The volume of the book is open, the Angel waiteth without, for the summer is at hand. Come away! For the Aeon is measured, and thy span allotted. Come away! For the mighty sounds have entered into every angle. And they have awakened the Angels of the Aethyrs that slept these three hundred years.

For in the Holy letter Shin, that is the Resurrection in the Book of Thoth, that is the Holy Spirit in the Trinity, that is three hundred in the tale of the years, hath the tomb been opened, so that this great wisdom might be revealed.

Come away! For the Second Triad is completed, and there remaineth only the Lord of the Aeon, the Avenger, the Child both Crowned and Conquering, the Lord of the Sword and the Sun, the Babe in the Lotus, pure from his birth, the Child of suffering, the Father of justice, unto whom be the glory throughout all the Aeon![20]

Come away! For that which was to be accomplished is accomplished, seeing that thou hadst faith unto the end of all.

In the letter N the Voice of the Aethyr is ended.

BISKRA, ALGERIA.
December 20, 1909. 8:35–9:35 P.M.

THE CRY OF THE 1ST AETHYR WHICH IS CALLED LIL

First, let praise and worship and honour and glory and great thanks be given unto the Holy One, who hath permitted us to come thus far, who hath revealed unto us the ineffable mysteries, that they might be disclosed before men. And we humbly beseech His infinite goodness that he will be pleased to manifest unto us even the Mystery of the First Aethyr.

(Here followeth the Call of the Aethyr.)

The veil of the Aethyr is like the veil of night, dark azure, full of countless stars. And because the veil is infinite, at first one seeth not the winged globe of the sun that burneth in the centre thereof. Profound peace filleth me—beyond ecstasy, beyond thought, beyond being itself, IAIDA. (This word means "I am," but in a sense entirely beyond being.)

(*Note:* In Hebrew letters it adds to 26. In Hebrew letters the name of the Aethyr is 70, ayin; but by turning the Yetziratic attributions of the letters into Hebrew, it gives 66, and 66 is the sum of the numbers from 0 to 11.)

Yes; there is peace. There is no *tendency* of any sort,

20. The Seer had absolutely forgotten this prophecy, and was amazed at the final identification of the Child in LIL with Hoor.

much less any observation or feeling or impression. There is only a faint consciousness, like the scent of jasmine.

The body of the Seer is rested in a waking sleep that is deeper than sleep, and his mind is still; he seems like a well in the desert, shaded by windless palms.

And it is night; and because the night is the whole night of space, and not the partial night of earth, there is no thought of dawn. For the light of the Sun maketh illusion, blinding man's eyes to the glory of the stars. And unless he be in the shadow of the earth, he cannot see the stars. So, also, unless he be hidden from the light of life, he cannot behold Nuit. Here, then, do I abide in unalterable midnight, utterly at peace.

I have forgotten where I am, and who I am. I am hanging in nothing.

Now the veil opens of itself. (To Scribe: Come nearer; I don't want to have to speak so loudly.)

It is a little child covered with lilies and roses. He is supported by countless myriads of Archangels. The Archangels are all the same colourless brilliance, and every one of them is blind. Below the Archangels again are many, many other legions, and so on far below, so far that the eye cannot pierce. And on his forehead, and on his heart, and in his hand, is the secret sigil of the Beast. And of all this the glory is so great that all the spiritual senses fail, and their reflections in the body fail.

It is very strange. In my heart is rapture, holy and ineffable, absolutely beyond emotion; beyond even that bliss called Ananda, infinitely calm and pure. Yet at the gates of mine eyes stand tears, like warriors upon the watch, that lean on their spears, listening.[21]

21. There are long intervals between many of these paragraphs, the Seer having been lost to Being. The reader will note that "The Great and Terrible Angel" has not been mentioned, but comes in suddenly. This was because the Seer's speech was inaudible, or never occurred. This angel was the "Higher Genius" of the Seer.

The great and terrible Angel keeps on looking at me, as if to bar me from the vision. There is another blinding my mind. There is another forcing my head down in sleep.

(It's very difficult to talk at all, because an impression takes such an immense time to travel from the will to the muscles. Naturally, I've no idea of time.)

I have gone up again to the child, led by two Angels, abasing my head.

This child seems to be the child that one attempted to describe in "The Garden of Janus."

Every volition is inhibited. I have tried to say a lot, and it has always got lost on the way.

Holy art thou, O more beautiful than all the stars of the Night!

There has never been such peace, such silence. But these are *positive* things. Singing praises of things eternal amid the flames of first glory, and every note of every song is a fresh flower in the garland of peace.

This child danceth not, but it is because he is the soul of the two dances—the right hand and the left hand, and in him they are one dance, the dance without motion.

There is dew on all the fire. Every drop is the quintessence of the ecstasy of stars.

Yet a third time am I led to him, prostrating myself seven times at every step. There is a perfume in the air, reflected down even to the body of the seer. That perfume thrills his body with an ecstasy that is like love, like sleep.

And this is the song:

I am the child of all who am the father of all, for from me came forth all things, that I might be. I am the fountain in the snows, and I am the eternal sea. I am the lover, and I am the beloved, and I am the first-fruits of their love. I am the first faint shuddering of the light, and I am the loom wherein night weaveth her impenetrable veil.

I am the captain of the hosts of eternity; of the swordsmen and the spearmen and the bowmen and the charioteers. I have led the armies of the east against the armies of the west, and the armies of the west against the armies of the east. For I am Peace.

My groves of olive were planted by an harlot, and my horses were bred by a thief. I have trained my vines upon the spears of the Most High, and with my laughter have I slain a thousand men.

With the wine in my cup have I mixed the lightnings, and I have carved my bread with a sharp sword.

With my folly have I undone the wisdom of the Magus, even as with my judgments I have overwhelmed the universe. I have eaten the pomegranate in the House of Wrath, and I have crushed out the blood of my mother between mill-stones to make bread.

There is nothing that I have not trampled beneath my feet. There is nothing that I have not set a garland on my brow. I have wound all things about my waist as a girdle. I have hidden all things in the cave of my heart. I have slain all things because I am Innocence. I have lain with all things because I am Untouched Virginity. I have given birth to all things because I am Death.

Stainless are my lips, for they are redder than the purple of the vine, and of the blood wherewith I am intoxicated. Stainless is my forehead, for it is whiter than the wind and the dew that cooleth it.

I am light, and I am night, and I am that which is beyond them.

I am speech, and I am silence, and I am that which is beyond them.

I am life, and I am death, and I am that which is beyond them.

I am war, and I am peace, and I am that which is beyond them.

I am weakness and I am strength, and I am that which is beyond them.

Yet by none of these can man reach up to me. Yet by each of them must man reach up to me.

Thou shalt laugh at the folly of the fool. Thou shalt learn the wisdom of the wise. And thou shalt be initiate in holy things. And thou shalt be learned in the things of love. And thou shalt be mighty in the things of war. And thou shalt be adept in things occult. And thou shalt interpret the oracles. And thou shalt drive all these before thee in thy car, and though by none of these canst thou reach up to me, yet by each of these must thou attain to me. And thou must have the strength of the lion, and the secrecy of the hermit. And thou must turn the wheel of life. And thou must hold the balances of Truth. Thou must pass through the great Waters, a Redeemer. Thou must have the tail of the scorpion, and the poisoned arrows of the Archer, and the dreadful horns of the Goat. And so shalt thou break down the fortress that guardeth the Palace of the King my son. And thou must work by the light of the Star and of the Moon and of the Sun, and by the dreadful light of judgment that is the birth of the Holy Spirit within thee. When these shall have destroyed the universe, then mayest thou enter the palace of the Queen my daughter.

Blessed, blessed blessed; yea, blessed; thrice and four times blessed is he that hath attained to look upon thy face. For I will hurl thee forth from my presence as a whirling thunderbolt to guard the ways, and whom thou smitest shall be smitten indeed. And whom thou lovest shall be loved indeed. And whether by smiting or by love thou workest, each one shall see my face, a glimmer through a thousand veils. And they shall rise up from love's sleep or death's, and gird themselves with a girdle of snake-skin for wisdom, and they shall wear the white tunic of purity, and the apron of flaming orange for will, and over their shoulders shall they cast the panther's skin of courage. And they shall wear the nemyss of secrecy and the ateph crown of truth. And on their feet shall they put sandals made of the skin of beasts, that they may trample upon all they were, yet also that its toughness shall support them, and protect their feet, as they pass upon the mystical way that lieth through the pylons. And upon their breasts shall be the Rose and Cross of light and life, and in their hands the hermit's staff and lamp. Thus shall they set out upon the never-ending journey, each step of which is an unutterable reward.

Holy, Holy, Holy, Holy; yea, thrice and four times holy art thou, because thou hast attained to look upon my face; not by my favour only, not by thy magick only, may this be won. Yet it is written: "Unto the persevering mortal the blessed Immortals are swift."

Mighty, mighty, mighty, mighty; yea, thrice and four times mighty art thou. He that riseth up against thee shall be thrown down, though thou raise not so much as thy little finger against him. And he that speaketh evil against thee shall be put to shame, though thy lips utter not the littlest syllable against him. And he that thinketh evil concerning thee shall be confounded in his thought, although in thy mind arise not the least thought of him. And they shall be brought unto subjection unto thee, and serve thee, though thou willest it not. And it shall be unto them a grace and a sacrament, and ye shall all sit down together at the supernal banquet, and ye shall feast upon the honey of the gods, and be drunk upon the dew of immortality—FOR I AM HORUS, THE CROWNED AND CONQUERING CHILD, WHOM THOU KNEWEST NOT!

Pass thou on, therefore, O thou Prophet of the Gods,

unto the Cubical Altar of the Universe; there shalt thou receive every tribe and kingdom and nation into the mighty Order that reacheth from the frontier fortresses that guard the Uttermost Abyss unto My Throne.

This is the formula of the Aeon, and with that the voice of LIL, that is the Lamp of the Invisible Light, is ended. Amen.

BISKRA, ALGERIA.
December 19, 1909. 1:30–3:30 P.M.

A COMMENT UPON THE NATURES OF THE AETHYRS

30. Without the cube—the material world—is the sphere-system of the spiritual world enfolding it. The Cry seems to be a sort of Exordium, an external showing forth of the coming of the new Aeon, the Aeon of Horus the crowned child.

29. The disturbance of Equilibrium caused by the Coming of the Aeon.

28. Now is a further and clearer shadowing-forth of the Great Mystery of the Aeon which is to be led up to by the Aethyrs. Note however that the King of the New Aeon never appears until the very first Aethyr.

27. Hecate appears—her son, the son of a Virgin, a magus, is to bring the Aeon to pass. And she, the herald, her function fulfilled, withdraws within her mystic veil.

26. The death of the past Aeon, that of Jehovah and Jesus; ends with adumbration of the new, the vision of the Stele of Ankh-f-n-khonsu, whose discovery brought about in a human consciousness the knowledge of the Equinox of the Gods, 21/3/04.

25. Appearance of the Lion God of Horus, the child of Leo that incarnates him.

The first Angel is Isis its mother.

24. Now appears his mate, the heavenly Venus, the Scarlet Woman, who by men is thought of as Babalon as he is thought of as Chaos.

23. Here appear the Cherubim, the other officers of the new Temple, the earth and water assistants of the fire and air Beast and Scarlet Woman.

22. Here is the First Key to the formula of Horus, a sevenfold arrangement. A shadow of Horus declares his nature.

21. This seems to be the Vision of God face to face that is the necessary ordeal for him who would pass the Abyss, as it were. A commission to be the prophet of the Aeon arising is given to the Seer. The God is the Hierophant in the Ceremony of Magister Templi.

20. A guide is given to the Seer, his Holy Guardian Angel. And this is attained by a mastery of the Universe conceived as a wheel. The Hiereus in the Ceremony of Magister Templi.

19. Now cometh forth the Angel who giveth instruction, in the lowest form. The Hegemone in the Ceremony of Magister Templi which the Seer is about to undergo.

18. The Vault of preparation for the Ceremony of M.T. The Veil is the Crucifixion, symbol of the dead Aeon. The first ordeal is undergone.

17. The symbol of the Balance is now given unto the Aspirant.

16. The sacrifice is made. The High Priestess (image of Babalon) cometh forth upon her Beast and maketh this.

15. The mystic dance by Salome. The new Temple, the signs of the grades are received and the A.E. rejected.

14. The Shrine of Darkness. Final initiation into grade of M.T.

13. The emergence of Nemo into the world; his work therein. This is the first mystery revealed to a M.T.

12. The Second Mystery: the cup-bearer of Babalon

the beautiful. The Holy Grail manifested to the M.T., with the first knowledge of the Black Brothers.

11. Now cometh the Frontier of the Holy City; the M.T. is taken into the Abyss.

10. The Abyss.

9. The M.T. hath passed the Abyss, and is led to the Palace of the Virgin redeemed from Malkuth unto Binah.

8. The fuller manifestation of the Holy Guardian Angel.

7. The Virgin become the Bride, the great Reward of the Ceremony. Also an adumbration of the Further Progress.

6. A shadowing-forth of the grade of Magus.

5. The reception of the M.T. among the Brethren of the A ∴ A ∴. The manifestion of the Arrow.

4. Further concerning the Magus. The marriage of Chaos with the purified Virgin.

3. The Magician. Exhibition of the Guards to the Higher Knowledge.

2. The understanding of the Curse, that is become a Blessing. The final reward of the M.T., his marriage even with Babalon Herself. The paean thereof.

1. The final manifestation. All leads up to the Crowned Child, Horus, the Lord of the New Aeon.

SECTION V

SEX MAGICK

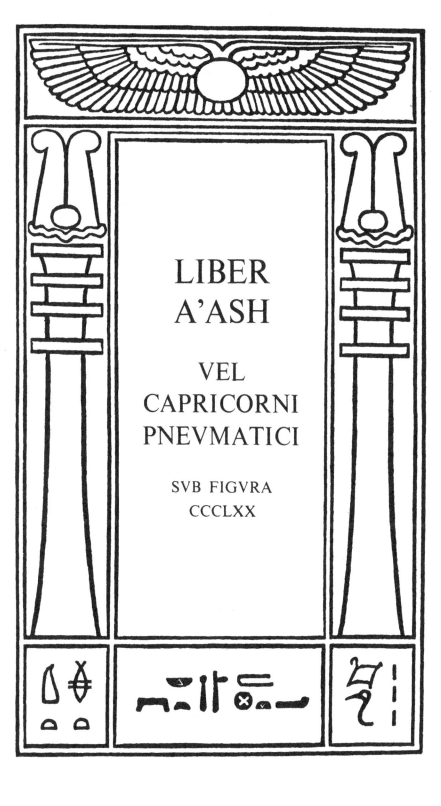

LIBER
A'ASH

VEL
CAPRICORNI
PNEVMATICI

SVB FIGVRA
CCCLXX

A ∴ A ∴
Publication in Class A
Imprimatur:
N. Fra ∴ A ∴ A ∴

LIBER A'ASH

0. Gnarled Oak of God! In thy branches is the lightning nested! Above thee hangs the Eyeless Hawk.

1. Thou art blasted and black! Supremely solitary in that heath of scrub.

2. Up! The ruddy clouds hang over thee! It is the storm.

3. There is a flaming gash in the sky.

4. Up.

5. Thou art tossed about in the grip of the storm for an aeon and an aeon and an aeon. But thou givest not thy sap; thou fallest not.

6. Only in the end shalt thou give up thy sap when the great God F. I. A. T. is enthroned on the day of Be-with-Us.

7. For two things are done and a third thing is begun. Isis and Osiris are given over to incest and adultery. Horus leaps up thrice armed from the womb of his mother. Harpocrates his twin is hidden within him. Set is his holy covenant, that he shall display in the great day of M. A. A. T., that is being interpreted the Master of the Temple of A .·. A .·. whose name is Truth.

8. Now in this is the magical power known.

9. It is like the oak that hardens itself and bears up against the storm. It is weather-beaten and scarred and confident like a sea-captain.

10. Also it straineth like a hound in the leash.

11. It hath pride and great subtlety. Yea, and glee also!

12. Let the magus act thus in his conjuration.

13. Let him sit and conjure; let him draw himself together in that forcefulness; let him rise next swollen and straining; let him dash back the hood from his head and fix his basilisk eye upon the sigil of the demon. Then let him sway the force of him to and fro like a satyr in silence, until the Word burst from his throat.

14. Then let him not fall exhausted, although the might have been ten thousandfold the human; but that which floodeth him is the infinite mercy of the Genitor-Genetrix of the Universe, whereof he is the Vessel.

15. Nor do thou deceive thyself. It is easy to tell the live force from the dead matter. It is no easier to tell the live snake from the dead snake.

16. Also concerning vows. Be obstinate, and be not obstinate. Understand that the yielding of the Yoni is one with the lengthening of the Lingam. Thou art both these; and thy vow is but the rustling of the wind on Mount Meru.

17. Now shalt thou adore me who am the Eye and the Tooth, the Goat of the Spirit, the Lord of Creation. I am the Eye in the Triangle, the Silver Star that ye adore.

18. I am Baphomet, that is the Eightfold Word that shall be equilibrated with the Three.

19. There is no act or passion that shall not be a hymn in mine honour.

20. All holy things and all symbolic things shall be my sacraments.

21. These animals are sacred unto me; the goat, and

the duck, and the ass, and the gazelle, the man, the woman and the child.

22. All corpses are sacred unto me; they shall not be touched save in mine eucharist. All lonely places are sacred unto me; where one man gathereth himself together in my name, there will I leap forth in the midst of him.

23. I am the hideous god; and who mastereth me is uglier than I.

24. Yet I give more than Bacchus and Apollo; my gifts exceed the olive and the horse.

25. Who worshippeth me must worship me with many rites.

26. I am concealed with all concealments; when the Most Holy Ancient One is stripped and driven through the marketplace I am still secret and apart.

27. Whom I love I chastise with many rods.

28. All things are sacred to me; no thing is sacred from me.

29. For there is no holiness where I am not.

30. Fear not when I fall in the fury of the storm; for mine acorns are blown afar by the wind; and verily I shall rise again, and my children about me, so that we shall uplift our forest in Eternity.

31. Eternity is the storm that covereth me.

32. I am Existence, the Existence that existeth not save through its own Existence, that is beyond the Existence of Existences, and rooted deeper than the No-Thing-Tree in the Land of No-Thing.

33. Now therefore thou knowest when I am within thee, when my hood is spread over thy skull, when my might is more than the penned Indus, and resistless as the Giant Glacier.

34. For as thou art before a lewd woman in Thy nakedness in the bazaar, sucked up by her slyness and smiles, so art thou wholly and no more in part before the symbol

of the beloved, though it be but a Pisacha or a Yantra
or a Deva.

35. And in all shalt thou create the Infinite Bliss, and
the next link of the Infinite Chain.

36. This chain reaches from Eternity to Eternity, ever
in triangles—is not my symbol a triangle?—ever in
circles—is not the symbol of the Beloved a circle? Therein
is all progress base illusion, for every circle is alike and
every triangle alike!

37. But the progress is progress, and progress is rapture,
constant, dazzling, showers of light, waves of dew, flames
of the hair of the Great Goddess, flowers of the roses
that are about her neck, Amen!

38. Therefore lift up thyself as I am lifted up. Hold
thyself in as I am master to accomplish. At the end, be
the end far distant as the stars that lie in the navel of
Nuit, do thou slay thyself as I at the end am slain, in the
death that is life, in the peace that is mother of war, in the
darkness that holds light in his hand, as a harlot that plucks
a jewel from her nostrils.

39. So therefore the beginning is delight and the end is
delight, and delight is in the midst, even as the Indus is
water in the cavern of the glacier, and water among the
greater hills and the lesser hills and through the ramparts
of the hills and through the plains, and water at the mouth
thereof when it leaps forth into the mighty sea, yea, into
the mighty sea.

(The Interpretation of this Book will be given to
members of the Grade of Dominus Liminis on application, each to his Adeptus.)

LIBER
CHETH

VEL
VALLVM
ABIEGNI

SVB FIGVRA
CLVI

A∴ A∴
Publication in Class A
Imprimatur:
N. Fra A∴ A∴

LIBER CHETH

1. This is the secret of the Holy Graal, that is the sacred vessel of our Lady the Scarlet Woman, Babalon the Mother of Abominations, the bride of Chaos, that rideth upon our Lord the Beast.

2. Thou shalt drain out thy blood that is thy life into the golden cup of her fornication.

3. Thou shalt mingle thy life with the universal life. Thou shalt keep not back one drop.

4. Then shall thy brain be dumb, and thy heart beat no more, and all thy life shall go from thee; and thou shalt be cast out upon the midden, and the birds of the air shall feast upon thy flesh, and thy bones shall whiten in the sun.

5. Then shall the winds gather themselves together, and bear thee up as it were a little heap of dust in a sheet that hath four corners, and they shall give it unto the guardians of the abyss.

6. And because there is no life therein, the guardians of the abyss shall bid the angels of the winds pass by. And the angels shall lay thy dust in the City of the Pyramids, and the name thereof shall be no more.

7. Now therefore that thou mayest achieve this ritual of the Holy Graal, do thou divest thyself of all thy goods.

8. Thou hast wealth; give it unto them that have need thereof, yet no desire toward it.

9. Thou hast health; slay thyself in the fervour of thine abandonment unto Our Lady. Let thy flesh hang loose upon thy bones, and thine eyes glare with thy quenchless lust unto the Infinite, with thy passion for the Unknown, for Her that is beyond Knowledge the accursed one.

10. Thou hast love; tear thy mother from thine heart, and spit in the face of thy father. Let thy foot trample the belly of thy wife, and let the babe at her breast be the prey of dogs and vultures.

11. For if thou dost not this with thy will, then shall We do this despite thy will. So that thou attain to the Sacrament of the Graal in the Chapel of Abominations.

12. And behold! if by stealth thou keep unto thyself one thought of thine, then shalt thou be cast out into the abyss for ever; and thou shalt be the lonely one, the eater of dung, the afflicted in the Day of Be-with-Us.

13. Yea! verily this is the Truth, this is the Truth, this is the Truth. Unto thee shall be granted joy and health and wealth and wisdom when thou art no longer thou.

14. Then shall every gain be a new sacrament, and it shall not defile thee; thou shalt revel with the wanton in the market-place, and the virgins shall fling roses upon thee, and the merchants bend their knees and bring thee gold and spices. Also young boys shall pour wonderful wines for thee, and the singers and the dancers shall sing and dance for thee.

15. Yet shalt thou not be therein, for thou shalt be forgotten, dust lost in dust.

16. Nor shall the aeon itself avail thee in this; for from the dust shall a white ash be prepared by Hermes the Invisible.

17. And this is the wrath of God, that these things should be thus.

18. And this is the grace of God, that these things should be thus.

19. Wherefore I charge you that'ye come unto me in the Beginning; for if ye take but one step in this Path, ye must arrive inevitably at the end thereof.

20. This Path is beyond Life and Death; it is also beyond Love; but that ye know not, for ye know not Love.

21. And the end thereof is known not even unto Our Lady or to the Beast whereon She rideth; nor unto the Virgin her daughter nor unto Chaos her lawful Lord; but unto the Crowned Child is it known? It is not known if it be known.

22. Therefore unto Hadit and unto Nuit be the glory in the End and the Beginning; yea, in the End and the Beginning.

LIBER
STELLAE
RUBEAE

A SECRET RITUAL
OF APEP
THE HEART OF
IAO-OAI
DELIVERED UNTO
V.V.V.V.V.
FOR HIS USE IN
A CERTAIN MATTER
OF
LIBER LEGIS
AND WRITTEN DOWN
UNDER THE FIGURE

LXVI

A ∴ A ∴
Publication Class A

Imprimatur:
N. Fra A ∴ A ∴

LIBER STELLAE RUBEAE

1. Apep deifieth Asar.

2. Let excellent virgins evoke rejoicing, son of Night!

3. This is the book of the most secret cult of the Ruby Star. It shall be given to none, save to the shameless in deed as in word.

4. No man shall understand this writing—it is too subtle for the sons of men.

5. If the Ruby Star have shed its blood upon thee; if in the season of the moon thou hast invoked by the Iod and the Pe, then mayst thou partake of this most secret sacrament.

6. One shall instruct another, with no care for the matters of men's thought.

7. There shall be a fair altar in the midst, extended upon a black stone.

8. At the head of the altar gold, and twin images in green of the Master.

9. In the midst a cup of green wine.

10. At the foot the Star of Ruby.

11. The altar shall be entirely bare.

12. First, the ritual of the Flaming Star.

13. Next, the ritual of the Seal.

14. Next, the infernal adorations of Oai.

Mu pa telai,
Tu wa melai
ā, ā, ā.
Tu fu tulu!
Tu fu tulu
Pa, Sa, Ga.

Qwi Mu telai
Ya Pu melai;
ū, ū, ū.
'Se gu malai;
Pe fu telai,
Fu tu lu.

O chi balae
Wa pa malae:—
Ūt! Ūt! Ūt!
Ge; fu latrai,
Le fu malai
Kūt! Hūt! Nūt!

Al Ōāī
Rel moai
Ti—Ti—Ti!
Wa la pelai
Tu fu latai
Wi, Ni, Bi.

15. Also thou shalt excite the wheels with the five wounds and the five wounds.

16. Then thou shalt excite the wheels with the two and the third in the midst; even ♄ and ♃, ☉ and ☽, ♂ and ♀, and ☿.

17. Then the five—and the sixth.

18. Also the altar shall fume before the master with incense that hath no smoke.

19. That which is to be denied shall be denied; that

which is to be trampled shall be trampled; that which is to be spat upon shall be spat upon.

20. These things shall be burnt in the outer fire.

21. Then again the master shall speak as he will soft words, and with music and what else he will bring forward the Victim.

22. Also he shall slay a young child upon the altar, and the blood shall cover the altar with perfume as of roses.

23. Then shall the master appear as He should appear—in His glory.

24. He shall stretch himself upon the altar, and awake it into life, and into death.

25 (For so we conceal that life which is beyond.)

26. The temple shall be darkened, save for the fire and the lamp of the altar.

27. There shall he kindle a great fire and a devouring.

28. Also he shall smite the altar with his scourge, and blood shall flow therefrom.

29. Also he shall have made roses bloom thereon.

30. In the end he shall offer up the Vast Sacrifice, at the moment when the God licks up the flame upon the altar.

31. All these things shalt thou perform strictly, observing the time.

32. And the Beloved shall abide with Thee.

33. Thou shalt not disclose the interior world of this rite unto any one: therefore have I written it in symbols that cannot be understood.

34. I who reveal the ritual am Iao and Oai; the Right and the Averse.

35. These are alike unto me.

36. Now the Veil of this operation is called Shame, and the Glory abideth within.

37. Thou shalt comfort the heart of the secret stone

with the warm blood. Thou shalt make a subtle decoction of delight, and the Watchers shall drink thereof.

38. I, Apep the Serpent, am the heart of Iao. Isis shall await Asar, and I in the midst.

39. Also the Priestess shall seek another altar, and perform my ceremonies thereon.

40. There shall be no hymn nor dithyramb in my praise and the praise of the rite, seeing that it is utterly beyond.

41. Thou shalt assure thyself of the stability of the altar.

42. In this rite thou shalt be alone.

43. I will give thee another ceremony whereby many shall rejoice.

44. Before all let the Oath be taken firmly as thou raisest up the altar from the black earth.

45. In the words that Thou knowest.

46. For I also swear unto thee by my body and soul that shall never be parted in sunder that I dwell within thee coiled and ready to spring.

47. I will give thee the kingdoms of the earth, O thou Who hast mastered the kingdoms of the East and of the West.

48. I am Apep, O thou slain One. Thou shalt slay thyself upon mine altar: I will have thy blood to drink.

49. For I am a mighty vampire, and my children shall suck up the wine of the earth which is blood.

50. Thou shalt replenish thy veins from the chalice of heaven.

51. Thou shalt be secret, a fear to the world.

52. Thou shalt be exalted, and none shall see thee; exalted, and none shall suspect thee.

53. For there are two glories diverse, and thou who hast won the first shalt enjoy the second.

54. I leap with joy within thee; my head is arisen to strike.

55. O the lust, the sheer rapture, of the life of the snake in the spine!

56. Mightier than God or man, I am in them, and pervade them.

57. Follow out these my words.

58. Fear nothing.
Fear nothing.
Fear nothing.

59. For I am nothing, and me thou shalt fear, O my virgin, my prophet within whose bowels I rejoice.

60. Thou shalt fear with the fear of love: I will overcome thee.

61. Thou shalt be very nigh to death.

62. But I will overcome thee; the New Life shall illumine thee with the Light that is beyond the Stars.

63 Thinkest thou? I, the force that have created all, am not to be despised.

64. And I will slay thee in my lust.

65. Thou shalt scream with the joy and the pain and the fear and the love—so that the ΛΟΓΟΣ of a new God leaps out among the Stars.

66. There shall be no sound heard but this thy lion-roar of rapture; yea, this thy lion-roar of rapture.

Translation of Invocation in Moon Language

Silence! the moon ceaseth (her motion),
That also was sweet
In the air, in the air, in the air!
Who Will shall attain!
Who Will shall attain
By the Moon, and by Myself, and by the Angel of the Lord!

Now Silence ceaseth
And the moon waxeth sweet;
(It is the hour of) Initiation, Initation, Initiation.
The kiss of Isis is honeyed;

My own Will is ended,
For Will hath attained.

Behold the lion-child swimmeth (in the heaven)
And the moon reeleth:—
(It is) Thou! (It is) Thou! (It is) Thou!
Triumph; the Will stealeth away (like a thief),
The Strong Will that staggered
Before Ra Hoor Khuit!—Hadit!—Nuit!

To the God OAI
Be praise
In the end and the beginning!
And may none fall
Who Will attain
The Sword, the Balances, the Crown!

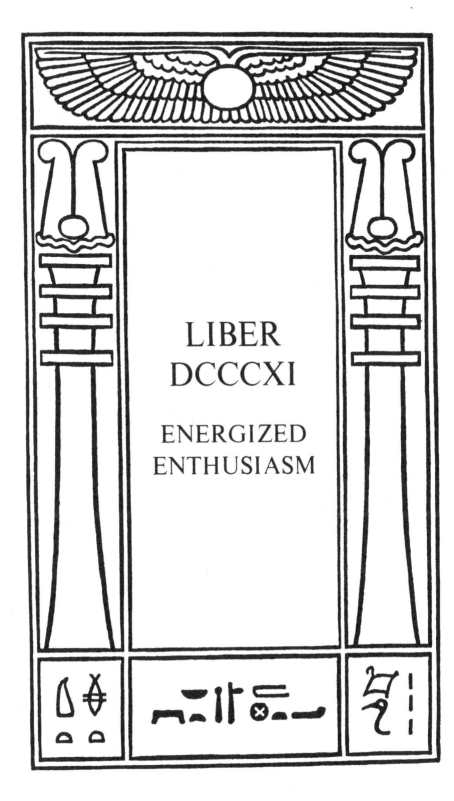

LIBER
DCCCXI

ENERGIZED
ENTHUSIASM

ENERGIZED ENTHUSIASM

A NOTE ON THEURGY

I

I A O the supreme One of the Gnostics, the true God, is
the Lord of this work. Let us therefore invoke Him by
that name which the Companions of the Royal Arch
blaspheme to aid us in the essay to declare the means
which He has bestowed upon us!

II

The divine consciousness which is reflected and re-
fracted in the works of Genius feeds upon a certain
secretion, as I believe. This secretion is analogous to
semen, but not identical with it. There are but few men
and fewer women, those women being invariably an-
drogyne, who possess it at any time in any quantity.

So closely is this secretion connected with the sexual
economy that it appears to me at times as if it might be a
by-product of that process which generates semen. That
some form of this doctrine has been generally accepted is
shown in the prohibitions of all religions. Sanctity has
been assumed to depend on chastity, and chastity has
nearly always been interpreted as abstinence. But I doubt
whether the relation is so simple as this would imply;

for example, I find in myself that manifestations of mental creative force always concur with some abnormal condition of the physical powers of generation. But it is not the case that long periods of chastity, on the one hand, or excess of orgies, on the other, are favourable to its manifestation or even to its formation.

I know myself, and in me it is extremely strong; its results are astounding.

For example, I wrote *Tannhäuser*, complete from conception to execution, in sixty-seven consecutive hours. I was unconscious of the fall of nights and days, even after stopping; nor was there any reaction of fatigue. This work was written when I was twenty-four years old, immediately on the completion of an orgie which would normally have tired me out.

Often and often have I noticed that sexual satisfaction so-called has left me dissatisfied and unfatigued, and let loose the floods of verse which have disgraced my career.

Yet, on the contrary, a period of chastity has sometimes fortified me for a great outburst. This is far from being invariably the case. At the conclusion of the K 2 expedition, after five months of chastity, I did no work whatever, barring very few odd lyrics, for months afterwards.

I may mention the year 1911. At this time I was living, in excellent good health, with the woman whom I loved. Her health was, however, variable, and we were both constantly worried.

The weather was continuously fine and hot. For a period of about three months I hardly missed a morning; always on waking I burst out with a new idea which had to be written down.

The total energy of my being was very high. My weight was 10 stone 8 lb., which had been my fighting weight when I was ten years younger. We walked some twenty miles daily through hilly forest.

The actual amount of MSS. written at this time is astounding; their variety is even more so; of their excellence I will not speak.

Here is a rough list from memory; it is far from exhaustive:

(1) Some dozen books of A ∴. A ∴. instruction, including *Liber Astarte,* and *The Temple of Solomon the King* for *The Equinox,* VII.

(2) Short Stories: "The Woodcutter"
"His Secret Sin"

(3) Plays: *His Majesty's Fiddler*
Elder Eel
Adonis ⎞ written straight off, one after
The Ghouls ⎠ the other
Mortadello

(4) Poems: "The Sevenfold Sacrament"
"A Birthday"

(5) Fundamentals of the Greek Qabalah (involving the collection and analysis of several thousand words).

I think this phenomenon is unique in the history of literature.

I may further refer to my second journey to Algeria, where my sexual life, though fairly full, had been unsatisfactory.

On quitting Biskra, I was so full of ideas that I had to get off the train at El-Kantara, where I wrote "The Scorpion." Five or six poems were written on the way to Paris; "The Ordeal of Ida Pendragon" during my twenty-four hours' stay in Paris, and "Snowstorm" and "The Electric Silence" immediately on my return to England.

To sum up, I can always trace a connection between my sexual condition and the condition of artistic creation, which is so close as to approach identity, and yet so loose that I cannot predicate a single important proposition.

It is these considerations which give me pain when I

am reproached by the ignorant with wishing to produce genius mechanically. I may fail, but my failure is a thousand times greater than their utmost success.

I shall therefore base my remarks not so much on the observations which I have myself made, and the experiments which I have tried, as on the accepted classical methods of producing that energized enthusiasm which is the lever that moves God.

III

The Greeks say that there are three methods of discharging the genial secretion of which I have spoken. They thought perhaps that their methods tended to secrete it, but this I do not believe altogether, or without a qualm. For the manifestation of force implies force, and this force must have come from somewhere. Easier I find it to say "subconsciousness" and "secretion" than to postulate an external reservoir, to extend my connotation of "man" than to invent "God."

However, parsimony apart, I find it in my experience that it is useless to flog a tired horse. There are times when I am absolutely bereft of even one drop of this elixir. Nothing will restore it, neither rest in bed, nor drugs, nor exercise. On the other hand, sometimes when after a severe spell of work I have been dropping with physical fatigue, perhaps sprawling on the floor, too tired to move hand or foot, the occurrence of an idea has restored me to perfect intensity of energy, and the working out of the idea has actually got rid of the aforesaid physical fatigue, although it involved a great additional labour.

Exactly parallel (nowhere meeting) is the case of mania. A madman may struggle against six trained athletes for hours, and show no sign of fatigue. Then he will suddenly collapse, but at a second's notice from the irritable idea will resume the struggle as fresh as ever. Until we discovered "unconscious muscular action" and its effects, it was rational to suppose such a man "possessed of a devil"; and the difference between the madman and the genius is not in the quantity but in the quality of their work. Genius is organized, madness chaotic. Often the organization of genius is on original lines, and ill-balanced and ignorant medicine-men mistake it for disorder. Time has shown that Whistler and Gauguin "kept rules" as well as the masters whom they were supposed to be upsetting.

IV

The Greeks say that there are three methods of discharging the Leyden Jar of Genius. These three methods they assign to three Gods.

These three Gods are Dionysus, Apollo, Aphrodite. In English: wine, woman and song.

Now it would be a great mistake to imagine that the Greeks were recommending a visit to a brothel. As well condemn the High Mass at St Peter's on the strength of having witnessed a Protestant revival meeting. Disorder is always a parody of order, because there is no archetypal disorder that it might resemble. Owen Seaman can parody a poet; nobody can parody Owen Seaman. A critic is a bundle of impressions; there is no ego behind it. All photographs are essentially alike; the works of all good painters essentially differ.

Some writers suppose that in the ancient rites of Eleusis the High Priest publicly copulated with the High Priestess. Were this so, it would be no more "indecent" than it is "blasphemous" for the priest to make bread and wine into the body and blood of God.

True, the Protestants say that it is blasphemous; but a Protestant is one to whom all things sacred are profane, whose mind being all filth can see nothing in the sexual act but a crime or a jest, whose only facial gestures are the sneer and the leer.

Protestantism is the excrement of human thought, and accordingly in Protestant countries art, if it exist at all, only exists to revolt. Let us return from this unsavoury allusion to our consideration of the methods of the Greeks.

V

Agree then that it does not follow from the fact that wine, woman and song make the sailor's tavern that these ingredients must necessarily concoct a hell-broth.

There are some people so simple as to think that, when they have proved the religious instinct to be a mere efflorescence of the sex-instinct, they have destroyed religion.

We should rather consider that the sailor's tavern gives him his only glimpse of heaven, just as the destructive criticism of the phallicists has only proved sex to be a sacrament. Consciousness, says the materialist, axe in hand, is a function of the brain. He has only re-formulated the old saying, "Your bodies are the temples of the Holy Ghost."!

Now sex is justly hallowed in this sense, that it is the eternal fire of the race. Huxley admitted that "some of the lower animalculae are in a sense immortal," because they go on reproducing eternally by fission, and however often you divide x by 2 there is always something left. But he never seems to have seen that mankind is immortal in exactly the same sense, and goes on reproducing itself with similar characteristics through the ages, changed by circumstance indeed, but always identical in itself. But the spiritual flower of this process is that at the moment of discharge a physical ecstasy occurs, a spasm analogous to the mental spasm which meditation gives. And further, in the sacramental and ceremonial use of the sexual act, the divine consciousness may be attained.

VI

The sexual act being then a sacrament, it remains to consider in what respect this limits the employment of the organs.

First, it is obviously legitimate to employ them for their natural physical purpose. But if it be allowable to use them ceremonially for a religious purpose, we shall find the act hedged about with many restrictions.

For in this case the organs become holy. It matters little to mere propagation that men should be vicious; the most debauched roué might and almost certainly would beget more healthy children than a semi-sexed prude. So the so-called "moral" restraints are not based on reason; thus they are neglected.

But admit its religious function, and one may at once lay down that the act must not be profaned. It must not be undertaken lightly and foolishly without excuse.

It may be undertaken for the direct object of continuing the race.

It may be undertaken in obedience to real passion; for passion, as its name implies, is rather inspired by a force of divine strength and beauty without the will of the individual, often even against it.

It is the casual or habitual—what Christ called "idle"— use or rather abuse of these forces which constitutes their profanation. It will further be obvious that, if the act in itself is to be the sacrament in a religious ceremony, this act must be accomplished solely for the love of God. All personal considerations must be banished utterly. Just as any priest can perform the miracle of transubstantiation, so can any man, possessing the necessary qualifications, perform this other miracle, whose nature must form the subject of a subsequent discussion.

Personal aims being destroyed, it is *à fortiori* necessary to neglect social and other similar considerations.

Physical strength and beauty are necessary and desirable for aesthetic reasons, the attention of the worshippers being liable to distraction if the celebrants are ugly, deformed, or incompetent. I need hardly emphasize the necessity for the strictest self-control and concentration on their part. As it would be blasphemy to enjoy the gross taste of the wine of the sacrament, so must the celebrant suppress even the minutest manifestion of animal pleasure.

Of the qualifying tests there is no necessity to speak; it is sufficient to say that the adepts have always known how to secure efficiency.

Needless also to insist on a similar quality in the assistants; the sexual excitement must be suppressed and transformed into its religious equivalent.

VII

With these preliminaries settled in order to guard against foreseen criticisms of those Protestants who, God having made them a little lower than the Angels, have made themselves a great deal lower than the beasts by their consistently bestial interpretation of all things human and divine, we may consider first the triune nature of these ancient methods of energizing enthusiasm.

Music has two parts; tone or pitch, and rhythm. The latter quality associates it with the dance, and that part of dancing which is not rhythm is sex. Now that part of sex which is not a form of the dance, animal movement, is intoxication of the soul, which connects it with wine. Further identities will suggest themselves to the student.

By the use of the three methods in one the whole being of man may thus be stimulated.

The music will create a general harmony of the brain, leading it in its own paths; the wine affords a general stimulus of the animal nature; and the sex-excitement elevates the moral nature of the man by its close analogy with the highest ecstasy. It remains, however, always for him to make the final transmutation. Unless he have the special secretion which I have postulated, the result will be commonplace.

So consonant is this system with the nature of man that it is exactly parodied and profaned not only in the sailor's tavern, but in the Society ball. Here, for the lowest natures the result is drunkenness, disease and death; for the middle natures a gradual blunting of the finer feelings; for the higher, an exhilaration amounting at the best to the foundation of a life-long love.

If these Society "rites" are properly performed, there should be no exhaustion. After a ball, one should feel the need of a long walk in the young morning air. The weariness or boredom, the headache or somnolence, are Nature's warnings.

VIII

Now the purpose of such a ball, the moral attitude on entering, seems to me to be of supreme importance. If you go with the idea of killing time, you are rather killing yourself. Baudelaire speaks of the first period of love when the boy kisses the trees of the wood, rather than kiss nothing. At the age of thirty-six I found myself at Pompeii, passionately kissing that great grave statue of a woman that stands in the avenue of the tombs. Even now, as I wake in the morning, I sometimes fall to kissing my own arms.

It is with such a feeling that one should go to a ball, and

with such a feeling intensified, purified and exalted, that one should leave it.

If this be so, how much more if one go with the direct religious purpose burning in one's whole being! Beethoven roaring at the sunrise is no strange spectacle to me, who shout with joy and wonder, when I understand (without which one cannot really be said ever to see) a blade of grass. I fall upon my knees in speechless adoration at the moon; I hide my eyes in holy awe from a good Van Gogh.

Imagine then a ball in which the music is the choir celestial, the wine the wine of the Graal, or that of the Sabbath of the Adepts, and one's partner the Infinite and Eternal One, the True and Living God Most High!

Go even to a common ball—the Moulin de la Galette will serve even the least of my magicians—with your whole soul aflame within you, and your whole will concentrated on these transubstantiations, and tell me what miracle takes place!

It is the hate of, the distaste for, life that sends one to the ball when one is old; when one is young one is on springs until the hour falls; but the love of God, which is the only true love, diminishes not with age; it grows deeper and intenser with every satisfaction. It seems as if in the noblest men this secretion constantly increases—which certainly suggests an external reservoir—so that age loses all its bitterness. We find "Brother Lawrence," Nicholas Herman of Lorraine, at the age of eighty in continuous enjoyment of union with God. Buddha at an equal age would run up and down the Eight High Trances like an acrobat on a ladder; stories not too dissimilar are told of Bishop Berkeley. Many persons have not attained union at all until middle age, and then have rarely lost it.

It is true that genius in the ordinary sense of the word has nearly always showed itself in the young. Perhaps we should regard such cases as Nicholas Herman as cases of acquired genius.

Now I am certainly of opinion that genius can be acquired, or, in the alternative, that it is an almost universal possession. Its rarity may be attributed to the crushing influence of a corrupted society. It is rare to meet a youth without high ideals, generous thoughts, a sense of holiness, of his own importance, which, being interpreted, is, of his own identity with God. Three years in the world, and he is a bank clerk or even a government official. Only those who intuitively understand from early boyhood that they must stand out, and who have the incredible courage and endurance to do so in face of all that tyranny, callousness, and the scorn of inferiors can do; only these arrive at manhood uncontaminated.

Every serious or spiritual thought is made a jest; poets are thought "soft" and "cowardly," apparently because they are the only boys with a will of their own and courage to hold out against the whole school, boys and masters in league as once were Pilate and Herod; honour is replaced by expediency, holiness by hypocrisy.

Even where we find thoroughly good seed sprouting in favourable ground, too often is there a frittering away of the forces. Facile encouragement of a poet or painter is far worse for him than any amount of opposition. Here again the sex question (S.Q. so-called by Tolstoyans, chastity-mongers, nut-fooders, and such who talk and think of nothing else) intrudes its horrid head. I believe that every boy is originally conscious of sex as sacred. But he does not know what it is. With infinite diffidence he asks. The master replies with holy horror; the boy with a low leer, a furtive laugh, perhaps worse.

I am inclined to agree with the Head Master of Eton that paederastic passions among schoolboys "do no

harm"; further, I think them the only redeeming feature
of sexual life at public schools.

The Hindoos are wiser. At the well-watched hour of
puberty the boy is prepared as for a sacrament; he is led to
a duly consecrated temple, and there by a wise and holy
woman, skilled in the art, and devoted to this end, he is
initiated with all solemnity into the mystery of life.

The act is thus declared religious, sacred, impersonal,
utterly apart from amorism and eroticism and animalism
and sentimentalism and all the other vilenesses that
Protestantism has made of it.

The Catholic Church did, I believe, to some extent
preserve the Pagan tradition. Marriage is a sacrament.[1]
But in the attempt to deprive the act of all accretions which
would profane it, the Fathers of the Church added in
spite of themselves other accretions which profaned it
more. They tied it to property and inheritance. They
wished it to serve both God and Mammon.

Rightly restraining the priest, who should employ his
whole energy in the miracle of the Mass, they found their
counsel a counsel of perfection. The magical tradition was
in part lost; the priest could not do what was expected of
him, and the unexpended portion of his energy turned
sour.

Hence the thoughts of priests, like the thoughts of
modern faddists, revolved eternally around the S.Q.

A special and Secret Mass, a Mass of the Holy Ghost, a
Mass of the Mystery of the Incarnation, to be performed
at stated intervals, might have saved both monks and
nuns, and given the Church eternal dominion of the
world.

1. Of course there has been a school of devilish ananders that has held the
act in itself to be "wicked." Of such blasphemers of Nature let no further word
be said.

IX

To return. The rarity of genius is in great part due to the destruction of its young. Even as in physical life that is a favoured plant one of whose thousand seeds ever shoots forth a blade, so do conditions kill all but the strongest sons of genius.

But just as rabbits increased apace in Australia, where even a missionary has been known to beget ninety children in two years, so shall we be able to breed genius if we can find the conditions which hamper it, and remove them.

The obvious practical step to take is to restore the rites of Bacchus, Aphrodite and Apollo to their proper place. They should not be open to every one, and manhood should be the reward of ordeal and initiation.

The physical tests should be severe, and weaklings should be killed out rather than artificially preserved. The same remark applies to intellectual tests. But such tests should be as wide as possible. I was an absolute duffer at school in all forms of athletics and games, because I despised them. I held, and still hold, numerous mountaineering world's records. Similarly, examinations fail to test intelligence. Cecil Rhodes refused to employ any man with a University degree. That such degrees lead to honour in England is a sign of England's decay, though even in England they are usually the stepping stones to clerical idleness or pedagogic slavery.

Such is a dotted outline of the picture that I wish to draw. If the power to possess property depended on a man's competence, and his perception of real values, a new aristocracy would at once be created, and the deadly fact that social consideration varies with the power of purchasing champagne would cease to be a fact. Our pluto-hetairo-politicocracy would fall in a day.

But I am only too well aware that such a picture is not likely to be painted. We can then only work patiently and in secret. We must select suitable material and train it in utmost reverence to these three master-methods, or aiding the soul in its genial orgasm.

X

This reverent attitude is of an importance which I cannot over-rate. Normal people find normal relief from any general or special excitement in the sexual act.

Commander Marston, R.N., whose experiments in the effect of the tom-tom on the married Englishwoman are classical and conclusive, has admirably described how the vague unrest which she at first shows gradually assumes the sexual form, and culminates, if allowed to do so, in shameless masturbation or indecent advances. But this is a natural corollary of the proposition that married Englishwomen are usually unacquainted with sexual satisfaction. Their desires are constantly stimulated by brutal and ignorant husbands, and never gratified. This fact again accounts for the amazing prevalence of Sapphism in London Society.

The Hindus warn their pupils against the dangers of breathing exercises. Indeed the slightest laxness in moral or physical tissues may cause the energy accumulated by the practice to discharge itself by involuntary emission. I have known this happen in my own experience.

It is then of the utmost importance to realize that the relief of the tension is to be found in what the Hebrews and the Greeks called prophesying, and which is better when organized into art. The disorderly discharge is mere waste, a wilderness of howlings; the orderly discharge is a "Prometheus unbound," or a "L'age d'airain," according to the special aptitudes of the enthused person. But it must be remembered that special aptitudes are very easy to acquire if the driving force of enthusiasm be great. If you cannot keep the rules of others, you make rules of your own. One set turns out in the long run to be just as good as another.

Henri Rousseau, the douanier, was laughed at all his life. I laughed as heartily as the rest; though, almost despite myself, I kept on saying (as the phrase goes) "that I felt something; couldn't say what."

The moment it occurred to somebody to put up all his paintings in one room by themselves, it was instantly apparent that his *naiveté* was the simplicity of a Master.

Let no one then imagine that I fail to perceive or underestimate the dangers of employing these methods. The occurrence even of so simple a matter as fatigue might change a Las Meninas into a stupid sexual crisis.

It will be necessary for most Englishmen to emulate the self-control of the Arabs and Hindus, whose ideal is to deflower the greatest possible number of virgins—eighty is considered a fairly good performance—without completing the act.

It is, indeed, of the first importance for the celebrant in any phallic rite to be able to complete the act without even once allowing a sexual or sensual thought to invade his mind. The mind must be as absolutely detached from one's own body as it is from another person's.

XI

Of musical instruments few are suitable. The human voice is the best, and the only one which can be usefully employed in chorus. Anything like an orchestra implies infinite rehearsal, and introduces an atmosphere of artificiality. The organ is a worthy solo instrument, and is an orchestra in itself, while its tone and associations favour the religious idea.

The violin is the most useful of all, for its every mood

expresses the hunger for the infinite, and yet it is so mobile that it has a greater emotional range than any of its competitors. Accompaniment must be dispensed with, unless a harpist be available.

The harmonium is a horrible instrument, if only because of its associations; and the piano is like unto it, although, if unseen and played by a Paderewski, it would serve.

The trumpet and the bell are excellent, to startle, at the crises of a ceremony.

Hot, drubbing, passionate, in a different class of ceremony, a class more intense and direct, but on the whole less exalted, the tom-tom stands alone. It combines well with the practice of mantra, and is the best accompaniment for any sacred dance.

XII

Of sacred dances the most practical for a gathering is the seated dance. One sits cross-legged on the floor, and sways to and fro from the hips in time with the mantra. A solo or duet of dancers as a spectacle rather distracts from this exercise. I would suggest a very small and very brilliant light on the floor in the middle of the room. Such a room is best floored with mosaic marble; an ordinary Freemason's Lodge carpet is not a bad thing.

The eyes, if they see anything at all, see then only the rhythmical or mechanical squares leading in perspective to the simple unwinking light.

The swinging of the body with the mantra (which has a habit of rising and falling as if of its own accord in a very weird way) becomes more accentuated; ultimately a curiously spasmodic stage occurs, and then the consciousness flickers and goes out; perhaps breaks through into the divine consciousness, perhaps is merely recalled to itself by some variable in external impression.

The above is a very simple description of a very simple and earnest form of ceremony, based entirely upon rhythm. It is very easy to prepare, and its results are usually very encouraging for the beginner.

XIII

Wine being a mocker and strong drink raging, its use is more likely to lead to trouble than mere music.

One essential difficulty is dosage. One needs exactly enough; and, as Blake points out, one can only tell what is enough by taking too much. For each man the dose varies enormously; so does it for the same man at different times.

The ceremonial escape from this is to have a noiseless attendant to bear the bowl of libation, and present it to each in turn, at frequent intervals. Small doses should be drunk, and the bowl passed on, taken as the worshipper deems advisable. Yet the cup-bearer should be an initiate, and use his own discretion before presenting the bowl. The slightest sign that intoxication is mastering the man should be a sign to him to pass that man. This practice can be easily fitted to the ceremony previously described.

If desired, instead of wine, the elixir introduced by me to Europe may be employed. But its results, if used in this way, have not as yet been thoroughly studied. It is my immediate purpose to repair this neglect.

XIV

The sexual excitement, which must complete the harmony of method, offers a more difficult problem.

It is exceptionally desirable that the actual bodily movements involved should be decorous in the highest sense, and many people are so ill-trained that they will be unable to regard such a ceremony with any but critical or lascivious eyes; either would be fatal to all the good already done. It is presumably better to wait until all present are greatly exalted before risking a profanation.

It is not desirable, in my opinion, that the ordinary worshippers should celebrate in public.

The sacrifice should be single.

Whether or no . . .

XV

Thus far had I written when the distinguished poet, whose conversation with me upon the Mysteries had incited me to jot down these few rough notes, knocked at my door. I told him that I was at work on the ideas suggested by him, and that—well, I was rather stuck. He asked permission to glance at the MS. (for he reads English fluently, though speaking but a few words), and having done so, kindled and said: "If you come with me now, we will finish your essay." Glad enough of any excuse to stop working, the more plausible the better, I hastened to take down my coat and hat.

"By the way," he remarked in the automobile, "I take it that you do not mind giving me the Word of Rose Croix." Surprised, I exchanged the secrets of I.N.R.I. with him. "And now, very excellent and perfect Prince," he said, "what follows is under this seal." And he gave me the most solemn of all Masonic tokens. "You are about," said he, "to compare your ideal with our real."

He touched a bell. The automobile stopped, and we got out. He dismissed the chauffeur. "Come," he said, "we have a brisk half-mile." We walked through thick woods to an old house, where we were greeted in silence by a gentleman who, though in court dress, wore a very "practicable" sword. On satisfying him, we were passed through a corridor to an anteroom, where another armed guardian awaited us. He, after a further examination, proceeded to offer me a court dress, the insignia of a Sovereign Prince of Rose Croix, and a garter and mantle, the former of green silk, the latter of green velvet, and lined with cerise silk. "It is a low mass," whispered the guardian. In this anteroom were three or four others, both ladies and gentlemen, busily robing.

In a third room we found a procession formed, and joined it. There were twenty-six of us in all. Passing a final guardian we reached the chapel itself, at whose entrance stood a young man and a young woman, both dressed in simple robes of white silk embroidered with gold, red and blue. The former bore a torch of resinous wood, the latter sprayed us as we passed with attar of roses from a cup.

The room in which we now were had at one time been a chapel; so much its shape declared. But the high altar was covered with a cloth that displayed the Rose and Cross, while above it were ranged seven candelabra, each of seven branches.

The stalls had been retained; and at each knight's hand burned a taper of rose-coloured wax, and a bouquet of roses was before him.

In the centre of the nave was a great cross—a "calvary cross of ten squares," measuring, say, six feet by five—painted in red upon a white board, at whose edge were rings through which passed gilt staves. At each corner was a banner, bearing lion, bull, eagle and man, and from the top of their staves sprang a canopy of blue, wherein were figured in gold the twelve emblems of the Zodiac.

Knights and Dames being installed, suddenly a bell tinkled in the architrave. Instantly all rose. The doors opened at a trumpet peal from without, and a herald advanced, followed by the High Priest and Priestess.

The High Priest was a man of nearly sixty years, if I

may judge by the white beard; but he walked with the springy yet assured step of the thirties. The High Priestess, a proud, tall sombre woman of perhaps thirty summers, walked by his side, their hands raised and touching as in the minuet. Their trains were borne by the two youths who had admitted us.

All this while an unseen organ played an Introit.

This ceased as they took their places at the altar. They faced West, waiting.

On the closing of the doors the armed guard, who was clothed in a scarlet robe instead of green, drew his sword, and went up and down the aisle, chanting exorcisms and swinging the great sword. All present drew their swords and faced outward, holding the points in front of them. This part of the ceremony appeared interminable. When it was over the girl and boy reappeared; bearing, the one a bowl, the other a censer. Singing some litany or other, apparently in Greek, though I could not catch the words, they purified and consecrated the chapel.

Now the High Priest and High Priestess began a litany in rhythmic lines of equal length. At each third response they touched hands in a peculiar manner; at each seventh they kissed. The twenty-first was a complete embrace. The bell tinkled in the architrave; and they parted. The High Priest then took from the altar a flask curiously shaped to imitate a phallus. The High Priestess knelt and presented a boat-shaped cup of gold. He knelt opposite her, and did not pour from the flask.

Now the Knights and Dames began a long litany; first a Dame in treble, then a Knight in bass, then a response in chorus of all present with the organ. This Chorus was:

EVOE HO, IACCHE! EPELTHON,
EPELTHON, EVOE, IAO!

Again and again it rose and fell. Towards its close, whether by "stage effect" or no I could not swear, the light over the altar grew rosy, then purple. The High Priest sharply and suddenly threw up his hand; instant silence.

He now poured out the wine from the flask. The High Priestess gave it to the girl attendant, who bore it to all present.

This was no ordinary wine. It has been said of vodka that it looks like water and tastes like fire. With this wine the reverse is the case. It was of a rich fiery gold in which flames of light danced and shook, but its taste was limpid and pure like fresh spring water. No sooner had I drunk of it, however, than I began to tremble. It was a most astonishing sensation; I can imagine a man feel thus as he awaits his executioner, when he has passed through fear, and is all excitement.

I looked down my stall, and saw that each was similarly affected. During the libation the High Priestess sang a hymn, again in Greek. This time I recognized the words; they were those of an ancient Ode to Aphrodite.

The boy attendant now descended to the red cross, stooped and kissed it; then he danced upon it in such a way that he seemed to be tracing the patterns of a marvellous rose of gold, for the percussion caused a shower of bright dust to fall from the canopy. Meanwhile the litany (different words, but the same chorus) began again. This time it was a duet between the High Priest and Priestess. At each chorus Knights and Dames bowed low. The girl moved round continuously, and the bowl passed.

This ended in the exhaustion of the boy, who fell fainting on the cross. The girl immediately took the bowl and put it to his lips. Then she raised him, and, with the assistance of the Guardian of the Sanctuary, led him out of the chapel.

The bell again tinkled in the architrave.

The herald blew a fanfare.

The High Priest and High Priestess moved stately to

each other and embraced, in the act unloosing the heavy golden robes which they wore. These fell, twin lakes of gold. I now saw her dressed in a garment of white watered silk, lined throughout (as it appeared later) with ermine.

The High Priest's vestment was an elaborate embroidery of every colour, harmonized by exquisite yet robust art. He wore also a breastplate corresponding to the canopy; a sculptured "beast" at each corner in gold, while the twelve signs of the Zodiac were symbolized by the stones of the breastplate.

The bell tinkled yet again, and the herald again sounded his trumpet. The celebrants moved hand in hand down the nave while the organ thundered forth its solemn harmonies.

All the Knights and Dames rose and gave the secret sign of the Rose Croix.

It was at this part of the ceremony that things began to happen to me. I became suddenly aware that my body had lost both weight and tactile sensibility. My consciousness seemed to be situated no longer in my body. I "mistook myself," if I may use the phrase, for one of the stars in the canopy.

In this way I missed seeing the celebrants actually approach the cross. The bell tinkled again; I came back to myself, and then I saw that the High Priestess, standing at the foot of the cross, had thrown her robe over it, so that the cross was no longer visible. There was only a board covered with ermine. She was now naked but for her coloured and jewelled head-dress and the heavy torque of gold about her neck, and the armlets and anklets that matched it. She began to sing in a soft strange tongue, so low and smoothly that in my partial bewilderment I could not hear all; but I caught a few words, Io Pan! Io Pan! and a phrase in which the words Iao Sabao ended emphatically a sentence in which I caught the words Eros, Thelema and Sebazo.

While she did this she unloosed the breastplate and gave it to the girl attendant. The robe followed; I saw that they were naked and unashamed. For the first time there was absolute silence.

Now, from an hundred jets surrounding the board poured forth a perfumed purple smoke. The world was wrapt in a fond gauze of mist, sacred as the clouds upon the mountains.

Then at a signal given by the High Priest, the bell tinkled once more. The celebrants stretched out their arms in the form of a cross, interlacing their fingers. Slowly they revolved through three circles and a half. She then laid him down upon the cross, and took her own appointed place.

The organ now again rolled forth its solemn music.

I was lost to everything. Only this I saw, that the celebrants made no expected motion. The movements were extremely small and yet extremely strong.

This must have continued for a great length of time. To me it seemed as if eternity itself could not contain the variety and depth of my experiences. Tongue nor pen could record them; and yet I am fain to attempt the impossible.

1. I was, certainly and undoubtedly, the star in the canopy. This star was an incomprehensibly enormous world of pure flame.

2. I suddenly realized that the star was of no size whatever. It was not that the star shrank, but that it ($=$ I) became suddenly conscious of infinite space.

3. An explosion took place. I was in consequence a point of light, infinitely small, yet infinitely bright, and this point was *without position*.

4. Consequently this point was ubiquitous, and there was a feeling of infinite bewilderment, blinded after a very long time by a gush of infinite rapture. (I use the word "blinded" as if under constraint; I should have preferred to use the words "blotted out" or "overwhelmed" or "illuminated.")

5. This infinite fullness—I have not described it as such, but it was that—was suddenly changed into a feeling of infinite emptiness, which became conscious as a yearning.

6. These two feelings began to alternate, always with suddenness, and without in any way overlapping, with great rapidity.

7. This alternation must have occurred fifty times—I had rather have said an hundred.

8. The two feelings suddenly became one. Again the word explosion is the only one that gives any idea of it.

9. I now seemed to be conscious of everything at once, that it was at the same time *one* and *many*. I say "at once," that is, I was not successively all things, but instantaneously.

10. This being, if I may call it being, seemed to drop into an infinite abyss of Nothing.

11. While this "falling" lasted, the bell suddenly tinkled three times. I instantly became my normal self, yet with a constant awareness, which has never left me to this hour, that the truth of the matter is not this normal "I" but "That" which is still dropping into Nothing. I am assured by those who know that I may be able to take up the thread if I attend another ceremony.

The tinkle died away. The girl attendant ran quickly forward and folded the ermine over the celebrants. The herald blew a fanfare, and the Knights and Dames left their stalls. Advancing to the board, we took hold of the gilded carrying poles, and followed the herald in procession out of the chapel, bearing the litter to a small side-chapel leading out of the middle anteroom, where we left it, the guard closing the doors.

In silence we disrobed, and left the house. About a mile through the woods we found my friend's automobile waiting.

I asked him, if that was a low mass, might I not be permitted to witness a High Mass?

"Perhaps," he answered with a curious smile, "if all they tell of you is true."

In the meanwhile he permitted me to describe the ceremony and its results as faithfully as I was able, charging me only to give no indication of the city near which it took place.

I am willing to indicate to initiates of the Rose Croix degree of Masonry under proper charter from the genuine authorities (for there are spurious Masons working under a forged charter) the address of a person willing to consider their fitness to affiliate to a Chapter practising similar rites.

XVI

I consider it supererogatory to continue my essay on the Mysteries and my analysis of *Energized Enthusiasm*.

SECTION VI

MISCELLANEOUS

LIBER
B

VEL
MAGI

SVB FIGVRA
I

A∴A∴
Publication in Class A

LIBER B VEL MAGI

00. One is the Magus: twain His forces: four His weapons. These are the Seven Spirits of Unrighteousness; seven vultures of evil. Thus is the art and craft of the Magus but glamour. How shall He destroy Himself?

0. Yet the Magus hath power upon the Mother both directly and through Love. And the Magus is Love, and bindeth together That and This in His Conjuration.

1. In the beginning doth the Magus speak Truth, and send forth Illusion and Falsehood to enslave the soul. Yet therein is the Mystery of Redemption.

2. By His Wisdom made He the Worlds; the Word that is God is none other than He.

3. How then shall He end His speech with Silence? For He is Speech.

4. He is the First and the Last. How shall He cease to number Himself?

5. By a Magus is this writing made known through the mind of a Magister. The one uttereth clearly, and the other understandeth; yet the Word is falsehood, and the Understanding darkness. And this saying is Of All Truth.

6. Nevertheless it is written; for there be times of darkness, and this as a lamp therein.

7. With the Wand createth He.

8. With the Cup preserveth He.

9. With the Dagger destroyeth He.

10. With the Coin redeemeth He.

11. His weapons fulfil the wheel; and on What Axle that turneth is not known unto Him.

12. From all these actions must He cease before the curse of His Grade is uplifted from Him. Before He attain to That which existeth without Form.

13. And if at this time He be manifested upon earth as a Man, and therefore is this present writing, let this be His method, that the curse of His grade, and the burden of His attainment, be uplifted from Him.

14. Let Him beware of abstinence from action. For the curse of His grade is that He must speak Truth, that the Falsehood thereof may enslave the souls of men. Let Him then utter that without Fear, that the Law may be fulfilled. And according to His Original Nature will that law be shapen, so that one may declare gentleness and quietness, being an Hindu; and another fierceness and servility, being a Jew; and yet another ardour and manliness, being an Arab. Yet this matter toucheth the mystery of Incarnation, and is not here to be declared.

15. Now the grade of a Magister teacheth the Mystery of Sorrow, and the grade of a Magus the Mystery of Change, and the grade of Ipsissimus the Mystery of Selflessness, which is called also the Mystery of Pan.

16. Let the Magus then contemplate each in turn, raising it to the ultimate power of Infinity. Wherein Sorrow is Joy, and Change is Stability, and Selflessness is Self. For the interplay of the parts hath no action upon the whole. And this contemplation shall be performed not by simple meditation—how much less then by reason?

but by the method which shall have been given unto Him in His initiation to the Grade.

17. Following which method, it shall be easy for Him to combine that trinity from its elements, and further to combine Sat-Chit-Ananda, and Light, Love, Life, three by three into nine that are one, in which meditation success shall be That which was first adumbrated to Him in the grade of Practicus (which reflecteth Mercury into the lowest world) in *Liber XXVII*, "Here is Nothing under its three Forms."

18. And this is the Opening of the Grade of Ipsissimus, and by the Buddhists it is called the trance Nerodha-Samapatti.

19. And woe, woe, woe, yea woe, and again woe, woe, woe unto seven times be His that preacheth not His law to men!

20. And woe also be unto Him that refuseth the curse of the grade of a Magus, and the burden of the Attainment thereof.

21. And in the word CHAOS let the Book be sealed; yea, let the Book be sealed.

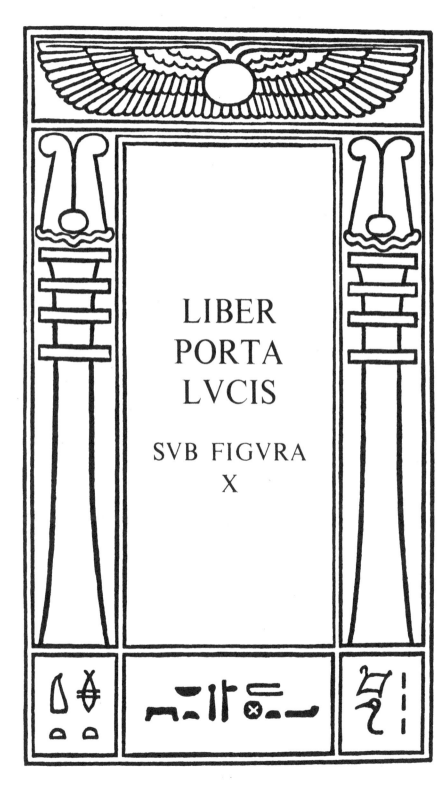

LIBER
PORTA
LVCIS

SVB FIGVRA
X

A∴A∴
Publication Class A

Imprimatur:
N. Fra A∴A∴

LIBER PORTA LVCIS

1. I behold a small dark orb, wheeling in an abyss of infinite space. It is minute among a myriad vast ones, dark amid a myriad bright ones.

2. I who comprehend in myself all the vast and the minute, all the bright and the dark, have mitigated the brilliance of mine unutterable splendour, sending forth V.V.V.V.V. as a ray of my light, as a messenger unto that small dark orb.

3. Then V.V.V.V.V. taketh up the word, and sayeth:

4. Men and women of the Earth, to you am I come from the Ages beyond the Ages, from the Space beyond your vision; and I bring to you these words.

5. But they heard him not, for they were not ready to receive them.

6. But certain men heard and understood, and through them shall this Knowledge be made known.

7. The least therefore of them, the servant of them all, writeth this book.

8. He writeth for them that are ready. Thus is it known if one be ready, if he be endowed with certain gifts, if he be fitted by birth, or by wealth, or by intelli-

gence, or by some other manifest sign. And the servants of the master by his insight shall judge of these.

9. This Knowledge is not for all men; few indeed are called, but of these few many are chosen.

10. This is the nature of the Work.

11. First, there are many and diverse conditions of life upon this earth. In all of these is some seed of sorrow. Who can escape from sickness and from old age and from death?

12. We are come to save our fellows from these things. For there is a life intense with knowledge and extreme bliss which is untouched by any of them.

13. To this life we attain even here and now. The adepts, the servants of V.V.V.V.V., have attained thereunto.

14. It is impossible to tell you of the splendours of that to which they have attained.

Little by little, as your eyes grow stronger, will we unveil to you the ineffable glory of the Path of the Adepts, and its nameless goal.

15. Even as a man ascending a steep mountain is lost to sight of his friends in the valley, so must the adept seem. They shall say: He is lost in the clouds. But he shall rejoice in the sunlight above them, and come to the eternal snows.

16. Or as a scholar may learn some secret language of the ancients, his friends shall say: "Look! he pretends to read this book. But it is unintelligible—it is nonsense." Yet he delights in the Odyssey, while they read vain and vulgar things.

17. We shall bring you to Absolute Truth, Absolute Light, Absolute Bliss.

18. Many adepts throughout the ages have sought to do this; but their words have been perverted by their

successors, and again and again the Veil has fallen upon the Holy of Holies.

19. To you who yet wander in the Court of the Profane we cannot yet reveal all; but you will easily understand that the religions of the world are but symbols and veils of the Absolute Truth. So also are the philosophies. To the adept, seeing all these things from above, there seems nothing to choose between Buddha and Mohammed, between Atheism and Theism.

20. The many change and pass; the one remains. Even as wood and coal and iron burn up together in one great flame, if only that furnace be of transcendent heat; so in the alembic of this spiritual alchemy, if only the zelator blow sufficiently upon this furnace all the systems of earth are consumed in the One Knowledge.

21. Nevertheless, as a fire cannot be started with iron alone, in the beginning one system may be suited for one seeker, another for another.

22. We therefore who are without the chains of ignorance, look closely into the heart of the seeker and lead him by the path which is best suited to his nature unto the ultimate end of all things, the supreme realization, the Life which abideth in Light, yea, the Life which abideth in Light.

LIBER
TZADDI

VEL
HAMVS
HERMETICVS

SVB FIGVRA
XC

A∴A∴
Publication in Class A
Imprimatur:
N. Fra A∴A∴

LIBER TZADDI

0. In the name of the Lord of Initiation, Amen.

1. I fly and I alight as an hawk: of mother-of-emerald are my mighty-sweeping wings.

2. I swoop down upon the black earth; and it gladdens into green at my coming.

3. Children of Earth! rejoice! rejoice exceedingly; for your salvation is at hand.

4. The end of sorrow is come; I will ravish you away into mine unutterable joy.

5. I will kiss you, and bring you to the bridal: I will spread a feast before you in the house of happiness.

6. I am not come to rebuke you, or to enslave you.

7. I bid you not turn from your voluptuous ways, from your idleness, from your follies.

8. But I bring you joy to your pleasure, peace to your languor, wisdom to your folly.

9. All that ye do is right, if so be that ye enjoy it.

10. I am come against sorrow, against weariness, against them that seek to enslave you.

11. I pour you lustral wine, that giveth you delight both at the sunset and the dawn.

12. Come with me, and I will give you all that is desirable upon the earth.

13. Because I give you that of which Earth and its joys are but as shadows.

14. They flee away, but my joy abideth even unto the end.

15. I have hidden myself beneath a mask: I am a black and terrible God.

16. With courage conquering fear shall ye approach me: ye shall lay down your heads upon mine altar, expecting the sweep of the sword.

17. But the first kiss of love shall be radiant on your lips; and all my darkness and terror shall turn to light and joy.

18. Only those who fear shall fail. Those who have bent their backs to the yoke of slavery until they can no longer stand upright; them will I despise.

19. But you who have defied the law; you who have conquered by subtlety or force; you will I take unto me, even I will take you unto me.

20. I ask you to sacrifice nothing at mine altar; I am the God who giveth all.

21. Light, Life, Love; Force, Fantasy, Fire; these do I bring you: mine hands are full of these.

22. There is joy in the setting-out; there is joy in the journey; there is joy in the goal.

23. Only if ye are sorrowful, or weary, or angry, or discomforted; then ye may know that ye have lost the golden thread, the thread wherewith I guide you to the heart of the groves of Eleusis.

24. My disciples are proud and beautiful; they are strong and swift; they rule their way like mighty conquerors.

25. The weak, the timid, the imperfect, the cowardly, the poor, the tearful—these are mine enemies, and I am come to destroy them.

26. This also is compassion: an end to the sickness of earth. A rooting-out of the weeds: a watering of the flowers.

27. O my children, ye are more beautiful than the flowers: ye must not fade in your season.

28. I love you; I would sprinkle you with the divine dew of immortality.

29. This immortality is no vain hope beyond the grave: I offer you the certain consciousness of bliss.

30. I offer it at once, on earth; before an hour hath struck upon the bell, ye shall be with Me in the Abodes that are beyond Decay.

31. Also I give you power earthly and joy earthly; wealth, and health, and length of days. Adoration and love shall cling to your feet, and twine around your heart.

32. Only your mouths shall drink of a delicious wine— the wine of Iacchus; they shall reach ever to the heavenly kiss of the Beautiful God.

33. I reveal unto you a great mystery. Ye stand between the abyss of height and the abyss of depth.

34. In either awaits you a Companion; and that Companion is Yourself.

35. Ye can have no other Companion.

36. Many have arisen, being wise. They have said "Seek out the glittering Image in the place ever golden, and unite yourselves with It."

37. Many have arisen, being foolish. They have said, "Stoop down unto the darkly splendid world, and be wedded to that Blind Creature of the Slime."

38. I who am beyond Wisdom and Folly, arise and say unto you: achieve both weddings! Unite yourselves with both!

39. Beware, beware, I say, lest ye seek after the one and lose the other!

40. My adepts stand upright; their head above the heavens, their feet below the hells.

41. But since one is naturally attracted to the Angel, another to the Demon, let the first strengthen the lower link, the last attach more firmly to the higher.

42. Thus shall equilibrium become perfect. I will aid my disciples; as fast as they acquire this balanced power and joy so faster will I push them.

43. They shall in their turn speak from this Invisible Throne; their words shall illumine the worlds.

44. They shall be masters of majesty and might; they shall be beautiful and joyous; they shall be clothed with victory and splendour; they shall stand upon the firm foundation; the kingdom shall be theirs; yea, the kingdom shall be theirs.

In the name of the Lord of Initiation. Amen.

LIBER
ARCANORVM
τῶν
ATV
τοῦ
TAHVTI
QUAS VIDIT
ASAR IN
AMENNTI

SVB FIGVRA
CCXXXI

A ∴ A ∴

Publication in Class A

Imprimatur:
N. Fra A ∴ A ∴

Liber XXII Carcerorum Qliphoth
Cum Suis Geniis

Liber XXII Domarum Mercurii
Cum Suis Geniis

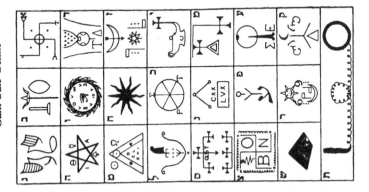

Compare
with

LIBER CCXXXI

This book is true up to the grade of Adeptus Exemptus.
—V.V.V.V.V. 8°, 3□.

0. A, the heart of IAO, dwelleth in ecstasy in the secret place of the thunders. Between Asar and Asi he abideth in joy.

1. The lightnings increased and the Lord Tahuti stood forth. The Voice came from the Silence. Then the One ran and returned.

2. Now hath Nuit veiled herself, that she may open the gate of her sister.

3. The Virgin of God is enthroned upon an oyster-shell; she is like a pearl, and seeketh Seventy to her Four. In her heart is Hadit the invisible glory.

4. Now riseth Ra-Hoor-Khuit, and dominion is established in the Star of the Flame.

5. Also is the Star of the Flame exalted, bringing benediction to the universe.

6. Here then beneath the winged Eros is youth, delighting in the one and the other.

He is Asar between Asi and Nephthi; he cometh forth from the veil.

7. He rideth upon the chariot of eternity; the white and

667

the black are harnessed to his car. Therefore he reflecteth the Fool, and the sevenfold veil is reveiled.

8. Also came forth mother Earth with her lion, even Sekhet, the lady of Asi.

9. Also the Priest veiled himself, lest his glory be profaned, lest his word be lost in the multitude.

10. Now then the Father of all issued as a mighty wheel; the Sphinx, and the dog-headed god, and Typhon, were bound on his circumference.

11. Also the lady Maat with her feather and her sword abode to judge the righteous.

For Fate was already established.

12. Then the holy one appeared in the great water of the North; as a golden dawn did he appear, bringing benediction to the fallen universe.

13. Also Asar was hidden in Amennti; and the Lords of Time swept over him with the sickle of death.

14. And a mighty angel appeared as a woman, pouring vials of woe upon the flames, lighting the pure stream with her brand of cursing. And the iniquity was very great.

15. Then the Lord Khem arose, He who is holy among the highest, and set up his crowned staff for to redeem the universe.

16. He smote the towers of wailing; he brake them in pieces in the fire of his anger, so that he alone did escape from the ruin thereof.

17. Transformed, the holy virgin appeared as a fluidic fire, making her beauty into a thunderbolt.

18. By her spells she invoked the Scarab, the Lord Kheph-Ra, so that the waters were cloven and the illusion of the towers was destroyed.

19. Then the sun did appear unclouded, and the mouth of Asi was on the mouth of Asar.

20. Then also the Pyramid was builded so that the Initiation might be complete.

21. And in the heart of the Sphinx danced the Lord Adonai, in His garlands of roses and pearls making glad the concourse of things; yea, making glad the concourse of things.

THE GENII OF THE 22 SCALES OF THE SERPENT AND OF THE QLIPHOTH

א	Aç u-iao-uça [ç = y]	Amprodias
ב	Beç θaoooabitiom	Baratchial
ג	Gitωnosapφωllois	Gargophias
ד	Dηnaᶎartarωθ[ᶎ =st]	Dagdagiel
ה	Hoo-oor ω-iᶎ	Hemethterith
ו	Vuaretza—[a secret name follows]	Uriens
ז	Zoowasar	Zamradiel
ח	Chiva-abrahadabra-cadaxviii	Characith
ט	Θalç ᶎer-a-dekerval	Temphioth
י	Iehuvaha ᶎan çθ atan	Yamatu
כ	Kerugunaviel	Kurgasiax
ל	Lusanaherandraton	Lafcursiax
מ	Malai	Malkunofat
נ	Nadimraphoroiozçθ alai	Niantiel
ס	Salaθlala-amrodnaθ çiᶎ	Saksaksalim
ע	Oaoaaaooç-iᶎ	A'ano'nin
פ	Puraθmetai-ap ηmetai	Parfaxitas
צ	Xanθaᶎeran ϵϙ-iᶎ [ϵϙ=sh, q]	Tzuflifu
ק	QaniΔnayx-ipamai	Qulielfi
ר	Ra-a-gioselahladnaimawa-iᶎ	Raflifu
ש	Shabnax-odobor	Shalicu
ת	Thath'th'thithçthuth-thi ᶎ	Thantifaxath

NOTE BY H. FRA. P. 4°=7□ (1899)
ON THE R.O.T.A.
BY THE
QABALAH OF NINE CHAMBERS

Units are divine—The upright Triangle.

Tens reflected—The averse Triangle.

Hundreds equilibrated—The Hexagram their combination.

1. *Light.* (Here can be no evil.) א The hidden light—the "wisdom of God foolishness with men."

> י The Adept bearing Light.
> The Light in darkness and illusion.
> ק (Khephra about to rise.)

2. *Action.* ב Active and Passive—dual current, etc.—the Alternating Forces in Harmony.

> כ The Contending Forces—fluctuation of earth-life.
> ר The Twins embracing—eventual glory of harmonised life under ☉.

3. *The Way.* (Here also no evil.) ג The Higher Self.

> ל The severe discipline of the Path.
> ט The judgment and resurrection.
> (0° = and 5° = 6 rituals)

4. *Life.* ד The Mother of God. Aima.

מ The Son Slain.

ת The Bride.

5. *Force* (Purification). ה The Supernal Sulphur purifying by fire.

> נ The Infernal Water ♏ purifying by putrefaction.
> This work is not complete;

therefore is there no equilibration.

6. *Harmony.* ו The Reconciler (ו of יהוה) above.

ם The Reconciler below (lion and eagle, etc.).

This work also unfinished.

7. *Birth.* ז The Powers of Spiritual Regeneration.

(The Z.A.M. as Osiris risen between Isis and Nephthys. The path of ג, Diana, above his head.)

ע The gross powers of generation.

8. *Rule.* ח The Orderly Ruling of diverse forces.

פ The Ruin of the Unbalanced Forces.

9. *Stability.* ט The Force that represses evil.

צ The Force that restores the world ruined by evil.

LIBER TAV

VEL

KABBALAE TRIVM LITERARUM

SVB FIGVRA
CD

A∴A∴
Publication in Class B

Imprimatur:
N. Fra A∴A∴

אבס
עגפ
רחת
קלמ
נוז
ש

The Magister Templi, the Adeptus, the Neophyte (8°=3°▢, 5°=6▢, 0°=0▢).

The Ultimate Illusion, the Illusion of Force, the Illusion of Matter.

The Functions of the 3 Orders: Silence in Speech; Silence; Speech in Silence: Construction, Preservation, Destruction.

The Supreme Unveiling (or Unveiling of Light), the Unveiling of Life, the Unveiling of Love.

Equilibrium; on the Cubic Stone, on the Path, and among the Shells.

The Rituals of Initiation, 8°=3°▢, 5°=6▢, 0°=0▢: Asar, as Bull, as Man, as Sun.

The Ordeals of Initiation, 8°=3°▢, 5°=6▢, 0°=0▢: Birth, Death, Resurrection.

(This analysis may be checked by adding the columns vertically, 69, 81, 93, 114, 135, 246, 357. Dividing by 3 we get 23, 27, 31, 38, 45, 82, 119, which in the Sepher Sephiroth mean respectively Life, Purity, Negation, "38 × 11 = 418," Innocent, Formation, Prayer, Weeping. The analogies are obvious.)

LIBER VIARVM VIAE

SVB FIGVRA
DCCCLXVIII

A∴A∴
Publication in Class A
Imprimatur:
N. Fra∴A∴A∴

LIBER VIARVM VIAE

Nine locks of the Inferior Beard	21.	Nine paths below Adeptus	פ The Formulation of the Body of Light. *Liber O.*
	20.		ע The Passage of the King's Chamber. *Liber H H H.*
	19.		ר The Illumination of the Sphere. *Liber H H H.*
	18.		ק The Divining of Destiny. *Liber Memoriae Viae CMXIII.*
	17.		צ The Adoration under the Starry Heaven. *Liber XI, NV* (from *Liber CCXX*).
	16.		כ The Destruction of the House of God. *Liber XVI.*
	15.		י The Sabbath of the Adepts. *Liber CCCLXX.*
	14.		ס Skrying in the Spirit Vision: The Ladder of Jacob. *Liber O.*
	13.		נ The Preparation of the Corpse for the Tomb. *Liber XXV.*

Thirteen locks of the Superior Beard	12.	Three below I.	מ The Sleep of Siloam. *Liber CDLI.*
	8.		ט The Protection of the Sphere. *Liber O.*
	10.		כ The Evocation of the Mighty Ones. *Liber . . .*
	9.		י The Absorption of the Emanations. *Liber DCCCXI.*
	11.		ל The Passing of the Hall of the Balances. *Liber XXX.*
	7.		ח The Ritual of the Holy Graal. *Liber CLVI.*
	6.		ז The Utterance of the Pythoness. *Liber MCXXXIX.*
	5.	Three below M.	ו The Forthcoming of the Hierophant. *Liber VIII* (8th Aethyr in *Liber 418*).
	4.		ה The Formulation of the Flaming Star. *Liber V.*
	3.		ד The Incarnation of the Inmost Light. *Liber DLV Had* (from *Liber CCXX*).
	2.	Seven paths below M. T.	ג The Supreme Ecstasy of Purity. *Liber LXXIII.*
	1.		ב The Universal Affirmations and Denials. *Liber B (I).*
	0.		א The transcending of all these; yea, the transcending of all these.

Seven Inferiors: Seven Superiors: Seven above All:
and Seven Interpretations of every Word.

LIBER CLXV

A MASTER OF THE TEMPLE

BEING AN ACCOUNT
OF THE
ATTAINMENT
OF
FRATER
VNVS IN OMNIBVS

ABRIDGED FROM HIS
MAGICAL RECORD

A ∴ A ∴ Publication in Class B

93	$10° = 1^\square$	
666	$9° = 2^\square$	Pro Coll.
777	$8° = 3^\square$	Summ.
D. D. S.	$7° = 4^\square$	
O. M.	$7° = 4^\square$	Pro Coll.
O. S. V.	$6° = 5^\square$	Int.
Parzival	$5° = 6^\square$	
V. N.	Praemonstrator	
P.	Imperator	Pro Coll.
Achad	Cancellarius	Ext.

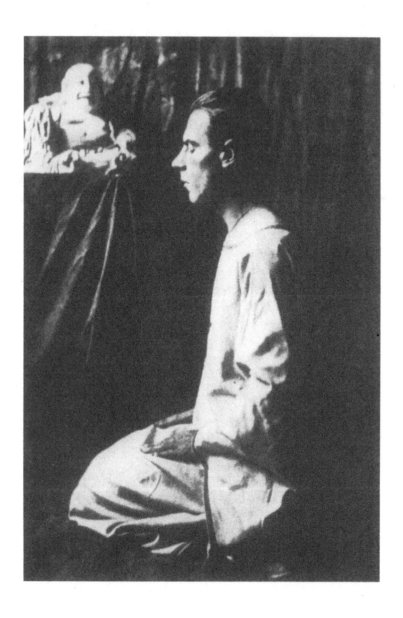

Frater VNVS in Omnibvs
From the Photograph by Henry B. Camp

The Master is represented in the Robe of, and described by His
name as, a Probationer, as if to assert His Simplicity. He is in His
favourite Asana, the Dragon, in profound holy meditation.

A MASTER
OF THE TEMPLE

Section I
April 2, 1886, to December 24, 1909

Charles Stansfeld Jones, whom I shall usually mention by the motto V.I.O., which he took on becoming a Probationer of the A ∴ A ∴, made his entry into this World by the usual and approved method, on April 2nd 1886 E. V., having only escaped becoming an April Fool by delaying a day to summon up enough courage to turn out once more into this cold and uninviting World. Having been oiled, smacked and allowed to live, we shall trouble no further about the details of his career until 1906, when, having reached the age of 20 years, he began to turn his attention toward the Mysteries, and to investigate Spiritualism, chiefly with the idea of disproving it. From this year his interest in the Occult seems to date, and it was about this time that he first consciously aspired to find, and get into touch with, a True Occult Order. This aspiration was, as we shall see, fulfilled three years later, when he had an opportunity to become a Probationer of the A ∴ A ∴, and immediately grasped it; but during those three years his researches led him into varied paths: Spiritualism, Faithism and other Isms on the one hand, and "The Europe," "The Leicester," and "The Cosy

685

Corner" on the other: last, but not least, into Marriage, a difficult thing to put on one side and perhaps best left on the other. Having then plunged wholeheartedly into this final experiment, becoming as it were "Omnia in Uno" for a time, he emerged in a frame of mind well suited to the study of Scientific Illuminism, of which he was much in need, and, having signed the Probationer's Pledge Form on December 24th, 1909, E.V., he took— after careful thought—the Motto "Unus in Omnibus" and has been riding very comfortably ever since.

From this time onward, according to the Rules of the Order, he began keeping a written record of his Work, and this makes our task easier; but since he himself became more serious from that moment, we must to a certain extent follow his example and treat what is recorded as the attempt of a struggling soul to obtain Light for himself and others. Whatever his mistakes, however poor his results, or laughable his failures, there is this much to be said for him, that he never turned back.

Section II
December 24, 1909, to May 14, 1910

Frater V.I.O. started off bravely enough. As soon as he had read the first number of *The Equinox,* and before he got into touch with any Member of the A∴ A∴ he made an attempt at Asana. The earliest record I can find reads as follows:

Thursday, Nov. 4th, 1909.   11:20 P.M. to 11:41 P.M.
Asana. Position I. The God.

Inclination for back to bend, just above hips, had to straighten up several times.

Opened eyes once and moved head, after about five minutes.

Breathed fairly regularly after the first few minutes, counting 9 in, holding 4, 9 out, holding 4.

Saw various colours in clouds, and uncertain figures, during the latter part of the time.

On December 19th his practice lasted 46 minutes. He hoped to do 60 minutes next time. But he does not appear to have done so, for after signing his Probationer's Oath on December 24th I find no record till January 11th, 1910, E.V., the day he received his first written instructions from his Neophyte, Frater P.A. As those instructions represent the basis upon which he worked for a considerable period, I shall include them here, in spite of the fact that it may have been out of order for him to work on definite instructions at all, since the Probationer is supposed to choose for himself those practices which please him best, and to experiment therewith for himself. Since however he did not know this at the time, he cannot be blamed for doing his best along the lines laid down by his Neophyte.[1] In any case he might have done far worse than to strive to carry out these few simple rules which are as follows:

THE RULES

1. Ever be moderate and follow the middle path; rather be the tortoise than the hare; do not rush wildly into anything; but do not abandon what you have taken up, without much forethought.

2. Always keep your body and mind in a healthy and fit condition; and never carry out an exercise, whether mental or physical, when you are fatigued.

3. In an ideal country the hours in which to practice are: at sunrise, sunset, noon and midnight (and always before a meal never immediately after one). As this cannot be done with comfort,

1. It is presumptuous for a Neophyte to lay down rules; for (a) he cannot possibly know what his Probationer needs, having no record to guide him; (b) the Probationer's task is to explore his own nature, not to follow any prescribed course. A third objection is that by putting the Probationer in Corsets, an entirely flabby person may sneak through his year, and become a Neophyte, to the shame of the Order. But this objection is theoretical; for Initiation is overseen from the Third Order, where no Error may endure.—O.M.

in this country (England), let your chief practice take place an hour or half an hour before your breakfast hour.

4. If possible set apart a room wherein to carry out your exercises; keep it clean, and only keep in it objects which please you; burn a little incense in the room before beginning an exercise; keep the room holy to yourself, and do not allow yourself or another to do anything unbalanced in thought or action in it. In will and deed make this room a temple and a symbol of that greater Temple which is your HIGHER SELF.

THE EXERCISES

The First Exercise

Rise to time, and without undue haste, wash and dress, robe yourself and enter the room you have set apart; burn a little incense and turning to the East repeat some simple orison such as: "May the light of Adonai arise within me, may it guide me through this day and be as a lamp to lighten my darkness." Then make a general confession, as shortly as possible, of your last day's work and enter it in your diary, after which sit down in a comfortable position and do the following.

With your hands upon your knees and your head straight, take in a breath in measured time inwards and concentrate the whole of your thought on that breath as it flows into your lungs, cutting away all other thoughts that may arise at the time; then exhale the breath, still keeping your thought fixed on it. Do this for some ten minutes or a quarter of an hour, and mark down in your diary the number of "breaks," or any result. The whole of this practice must be performed rhythmically and harmoniously.

The Second Exercise

As the rush of daily work tends to undo what the morning exercise has done, try your utmost to turn every item of your professional work into a magical exercise. Do all, even the smallest work, in honour and glory of Adonai: excel in your special duties in life, because He is of you, and you of Him; do not think of Him as Adonai, but think of Adonai as the work; and of your daily work create a symbol of the Symbol of "The Great Work which is TO BE."

The Third Exercise

As the rush of your daily work tends to unbalance you, so do the pleasures you indulge in. Cultivate joyfulness in all your amusements; and, when joyful, break out into silent and inward praise of the joy within you. Do not make a prudish exercise of it, work silently and joyously, and do not discuss your results with casual friends. And above all do everything for the honour and glory of Adonai, so that of your daily pleasures you may construct a symbol of that Unchanging Joy that IS.

These instructions were accompanied by a letter from which I quote the following: "The enclosed exercises perform regularly, say to yourself: 'I will do these for three months; even if I get no benefit from them, yet I am *determined* to do them.' Write to me whenever you like, but don't consider any result that you may get as worth much; for these little exercises are only to produce an equilibrium which is essential before really setting out. If you add any exercise of your own then do it at a definite hour daily and do it continuously; to take up an exercise and then drop it is worse than useless, for it is unbalancing."

Now, as any Probationer knows, as soon as one sets out to do the simplest task regularly and with magical intent, that task becomes not only difficult, but well nigh impossible of performance. This is just what V.I.O. found, and no sooner had his task been set than all kinds of difficulties presented themselves, like the dog-faced demons mentioned by Zoroaster, to prevent its fulfilment. He tried, but at the end of January he writes: "I cannot get on under these conditions. Had plenty of time to do exercises this morning, but was continually interrupted. Did not robe myself as I have no place fit to call a temple." How little did he know at that time how well off he really was in the latter respect! He was living in comfort in a Kensington Flat with every convenience of civilization; a few years later he was glad to do Asana and perform his meditations out in the rain, clad in pyjamas, because his tiny tent in British Columbia was too small to allow of work inside. But we digress. At this point his record breaks off abruptly. He remained in London until May of 1910, when circumstances arose which made it possible for him to visit British Columbia.

Armed then with his instruction paper, *The Equinox*, and a few Occult books, he sailed for Canada, alone, to start again in new and unploughed fields.

Section III
July 25, 1910, to April 30, 1911

The next entry in his diary is dated July 25th, 1910. It is a general confession of the previous six months. Half of his year of Probation had passed away, and he has not reported to, or received any communication from, the Order. He laments his negligence in this respect, but writes: "Yet know I well that I alone have suffered and shall suffer from this negligence, and I must humbly take any results that may arise out of my failure. Still, even though I may have neglected the advice given me when I first became a Probationer, I feel that I have progressed, be it never so slightly, along the Path which from the first I set out to tread. May it not be, O Adonai, that even now the second six months may be made to balance the first six, and that what is passed may yet be for the best?"

At that time he had not found out that things always turn out for the best; it took him a long while to realize this, but it is evident that soon afterwards his efforts produced some result; for we find an entry on Sunday, August 7th, 1910. "I have found (for a few moments) the Peace which passeth all understanding. Amen." This was evidently the foreshadowing of his first really notable result, the first Dawning of L.V.X. which he experienced on August 29th. There is an entry on September 2nd, full of joy and gladness and wonder at his first Illumination; and then, three days later, he had evidently recognised that this alone was not enough, and this was evidently the reason for the next somewhat curious entry of September 5th, 7:53 P.M., which I shall quote practically in full:

I am calm now, as I commence to write what may be the last entry in this diary. All that I can remember of my life on this planet has, as I look back upon it, been guided by an unseen hand. For so short a life (24 years and six months) it has been filled with an unusual number of incidents, some painful, some joyful and some of a purely spiritual nature. I regret nothing. Again three days have passed since I made entry in this book. I cannot talk of what has happened during those three days, it seems useless to try and do so, in fact it seems useless to make this entry at all except that *I know not what is before me*, and I feel that had I (or if I) lived longer upon this planet it would have been my life work, indeed it must have been, to help others to the Path. Therefore to those who follow after are these lines written in the hope that they may be saved one drop of the anguish I now suffer. Whatever may have happened in this last three days, the results of my thoughts amount to this. I who have found the heart of the shining triangle, who have indeed become one with the Great White Brotherhood, who have heard the Voice of God in all Its sweetness, who have made that message a part (nay all) of my being, who have held my Beloved in my arms, who have Become my Beloved and lost myself therein, who have for ever given up my lower self, who have conquered Death, who have felt the Pain of the whole World, who have found Wisdom, Love and Power, who have given up All to become Nothing, I who have seen the need of the World, have found that books (hitherto my dearest companions) have no longer any word to say to me—have found that knowledge (relative) or what I thought was knowledge, is of no avail to supply the need of all that other part of my Being that my great God-love would give it. I who have conquered Fear and Death, am now confronted with the fact that without Absolute Knowledge all is vain. I am going to ask the One Last Question. WHY? I have written it. An awful stillness falls. I am alone in my lodgings, I have no money, and I cannot use my Will to demand it from others if I can give nothing in return to help them to find what they really seek. I have cried with Christ "Eli, Eli, Lama Sabacthani." I have suffered the Bloody Sweat with Him on the Cross, and now I say with Him "It is finished" Amen. One last note occurs to me before I wrap up this book and seal it and address it to F... in whose hands it will be safe. I looked into the eyes of a little child this evening. Does the answer lie there?

Sep. 5th, 12:26 P.M. It is over. I have unsealed the package and once more opened the book. This time it will be but a short entry. Very quietly I knelt; I did not robe or burn incense. I just took with me the memory of the little child who had looked into my eyes as I kissed its forehead. Very quietly I asked my question. I rose and lay upon the bed, and soon the answer came. It came quite silently, and at first I thought I must be mistaken, I had (it seemed) heard it so many times before. No other answer came, so I went out into the streets and along my way. Gradually the fuller meaning has dawned on me, and I have returned to make this entry. I need not add much more. I do not put the answer down. It was given in silence and must remain in Silence. Still there seemed to be just one little ripple of joy in the Great Silent Sea as another sould gently sank to its rest, and the silent voices whispered "Welcome brother." Then all was calm and Peace as before. The little ripple flowed on to let the whole world know, then, having delivered its message, all was still. Amen.

Whatever the nature of this Illumination, probably a state of Dhyana, it left a very marked result on the consciousness of Frater V.I.O., and gave him the necessary energy to continue his Work through many a dark and dismal period. He himself could not gauge its value at all at the time. He was alone in Vancouver and out of touch with the Order, having received no further word from his Neophyte since he left England. In fact he heard nothing till January of the following year. He however sent a post-card to say that he had obtained some result.

About this same time I find an entry called "The

Philosophy of V.I.O." which seems of interest on account of some similarities to the Law of Thelema, of which he had heard nothing at that time. It reads as follows:

Man is bound by but *One Law*.
If he breaks a part of it, he hurts no one but himself.
While he lives in unity with It, he is God.
While he does not live in unity with It he is Man.
While he lives in unity with it he becomes the Law.
To realise the Law and live it is the Great Work.
To break the Law after he has realized it is Sin.
To endeavour to bring all to the knowledge of the Law, is to keep the Law.
Seek ye the Law that ye may be Free.
Wisdom, Love and Power, these three are One. That these should be One is the Law.
By finding the Point from which these three become equal, and there remaining, by this means only, can the Law be Known.
If ye know this, ye know All.
If ye know not this, ye know less than All.
Seek ever for the Absolute, and be content with Nothing less.

By the end of September the immediate results of this first Illumination seem to have worn off, and we find Frater V.I.O. striving desperately to estimate the value of what had happened to him. He was certainly in a mental muddle, as the following entry shows, yet at the same time his one thought seems to have been to find a means of helping others to find that Light which had so transformed his whole being.

Sept. 24th, 1910. Driad Hotel. Victoria, B. C.
I sit here with the idea of attempting to classify the results lately obtained. (Since L.V.X. entry.)
I may mention that during the interval I have carefully read and studied Crowley's *Tannhäuser, The Sword of Song, Excluded Middle, Time, Berashith, Science and Buddhism, Three Characteristics*, etc. In the Light of Understanding, all these works have

taken on a very different aspect to when I read them previously. Also the Purpose of *Liber LXV* is clear. The result of all this gives me a feeling that I have arrived at the End and also at the Beginning at the same time.

This (by the way) seems the usual experience of the beginner; no sooner does he get a result, any result, than he immediately thinks he is at the end. But V.I.O. is evidently not to be deceived in that way, for he goes on:

Now, had I really arrived at the End, it seems reasonable to suppose I should not be here writing this. My body and mind are at any rate still in existence as a body and mind. But, as these are admittedly impermanent, does it matter much that they continue to exist in this form or no? What has that to do with the Consciousness of the Existence of That which transcends both? Now, had not some part of my present State of Existence *realized* the possibility of another and higher state of Consciousness, should I not still be in that state of uncertainly in which I lived before this realization came? This *realization* having come about has at any rate remained as a glimpse of Being, different from the previous not-being.

The result of his mental analysis appears to amount to this, that he had experienced within himself a state of consciousness full of Peace and Joy, yet which more nearly approximated to Zero than any other term. He can find nothing with which to compare this state, but he recognizes its immense superiority over normal consciousness, and feels an intense desire to make it possible for others to share his experience. Since however he finds it impossible to explain it in words, he recognises that he must obtain the knowledge of some definite System of producing the state scientifically, but since he is not even a Neophyte of the A ∴ A ∴, he wonders if They will recognise him as qualified to demand the right to know and spread Their teachings. He determines in any case to reduce the wants of the Ego as a separate being as far as possible, by forgetting self in his efforts to do all he can for others according to the Light he had obtained.

He found however that the destruction of the Ego was not thus easily accomplished at the first assault. Nevertheless he learned, not from books but from experience, that the Goal was to be found within himself, and that the nearer he could approach to the Consciousness of Nothingness the nearer he got to the Realization of Pure Existence. This reduction of consciousness to Zero then became the fixed aim of his Meditations; and any other experiments he entered upon, were, from that time onward, looked upon as necessary in order that he might fit himself to help others, rather than for his personal development.

On January 7th, 1911, he received No. 4 of *The Equinox,* and on seeing the Frontispiece to *Liber Jvgorvm* he experienced a feeling of decided aversion to cutting his arm in the prescribed manner. But, said he, "Fear is failure and the forerunner of failure"; and it will no doubt be best to undertake a week of this work so as to get used to it, after which I shall probably have no more trouble in this respect. He decided therefore to omit the word AND from his conversation for that period. His record of this experiment is kept in detail[2] and may prove interesting to other Students; so I shall transcribe it in full.

Saturday, Jan. 7th, 1911.   Vancouver, B. C.

4 P.M. Have just received *The Equinox* and am going to experiment with the Control of Speech by not using the word "AND" for one week. May My Lord Adonai assist me. Amen.

2. The reader is asked to note that only a very few of very many practices are transcribed in this abridged record. This note is especially important, because a casual reader might be led to suppose that V.I.O. got a great deal for very little. On the contrary, he is the hardest worker of all the Brethren, and well deserved his unprecedented success.—O.M.

Sat. 7th., 12 Midnight.

Although continually watchful, have had to chastise myself 15 times since 4 o'c. Will try and make a better record to-morrow. (I am certain that I have not missed cutting arm immediately after using the word.)

Sun. 8th, 11:30 P.M.
  Said prohibited word
    2 before rising in morning.
    1 during conversation.
    3 during singing practice.
    1 at tea.
    1 in evening.
    1 Supper.
    —

  Total 9

This is certainly better. The three times during singing practice occurred while trying over new music with the choir of which I am a member, and it is very hard to leave out a word when singing. I find this practice makes one speak much less. The word chosen being a conjunction often results in the second part of a sentence remaining unspoken. I never before noticed how unnecessary some of our speech is; in fact I have now no doubt that a great many things are better left unsaid.

Monday, Jan. 9th. Bedtime.
  Said word to-day for the first time at Lunch.
    1 at 1:20 P.M. Lunch.
    1 at 2:25 P.M. at Office.
    2 at 4 P.M. { Was careless enough to repeat a sentence con-
               { taining it. Give extra sharp cut.
    1 at 5:10 P.M.
    1 at 5:30 P.M.
    —

  Total 6

I am glad this shows further improvement. I was working and taking at the Office all the evening up to 10 o'c. and then had some conversation at home.

Tuesday, Jan. 10th. 12:35 P.M.

I am annoyed with myself, have been very careless. Had a talk with a man this morning for about 7 minutes, and forgot all about concentration. However, I have more or less formed a habit of speaking in short sentences; so I don't think I said the word more than twice. However am just going to give an extra cut in case, for being careless.

  1 before leaving home in morning.
  2 during conversation (as above) 12:10 A.M.
  1 during Lunch. (This only half sounded, but have recorded
        it.)
  1 at 7:45 P.M. (arm begins to feel sore)
  1 at 10:30 P.M. (speaking too quickly to M.)
  —   Went to bed at 11:10 P.M.
Total 6

Wednesday, Jan. 11. 6:45 P.M.

           1 at 9:50 A.M. at Office.
Lunch 1 while talking to my brother C.
Hour   1 while talking to my wife.
12–1 o'c. 1 while talking to my barber.

I consider the above *very bad*; but the explanation is that this particular hour was a great "rush" as I had to call at my brother's Office, go home for lunch, do some shopping for lunch, and back again to eat same, also get shaved, in one hour. I evidently got flurried and lost control a bit. (Note the time when talking to my brother is doubtful, but have included it.) I think I should here note that on Saturday evening, Sunday and Monday I was quite aware of my task practically *all the time*; even when I made mistakes, they were in almost every case caused through *trying too hard*. Probably, having got over a difficult bit of conversation successfully, I was seduced into the error. Tuesday and to-day have been rather different. I have lapsed a little in vigilance, but attained a certain subconscious wariness. This makes conversation easier, but is not established enough to make me free from errors. In fact I am not sure if I am not getting more careless.

  1 at 5:20 P.M. office.
  1 at 8:30 P.M. to wife.

1 at 10:00 P.M. Singing.
1 10:50 talking to wife.

—

Total for day, 9

Note. I felt terribly restless all the evening, and had an intense desire to talk freely. Went to a Smoking Concert at 8:45, but left again at 10:5, as I could not stand it any longer. I wanted to sing very much, and in fact did join in one song and made slip noted above. I find it very difficult to leave out a word throughout a song, even if singing with others.

Thursday, Jan. 12, 7:35 P.M.
Have felt much better to-day and had much more control so far. At 8:58 A.M. I recorded one failure, but this time not spoken audibly; the meaning however was in mind, so I count it. I was repeating the time after being told it by a friend, viz., one *and* a half minutes to nine. Again at 6:35 P.M. once, but also inaudible.
I completed the day successfully with a total of 2 (inaudible).

Friday, Jan. 13, 6:20 P.M.
    1 during morning at office. ⎫
    1 at 2:35 P.M.   ⎬ all inaudible
    1 at 4:30 P.M.   ⎭
    1 at 6:10 P.M. Aloud.

I hardly know whether to count the inaudible ones, but would rather make failure appear worse than to try and deceive myself.

    1 at 7:10 P.M. to Mrs. R. (*loud*)
    1 at 9:00 P.M. Office.
    1 at 10:30 P.M. to wife.
    1 at 11:30 P.M. to wife.

—

8 Total for day
This was a very bad day; and I had so much hoped to get through one clear day without a break! Never mind, better results next experiment.

Saturday, Jan. 14, 6:30 P.M.
Results very poor again.

1 during morning.
1 at 1:45 P.M. to wife.
1 at 3:00 P.M. to wife.

——

3
Saturday eveing, Jan. 7   15
Sunday   9
Monday   6
Tuesday   6
Wednesday   9
Thursday   2
Friday   8
Sat. till 4 P.M.   3

——

Total for week   58

Thus ends first experiment in control of Speech. It has been somewhat disappointing as regards results; but has proved to me how much I needed the exercise. I am very glad I undertook it, and shall try again in the near future.

Note. I have got over the feeling of shrinking at cutting myself. The first cuts were quite short and about half an inch long, afterwards I increased them to as much as 3 inches in length.

From Jan. 21 to 28th, Frater V.I.O. experimented with control of body, by not crossing legs. Same penalty as before. Total breaks for week, 24. On Feb. 25th, he records the fact that he had succeeded in performing this practice for a clear week with one doubtful break only during sleep.

The result of these practices on Frater V.I.O. was a marked one. For one thing, the cutting of his arm during the first practice in the control of speech resulted in a subconscious wariness, for during the second—the details of which I have not recorded—he noticed that although the object of the practice was the control of the body by not crossing the legs, yet the attempt of the legs to drop into their old habits often had the effect of making him suddenly more careful in his speech, thus showing that there was an underlying connection in his subconscious mind resulting from his former work. These practices may then be said to have a cumulative effect, which makes them all the more valuable in helping towards the general control of body and mind.

But what is of still greater importance as far as Frater V.I.O. was concerned, they evidently had the effect—heightened perhaps by a letter from his Neophyte—of causing him to make a fresh and more determined effort to perform the Mystical Exercises for a definite period and with regularity, according to his original A .·. A .·. instructions. From January 30th, 1911, to April 30th of that year, he kept a scientifically tabulated diary and during the prescribed three months he never missed a day in the performance of his appointed task.

His results, during this period, were perhaps not of a very startling nature, but, as any true Student learns, it is the long and continued "grind," the determined effort to carry out the work in hand or task set, in spite of every obstacle that may arise, that really counts when it comes to lasting results. It is the Will that needs training, and the accomplishment of such work, particularly if uninteresting and tedious in itself, goes far towards that end.

Jan. 30th, 1911. Letter from Frater P.A. his Neophyte. From this letter he learned that many changes had transpired since he left England, and among them that Frater P.A. had severed his connection with the Outer Order, but was willing to continue in charge of him.

Feb. 5th. He wondered if Frater P.A. had only told him this as a test. It must be remembered that all this while he had worked on alone, and had had no news to speak of, and this he attributed to his own failure to carry out his task in detail. In this he was no doubt right to a great extent, for unless any Probationer does what he is instructed, he can expect no further help, which would only mean that the Master concurred in his laziness or weakness.

March 6th, 1911. Up to this time, although he had done the exercises regularly no particular result had occurred, and we find this note: "I do not really look for any results now, or expect any, since control of 'self' is the object of these exercises."

Now it is to be noted that when one really gets to a state when having worked one is content to continue to do so, expecting no results, one often obtains them. (Of course it's no use trying to fool oneself on these things, you can't get a result by just saying you don't care a damn.) Something of the sort seems to have happened in this case, as the following shows.

March 12th. During Lecture on "Parsifal," I felt illumination within which permeated my whole being, and I became *conscious once more* of the Truth of *my previous Illumination* which I had lost, as it were.

This entry is interesting. Illumination comes, and at the time there is no doubt about it. IT IS. Then, perhaps, life goes on much as before, except for the ever present remembrance of "Something that happened"; and, having nothing with which to compare it, that Something is difficult to describe or even to formulate. However, immediately one approaches another period one can recognise the symptoms, almost in advance, and the new Illumination is as it were added to the old, and there is fresh wonder and joy in both.

March 15th. I feel as if I were a highly strung musical instrument. My Will runs over the strings, causing complete and harmonious vibrations in my being, which seems to give forth at times an unformulated and therefore most delightful melody.

March 28th. How can I write it, how put into words the least idea of that which is unformed? Yet I will try while yet a vestige of the thought remains. I have conceived within my womb a child. Or is it that I have for the first time realized that I have a womb? Yet it is so, that "blank" within, into which I have projected my thoughts, and from which they have come forth again "living" is for a greater purpose. Can I not form therein a child that shall be MYSELF made from the highest ideals, the essence of my pains, refined and purified, freed from dross by the living fire? This life of Service must be lived till I am "selfless" in all that I knew as myself; but all the time will not my "child" be growing within me, composed of finer materials? And by complete union therwith . . . I cannot formulate any more now.

This entry indicates a recognition of the "formulation of the negative in the ego" which shall eventually destroy it. Is it not written in *Liber LXV* "As an acid eats into steel, and as a cancer utterly corrupts the body, so am I unto the spirit of Man. I shall not rest until I have destroyed it utterly"?

Sunday, April 2nd. [Fra V.I.O.'s 25th Birthday.] During practice I had a distinct consciousness of the "centre of consciousness" being not "within" as usual, but above head.

April 3rd. I alternate between a state of "enjoying any task or position because it is the first that comes to hand and therefore the simplest and best course of action," and "a feeling of absolute mental torture caused by the necessity of existing at all." The first appears to give the chance of continually "enlarging" until one becomes That which I can "consciously be" for a short period at a time, and the other seems to lead to annihilation. Probably the multiplication of one state by the other is the solution. (Crowley's $0 \times \infty$.)

Sat., April 8th. During the last three days have gradually been nearing another "climax" which reached, shall I say, its height on Saturday, when I arrived at a state of Illumination which was, as it were "added to my previous state." I seized a scrap of paper and wrote "Amid all the complications and perplexity there remains, back of all, the Will. The Will to Be. The Will to Be Nothing, which is the only state inconceivable to the mind. The old God willed to be something, and the Universe appeared; The New God wills to be Nothing and becomes ? ? ? ? ?" After writing the foregoing, there was a state of bliss the reflection of which was caught by the body. So joyful it became that it whirled round in a mad dance, and was filled with music. It was stifled by the confines of the room; but "I" was Free, so it couldn't matter much. (This is the second experience of rhythm filling the body, and causing it to whirl and dance in order to find expression somehow.)

April 9th. Started to read about 8:30 this morning. Sometime during morning lost idea of "ego" to realize All as Self. (Left notes for a couple of hours.) I find terrible difficulty in expressing the slightest idea of that which occurred during this state, yet it would seem of importance to do the best I can. That *there is no soul* struck me as a horrible blank. That *I do not, and never have existed as "I"* comes as a wonderful realization while the consciousness of the unreality of the "I" lasts. With the loss of "the ego" comes the consciousness that the whole universe of things and people is but a part of the State then arrived at. That if this little body dies, existence still remains in all the other part of the Universe and therefore the change called Death, occurring in different atoms, all the time, makes no difference. Is there any reason why one should not look upon every thing and everybody as parts of Oneself, since one is equally willing to allow any other body to consider you as a part of their imagination only? It would seem that one tiny part—self—has been fondly cherished, while in reality that tiny part is but a reflex of the Whole which is really You, but even this state must in the end give way before the Power of Nothing.

April 16th, 8:30 A.M. Finished reading *The Life of Buddha,* and then, lying down, composed myself for Meditation. Breathed regularly and deeply for a time, afterwards stopping all entries two or three times. (Shanmukhi Mudra.) Presently I passed into a state which was practically desireless. I could feel the Goal, but the wish to help others made it impossible to Become the State I contemplated. After this, I was surprised, on letting all breath out of the body, to feel a sudden lightness, as if I were about to float. This being unexpected, caused me to turn my thoughts to the body, after which, although I tried, I could not get back to the previous state. I estimate that I remained in the condition mentioned for over an hour, as it was 12 o'c. when I looked at the time. In fact, it may have been nearer two hours.

The above meditation left Frater V.I.O. with a feeling of "Nearly but not Quite." He had, to some extent, gazed at the Goal of Nothingness, but had failed to Become that Goal. The following day there is despondency and dissatisfaction. On April 22nd reason again holds sway, and he tries to use it to discover just where he is, of course without success, since Reason can never explain that which is Beyond Reason. I think at this point he also began to make another grave error; he tried to compare his experiences with those of *John St. John,* with the result that, later on, when he undertook a Retirement, that of J. St. J. subconsciously influenced him to a great extent, although he would not and could not have admitted it at the time. In these things one must be Oneself, not try to be another. His entry of April 22 is a long one, and I quote it in part.

I wish I could express myself better. On reading *J. St. J.* again I find that I can comprehend it ever so much better than when I first read it some three months after its publication. Then, it seemed like a dream of the far distant future; now, many parts seem like records of my own experiences, only expressed infinitely better than I have been able to put them. Now, of what value are the experiences I have gained? Why is the state of Oneness with Adonai not lasting, or rather, is it possible to remain always conscious of that State? How is it when reading an account like J. St. John's that I *know* what he is talking about, and can *feel* with him the difficulty of putting these things into words? I could not have *realized* this a year ago, before I entered into certain states of which I cannot gauge the value at all, while in normal consciousness. There is no Doubt Then. But how may I be Sure always? I will fetch *The Equinox*, and put down the points as they come to me. Let me quote page 87. "Well, one thing I got (again!) that is that when all is said and done I am that I am, all these thoughts of mine, angels and devils both, are only fleeting moods of me. The one true self of me is Adonai. Simple! Yet I cannot remain in that simplicity." I can realize that state perfectly, but I am not a Magician, I know little or nothing of Ceremonial Magick, except from reading; my results have not been accompanied by visions. What results I have obtained have been in the nature of becoming the thing itself, not seeing it. However, to pass on: Is the idea of coming back to help others (see Sun. Apr. 16) only a form of the Dweller on the Threshold and caused through *fear* of annihilation or madness? Or is it a concession to my own weakness, a pandering to my "self" because I am really nowhere near ready to hurl myself into the Gulf, instead of which I come back to normal consciousness, and try and make myself believe I have "given up" what I "could not get" for the sake of "others" which do not exist at the time (for me)? This is certainly a difficult one to tackle; I am entering it so as to try and formulate the proposition clearly. Now, the doubt enters my mind, that I have only put it down in order to *appear honest* to Fra. P.A., or anyone who may read this record. NO..... The foregoing thought seems to have a parallel in *J. St. J.* Again on page 96 "I must attain or . . . an end to J. St. J." seems similar to the state arrived at one Sept. 5, 1910, when I determined to ask the last WHY? and afterwards entered into Peace. On page 133 he says "subtly, simply, imperceptibly gliding I passed away into nothing. . . . I felt the interior trembling kindle itself into a kiss . . . also I was given to enjoy the subtle Presence of my Lord interiorly during the whole of the twelfth day. But he withdrew Himself . . . yet leaving a comfort not to be told, a Peace . . . The Peace." Yes, with me also the Peace has remained, but sometimes I cannot connect myself with It, or fail to do so, being led away by Maya. Then comes the entry of the Thirteenth Day: "Being entered into the Silence let me abide in the Silence. Amen." And here I am puzzled. Either J. St. J. attained permanently to a State such that he was never again annoyed by the silly mistake of identifying Himself with the body, or he did not.[3] But after all, what has that to do with V.I.O.? It has certainly nothing to

3. He had finished his immediate work, and went back into the world, as per *Liber VII*, II: 51–53, bestowing on himself this Benediction as he did so.—O.M.

do with C.S.J. But how do I stand? This seems to be the position.
While in normal consciousness I know that I (or Not I) am ever
in the state of which I sometimes catch the reflection when I
realize that I am *not* I. There, that is the clearest original thought
I have expressed this afternoon, and bad at that. Of course, I
am really quite content, it is only when I begin to think and reason
about things that I begin to become discontented. It's about time
I shut up.

And on April 30th the three months prescribed by his
Neophyte came to an end. He writes: "I feel they have
been well spent, and that I have gained a more certain
control of my body and mind, but realize *how much is*
needed before . . . $0 \times \infty$. Peace unto all beings. Amen."

Section IV
April 30th, 1911, to October 13th, 1912

Frater V.I.O. next experienced a state of "Dryness"
such as almost invariably follows a partial success. On
Sunday, May 7th he writes:

I have not made an entry in this record for a whole week. I seem
to be losing control, and my diary, lying untouched in my drawer,
is becoming like a horrible fiend. It worries me when I do not
enter it; and yet it requires a great effort even to touch it or take
it out, while to enter it daily appears an almost superhuman task.
Why is this? I have done exercises this week as usual, but a little
earlier than previously, because I have to be at the office by
8:30 A.M. instead of nine o'c. as heretofore. I think Fra. P.A.
might write to me. I feel that he is testing me, and have tried to
hold to that idea. I know that *really* it does not matter, but I am
weak yet, and should so like a little friendly push and a few words
of advice. I feel like dropping it all for a time; but that is perhaps
the very thing that is so difficult, in fact, the whole trick! O dear,
I am certainly having a spell of "dryness." But I will plod on,
On, ON, and in, In, IN. O for one kiss, or the echo of a Kiss,
My Lord Adonai. I yearn for Thee, I am Parched for Thee. Let
me be utterly consumed in Thee! Amen.

Saturday, June 10, 1911. Tonight I must write an entry. I MUST. And it is time. Why have I not done so before? Because I have experienced a "dryness" for the last month, and have made no definite effort to overcome it, but have just kept a firm hold on the little atom of real Knowledge I have obtained, & setting my face still towards the East, have plodded on with this material existence and the office work I have undertaken. I have experienced an incessant yearning for that "Something" or "Nothing" of which a glimpse had been vouchsafed unto me, and *Waited*. Maybe I should have *Worked and waited*, but I did not. I have not heard from Frater P.A. yet, but I wrote again during the month, saying I wanted to do something to help others a little, and asking if he could spare time to advise me on that score. To-day, I received *The Equinox* ordered last April. It had been sent to my brother's Club and had been lying there for a month, and all the while I had been waiting and hoping for its arrival. Then, when hope was about dead, I obtained a trace of it. It came as a drink of sweet nectar to a thirsty pilgrim, and it is wonderful how much better I feel. The note *re* Neophytes and Probationers has set me at rest about the silence of Fra P.A.; and confirms, what all the while I have suspected, that his delay in answering is a test. This confirmation is cheering, however hard the trial may have been, in so far as I had made up my mind to work on, whether he writes or not, and had got quite used to the idea of having to work out my own Path, without outside aid or encouragement.

He was also pleased to find some of his own experiments more or less confirmed in *Liber HHH* of which he writes:

M.M.M. 2, "mentions the breath playing upon the skin, etc." I have experienced this, and asked Fra P.A. for instructions thereon. Sometimes, after hard breathing, I have been filled with the sensation. I think I understand the "lightning flash," but shall experiment. My present knowledge is more as a sheet of summer lightning. The minute point of light has often appeared to me, and I had come to the conclusion that it should be held in the zenith. The radiating cone, I have not experienced. II. A.A.A. The idea of considering one's own death is mentioned. This occurred to me and was carried out before my first Illumination;

this serves as a confirmation that I was on the right track. I should have no doubt mentioned these meditations more fully at the time.[4] I have often wondered *how* I got into the state I then experienced, and this copy of *The Equinox* has revived the memory and gives instruction for obtaining, no doubt, a very much fuller result, only I shall have to work with a big W.

June 12, 1911. On Saturday night, in bed I attempted "thinking backwards" and successfully managed two days, with no breaks in the first day, and practically none for the day before, except a few little incidents during office hours in the morning. When I came to thoughts on waking of Saturday morning and got to the "blank" I experienced some mental visions and "telephone-cross voices," but cannot say if they were connected with any dream; then suddenly I found myself lying in bed with the last thoughts of the previous night in mind. Yesterday, I read the article on the subject (Training of the Mind) carefully, also learnt the formula of the four great meditations on Love, Pity, Happiness and Indifference. At night, I again attempted "thinking backwards," but experienced rather more difficulty as conditions were bad. However, once started, I got back through Sunday and very nearly, if not quite as fully, over the two previous days; then, having got into the swing, I roughly attempted a short and incomplete review of my whole life, which although brief, was much fuller than I expected. I remembered things connected with early childhood quite accurately, but of course not with full connections. Then something occurred that I really did not expect, and only later trials will prove if it was an illusion or not. Having tried hard to pierce the blank, back of all, I had a sudden clear sensation of lying on a bed with people around, and in particular an elderly man in black velvet and knee breeches, whom I at once felt was my Tutor, leaning over me. The ideas that came with this were that I was quite young, and had some disease like consumption, that the family was wealthy, and the house a Country Residence. These impressions were very real and quite unexpected, but as I used to have a dread of consumption, and still young, and meditation took place lying down, it would seem that very little imagination would make up the rest. However, I mention it, as the experience was different from anything I can previously remember.

4. Observe how the least slackness in writing up the Record avenges itself. The Record is both chart and log to the bold Sea-Captains of The Voyage Marvelous!

July 8th, 1911. About a fortnight ago, I received a letter from Frater P.A.[5] in answer to my previous two. I was pleased to hear from him, but he gave me a good talking to, also some new instructions. He wanted to know, what I meant by making a claim to having attained Samadhi, or something very like it, in August last, and then shortly afterwards started cutting my arm, etc. I have not answered it yet, but this much for reference: (1) I never mentioned Samadhi, nor can I remember claiming to have attained it. (2) I did attain a state of consciousness which has had a lasting effect upon my life and made my viewpoint entirely different from that time. (3) The language I used to describe the state, came perfectly naturally to me, as the most convenient to describe a state foreign to any previous experience. (4) I might have used language of a higher plane than I was on, but I don't see why. (5) I started control of body some months later when I had in some measure lost the complete recollection of the state, or rather when it was little more than a recollection, also when I first saw picture of man's arm in *The Equinox*, I rather dreaded to cut mine, so thought it best to carry out exercise and get over bodily dread of a little pain. I did so and am not sorry.

This letter from Fra P. A. giving new practice, etc., combined with some considerable dissatisfaction on Frater V.I.O.'s part, regarding his present state, caused him to undertake another regular spell of work for 32 days, after which he seems to have recorded very little

5. Frater P.A. was not a Neophyte, but had been appointed to receive other Probationers for administrative convenience. This was a plain breach of the regulations of the Order, and the result was this comic letter. Frater P.A. was apparently under the impression that as soon as any one happened along into Samadhi, he was to yawn his "Nunc dimittis."

This incident should be a warning to all those in charge of authority that they must in no wise vary the strict instructions of the Order, however obvious may appear the advantages of doing so.

The result of Frater P.A.'s presumption in trying to train Frater V.I.O., instead of pressing on to the mark of his own high calling, was that he simply dropped out of the Order altogether, leaving himself as a memorial only this ridiculous episode, in which he appears as a small boy who should have hooked a tarpon when he was fishing for catfish.

Had he adhered to the rules of the Order, attended solely to his own business, and forwarded V.I.O.'s record to his superiors, who were competent to interpret it, we should not have had this excellent example of the results of presumption and folly to guide us for the future, and to enliven our perusal of the record of our conscientious V.I.O. with a touch of timely merriment.—O.M.

until March 25 in the following year, viz., 1912. He then experimented with SSS section of *Liber HHH*, from *The Equinox*, vol. V and obtained automatic rigidity. He writes: "(1) Brain became charged with electric fluid or Prana, in fact whole face and hands became as if connected with an electric battery, also brain seemed luminous but void. (2) Could not awaken spine from 'yoni'; but, after persisting, the part just below small of back became enlivened, then under ribs, then breast and nape of neck. The current became very strong and almost unbearable. Whole body became perfectly and automatically rigid. Hands seemed to feel gnarled and misshapen, contorted by the force in them (I noticed this as a side issue). Feet also became filled with life, etc." He had had some experience with Pranic Currents in his body before, in fact in 1910, but never so fully and completely. He then reported this, and his general progress, to Fra P.A.

In July, he received a letter from Fra P.A., saying that he had now arrived at a stage when he might undertake an Operation for the Invocation of Adonai,[6] which would require six weeks' work, the last twelve days of which must be in complete Retirement. At first he could see no possible way to undertake this, owing to, (1) Family Affairs, (2) Office work, (3) Lack of money. He determined however to go ahead in spite of apparent obstacles, and duly made a start at Midnight, August 31. From that time until September 18th he was occupied by the Preparatory work, and from Midnight September 18th to Midnight September 30th by the Purity Section. October 1st to October 12th Proper Retirement, and on October 12th Invocation of Holy Guardian Angel. All this meant a great deal of work and trouble, and much new

6. No man has the right to make the slightest suggestion to another as to when he should or should not undertake this critical and central Operation. To interfere in any way between a man and his Holy Guardian Angel is the most intolerable presumption.—O.M.

experience gained, but was on the whole a failure, though a Step on the Path. During this retirement he cut a Wand, as a Symbol not of his will but of the Will of Adonai in him. It would be hardly right to say that this Magical Retirement produced no results, though it may not have produced the One Desired Result. By the time a man has made 671 entries in his Magical Record (as Frater V.I.O. did during those six weeks) and each of those entries has a direct bearing on the matter in hand, he is bound to have produced a state of mind somewhat different from normal consciousness. (It is interesting to note that 671, by a curious coincidence, is the numeration of Adonai, spelt in full, the Central idea of the Invocation.)

We shall not enter into the details of the various practices he performed during this period, but we may mention, for the sake of completeness, a few fragments recorded during the last few days of the Retirement.

October 9, 9:6 P.M. (This was the 9th day of Section C, and the 39th day of the complete Operation.)

The "state" is getting more and more difficult to describe, in fact I don't know what to make of it. I might almost say I feel "normal"; and yet there is a subtle difference. There is (I think) an entire absence of fear, worry, disgust, joy, sorrow, pain, or any of the old states, and this seems to be a condition of *calm observation* without any desire to criticise anything. I suppose, as a matter of fact, it is a state of equilibrium. I think I have it. It is the empty shrine awaiting the in-dwelling of the God.

10 P.M. I experienced another peculiar state just now. Having closed my eyes for a few moments (concentrating), I thought I would try and think backwards over the last few things I had been doing, but found, try as I would, I could not think of things done *even a moment before*. All was the "present peculiar experience," and there was no getting away from it. The concentration acted just like a magnet, and became automatic. Again, on trying to look back over this retirement, it appears as a "Single

state of consciousness," not as a number of events. I should really have to read my diary if I wanted to know any details in succession just now.

At the end of the 10th day of this Section C and the beginning of the 11th day I think the true climax of the Operation took place, for he writes:

Oct. 11, 12:30. So did the day start and I knelt at the altar from 12 Midnight until 12:28. During this time did my Lord Adonai begin to manifest within me, so that my being was wrapped away in bliss ineffable. And my body was filled with rapture of His coming until the cry burst from my lips "My Lord and my God." There are no words to describe Thee, my Beloved, though I yet tremble with the joy of Thy presence, yet do I feel that this is but the beginning of the reflection of Thee. O God, wrap me utterly away, beyond even this Bliss. Let me be utterly consumed in Thine Essence. Amen.

However, on The DAY, the 12th of October, when he came actually to use his Invocation (prepared and illuminated during his retirement) expecting the Result might occur, he writes as follows:

At precisely 6:50 I entered the Temple, lit the incense and robed. All being in order I knelt in prayer and at 7 P.M. I arose and performed the Banishing Ritual of the Pentagram, then, taking the ritual in my left hand and raising the wand in my right, I slowly and clearly read the Oath and the Invocation. Afterwards, I was impressed to make a certain Sign with the wand. And the Word that came to me was . . . Kneeling, I felt very calm, and I waited . . . afterwards, according to my understanding, I turned off the light, leaving only the lamp of olive Oil, and I lay down upon the place prepared and waited . . . and all was very dark and still, with a feeling of absolute calm and control, and I waited . . . And nothing happened. Then something seemed to tell me to get up and to kneel again at the altar, yet I waited, but presently I arose and stood at the altar, and I felt "I am that I am"; but there seemed not much joy in the thought, and yet, I knew that I had done all, even the least thing, to the best of mine understanding and ability. . . . And it began to dawn upon me that I had failed, but where and how, I know not.

I have been dazzled with no illusionary success, I have overcome the fear of failure, and now, even as a tired warrior, I will go back into the world—and STRIVE.

The Next day. Chaos. Reason is quite inadequate to solve the problem. Here followeth a certain passage from Ezekiel.

"Son of man, behold, I take away from thee the desire of thine eyes with a stroke: yet neither shalt thou mourn nor weep, neither shalt thy tears run down. Forbear to cry, make no mourning for the dead, bind the tire of thine head upon thee, and put on thy shoes upon thy feet, and cover not thy lips, and eat not the bread of men. So I spake unto the people in the morning; and at even my wife died: and I did in the morning as I was commanded. And the people said unto me: Wilt thou not tell us what these things are to us, that thou doest so? Then I answered them. The word of the Lord came unto me saying: Speak unto the house of Israel: Thus saith the Lord God . . . Ezekiel is unto you a sign: according to all that he hath done, shall ye do; and when this cometh, ye shall know that I am the Lord. Also, son of man, shall it not be in the day when I take from them their strength, the joy of their glory, the desire of their eyes, and that whereon they set their minds . . . In that day shall thy mouth be opened . . . and thou shalt speak . . . and thou shalt be a sign unto them, and they shall know that I am the Lord." Amen.

A last note: TRUTH must ever be One. Whatever I expected, I found not. But why should I grieve because of having exposed some of my illusions? I have held to the truth, and the Truth remains, for the Truth is ever One, yea, the Truth is Ever One. Amen.

Section V

January 1st, 1913, to December 31st, 1913

We must now pass on to Fra V.I.O.'s diary for the year 1913, E.V. I can find no written records of the period between October 13th, 1912, when he finished the Retirement, and March 2nd, 1913, when he again began to keep a regular summary of his work. On that date he writes:

During the last few days some important events have taken place. First however I must mention that I have heard nothing from Frater P.A. since the retirement except a P.C. to say that he had received my record. On ... I received a letter dated in London, Jan. 10th, from the Chancellor of A ∴ . A ∴ ., asking the results of my work since I became a Probationer. Answered same on Jan. 26th, and was surprised and pleased on Feb. 26th, to receive a reply passing me to the Grade of Neophyte, followed by the necessary documents. Answered this on Feb. 28th.

This letter from the Chancellor of A ∴ . A ∴ . passing Frater V.I.O. to the grade of Neophyte, contained the following passage, which is important, in the light of later events: "We wish our Body to be a Body of Servants of Humanity. A time will come when you will obtain the experience of the 14th Aethyr. You will become a Master of the Temple. That experience must be followed by that of the 13th Aethyr, in which, the Master, wholly casting aside all ideas of personal attainment, busies himself exclusively with the care of others."

The year 1913 was an important one for Frater V.I.O. in many ways. For one thing, it was during this period that he was forced to stand alone, and to rely upon himself and his own judgment of what was the right course of action for the governance of his life and the solution of his family difficulties as well as his occult problems. Hitherto, as before remarked, he had been under the guidance of one upon whom he had looked as his Neophyte, and in whom he had placed the utmost confidence. He now found himself in one of the most trying situations that had up to that time been his lot to cope with, viz.: that he must choose between the continuance of that guidance, and the regular course of training mapped out in the Outer Order of the A ∴ A ∴. He must either resign the grade of Neophyte just conferred upon him, severing his connection with the Outer Order, or cease to work under Frater P.A. altogether. The reasons for this cannot be dealt with fully in this place, nor would they be of the slightest interest to our readers. Suffice it to say that Frater V.I.O. had pledged himself to work on certain lines for six months and that these lines had been laid down by Frater P.A. His duty was then fairly clear, so he practically severed himself from obtaining guidance from either his old Neophyte or his newly appointed Zelator, until that period of work, to which he felt bound by his own oath to himself, was over, and at the end of that time, having worked hard and well, Those who were guiding and directing his life made the way clear for him, and he found himself in a position to accept the instruction of the A ∴ A ∴, coming under the direct guidance of Frater O.M. This event must not be supposed to reflect in any way on Frater P.A. for whom he always felt and will feel great love and respect; the circumstances leading up to this change were outside the sphere of influence of Fra V.I.O. and the more difficult to judge owing to his isolation in Canada. With this brief allusion to the change in his occult affairs, we may pass on to a corresponding change in his material surroundings, for although he continued with his usual office work, he lived during the best part of this year under canvas in a small tent by the sea shore, necessitating some miles of walking every day, and throwing him a good deal more in touch with Nature than formerly; also the addition of a "little stranger" to his family had a marked effect on his home affairs, being as it were the key to the solution of certain problems that had been puzzling him in that direction.

During the period from March 2nd to September 4th,

when we might say he was working on alone, his record shows some 340 Meditation practices, mostly in the Asana known as the Dragon, the periods ranging from a few minutes to something over an hour, but most of them comparatively short, the average perhaps being twenty minutes.

After this there is a gap, during which he worked morning and evening most days, but made no further record till November 9, from which date to December 31 over eighty practices are recorded.

Of the details of all this early work it is not necessary to treat very fully, but since, on sending in his record at the end of the year, it was returned by Frater O.M. with various notes and comments of the greatest help and value to Fra V.I.O., I am selecting those passages so commented upon as likely to be of most interest and help to other students. The comments of Fra O.M. (in brackets) follow entries.

March 2, 1913. I have got a zeal for service since the retirement, wanted to take for new Motto "I aspire to serve" but cannot find Latin equivalent.

["Volo servare" would do. But a better idea is "I want to help" rather than "serve."—O.M.]

March 22. Feel sorry I missed exercise this morning through slackness.

[When you *detect* slackness, double the exercise, if it kills you. Sure cure!—O.M.]

March 25. Dragon Asana. Mantra A.M.P.H. 9:39 to 10:34 P.M.=55 mins, Breaks 14 to 18, mostly very slight. Interruptions none. Results: Dharana, got feeling on skin and automatic rigidity. Lost all personality most of the time, but only found this out by "break" which revived it. Brain soon took up Mantra automatically. Illumination in brain after a while. Towards the last saw some

visions of sea, &c. (very slight). Space and time annihilated during most of the practice. Good.
[Beginning good—end bad.—O.M.]

Mar. 30, 5:15 to 5:46 P.M.=31 Mins. Counted first seven breaks, then became concentrated and lost count. Interruptions. (1) A safety pin, falling on floor, made me start violently. (2) R. called. Results: Breath arose on skin and the "light" arose. Started to concentrate on spine. Towards the end started a sort of automatic chant of apparently senseless words. Have noticed before that when this occur, it leads to a kind of ecstasy. Had to leave off, as was called to tea by Ruby.
[Good, but a virtuous woman is above Rubies, and never calls holy men to tea.—O.M.]

Apr. 4. Control of Body. While at office kept left elbow at side for 3 hours. Wished to see if this would be quite easy and found I had no difficulty in remembering.
[Good: try something harder.—O.M.]

Apr. 6, 9:20–10 P.M. Dragon. This meditation was the best lately. Quickly felt the Prana gripping the body. Conceived the blackness of Understanding become penetrated by Wisdom. Brain became luminous. Body rigid. Tension passed and force concentrated at bridge of nose. Concentrated on Ajna. Personality gone. Tried to project consciousness straight up. Was suddenly interrupted by R. who was in bed just by my side. Hardly knew where I was for the moment and had to concentrate on body to regain normal.
[Too big a handicap, having anyone in the room.—O.M.]

Apr. 8, 9:25 to 10:11 P.M.=46 Mins. Dragon. The mind and seer alone remain. Turning back on the seer there seem intervals of blank. This is accompanied with no illumination or joy, and one almost wonders why one has gone so far to obtain this. Probably desire not entirely obliterated. Some disinclination to leave the state.
[This sounds better.—O.M.]

Apr. 13, 11:21–11:36 P.M. Dragon. A certain bliss arose at the

thought that I was but a little child of the Great Father. Joy. Joy.
[Yes: too emotional.—O.M.]

Apr. 19, 7:07 A.M. to 7:20 A.M. Not anything very definite. There
is a certain quality of bliss about these practices which is peculiar
to concentration but otherwise indescribable.
[This is bad. You do things well, and work hard; but your point
of view is all wrong. I feel a sort of sentimentality injuring your
scientific attitude.—O.M.]

April 20, 2:40–3:10 P.M. Having left home about 2:15 I climbed
up towards the mountain till I found a secluded spot; there I
knelt down and did breathing exercise. Felt Prana all over body.
Invoked Adonai and tried to unite with Him. A brilliant White
light filled sphere of consciousness. Arose as Adonai performed the
Ritual of Pentagram, then prayed aloud and fluently, trying to
unite consciousness with all Nature. Knelt again in Meditation,
and arose much strengthened and with a feeling of the Divine
Presence.
[This is excellent for a beginner. But remember—all these
divine illuminations are mere Breaks.—O.M.]
Note: I find more and more difficulty in remembering any
details of these practices the next day. Concentration was good.
In this instance at end of practice could not remember what time
I started, although I believe I am correct. I have thought several
times lately about this loss of memory. Is it a result, or is it a
fault?
[It's a good sign, as a rule.—O.M.]

May 9, 10:21–10:43 P.M. Dragon. Astral journey of no particulra
import. Cannot properly identify with image. Seem to see the
image while acting in it.
[This isn't as bad as it sounds. Don't worry, so long as the
Image is quite sure of itseef.—O.M.]
[This, by the way, would have been particularly helpful information, and if Fra. V.I.O. had had it at the time he might have
done a good many more Astral journeys. This lack of confidence
at first seems to hold back many Students who could otherwise
travel on the Astral quite successfully.—Ed.]
May 21, 8:45 to 9:34 P.M.=49 Mins. Thumbs in ears; first 25

mins in Dragon. Then lying flat on back. Cramp in left foot on change of position. After the loud sounds subsided, became concentrated on ringing sound in left ear. Mind became calmer, and I heard the sound of a little silver bell, very clear and sweet, struck a number of times. This still in left ear. Then heard sound of metallic throbbing (if I can use the term) very faintly in right ear. Mind must have been well concentrated as time passed quickly.

[Sounds rather good.—O.M.]

July 7. *Note.* This afternoon, while reclining in an easy chair, nearly fell asleep; instead, however, I concentrated for some while. On being asked by R. to go and do some little thing for her, I put hands over eyes before rising, and saw a light so peculiar that it is worth mentioning. It had the appearance of being three distinct things at once. Dead black, a beautiful night-sky-blue, but at the same time the very essence of it was *brilliant light.* Quite indescribable in words.

[Seems very good.—O.M.]

[It may be remarked that Fra. V.I.O. had occupied himself with the contemplation of the Stélé of Revealing, completed therefrom a Pantacle of Nuit, and had obtained a sigil for same, during this day. This peculiar light is stigmatically characteristic of the Stélé.—O.M.]

June 18th, 10:34 to 10:53 P.M.=19 mins. 14 mins Pranayama 10,20,20. Regular and easy. 5 Mins. Meditation. Mind cleared and became calm. It perhaps appears that little progress is made, and some slackness exists as regards exercises. The truth is, I more and more use the true essence. If a little worry occurs, automatically, I turn to That within which dissolves it at once and restores the balance. It is that NOTHING with which I come into closest contact during meditation, but It is ever present, and I recognize the fact. I believe it to be the true Stone of the Wise which turns everything to gold. I call it Adonai when I give it a name at all. Most often the mind slips into that state without reason or argument.

[Yes: it does appear that more time ought to be given to the Work. But the Progress is not bad for all that. However, I don't quite like the complacent feeling. Nothing replaces hard work. Somebody I know (or don't know) does more actual grind than he ever did. 24 full dress Magick ceremonies in the first 5 weeks of 1914, and about 2 hours every morning writing up the records. And in this please include 2 bad goes of influenza and bronchitis!— O.M.]

July 9, 7:20–7:24 A.M. Dragon. Rather bad. Tried to do practice outside in the rain, there being no room in the tent. *Note*: Man, wife and baby together with all one's earthly belongings in a tent 12′x10′ in wet weather, is certainly a record.

[I've been one of 5 big men in a tent 7′6x6′ in a hurricane blizzard on a glacier. But you win.—O.M.]

Aug. 8. *Note*. I begin to feel the fuller life again. These few pages of Edward Carpenter have acted like a draught of living water and revived me a great deal. I feel a secret Joy to-night. The unaccountable inner Joy which transforms everything and frees the soul from its shackles. All seems so good to-night, this simple life, the tent by the sea, the night air, the happy tired feeling after the day's work, the presence of my two dear ones, and all the dear ones of which I am a part, the presence of Adonai within and without. It is good to have lived for this.

[This is dreadful! You must not mistake "feeling good" for a mystic state.—O.M.]

Aug. 9, 9:59 to 10:26 P.M. During this meditation a certain magical understanding arose whereby it was easy to interpret any common object into a symbol of the Work.

[A bit better.—O.M.]

Aug. 18, 11:07 to 11:13 P.M. Even 6 mins is a difficulty now. When will the tide turn again!

[The tides are due to the pull of the Sun and Moon.—O.M.]

Aug. 19, 7:32 to 7:42 P.M. Slight feeling of Joy.

[Bother joy!—O.M.]

Aug. 25, 1:33 to 10:55 P.M. Changed my Asana once during practice and found I could move body without affecting the particular part which was in the calm state.

[Good.—O.M.]

Aug. 26. A quiet evening at home, for which I am grateful. It seems as if so little is entered in this diary and so much remains unsaid. How one longs sometimes to *express* things and thoughts and generally ends by some commonplace entry. I think to-night I will try a little more than usual. All this time I have been plodding on, having made up my mind to a course of action in accordance with my aspiration. Day after day I have continued until this round of existence has become almost a fixed habit. My times of meditation and practice have dwindled till they are somewhat short, but for all that, the main idea has never become clouded. I feel far more determined in every way than I did, although less certain of any fixed goal. I know also that I have problems to face, now, or in the future, but have learnt to keep doing what comes to hand, without wavering or despairing. I do not seem to have made much definite progress, yet there are signs which give me to understand that all is as it should be; perhaps I am more in tune and so do not notice such vivid changes. I have found nature very fair and beautiful, this summer. I have got to love Her so much more than formerly. Then again, I have mastered Her a little more; I have learnt more of swimming, climbing, walking and other exercises through daily practice. I have made new friends, have learnt from them and taught them in return. All this, in spite of the limited existence of living in a tiny tent and often being very hard up. The power to retreat into that part of me which is Peace, free from all strife, remains with me. To be an onlooker at my thoughts and actions and remain the while in perfect rest—very seldom disturbed by outside influences—this is indeed something. Another important thing I would mention. I have an intense longing for more Love, a sort of unsatisfied craving to embrace people, particularly women, and sometimes natural things (this was not meant for sarcasm) such as the earth, the grass, etc. I do not think I expect and ask the love of others so much as I feel the need of entire freedom to love without barrier or restraint; but always there seems a something holding me back, invisible, formless, but of great strength, so that I yearn and open my arms (as it were) but am not satisfied; and so I turn and direct it towards that formless vision of Adonai within. Maybe, some day a spark will fire it and it will break loose; & then?

[This sounds very good indeed.—O.M.]

Aug. 27. The most perfect peace I have experienced for a long time.

Sep. 1. This is the last day of the six months.

Nov. 9. Nearly two months since I made an entry. Will write down a few of the events that I remember during that time. Have done some slight morning and evening practice almost every day. Have occupied a fair amount of time in giving what instructions I can on occult matters to those who have requested information.

S. and L. have become sufficiently interested to apply for Studentship, and W. has at last written and asked *re* Probationership.

Have heard finally from Fra P.A. and answered his letter.

Nov. 26, 11:40 to 11:55 P.M. Meditation on Love. Commenced with sending Love to the six directions of space (See *Training of the Mind, The Equinox,* vol. 5). Became identified with Love to the exclusion of all other ideas. It is verily a dew which dissolves thought.

[Dangerous, though, for a beginner. Often means little more than the maudlin benevolence of one who has dined too well. Fill yourself with Love, and it will flow out of its own accord.—O.M.]

Nov. 27. Letter from Chancellor of A ∴ A ∴. Was glad to receive this, as it cleared up a point that had long troubled me. *Note*: This was the point *re* Astral journeys, mentioned before.

[This gave Fra. V.I.O. fresh confidence, and we find records of experiments at once.—Ed.]

Nov. 27, 11:6 to 11:28 P.M. Astral Journey. Rising on the Planes. Will try and recount this experience in detail as it was somewhat different from any previous experiment. After prayer, formulated astral enclosing body and began to rise. Tried to ascend Middle Pillar. Dark Blue, then more Purple. Presently found my astral body in a sort of open Temple Square with 4 pillars for corners, open sides and a high domed roof. In the centre of the floor was a circular basin of water. Someone said (of the water) "It is Thyself" (or thy mind). Could distinguish nothing for some time. Presently a star appeared in the centre of the pool, evidently reflected through a circular hole in centre of roof. Looking up, could not see this star from where I was standing on the step at front of Temple. Someone said: "Enter the water." Did so, finding it reached to the neck. Looked up, and could discern the star clearly. Someone said "You must travel up through the roof to the star." Did so, and discovered I was without clothes. Some time elapsed before I could get near the star, but on doing so I was whirled round it three times and alighted. Then became conscious that the body had given place to a flame only. Ascended as a flame into the air. Became dimly conscious that the flame was in the heart of a larger body. Strove still to rise, but came to blackness. Returned and disrobed. Gave thanks and entered diary.

[This is very good indeed, as a start. It should be repeated with ever-increasing persistence. The time occupied tells me its faults more than the text. A good "rising" should take 1? to ½ hours.— O.M.]

Nov. 28, 11:5 to 11:27 P.M. Astral Journey.

Drew, with wand, in front of me, a circle (three times round) and formed astral in that. Rose to a great height. Suddenly, as it were, a rope flashed round me and fell, forming a spiral, ever widening, at the top of which I sat. Stood up on this, only to fall, down, down, down, not quite vertically into the water. Rising again, and striking out, I after a short while perceived a boat, something like a gondola, and swam towards it. It was rowed by a dark-skinned man, old and wrinkled, whom I at first thought to be an Indian. As I reached the boat and put my hand on the side, it seemed as if he would strike at me with his oar, but no, he grinned, and I drew myself into the boat and sat in the fore part, which was high and covered by a sort of hood. Presently, it struck me that the man was not living but dead. Death. We then drifted in a mist, and all became blank for a while; the memory of boat, man and self, *were all but lost.* When the mist cleared I realized that the man was no longer there, and I myself guided the boat. Coming back out of the mist the waters were blue and no longer black, and I realized that day was breaking. Gradually I watched the Sunrise, and set the boat in that direction, rowing so as to keep my face to the Sun. It seemed like a Portal; but, keeping on, it presently rose, and by the time it was getting high in the heavens I perceived a fair City ahead. Domes, Minarets, etc. Arriving there, I for the first time noticed I was dark skinned and clad in a loincloth. Landing, I was surrounded with men in an Eastern costume, Arabs or Turks I thought. One old man took me by the hand, I made the sign of the Pentagram over him, but he smiled and said "Come along, it's all right," and led me along a street paved with cobbles, the houses of which overhung, till we reached a sort of a mosque. Entering this he led me to the altar, which was supported by brackets from the wall, and above which was a beautiful stained window. At the sides were thin columns and sort of boxes, similar to theatre boxes. We knelt at the altar; and he took my hand and said: "Raise your consciousness." I perceived a star and crescent above me, and a cross dimly formulated in the background. After this, the astral seemed to coincide with the body; but consciousness of the astral surroundings was still clear. Continued to raise consciousness, and to send out thoughts of Love. Perceived around me innumerable streams of thought, interlacing and like a net-work, and when the Love-thought was sent out, the whole net sparkled, as with little specks of gold. Continued in this thought for some minutes, and gradually returned to normal. Gave thanks and entered diary.

[Very nearly in serious trouble, my young and rash friend! It seems that you must go up well outside earth-attraction if you wish to get good astrals. It sounds Sunday-school-talk, and I can give no reason. But I've tried repeatedly going horizontally and downwards, always with the same result. Gross and hostile things are below, pure beings above. The vision is good enough for what it is; it is clear and coherent. But I see no trace of scientific method in directing the vision. I explain further in the general comment.—O.M.]

About this time Frater V.I.O. appears to have been studying Jnana Yoga. There is a simple entry on November 30th, "THOU ART THAT," without any attempt at comment, and on the following day "Ditto, but in a less degree." On December 4 we find this entry:

The reading of "Jnana Yoga" revives very clearly the state of Unity produced by the practice of Raja Yoga. There is a clearer conception, and the feeling of being very near the Truth. N.B. During meditation the Light above head was beginning to envelope the mind, but was disturbed by R. calling me to come to bed.

[R. must be told not to call you to come to bed. The feeling that she may possibly do so is enough to prevent concentration. Also, as a general rule, it's very bad to sleep with another person in the room.—O.M.]

Dec. 5th. More and More realization of the One Truth. THOU ART THAT. Got some idea that there was only one "plane" in reality, not many.

Dec. 6th, 11:22 A.M. Started Neti, Neti' again. (Very near, not quite. V.I.O.)

10:45 P.M.

Oh Thou Ever-present, Eternal Silence, wherein all vanishes and emerges clothed in Bliss. I Invoke Thee.

Oh Thou elusive Self of my self, Thou All, wherein all dissolves and becomes Thy Being. I invoke Thee.

Oh Thou Existence of Existences, Thou Knower of Knowledge, wherein knowledge of all else is lost. I Invoke Thee.

Oh Thou Bliss Absolute, Thou One without a second, Thou in Whom Time and Space no longer exist. I invoke Thee.

Oh Thou, who when I think of Thee art God, who when I cease to think of Thee art My self, may I be lost in THEE.

Yet never shall I be lost, for Thou Art, who art not.

Oh Beloved, I come to Thee when I realize that never have I *moved* through all Eternity.

Oh Thou, on Whom man looks through the senses, and sees as the world.

Oh Thou, on Whom man looks through the mind and sees as the world of thought.

Oh Thou on Whom man looks as Thyself and becomes Infinite Bliss, let there be no thought of separateness, for there is none other. Thou Art That.

If I call Thee a Point, Thou laughest, saying: "I am the Infinite Circle."

If I worship the Circle, Thou laughest, saying: "I am concealed in the Point."

Only if I claim Thee Wholly, may I define Thee. Then who cares, Aye or Nay?

If I attempt to name Thee, I lose Thee, Oh Thou Nameless

7. "Not this, not this!" a Hindoo phrase used in the practice of rejecting all thoughts as they arise.

unto Eternity. To Whom shall I reveal Thee, who wast never known but to Thyself?

Surely words are vain, O Thou who art beyond the Silence. Aum.

[This is very good.—O.M.]

Dec. 11th, 9:52–10:37 P.M. Meditation in Asana. Dragon as usual.

Took a few long breaths, filling the body and mind with Love, and then expelling it till it flowed through me. Used Mantra: "The Self is Love. That Self am I" first part of the time, afterwards changing to "The Self is THAT, that Self am I."

Eyes half closed, fixed on nose. Shut them about the middle of the meditation and turned them to Ajna. Very few invading thoughts.

Presently all became brilliant light, with which I became identified.

Realization of Oneness. No doubt remained that this was indeed the Union with the Higher Self. Then again arose the question "What about the Others when this state subsides again?" Then it seemed that a voice spoke clearly to the brain, saying: "Truly when united so thou art one with the Holy Guardian Angel that speaks unto thee now. Therefore worry no more about attaining. In future it is thy work to see that not only the *part* attain, but that other parts, those that are called 'others' in ordinary consciousness, realize the Oneness also." N. B. These are not the words, and do not properly express the meaning. The experience itself was in the nature of *realization* rather than in any language.

[Not at all bad.—O.M.]

Dec. 12. To-night, while walking, I thought that some time, when I can find the right person, it would be well to get him to record for me one of these experiences such as that of last night, during its occurrence; (1) providing I could speak without altering the state of consciousness; (2) providing I could find the necessary person.

[No good.—O.M.]

Dec. 15th, 11:50 to 12:9 P.M. Astral Journey.

On first trying to project astral it went rapidly off in a N.E. direction [Bad.— O.M.] then described a curve to the North and so round twice, and became normal again. Second attempt.

Enclosed astral in egg of light, sent it straight up. Egg opened; and I opened eyes in space. I saw above me a shining object, oblong in shape, and travelling to it, found it almost like a kite. Leaning upon it, I was carried backwards for some distance, during which time I watched a changing landscape below. Wishing to descend, I dropped towards the Earth, and found body supported by another. When near the ground, skimmed over the earth and eventually came to a dark gateway or tunnel. Walked into this and proceeded, lighted by a silver star on brow, till I arrived at a circular room at the end, lit by one candle placed on a round table at which sat an old white-bearded man writing in a book. I approached him, and said: "Why writest thou, Father?" and he replied "That those who read may live." (I seem to have asked him another question, but cannot remember what.) Then I said: "What writest thou, Father?" And he replied: "Death, always Death," And I said: "Show me thy writing, Father" and looking he wrote the word HARTHA. And I said "This is a mystery to me" so he pointed to it letter by letter and I tried to interpret it Qabalistically, but was not successful. It seemed that the value of the letters was 507. He said I should understand, and with that I left him and returned.

8 P.M., Dec. 16. Have just been working out the meaning of the word obtained last night. I then *thought* the value was 507="That which causes ferment" or 5 plus 7=12=He longed for, missed, etc. This shows how I went astray. I find however that the word actually adds to 607=Adam Primus. But 6 plus 7=13 Unity, Love, and The Tarot Trump is DEATH, and this is what he said he was writing. (Note Apr. 21, 1917. Ha=The Sun; tha=The Moon, as stated in the Hatha-Yoga Pradipika.)

[Well worked out, method good; but not much of a place to have reached. You should have got more of the book, too.—O.M.]

Dec. 18th. *Note.* There is one thing I had intended to mention before. Instead of sleeping deeply, as was my former habit, I have lately noticed quite a change in this respect. Sometimes, though resting, I retain consciousness most of the night. In this state I appear to think very much along the same lines as I do in ordinary waking consciousness. In the morning I have the ability to change from one state to the other quite easily, but on leaving the bed and becoming fully awakened I can seldom remember any particulars of what occurred during sleep.

[This sounds good, as if the Tamo-Guna were breaking up.— O.M.]

Dec. 19, 11:38. Prayer and Meditation. Felt "informed" by that Greater Self that Humility, Patience and Selflessness would bring the condition required. Dwelt for awhile in that Boundless Silence of which words can express nothing.

[Humility, like Pride, implies a self.—O.M.]

Dec. 26th, 11:3 to 11:20 P.M. Meditation. Gradually separating the Self from the body, mind, life, death, etc., till an entirely impersonal state resulted.

[These things don't mean much, as a rule. They are only what we call "reverie," a dulcet meandering of the mind.—O.M.]

Dec. 27th, 11:13 to 11:30 P.M. Meditation. After striving to unite consciousness completely with Adonai, the sphere of Consciousness widened out and became one with the Many; so that, when asking of the Self: "What am I? Who am I?" this no longer seemed an individual question, but to be taken up by many units in all parts of space, yet upon a formless plane. I rose higher and tried to unify all these; this resulted in an absolutely impersonal state which continued even after the meditation was over until about 12 o'clock. While it lasted it was distinctly different from any former experience, especially the earlier part.

[Not very good; seems too much like thinking.—O.M.]

Dec. 31, 11:30 to 11:46 P.M. L.B.R. Dragon. Meditation on Love.[8] Afterwards I imagined the dim figure of Nuith overshadowed the Universe. Amen. And now I will go out and wish R. and baby a Happy New Year.

A Summary Comment. By Fra O.M. 7°=4□

I think you are the real man, and will attain. You work hard and regularly, and keep the record well. And you have the Root of

8. [This sort of thing is all wrong. It isn't really meditation at all. You let your mind rove about, instead of pinning it down to a single, simple object. Samadhi never occurs in such conditions.—O.M.]

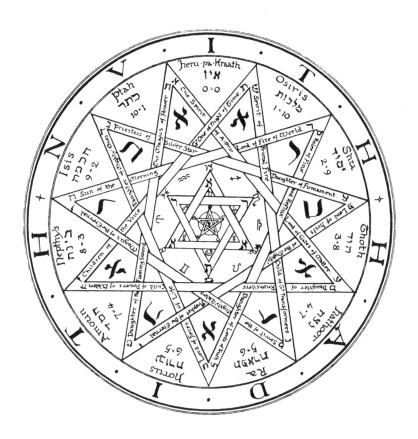

The Pantacle of Frater V. I. O.

This Pantacle is a symbolical map of the Universe, as understood
by Frater V. I. O. when a Neophyte of A . ·. A . ·., and offered by
him for the Examination of that Grade.

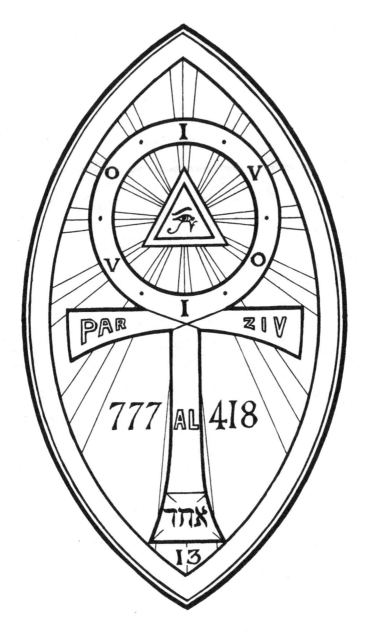

The Lamen of Frater V. I. O.

This Lamen is symbolical of the Master's Attainment, the Great Work which He brought to fulfilment.

the Matter in you. These are your dangers. (1) You are emotional. This is very bad, and must be got rid of. It's a form of Egoism, and leads to the Left-hand Path. You say: "I object to my wife being run over by a motor-car," and think you are stating an Eternal Truth. Now no elephant in Siam cares whether she is run over or not. Say then: "It is (relatively to V.I.O.) right that he should object, etc., etc." Use this analysis with all emotions. Don't allow yourself to think that your own point of view is the only one. Read *Liber LXV*, Cap. I: 32–40 and 57–61. This is extremely important: for one thing, if you fail to understand, you will go mad when you come to a certain Gate. (2) You are inclined to vagueness. This is evidently partly caused by the fog of emotion. Before you can pass to Zelator, you must know and rule the Astral Plane throughout. Astral journeys, however interesting and even splendid and illuminating, don't count unless they are willed. If you want to go to your office, and find yourself at the Town Hall instead, it's no excuse that the Town Hall has fine columns! You should drop all "Meditations on Love." What's the matter with Hate, anyway? From beyond the Abyss, they look as like each other as two new pennies. You really mean "Reflection on Love": "Jones' Night Thoughts": "Idle thoughts of an idle fellow." It's a soul-destroying, mind-fuddling practice. If indulged in, it will absolutely ruin all power of concentration.

Now here is your Examination for the Grade of Zelator.[9]

(*a*) Go through a door on which is engraved this figure and explain the figure in detail by means of your visions.

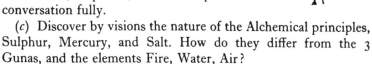

(*b*) Invoke Mercury and Hod, and travel till you meet the Unicorn mentioned in *Liber LXV*, Cap. III, verse 2. Report its conversation fully.

(*c*) Discover by visions the nature of the Alchemical principles, Sulphur, Mercury, and Salt. How do they differ from the 3 Gunas, and the elements Fire, Water, Air?

(*d*) Give an account of the sign Aquarius in the 4 Worlds, Assiah, Yetzirah, Briah, and Atziluth.

(*e*) Visit and describe fully the Qliphoth of Aries.

9. [This Examination is a subtle compliment, amounting almost to Flattery. It is a much harder paper than would be set in most cases.—O.M.]

(*f*) Visit Iophiel and Hismael, and report their appearance, mode of life, and conversation.

Observe. The A .˙. A .˙. work throughout is definite and directed. There is no room for a single loose thought.

(3) You must be perfectly stern and austere about the sanctity of the Work. You wouldn't allow your wife to come to the office and talk: you must make her respect your hour of work at home. Here I foresee trouble: with rarest exceptions a woman objects to a man doing anything of which she is not the centre. His business is only allowable because it provides for her. Herein no compromise is possible. You must be master or slave; and the truest kindness is to be master once and for all, whatever the cost.—O.M.

In this defile we must leave our Pilgrim for the present. He is about to confront the denizens of the Astral World, menacing or seducing in turn; and, following the bold Rosicrucian rule, he remains in the current of life, without the safeguard of an absolute external retirement and renunciation, such as is advocated by Eastern teachers. But in the Way of the A .˙. A .˙. externals are of less account than essentials, and V.I.O. was under the guidance and guardianship of an Order whose Omniscience is impeccable, and Its ward sure.

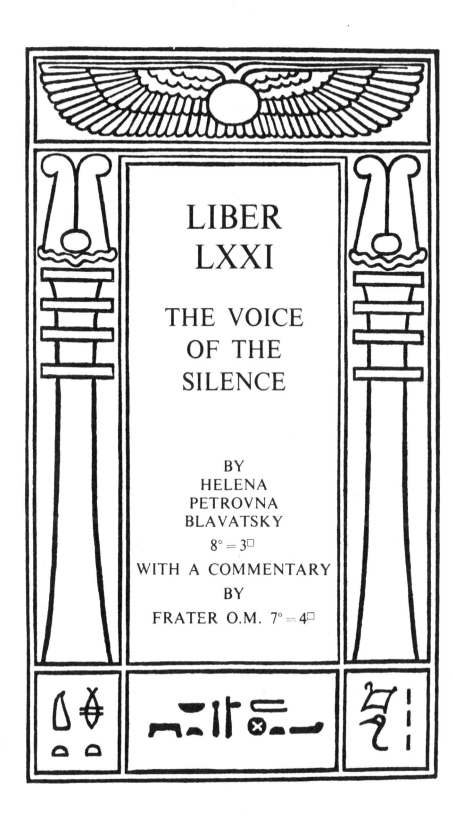

LIBER
LXXI

THE VOICE
OF THE
SILENCE

BY
HELENA
PETROVNA
BLAVATSKY

$8° = 3^{\square}$

WITH A COMMENTARY
BY
FRATER O.M. $7° = 4^{\square}$

A ∴ . A ∴. Publication in Class B

93	10° = 1□		
666	9° = 2□		Pro Coll.
777	8° = 3□		Summ.
D. D. S.	7° = 4□		
O. M.	7° = 4□		Pro Coll.
O. S. V.	6° = 5□		Int.
Parzival	5° = 6□		
V. N.	Praemonstrator		
P.	Imperator		Pro Coll.
Achad	Cancellarius		Ext.

THE VOICE
OF THE SILENCE

PREFATORY NOTE

Do what thou wilt shall be the whole of the Law.

It is not very difficult to write a book, if one chance to possess the necessary degree of Initiation, and the power of expression. It is infernally difficult to comment on such a Book. The principal reason for this is that every statement is true and untrue, alternately, as one advances upon the Path of the Wise. The question always arises: For what grade is this Book meant? To give one simple concrete example, it is stated in the third part of this treatise that Change is the great enemy. This is all very well as meaning that one ought to stick to one's job. But in another sense Change is the Great Friend. As it is marvelous well shewed forth by The Beast Himself in *Liber Aleph,* Love is the law, and Love is Change, by definition. Short of writing a separate interpretation suited for every grade, therefore, the commentator is in a bog of quandary which makes Flanders Mud seem like polished granite. He can only do his poor best, leaving it very much to the intelligence of each reader to get just what he needs. These remarks are peculiarly applicable to the present treatise; for the issues are presented in so confused a manner that one almost wonders whether Madame

Blavatsky was not a reincarnation of the Woman with the Issue of Blood familiar to readers of the gospels. It is astonishing and distressing to notice how the Lanoo, no matter what happens to him, soaring aloft like the Phang, and sailing gloriously through innumerable Gates of High Initiation, nevertheless keeps his original Point of View, like a Bourbon. He is always getting rid of Illusions, but, like the entourage of the Cardinal Lord Archbishop of Rheims after he cursed the thief, nobody seems one penny the worse—or the better.

Probably the best way to take the whole treatise is to assume that it is written for the absolute tyro, with a good deal between the lines for the more advanced mystic. This will excuse, to the mahatma-snob, a good deal of apparent triviality and crudity of standpoint. It is of course necessary for the commentator to point out just those things which the novice is not expected to see. He will have to shew mysteries in many grades, and each reader must glean his own wheat.

At the same time, the commentator has done a good deal to uproot some of the tares in the mind of the tyro aforesaid, which Madame Blavatsky was apparently content to let grow until the day of judgment. But that day is come since she wrote this Book; the New Aeon is here, and its Word is Do what thou wilt. It is certainly time to give the order: "Chautauqua est delenda."

Love is the law, love under will.

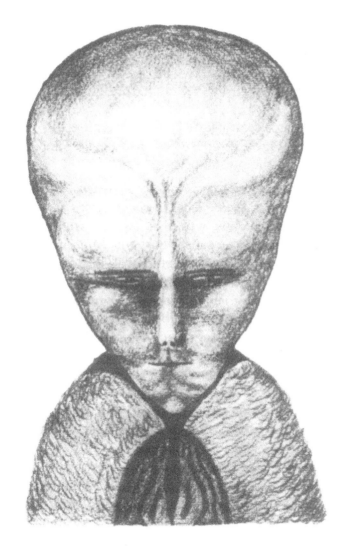

The Way

Lam is the Tibetan word for Way or Path, and Lama is He who
Goeth, the specific title of the Gods of Egypt, the Treader of the
Path, in Buddhistic phraseology. Its numerical value is 71, the
number of this book.

FRAGMENT I FROM THE
BOOK OF THE GOLDEN PRECEPTS

[Madame Blavatsky's notes are omitted in this edition, as they are diffuse, full of inaccuracies, and intended to mislead the presumptuous.—Ed.]

1. *These instructions are for those ignorant of the dangers of the lower Iddhi (magical powers).*

Do what thou wilt shall be the whole of the Law. Nothing less can satisfy than this Motion in your orbit.

It is important to reject any Iddhi of which you may become possessed. Firstly, because of the wasting of energy, which should rather be concentrated on further advance; and secondly, because Iddhi are in many cases so seductive that they lead the unwary to forget altogether the real purpose of their endeavours.

The Student must be prepared for temptations of the most extraordinary subtlety; as the Scriptures of the Christians mystically put it, in their queer but often illuminating jargon, the Devil can disguise himself as an Angel of Light.

A species of parenthesis is necessary thus early in this Comment. One must warn the reader that he is going to swim in very deep waters. To begin with, it is assumed throughout that the student is already familiar with at least the elements of Mysticism. True, you are supposed to be ignorant of the dangers of the lower Iddhi; but there are really quite a lot of people, even in Boston, who do not know that there are any Iddhi at all, low or high. However, one who has been assiduous with *Book 4,* by Frater Perdurabo, should have no difficulty so far as a general comprehension of the subject-matter of the book is concerned. Too ruddy a cheerfulness on the part of the assiduous one will however be premature, to say the least. For the fact is that this treatise does not contain an intelligible and coherent cosmogony. The unfortunate Lanoo is in the position of a sea captain who is furnished with the most elaborate and detailed sailing-instructions, but is not allowed to have the slightest idea of what port he is to make, still less given a chart of the Ocean. One finds oneself accordingly in a sort of "Childe Roland to the Dark Tower came" atmosphere. That poem of Browning owes much of its haunting charm to this very circumstance, that the reader is never told who Childe Roland is, or why he wants to get to the Dark Tower, or what he expects to find when he does get there. There is a skilfully constructed atmosphere of Giants, and Ogres, and Hunchbacks, and the rest of the apparatus of fairy tales; but there is no trace of the influence of Baedeker in the style. Now this is really very irritating to anybody who happens to be seriously concerned to get to that tower. I remember, as a boy, what misery I suffered over this poem. Had Browning been alive, I think I would have sought him out, so seriously did I take the Quest. The student of Blavatsky is equally handicapped. Fortunately, *Book 4,* Part III, comes to the rescue once more with a rough sketch of the Universe as it is conceived by Those who know it; and a regular investigation of that book, and the companion volumes ordered in the Curriculum of the A ∴ A ∴, fortified by steady persistence in practical personal exploration, will enable this Voice of the Silence to become a serious guide in some of the subtler obscurities which weigh upon the Eyelids of the Seeker.

2. *He who would hear the voice of Nâda, the "Soundless Sound," and comprehend it, he has to learn the nature of Dhâranâ (concentrated thought).*

The voice of Nada is very soon heard by the beginner, especially during the practice of Pranayama (control of breath-force). At first it resembles distant surf, though in the adept it is more like the twittering of innumerable nightingales; but this sound is premonitory, as it were, the veil of more distinct and articulate sounds which come later. It corresponds in hearing to that dark veil which is seen when the eyes are closed, although in this case a certain degree of progress is necessary before anything at all is heard.

3. *Having become indifferent to objects of perception, the pupil must seek out the Râjah (king) of the senses, the Thought-Producer, he [sic] who awakes illusion.*

The word "indifferent" here implies 'able to shut out.' The Rajah referred to is in that spot whence thoughts spring. He turns out ultimately to be Mayan, the great Magician described in the 3rd Aethyr. (See *The Equinox*, vol. I, no. 5, Supplement.) Let the Student notice that in his early meditations, all his thoughts will be under the Tamo-Guna, the principle of Inertia and Darkness. When he has destroyed all those, he will be under the dominion of an entirely new set of the type of Rajo-Guna, the principle of Activity, and so on. To the advanced Student a simple ordinary thought, which seems little or nothing to the beginner, becomes a great and terrible fountain of iniquity, and the higher he goes, up to a certain point, the point of definitive victory, the more that is the case. The beginner can think, "It is ten o'clock," and dismiss the thought. To the mind of the adept this sentence will awaken all its possible correspondences, all the reflections he has ever made on time, as also accidental sympathetics like Mr Whistler's essay; and if he is sufficiently far advanced, all these thoughts in their hundreds and thousands diverging from the one thought, will again converge, and become the resultant of all those thoughts. He will get

Samadhi upon that original thought, and this will be a terrible enemy to his progress.

4. *The Mind is the great Slayer of the Real.*

In the word "Mind" we should include all phenomena of Mind, including Samadhi itself. Any phenomenon has causes and produces results, and all these things are below the "REAL." By the REAL is here meant the NIB-BANA-DHATU.

5. *Let the Disciple slay the Slayer. For—*

This is a corollary of Verse 4. These texts may be interpreted in a quite elementary sense. It is of course the object of even the beginner to suppress mind and all its manifestations, but only as he advances will he discover what Mind means.

6. *When to himself his form appears unreal, as do on waking all the forms he sees in dreams;*

This is a somewhat elementary result. Concentration on any subject leads soon enough to a sudden and overwhelming conviction that the object is unreal. The reason of this may perhaps be—speaking philosophically—that the object, whatever it is, has only a relative existence. (See *The Equinox*, vol. 1, no. 4, p. 159.)

7. *When he has ceased to hear the many, he may discern the ONE—the inner sound which kills the outer.*

By the "many" are meant primarily noises which take place outside the Student, and secondly, those which take place inside him. For example, the pulsation of the blood in the ears, and later the mystic sounds which are described in Verse 40.

8. *Then only, not till then, shall he forsake the region of ASAT, the false, to come unto the realm of SAT, the true.*

By "SAT, the true," is meant a thing previous to the "REAL" referred to above. SAT itself is an illusion. Some schools of philosophy have a higher ASAT, Not-Being, which is beyond SAT, and consequently is to Shivadarshana as SAT is to Atmadarshana. Nirvana is beyond both these.

9. *Before the Soul can see, the Harmony within must be attained, and fleshly eyes be rendered blind to all illusion.*

By the "Harmony within" is meant that state in which neither objects of sense, nor physiological sensations, nor emotions, can disturb the concentration of thought.

10. *Before the Soul can hear, the image (man) has to become as deaf to roarings as to whispers, to cries of bellowing elephants as to the silvery buzzing of the golden firefly.*

In the text the image is explained as "Man," but it more properly refers to the consciousness of man, which consciousness is considered as being a reflection of the Non-Ego, or a creation of the Ego, according to the school of philosophy to which the Student may belong.

11. *Before the Soul can comprehend and may remember, she must unto the Silent Speaker be united, just as the form to which the clay is modelled is first united with the potter's mind.*

Any actual object of the senses is considered as a precipitation of an ideal. Just as no existing triangle is a pure triangle, since it must be either equilateral, isosceles, or scalene, so every object is a miscarriage of an ideal. In the course of practice one concentrates upon a given thing, rejecting this outer appearance and arriving at that ideal, which of course will not in any way resemble any of the objects which are its incarnations. It is with this in view that the verse tells us that the Soul must be united to the Silent Speaker. The words "Silent Speaker" may be considered as a hieroglyph of the same character as LOGOS, אזני, or the Ineffable Name.

12. *For then the Soul will hear and will remember.*

The word "hear" alludes to the tradition that hearing is the organ of Spirit, just as seeing is that of Fire. The word "remember" might be explained as "will attain to memory." Memory is the link between the atoms of consciousness, for each successive consciousness of Man is a single phenomenon, and has no connection with any other. A looking-glass knows nothing of the different people that look into it. It only reflects one at a time. The brain is however more like a sensitive plate, and memory is the faculty of bringing up into consciousness any picture required. As this occurs in the normal man with his own experiences, so it occurs in the Adept with all experiences. (This is one more reason for His identifying Himself with others.)

13. *And then to the inner ear will speak—THE VOICE OF THE SILENCE, And say:*

What follows must be regarded as the device of the poet, for of course the "Voice of the Silence" cannot be interpreted in words. What follows is only its utterance in respect of the Path itself.

14. *If thy Soul smiles while bathing in the Sunlight of thy Life; if thy Soul sings within her chrysalis of flesh and matter; if thy Soul weeps inside her castle of illusion; if thy Soul struggles to break the silver thread that binds her to the MASTER; know, O Disciple, thy Soul is of the earth.*

In this verse the Student is exhorted to indifference to everything but his own progress. It does not mean the indifference of the Man to the things around him, as it has often been so unworthily and wickedly interpreted. The indifference spoken of is a kind of inner indifference. Everything should be enjoyed to the full, but always with the reservation that the absence of the thing enjoyed shall not cause regret. This is too hard for the beginner, and in many cases it is necessary for him to abandon pleasures in order to prove to himself that he is indifferent to them, and it may be occasionally advisable even for the Adept to do this now and again. Of course during periods of actual concentration there is no time whatever for any-

thing but the work itself; but to make even the mildest
asceticism a rule of life is the gravest of errors, except
perhaps that of regarding Asceticism as a virtue. This
latter always leads to spiritual pride, and spiritual pride is
the principal quality of the brother of the Left-hand Path.

"Ascetic" comes from the Greek *Askio*, 'to work curiously, to adorn, to exercise, to train.' The Latin *Ars* is
derived from this same word. Artist, in its finest sense of
creative craftsman, is therefore the best translation. The
word has degenerated under Puritan foulness.

15. *When to the World's turmoil thy budding Soul lends
ear; when to the roaring voice of the Great Illusion thy
Soul responds; when frightened at the sight of the hot tears of
pain; when deafened by the cries of distress, thy Soul withdraws like the shy turtle within the carapace of SELF-
HOOD, learn, O Disciple, of her Silent "God" thy Soul
is an unworthy shrine.*

This verse deals with an obstacle at a more advanced
stage. It is again a warning not to shut one's self up in
one's own universe. It is not by the exclusion of the Non-
Ego that saintship is attained, but by its inclusion. Love
is the law, love under will.

16. *When waxing stronger thy Soul glides forth from her
secure retreat; and breaking loose from the protecting
shrine, extends her silver thread and rushes onward; when
beholding her image on the waves of Space she whispers,
"This is I"—declare, O Disciple, that thy Soul is caught in
the webs of delusion.*

An even more advanced instruction, but still connected
with the question of the Ego and the non-Ego. The
phenomenon described is perhaps Atmadarshana, which
is still a delusion, in one sense still a delusion of personality; for although the Ego is destroyed in the Universe,
and the Universe in it, there is a distinct though exceedingly subtle tendency to sum up its experience as Ego.

These three verses might be interpreted also as quite elementary; v. 14 as blindness to the First Noble Truth "Everything is Sorrow"; v. 15 as the coward's attempt to escape Sorrow by Retreat; and v. 16 as the acceptance of the Astral as SAT.

17. *This earth, Disciple, is the Hall of Sorrow, wherein are set along the Path of dire probations, traps to ensnare thy EGO by the delusion called "Great Heresy."*

Develops still further these remarks.

18. *This earth, O ignorant Disciple, is but the dismal entrance leading to the twilight that precedes the valley of true light—that light which no wind can extinguish, that light which burns without a wick or fuel.*

"Twilight" here may again refer to Atmadarshana. The last phrase is borrowed from Eliphas Levi, who was not (I believe) a Tibetan of antiquity. [Madame Blavatsky humorously pretended that this Book is an ancient Tibetan writing.—Ed.]

19. *Saith the Great Law: "In order to become the knower of ALL-SELF, thou hast first of SELF to be the knower." To reach the knowledge of that SELF, thou hast to give up Self to Non-Self, Being to Non-Being, and then thou canst repose between the wings of the GREAT BIRD. Aye, sweet is rest between the wings of that which is not born, nor dies, but is the AUM throughout eternal Ages.*

The words "give up" may be explained as "yield" in its subtler or quasi-masochistic erotic sense, but on a higher plane. In the following quotation from the "Great Law" it explains that the yielding is not the beginning but the end of the Path.

> Then let the End awake. Long hast thou slept, O great God Terminus! Long ages hast thou waited at the end of the city and the roads thereof.
> Awake Thou! Wait no more!
> Nay, Lord! but I am come to Thee. It is I that wait at last.

The prophet cried against the mountain; come thou hither, that I may speak with thee!

The mountain stirred not. Therefore went the prophet unto the mountain, and spake unto it. But the feet of the prophet were weary, and the mountain heard not his voice.

But I have called unto Thee, and I have journeyed unto Thee, and it availed me not.

I waited patiently, and Thou wast with me from the beginning.

This now I know, O my beloved, and we are stretched at our ease among the vines.

But these thy prophets; they must cry aloud and scourge themselves; they must cross trackless wastes and unfathomed oceans; to await Thee is the end, not the beginning.

AUM is here quoted as the hieroglyph of the Eternal. "A" the beginning of sound, "U" its middle, and "M" its end, together form a single word or Trinity, indicating that the Real must be regarded as of this three-fold nature, Birth, Life and Death, not successive, but one. Those who have reached trances in which "time" is no more will understand better than others how this may be.

20. *Bestride the Bird of Life if thou wouldst know.*

The word "know" is specially used here in a technical sense. Avidya, ignorance, the first of the fetters, is moreover one which includes all the others.

With regard to this Swan "Aum" compare the following verses from the "Great Law," *Liber LXV*, II: 17–25.

Also the Holy One came upon me, and I beheld a white swan floating in the blue.

Between its wings I sate, and the aeons fled away.

Then the swan flew and dived and soared, yet no whither we went.

A little crazy boy that rode with me spake unto the swan, and said:

Who art thou that dost float and fly and dive and soar in the inane? Behold, these many aeons have passed; whence camest thou? Whither wilt thou go?

And laughing I chid him, saying: No whence! No whither!
The swan being silent, he answered: Then, if with no goal,
why this eternal journey?

And I laid my head against the Head of the Swan, and
laughed, saying: Is there not joy ineffable in this aimless
winging? Is there not weariness and impatience for who
would attain to some goal?

And the swan was ever silent. Ah! but we floated in the
infinite Abyss. Joy! Joy!

White swan, bear thou ever me up between thy wings!

21. *Give up thy life, if thou wouldst live.*

This verse may be compared with similar statements in
the Gospels, in *The Vision and the Voice,* and in the Books
of Thelema. It does not mean asceticism in the sense
usually understood by the world. The 12th Aethyr (see
The Equinox, vol. 1, no. 5, Supplement) gives the clearest
explanation of this phrase.

22. *Three Halls, O weary Pilgrim, lead to the end of toils.
Three Halls, O conqueror of Mâra, will bring thee through
three states into the fourth, and thence into the seven
Worlds, the Worlds of Rest Eternal.*

If this had been a genuine document I should have taken
the three states to be Srotapatti, etc., and the fourth Arhat,
for which the reader should consult *Science and Buddhism*
and similar treatises. But as it is better than "genuine,"
being, like *The Chymical Marriage of Christian Rosencreutz,* the forgery of a great adept, one cannot too confidently refer it thus. For the "Seven Worlds" are not
Buddhism.

23. *If thou would'st learn their names, then hearken, and
remember. The name of the first Hall is IGNORANCE—
Avidyâ. It is the Hall in which thou saw'st the light, in
which thou livest and shalt die.*

These three Halls correspond to the Gunas: Ignorance,
Tamas; Learning, Rajas; Wisdom, Sattvas.

Again, Ignorance corresponds to Malkuth and Nephesh (the animal soul), Learning to Tiphareth and Ruach (the mind), and Wisdom to Binah and Neshamah (the aspiration or Divine Mind).

24. *The name of Hall the second is the Hall of LEARNING. In it thy Soul will find the blossoms of life, but under every flower a serpent coiled.*

This Hall is a very much larger region than that usually understood by the Astral World. It would certainly include all states up to Dhyana. The Student will remember that his "rewards" immediately transmute themselves into temptations.

25. *The name of the third Hall is Wisdom, beyond which stretch the shoreless waters of AKSHARA, the indestructible Fount of Omniscience.*

Akshara is the same as the Great Sea of the Qabalah. The reader must consult *The Equinox* for a full study of this Great Sea.

26. *If thou would'st cross the first Hall safely, let not thy mind mistake the fires of lust that burn therein for the sunlight of life.*

The metaphor is now somewhat changed. The Hall of Ignorance represents the physical life. Note carefully the phraseology, "Let not thy mind mistake the fires of lust." It is legitimate to warm yourself by those fires so long as they do not deceive you.

27. *If thou would'st cross the second safely, stop not the fragrance of its stupefying blossoms to inhale. If freed thou would'st be from the Karmic chains, seek not for thy Guru in those Mâyâvic regions.*

A similar lesson is taught in this verse. Do not imagine that your early psychic experiences are Ultimate Truth. Do not become a slave to your results.

28. *The WISE ONES tarry not in pleasure grounds of senses.*

This lesson is confirmed. The wise ones tarry not. That is to say, they do not allow pleasure to interfere with business.

29. *The WISE ONES heed not the sweet-tongued voices of illusion.*

The wise ones heed not. They listen to them, but do not necessarily attach importance to what they say.

30. *Seek for him who is to give thee birth, in the Hall of Wisdom, the Hall which lies beyond, wherein all shadows are unknown, and where the light of truth shines with unfading glory.*

This apparently means that the only reliable Guru is one who has attained the grade of Magister Templi. For the attainments of this grade consult *The Equinox,* vol. 1, no. 5, Supplement, etc.

31. *That which is uncreate abides in thee, Disciple, as it abides in that Hall. If thou would'st reach it and blend the two, thou must divest thyself of thy dark garments of illusion. Stifle the voice of flesh, allow no image of the senses to get between its light and thine, that thus the twain may blend in one. And having learnt thine own Agnyâna, flee from the Hall of learning. This Hall is dangerous in its perfidious beauty, is needed but for thy probation. Beware, Lanoo, lest dazzled by illusive radiance thy Soul should linger and be caught in its deceptive light.*

This is a résumé of the previous seven verses. It inculcates the necessity of unwavering aspiration, and in particular warns the advanced Student against accepting his rewards. There is one method of meditation in which the Student kills thoughts as they arise by the reflection, "That's not it." Frater P. indicated the same by taking as his motto, in the Second Order which reaches from Yesod to Chesed, "ΟΥ ΜΗ," "No, certainly not!"

32. *This light shines from the jewel of the Great Ensnarer (Mâra). The senses it bewitches, blinds the mind, and leaves*

the unwary an abandoned wreck.

I am inclined to believe that most of Blavatsky's notes are intended as blinds. "Light" such as is described has a technical meaning. It would be too petty to regard Mara as a Christian would regard a man who offered him a cigarette. The supreme and blinding light of this jewel is the great vision of Light. It is the light which streams from the threshold of Nirvana, and Mara is the "dweller on the threshold." It is absurd to call this light "evil" in any commonplace sense. It is the two-edged sword, flaming every way, that keeps the gate of the Tree of Life. And there is a further Arcanum connected with this which it would be improper here to divulge.

33. *The moth attracted to the dazzling flame of thy night lamp is doomed to perish in the viscid oil. The unwary Soul that fails to grapple with the mocking demon of illusion, will return to earth the slave of Mâra.*

The result of failing to reject rewards is the return to earth. The temptation is to regard oneself as having attained, and so do no more work.

34. *Behold the Hosts of Souls. Watch how they hover o'er the stormy sea of human life, and how, exhausted, bleeding, broken-winged, they drop one after another on the swelling waves. Tossed by the fierce winds, chased by the gale, they drift into the eddies and disappear within the first great vortex.*

In this metaphor is contained a warning against identifying the Soul with human life, from the failure of its aspirations.

35. *If through the Hall of Wisdom, thou would'st reach the Vale of Bliss, Disciple, close fast thy senses against the great dire heresy of Separateness that weans thee from the rest.*

This verse reads at first as if the heresy were still possible in the Hall of Wisdom, but this is not as it seems. The

Disciple is urged to find out his Ego and slay it even in the beginning.

36. *Let not that "Heaven-Born," merged in the sea of Mâyâ, break from the Universal Parent (SOUL), but let the fiery power retire into the inmost chamber, the chamber of the Heart, and the abode of the World's Mother.*

This develops verse 35. The heaven-born is the human consciousness. The chamber of the Heart is the Anahata lotus. The abode of the World's Mother is the Muladhara lotus. But there is a more technical meaning yet—and this whole verse describes a particular method of meditation, a final method, which is far too difficult for the beginner. (See, however, *The Equinox*, on all these points.)

37. *Then from the heart that Power shall rise into the sixth, the middle region, the place between thine eyes, when it becomes the breath of the ONE-SOUL, the voice which filleth all, thy Master's voice.*

This verse teaches the concentration of the Kundalini in the Ajna Cakra. "Breath" is that which goes to and fro, and refers to the uniting of Shiva with Sakti in the Sahasrara. (See *The Equinox*.)

38. *'Tis only then thou canst become a "Walker of the Sky," who treads the winds above the waves, whose step touches not the waters.*

This partly refers to certain Iddhi, concerning Understanding of Devas (gods) etc.; here the word "wind" may be interpreted as "spirit." It is comparatively easy to reach this state, and it has no great importance. The "walker of the sky" is much superior to the mere reader of the minds of ants.

39. *Before thou sett'st thy foot upon the ladder's upper rung, the ladder of the mystic sounds, thou hast to hear the voice of thy INNER God in seven manners.*

The word "seven" is here, as so frequently, rather poetic than mathematic; for there are many more. The verse also reads as if it were necessary to hear all the seven, and this is not the case—some will get one and some another. Some students may even miss all of them.

(This might happen as the result of his having conquered, and uprooted them, and "fried their seeds" in a previous birth.)

40. *The first is like the nightingale's sweet voice chanting a song of parting to its mate.*

The second comes as the sound of a silver cymbal of the Dhyânis, awakening the twinkling stars.

The next is as the plaint melodious of the ocean-sprite imprisoned in its shell.

And this is followed by the chant of Vına (the Hindu lute).

The fifth like sound of bamboo-flute shrills in thine ear.

It changes next into a trumpet-blast.

The last vibrates like the dull rumbling of a thunder-cloud.

The seventh swallows all the other sounds. They die, and then are heard no more.

The first four are comparatively easy to obtain, and many people can hear them at will. The last three are much rarer, not necessarily because they are more difficult to get, and indicate greater advance, but because the protective envelope of the Adept is become so strong that they cannot pierce it. The last of the seven sometimes occurs, not as a sound, but as an earthquake, if the expression may be permitted. It is a mingling of terror and rapture impossible to describe, and as a general rule it completely discharges the energy of the Adept, leaving him weaker than an attack of Malaria would do; but if the practice has been right, this soon passes off, and the experience has this advantage, that one is far less troubled with minor phenomena than before. It is just possible that this is referred to in the Apocalypse XVI, XVII, XVIII.

41. *When the six are slain and at the Master's feet are*

laid, then is the pupil merged into the ONE, as becomes that One and lives therein.

The note tells that this refers to the six principles, so that the subject is completely changed. By the slaying of the principles is meant the withdrawal of the consciousness from them, their rejection by the seeker of truth. Sabapaty Swami has an excellent method on these lines: it is given, in an improved form, in *Liber HHH*. (See *The Equinox*, vol. I, no. 5, p. 5.)

42. *Before that path is entered, thou must destroy thy lunar body, cleanse thy mind body, and make clean thy heart.*

The Lunar body is Nephesh, and the Mind body Ruach. The heart is Tiphareth, the centre of Ruach.

43. *Eternal life's pure waters, clear and crystal, with the monsoon tempest's muddy torrents cannot mingle.*

We are now again on the subject of suppressing thought. The pure water is the stilled mind, the torrent the mind invaded by thoughts.

44. *Heaven's dew-drop glittering in the morn's first sunbeam within the bosom of the lotus, when dropped on earth becomes a piece of clay; behold, the pearl is now a speck of mire.*

This is not a mere poetic image. This dew-drop in the lotus is connected with the mantra "Aum Mani Padmen Hum," and to what this verse really refers is known only to members of the ninth degree of O.T.O.

45. *Strive with thy thoughts unclean before they overpower thee. Use them as they will thee, for if thou sparest them and they take root and grow, know well, these thoughts will overpower and kill thee. Beware, Disciple, suffer not, e'en though it be their shadow, to approach. For it will grow, increase in size and power, and then this thing of darkness will absorb thy being before thou hast well realized the black foul monster's presence.*

The text returns to the question of suppressing thoughts. Verse 44 has been inserted where it is in the hope of deluding the reader into the belief that it belongs to verses 43 and 45, for the Arcanum which it contains is so dangerous that it must be guarded in all possible ways. Perhaps even to call attention to it is a blind intended to prevent the reader from looking for something else.

46. *Before the "mystic Power" can make of thee a God, Lanoo, thou must have gained the faculty to slay thy lunar form at will.*

It is now evident that by destroying or slaying is not meant a permanent destruction. If you can slay a thing at will it means that you can revive it at will, for the word "faculty" implies repeated action.

47. *The Self of Matter and the SELF of Spirit can never meet. One of the twain must disappear; there is no place for both.*

This is a very difficult verse, because it appears so easy. It is not merely a question of Advaitism, it refers to the spiritual marriage. [Advaitism is a spiritual Monism. —Ed.]

48. *Ere thy Soul's mind can understand, the bud of personality must be crushed out; the worm of sense destroyed past resurrection.*

This is again filled with deeper meaning than that which appears on the surface. The words "bud" and "worm" form a clue.

49. *Thou canst not travel on the path before thou hast become that Path itself.*

Compare the scene in *Parsifal*, where the scenery comes to the knight instead of the knight going to the scenery. But there is also implied the doctrine of the Tao, and only one who is an accomplished Taoist can hope to understand this verse. (See "The Hermit of Esopus Island," part of *The Magical Record of 666*, to be published in *The*

Equinox, vol. III.)

50. *Let thy Soul lend its ear to every cry of pain like as the lotus bares its heart to drink the morning sun.*

51. *Let not the fierce sun dry one tear of pain before thyself hast wiped it from the sufferer's eye.*

52. *But let each burning human tear drop on thy heart and there remain; nor ever brush it off, until the pain that caused it is removed.*

This is a counsel never to forget the original stimulus which has driven you to the Path, the "first noble truth." Everything is now "good." This is why verse 53 says that these tears are the streams that irrigate the fields of charity immortal. (Tears, by the way. Think!)

53. *These tears, O thou of heart most merciful, these are the streams that irrigate the fields of charity immortal. 'Tis on such soil that grows the midnight blossom of Buddha, more difficult to find, more rare to view, than is the flower of the Vogay tree. It is the seed of freedom from rebirth. It isolates the Arhat both from strife and lust, it leads him through the fields of Being unto the peace and bliss known only in the land of Silence and Non-Being.*

The "midnight blossom" is a phrase connected with the doctrine of the Night of Pan, familiar to Masters of the Temple. "The Poppy that flowers in the dusk" is another name for it. A most secret Formula of Magick is connected with this "Heart of the Circle."

54. *Kill out desire; but if thou killest it, take heed lest from the dead it should again rise.*

By "desire" in all mystic treatises of any merit is meant tendency. Desire is manifested universally in the law of gravitation, in that of chemical attraction, and so on; in fact, everything that is done is caused by the desire to do it, in this technical sense of the word. The "midnight blossom" implies a certain monastic Renunciation of all desire, which reaches to all planes. One must however distinguish between desire, which means unnatural attraction to an ideal, and love, which is natural Motion.

55. *Kill love of life; but if thou slayest Tanhâ, let this not be for thirst of life eternal, but to replace the fleeting by the everlasting.*

This particularises a special form of desire. The English is very obscure to any one unacquainted with Buddhist literature. The "everlasting" referred to is not a life-condition at all. (Tanha is the instinct of self-preservation.)

56. *Desire nothing. Chafe not at Karma, nor at Nature's changeless laws. But struggle only with the personal, the transitory, the evanescent and the perishable.*

The words "desire nothing" should be interpreted positively as well as negatively. The main sense of the rest of the verse is to advise the Disciple to work, and not to complain.

57. *Help Nature and work on with her; and Nature will regard thee as one of her creators and make obeisance.*

Although the object of the Disciple is to transcend Law, he must work through Law to attain this end.

It may be remarked that this treatise—and this comment for the most part—is written for disciples of certain grades only. It is altogether inferior to such books as *Liber CXI Aleph;* but for that very reason, more useful, perhaps, to the average seeker.

58. *And she will open wide before thee the portals of her secret chambers, lay bare before thy gaze the treasures hidden in the depths of her pure virgin bosom. Unsullied by the hand of matter, she shows her treasures only to the eye of spirit—the eye which never closes, the eye for which there is no veil in all her kingdoms.*

This verse reminds one of the writings of Alchemists; and it should be interpreted as the best of them would have interpreted it.

59. *Then will she show thee the means and way, the first*

gate and the second, the third, up to the very seventh. And then, the goal; beyond which lie, bathed in the sunlight of the Spirit, glories untold, unseen by any save the eye of Soul.

These gates are described in the third treatise. The words "spirit" and "soul" are highly ambiguous, and had better be regarded as poetic figures, without a technical meaning being sought.

60. There is but one road to the Path: at its very end alone the voice of Silence can be heard. The ladder by which the candidate ascends is formed of rungs of suffering and pain: these can be silenced only by the voice of virtue. Woe, then, to thee, Disciple, if there is one single vice thou hast left behind; for then the ladder will give way and overthrow thee; its foot rests in the deep mire of thy sins and failings, and ere thou canst attempt to cross this wide abyss of matter, thou hast to lave thy feet in Waters of Renunciation. Beware lest thou shouldst set a foot still soiled upon the ladder's lowest rung. Woe unto him who dares pollute one rung with miry feet. The foul and viscous mud will dry, become tenacious, then glue his feet unto the spot; and like a bird caught in the wily fowler's lime, he will be stayed from further progress. His vices will take shape and drag him down. His sins will raise their voices like as the jackal's laugh and sob after the sun goes down; his thoughts become an army, and bear him off a captive slave.

A warning against any impurity in the original aspiration of the Disciple. By impurity is meant, and should always be meant, the mingling (as opposed to the combination) of two things. Do one thing at a time. This is particularly necessary in the matter of the aspiration. For if the aspiration be in any way impure, it means divergence in the will itself; and this is will's one fatal flaw. It will however be understood that aspiration constantly changes and develops with progress. The beginner can only see a certain distance. Just so with our first telescopes we discovered many new stars, and with each improvement in the instrument we have discovered more. The second and more obvious meaning in the verse preaches the practice of Yama, Niyama, before serious practice is started, and this in actual life means, map out your career as well as you can. Decide to do so many hours' work a day in such conditions as may be possible. It does not mean that you should set up neuroses and hysteria by suppressing your natural instincts, which are perfectly right on their own plane, and only wrong when they invade other planes, and set up alien tyrannies.

61. *Kill thy desires, Lanoo, make thy vices impotent, ere the first step is taken on the solemn journey.*

By "desires" and "vices" are meant those things which you yourself think to be inimical to the work; for each man they will be quite different, and any attempt to lay down a general rule leads to worse than confusion.

62. *Strangle thy sins and make them dumb for ever, before thou dost lift one foot to mount the ladder.*

This is merely a repetition of verse 61 in different language. But remember: "The word of Sin is Restriction." "Do what thou wilt shall be the whole of the Law."

63. *Silence thy thoughts and fix thy whole attention on thy Master, whom yet thou dost not see, but whom thou feelest.*

This again commands the stilling of thoughts. The previous verses referred rather to emotions, which are the great stagnant pools on which the mosquito thought breeds. Emotions are objectionable, as they represent an invasion of the mental plane by sensory or moral impressions.

64. *Merge into one sense thy senses, if thou would'st be secure against the foe. 'Tis by that sense alone which lies concealed within the hollow of thy brain, that the steep Path*

which leadeth to thy Master may be disclosed before thy Soul's dim eyes.

This verse refers to a Meditation practice somewhat similar to those described in *Liber 831*. (See *The Equinox*.)

65. *Long and weary is the way before thee, O Disciple. One single thought about the past that thou hast left behind, will drag thee down, and thou wilt have to start the climb anew.*

Remember Lot's wife.

66. *Kill in thyself all memory of past experiences. Look not behind or thou art lost.*

Remember Lot's wife.

It is a division of Will to dwell in the past. But one's past experiences must be built into one's Pyramid, as one advances, layer by layer. One must also remark that this verse only applies to those who have not yet come to reconcile past, present, and future. Every incarnation is a Veil of Isis.

67. *Do not believe that lust can ever be killed out if gratified or satiated, for this is an abomination inspired by Mâra. It is by feeding vice that it expands and waxes strong, like to the worm that fattens on the blossom's heart.*

This verse must not be taken in its literal sense. Hunger is not conquered by starvation. One's attitude to all the necessities which the traditions of earthly life involve should be to rule them, neither by mortification nor by indulgence. In order to do the work you must keep in proper physical and mental condition. Be sane. Asceticism always excites the mind, and the object of the Disciple is to calm it. However, ascetic originally meant athletic, and it has only acquired its modern meaning on account of the corruptions that crept into the practices used by those in "training." The prohibitions, relatively valuable, were exalted into general rules. To "break training" is not a sin for any one who is not in training. Incidentally, it takes all sorts to make a world. Imagine the stupidity of a universe full of Arhans! All work and no play makes Jack a dull boy.

68. *The rose must re-become the bud, born of its parent stem, before the parasite has eaten through its heart and drunk its life sap.*

The English is here ambiguous and obscure, but the meaning is that it is important to achieve the Great Work while you have youth and energy.

69. *The golden tree puts forth its jewel-buds before its trunk is withered by the storm.*

Repeats this in clearer language.

70. *The Pupil must regain THE CHILD-STATE HE HAS LOST ere the first sound can fall upon his ear.*

Compare the remark of "Christ," "Except ye become as little children ye shall in no wise enter into the Kingdom of Heaven," and also, "Ye must be born again." It also refers to the overcoming of shame and of the sense of sin. If you think the Temple of the Holy Ghost to be a pig-stye, it is certainly improper to perform therein the Mass of the Graal. Therefore purify and consecrate yourselves; and then, Kings and Priests unto God, perform ye the Miracle of the One Substance.

Here is written also the Mystery of Harpocrates. One must become the "Unconscious" (of Jung), the Phallic or Divine Child or Dwarf-Self.

71. *The light from the ONE MASTER, the one unfading golden light of Spirit, shoots its effulgent beams on the Disciple from the very first. Its rays thread through the thick, dark clouds of Matter.*

The Holy Guardian Angel is already aspiring to union with the Disciple, even before his aspiration is formulated in the latter.

72. *Now here, now there, these rays illumine it, like sun-sparks light the earth through the thick foliage of jungle*

growth. But, O Disciple, unless the flesh is passive, head cool, the Soul as firm and pure as flaming diamond, the radiance will not reach the CHAMBER, its sunlight will not warm the heart, nor will the mystic sounds of Akâshic heights reach the ear, however eager, at the initial stage.

The uniting of the Disciple with his Angel depends upon the former. The Latter is always at hand. "Akashic Heights"—the dwelling-place of Nuith.

73. *Unless thou hear'st, thou canst not see. Unless thou seest, thou canst not hear. To hear and see, this is the second stage.*

. . . .

This is an obscure verse. It implies that the qualities of fire and Spirit commingle to reach the second stage. There is evidently a verse missing, or rather omitted, as may be understood by the row of dots; this presumably refers to to the third stage. This third stage may be found by the discerning in *Liber 831.*

74. *When the Disciple sees and hears, and when he smells and tastes, eyes closed, ears shut, with mouth and nostrils stopped; when the four senses blend and ready are to pass into the fifth, that of the inner touch—then into stage the fourth he hath passed on.*

The practice indicated in verse 74 is described in most books upon the Tatwas. The orifices of the face being covered with the fingers, the senses take on a new shape.

75. *And in the fifth, O slayer of thy thoughts, all these have to be killed beyond re-animation.*

It is not sufficient to get rid temporarily of one's obstacles. One must seek out their roots and destroy them, so that they can never rise again. This involves a very deep psychological investigation, as a preliminary. But the whole matter is one between the Self and its modifications, not at all between the Instrument and its gates. To kill out the sense of sight is not achieved by removing the eyes. This mistake has done more to obscure the Path than any other, and has been responsible for endless misery.

76. *Withhold thy mind from all external objects, all external sights. Withhold internal images, lest on thy Soul-light a dark shadow they should cast.*

This is the usual instruction once more, but, going further, it intimates that the internal image or reality of the object must be destroyed as well as the outer image and the ideal image.

77. *Thou art now in DHARANA, the sixth stage.*

DHARANA has been explained thoroughly in *Book 4,* q. v.

78. *When thou hast passed into the seventh, O happy one, thou shalt perceive no more the sacred Three, for thou shalt have become that Three thyself. Thyself and mind, like twins upon a line, the Star which is thy goal burns overhead. The Three that dwell in glory and in bliss ineffable, now in the World of Mâyâ have lost their names. They have become one Star, the fire that burns but scorches not, that fire which is the Upâdhi of the Flame.*

It would be a mistake to attach more than a poetic meaning to these remarks upon the sacred Three; but Ego, non-Ego, and That which is formed from their wedding, are here referred to. There are two Triangles of especial importance to mystics; one is the equilateral, the other that familiar to the Past Master in Craft Masonry. The last sentence in the text refers to the "Seed" of Fire, the "Ace of Wands," the "Lion-Serpent," the "Dwarf-Self," the "Winged Egg," etc.

79. *And this, O Yogi of success, is what men call Dhyâna, the right precursor of Samâdhi.*

These states have been sufficiently, and much better, described in *Book 4,* q. v.

80. *And now thy Self is lost in SELF, Thyself unto*

THYSELF, merged in THAT SELF from which thou first didst radiate.

In this verse is given a hint of the underlying philosophical theory of the Cosmos. See *Liber CXI* for a full and proper account of this.

81. *Where is thy individuality, Lanoo, where the Lanoo himself? It is the spark lost in the fire, the drop within the ocean, the ever-present ray become the ALL and the eternal radiance.*

Again principally poetical. The man is conceived as a mere accretion about his "Dwarf-Self," and he is now wholly absorbed therein. For IT is also ALL, being of the Body of Nuith.

82. *And now, Lanoo, thou art the doer and the witness, the radiator and the radiation, Light in the Sound, and the Sound in the Light.*

Important, as indicating the attainment of a mystical state, in which you are not only involved in an action, but apart from it. There is a higher state described in the *Bhagavad Gita.* "I who am all, and made it all, abide its separate Lord."

83. *Thou art acquainted with the five impediments, O blessed one. Thou art their conqueror, the Master of the sixth, deliverer of the four modes of Truth. The light that falls upon them shines from thyself, O thou who wast Disciple, but art Teacher now.*

The five impediments are usually taken to be the five senses. In this case the term "Master of the sixth" becomes of profound significance. The "sixth sense" is the race-instinct, whose common manifestation is in sex; this sense is then the birth of the Individual or Conscious Self with the "Dwarf-Self," the Silent Babe, Harpocrates. The "four modes of Truth" (noble Truths) are adequately described in *Science and Buddhism.* (See Crowley, *Collected Works.*)

84. *And of these modes of Truth:*
   Hast thou not passed through knowledge of all misery—truth the first?

85. *Hast thou not conquered the Mârâs' King at Tsi, the portal of assembling—truth the second?*

86. *Hast thou not sin at the third gate destroyed, and truth the third attained?*

87. *Hast thou not entered Tau, the "Path" that leads to knowledge—the fourth truth?*

The reference to the "Maras' King" confuses the second truth with the third. (See *Science and Buddhism.*) The third Truth is a mere corollary of the Second, and the Fourth a Grammar of the Third.

88. *And now rest 'neath the Bodhi tree, which is perfection of all knowledge, for, know, thou art the Master of SAMADHI—the state of faultless vision.*

This account of Samadhi is very incongruous. Throughout the whole treatise Hindoo ideas are painfully mixed with Buddhist, and the introduction of the "four noble truths" comes very strangely as the precursor of verses 88 and 89.

89. *Behold! thou hast become the Light, thou hast become the Sound, thou art thy Master and thy God. Thou art THY-SELF the object of thy search: the VOICE unbroken, that resounds throughout eternities, exempt from change, from sin exempt, the Seven Sounds in one,*

THE VOICE OF THE SILENCE
Om   Tat   Sat.

This is a pure peroration, and clearly involves an egocentric metaphysic.

The style of the whole treatise is characteristically occidental.

FRAGMENT II
THE TWO PATHS

1. *And now, O Teacher of Compassion, point thou the way to other men. Behold all those who, knocking for admission, await [sic] in ignorance and darkness to see the gate of the Sweet Law flung open!*

This begins with the word "And," rather as if it were a sequel to *The Voice of the Silence.* It should not be assumed that this is the case. However, assuming that the first Fragment explains the Path as far as Master of the Temple, it is legitimate to regard this second Fragment, so called, as the further instruction; for the Master of the Temple must leave his personal progress to attend to that of other people, a task from which, I am bound to add, even the most patient of Masters feels at times a tendency to revolt!

2. *The voice of the Candidates :*

Shalt not thou, Master of thine own Mercy, reveal the doctrine of the Heart? Shalt thou refuse to lead thy Servants unto the Path of Liberation?

One is compelled to remark a certain flavour of sentimentality in the exposition of the "Heart doctrine," perhaps due to the increasing age and weight of the Authoress. The real reason of the compassion (so-called) of the Master is a perfectly practical and sensible one. It has nothing to do with the beautiful verses, "It is only the sorrows of others Cast their shadows over me." The Master has learnt the first noble truth: "Everything is sorrow," and he has learnt that there is no such thing as separate existence. Existence is one. He knows these things as facts, just as he knows that two and two make four. Consequently, although he has found the way of escape for that fraction of consciousness which he once called "I," and although he knows that not only that consciousness, but all other consciousnesses, are but part of an illusion, yet he feels that his own task is not accomplished while there remains any fragment of consciousness thus unemancipated from illusion. Here we get into very deep metaphysical difficulties, but that cannot be helped, for the Master of the Temple knows that any statement, however simple, involves metaphysical difficulties which are not only difficult, but insoluble. On the plane of which Reason is Lord, all antinomies are irreconcilable. It is impossible for any one below the grade of Magister Templi even to begin to comprehend the resolution of them. This fragment of the imaginary *Book of the Golden Precepts* must be studied without ever losing sight of this fact.

3. *Quoth the Teacher:*
The Paths are two; the great Perfections three; six are the Virtues that transform the body into the Tree of Knowledge.

The "Tree of Knowledge" is of course another euphemism, the "Dragon Tree" representing the uniting of the straight and the curved. A further description of the Tree under which Gautama sat and attained emancipation is unfit for this elementary comment. Aum Mani Padmen Hum.

4. *Who shall approach them?*
Who shall first enter them?
Who shall first hear the doctrine of two Paths in one, the truth unveiled about the Secret Heart? The Law which, shunning learning, teaches Wisdom, reveals a tale of woe!

This expression "two Paths in one" is intended to convey a hint that this fragment has a much deeper meaning than is apparent. The key should again be sought in Alchemy.

5. *Alas, alas, that all men should possess Alaya, be one with the Great Soul, and that, possessing it, Alaya should so little avail them!*

6. *Behold how like the moon, reflected in the tranquil waves, Alaya is reflected by the small and by the great, is mirrored in the tiniest atoms, yet fails to reach the heart of all. Alas, that so few men should profit by the gift, the priceless boon of learning truth, the right perception of existing things, the knowledge of the non-existent!*

This is indeed a serious metaphysical complaint. The solution of it is not to be found in reason.

7. *Saith the Pupil:*
O Teacher, what shall I do to reach Wisdom?
O Wise One, what, to gain perfection?

8. *Search for the Paths. But, O Lanoo, be of clean heart before thou startest on thy journey. Before thou takest thy first step, learn to discern the real from the false, the ever-fleeting from the ever-lasting. Learn above all to separate Head-learning from Soul-wisdom, the "Eye" from the "Heart" doctrine.*

The Authoress of these treatises is a little exacting in the number of things that you have to do before you take your first step, most of them being things which more nearly resemble the difficulties of the last step. But by learning to distinguish the "real from the false" is only meant a sort of elementary discernment between things that are worth having and those that are not worth having, and, of course, the perception will alter with advance in knowledge. By "Head-learning" is meant the contents of the Ruach (mind) or Manas. Chiah is sub-consciousness in its best sense, that subliminal which is sublime. The "Eye" doctrine then means that exoteric, the "Heart" doctrine the esoteric. Of course, in a more secret doctrine still, there is an Eye Doctrine which transcends the Heart Doctrine as that transcends this lesser Eye Doctrine.

9. *Yea, ignorance is like unto a closed and airless vessel;
the soul a bird shut up within. It warbles not, nor can it stir
a feather; but the songster mute and torpid sits, and of
exhaustion dies.*

The Soul, Atma, despite its possession of the attributes
omniscience, omnipotence, omnipresence, etc., is entirely
bound and blindfolded by ignorance. The metaphysical
puzzle to which this gives rise cannot be discussed here—
it is insoluble by reason, though one may call attention to
the inherent incommensurability of a postulated absolute
with an observed relative.

10. *But even ignorance is better than Head-learning with
no Soul-wisdom to illumine and guide it.*

The word "better" is used rather sentimentally, for, as
"It is better to have loved and lost than never to have loved
at all," so it is better to be a madman than an idiot. There
is always a chance of putting wrong right. As, however,
the disease of the age is intellectualism, this lesson is
well to teach. Numerous sermons on this point will be
found in many of the writings of Frater Perdurabo.

11. *The seeds of Wisdom cannot sprout and grow in airless space. To live and reap experience, the mind needs
breadth and depth and points to draw it towards the Diamond Soul. Seek not those points in Mâyâ's realm; but soar
beyond illusions, search the eternal and the changeless SAT,
mistrusting fancy's false suggestions.*

Compare what is said in *Book 4*, Part II, about the
Sword. In the last part of the verse the adjuration is
somewhat obvious, and it must be remembered that with
progress the realm of Maya constantly expands as that of
Sat diminishes. In orthodox Buddhism this process continues indefinitely. There is also the resolution SAT =
ASAT.

12. *For mind is like a mirror; it gathers dust while
it reflects. It needs the gentle breezes of Soul-wisdom to*

brush away the dust of our illusions. Seek, O Beginner, to blend thy Mind and Soul.

The charge is to eliminate rubbish from the Mind, and teaches that Soul-wisdom is the selective agent. But these Fragments will be most shamefully misinterpreted if a trace of sentimentality is allowed to creep in. "Soul-wisdom" does not mean "piety" and "nobility" and similar conceptions, which only flourish where truth is permanently lost, as in England. Soul-wisdom here means the Will. You should eliminate from your mind anything which does not subserve your real purpose. It was, however, said in verse 11 that the "mind needs breadth," and this also is true, but if all the facts known to the Thinker are properly co-ordinated and connected causally, and by necessity, the ideal mind will be attained, for although complex it will be unified. And if the summit of its pyramid be the Soul, the injunction in this verse 12 to the Beginner will be properly observed.

13. *Shun ignorance and likewise shun illusion. Avert thy face from world deceptions: mistrust thy senses; they are false. But within thy body—the shrine of thy sensations—seek in the Impersonal for the "Eternal Man"; and having sought him out, look inward: thou art Buddha.*

"Shun ignorance": Keep on acquiring facts.

"Shun illusion": Refer every fact to the ultimate reality. "Interpret every phenomenon as a particular dealing of God with your Soul."

"Mistrust thy senses": Avoid superficial judgment of the facts which they present to you.

The last paragraph gives too succinct a statement of the facts. The attainment of the knowledge of the Holy Guardian Angel is only the "next step." It does not imply Buddhahood by any means.

14. *Shun praise, O Devotee. Praise leads to self-delusion. Thy body is not Self, thy SELF is in itself without a body,*

and either praise or blame affects it not.

Pride is an expansion of the Ego, and the Ego must be destroyed. Pride is its protective sheath, and hence exceptionally dangerous, but this is a mystical truth concerning the inner life. The Adept is anything but a "creeping Jesus."

15. *Self-gratulation, O Disciple, is like unto a lofty tower, up which a haughty fool has climbed. Thereon he sits in prideful solitude and unperceived by any but himself.*

Develops this: but, this treatise being for beginners as well as for the more advanced, a sensible commonplace reason is given for avoiding pride, in that it defeats its own object.

16. *False learning is rejected by the Wise, and scattered to the Winds by the Good Law. Its wheel revolves for all, the humble and the proud; the "Doctrine of the Heart" for the elect. The first repeat in pride: "Behold, I know"; the last, they who in humbleness have garnered, low confess: "Thus have I heard."*

Continues the subject, but adds a further Word to discriminate from Daath (knowledge) in favour of Binah (understanding).

17. *"Great Sifter" is the name of the "Heart Doctrine," O Disciple.*

This explains the "Heart Doctrine" as a process of continual elimination which refers both to the aspirants and to the thoughts.

18. *The wheel of the Good Law moves swiftly on. It grinds by night and day. The worthless husks it drives from out the golden grain, the refuse from the flour. The hand of Karma guides the wheel; the revolutions mark the beatings of the Karmic heart.*

The subject of elimination is here further developed. The favourite Eastern image of the Wheel of the Good Law is difficult to Western minds, and the whole metaphor appears to us somewhat confused.

19. *True knowledge is the flour, false learning is the husk. If thou would'st eat the bread of Wisdom, thy flour thou hast to knead with Amrita's clear waters. But if thou kneadest husks with Mâyâ's dew, thou canst create but food for the black doves of death, the birds of birth, decay and sorrow.*

"Amrita" means not only Immortality, but is the technical name of the Divine force which descends upon man, but which is burnt up by his tendencies, by the forces which make him what he is. It is also a certain Elixir which is the Menstruum of Harpocrates.

Amrita here is best interpreted thus, for it is in opposition to "Maya." To interpret illusion is to make confusion more confused.

20. *If thou art told that to become Arhan thou hast to cease to love all beings—tell them they lie.*

Here begins an instruction against Asceticism, which has always been the stumbling block most dreaded by the wise. "Christ" said that John the Baptist came neither eating nor drinking, and the people called him mad. He himself came eating and drinking; and they called him a gluttonous man and a wine bibber, a friend of publicans and sinners. The Adept does what he likes, or rather what he wills, and allows nothing to interfere with it, but because he is ascetic in the sense that he has no appetite for the stale stupidities which fools call pleasure, people expect him to refuse things both natural and necessary. Some people are so hypocritical that they claim their dislikes as virtue, and so the poor, weedy, unhealthy degenerate who cannot smoke because his heart is out of order, and cannot drink because his brain is too weak to stand it, or perhaps because his doctor has forbidden him to do either for the next two years, the man who is afraid of life, afraid to do anything lest some result should follow, is acclaimed as the best and greatest of mankind.

It is very amusing in England to watch the snobbishness, particularly of the middle classes, and their absurd aping of their betters, while the cream of the jest is that the morality to which the middle classes cling does not exist in good society. Those who have Master Souls refuse to be bound by anything but their own wills. They may refrain from certain actions because their main purpose would be interfered with, just as a man refrains from smoking if he is training for a boat-race; and those in whom cunning is stronger than self-respect sometimes dupe the populace by ostentatiously refraining from certain actions, while, however, they perform them in private. Especially of recent years, some Adepts have thought it wise either to refrain or to pretend to refrain from various things in order to increase their influence. This is a great folly. What is most necessary to demonstrate is that the Adept is not less but more than a man. It is better to hit your enemy and be falsely accused of malice, than to refrain from hitting him and be falsely accused of cowardice.

21. *If thou art told that to gain liberation thou hast to hate thy mother and disregard thy son; to disavow thy father and call him "householder"; for man and beast all pity to renounce—tell them their tongue is false.*

This verse explains that the Adept has no business to break up his domestic circumstances. The Rosicrucian Doctrine that the Adept should be a man of the world, is much nobler than that of the hermit. If the Ascetic Doctrine is carried to its logical conclusion, a stone is holier than Buddha himself. Read, however, *Liber CLVI.*

22. *Thus teach the Tirthikas, the unbelievers.*

It is a little difficult to justify the epithet "unbeliever"— it seems to me that on the contrary they are the believers. Scepticism is sword and shield to the wise man.

But by scepticism one does not mean the sneering in-
fidelity of a Bolinbroke, or the gutter-snipe agnosticism
of a Harry Boulter, which are crude remedies against a
very vulgar colic.

23. *If thou art taught that sin is born of action and bliss
of absolute inaction, then tell them that they err. Non-per-
manence of human action, deliverance of mind from thraldom
by the cessation of sin and faults, are not for "Deva Egos."
Thus saith the "Doctrine of the Heart."*

This Doctrine is further developed. The term "Deva
Egos" is again obscure. The verse teaches that one should
not be afraid to act. Action must be fought by reaction,
and tyranny will never be overthrown by slavish submission to it. Cowardice is conquered by a course of
exposing oneself unnecessarily to danger. The desire of
the flesh has ever grown stronger for ascetics, as they
endeavoured to combat it by abstinence, and when with
old age their functions are atrophied, they proclaim vain-
gloriously "I have conquered." The way to conquer any
desire is to understand it, and freedom consists in the
ability to decide whether or no you will perform any given
action. The Adept should always be ready to abide by the
toss of a coin, and remain absolutely indifferent as to
whether it falls head or tail.

24. *The Dharma (law) of the "Eye" is the embodiment
of the external, and the non-existing.*

By "non-existing" is meant the lower Asat. The word
is used on other occasions to mean an Asat which is
higher than, and beyond, Sat.

25. *The Dharma of the "Heart" is the embodiment of
Bodhi, the Permanent and Everlasting.*

"Bodhi" implies the root "Light" in its highest sense of
L.V.X. But, even in Hindu Theory, πανта ρει.

26. *The Lamp burns bright when wick and oil are clean.
To make them clean a cleaner is required. The flame feels*

*not the process of the cleaning. "The branches of the tree
are shaken by the wind; the trunk remains unmoved."*

This verse again refers to the process of selection and
elimination already described. The aspiration must be
considered as unaffected by this process except in so far
as it becomes brighter and clearer in consequence of it.
The last sentence seems again to refer to this question of
asceticism. The Adept is not affected by his actions.

27. *Both action and inaction may find room in thee; thy
body agitated, thy mind tranquil, thy Soul as limpid as a
mountain lake.*

This repeats the same lesson. The Adept may plunge
into the work of the world, and undertake his daily duties
and pleasures exactly as another man would do, but he
is not moved by them as the other man is.

28. *Wouldst thou become a Yogi of "Time's Circle"?
Then, O Lanoo:*

29. *Believe thou not that sitting in dark forests, in proud
seclusion and apart from men; believe thou not that life on
roots and plants, that thirst assuaged with snow from the
great Range—believe thou not, O Devotee, that this will
lead thee to the goal of final liberation.*

30. *Think not that breaking bone, that rending flesh and
muscle, unites thee to thy "Silent Self." Think not that when
the sins of thy gross form are conquered, O Victim of thy
Shadows, thy duty is accomplished by nature and by
man.*

Once again the ascetic life is forbidden. It is moreover
shown to be a delusion that the ascetic life assists liberation. The ascetic thinks that by reducing himself to the
condition of a vegetable he is advanced upon the path of
Evolution. It is not so. Minerals have no inherent power of
motion save intramolecularly. Plants grow and move,
though but little. Animals are free to move in every direction, and space itself is no hindrance to the higher prin-

ciples of man. Advance is in the direction of more continuous and more untiring energy.

31. *The blessed ones have scorned to do so. The Lion of the Law, the Lord of Mercy, perceiving the true cause of human woe, immediately forsook the sweet but selfish rest of quiet wilds. From Aranyani He became the Teacher of mankind. After Julai had entered the Nirvana, He preached on mount and plain, and held discourses in the cities, to Devas, men and Gods.*

Reference is here made to the attainment of the Buddha. It was only after he had abandoned the Ascetic Life that he attained, and so far from manifesting that attainment by non-action, he created a revolution in India by attacking the Caste system, and by preaching his law created a Karma so violent that even to-day its primary force is still active. The present "Buddha," the Master Therion, is doing a similar, but even greater work, by His proclamation: Do what thou wilt shall be the whole of the Law.

32. *Sow kindly acts and thou shalt reap their fruition. Inaction in a deed of mercy becomes an action in a deadly sin. Thus saith the Sage.*

This continues the diatribe against non-action, and points out that the Ascetic is entirely deluded when he supposes that doing nothing has no effect. To refuse to save life is murder.

33. *Shalt thou abstain from action? Not so shall gain thy Soul her freedom. To reach Nirvana one must reach Self-Knowledge, and Self-Knowledge is of loving deeds the child.*

Continues the subject. The basis of knowledge is experience.

34. *Have patience, Candidate, as one who fears no failure, courts no success. Fix thy Soul's gaze upon the star whose ray thou art, the flaming star that shines within the*

lightless depths of ever-being, the boundless fields of the Unknown.

The Candidate is exhorted to patience and one-pointedness, and, further, to an indifference to the result which comes of true confidence that that result will follow. Cf. *Liber CCXX*, I: "For pure will, unassuaged of purpose, delivered from the lust of result, is every way perfect."

35. *Have perseverance as one who doth for evermore endure. Thy shadows live and vanish; that which in thee shall live for ever, that which in thee knows, for it is knowledge, is not of fleeting life: it is the Man that was, that is, and will be, for whom the hour shall never strike.*

Compare Levi's aphorism, "The Magician should work as though he had omnipotence at his command and eternity at his disposal." Do not imagine that it matters whether you finish the task in this life or not. Go on quietly and steadily, unmoved by anything whatever.

36. *If thou wouldst reap sweet peace and rest, Disciple, sow with the seeds of merit the fields of future harvests. Accept the woes of birth.*

Accept the Laws of Nature and work with them. Do not be always trying to take short cuts. Do not complain, and do not be afraid of the length of the Path. This treatise being for beginners, reward is offered. And—it is really worth while. One may find oneself in the Office of a Buddha.

"Yea, cried the Holy One, and from Thy spark will I the Lord kindle a great light; I will burn through the grey city in the old and desolate land; I will cleanse it from its great impurity.

"And thou, O prophet, shalt see these things, and thou shalt heed them not.

"Now is the Pillar established in the Void; now is Asi fulfilled of Asar; now is Hoor let down into the Animal Soul of Things like a fiery star that falleth upon the darkness of the earth.

"Through the midnight thou art dropt, O my child, my conqueror, my sword-girt captain, O Hoor! and they shall find thee as a black gnarl'd glittering stone, and they shall worship thee."

37. *Step out from sunlight into shade, to make more room for others. The tears that water the parched soil of pain and sorrow bring forth the blossoms and the fruits of Karmic retribution. Out of the furnace of man's life and its black smoke, winged flames arise, flames purified, that soaring onward, 'neath the Karmic eye, weave in the end the fabric glorified of the three vestures of the Path:*

Now the discourse turns to the question of the origin of Evil. The alchemical theory is here set forth. The first matter of the work is not so worthy as the elixir, and it must pass through the state of the Black Dragon to attain thereto.

38. *These vestures are: Nirmânakâya, Sambhogakâya, Dharmakâya, robe Sublime.*

The Nirmanakaya body is the "Body of Light" as described in *Book 4*, Part III. But it is to be considered as having been developed to the highest point possible that is compatible with incarnation.

The Sambhogakaya has "three perfections" added, so-called. These would prevent incarnation.

The Dharmakaya body is what may be described as the final sublimation of an individual. It is a bodiless flame on the point of mingling with the infinite flame. A description of the state of one who is in this body is given in "The Hermit of Aesopus Island."

Such is a rough account of these "robes" according to Mme. Blavatsky. She further adds that the Dharmakaya body has to be renounced by anyone who wants to help humanity. Now, helping humanity is a very nice thing for those who like it, and no doubt those who do so deserve well of their fellows. But there is no reason whatever for imagining that to help humanity is the only kind of work worth doing in this universe. The feeling of desire to do so is a limitation and a drag just as bad as any other; and it is not at all necessary to make all this fuss about Initiation and all the rest of it. The universe is exceedingly elastic, especially for those who are themselves elastic. Therefore, though of course one cannot remember humanity when one is wearing the Dharmakaya body, one can hang the Dharmakaya body in one's magical wardrobe, with a few camphor-balls to keep the moths out, and put it on from time to time when feeling in need of refreshment. In fact, one who is helping humanity is constantly in need of a wash and brush-up from time to time. There is nothing quite so contaminating as humanity, especially Theosophists, as Mme. Blavatsky herself discovered. But the best of all lustrations is death, in which all things unessential to progress are burned up. The plan is much better than that of the Elixir of Life. It is perfectly all right to use this Elixir for energy and youth, but despite all, impressions keep on cluttering up the mind, and once in a while it is certainly a splendid thing for everybody to have the Spring Cleaning of death.

With regard to one's purpose in doing anything at all, it depends on the nature of one's Star. Blavatsky was horribly hampered by the Trance of Sorrow. She could see nothing else in the world but helping humanity. She takes no notice whatever of the question of progress through other planets.

Geocentricity is a very pathetic and amusingly childish characteristic of the older schools. They are always talking about the ten thousand worlds, but it is only a figure of speech. They do not believe in them as actual realities. It is one of the regular Oriental tricks to exaggerate all sorts of things in order to impress other people with one's knowledge, and then to forget altogether to weld this particular piece of information on to the wheel of the Law. Consequently, all Blavatsky's talk about the sublimity of the Nirmanakaya body is no more than the speech of a politician who is thanking a famous general for having done some of his dirty work for him.

39. *The Shangna robe, 'tis true, can purchase light eternal. The Shangna robe alone gives the Nirvâna of destruction; it stops rebirth, but O Lanoo, it also kills compassion. No longer can the perfect Buddhas, who don the Dharmakâya glory, help man's salvation. Alas! shall SELVES be sacrificed to Self; mankind, unto the weal of Units?*

The sum of misery is diminished only in a minute degree by the attainment of a Pratyeka-Buddha. The tremendous energy acquired is used to accomplish the miracle of destruction. If the keystone of an arch is taken away the other stones are not promoted to a higher place. They fall. [A Pratyeka-Buddha is one who attains emancipation for himself alone.—Ed.]

("Nirvana of destruction"! *Nirvana* means 'cessation'. What messy English!)

40. *Know, O beginner, this is the Open PATH, the way to selfish bliss, shunned by the Bodhisattvas of the "Secret Heart," the Buddhas of Compassion.*

The words "selfish bliss" must not be taken in a literal sense. It is exceedingly difficult to discuss this question. The Occidental mind finds it difficult even to attach any meaning to the conditions of Nirvana. Partly it is the fault of language, partly it is due to the fact that the condition of Arhat is quite beyond thought. He is beyond the Abyss, and there a thing is only true in so far as it is self-contradictory. The Arhat has no self to be blissful. It is much simpler to consider it on the lines given in my commentary to the last verse.

41. *To live to benefit mankind is the first step. To practise the six glorious virtues is the second.*

42. *To don Nirmânakâya's humble robe is to forego eternal bliss for Self, to help on man's salvation. To reach Nirvâna's bliss but to renounce it, is the supreme, the final step—the highest on Renunciation's Path.*

All this about Gautama Buddha having renounced Nirvana is apparently all a pure invention of Mme. Blavatsky, and has no authority in the Buddhist canon. The Buddha is referred to, again and again, as having "passed away by that kind of passing away which leaves nothing whatever behind." The account of his doing this is given in the Mahaparinibbana Sutta; and it was the contention of the Theosophists that this "great, sublime, Nibbana story" was something peculiar to Gautama Buddha. They began to talk about Parinibbana, super-Nibbana, as if there were some way of subtracting one from one which would leave a higher, superior kind of a nothing, or as if there were some way of blowing out a candle which would leave Moses in a much more Egyptian darkness than we ever supposed when we were children.

This is not science. This is not business. This is American Sunday journalism. The Hindu and the American are very much alike in this innocence, this naiveté which demands fairy stories with ever bigger giants. They cannot bear the idea of anything being complete and done with. So, they are always talking in superlatives, and are hard put to it when the facts catch up with them, and they have to invent new superlatives. Instead of saying that there are bricks of various sizes, and specifying those sizes, they have a brick, and a super-brick, and "one" brick, and "some" brick; and when they have got to the end, they chase through the dictionary for some other epithet to brick, which shall excite the sense of wonder at the magnificent progress and super-progress—I present the American nation with this word—which is supposed to have been made. Probably the whole thing is a bluff without a single fact behind it. Almost the whole of the Hindu psychology is an example of this kind of journalism. They are not content with the supreme God. The other man wishes to show off by having a supremer God than that, and when a third man comes along and finds them disputing, it is up to him to invent a supremest super-God.

It is simply ridiculous to try to add to the definition of Nibbana by this invention of Parinibbana, and only talkers busy themselves with these fantastic speculations. The serious student minds his own business, which is the business in hand. The President of a Corporation does not pay his bookkeeper to make a statement of the countless billions of profit to be made in some future year. It requires no great ability to string a row of zeros after a significant figure until the ink runs out. What is wanted is the actual balance of the week.

The reader is most strongly urged not to permit himself to indulge in fantastic flights of thought, which are the poison of the mind, because they represent an attempt to run away from reality, a dispersion of energy and a corruption of moral strength. His business is, firstly, to know himself; secondly, to order and control himself; thirdly, to develop himself on sound organic lines little by little. The rest is only leather and Prunella.

There is, however, a sense in which the service of humanity is necessary to the completeness of the Adept. He is not to fly away too far.

Some remarks on this course are given in the note to the next verse.

The student is also advised to take note of the conditions of membership of the A ∴ A ∴.

43. *Know, O Disciple, this is the Secret PATH, selected*

by the Buddhas of Perfection, who sacrificed the SELF to weaker Selves.

This is a statement of the conditions of performing the Alchemical operation indicated in the injunction: "Coagula." In "Solvé" the Adept aspires upward. He casts off everything that he has or is. But after reaching the supreme triad, he aspires downward. He keeps on adding to all that he has or is, but after another manner.

This part of our treatise is loathsomely sentimental twaddle, what America (God bless her!) calls "sob-stuff." When tipsy old ladies become maudlin, it is time to go.

44. *Yet, if the "Doctrine of the Heart" is too high-winged for thee, if thou needest help thyself and fearest to offer help to others—then, thou of timid heart, be warned in time: remain content with the "Eye Doctrine" of the Law. Hope still. For if the "Secret Path" is unattainable this "day," it is within thy reach "To-morrow." Learn that no efforts, not the smallest—whether in right or wrong direction—can vanish from the world of causes. E'en wasted smoke remains not traceless. "A harsh word uttered in past lives is not destroyed, but ever comes again." The pepper plant will not give birth to roses, nor the sweet jessamine's silver star to thorn or thistle turn.*

Behold what is written for a Parable in the "Great Law":

> Let not the failure and the pain turn aside the worshippers. The foundations of the pyramid were hewn in the living rock ere sunset; did the king weep at dawn that the crown of the pyramid was yet unquarried in the distant land?
>
> There was also an humming-bird that spake unto the horned cerastes, and prayed him for poison. And the great snake of Khem the Holy One, the royal Uraeus serpent, answered. him and said:
>
> I sailed over the sky of Nu in the car called Millions-of-Years, and I saw not any creature upon Seb that was equal to me.

The venom of my fang is the inheritance of my father, and of my father's father; and how shall I give it unto thee? Live thou and thy children as I and my fathers have lived, even unto an hundred millions of generations, and it may be that the mercy of the Mighty Ones may bestow upon thy children a drop of the poison of eld.

Then the humming-bird was afflicted in his spirit, and he flew unto the flowers, and it was as if naught had been spoken between them. Yet in a little while a serpent struck him that he died.

But an Ibis that meditated upon the bank of Nile the beautiful God listened and heard. And he laid aside his Ibis ways, and became as a serpent, saying Peradventure in an hundred millions of millions of generations of my children, they shall attain to a drop of the poison of the fang of the Exalted One.

And behold! ere the moon waxed thrice he became an Uraeus serpent, and the poison of the fang was established in him and his seed even for ever and for ever.

45. *Thou canst create this "day" thy chances for thy "to-morrow." In the "Great Journey," causes sown each hour bear each its harvest of effects, for rigid Justice rules the World. With mighty sweep of never-erring action, it brings to mortals lives of weal or woe, the Karmic progeny of all our former thoughts and deeds.*

46. *Take them as much as merit hath in store for thee, O thou of patient heart. Be of good cheer and rest content with fate. Such is thy Karma, the Karma of the cycle of thy births, the destiny of those who, in their pain and sorrow, are born along with thee, rejoice and weep from life to life, chained to thy previous actions.*

47. *Act thou for them "to-day," and they will act for thee "to-morrow."*

These verses confirm what was said above with regard to perseverance. Every cause has its effect. There is no waste. There is no evasion.

48. *'Tis from the bud of Renunciation of the Self, that springeth the sweet fruit of final Liberation.*

This is again obscure, as the word "Self" means so many things, and though many kinds of type have been employed to spell it, clear definitions of what each type indicates are lacking. It is here, however, the doctrine of the Two Paths which is taught. On reaching the highest grade of the second Order, that of Exempt Adept, there are two Paths open, the right hand and the left. These are described at length in *Liber 418*, and we must refer the Student to that book. But the main point is that on the right hand path, stripping self, the Adept becomes Nemo, the Master of the Temple, and returns across the abyss, or rather is flung forth, and appears in the Heaven of Jupiter—or sphere of another planet—as a morning Star or an evening Star to bring light to them that dwell upon the earth. On the left hand Path, the Adept, wishing to keep all that he has, shuts himself up in a Tower of Silence, there to suffer the progressively degrading agony of slow dispersion. For on the right hand Path the Master of the Temple is—momentarily—after a fashion—at rest. His intellectual and physical forces are acting in the world, but his blood is in the Cup of Babalon, a draught to awaken the Eld of the All-Father, and all that remains of him is a little pile of dust which only waits the moment when it shall be burnt to ashes.

49. *To perish doomed is he, who out of fear of Mâra refrains from helping man, lest he should act for Self. The pilgrim who would cool his weary limbs in running water, yet dares not plunge for terror of the stream risks to succumb from heat. Inaction based on selfish fear can bear but evil fruit.*

A further warning against the doctrine of inaction. It is extraordinary how the Author insists again and again on this point. Orthodox Buddhism ostensibly teaches that creation of any Karma whatever merely perpetuates "Sorrow."

50. *The selfish devotee lives to no purpose. The man who does not go through his appointed work in life—has lived in vain.*

This verse repeats this lesson yet once more. It is another way of saying: Do what thou wilt shall be the whole of the Law.

51. *Follow the wheel of life; follow the wheel of duty to race and kin, to friend and foe, and close thy mind to pleasures as to pain. Exhaust the law of Karmic retribution. Gain Siddhis for thy future birth.*

This again states the same thing, urges the aspirant to live his life fully on every plane, preserving, it is true, an indifference to all that he does, but only the inner indifference of contempt, not the outer indifference of atrophy. Madame Blavatsky herself smoked like a volcano, drank like a fish, swore like a trooper, loved like a Cleopatra. She was right. Read the Taoist instructions to this effect.

52. *If Sun thou canst not be, then be the humble planet. Aye, if thou art debarred from flaming like the noonday Sun upon the snow-capped mount of purity eternal, then choose, O Neophyte, a humbler course.*

There are a great many people who not only are without marked capacity, but are obviously without any capacity at all, for attainment even on a very modest scale. The question then arises as to whether they can "be any good." Unless they are made to do something, they are likely to slip back rather than to make progress. Fortunately, there is a way through which they can make sure of acquiring the capacity in their next incarnation. This way is Karma Yoga: devotion through work to the Work.

53. *Point out the "Way"—however dimly, and lost among the host—as does the evening star to those who tread*

their path in darkness.

The principal method of Karma Yoga indicated is the preaching of the good Law. Of course it will be understood that anyone thus unfortunately situated cannot understand the Law, but the Law is of such virtue that this is not a fatal disadvantage. See *Liber CCC*.

54. *Behold Migmar (Mars), as in his crimson veils his "Eye" sweeps over slumbering Earth. Behold the fiery aura of the "Hand" of Lhagpa (Mercury) extended in protecting love over the heads of his ascetics. Both are now servants to Nyima (the Sun), left in his absence silent watchers in the night. Yet both in Kalpas past were bright Nyimas, and may in future "Days" again become two Suns. Such are the falls and rises of the Karmic Law in Nature.*

The astronomy of the Author of this book is not equal to her poetic prose. Mercury can hardly be said to have a fiery aura, or to be a silent watcher in the night. Nor is it easy to attach any meaning to the statement that Mars and Mercury were once Suns. The theories of transmigration of personality involved are a little difficult!

55. *Be, O Lanoo, like them. Give light and comfort to the toiling pilgrims, and seek out him who knows still less than thou; who in his wretched desolation sits starving for the bread of Wisdom and the bread which feeds the shadow, without a Teacher, hope or consolation, and—let him hear the Law.*

This charge is very important to all Students of whatever grade. Everyone's first duty is to himself, and to his progress in the Path; but his second duty, which presses the first hard, is to give assistance to those not so advanced.

56. *Tell him, O Candidate, that he who makes of pride and self-regard bondmaidens to devotion; that he, who, cleaving to existence, still lays his patience and submission to the Law, as a sweet flower at the feet of Shâkya-Thub-pa, becomes a Srotâpatti in this birth. The Siddhis of perfection*

may loom far, far away; but the first step is taken, the stream is entered, and he may gain the eyesight of the mountain eagle, the hearing of the timid doe.

It seems rather a bold assertion that Srotapatti is so easily attained, and I know of no Canonical Buddhist authority for this statement. (A Srotapatti becomes an Arahat in seven more incarnations. "Siddhis"—magic powers.)

57. *Tell him, O Aspirant, that true devotion may bring him back the knowledge, that knowledge which was his in former births. The deva-sight and deva-hearing are not obtained in one short birth.*

The promise in this verse is less difficult to believe. By true devotion is meant a devotion which does not depend upon its object. The highest kind of love asks for no return. It is however misleading to say that "deva-sight and deva-hearing are not obtained in one short birth," as that appears to mean that unless you are born with them you can never acquire them, which is certainly untrue. It is open to any one to say to any one who has acquired them, that he must have acquired them in a previous existence, but a more stupid argument can hardly be imagined. It is an ex-cathedrâ statement, and it begs the question, and it contains the same fallacy as is committed by those who suppose that an uncreated God can explain an uncreated Universe.

58. *Be humble, if thou would'st attain to Wisdom.*

By humility is meant the humility of the scientific man.

59. *Be humbler still, when Wisdom thou hast mastered.*

This is merely a paraphrase of Sir Isaac Newton's remark about the child picking up shells.

60. *Be like the Ocean which receives all streams and rivers. The Ocean's mighty calm remains unmoved; it feels them not.*

This verse has many possible interpretations, but its

main meaning is that you should accept the universe without being affected by it.

61. *Restrain by thy Divine thy lower Self.*

"Divine" refers to Tiphareth. (See *The Equinox.*)

62. *Restrain by the Eternal the Divine.*

"Eternal" refers to Kether. In these two verses the Path is explained in language almost Qabalistic.

63. *Aye [sic], great is he who is the slayer of desire.*

By "desire" is again meant "tendency" in the technical Buddhist sense. The Law of Gravitation is the most universal example of such a tendency.

64. *Still greater he, in whom the Self Divine has slain the very knowledge of desire.*

This verse refers to a stage in which the Master has got entirely beyond the Law of cause and effect. The words "Self Divine" are somewhat misleading in view of the sense in which they have been used previously.

65. *Guard thou the Lower lest it soil the Higher.*

The Student is told to "guard" the lower, that is to say he should protect and strengthen it in every possible way, never allowing it to grow disproportionately or to overstep its boundaries.

66. *The way to final freedom is within thy SELF.*

In this verse we find the "SELF" identified with the Universe.

67. *That way begins and ends outside of Self.*

The Ego, i.e., that which is opposed by the non-Ego, has to be destroyed.

68. *Unpraised by men and humble is the mother of all rivers, in Tirthika's proud sight; empty the human form though filled with Amrita's sweet waters, in the sight of fools. Withal, the birthplace of the sacred rivers is the sacred land, and he who Wisdom hath, is honoured by all men.*

This verse appears to employ a local metaphor, and as

Madame Blavatsky had never visited Tibet, the metaphor is obscure, and the geography doubtful.

69. *Arhans and Sages of the boundless Vision are rare as is the blossom of the Udumbara tree. Arhans are born at midnight hour, together with the sacred plant of nine and seven stalks, the holy flower that opens and blooms in darkness, out of the pure dew and on the frozen bed of snow-capped heights, heights that are trodden by no sinful foot.*

We find the talented Author again in difficulties, this time with Botany. By the "boundless Vision" is not meant the stupid Siddhi, but one of the forms of Samadhi, perhaps that upon the snake Ananta, the great green snake that bounds the Universe.

70. *No Arhan, O Lanoo, becomes one in that birth when for the first time the Soul begins to long for final liberation. Yet, O thou anxious one, no warrior volunteering fight in the fierce strife between the living and the dead, not one recruit can ever be refused the right to enter on the Path that leads toward the field of Battle. For either he shall win, or he shall fail.*

It is most important that the Master should not reject any pupil. As it is written in *Liber Legis,* "He must teach, but he may make severe the ordeals." Compare also the 13th Aethyr, in *Liber 418,* where it is shown that Nemo has no means of deciding which of his flowers is the really important one, although assured that all will one day bloom.

71. *Yea, if he conquers, Nirvâna shall be his. Before he casts his shadow off, his mortal coil, that pregnant cause of anguish and illimitable pain—in him will men a great and holy Buddha honour.*

The words "mortal coil" suggest Stratford-on-Avon rather than Lhassa. The meaning of the verse is a little obscure. It is that the conqueror will be recognised as a Buddha sooner or later. This is not true, but does not matter. My God! if one wanted "recognition" from "men"! Help!

72. *And if he falls, e'en then he does not fall in vain; the enemies he slew in the last battle will not return to life in the next birth that will be his.*

Further encouragement to proceed; for although you do not attain everything, yet the enemies you have conquered will not again attack you. In point of fact this is hardly true. The conquest must be very complete for it to be so; but they certainly recur with very diminished intensity. Similar is the gradual immunization of man to syphilis, which was a rapidly fatal disease when fresh. Now we all have it in our blood, and are protected (to some extent, at least) against the ladies.

73. *But if thou would'st Nirvana reach, or cast the prize away, let not the fruit of action and inaction be thy motive, O thou of dauntless heart.*

This verse is again very obscure, from overloading. The "fruit" and the "prize" both refer to Nirvana.

74. *Know that the Bodhisattva who Liberation changes for Renunciation to don the miseries of "Secret Life," is called "thrice Honoured," O thou candidate for woe throughout the cycles.*

This verse must not be interpreted as offering the inducement of the title of "thrice Honoured" to a Bodhisattva. It is a mere eloquent appeal to the Candidate. This about woe is awful. It suggests a landlady in Dickens who 'as seen better days.

75. *The PATH is one, Disciple, yet in the end, twofold. Marked are its stages by four and seven Portals. At one end —bliss immediate, and at the other—bliss deferred. Both are of merit the reward; the choice is thine.*

The "four and seven Portals" refer, the first to the four stages ending in Arhat, the second to the Portals referred to in the third Fragment.

76. *The One becomes the two, the Open and the Secret. The first one leadeth to the goal, the second, to Self-Immolation.*

The obvious meaning of the verse is the one to take. However, I must again warn the reader against supposing that "Self-Immolation" has anything to do with Sir Philip Sidney, or the Sati of the Brahmin's widow.

77. *When to the Permanent is sacrificed the Mutable, the prize is thine : the drop returneth whence it came. The Open PATH leads to the changeless change—Nirvâna, the glorious state of Absoluteness, the Bliss past human thought.*

78. *Thus, the first Path is LIBERATION.*

79. *But Path the second is RENUNCIATION, and therefore called the "Path of Woe."*

There is far too much emotionalism in this part of the treatise, though perhaps this is the fault of the language; but the attitude of contemplating the sorrow of the Universe eternally is unmanly and unscientific. In the practical attempt to aid suffering, the consciousness of that suffering is lost. With regard to the Doctrine of Karma, argument is nugatory. In one sense Karma cannot be interfered with, even to the smallest extent, in any way, and therefore all action is not truly cause, but effect. In another sense Zoroaster is right when he says "Theurgists fall not so low as to be ranked among the herd that are in subjection to fate." Even if the will be not free, it must be considered as free, or the word loses its meaning. There is, however, a much deeper teaching in this matter.

80. *That Secret Path leads the Arhan to mental woe unspeakable; woe for the living Dead, and helpless pity for the men of Karmic sorrow; the fruit of Karma Sages dare not still.*

Mental woe unspeakable—Rats! If we were to take all this *au grand sérieux,* we should have to class H. P. B.

with Sacher-Masoch. She does not seem to have any idea of what an Arhan is, as soon as she plunges into one of these orgies of moral flagellation! Long before one becomes an Arhan, one has completely cured the mind. One knows that it is contradiction and illusion. One has passed by the Abyss, and reached Reality. Now, although one is flung forth again across the Abyss, as explained in *Liber CDXVIII*, and undergoes quite normal mental experiences, yet they are no longer taken seriously, for they have not the power to delude.

There is no question of Sages daring to still the fruit of Karma. I do not quite know how one would set about stilling a fruit, by the way. But the more sage one is, the less one wants to interfere with law. There is a special comment upon this point in *Liber Aleph*. Most of the pleasures in life, and most of the education in life, are given by superable obstacles. Sport, including love, depends on the overcoming of artificial or imaginary resistance. Golf has been defined as trying to knock a little ball into a hole with a set of instruments very ill-adapted for the purpose. In Chess one is bound by purely arbitrary rules. The most successful courtesans are those who have the most tricks in their bags. I will not argue that this complexity is better than the Way of the Tao. It is probably a perversion of taste, a spiritual caviar. But as the poet says:

> It may seem to you strange:
> The fact is—I like it!

81. *For it is written: "Teach to eschew all causes; the ripple of effect, as the great tidal wave, thou shalt let run its course."*

This verse apparently contradicts completely the long philippic against inaction, for the Object of those who counsel non-action is to prevent any inward cause arising, so that when the old causes have worked this out there is nothing left. But this is quite unphilosophical, for every effect as soon as it occurs becomes a new cause, and it is always equal to its cause. There is no waste or dissipation. If you take an atom of hydrogen and combine it with one hundred thousand other atoms in turn, it still remains hydrogen, and it has not lost any of its qualities.

The harmony of the doctrines of Action and Non-Action is to be found in The Way of the Tao. One should do what is perfectly natural to one; but this can only be done when one's consciousness is merged in the Universal or Phallic Consciousness.

82. *The "Open Way," no sooner hast thou reached its goal, will lead thee to reject the Bodhisattvic body, and make thee enter the thrice glorious state of Dharmakâya, which is oblivion of the world and men for ever.*

The collocation called "I" is dissolved. One "goes out" like the flame of a candle. But I must remark that the final clause is again painfully geocentric.

83. *The "Secret Way" leads also to Paranirvânic bliss— but at the close of Kalpas without number; Nirvânas gained and lost from boundless pity and compassion for the world of deluded mortals.*

This is quite contrary to Buddhist teaching. Buddha certainly had "Parinirvana," if there be such a thing, though, as *Nirvana* means 'Annihilation' and *Parinirvana* 'complete Annihilation' it requires a mind more metaphysical than mine to distinguish between these. It is quite certain that Buddha did not require any old Kalpas to get there, and to suppose that Buddha is still about, watching over the world, degrades him to a common Deity, and is in flat contradiction to the statements in the Mahaparinibbana Sutta, where Buddha gravely explains that he is passing away by that kind of passing away which leaves nothing whatever behind, and compares his death to the extinction of a lamp. Canonical Buddhism is certainly the only thing upon which we can rely as a guide to the teachings of the Buddha, if there ever was a Buddha. But we are in no wise bound to accept such teachings blindly, however great our personal reverence for the teacher.

84. *But it is said: "The last shall be the greatest."*
Samyak Sambuddha, the Teacher of Perfection, gave up his
SELF for the salvation of the World, by stopping at the
threshold of Nirvâna—the pure state.

Here is further metaphysical difficulty. One kind of nothing, by taking its pleasures sadly, becomes an altogether superior kind of nothing.

It is with no hope of personal advancement that the Masters teach. Personal advancement has ceased to have any meaning long before one becomes a Master. Nor do they teach because they are such Nice Kind People. Masters are like Dogs, which "bark and bite, for 'tis their nature to." We want no credit, no thanks; we are sick of you; only, we have to go on.

This verse is, one must suppose, an attempt to put things into the kind of language that would be understood by beginners. Compare Chapter Thirteen of *The Book of Lies*, where it explains how one is induced to follow the Path by false pretences. Compare also the story of "The Dolphin and the Prophet" in *Liber LXV*.

37. Behold! the Abyss of the Great Deep. Therein is a mighty dolphin, lashing his sides with the force of the waves.
38. There is also an harper of gold, playing infinite tunes.
39. Then the dolphin delighted therein, and put off his body, and became a bird.
40. The harper also laid aside his harp, and played infinite tunes upon the Pan-pipe.
41. Then the bird desired exceedingly this bliss, and

laying down its wings became a faun of the forest.

42. The harper also laid down his Pan-pipe, and with the human voice sang his infinite tunes.

43. Then the faun was enraptured, and followed far; at last the harper was silent, and the faun became Pan in the midst of the primal forest of Eternity.

44. Thou canst not charm the dolphin with silence, O my Prophet!

85. *Thou hast the knowledge concerning the two Ways. Thy time will come for choice, O thou eager Soul, when thou hast reached the end and passed the seven Portals. Thy mind is clear. No more art thou entangled in delusive thoughts, for thou hast learned all. Unveiled stands Truth and looks thee sternly in the face. She says: "Sweet are the fruits of Rest and Liberation for the sake of Self; but sweeter still the fruits of long and bitter duty. Aye [sic], Renunciation for the sake of others, of suffering fellow-men."*

86. *He, who becomes Pratyeka-Buddha, makes his obeisance but to his Self. The Bodhisattva who has won the battle, who holds the prize within his palm, yet says in his divine compassion:*

87. *"For others' sake this great reward I yield"—accomplishes the greater Renunciation.*

A SAVIOUR OF THE WORLD is he.

.   .   .   .

Here again we are told of the sweetness of the fruits. But even in the beginning the Magician has had to work entirely regardless of any fruits, and his principal method has been to reject any that may come his way. Again all this about the "sake of others" and "suffering fellow-men," is the kind of sentimental balderdash that assures one that this book was intended to reach the English and not the Tibetan public. The sense of separateness from others has been weeded out from the consciousness long, long ago. The Buddha who accomplishes the greater Renunciation is a Saviour of the World—it is the dogginess of a dog that makes it doggy. It is not the virtue of a dog to be doggy. A dog does not become doggy by the renunciation of non-dogginess. It is quite true that you and I value one kind of a Buddha more than another kind of a Buddha, but the Universe is not framed in accordance with what you and I like. As Zoroaster says: "The progression of the Stars was not generated for your sake," and there are times when a Dhamma-Buddha reflects on the fact that he is no more and no less than any other thing, and wishes he were dead. That is to say, that kind of a Dhamma-Buddha in whom such thoughts necessarily arise, thinks so; but this of course does not happen, because it is not in the nature of a Dhamma-Buddha to think anything of the sort, and he even knows too much to think that it would be rather natural if there were some kinds of Dhamma-Buddha who did think something of the kind. But he is assuredly quite indifferent to the praise and blame of the "suffering fellow-men." He does not want their gratitude. We will now close this painful subject.

88. *Behold! The goal of bliss and the long Path of Woe are at the furthest end. Thou canst choose either, O aspirant to Sorrow, throughout the coming cycles!*

Om Vajrapani Hum

With this eloquent passage the Fragment closes. It may be remarked that the statement "thou canst choose" is altogether opposed to that form of the theory of determinism which is orthodox Buddhism. However, the question of Free Will has been discussed in a previous Note.

OM VAJRAPANI HUM. Vajrapani was some kind of a universal deity in a previous Manvantara who took an oath:

Ere the Cycle reach to utter darkness,

Work I so that every living being
Pass beyond this constant chain of causes.
If I fail, may all my being shatter
Into millions of far-whirling pieces!

He failed, of course, and blew up accordingly; hence
the Stars.

FRAGMENT III
THE SEVEN PORTALS

1. *"Upâdhâya, the choice is made, I thirst for Wisdom. Now hast thou rent the veil before the secret Path and taught the greater Yâna.* [Mahayana, the Big Path; a term for the Hinduized Buddhism of Tibet.—Ed.] *Thy servant here is ready for thy guidance."*

This fragment again appears to be intended to follow on immediately after the last, and yet the Chela says to the Guru that the choice is made. Obviously it does not refer to the great choice referred to in Fragment II, verse 88. One is inclined further to suspect that Madame Blavatsky supposes Mahayana and Hinayana to refer in some way or other to the two Paths previously discussed. They do not. Madame Blavatsky's method of exegesis, in the absence of original information, was to take existing commentators and disagree with them, her standard being what the unknown originals ought, in her opinion, to have said. This method saves much of the labour of research, and with a little luck it ought to be possible to discover subsequently much justification in the originals as they become known. Madame Blavatsky was justified in employing this method because she really did know the subject better than either commentator or original. She merely used Oriental lore as an Ostrich hunter uses the skin of a dead bird. She was Ulysses, and the East her Wooden Horse. [Maha (great) and Hina (little) are quite meaningless epithets, only serving to distinguish Hinduized Tibetan Buddhism from canonical Cingalese-Burmese-Siamese Buddhism.—Ed.]

2. *'Tis well, Shrâvaka. Prepare thyself, for thou wilt*

have to travel on alone. The Teacher can but point the way. The path is one for all, the means to reach the goal must vary with the Pilgrims.

It is here admitted that there are many ways of reaching the same end. In order to assist a pupil, the Teacher should know all these ways by actual experience. He should know them in detail. There is a great deal of pious gassing about most Teachers—it is very easy to say "Be good and you will be happy," and I am afraid that even this book itself has been taken as little better by the majority of its admirers. What the pupil wants is not vague generalisations on virtue, not analyses of Nirvana and explorations in Hindu metaphysics, but a plain straightforward statement of a practical character. When a man is meditating and finds himself interfered with by some particular class of thought, he does not want to know about the glory of the Buddha and the advantages of the Dhamma and the fraternal piety of the Sangha. He wants to know how to stop those thoughts arising, and the only person who can help him to do that is a Teacher who has been troubled by those same thoughts, and learnt how to stop them in his own case. For one Teacher who knows his subject at all, there are at least ten thousand who belch pious platitudes. I wish to name no names, but Annie Besant, Prentice Mulford, Troward, Ella Wheeler Wilcox, and so on, down—right down—to Arthur Edward Waite, immediately occur to the mind. What does not occur to the mind is the names of people now living who know their subject from experience. The late Swami Vivekananda did know his. Sabapaty Swami did so. Shri Parananda Swami did so, and of course above all these stands Bhikkhu Ananda Metteya. Outside these, one can think of no one, except the very reticent Rudolf Steiner, who betrays practical acquaintance with the Path. The way to discover whether a Teacher knows anything about it or not is to do the work yourself, and see if your understanding of him improves, or whether he fobs you off in your hour of need with remarks on Virtue.

3. *Which wilt thou choose, O thou of dauntless heart? The Samtan of "Eye Doctrine," fourfold Dhyâna, or thread thy way through Pâramitâs, six in number, noble gates of virtue leading to Bodhi and to Pragnyâ, seventh step of Wisdom?*

It must not be supposed that the Paths here indicated are all. Apparently the writer is still harping on the same old two Paths. It appears that "fourfold Dhyana" is a mere extension of the word Samtan. There are, however, eight, not four, four of these being called Low and four High. They are defined in Rhys-Davids' *Buddhism,* p. 174–6.

The Buddha just before his death went through all these stages of meditation which are described in the paragraph here quoted:

> Then the blessed One addressed the Brethren, and said: "Behold now, brethren, I exhort you, saying, 'Decay is inherent in all component things! Work out your salvation with diligence!'"
> This was the last word of the Tathagata!
> Then the Blessed One entered into the first stage of deep meditation. And rising out of the first stage he passed into the second. And rising out of the second he passed into the third. And rising out of the third stage he passed into the fourth. And rising out of the fourth stage of deep meditation he entered into the state of mind to which the infinity of space is alone present. And passing out of the mere consciousness of the infinity of space he entered into the state of mind to which the infinity of thought is alone present. And passing out of the mere consciousness of the infinity of thought he entered into a state of mind to which nothing at all was specially present. And passing out of the consciousness of no special object he fell into a state between consciousness

and unconsciousness. And passing out of the state between consciousness and unconsciousness he fell into a state in which the unconsciousness both of sensations and of ideas had wholly passed away.

What rubbish! Here we have a man with no experience of the states which he is trying to describe; for Prof. Rhys-Davids, many though are his virtues, is not Buddha, and this man is attempting to translate highly technical terms into a language in which those technical terms not only have no equivalent, but have nothing in the remotest degree capable of being substituted for an equivalent. This is characteristic of practically all writing on Eastern thought. What was wanted was a Master of some Occidental language to obtain the experiences of the East by undertaking the practices of the East. His own experience put into words would then form a far better translation of Oriental works on the same subject, than any translation which a scholar might furnish. I am inclined to think that this was Blavatsky's method. So obvious a forgery as this volume only contains so much truth and wisdom because this is the case. The Master— alike of Language and of Experience—has at last arisen; it is the Master Therion—The Beast—666—the Logos of the Aeon—whose Word is "Do what thou wilt shall be the whole of the Law."

4. *The rugged Path of fourfold Dhyâna winds on uphill. Thrice great is he who climbs the lofty top.*

5. *The Pâramita heights are crossed by a still steeper path. Thou hast to fight thy way through portals seven, seven strongholds held by cruel, crafty Powers—passions incarnate.*

The distinction between the two Paths is now evident; that of Dhyana is intellectual, or one might better say, mental, that of Paramita, moral. But it may well be asked whether these Paths are mutually exclusive, whether a good man is always an idiot and a clever man always a brute, to put the antithesis on a somewhat lower plane. Does anyone really think that one can reach supreme mental control while there are "seven cruel, crafty powers, passions incarnate," worrying you? The fact is that this dichotomy of the Path is rather dramatic than based on experience.

6. *Be of good cheer, Disciple; bear in mind the golden rule. Once thou hast passed the gate Srotâpatti, "he who the stream hath entered"; once thy foot hath pressed the bed of the Nirvânic stream in this or any future life; thou hast but seven other births before thee, O thou of adamantine Will.*

The author does not state what is meant by the "golden rule." A Srotapatti is a person in such a stage that he will become Arhan after seven more incarnations.[1] There is nothing in Buddhism about the voluntary undertaking of incarnations in order to help mankind. And of course the talk about "Nirvanic bliss" is misleading when one reflects that this quality of bliss or Ananda arising with the first Jhana, has already disappeared, never to return, in the second. The whole question of Nibbana is hopelessly entangled with moonshine metaphysic and mis-interpretation and false tradition. It must be remembered that Nibbana is merely the Pali, the vulgar dialect, for the Sanskrit NIRVANA, and that Nirvana is a state characterising Moksha, which is the liberation resulting from Nirvikalpa-Samâdhi. But then Moksha is defined by the Hindus as unity with Parabrahman; and Parabrahman is without quantity or quality, not subject to change in any way, altogether beyond Manvantara and Pralaya; and so on. In one sense he is pure Atman.

Now the Buddhist rejects Atman, saying there is no such thing. Therefore—to him—there is no Parabrah-

---

1. See Crowley's "The Three Characteristics" in his *The Sword of Song* for an amusing but illuminated story on this state.

man. There is really Maha Brahma, who is (ultimately) subject to change, and, when the Karma which has made him Maha Brahma is exhausted, may be reincarnated as a pig or a Pisacha. Consequently Moksha is not liberation at all, for Nirvana means cessation of that which, after however long a period, may change. This is all clear enough, but then the Buddhist goes on and takes the word Nibbana to mean exactly that which the Hindus meant by Nirvana, insisting strenuously that it is entirely different. And so indeed it is. But if one proceeds further to enquire, "Then what is it?" one finds oneself involved in very considerable difficulty. It is a difficulty which I cannot pretend to solve, even by the logic which obtains above the abyss. I can, however, exhibit the difficulty by relating a conversation which I had with Bhikkhu Ananda Metteya in November, 1906, while I was staying with him in his Monastery outside Rangoon. I was arguing that result was the direct effect of the work of the student. If he went on long enough he was bound to succeed, and he might reasonably infer a causal connection between his work and its result. The Bhikkhu was not unwilling to admit that this might be so in such elementary stages as Jhana, but with regard to the attaining of Arhatship he argued that it depended rather on universal Karma than on that created by the aspirant. Avoiding metaphysical quibbles as to whether these two kinds of Karma are not identical, he figured the situation in this manner. There are two wheels, one of which is the wheel of Nibbana, and the other that of the attainment of the Adept. These two wheels only touch at one point. Now the Arhat may reach the circumference of his wheel, that is, the summit of his attainment, as often as he likes, but unless he happens to do so at the moment when that point touches the wheel of Nibbana, he will not become an Arhat, and it is therefore necessary for him to remain at that summit as long as possible, in fact always, in order that bye and bye—it might be after many incarnations of perfection—these two might coincide. This perfection he regarded not as that of spiritual experience, but as the attainment of Sila, and by Sila he meant the strict observance of all the rules laid down by the Buddha for the Bhikkhu. He continued that the Buddha had apparently attached far more importance to virtue than to any degree of spiritual attainment, placing the well-behaved Bhikkhu not only above the gods, but above the greatest Yogis. (It is obvious, to the Buddhist, that Hindu Yogis, however eminent, are not Arhats.) He said that the rules laid down for Bhikkhus created the conditions necessary. A good Bhikkhu, with no spiritual experience, had at least some chance, whereas the bad Bhikkhu or non-Bhikkhu, although every form of Samadhi was at his fingers' ends, had none. The point is very important, because on this theory the latter, after all his attainments, might pass through all the Dhyana-Lokas and through the Arupa-Brahma-Lokas, exhaust that Karma, be re-incarnated as a Spirochaetes Pallida, and have to begin all over again. And the most virtuous Bhikkhu might be so unfortunate as to fall from Virtue the millionth part of a second before his point on the circumference of the sphere was going to touch that of the wheel of Nibbana, regain it two-millionths of a second later, and thus find Arhatship indefinitely postponed.

I then said: O most excellent expounder of the good Law, prithee explain to me the exact difference between this Doctrine and that which we heard from Shri Parananda that the attainment of Samadhi, though it depended to some extent upon the attainment of the Yogi, depended also upon the grace of the Lord Shiva, and that Yoga did us all no good unless the Lord Shiva happened to be in a good temper. Then the Bhikkhu replied in a dramatic whisper, "There is no difference, except that it is not Buddhism." From this example the Student will understand that he had better not worry about Nibbana and its nature, but confine himself to controlling his thoughts.

7. *Look on. What seest thou before thine eye, O aspirant to Godlike Wisdom?*

8. *"The cloak of darkness is upon the deep of matter; within its folds I struggle. Beneath my gaze it deepens, Lord; it is dispelled beneath the waving of thy hand. A shadow moveth, creeping like the stretching serpent coils . . . It grows, swells out, and disappears in Darkness."*

In this passage a definite vision is presented to the Lanoo. This can be done by an Adept, and sometimes it is a useful method.

9. *It is the shadow of thyself outside the PATH, cast on the darkness of thy sins.*

This charming poetic image should not be taken literally.

10. *"Yea, Lord; I see the PATH; its foot in mire, its summit lost in glorious light Nirvânic. And now I see the ever-narrowing Portals on the hard and thorny way to Gnyâna."*

This continues a vision which resembles, only too painfully, the coloured prints of the Broad and Narrow Ways so familiar to those unfortunates whose business takes them through Paternoster Row.

11. *Thou seest well, Lanoo. These Portals lead the aspirant across the waters on "to the other shore." Each Portal hath a golden key that openeth its gate; and these keys are:*

The expression "the other shore" is particularly unfortunate, owing to its associations in English minds with the hymn usually known as "The sweet bye and bye." It is a metaphor for which there is little justification. Nirvana is frequently spoken of as an island in Buddhist writings, but I am not familiar with any passage in which the metaphor is that of a place at the other end of a journey. The metaphor moreover is mixed. In the last verse he was climbing a ladder; now he is going across the waters, and neither on ladders nor in journeys by water does one usually pass through Portals.[2]

12. 1. *DANA, the key of charity and love immortal.*

2. *SHILA, the key of Harmony in word and act, that counterbalances the cause and the effect, and leaves no further room for Karmic action.*

3. *KSHANTI, patience sweet, that nought can ruffle.*

4. *VAIRAGYA, indifference to pleasure and to pain, illusion conquered, truth alone perceived.*

5. *VIRYA, the dauntless energy that fights its way to the supernal TRUTH, out of the mire of lies terrestrial.*

6. *DHYANA, whose golden gate once opened leads the Narjol toward the realm of Sat eternal and its ceaseless contemplation.*

7. *PRAJNA, the key to which makes of a man a God, creating him a Bodhisattva, son of the Dhyânis. Such to the Portals are the golden keys.*

(Subsection I.) Charity and love are here used in their technical sense, Agape. "Love is the law, love under will." Both Agape and Thelema (will) add to 93, which identifies them qabalistically. This love is not a sloppy feeling of maudlin sentimental kindness. The majority of people of the Christian Science, Theosophical, New Thought type, think that a lot of flabby thoughts, sending out streams of

---

2. During World War 1, when Crowley wrote this Commentary in the United States, the Mahaprajna Paramita Texts had not yet been translated into English. Or else, they had not come to Crowley's notice since his interest in Buddhism had long since lapsed. At any rate, here it must be stated that these texts do speak of "the other shore." Blavatsky was right and Crowley was wrong in this particular instance, despite his claim, sometimes justified, that her thinking was muddled in other respects.

love in the Six Quarters, and so on, will help them. It won't. Love is a pure flame, as swift and deadly as the lightning. This is the kind of love that the Student needs.

(Subsection II.) The "key" here spoken of has been thoroughly explained in Thien Tao in *Konx Om Pax*, but there is a peculiar method, apart from this plane, and easily understood by the equilibrium by which things can be done which bear no fruit. And this method it is quite impossible to explain.

The nearest I can come to intelligibility, is to say that you get very nearly the same sort of feeling as you do when you are making yourself invisible.

Shila is in no way connected with the charming Irish colleen of the same name.

(Subsection III.) The "patience" here spoken of seems to imply courage of a very active kind. It is the quality which persists in spite of all opposition. It must not be forgotten that the word "patience" is derived from *Patior*, 'I suffer.' But, especially with the ancients, suffering was not conceived of as a purely passive function. It was keenly active and intensely enjoyable. There are certain words today still extant in which the original meaning of this word lingers, and consideration may suggest to the Student the true and secret meaning of this passage, "Accendat in nobis Dominus ignem sui amoris et flammam aeternae caritatis," a phrase with the subtle ambiguity which the classics found the finest form of wit.

(Subsection IV.) This indifference is very much the same as what is usually spoken of as non-attachment. The Doctrine has been rediscovered in the West, and is usually announced as "Art for Art's sake." This quality is most entirely necessary in Yoga. In times of dryness the "Devil" comes to you and persuades you that if you go on meditating or doing Pranayama, or whatever it is you may be at, you will go mad. He will also prove to you that it is most necessary for your spiritual progress to repose. He will explain that, by the great law of action and re-action, you should alternate the task which you have set out to do with something else, that you should, in fact, somehow or other change your plans. Any attempt to argue with him will assuredly result in defeat. You must be able to reply, "But I am not in the least interested in my spiritual progress; I am doing this because I put it down in my programme to do it. It may hurt my spiritual progress more than anything in the world. That does not matter. I will gladly be damned eternally, but I will not break my obligation in the smallest detail." By doing this you come out at the other end, and discover that the whole controversy was illusion. One does become blind; one does have to fight one's way through the ocean of asphalt. Hope and Faith are no more. All that can be done is to guard Love, the original source of your energy, by the mask of indifference. This image is a little misleading, perhaps. It must not be supposed that the indifference is a cloak; it must be a real indifference. Desire of any kind must really be conquered, for of course every desire is as it were a string on you to pull you in some direction, and it must be remembered that Nirvana lies (as it were) in no direction, like the fourth dimension in space.

(Subsection V.) *Virya* is, etymologically, 'Manhood'. It is that quality which has been symbolised habitually by the Phallus, and its importance is sufficient to have made the Phallus an universal symbol, apart altogether from reasons connected with the course of nature. Yet these confirm the choice. It is free—it has a will of its own quite independent of the conscious will of the man bearing it. It has no conscience. It leaps. It has no consideration for anything but its own purpose. Again and again this symbol in a new sense will recur as the type of the ideal. It is a symbol alike of the Beginning, the Way and the End. In this particular passage it is however principally synonymous with Will, and Will has been so fully dealt with in *Book 4*, Part II, that it will save trouble if we assume that the reader is familiar with that masterpiece.

(Subsection VI.) This, too, has been carefully described in *Book 4*, Part I.

There is a distinction between Buddhist "Jhana" and Sanskrit "Dhyana," though etymologically the former is a corruption of the latter.

The craze for classification which obsesses the dull minds of the learned has been peculiarly pernicious in the East. In order to divide states of thought into 84 classes, which is—to their fatuity!—an object in itself, because 84 is seven times twelve, they do not hesitate to invent names for quite imaginary states of mind, and to put down the same state of mind several times. This leads to extreme difficulty in the study of their works on psychology and the like. The original man, Buddha, or whoever he may have been, dug out of his mind a sufficient number of jewels, and the wretched intellectuals who edited his work have added bits of glass to make up the string. The result has been that many scholars have thought that the whole psychology of the East was pure bluff. A similar remark is true of the philosophy of the West, where the Schoolmen produced an equal obfuscation. Even now people hardly realize that they did any valuable work at all, and quote their controversies, such as that concerning the number of angels who can dance on the point of a needle, as examples of their complete fatuity and donnishness. In point of fact, it is the critic who is stupid. The question about the angels involves the profoundest considerations of metaphysics, and it was about these that the battle raged. I fancy that their critics imagine the Schoolmen disputing whether the number was 25 or 26, which argues their own shallowness by the readiness with which they attribute the same quality to others. However, a great deal of mischief has been done by the pedant, and the distinctions between the various Jhanas will convey little to the Western mind, even of a man who has some experience of them. The question of mistranslation alone renders the majority of Buddhist documents, if not valueless, at least unreliable. We, however, taking this book as an original work by Blavatsky, need not be bothered by any doubts more deadly than that as to whether her command of English was perfect; and in this treatise, in spite of certain obvious sentimentalities and bombasticisms, we find at least the foundations of a fairly fine style. I think that what she says in this sub-section refers to a statement which I got from my Guru in Madura to the effect that there was a certain point in the body suitable for meditation, which, if once discovered, drew the thought naturally towards itself, the difficulty of concentration consequently disappearing, and that the knowledge of this particular point could be communicated by the Guru to his approved disciples.

(Subsection VII.) We now find a muddle between the keys and the gates. The first five are all obviously keys. The last two seem to be gates, in spite of the statements in the text. We also find the term Bodhisattva in a quite unintelligible sense. We shall discuss this question more fully a little later on.

The Dhyanis are gods of sorts, either perfect men or what one may call natural gods, who occupy eternity in a ceaseless contemplation of the Universe. The Master of the Temple, as he is in himself, is a rather similar person.

Narjol is the Path-Treader, not a paraffin-purgative.

13. *Before thou canst approach the last, O weaver of thy freedom, thou hast to master these Pâramitâs of perfection—*

the virtues transcendental six and ten in number—along the weary Path.

We now get back to the Paramitas, and this treatise is apparently silent with regard to them. Does any one regret it? It isn't the Path that is weary: it is the Sermons on the way.

14. *For, O Disciple! before thou wert made fit to meet thy Teacher face to face, thy MASTER light to light, what wert thou told?*

The old trouble recurs. We cannot tell quite clearly in what stage the Disciple is supposed to be with regard to any given piece of instruction.

15. *Before thou canst approach the foremost gate thou hast to learn to part thy body from thy mind, to dissipate the shadow, and to live in the eternal. For this, thou hast to live and breathe in all, as all that thou perceivest breathes in thee; to feel thyself abiding in all things, all things in self.*

In verse 13 we were told to master the Paramitas before approaching the last gate. Now the author harks back to what he had to do before he approached the first gate, but this may be regarded as a sort of a joke on the part of the Guru. The Guru has a weary time, and frequently amuses himself by telling the pupil that he must do something obviously impossible before he begins. This increases the respect of the pupil for the Guru, and in this way helps him, while at the same time his air of hopelessness is intensely funny—to the Guru. So we find in this verse that the final result, or something very like it, is given as a qualification antecedent to the starting point; as if one told a blind man that he must be able to see through a brick wall before regaining his eyesight.

16. *Thou shalt not let thy senses make a playground of thy mind.*

Following on the tremendous task of verse 15 comes the obvious elementary piece of instruction which one gives to a beginner. The best way out of the dilemma is to take verse 15 in a very elementary sense. Let us paraphrase that verse. "Try to get into the habit of thinking of your mind and body as distinct. Attach yourself to matters of eternal importance, and do not be deluded by the idea that the material universe is real. Try to realise the unity of being." That is a sensible and suitable instruction, a kind of adumbration of the goal. It harmonises emotional and intellectual conceptions to—that which subsequently turns out not to be reality.

17. *Thou shalt not separate thy being from BEING, and the rest, but merge the Ocean in the deep, the drop within the Ocean.*

This too can be considered in an elementary light as meaning: "Begin even at once to destroy the sense of separateness."

18. *So shalt thou be in full accord with all that lives; bear love to men as though they were thy brother-pupils, disciples of one Teacher, the sons of one sweet mother.*

It now becomes clear that all this is meant in an elementary sense, for verse 18 is really little more than a statement that an irritable frame of mind is bad for meditation. Of course anybody who really "bore love," etc., as requested would be suffering from softening of the brain. That is, if you take all this in its obvious literal sense. There is a clean way of Love, but it is not this toshy slop treacle-goo.

19. *Of teachers there are many; the MASTER-SOUL is one, Alaya, the Universal Soul. Live in that MASTER as ITS ray in thee. Live in thy fellows as they live in IT.*

Here the killing of the sense of separateness is further advised. It is a description of the nature of Atma, and Atma is, as elsewhere stated, not a Buddhist, but a Hindu idea. The teaching is here to refer everything to Atma, to regard everything as a corruption of Atma, if you please, but a corruption which is unreal, because Atma is the only real thing. There is a similar instruction in *Liber Legis:* "Let there be no difference made among you between any one thing and any other thing"; and you are urged not to "confound the space marks," saying "they are one," or "they are many."

20. *Before thou standest on the threshold of the Path; before thou crossest the foremost gate, thou hast to merge the two into the One and sacrifice the personal to SELF impersonal and thus destroy the "path" between the two—Antaskarana.*

Here is again the confusion noted with regard to verse 15—for the destruction of the lower Manas implies an attainment not less than that of a Master of the Temple.

21. *Thou hast to be prepared to answer Dharma, the stern law, whose voice will ask thee first at thy initial step:*

22. *"Hast thou complied with all the rules, O thou of lofty hopes?*

"Hast thou attuned thy heart and mind to the great mind and heart of all mankind? For as the sacred River's roaring voice whereby all Nature-sounds are echoed back, so must the heart of him 'who in the stream would enter,' thrill in response to every sigh and thought of all that lives and breathes."

Here is another absurdity. What is the sense of asking a man at his initial step if he has complied with all the rules? If the disciple were in the condition mentioned, he would be already very far advanced. But of course if we were to take the words

"The threshold of the Path"
"The foremost gate"
"The stream"

as equivalent to Srotapatti, the passage would gain in intelligibility. But, just as in the noble eight-fold Path, the steps are concurrent, not consecutive, so, like the

Comte de Saint Germain, when he was expelled from
Berlin, one can go through all the seven Gates at once.

23. *Disciples may be likened to the strings of the soul-
echoing Vinâ; mankind, unto its sounding-board; the hand
that sweeps it to the tuneful breath of the GREAT WORLD-
SOUL. The string that fails to answer 'neath the Master's
touch in dulcet harmony with all the others, breaks—and is
cast away. So the collective minds of Lanoo-Shravakas.
They have to be attuned to the Upâdhyâya's mind—one with
the Over-Soul,—or, break away.*

This is a somewhat high-flown description—it is little
more than an advocacy of docility, a quiet acceptance of
the situation as it is, and an acquiescence in the ultimate
sublime purpose. The question of the crossing of the
abyss now arises, and we reach a consideration of the
Brothers of the Left Hand Path.

24. *Thus do the "Brothers of the Shadow"—the murder-
ers of their Souls, the dread Dad-Dugpa clan.*

"The Brothers of the Shadow" or of the Left Hand
Path are very carefully explained in *Liber 418*. The Exempt
Adept, when he has to proceed, has a choice either to fling
himself into the Abyss by all that he has and is being torn
away, or to shut himself up to do what he imagines to be
continuing with his personal development on very much
the original lines. This latter course does not take him
through the Abyss; but fixes him in Daath, at the crown
of a false Tree of Life in which the Supernal Triad is
missing. Now this man is also called a Black Magician,
and a great deal of confusion has arisen in connection with
this phrase. Even the Author, to judge by the Note,
seems to confuse the matter. Red Caps and Yellow Caps
alike are in general altogether beneath the stage of which
we have been speaking. And from the point of view of the
Master of the Temple, there is very little to choose
between White and Black Magic as ordinarily understood

by the man in the street, who distinguishes between them according as they are helpful or hurtful to himself. If the Magician cures his headache, or gives him a good tip on the Stock Exchange, he is a White Magician. If he suspects him of causing illness and the like, he is Black. To the Master of the Temple either proceeding appears blind and stupid. In the lower stages there is only one way right, and all the rest wrong. You are to aspire to the Knowledge and Conversation of the Holy Guardian Angel, and of course to do any other things which may subserve that one purpose; but nothing else. And of course it is a mistake, unless under very special circumstances, to perform any miracles, on the ground that they diminish the supreme energy reserved for the performance of the Main Task. It will be remembered that the Knowledge and Conversation of the Holy Guardian Angel is attributed to Tiphareth, while the Exempt Adept is in Chesed; how is it then that a Black Magician, a Brother of the Left Hand Path, can ever reach that grade? The answer is given in the eleventh Aethyr; when the Exempt Adept reaches the Frontier of the Abyss, his Holy Guardian Angel leaves him, and this is the one supreme terror of that passage. It seems extraordinary that one who has ever enjoyed His Knowledge and Conversation should afterwards fall away into that blind horror whose name is Choronzon. But such is the case. Some of the problems, or rather, mysteries, connected with this are too deep to enter upon in this place, but the main point to remember is this, that in the Outer Order, and in the College of Adepts itself, it is not certain to what end any one may come. The greatest and holiest of the Exempt Adepts may, in a single moment, become a Brother of the Left Hand Path. It is for this reason that the Great White Brotherhood admits no essential connection with the lower branches affiliated to The Order. At the same time, The Brothers of the

A ∴. A ∴. refuse none. They have no objection to any one claiming to be one of Themselves. If he does so, let him abide by it.

25. *Hast thou attuned thy being to Humanity's great pain, O candidate for light?*

Thou hast? . . . Thou mayest enter.

Yet, ere thou settest foot upon the dreary Path of Sorrow, 'tis well thou should'st first learn the pitfalls on thy way.

.   .   .   .

It appears as if the condition of entering the Path was the Vision of Sorrow, and of course the present Commentator might be inclined to support this theory, since, in his own experience, it was this Vision of Sorrow which caused him to take the First Great Oath. He had suddenly presented to him the perception of the Three Characteristics.[This is fully narrated in *Book 4, Part IV*. This is now known as *The Equinox of the Gods.* — I. R.] It is also evident that aspiration implies dissatisfaction of some sort. But at the same time I do not think that in all cases it is necessary that this dissatisfaction should be so conscious and so universal as appears to be implied in the text.

26. *Armed with the key of Charity, of love and tender mercy, thou art secure before the gate of Dâna, the gate that standeth at the entrance of the Path.*

27. *Behold, O happy Pilgrim! The Portal that faceth thee is high and wide, seems easy of access. The road that leads there-through is straight and smooth and green. 'Tis like a sunny glade in the dark forest depths, a spot on earth mirrored from Amitâbha's paradise. There nightingales of hope and birds of radiant plumage sing, perched in green bowers, chanting success to fearless Pilgrims. They sing of Bodhisattva's virtues five, the fivefold source of Bodhi power, and of the seven steps in Knowledge.*

28. *Pass on! For thou hast brought the key; thou art secure.*

The row of dots in the text (after verse 25) appears to imply complete change of subject, though on other occasions it did not do so. I have already explained one of the technical meanings of Dana, and undoubtedly the Path seems attractive at this stage. One thinks of the joyous reception into the Company of Adepts. One goes almost as a boy goes to meet his first sweetheart.

But there is here another allusion to the beginnings of Meditation, when everything seems so simple and straightforward, and withal so easy and pleasant. There is something intensely human about this. Men set out upon the most dangerous expeditions in high spirits.

29. *And to the second gate the way is verdant too. But it is steep and winds up hill; yea, to its rocky top. Grey Mists will overhang its rough and stony height, and all be dark beyond. As on he goes, the song of hope soundeth more feeble in the pilgrim's heart. The thrill of doubt is now upon him; his step less steady grows.*

Following the last comment a description of this Path refers to the beginning of "dryness" in the course of Meditation.

30. *Beware of this, O Candidate! Beware of fear that spreadeth, like the black and soundless wings of midnight bat, between the moonlight of thy Soul and thy great goal that loometh in the distance far away.*

This passage also appears to have reference to the early life of the Student—hence he is specially warned against fear. Fear is, of course, the first of the pylons through which one passes in the Egyptian system. It is important then to arrange one's life in such a way that one never allows one thing to interfere with another, and one never makes trouble for oneself. The method given in "Thien Tao" is the best to employ.

31. *Fear, O Disciple, kills the will and stays all action. If lacking in the Shila virtue—the pilgrim trips, and*

Karmic pebbles bruise his feet along the rocky path.

The objection to fear is not only the obvious one. Fear is only one of the things which interfere with concentration. The re-action against fear leads to over-boldness. Anything which interferes with the perfect unconscious simplicity of one's going leads to bruises. Troubles of this kind may be called Karmic, because it is events in the past which give occasion for trouble.

32. *Be of sure foot, O Candidate. In Kshânti's essence bathe thy Soul; for now thou dost approach the Portal of that name, the gate of fortitude and patience.*

We now come to the third gate. Notice that this is a further confusion of the Portal with the Key. As previously said, patience here implies rather self-control, a refusal to accept even favours until one is ready for them.

33. *Close not thine eyes, nor lose thy sight of Dorje (the Svastika); Mâra's arrows ever smite the man who has not reached Vairâga.*

"Close not thine eyes" may refer to sleep or to ecstasy, perhaps to both. Dorje is the whirling power which throws off from itself every other influence.

Vairaga is a very definite stage in moral strength. The point is that it is one's intense longing for ecstasy which makes one yield to it. If one does so, one is overwhelmed with the illusion, for even the highest ecstasy is still illusion. The result, in many cases, of obtaining Dhyana is that the workers cease to work. Vairaga is an indifference approaching disgust for everything. It reminds one a good deal of the Oxford Manner. Cambridge men have this feeling, but do not think other people worth the trouble of flattering.

34. *Beware of trembling. 'Neath the breath of fear the key of Kshânti rusty grows: the rusty key refuseth to unlock.*

The word "trembling" seems to imply that it is giddy ecstasy which is referred to, and the "fear" here spoken of may perhaps be the Panic Fear, possibly some feeling analogous to that which produces what is called psychical impotence.

35. *The more thou dost advance, the more thy feet pitfalls will meet. The Path that leadeth on is lighted by one fire— the light of daring burning in the heart. The more one dares, the more he shall obtain. The more he fears, the more that light shall pale—and that alone can guide. For as the lingering sunbeam, that on the top of some tall mountain shines, is followed by black night when out it fades, so is heart-light. When out it goes, a dark and threatening shade will fall from thine own heart upon the Path, and root thy feet in terror to the spot.*

It is true that the further one advances the more subtle and deadly are the enemies, up to the crossing of the Abyss; and, as far as one can judge, the present discourse does not rise above Tiphareth. I am very sorry to have to remark at this point that Madame Blavatsky is now wholly obsessed by her own style. She indulges, much more than in the earlier part of this treatise, in poetic and romantic imagery, and in Miltonic inversion. (I do not here refer to *Lycidas.*) Consequently we get quite a long passage on a somewhat obvious point, and the Evil Persona or Dweller of the Threshold is introduced. However, it is a correct enough place. That Dweller is Fear—his form is Dispersion. It is in this sense that Satan, or rather Samael, a totally different person, the accuser of the Brethren, is the Devil.

36. *Beware, Disciple, of that lethal shade. No light that shines from Spirit can dispel the darkness of the nether Soul unless all selfish thought has fled therefrom, and that the pilgrim saith: "I have renounced all this passing frame: I have destroyed the cause: the shadows cast can, as effects, no longer be." For now the last great fight, the final war between the Higher and the Lower Self, hath taken place.*

Behold, the very battlefield is now engulfed in the great war, and is no more.

The quotation is only proper in the mouth of a Buddha, from whom it is taken. At this point the Higher and Lower Selves are united. It is a mistake to represent their contest as a war—it is a wedding.

37. *But once thou hast passed the gate of Kshânti, step the third is taken. Thy body is thy slave. Now, for the fourth prepare, the Portal of temptations which do ensnare the inner man.*

We are now on a higher plane altogether. The Higher and Lower Selves are made One. It is that One whose further progress from Tiphareth to Binah is now to be described.

38. *Ere thou canst near that goal, before thine hand is lifted to upraise the fourth gate's latch, thou must have mastered all the mental changes in thy Self and slain the army of the thought sensations that, subtle and insidious, creep unasked within the Soul's bright shrine.*

It is the mental changes and the invading thoughts which distress us. These are to be understood in a rather advanced sense, for of course thought must have been conquered earlier than this, that is to say, the self must have been separated from its thoughts, so that they no longer disturb that self. Now, however, the fortress walls must be thrown down, and the mind slain in the open field.

39. *If thou would'st not be slain by them, then must thou harmless make thy own creations, the children of thy thoughts unseen, impalpable, that swarm round humankind, the progeny and heirs to man and his terrestrial spoils. Thou hast to study the voidness of the seeming full, the fulness of the seeming void. O fearless Aspirant, look deep within the well of thine own heart, and answer. Knowest thou of Self the powers, O thou perceiver of external shadows? If thou*

dost not—then art thou lost.

The way to make thoughts harmless is by the equilibrium of contradictions—this is the meaning of the phrase, "Thou hast to study the voidness of the seeming full, the fulness of the seeming void." This subject has been dealt with at some length in "The Soldier and the Hunchback" in *The Equinox,* vol. I, no. I, and many other references are to be found in the works of Mr Aleister Crowley.

A real identification of the Self with the Not-Self is necessary.

40. *For, on Path fourth, the lightest breeze of passion or desire will stir the steady light upon the pure white walls of Soul. The smallest wave of longing or regret for Mâyâ's gifts illusive, along Antaskarana—the path that lies between thy Spirit and thy Self, the highway of sensations, the rude arousers of Ahankâra (the faculty that makes the illusion called the Ego)—a thought as fleeting as the lightning flash will make thee thy three prizes forfeit—the prizes thou hast won.*

The meaning is again very much confused by the would-be poetic diction, but it is quite clear that desire of any kind must not interfere with this intensely intellectual meditation; and of course the whole object of it is to refrain from preferring any one thing to any other thing. When it says that "A thought as fleeting as the lightning flash will make thee thy three prizes forfeit—the prizes thou hast won," this does not mean that if you happen to make a mistake in meditation you have to begin all over again as an absolute beginner, and yet, of course, in any meditation the occurrence of a single break destroys, for the moment, the effect of what has gone immediately before. Whenever one is trying for cumulative effect, something of this sort is true. One gets a sort of Leyden Jar effect; but the sentence as it stands is misleading, as she explains further on in verse 70—"Each failure is success, and each sincere attempt wins its reward in time."

41. *For know, that the ETERNAL knows no change.*

Here again we have one subject "THE ETERNAL," and one predicate "the knower of no change"; the Hindu statement identical with the Buddhist, and the identity covered by crazy terminology. X = A says the Hindu, Y = A says the Buddhist. X = Y is furiously denied by both, although these two equations are our only source of information about either X or Y. Metaphysics has always been full of this airy building. We must postulate an Unseen behind the Seen; and when we have defined the Unseen as a round square, we quarrel with our fellow-professors who prefer to define it as a quadrilateral circle. The only way to avoid this is to leave argument altogether alone, and pay attention only to concentration, until the time comes to tackle mental phenomena once for all, by some such method as that of *Liber 474*.

42. *"The eight dire miseries forsake for evermore; if not, to wisdom, sure, thou canst not come, nor yet to liberation,"* saith the great Lord, the Tathâgata of perfection, *"he who has followed in the footsteps of his predecessors."*

"The eight dire miseries" are the five senses plus the threefold fire of Lust, Hatred and Dullness. But the quotation is not familiar. I feel sure He did not say "sure."

43. *Stern and exacting is the virtue of Vairâga. If thou its Path would'st master, thou must keep thy mind and thy perceptions far freer than before from killing action.*

The English is getting ambiguous. The word *killing* is, I suppose, an adjective implying 'fatal to the purpose of the Student'. But even so, the comment appears to me out of place. On this high Path action should already have been made harmless; in fact, the second Path had this as its principal object. It is very difficult to make out what the Authoress really wants you to do.

44. *Thou hast to saturate thyself with pure Alaya, become as one with Nature's Soul-Thought. At one with it thou art invincible; in separation, thou becomest the playground of Sauvritti, origin of all the world's delusions.*

This means, acquire sympathy with the universal Soul of Nature. This Soul of Nature here spoken of is of course imagined as something entirely contrary to anything we really know of Nature. In fact, it would be difficult to distinguish it from a pious fiction. The only reason that can be given for assuming the Soul of Nature to be pure, calm, kind, and all the other tea-party virtues, is *Lucus a non lucendo*. To put it in some kind of logical form, the Manifested is not the Unmanifested; therefore the Manifested is that which the Unmanifested is not. Nature, as we know it, is stupid, brutal, cruel, beautiful, extravagant, and above all the receptacle or vehicle of illimitable energy. However, by meditation one comes to a quite different view of Nature. Many of the stupidities and brutalities are only apparent. The beauty, the energy, and the majesty, or, if you prefer it, the love, remain undeniable. It is the first reversed triangle of the Tree of Life.

What is said of "Samvritti" is nonsense. The Vrittis are impressions or the causes of impressions. Samvritti is simply the sum of these.

45. *All is impermanent in man except the pure bright essence of Alaya. Man is its crystal ray; a beam of light immaculate within, a form of clay material upon the lower surface. That beam is thy life-guide and thy true Self, the Watcher and the silent Thinker, the victim of thy lower Self. Thy Soul cannot be hurt but through thy erring body; control and master both, and thou art safe when crossing to the nearing "Gate of Balance."*

Here we have Alaya identified with Atma. The rest of the verse is mostly poetic nothing, and there is no guide to the meaning of the word "Soul." It is a perfectly absurd theory to regard the body as capable of inflicting wounds upon the Soul, which is apparently the meaning here. The definition of Atma gives impassibility as almost its prime condition.

From the phrase "control and master both" we must suppose that the Soul here spoken of is some intermediate principle, presumably Nephesh.

46. *Be of good cheer, O daring pilgrim "to the other shore." Heed not the whisperings of Mâra's hosts; wave off the tempters, those ill-natured Sprites, the jealous Llamayin in endless space.*

This verse may be again dismissed as too easily indulgent in poetic diction. A properly controlled mind should not be subject to these illusions. And although it may be conceded that these things, although illusions, do correspond with a certain reality, anything objective should have been dismissed at an earlier stage. In the mental struggles there should be no place for demons. Unless my memory deceives me, that was just the one trouble that I did not have. The reason may possibly have been that I had mastered all external demons before I took up meditation.

47. *Hold firm! Thou nearest now the middle Portal, the gate of Woe, with its ten thousand snares.*

No explanation is given as to why the fifth should be called the "middle Portal" of seven.

48. *Have mastery o'er thy thoughts, O striver for perfection, if thou would'st cross its threshold.*

From here to verse 71 is the long description of this fifth gate, the key to which (it will be remembered) was Virya—that is, energy and will, Manhood in its most secret sense.

It seems rather useless to tell the Student to have mastery over his thoughts in this verse, because he has been doing nothing else in all the previous Gates.

49. *Have mastery o'er thy Soul, O seeker after truths undying, if thou would'st reach the goal.*

The pupil is also told to have mastery over his Soul, and again there is no indication as to what is meant by "Soul."

Bhikkhu Ananda Metteya once remarked that Theosophists were rather absurd to call themselves Buddhists, as the Buddhist had no Soul, and the Theosophist, not even content with having one, insisted on possessing seven different kinds.

If it means Nephesh, of course this ought to have been mastered long ago. It probably means Neshamah. If we take this to be so, the whole passage will become intelligible. In the beginning of progress we have the automatic Ego, the animal creator or generator of Nephesh in Yesod, the lowest point of the Ruach, and the marriage between these is the first regeneration. Nephesh is Syrinx, and Yesod is Pan. Nephesh is the elemental Soul which seeks redemption and immortality. In order to obtain it, it must acquire a Soul such as is possessed by men. Now the elemental is said to be afraid of the sword with its cross hilt, of the Cross, that is to say of the Phallus, and this is what is called Panic fear, which, originally an individual thing, is applied to a mob, because a mob has no Soul. A very great many elementals are to be found in human form to-day; they are nearly always women, or such men as are not men. Such beings are imitative, irresponsible, always being shocked, without any standard of truth, although often extremely logical; criminal without a sense of right and wrong, and as shameless as they are prudish. Truth of any kind frightens them. They are usually Christian Scientists, Spiritualists, Theosophists, or what not. They reflect the personality of a man with extraordinary ease, and frequently deceive him into thinking that they know what they are saying. Levi remarks that "the love of the Magus for such beings is insensate, and may destroy him." He had had some. This doctrine is magnificently expounded in Wagner's *Parsifal*. The way to redeem such creatures is to withstand them, and their Path of Redemption is the Path of Service to the man who has withstood them. However, when at the right moment the crucified one, the extended one, the Secret Saviour, consents to redeem them, and can do so without losing his power, without in any way yielding to them, their next step is accomplished, and they are re-born as men. This brings us back to our subject, for the lower man, of whom we are still speaking, possesses, above Yesod, five forms of intellect and Daath their Crown.

We then come to another marriage on a higher plane, the redemption of Malkuth by Tiphareth; the attaining of the Knowledge and Conversation of the Holy Guardian Angel.

The next critical step is the sacrificing of this whole organism to the Mother, Neshamah, a higher Soul which is as spiritually dark and lonely as Nephesh was materially. Neshamah is beyond the Abyss, has no concern with that bridal, but to absorb it; and by offering the blood of her Son to the All-Father, that was her husband, she awakes Him. He, in His turn, vitalizes the original Daughter, thus completing the cycle. Now on the human plane this All-Father is the true generative force, the real Ego, of which all types of conscious Ego in a man are but Eidola, and this true creative force is the Virya of which we are now speaking.

50. *Thy Soul-gaze centre on the One Pure Light, the Light that is free from affection, and use thy golden key.*

.   .   .   .

This Virya is the one pure light spoken of in this verse. It is called "free from affection." It creates without desire, simply because it is its nature to create. It is this force in one's self of which one must become conscious in this stage.

. . . .

51. *The dreary task is done, thy labour well-nigh o'er.*
The wide abyss that gaped to swallow thee is almost spanned.

. . . .

It should be noticed that this verse has rows of dots both above and below it. There is a secret meaning to verse 51 which will be evident to anyone who has properly understood our comment on verse 49. The highest marriage, that between Neshamah and Chiah, is accomplished—again, after another manner!

52. *Thou hast now crossed the moat that circles round the gate of human passions.*

By "human passions" must be understood every kind of attraction, not merely gross appetites—which have been long ago conquered, not by excluding, but by regulating them. On the plane of mind itself all is in order; everything has been balanced by its opposite.

53. *Thou hast now conquered Mâra and his furious host.*

The seeker has now passed through the Abyss where dwells Choronzon whose name is Legion. All this must be studied most carefully in *Liber 418.*

54. *Thou hast removed pollution from thine heart and bled it from impure desire. But, O thou glorious Combatant, thy task is not yet done. Build high, Lanoo, the wall that shall hedge in the Holy Isle, the dam that will protect thy mind from pride and satisfaction at thoughts of the great feat achieved.*

Here again is one of those unfortunate passages which enable the superficial to imagine that the task of the Adept is to hunger-strike, and wear the blue ribbon, and give up smoking. The first paragraph of this verse rather means that filling of the cup of Babalon with every drop of blood, which is explained in *Liber 418.*

The higher Ego—"Holy Isle"—is not the thinking self; it is the "Dwarf-Self," the self which is beyond thinking. The aspirant is now in fact beyond all thought, and this talk of building high the wall or dam is too much like poetry to be good sense. What it means is, "Beware lest the re-awakened Ego, the Chiah, should become self-conscious, as it is liable to do owing to its wedding with Neshamah."

Or, shall we say, with Nephesh? For the organism has now been brought to perfect harmony in all its parts. The Adept has a strong, healthy, vigorous body, and a mind no less perfect; he is a very different person from the feeble emasculate cabbage-chewing victim of anaemia, with its mind which has gained what it calls emancipation by forgetting how to think. Little as it ever knew! Not in such may one find the true Adept. Read *Liber Legis,* chap. II, verse 24, and learn where to look for hermits.

55. *A sense of pride would mar the work. Aye, build it strong, lest the fierce rush of battling waves, that mount and beat its shore from out the great World Maya's Ocean, swallow up the pilgrim and the isle—yea, even when the victory's achieved.*

We now perceive more clearly the meaning of this passage. Just as the man, in order to conquer the woman, used restraint, so also must this true Soul restrain itself, even at this high stage, although it gives itself completely up. Although it creates without thought and without desire, let it do that without losing anything. And because the surrender must be complete, it must beware of that expansion which is called pride; for it is destroying duality, and pride implies duality.

56. *Thine "isle" is the deer, thy thoughts the hounds that weary and pursue his progress to the stream of Life. Woe to the deer that is o'ertaken by the barking fiends before he reach the Vale of Refuge—Dhyâna-Mârga, "path of pure knowledge" named.*

Once more the passage harks back to the Abyss where thoughts prevail. It is another poetic image, and not a good one. Extraordinary how liable this unassailable Alaya-Soul is to catch cold! It isn't woe to him; it's woe to YOU!

57. *Ere thou canst settle in Dhyâna-Mârga and call it thine, thy Soul has to become as the ripe mango fruit; as soft and sweet as its bright golden pulp for others' woes, as hard as that fruit's stone for thine own throes and sorrows, O conqueror of weal and woe.*

More trouble, more poetic image, more apparent sentimentality. Its true interpretation is to be found in the old symbolism of this marriage of Chiah and Neshamah. Chiah is the male, proof against seduction; Neshamah the female that overcomes by weakness. But in actual practice the meaning may be explained thus, you yourself have conquered, you have become perfectly indifferent, perfectly energetic, perfectly creative, but, having united yourself to the Universe, you become acutely conscious that your own fortunate condition is not shared by that which you now are. It is then that the adept turns his face downwards, changes his formula from *solve* to *coagula*. His progress on the upward path now corresponds exactly with his progress on the downward path; he can only save himself by saving others, for if it were not so he would be hardly better than he who shuts himself in his black tower of illusion, the Brother of the Left Hand, the Klingsor of "Parsifal."

58. *Make hard thy Soul against the snares of* Self; *deserve for it the name of "Diamond-Soul."*

Here is another muddle, for the words "Soul" and "Self" have previously been used in exactly the opposite meaning. If any meaning at all is to be attached to this verse and to verse 59, it is that the progress downwards, the progress of the Redeemer of the Sun as he descends from the Zenith, or passes from the Summer Solstice to his doom, must be a voluntary absorption of Death in order to turn it into life. Never again must the Adept be deceived by his impressions, though there is that part of him which suffers.

59. *For, as the diamond buried deep within the throbbing heart of earth can never mirror back the earthly lights, so are thy mind and Soul; plunged in Dhyâna-Mârga, these must mirror nought of Mâyâ's realm illusive.*

It is now evident that a most unfortunate metaphor has been chosen. A diamond is not much use when it is buried deep within the throbbing heart of earth. The proper place for a diamond is the neck of a courtesan.

60. *When thou hast reached that state, the Portals that thou hast to conquer on the Path fling open wide their gates to let thee pass, and Nature's strongest mights possess no power to stay thy course. Thou wilt be master of the seven-fold Path; but not till then, O Candidate for trials passing speech.*

That we have correctly interpreted these obscure passages now becomes clear. No further personal effort is required. The gates open of themselves to the Master of the Temple.

61. *Till then, a task far harder still awaits thee : thou hast to feel thyself ALL-THOUGHT, and yet exile all thoughts from out thy SOUL.*

The discourse again reverts to another phase of this task of Vairaga. It is just as in the "Earth-Bhavana," where you have to look at a frame of earth, and reach that impression of Earth in which is no Earthly quality, "that earth which is not earth," as the Qabalah would say. So on this higher plane you must reach a quintessence of thought, of which all thoughts are perhaps debased images, but which in no way partakes of anything concerning them.

62. *Thou hast to reach that fixity of mind in which no breeze, however strong, can waft an earthly thought within. Thus purified, the shrine must of all action, sound, or earthly light be void; e'en as the butterfly, o'ertaken by the frost, falls lifeless at the threshold—so must all earthly thoughts fall dead before the fane.*

Again another phase of this task. Complete detachment, perfect silence, absolute will; this must be that pure Chiah which is utterly removed from Ruach.

63. *Behold it written :*

"Ere the gold flame can burn with steady light, the lamp must stand well guarded in a spot free from all wind." Exposed to shifting breeze, the jet will flicker and the quivering flame cast shades deceptive, dark and ever-changing, on the Soul's white shrine.

This familiar phrase is usually interpreted to mean the mere keeping of the mind free from invading thoughts. It has also that secret significance at which we have several times already hinted.

These unfortunate poetic images again bewilder us. Blavatsky's constant use of the word "Soul" without definition is very annoying. These verses 63 and 64 must be taken as dealing with a state preliminary to the attainment of this Fifth Gate. If the lance shakes in the hand of the warrior, whatever the cause, the result is fumbling and failure.

64. *And then, O thou pursuer of the Truth, thy Mind-Soul will become as a mad elephant, that rages in the jungle. Mistaking forest trees for living foes, he perishes in his attempts to kill the ever-shifting shadows dancing on the wall of sunlit rocks.*

This verse explains the state of the mind which has failed in the Abyss—the student becomes insane.

65. *Beware, lest in the care of Self thy Soul should lose her foothold on the soil of Deva-knowledge.*

66. *Beware, lest in forgetting SELF, thy Soul lose o'er its trembling mind control, and forfeit thus the due fruition of its conquests.*

These two verses seem to mean that any attention to Self would prevent one crossing the Abyss, while in the event of any inattention to Self the mind would revolt. In other words, "Soul" means Neshamah, and it is important for Neshamah to fix its attention on Chiah, rather than on Ruach.

67. *Beware of change! For change is thy great foe. This change will fight thee off, and throw thee back, out of the Patch thou threadest, deep into viscous swamps of doubt.*

The only difficulty in this verse is the word "change." People who are meditating often get thrown off by the circumstances of their lives, and these circumstances must be controlled absolutely. It should, however, also be taken to refer to any change in one's methods of meditation. You should make up your mind thoroughly to a given scheme of action, and be bound by it. A man is perfectly hopeless if, on finding one Mantra unsuccessful, he tries another. There is cumulative effect in all mystic and magical work; and the Mantra you have been doing, however bad, is the best one to go on with.

68. *Prepare, and be forewarned in time. If thou hast tried and failed, O dauntless fighter, yet lose not courage: fight on and to the charge return again, and yet again.*

Verse 68 confirms our interpretation of these verses.

69. *The fearless warrior, his precious life-blood oozing from his wide and gaping wounds, will still attack the foe, drive him from out his stronghold, vanquish him, ere he himself expires. Act then, all ye who fail and suffer, act like him; and from the stronghold of your Soul chase all your foes away—ambition, anger, hatred, e'en to the shadow of desire—when even you have failed.*

70. *Remember, thou that fightest for man's liberation,*

each failure is success, and each sincere attempt wins its reward in time. The holy germs that sprout and grow unseen in the disciple's soul, their stalks wax strong at each new trial, they bend like reeds but never break, nor can they e'er be lost. But when the hour has struck they blossom forth.

. . . .

But if thou cam'st prepared, then have no fear.

. . . .

These verses explain the cumulative effect of which we spoke. It is very hard to persist, because very often we seem to make no progress. There is the water on the fire, and nothing whatever appears to be happening. But without warning it suddenly boils. You may get the temperature to 99° and keep it at 99° for a thousand years, and the water will not boil. It is the last step that does the trick.

One remark in this connection may be useful: "A watched pot never boils." The student must practise complete detachment—must reach the stage when he does not care twopence whether he attains or not, while at the same time he pursues eagerly the Path of attainment. This is the ideal attitude. It is very well brought out in *Parsifal.* Klingsor, on having his error pointed out to him, said "Oh, that's quite easy," took a knife, and removed all danger of his ever making the same mistake again. Returning, full of honest pride in his achievement, he found himself more ignominiously rejected than before. Ultimately the sacred lance is brought back into the Hall where is the Graal, and there, at the right moment, not moved by desire, not seduced by cunning Kundry, but of his own nature, the sacrifice may be accomplished.

So, as previously explained, it is important not to keep on worrying about one's progress; otherwise all the concentration is lost, and a mood of irritability rises, work is given up, and the student becomes angry with his

Teacher. His Mind-Soul becomes as a mad elephant that rages in the jungle. He may even obtain the Vision of the Demon Crowley. But by persistence in the appointed Path, by avoiding disappointment through not permitting the fiend Hope to set its suckers on your Soul, by quietly continuing the appointed discourse in spite of Mara and his hosts, the wheel comes full circle, the hour strikes, the talipot palm blossoms, and all is fun and feasting, like Alice when she got to the Eighth Square.

It is my daily prayer that I may be spared to write a complete commentary on the extremely mystical works of the Rev. C. L. Dodgson.

Please note the two lines of dots for the last paragraph of this verse. It is that final scene of *Parsifal*, which words are unfitted to express.

71. *Henceforth thy way is clear right through Virya gate, the fifth one of the Seven Portals. Thou art now on the way that leadeth to the Dhyâna haven, the sixth, the Bodhi Portal.*

72. *The Dhyâna gate is like an alabaster vase, white and transparent; within there burns a steady golden fire, the flame of Prajnâ that radiates from Atmâ.*

Thou art that vase.

73. *Thou hast estranged thyself from objects of the senses, travelled on the "Path of seeing," on the "Path of hearing," and standest in the light of Knowledge. Thou hast now reached Titikshâ state.*

O Narjol, thou art safe.

.   .   .   .

In these three verses the passage to the sixth Gate is made clear. There is no longer any struggle, there is but the golden fire within the alabaster vase, and thou art that vase. Male and female are again interchanged. Above Chiah and Neshamah is Yechidah, and in the lower aspect of that, one has again become the receptacle of the

Infinite, not that which penetrates the Infinite.

There are two formulae of making two things one. The active formula is that of the arrow piercing the rainbow, the Cross erected upon the Hill of Golgotha, and so on. But the passive formula is that of the cup into which the wine is poured, that of the cloud which wraps itself around Ixion. It is very annoying to hear that the Narjol is safe. This is all Oedipus-Complex. Why not "Safe in the arms of Jesus"? Devil fly away with this "eternal rest" stuff! Give me a night's rest now and again; a dip into the Tao, and then—off we go again!

74. *Know, Conqueror of Sins, once that a Sowani hath cross'd the seventh Path, all Nature thrills with joyous awe and feels subdued. The silver star now twinkles out the news to the night-blossoms, the streamlet to the pebbles ripples out the tale; dark ocean waves will roar it to the rocks surf-bound, scent-laden breezes sing it to the vales, and stately pines mysteriously whisper: "A Master has arisen, A MASTER OF THE DAY."*

There is a further terrible confusion between the personal progress of the man, and his progress in relation to his incarnations.

It cannot be too clearly understood that these things are altogether different. Blavatsky's attempt to mix up Hinduism and Buddhism is productive of constant friction. The first Path in Dhyana has nothing whatever to do with being a Srotapatti. It is perfectly clear that you could be Master of all the eight Jhanas with no more hope of becoming a Srotapatti than a Pwe-dancer.

However, this is an extremely poetical description of what happens on the seventh Path.

You must notice that there is a certain amount of confusion between the Paths and the Portals at the end of them. Apparently one does not reach the seventh Gate till the end of the treatise. "A Master of the Day" is said to refer to the Manvantara, but it is also an obvious phrase where *day* is equivalent to *Sun*.

75. *He standeth now like a white pillar to the west, upon whose face the rising Sun of thought eternal poureth forth its first most glorious waves. His mind, like a becalmed and boundless ocean, spreadeth out in shoreless space. He holdeth life and death in his strong hand.*

It is interesting to notice that he is still in the West. This is the penultimate stage. He is really now practically identical with Mayan himself. He has met and conquered the maker of illusion, become one with him, and his difficulty will then be so to complete that work, that it shall be centred on itself, and leave no seed that may subsequently germinate and destroy all that has been accomplished.

76. *Yea, he is mighty. The living power made free in him, that power which is HIMSELF, can raise the tabernacle of illusion high above the Gods, above great Brahm and Indra. Now he shall surely reach his great reward!*

The temptation at this point is to create an Universe. He is able: the necessity of so doing is strong within Him, and He may perhaps even imagine that He can make one which shall be free from the Three Characteristics. Evelyn Hall—an early love of mine—used to say: "God Almighty—or words to that effect—has no conscience"; and in the tremendous state of mind in which He is, a state of Cosmic priapism, He may very likely see red, care nothing for what may result to Himself or His victim, and, violently projecting Himself on the Akasa, may fertilize it, and the Universe begin once more.

In *Liber I* it seems as if this must be done, as if it were part of the Work, and *Liber Legis,* if I understand it aught, would inculcate the same. For to US the Three Characteristics and the Four Noble Truths are lies—the laws of Illusion. Ours is the Palace of the Graal, not

Klingsor's Castle.

77. *Shall he not use the gifts which it confers for his own rest and bliss, his well-earn'd weal and glory—he, the subduer of the Great Delusion?*

It is now seen that He should not do this, although He is able. He should on the contrary take up the burden of a Magus. This whole passage will be found in much clearer language in *Liber One, The Equinox*, no. 7.

78. *Nay, O thou candidate for Nature's hidden lore! If one would follow in the steps of holy Tathâgata, those gifts and powers are not for Self.*

It should be noticed that this is not quite identical with the way in which the Master of the Temple detaches the being that was once called "Self" to fling it down from the Abyss that it may "appear in the Heaven of Jupiter as a morning star or as an evening star, to give light to them that dwell upon the earth." This Magus is a much stronger person than the Master of the Temple. He is the creative force, while the Master is merely the receptive. But in these verses 78, 79, 80, it might be very easily supposed that it was merely a recapitulation of the former remarks, and I am inclined to think that there is a certain amount of confusion in the mind of the Author between these two grades. She attained only the lower. But careful study of these verses will incline the reader to perceive that it is a new creation which is here spoken of, not a mere amelioration.

The only really difficult verse on this interpretation is 86. There is a lot of sham sentiment in this verse. It gives an entirely false picture of the Adept, who does not whine, who does not play Pecksniff. All this business about protecting man from far greater misery and sorrow is absurd. For example, in one passage H. P. B. explains that the lowest hell is a man-bearing Planet.

There is a certain amount of melancholia with delusions

of persecution about this verse. Natural, perhaps, to one who was betrayed and robbed by Vittoria Cremers?

79. *Would'st thou thus dam the waters born on Sumeru? Shalt thou divert the stream for thine own sake, or send it back to its prime source along the crests of cycles?*

It is here seen that the ideal proposed by the Author is by no means rest or immobility. The Path, or rather the Goal, is symbolised as a swift and powerful stream, and the great mystery is revealed that the Path itself is the Goal.

> Were the world understood
> Ye would see it was good,
> A dance to a delicate measure.

This is also the doctrine indicated in all the works of Fra Perdurabo. You can see it in *Liber 418,* where, as soon as a certain stage is reached, the great curse turns into an ineffable blessing. In *The Book of Lies,* too, the same idea is stated again and again, with repetition only unwearying because of the beauty and variety of the form.

"Everything is sorrow," says the Buddha. Quite so, to begin with. We analyse the things we deem least sorrow, and find that by taking a long enough period, or a short enough period, we can prove them to be the most exquisite agony. Such is the attempt of all Buddhist writers, and their even feebler Western imitators. But once the secret of the universe is found, then everything is joy. The proposition is quite as universal.

80. *If thou would'st have that stream of hard-earn'd knowledge, of Wisdom heaven-born, remain sweet running waters, thou should'st not leave it to become a stagnant pond.*

Here we have the same thesis developed with unexpected force. So far from the Path being repose, the slightest slackening turns it stagnant.

81. *Know, if of Amitâbha, the "Boundless Age," thou would'st become co-worker, then must thou shed the light acquired, like to the Bodhisattvas twain, upon the span of all three worlds.*

The same doctrine is still further detailed, but I cannot give the authority by which Blavatsky speaks of Kwan-shiyin as a Bodhisattva. It will become abundantly evident in the comment to verse 97 that Blavatsky had not the remotest idea as to what a Bodhisattva was and is. But it is quite true that you have to shed light in the manner indicated if you are going to live the life of a Magus.

82. *Know that the stream of superhuman knowledge and the Deva-Wisdom thou hast won, must, from thyself, the channel of Alaya, be poured forth into another bed.*

Still further develops the same doctrine. You have acquired the supreme creative force. You are the Word, and it must be spoken (verse 83). There is a good deal of anti-climax in verse 83, and a peculiarly unnecessary split infinitive.

Blavatsky's difficulty seems to have been that although she is always talking of the advance of the good Narjol, he never seems to advance in point of view. Now, on the threshold of the last Path, he is still an ordinary person with vague visionary yearnings! It is true that He wishes the unity of all that lives, complete harmony in the parts, and perfect light in the whole. It is also true that He may spend a great deal of time in killing or otherwise instructing men, but He has not got at all the old conception. The ordinary Buddhist is quite unable to see anything but details. Bhikkhu Ananda Metteya once refused to undertake the superintendence of a coconut plantation, because he found that he would have to give orders for the destruction of vermin. But (with the best feeling in the world) he had to eat rice, and the people who cultivated

the rice had to destroy a lot of vermin too. One cannot
escape responsibility in this vicarious way. It is peculiarly
silly, because the whole point of Buddha's position is that
there is no escape. The Buddhist regulations are comparable to orders which might have been, but were not,
because he was not mad, given by the Captain of the
"Titanic" to caulk the planks after the ship had been cut
in two.

83. *Know, O Narjol, thou of the Secret Path, its pure
fresh waters must be used to sweeter make the Ocean's
bitter waves—that mighty sea of sorrow formed of the tears
of men.*

84. *Alas! when once thou hast become like the fix'd star
in highest heaven, that bright celestial orb must shine from
out the spatial depths for all—save for itself; give light to
all, but take from none.*

It is incomparably annoying to see this word "Alas!"
at the head of this verse as a pure oxymoron with the rest
of the text. Is stupid, unseeing selfishness so firmly fixed
in the nature of man that even at this height he still
laments? Do not believe it. It is interesting here to note
the view taken by Him who has actually attained the
Grade of Magus. He says:

> Do what thou wilt shall be the whole of the Law. It may
> be those three perfections of my Sambhogakaya Robe, but
> the fact is that one has reached a stage when the Path be-
> comes almost meaningless. The illusion of Sorrow has been
> exposed so ruthlessly that one can hardly realize that one,
> or any one else, can ever have been in such a silly muddle.
> It seems so perfectly natural that everything should be just
> as it is, and so right, that one is quite startled if one contem-
> plates the nature of one's Star, which led one into these
> "grave paths." The only "wrong" is the thinking about
> anything at all; this is of course the old "Thought is evil"
> on a higher plane. One gets to understand the Upanishad
> which tells us how The Original It made the error of con-

templating itself, of becoming self-conscious; and one also perceives the stupendous transcendentalism concealed in the phrase of *The Book of the Law*: "Enough of Because! Be he damned for a dog!" This Universe—the IO PAN PAN and the OIMOI TALAINOI too—is a Play of Our Merry Lady. It is as natural to have all this heavy stuff about the Weary Pilgrim's Bleeding Feet, and the Candidate for Woe, and all that, as it is for Theseus and Hippolyta to decide that Pyramus and Thisbe may amuse them. The Public will then kindly excuse the Magus if He be of a nature, and in a mood, to decline to take the tragedy too seriously, and to mock the crude buffooneries of Bottom. Perhaps it would be better taste in Him to draw the curtains of His box. But it is at least His pleasure to reward the actors. Love is the law, love under will.

85. *Alas! when once thou hast become like the pure snow in mountain vales, cold and unfeeling to the touch, warm and protective to the seed that sleepeth deep beneath its bosom—'tis now that snow which must receive the biting frost, the northern blasts, thus shielding from their sharp and cruel tooth the earth that holds the promised harvest, the harvest that will feed the hungry.*

Surely a better image would have been the Mother, and does the Mother complain or rejoice? It is also a bad image, this of the snow. Is snow in any way incommoded by the biting frosts, the northern blasts?

86. *Self-doomed to live through future Kalpas, unthanked and unperceived by men; wedged as a stone with countless other stones which form the "Guardian Wall," such is thy future if the seventh Gate thou passest. Built by the hands of many Masters of Compassion, raised by their tortures, by their blood cemented, it shields mankind, since man is man, protecting it from further and far greater misery and sorrow.*

Comment has already been made upon this verse.

87. *Withal man sees it not, will not perceive it, nor will he heed the word of wisdom . . . for he knows it not.*

Here indeed is the only sorrow that could seem, even for a moment, likely to touch the Adept. It is rather annoying that the great prize offered so freely to men is scorned by them. But this is only if the Adept fall for one moment to the narrower view, accept the conventional outlook on the universe. If only he remember that very simple and elementary instruction that the Magician must work as if he had Omnipotence at his command and Eternity at his disposal, He will not repine.

88. *But thou hast heard it, thou knowest all, O thou of eager guileless Soul . . . and thou must choose. Then hearken yet again.*

This verse introduces the climax of this treatise.

89. *On Sowan's Path, O Srotâpatti, thou art secure. Aye [sic], on that Mârga, where nought but darkness meets the weary pilgrim, where torn by thorns the hands drip blood, the feet are cut by sharp, unyielding flints, and Mâra wields his strongest arms—there lies a great reward immediately beyond.*

It is not at all clear to what stage of the Path this refers. In verse 91 it appears to refer to the Dhyana Path, but the Dhyana Path has been described in entirely different terms in verses 71 to 73, and it is certainly a quite bad description of the condition of Srotapatti.

I think the tragic note is struck for effect. Damn all these tortures and rewards! Has the Narjol no manhood at all?

90. *Calm and unmoved the Pilgrim glideth up the stream that to Nirvâna leads. He knoweth that the more his feet will bleed, the whiter will himself be washed. He knoweth well that after seven short and fleeting births Nirvâna will be his.*

Here is again a totally un-Buddhistic description.

It appears to me rather a paraphrase of the well-known

Sweeping through the gates of the New Jerusalem,
Washed in the Blood of the Lamb.

91. *Such is the Dhyâna Path, the haven of the Yogi, the blessed goal that Srotâpattis crave.*

Again the confusion of the attainment of the Student with regard to spiritual experience, and his attainment with regard to his grade. There is connection between these, but it is not a close and invariable one. A man might get quite a lot of Samadhi, and still be many lives away from Srotapatti.

92. *Not so when he hath crossed and won the Aryahata Path.*

From here to verse 95 is description of this last Path which leads to the last Gate.

93. *There Klesha is destroyed for ever, Tanhâ's roots torn out. But stay, Disciple . . . Yet one word. Canst thou destroy divine COMPASSION? Compassion is no attribute. It is the Law of LAWS—eternal Harmony, Alaya's SELF; a shoreless universal essence, the light of everlasting Right, and fitness of all things, the law of Love eternal.*

Here again is apparently a serious difficulty. The idea of Klesha, here identified with Love of worldly enjoyment, seems to put one back almost before the beginning. Is it now only that the almost-Arhat no longer wants to go to the theatre? It must not be interpreted in this low sense. At the same time, it is difficult to discover a sense high enough to fit the passage. With Tanha it is easier to find a meaning, for Madame seems to identify Tanha with the creative force of which we have spoken. But this is of course incompatible with the Buddhist teaching on the subject. Tanha is properly defined as the hunger of the individual for continuous personal existence, either in a material or a spiritual sense.

With regard to the rest of the verse, it certainly reads

as if yet again Blavatsky had taken the sword to a Gordian knot. By saying that Compassion is no attribute she is merely asserting what is evidently not true, and the therefore defines it in a peculiar way, and I am afraid that she does so in a somewhat misleading manner. It would be improper here to disclose what is presumably the true meaning of this verse. One can only commend it to the earnest consideration of members of the Sanctuary of the Gnosis, the IX° of the O.T.O.

94. *The more thou dost become at one with it, thy being melted in its BEING, the more thy Soul unites with that which IS, the more thou wilt become COMPASSION ABSOLUTE.*

This verse throws a little further light upon its predecessor. COMPASSION is really a certain Chinese figure whose names are numerous. One of them is BAPHOMET.

95. *Such is the Arya Path, Path of the Buddhas of perfection.*

This closes the subject.

96. *Withal, what mean the sacred scrolls which make thee say:*

"Om! I believe it is not all the Arhats that get of the Nirvânic Path the sweet fruition.

"Om! I believe that the Nirvâna-Dhârma is entered not by all the Buddhas."

Here, however, we come to the question of the final renunciation. It is undoubtedly true that one may push spiritual experience to the point of complete attainment without ever undertaking the work of a Dhamma-Buddha, though it seems hard to believe that at no period during that progress will it have become clear that the Complete Path is downwards as well as upwards.

97. *Yea; on the Arya Path thou art no more Srotapâtti, thou art a Bodhisattva. The stream is cross'd. 'Tis true thou*

hast a right to Dharmakâya vesture; but Sambhogakâya is greater than a Nirvâni, and greater still is a Nirmanakâya —the Buddha of Compassion.

Here once more we perceive the ignorance of the Author with reference to all matters of mystic terminology, an ignorance which would have been amusing indeed had she lived ten years later. A Bodhisattva is simply a being which has culminated in a Buddha. If you or I became Buddhas to-morrow, then all our previous incarnations were Bodhisattvas, and therefore, as there shall not be a single grain of dust which shall not attain to Buddhahood, every existing thing is in a way a Bodhisattva. But of course in practice the term is confined to these special incarnations of the only Buddha of whom we have any such record. It is, therefore, ridiculous to place Srotapatti as a Soul of inferior grade to Bodhisattva. Buddha did not become a Srotapatti until seven incarnations before he attained to Buddhahood.

The last part of the verse and the long note (of which we quote the gist) are nonsense. To describe a complete Buddha as "an ideal breath; Consciousness merged in the Universal Consciousness, or Soul devoid of every attribute," is not Buddhism at all, and is quite incompatible with Buddhism.

98. *Now bend thy head and listen well, O Bodhisattva— Compassion speaks and saith: "Can there be bliss when all that lives must suffer? Shalt thou be saved and hear the whole world cry?"*

Now thou hast heard that which was said.

Again we descend to the anti-climax of a somewhat mawkish sentimentality. Again we find the mistake of duality, of that opposition between self and others which, momentarily destroyed even in the most elementary periods of Samadhi, is completely wiped out by progress through the grades. The Path would indeed be a Treadmill if one always remained in this Salvation Army mood.

99. *Thou shalt attain the seventh step and cross the gate of final Knowledge, but only to wed woe—if thou would'st be Tathagata, follow upon thy predecessor's steps, remain unselfish till the endless end.*

Thou art enlightened—choose thy way.

. . . .

The anti-climax is now complete. Knowledge is by no means the last step. Knowledge has been finished with even by the Master of the Temple, and all this question of wedding woe, remaining unselfish till the endless end, is but poetic bombast, based upon misconception. It is as puerile as the crude conceptions of many Christian Sects.

100. *Behold, the mellow light that floods the Eastern sky. In signs of praise both heaven and earth unite. And from the four-fold manifested Powers a chant of love ariseth, both from the flaming Fire and flowing Water, and from sweet-smelling Earth and rushing Wind.*

Hark! . . . from the deep unfathomable vortex of that golden light in which the Victor bathes, ALL NATURE'S wordless voice in thousand tones ariseth to proclaim!

JOY UNTO YE, O MEN OF MYALBA.
A PILGRIM HATH RETURNED BACK
"FROM THE OTHER SHORE."
A NEW ARHAN IS BORN.
Peace to all Beings.

Here, however, we get something like real poetry. This, and not the Pi-Jaw, should be taken as the key to this Masterpiece.

Love is the law, love under will.

SECTION VII

REVIEWS

PART I

WISDOM
WHILE YOU WAITE

THE BOOK OF CEREMONIAL MAGIC.
— A. E. Waite

It would ill become us to review this book; which, when it was called *The Book of Black Magic and of Pacts,* was dismissed by the Editor of *The Goetia* as "a farrago of twenty-fifth-rate shoddy schoolboy journalism." And we are glad to see that in the new edition Mr Waite has corrected his logic by that Editor's light. But the introduction is new, and deserves comment.

Mr Waite still talks as if his mouth were full of hot potatoes. The length and obscurity of his archaisms renders him almost unintelligible to me, an affectation which I find intolerable. Such fools as it may impress are not worth having as followers, unless one is a swindler. In fact (let me whisper in Mr Waite's ear) no follower is worth having.

Mr Waite's central doctrine appears identical with that to which I personally assent; but I think he ruins its simplicity by his insistence on sectarian symbols and on the literalism which he would be the first to condemn in a Methodist.

As to the rituals of ceremonial magic which he condemns, he is right. But the Mass itself is a Magical

849

Ceremony, and he does not condemn the Mass. The ceremonies which might be practised by, say, a neophyte of the A ∴ A ∴ would be as sublime as, and less tainted than, the services of the Church. Of such rituals Mr Waite is ignorant, more ignorant than the author of *The King's Dole* should be, unless such ignorance be the result of envy, malice, and all uncharitableness.

Further, ceremonial magic, even of the low angelic order, may be a sort of divine trap. The utterance of the Logos is one, but he is heard by divers nations in divers languages. Cannot God deal with a soul even by allowing him to pass through the "Houses of Sin"? Mr Waite blasphemes if he denies it.

As a practical example, I know of a man who took up the blackest magic from sheer hatred of God and Christ, a hatred Shelleyan and Thomsonian. What happened? He found by practice that to call forth an evil spirit you must identify yourself with the god that commands him.

He then saw no use for the demon, and continued with the god. Reason next said: "If with the small god, why not with the great God of all?" And in the upshot he found himself practising exactly the same method as Molinos, St Teresa, Buddha, Father Poulain, St Paul, Meredith Starr, A. E. Waite, Aleister Crowley, and the rest—and getting the very same results.

Oh, my dear sir, a man is a man, and if you give whisky to A, B, and C, they all get drunk, with minor variations for the personal equation; and God is one, and when A, B, and C pray, meditate, concentrate, invoke, chant, mutter, watch, resign themselves, it is all one thing in different words. One is a little better, perhaps, for A; and another suits B. But God rewards all alike, in The End.

Mr Waite's grammar is as slovenly as ever: "The said three persons will draw lots among each other."

Mr Waite's scholarship is as slovenly as ever. He refers to Molinos as a Jesuit. I. Biss

I am learning Scotch (for legal purposes) at present. I know the meaning of "lovite," "compear," "furthcoming," "reponed," "Edictal," "the matter libelled," "effeirs," "teind," "condescendence," "decerned," "arrestments have been used," "diligence of arrestment," "addebted," "averments," "proof was led," "oath of calumny," "sist," "mandatory," "runrig and rundale," "The Record has been placed in the Roll for adjustment" (Not said of a Pianola).

So that I have no time to learn Waitese, such as "palmary," "the imputed standpoint," "scattermeal," "a writer of my known dedications," "in respect of diluted views," "in respect of the mystic term," "in fine," "signal presentations," "it offers an experiment in integration," "casually literate," "some more withdrawn condition," "ineffable typology," "an essence so uttermost," "anywise," "dilucid," "hypostatic," "super-incession," "all antecedents and warrants of precursors," and so on.

But where I can understand Mr Waite I am surprised to find him (as soon as he wishes to speak of the high states) borrowing without acknowledgement from my published works.

Waite (1911)	Crowley
The act or *state of being lost in God* is that which I have elsewhere described in a perfection of all similitudes — which is of my adaptation but not of my making [Is this his apology to me? —A.C.] when Christ delivers up the Kingdom of each soul to His Father, and	Man's vision goes, dissolves in God's. *(Aha!* 1909) All the illusion gone, behold The One that is. (Ib.) Thou fastenest on This soul of mine, that it is gone, Gone from all life, and rapt away. (Ib.)

God is all in all.

This I know, that I am gone
To the heart of God's great dia-
    mond.
            (*The Ladder,* 1909)

I climbed still inwards. At the move-
    less point
Where all power, life, light, motion
    concentrate
I found God dwelling. . . .
            He drank my breath,
Absorbed my life in His, dispersed
    me, gave me death.
            (*Aceldama,* 1898)

The First House (*i.e.* the Father's
House) is so brilliant that you can't
think; and there, too, is my lover
(the Son) and I (the soul) when we
are one. (*The Wake-World,* 1907)

This is the state beyond the
state when it is said that
"*they shall see His face.*"

reverent gaze
Upon the ancient One of Days,
Beyond which fancy lies the Truth.
            (*Pentecost,* 1902)

to us the rites of Eleusis should open
the doors of Heaven, and we shall
enter in and see God face to face!
(*Eleusis,* 1906)

ye also shall see God face to face.
(Ib.)

they do lead one to the Vision of
God face to face. (Ib.)

initiates — men who have themselves seen God face to face, and
lived. (Ib.)

the three ways to the Holy House
of the Old King . . . so that is his
House, he is the Old King himself,
and so are you. (*The Wake World,*
1907)

Leaping all the lesser bars, I shall become the One and All . . . and lose myself. (*Konx Om Pax,* 1907)

This were my guerdon; to fade utterly
Into the rose-heart of that sanguine vase,
And lose my purpose in its silent sea,
And lose my life, and find my life, and pass
Up to the sea that is as molten glass.
(*Tannhäuser,* 1901)

the ego is altogether abased, absorbed, in the Beloved. (*Time,* 1906)

in that love and in that joining together there is *no passage longer from subject to object.* But this is the Godhead. The Most Secret, Most Holy Temple, into which God and the soul go in [sic! I don't acknowledge Mr Waite as a disciple in grammar] and only one comes out.

(Of Dhyana)
The absolute identity
Of the beholder and the Vision.
(*Pentecost,* 1904)

If a single state of consciousness persist unchanged for a period exceeding a very few seconds, its duality is annihilated. (*Science and Buddhism,* 1904)

The object (*scil.* of meditation) disappears; in its stead arises a great glory, characterised by a feeling of calm, yet of intense, unimaginable bliss. . . it might be absurd to assert that either subject or object disappears in Dhyana to the disadvantage of the other. (*Time,* 1906)

He (the Black Magician) works in a circle. . . . He says; I am inside, and you can't get at me. He says One and One are Two! (By the "Black Magician" is here symbolised any person with the normal dualistic consciousness.) (*Ali Sloper,* 1907)

Destroy him, or be he! That is
enough; there is no more to say.
(*Konx Om Pax,* 1907)

Prostrate I wait upon Thy will,
Mine Angel, for this grace of union.
(Ib.)

nothing is
But the intensity of bliss.
Being is blasted. That exists.
(*Aha!* 1909)

All thoughts are evil. Thought is
two:
The seer and the seen. Eschew
That supreme blasphemy, my son,
Remembering that God is One.
(*Aha!* 1909)

In the astral visions the consciousness is hardly disturbed; in magical
evocations it is intensely exalted;
but it is still bound by its original
conditions. The Ego is still opposed
to the non-Ego. . . . All true mystical
phenomena contradict these conditions. In the first place, the Ego
and the non-Ego unite explosively...
&c., &c. (*The Psychology of Hashish,*
1909)

Samadhi (is) that state of mind in
which subject and object, becoming One, have disappeared. (Ib.)

The uniting of subject and object
which is Samadhi. (Ib.)

O thou sun
Of thought, of bliss transcending
thought,
Rise *where division dies!* Absorb
In glory of the glowing orb

Self and its shadow!

(Pentecost, 1904)

He (Huxley) denies the assertion of duality; he has no datum to assert the denial of duality. I have.

(Science and Buddhism, 1904)

Whosoever goes inward to find anything but the Divine in his centre is working on the side of his own loss . . . those who are seeking to exercise the powers of the soul apart from its graces are treading the downward path.

the quest of miraculous power (pertains to) the sciences of the abyss.

The tradition *à rebours* is definitely and clearly that of miraculous power in the quest and attainment thereof.

Miracles follow as a dower.
But ah! they used the fatal power
And lost the Spirit in the act.

(Pentecost, 1904)

Let then the student contradict every vision and refuse to enjoy it. *(Postcards to Probationers, 1909)*

It is waste of power (the most expensive kind of power) to "make the spirits bring us all kinds of food," etc. *(John St John, 1908)*

divination should be discarded from the start. (Ib.)

to use the spiritual forces to secure health is the vilest black magic. (Ib.)

He asked him (i.e. the Adept) frequently to dine,
Forgetting purposely the wine
(Though the Arcana of Nibbana
Ignore the very name of Cana).
He could not pass a herd of swine
Without a hint; in fact, in fine,
He took His Silence as a sign:
This is an enemy of mine!

(Konx Om Pax, 1907)

Fifth House, and mostly dream at that. (The Fifth House is that of Geburah, the house of Magical Power.) (Ib.)

But after all these wonders, rank after rank of the Bless-

Then subtly, easily, imperceptibly gliding, I passed away into nothing.

ed Angels, after all visions of the Great White Throne, it is as if a quiet centre opened unawares and through an immeasurable silence drew down the soul—from the many splendours into the one splendour . . . as if the soul saw there the one God and itself as the one worshipper. But after a little while the worshipper itself has dissolved, and from henceforth and for ever it has the consciousness of God only. . . .

And I was wrapped in the black brilliance of my Lord, that interpenetrated me in every part, fusing its light with my darkness, and leaving there no darkness, but pure light. . . . At once, automatically, the interior trembling began again, and again the subtle brilliance flowed through me. The consciousness again died and was reborn as the divine, always without shock or stress. . . . Being entered into the Silence, let me abide in the Silence! (*John St John*, 1909)

O petty purities and pale,
These visions I have spoken of!
The Infinite Lord of Light and
    Love
Breaks on the soul like dawn. . . .
In that fire the soul burns up.
One drop from that celestial cup
Is an abyss, an infinite sea
That sucks up immortality.
                    (*Aha!* 1909)
Lie open, a chameleon cup,
And let Him suck thine honey up.
                        (Ib.)

Dozens and scores of other parallel passages could be adduced; but I have sat up half the night already.

It follows that: *either* Mr Waite is a disciple of my own, *or* "the devil is quoting Holy Writ."

I'll risk a bob that he would rather be the devil!

Aleister Crowley

STEWED PRUNES
AND PRISM

THE TENNYSON CENTENARY

The judicious may possibly wonder why one should dig so deep into the tumulus of oblivion to rescue (though but for execration) the bones of so very dead a dog as Alfred Tennyson.

But the truth is not so near the surface. He can hardly be called dead who never lived; and a trodden worm writhes longer than a felled ox. So therefore Tennyson succumbed to contempt, not to hatred; men twitched their robes away from the contamination of the unclean thing—there was no fight, no bloodshed.

Now therefore the smirking approval of the neuters of England continues unashamed, until the younger generation (some of them) may be inclined to class Tennyson with the poets, rather than with the Longfellows and Cloughs.

They can hardly imagine any creature, however vile, so crapulous as to prostitute the noble legend of England herself to dust-licking before that amiable Teutonic prig, the late Prince Consort. Yet this busy buttock-groom gives the best part of his flunkey's life to the achievement. Even his own friendships—his friendships —are made but the pretext for a new servility.

And what an object for servility! The fashionable dilettante doubt, the fashionable dilettante faith, are neatly balanced in the scales of mid-Victorian pragmatism, whose coarse-fibred *affettuosi* bargain with God as with a huckster.

The British conception of the Noblest Man being that of a cheating tradesman, their God is fashioned in that image, and the ambition of them all is to cheat Him. So they avoid the sceptic's sneers by an affectation of doubt, the fanatic's thunders by an affectation of faith: between which two stools they fall to the ground.

In the end they are more sceptic than the sceptic. Hear how they try to be pious!

> Leave thou thy sister, when she prays,
> Her early Heaven, her happy views,

implies that the whole question of religion is so trivial that it is really not worth while disturbing any one about it.

So too the play at scepticism results in an insane excess of maudlin piety.

As we look back on that whole dreadful period, we sicken at its loathsome cant, its *laissez-faire,* its sweating, its commercialism, its respectability, its humanitarianism, its inhumanity.

Of this age we have two perfect relics.

If art be defined as the true reflection of the inmost soul of the age, then the works of Alfred Tennyson and the Albert Memorial are among our chiefest treasures.

How harmonious, too, they are! There is nothing in Tennyson which the Memorial does not figure in one or other of its gaudy features; no flatulence of the Memorial whose perfect parallel one cannot find in the shoddy sentimentalism of Tennyson.

Even where the vision is true and beautiful it is quite out of place.

The young gentleman waits in the park for his young lady; and sees, quite clearly and nicely:

> And like a ghost she glimmers on to me.

Apart from the villainous cacophony and bad taste of the wording, the vision is true enough; I was once young myself, in a park—and the rest of it; and that is exactly the vision. But what a point of view! The young gentleman must certainly have been a curate.

At such moments the heart should race, the veins swell, the breath quicken, the eyes strain, the foot—not a word of the struggle not to show impatience, the tenseness of the whole being of a man!

No! this is indeed a glimmering ghost, a bloodless, vacant phantom.

Note, too, the degradation of the symbols.

To compare a girl to a "ghost"; to disenchant the glow and glamour of her to a "glimmer."

To compare a volcano in eruption to the puffing of a steam engine; the sun in heaven at high noon to a farthing dip.

The vision is accurate enough; but the point of view is throughout that of a flunkey, of a tradesman, of a gelded toady, of a stewed prune!

So too the very perfection of form which marks Tennyson is a shocking fault, a guide to the governess' mind of the creature. He is so determined to keep all the rules that he utterly breaks the first (and last) rule: "Rules are the devil." He writes like a schoolboy for whom a false quantity means a basting. He counts his syllables on his fingers; he never writes by ear, as one whose ears are open to the heavenly melody of the Muses.

So we have all the artifice—and perhaps the worst artifice even invented—but no art, no humanity.

As a mountaineer (I have seen very many of the greatest mountains of the earth) I must admit that

> phantom fair
> Was Monte Rosa, hanging there,
> A thousand shadowy-pencilled valleys
> And dewy dells in a golden air

is a very decent word-picture of the great mountain. But a Man would have felt his muscles tighten; and the lust to match his force against the stern splendour of those glittering ridges would have sent him hot-foot after rope and axe.

A great artist would rarely see so tremendous a vision as that of a mountain without emotion of terror and wonder and rejoicing. Tennyson sees it as a mere sight—he ticks it off in his Baedeker. He sees the dolly side of everything. Everything he touches becomes petty, false, weak, a mirage. He degrades the courteous Gawain to a vulgar lecher—but his lechery is as mild as an old maid's Patience; he ruins women as a child plucks a daisy. Lancelot commits adultery with kid gloves on; and Enoch Arden moralises like a Sunday-School Teacher at a village treat.

In the mouth of this soft-spoken counter-jumper the wildest words take on the smoothest sense. By sheer dint of cadence

> Dragons of the prime
> That tare each other in their slime

sounds less terrible than a dog-fight.

> Nature, red in tooth and claw
> With ravine, shriek'd——

is but a termagant.

"Ring out, wild bells" suggests no tocsin (as it might, for they symbolise the stupendous world-tragedy of the Atonement) but at most the pastoral summons to a simple worship, at least the dinner-gong—a dinner whose Turkey cooed, not gobbled; a Plum Pudding innocent of brandy.

Yet these lines are the most forcible one can remember; and if these things are done in the green tree——?

Lady Clara Vere de Vere feels (or is supposed to feel) a ladylike repugnance to the sight of a suicide's scarred throat! She never is conceived of as rising either in joy or horror to the height of tragedy. Her atonement? To preside at the Dorcas Society!

This ridiculous monster!

Let us cover up these bones neatly and tidily and bury them yet deeper in their tumulus of oblivion.

Bones? Jelly!

A. Quiller, Jr.

THE DANGERS OF
MYSTICISM

A curious idea is being sedulously disseminated, and appears to be gaining ground, that mysticism is the "Safe" Path to the Highest, and magic the dangerous Path to the Lowest.

There are several comments to be made on this assertion. One may doubt whether anything worth doing at all is free from danger, and one may wonder what danger can threaten the man whose object is his own utter ruin. One may also smile a little grimly at the integrity of those who try to include all Magic under Black Magic, as is the present trick of the Mystic Militant here on earth.

Now, as one who may claim to a slight acquaintance with the literature of both paths, and to have been honoured by personal exposition from the adepts of both paths, I believe that I may be able to bring them fairly into the balance.

This is the magical theory, that the first departure from the Infinite must be equilibrated and so corrected. So the "great Magician," Mayan, the maker of Illusion, the Creator, must be met in combat. Then "if Satan be divided against Satan, how can his kingdom stand?"

863

Both vanish: the illusion is no more. Mathematically, $1+(-1)=0$. And this path is symbolised in the Taro under the figure of the Magus, the card numbered 1, the first departure from 0, but referred to Beth, 2, Mercury, the god of Wisdom, Magic and Truth.

And this Magus has the twofold aspect of the Magician himself and also of the "Great Magician" described in *Liber 418* (*The Equinox,* no. V, Special Supplement, p. 144).

Now the formula of the mystic is much simpler. Mathematically, it is $1-1=0$. He is like a grain of salt cast into the sea; the process of dissolution is obviously easier than the shock of worlds which the magician contemplates. "Sit down, and feel yourself as dust in the presence of God; nay, as less than dust, as nothing," is the all-sufficient simplicity of his method. Unfortunately, many people cannot do this. And when you urge your inability, the mystic is only too likely to shrug his shoulders and be done with you.

This path is symbolised by the "Fool" of the Tarot, who is alike the Mystic and the Infinite.

But apart from this question, it is by no means certain that the formula is as simple as it seems. How is the mystic to assure himself that "God" is really "God" and not some demon masquerading in His image? We find Gerson sacrificing Huss to his "God"; we find a modern journalist who has done more than dabble in mysticism writing, "This mystic life at its highest is undeniably selfish"; we find another writing like the old lady who ended her criticism of the Universe, "There's only Jock an' me'll be saved; an' I'm no that sure o' Jock"; we find another who at the age of ninety-nine foams at the mouth over an alleged breach of her alleged copyright; we find another so sensitive that the mention of his name by the present writer induces an attack of epileptic mania; if such are really "united with" or "absorbed in" God, what of God?

We are told in Galatians that the fruits of the Spirit are peace, love, joy, long-suffering, gentleness, goodness, faith, meekness, temperance; and somewhere else, "By their fruits ye shall know them."

Of these evil-doers then we must either think that they are dishonest, and have never attained at all, or that they have united themselves with a devil.

Such are "Brethren of the Left Hand Path," described so thoroughly in *Liber 418.* (*The Equinox,* no. V, Special Supplement, pp. 119 *sqq.*)

Of these the most characteristic sign is their exclusiveness. "We are the men. Ours is the only Way. All Buddhists are wicked," the insanity of spiritual pride.

The Magician is not nearly so liable to fall into this fearful mire of pride as the mystic; he is occupied with things outside himself, and can correct his pride. Indeed, he is constantly being corrected by Nature. He, the Great One, cannot run a mile in four minutes! The mystic is solitary and shut up, lacks wholesome combat. We are all schoolboys, and the football field is a perfect prophylactic of swelled head. When the mystic meets an obstacle, he "makes believe" about it. He says it is "only illusion." He has the morphino-maniac's feeling of *bien-etre,* the delusions of the general paralytic. He loses the power of looking any fact in the face; he feeds himself on his own imagination; he persuades himself of his own attainment. If contradicted on the subject, he is cross and spiteful and cattish. If I criticise Mr X, he screams, and tries to injure me behind my back; if I say that Madame Y is not exactly St Teresa, she writes a book to prove that she is.

Such persons "swollen with wind, and the rank mist they draw, Rot inwardly, and foul contagion spread," as Milton wrote of a less dangerous set of spiritual guides.

For their unhappy followers and imitators, no words of pity suffice. The whole universe is for them but "the glass of their fool's face"; only, unlike Sir Palamedes, they admire it. Moral and spiritual Narcissi, they perish in the waters of illusion. A friend of mine, a solicitor in Naples, has told me strange tales of where such self-adoration ends.

And the subtlety of the devil is shown particularly in the method by which such neophytes are caught by the Black Brothers. There is an exaggerated awe, a solemnity of diction, a vanity of archaic phrases, a false veil of holiness upon the unclean shrine. Stilted affectation masquerades as dignity; a rag-bag of mediaevalism apes profundity; jargon passes for literature; phylacteries increase about the hem of the perfect prig, prude, and Pharisee.

Corollary to this attitude is the lack of all human virtue. The greatest magician, when he acts in his human capacity, acts as a man should. In particular, he has learnt kindheartedness and sympathy. Unselfishness is very often his long suit. Just this the mystic lacks. Trying to absorb the lower planes into the higher, he neglects the lower, a mistake no magician could make.

The Nun Gertrude, when it came to her turn to wash up the dishes, used to explain that she was very sorry, but at that particular moment she was being married, with full choral service, to the Saviour.

Hundreds of mystics shut themselves up completely and for ever. Not only is their wealth-producing capacity lost to society, but so is their love and good-will, and worst of all, so is their example and precept. Christ, at the height of his career, found time to wash the feet of his disciples; any Master who does not do this on every plane is a Black Brother. The Hindus honour no man who becomes "Sannyasi" (nearly our "hermit") until he has faithfully fulfilled all his duties as a man and a citizen.

Celibacy is immoral, and the celibate shirks one of the greatest difficulties of the Path.

Beware of all those who shirk the lower difficulties: it's a good bet that they shirk the higher difficulties too.

Of the special dangers of the path there is here no space to write; each student finds at each step temptations reflecting his own special weaknesses. I have therefore dealt solely with the dangers inseparable from the path itself, dangers inherent in its nature. Not for one moment would I ask the weakest to turn back or turn aside from that path, but I would ask even the strongest to apply these correctives: first, the sceptical or scientific attitude, both in outlook and method; second, a healthy life, meaning by that what the athlete and the explorer mean; third, hearty human companionship, and devotion to life, work, and duty.

Let him remember that an ounce of honest pride is better than a ton of false humility, although an ounce of true humility is worth an ounce of honest pride; the man who works has no time to bother with either. And let him remember Christ's statement of the Law "to love God with all thy heart, and thy neighbour as thyself."

Aleister Crowley

THE
SHADOWY DILL-WATERS

OR

MR SMUDGE THE MEDIUM

'Tis like the howling of Irish wolves against the moon.

As You Like It

In our investigation of the trumpery tin Pantheon of Aunt Sallies which our courtesy calls "literary gents," one of the most striking figures is a certain lame duck that suggests a mixed ancestry of Brigand manqué and the Ghost in the Bab Ballads.

Historically, too, the subject has its advantage, for not only does the work of Weary Willie suggest primal Chaos, but himself recalls the Flood. He seems to have desired to emulate Noah, but the modern tendency to specialisation has led him to confine his attentions to the Insect World, and the remarkable jumping qualities of some of his specimens have their correspondence in the metre of those treacly emulsions which it is our present purpose to study.

Come with me! Behold the scene of action. What? You can see nothing? Of course not. It's out of focus, and the limelight is but a farthing dip. Never mind; take the slide, and hold it to the light! Ah! there's a well—a druid well; a wood—a druid wood; a boat (druid) on a druid sea. Why Druid? Because Willie is not a British workman. The expletive is harmless enough. Look! more wells and woods and boats and apple-blossoms. When in doubt, play apple-blossom. Try and scan it as a dactyl. You can't? He can.

Oh! there are some people in the boat. Druid people. A queen with hair like the casting-net of the stars. What's that? Never mind. There's nothing rude or offensive about the casting-net of the stars? Very good, then; let's get on. What are they doing? Drifting. That's dead sure, anyway. Drifting. Drifting. That's the beautiful Celtic glamour of it. Druidically drifting Druids on a druid sea of apple-blossom in the middle distance. Foreground, a well in a wood. Background, a casting-net of the stars. Dotted about, hounds of various colours, usually red. Let's have another slide. Same thing, with a fairy floating about. Tired? Yes. Well, sit down and talk about it. Tut! Tut! . . .

How on earth does anybody ever deliberately produce this sort of thing? He doesn't. It just happens. All the Gregory Powder in the world won't produce it; it's true Asiatic Cholera, and you can't imitate it. I didn't mean dill-waters; I meant rice-waters.

Now let no one think that we object to an atmosphere in Art. Maeterlinck is doubtless just as misty in his symbolism; equally he uses a leitmotiv; equally he relies on mystery to shroud his figures with fascination, terror, or glamour.

But the images are themselves perfectly clear and precise. In the mistiest of all, "Les Aveugles," one can condense the plot into a single phrase of simplest English. On this clean model, Greek in its simplicity, the master has thrown draperies of cleanly woven fabric, delicate and frail as spiders' webs—and as silvery and strong as they.

This is a craftsmanship exquisitely subtle and severe, a style of almost superhuman austerity.

In our shadowy choleraic we have the imitation of this,

its reflection in a dull and dirty mind.

Smudge.

When Ruskin reproached Whistler for his ability to distinguish between colours less violent than vermilion and emerald, he was no doubt a Philistine. But how much worse is the Bohemian who thinks—"Since I cannot see anything but muddiness in these silver-grey quarter-tones, I can easily rival Whistler." Forthwith he mixes up all the colours in his box, daubs a canvas with them and——? Certainly he deceives Ruskin, but he deceives nobody else.

Genius, O weary one, is not an infinite capacity for taking pains; but genius has to take pains to express itself, and expression is at least half the battle. You, I think, have neither genius nor application; neither a healthy skin nor the soap-travail which might reveal it. Still, one can never be sure; you might give a trial to the soap.

If we had not a sufficiency of hard work before us in interpreting the masters of old, we might be tempted to waste more time on you; but there is Blake. Blake is more obscure than you are; but we have this guarantee, based on experience, that when we do attain to his meaning, it starts up luminous, Titanic, splendid. With you, we discover only commonplace—the commonplace of a maudlin undertaker replying to the toast of the Ladies at the Annual Dinner of the Antique Order of Arch-Druids.

Blake fashioned his intricate caskets of symbol to conceal pearls; you pile up dead leaves to cover rotten apples.

You are Attis with a barren fig-leaf.

It is true that a sort of dreary music runs monotonously through your verses, only jarred by the occasional discords. It is as if an eternal funeral passed along, and the motor hearse had something wrong with the ignition—and the exhaust.

It is as if a man were lost upon a lonely marsh in the

flat country and constantly slipped and sat down with a splash in a puddle. These be ignoble images, my masters!

The fact is that you are both myopic and tone-deaf. You peer into the darkly splendid world, the abyss of light—for it is light, to the seer—and you see but "unintelligible images, unluminous, formless, and void." Then you return and pose as one who has trodden the eternal snows.

You are like a man who puts a penny into a mutoscope that is out of order; and, rather than admit that he has been swindled, pretends to have enjoyed it. You are like a parvenu with an ill-cooked chop at a swagger restaurant who eats it rather than incur the frown of the waiter.

Better abandon mysticism outright than this. But we suppose it is impossible; you must trim, and compromise, and try to get round the Boyg, O Peer Gynt without his courage and light-heartedness, O onion with many a stinking sheath, and a worm at the heart!

Yes, if nothing else were wrong with you—and everything else *is* wrong—you would still be damned for your toadying to Mrs Grundy and the Reverend Robert Rats.

We thought to sum you up on a page, and that page a page of but four corners; on mature consideration we think it could be done in a word, and that word a word of but four letters.

A. Quiller, Jr.

WAITE'S WET

OR

THE BACKSLIDER'S RETURN

All things come to him who Waites.
I waited patiently on the Lord; and He inclined unto me,
and heard my cry.

It was a brilliant May afternoon when the Prodigal
returned. At the offices of *The Equinox* the usual con-
stellation was assembled. Crowley lay lost in meditation
upon the 1500-guinea Persian rug, which he had received
from the executors of the late John Brown; Neuburg,
covered from head to foot with yellow paint and his own
post-prandial poetry, was yelling with laughter over a
telegram which informed him that his favourite uncle
had been disembowelled by a mad bull; Wieland, his
head among the fire-irons, his soul among the stars, was
trying to remember two important engagements which
he had written down in his note-book five minutes earlier;
Ethel Archer, talked to by Meredith Starr, but not listening
to him, sat pale and classical on the edge of a table in
default of a promontory, saying softly: "Bysses—aster—
kisses—caster—blisses—faster—this—is—master—misses
— disaster — Pisces — poetaster — Cambyses — chaster";
Madame Strindberg, still smarting under the description of
herself as "relict or derelict" of somebody, having tele-
graphed to the Bank to stop any cheques she might draw
in the next twelve months, was committing suicide with

the murmured apology: "After all, this isn't an hotel";
while "Boy Billy," tastefully costumed for walking in
Bond Street as an Egyptian *sais*, was romping with her
third best pal in spite of the broken heart which she had
left beneath the boots of Mr Hener Skene; Mr Austin
Harrison, who had dropped in for a quiet afternoon, was
quite failing to grasp the situation created by the Editor
herself, who, shaking in every chin, declared rather more
than less than aloud that, waiters or no waiters, she meant
to marry him, and the gentleman down-stairs could go—
my grandmother's hat!—and——

She was interrupted by the arrival of a telegraph boy,
who delivered a bulky envelope containing the following
message—

> Notwithstanding categorical imputations sacramentally
> integrated similitudes undedicated warrants antecedent
> Paulopetrine typology casually unworthy hypostaticism
> predecessorial superincession archidiaconal arch-amphibians
> osify elpidize redintegration status lymphaticus.

"A cipher telegram! How romantic!" cried the Editor,
releasing Austin Harrison for the fraction of a second.

"Oh no," said Crowley, "it's quite plain English; it's
from Arthur Edward Waite. He repents; he comes back
to the fold. He begs forgiveness. *Osify* means 'dare';
elpidize 'hope'; *redintegration* 'restoration'; *status* 'status.' "

"But he says 'status lymphaticus.' "

"It's a disease; he read about it in the *Daily Mail* on the
Underground between Aldgate and Blackfriars; but it
sounds better than plain "status"; so he damned the
extra ha'penny, and put it. To my mind it's the shortest
and plainest thing he's ever written. And I forgive him
all."

The company, overborne by authority, acquiesced. Only
Neuburg, always a pessimist, doubted. "It's unsigned!"

he groaned, his lips, blood-stained bolsters dipped in ink, writhing like half-boiled lobsters.

The Editor, with one shriek, one sob, and one sigh, thinking of the veil of the temple, tore a napkin in default of anything else to tear, and cried: "It is finished! Votes for Women!" Neuburg, his nose working feverishly, burst into hyena-howls. The Master arose; calling for hot water and sulphuric acid, he comparatively cleaned the victim's left ear, and bit another piece off. Calm was restored.[1]

Remembering Mr Waite's statement in *Who's Who* that he "holds nearly all degrees of Masonry known in England, and some which are here unknown," Crowley dictated the following telegram—

"Waite, Esquire, Etcetera, Sidmouth Lodge, South Ealing.

Yes.

Aleister Crowley"

"Apprentice, Companion, *Master*, Secret Master, Perfect Master, Intimate Secretary, Provost and Judge, Valiant Master, Elect of Nine, Elect of the Unknown, Elect of Fifteen, Perfect Elect, Illustrious, and in Scotland of the Holy Trinity, Companion, Master, Panissière, Master of the Triangle, of J.J.J., of the Sacred Vault, and of St. Andrew: Little Architect, Grand Architect, and Architect in Light and Perfection; Apprentice, Companion, and Master Perfect Architect, Perfect Architect, and in Scotland Sublime, and Sublime of Heredom; **Royal Arch,** Grand Axe, Sublime Knight of Choice, Knight of the Sublime Choice, Prussian Knight, *Knight of the Temple,* Knight of the Eagle, Knight of the Black Eagle, Knight of the Red Eagle, Knight of the White East, *Knight*

1. In the event, Neuburg proved to have been justified in his scepticism. The telegram was not from Waite; it was a practical joke of Dr Wynn Westcott's, possibly. But I can no more rewrite this article than Crowley can replace Neuburg's ear.—A. Q., Jr.

of the East, Commander of the East, Grand Commander of the East, **Sovereign Commander of the Temple,** and *Prince of Jerusalem*: **Sovereign Prince Rose Croix of Kilwinning and of Heredom,** Knight of the West, Sublime Philosopher, Discreet of Chaos, Sage of Chaos, Knight of the Sun, *Supreme Commander of the Stars,* Sublime Philosopher Knight Noachite, of all four grades of the Key of Masonry, True Mason Adept, Sovereign Elect, Sovereign of Sovereigns, Grand Master of the Symbolic Lodges, Very High and Very Powerful, Knight of Palestine, Knight of the White Eagle, **Grand Elected Knight Kadosch Sovereign Inspector,** and **Grand Inquisitor Commander,** Beneficent Knight, Knight of the Rainbow, Knight of Banuka, Very Wise Israelite Prince, Sovereign Prince Talmudim, Sovereign Prince Zadkim, Grand-Haram, Grand Prince Haram, Sovereign Prince Hasid, *Sovereign Grand Prince Hasid,* and **Grand Inspector Intendant Regulator of the Order:** Sovereign Prince of the 78th, 79th, 80th and 81st degrees; Sovereign Prince of the 82nd, 83rd, 84th, 85th and 86th degrees; *Sovereign Grand Prince of the 87th degree, Grand Master* **Constituent of the Order for the First Series,** *Sovereign Grand Prince of the 88th degree,* **Grand Master Constituent of the Order for the Second Series,** *Sovereign Grand Prince of the 89th degree,* **Grand Master Constituent of the Order for the Third Series,** and of the NINETIETH AND LAST DEGREE SUPREME GRAND CONSERVATOR AND ABSOLUTE GRAND SOVEREIGN AND PATRIARCH OF THE ANCIENT ORIENTAL RITE OF MIZRAIM: Pastophoris, Neocoris, and Melanophoris; Christophoris, Perfect Master Balahate, Sublime Master Just and Perfect, *Sublime Epopt,* and Knight of the Iris; Sublime Minerval, Knight of the Golden Fleece, Grand Elect Mysophilote, Knight of the Triangle, *Knight of the*

Sacred Arch, **Knight of the Secret Vault,** *Knight of the Sword,* Knight of Jerusalem, Knight of the East and **Knight of the Rose Croix:** Knight of the Red Eagle, *Knight of the Temple,* Sublime Aletophilote, Knight of Libanus, *Knight of Heredom,* Knight of the Tabernacle, *Knight of the Serpent,* Knight Sage of Truth, *Knight Hermetic Philosopher,* Knight of the Key, Knight of the White Eagle, KNIGHT KADOSCH, Knight of the Black Eagle, KNIGHT OF THE ROYAL MYSTERY, and KNIGHT GRAND INSPECTOR; Knight of Scandinavia, Sublime Commander of the Temple, Sublime Negotiate, Knight of Shota, Sublime Elect of Truth, *Grand Elect of the Aeons,* Sage Savaist, *Knight of the Arch of Seven Columns, Prince of Light,* Sublime Hermetic Sage, *Prince of the Zodiac,* Sublime Sage of the Mysteries, Sublime Pastor of the Huts, *Knight of the Seven Stars, Sublime Guardian of the Sacred Mount,* and *Sublime Sage of the Pyramids;* Sublime Philosopher of Samothrace, *Sublime Titan of the Caucasus,* Sage of the Labyrinth, *Knight of the Phoenix,* Sublime Scald, Sublime Orphic Doctor, Pontiff of Cadmia, Sublime Magus, Prince Brahmin, Grand Pontiff of Ogygia, *Sublime Guardian of the Three Fires, Sublime Unknown Philosopher, Sublime Sage of Eleusis, Sublime Kawi,* Sage of Mythras, *Grand Installator Guardian of the Sanctuary, Grand Consecrator Architect of the Mystic City, Grand Eulogist Guardian of the Ineffable Name, Patriarch of Truth, Knight of the Golden Branch of Eleusis,* Patriarch of the Planispheres, Patriarch of the Sacred Vedas, Supreme Master of Wisdom, *Doctor of the Sacred Fire,* Sublime Master of the Sloka, and Knight of the Lybic Chain: **Patriarch of Isis,** Sublime Knight Theosopher, *Grand Pontiff of the Thebaid,* Knight of the Redoubtable Sada, Sublime Elect of the Sanctuary of Mazias, **Patriarch of Memphis,** Grand Elect of the Temple of Midgard, Sublime Knight

of the Valley of Oddy, Doctor of the Izeds, Sublime
Knight of Kneph, Sublime Philosopher of the Valley of
Kabal, Sublime Prince of Masonry, *Grand Elect of the
Sacred Curtain, Prince Pontiff of the Mystic City, Sovereign
Master of Masonry,* and *Perfect Pontiff Sublime Master of
the Great Work: Grand Defender of the Order,* Sublime
Catechist, Adept of Sirius, Adept of Babylon, Companion
Banuke, Companion Zerdust, *Companion of the Luminous
Ring,* Sage of Elea, Sage of Delphi, Sublime Sage of
Symbols Intendant of Hieroglyphics, Sublime Sage of
Wisdom, Sublime Sage of the Mysteries, Sublime Sage of
the Sphinx, Priest of On, **Grand Inspector Regulator
General of the Order, Prince and Pontiff of Mem-
phis, Grand Administrator of the Order,** PATRI-
ARCH GRAND CONSERVATOR OF THE ORDER,
and a MEMBER OF THE SOVEREIGN SANC-
TUARY *of the* ANCIENT ORIENTAL RITE OF
MEMPHIS: *Apprentice, Companion,* and *Master*; Dis-
creet Master, Perfect Master, Intimate Secretary, Provost
and Judge, and Intendant of the Buildings; Elect of Nine,
Elect of Fifteen and Sublime Knight Elect; Grand Master
Architect, *Ancient Master of the Royal Arch,* and Grand
Elect Perfect and Sublime Mason; Knight of the Sword,
Prince of Jerusalem, Knight of the East and West, and
Knight of the Rose Croix of Heredom; Grand Pontiff,
Master ad Vitam, Knight, Prince of Libanus, Chief of the
Tabernacle, Prince of the Tabernacle, Knight of the
Brazen Serpent, Prince of Mercy and Grand Commander
of the Temple of Jerusalem; Knight of the Sun, Prince
Adept, Grand Sublime Knight of St. Andrew of Scotland,
GRAND ELECTED KNIGHT KADOSCH, **Grand
Inquisitor Commander, Sublime Prince of the
Royal Secret,** and SOVEREIGN GRAND INSPEC-
TOR GENERAL OF THE THIRTY-THIRD AND
LAST DEGREE OF THE ANCIENT AND AC-

CEPTED SCOTTISH RITE: etc., etc., etc., etc.,
etc., etc., etc., etc., etc., etc., etc., etc., etc.,
etc., etc., etc., etc., etc., etc., etc., etc., etc., etc.,
etc., etc., etc., etc., etc., etc., etc., etc., etc., etc., etc.,
etc., etc., etc., etc., etc., etc., etc."

"Send this," quoth he, "to the Flapper-haunted fields
where Prehistoric Peeps are frowned upon!"

To describe the scenes that followed would have
beggared the fertile or perhaps fertilized pen of the
Editor of the *Looking-Glass*; but he was in any case not
there, being busy in working out by applied mathematics
the problem as to which public man was worthiest of a
biography in his columns next week.

The words "blasphemous orgie" altogether fail to give
any idea of what occurred.

"Twenty-eight naked demi-mondaines now brimmed
the buckets with satyrion," hardly describes it.

"These loathsome and abominable creatures next
abandoned themselves to frenzied scenes unparalleled in
Degenerate Rome," conveys an altogether false impression.

Only my own pen can describe it accurately; and I
suppose the printer will refuse to set it up, and very likely
telephone the Public Prosecutor. However, I shall try and
sneak it through in Ciceronian Latin.

Crowleius dixit: Quid circa—(what on earth's the Latin
for "tea"?)?

Omnes biberunt.

(There must be some concealed horror in these words.
It *apparently* means "Crowley said—what about tea? They
all drank." With this reservation we prepare to fly to
Ostend, but print it. Printer.)

The good news ran through London like wildfire, doing
every hundred yards in even time.

Ralph Shirley, stirring uneasily in his office chair, stroked his pet rhinoceros, and murmured "Piles o' money"; Leopold Rothschild asked if the zebra could indeed change his stripes; and although ninety and nine just persons that needed no repentance had that very minute been presented to the angels in heaven, the subject was completely forgotten in the exuberance of the higher joy.

Waite's photograph, frock-coat and all, was carried in its red plush frame shoulder high by Mr Battiscombe Gunn; Kennedy took a tailor's bill from his bosom, and dropped a silent tear upon it, murmuring *"His* letter!" The Editor, bustling Austin Harrison aside, took a bottle of champagne and a taxi to South Ealing, ignorant or careless of the reception that she might expect from that mother of "one *d,*" née "Ada Lakeman, of Devonshire family and Greek extraction," with the words "Sidmouth Lodge—lickitysplit—my grandmother's hat!" while the stock of all those "public companies," of which Mr Waite is "in business secretary and director," soared beyond the clouds, and had subsequently to be watered with tears.

Brooklyn, N.Y., where he was born, organized a procession which, instead of taking so many hours to pass a given point, decided, in flattering imitation of its greatest son, to take several weeks to come to it. The "old family of Lovell," which boasts itself to be his ancestor through his mother, saw the culmination of its own fortunes in this great fortune of its fortune-telling scion, and gave itself the Glad Eye; the "earliest settlers in Connecticut," who were responsible for his father, wriggled with pleasure in their graves, like tickled children: the "orders and fraternities which are concealed within Masonry or have arisen out of it," with which he "is connected in particular," tyled themselves and gave themselves over to unbridled joy: the "Hermetic Text Society" recently established by him "for the production by experts of rare old books and MSS. belonging to the literatures of Christian Mysticism, Rosicrucianism, Kabalism, and Alchemy" (*more* commercial candour!) tried in its joy to sell the MS. of the Book of Deuteronomy at Sothebys': the very timbers of the ship in which he was "brought in infancy" to England shivered with ecstasy; the girls at the London Wall Exchange unanimously resolved never again to ring up 3469, however often and however angrily asked for, that the Restored-to-Favour might remain in the Adytum of God-nourished Silence for ever.

Neuburg himself wrote the following sonnet—

> They also serve who only stand, and—Waite,
> Sweeter than sugar and as soft as silk,
> You could not stand, you would not serve! What fate
> Threatened the hope of Horlick's Malted Milk?
> Graver than Gladstone, decenter than Dilke,
> You, called to be the Peter of the State,
> Tried in your agony to do a bilk:—
> Though you could handle rod, and master bait.
>
> Now all is changed. Offended Crowley cries
> Upon your shoulder. All's red nose, wet eyes.
> You shall be Mary now as well as Martha!
> The mystic quest is yours as well as mine,
> Dilucid: sacramentally, in fine,
> Victoria loved Albert: I love Arthur.

I shall now draw the Veil of Sanctimoniosity upon this touching scene.

A. Quiller, Jr.

GLAZIERS' HOUSES
OR
THE SHAVING OF SHAGPAT

I will write him a very taunting letter.

As You Like It

In these latter days, when (too often) a newspaper pro-
prietor is like a Buddhist monk, afraid to scratch his
head lest he should incommode his vermin, it is indeed a
joy for a young and nameless author to be presented with
a long sword by a cordial editor, with the injunction:
"There, my lad, sweep away, never mind what you hit—
I'll stand the racket."

Whoosh! off we go. One, two, three—crash! What's
that? "Aere perennius"? Or a perennial ass?

Let us see—a very curious problem.

A problem not to be solved by mere surface scraping.
Well then?

A thankless and invidious task it may seem to pierce
deeper than the "wolf in Dr Jaeger's clothing" of our
wittiest woman and most alluring *morphinomane*. That task
is ours. For last night in the visions of mine head upon
my bed I beheld, strangely interwoven with this striking
picture, the scene between Little Red Riding Hood and
her sick grandmother—how perverted! For in my dream
it seemed that the old lady had devoured the wolf and
that the scourge of the Tories was but a bed-ridden and

toothless hag, mumbling the senile curses and jests which she could no longer articulate.

True it is that the Word of Shaw is quick and powerful, sharper than a two-edged sword. Yet the habit of sword-swallowing is probably fatal to the suicidal intentions of a Brutus, and it has certainly grown on him until he can no longer slay either himself or another.

A dweller in the glass houses of Fad, he has thrown stones at the fishy god. A Society Shimei, he has spat against the wind, and his beard is befouled.

True, every thought of Shaw is a great thought; and so equable and far-seeing is the artist, that its contradictory appears with it. His births are all Siamese twins; his god is Janus; his sign is Gemini . . . but his end is (I fear) not to rise above the equilibrium of contraries by a praeter-Hegelian dialectic, but to sink wearily between his two stools, a lamentable loon. . . . This Nulli Secundus, inflated with fermenting Grape-Nuts!

For in all that mass of analysis lucid and terrible I cannot recall a single line of beauty, rarely a note of ecstasy; with one exception (John Tanner), hardly a hero. Even he not a little absurd.

He has seen through the shams of romance, and marriage, and free love, and literary pose, and medical Ju-Ju, and religious rant, and political twaddle, and Socialist Buncombe and—every phase of falsehood. . . . But he has hardly grasped that each such falsehood is but a shadow of some sun of truth. He does not perceive the ineffable glory of the Universe in its whole and in each part. He has smitten at the shadow of a shadow: it falls—the world is filth. Let him rather new-edge his sword for a deeper analysis, and cut away the veil from the face of our Mother. 'Sdeath, man, is there nothing we may love?

He is wrong, anyway, to gibe at Scripture. For, like

Balaam, I came to curse, and appear to be blessing him!
(with scarce a monitory word). And, like Balaam, too, I
have been reviewed by G. K. Chesterton.

To pass from this painful subject . . .

Let me rouse myself to a really resolute effort to
denounce Shaw as a niddering. Aha! I have it. The man
is a journalist after all. We have to thank him for semi-
educating a few of our noodles, for applying the caustic
of Ibsen (right) and Wagner (wrong—the book's drivel)
to that most indolent of ulcers, the British Public, but
for nothing more. His own work, bar *Man and Overman*
(why the hybrid Superman?) is a glib sham. If it proves
anything, it proves nothing.

But are we to writhe in the ecstasies of Pyrrhonism?
For this prophet claims to be Zoroaster.

Can we be sure even of that? He has educated the British
goat to caper to his discordant Pan-pipe, so that without
the nuisance of crucifixion he may scourge the money-
changers from the temple.

Yet is this true cynicism? Doth he delight, the surly
Diogenes, in his solitary gambols—that insult both Lydia
and Lalage? Or is he doing it to tempt them—to coquette
with them? Is he a man deadly serious in positive constructive aim, yet so sensitive to ridicule that he will
always seek to turn it off as a jest—and so a stultifier of
himself? A Christ crucified, not upon Calvary, but upon
Venusberg, and so no redeemer?

If so, *ave atque vale,* George Bernard Shaw, for a
redeemer from the Overmen we want, and we will have;
another we will not have. Rather than your mock-crucified
castrato-devilry, Barabbas!

But if it be your serious livelong purpose to slay all
ideas by ridicule . . . then we must claim you as an adept,
one fit for the scourge and the buffets, for the gibes and
the slaver of the lick-spittle English, whose only notion of

a jest is a smutty story.

There is room for another hand at my bench.

See! If thou be indeed Achilles, why should we be in doubt? The gilded arms of Pandarus—the speech of Thersites. Sir, these things trouble us!

Thou seest it! If thou art journalist, the very journalists may rise from their slime, bubbling with foul breath, and suck thee down to their mother ooze unspeakable; but if not, then I too (no journalist, God knows!) must praise thee.

Thee—not thy work. For the manner thereof is wholly abominable. What have all we done, that for Pegasus we have this spavined and hamstrung Rosinante, for Bucephalus this hydrocephalic hydropath?

Even as god Gilbert begat the devil-brood musical comedy, so hast thou begotten the tedious stage-sermons to which our priest-loving, sin-conscious slaves now flock. Refinement of cruelty! Thou hast replaced the Trappist cell by the Court Theatre!

For this, I, who prefer the study to the theatre, forgive thee; for I love not the badger-reek of Suburbia and Bohemia in my nostrils. But for this also I praise thee, that lion-like thou turnest at last upon the jackal-crowd at thy heels. That ungainly dragon, the Chesterbelloc, hast thou ridden against, good St George Bernard Shaw! With a spear thou hast pierced its side, and there floweth forth beer and water.

Turn also, gramercy, upon the others, even unto the lowest. As Ibsen hawked at carrion birds with a Wild Duck, so do thou create some harpy to torment them. Who is this that followeth thee? Behold this mumbler born to butcher the English language, and educated to hack it with a saw! This stuttering babbler, this Harpocrates by the compulsion of a Sloane Square Mammurra! Who is this hanger-on to the bedraggled petticoats of thy lousy Thalia—this beardless, witless filcher of thy fallen crab-apples? This housemaid of the Court Theatre, the Gittite slut whose bleary eyes weep sexless crocodile tears over the crassness of the daughters of the Philistines?

Arise, and speak to this palsied megalomaniac, this frowsy Moll Flanders of a degenerated Chelsea, this down-at-heel *flaneur* on the outer boulevards of a prostituted literature, this little mongrel dog that fawneth upon the ill-cut trousers of thee, O St Pancras Pulchinello —this little red-coated person that doth mouth and dance upon the kakophonous barrel-organ of New Thought fakirs and Modernity mountebanks.

Speak to this parasite—itself unspeakably verminous— of the long-haired brigade, who has "got on" for that it had neither sufficient talent to excite envy, nor manhood enough to excite apprehension, but wit well to comprehend the sycophancy of the self-styled court and the tittle-tattle of the servants' hall.

It is an Editor—dear Lord my God! it is an Editor; but he who employs it has an equally indefeasible title to employ the pronoun "We."

It hath never had aught to say; but, then, how affectedly it hath said it! . . .

Will not the late *New Quarterly* take note of this?

O these barbers, with their prattle, and their false expedients—and scarce even a safety razor among them!

For let each one who worships George Bernard Shaw, while ignorant of that magnificent foundation of literature and philosophy—the Cubical Stone of the Wise, on which a greater than Auguste Rodin hath erected the indomitable figure of Le Penseur—take these remarks individually to himself, and—oh! Thinker, think again. Let not posterity consider of this statue that its summit is no Overman, but a gibbering ape! Not filth, not sorrow, not laughter of the mocker is this universe; but laughter of a young god, a holy and beautiful god, a god of love and light.

And thou, since thou hast the ear of the British ass at thy lips, sing to it those starry songs. It can but bray. . . .

But why, as hitherto, shouldst thou bray also? Or if bray thou must, let us have the virile and portentous bray of the Ass of Apuleius, not (as hitherto) the plaintive bray of the proverbial ass who hesitated so long between the two thistles that he starved to death. I warn thee, ass! We who are gods have laughed with thee these many years; beware lest in the end we laugh at thee with the laughter of a mandrake torn up, whereat thou shouldst fall dead.

A. Quiller Jr.

A LITERATOORALOORAL
TREASURE-TROVE

The happiest of literary discoveries would presumably be the complete works of Sappho. In the meantime we have got along wonderfully well with the masterpiece of "G. Ragsdale M'Clintock" which Mark Twain unearthed in his matchless "Cure for the Blues." (He does not specify Oxford or Cambridge.) The phrase that chiefly sticks in my memory is one of which Mark Twain makes especial fun: "the topmast topaz of an ancient tower." But this is not funny, it is superb; it is pure early Maeterlinck, and better than the Belgian imitation at that. I admit, however, that the rest of the book is quite as absurd as Mark Twain makes out.

But after all this is no funnier than the "St Irvine; or, The Rosicrucian," and the "Zastrozzi" of Percy Bysshe Shelley; and I may modestly claim recognition as the finder of a rarer and more exquisite treasure. Modestly, for my treasure-trove was not the result of research; I followed up no clues; I deciphered no cryptogram. I claim only this degree of insight and moral courage: the minute I found it, I stole it.

I feel sure it was the author's own copy; for I cannot

believe that any one else would have had one. My a-
tonement be to give him belated recognition!

On the approved principles, let me describe my booty.
It is a small 4to about 6½″ × 4½,″ quietly bound in black
cloth. It is printed on very bad paper, and the edges have
been cut and marbled.

Unassuming, indeed, is this slim booklet of 207 pages.
But the author knew his business; for on the front cover
appear these words—it is like an obscure grey battleship
suddenly belching her broadside—

SONNETICAL
NOTES ON
PHILOSOPHY
By WM. HOWELL WILLIAMS

The first shot struck me between wind and water.
Sonnetical! There's glory for you! A beautiful new adjective; a perfect adjective; so simple, and yet nobody
ever thought of it before. Get smoked glasses and look at
it! No good; one cannot comment or criticize or weave a
word picture (as the D—— M—— might say) about it.
One can only bow down in reverent silence and adore.

But that is not all. That is only external barbaric
splendour. There is more behind. Think of all the things
that *might* be sonnetical—why, there isn't one. Nothing is
sonnetical but a sonnet. Aha! that is where your great
mind droops; where you stop, Wm. Howell Williams
begins.

Notes on Philosophy are to be sonnetical. Now one can
think of many things about which sonnets have been
written; there is just one which you would never think
of—Philosophy. That is where Wm. Howell Williams
has you every time.

In a stunned manner one opens the book. The author
pours in his second broadside, and leaves you but a

laughter-logged derelict. What *might* these Sonnetical
Notes on Philosophy be? It suggests Rousseau and
Shelley, in a kind of way. One might think of Bertram
Dobell—a mildly atheistic set of sonnets. Oh dear no!

There is one thing that could not be there—and there
it is. It is a reproduction of Holman Hunt's picture of the
Saviour with a stable lantern trying to look like Nana
Sahib in his more cynically cruel moments.

(I understand that the original of this picture has been
acquired by Manchester; and from what I am told of
Manchester, the penalty fits the crime.)

And opposite that is the text, "Behold, I stand at the
door and knock," etc.

You now begin to wonder if two books have not got
mixed up; but no.

The title-page then appears.

SONNETICAL
NOTES
ON
PHILOSOPHY
BY
WM. HOWELL WILLIAMS

No date; no publisher; no price. But on the reverse we
find, very small—

Copyrighted by
Wm. Howell Williams
April 1901

(It was in May 1906 that I stole this copy.)

Now one would have liked a preface, something to explain the astounding choice of form, and so on. Or to give
some idea of the scope and purpose of the treatise. No;
nothing of the sort. He butts right in with

INTRODUCTION

And no sooner does this begin than you see what the author is driving at. He is out to prove that no matter how simple language may seem, in his master hands it can be made absolutely unintelligible. He begins:

> Philosophy must knowledge be,
> Hence knowledge is philosophy.

Ponder that "hence." At least it must lead to something else. No. He continues:

> It matters not what savant say
> If somehow knowledge comes man's way.

You now see the beginning of his first great rule of grammar: "Never inflect a verb!"

But wait! he is going to lay a trap for the unwary. He is going to give us three couplets which seem consecutive, and possess a meaning—

> Supposing can be only fun,
> And knowledge never so begun.
> With supposition's wand laid by
> Hume, Berkley [sic], Kant and Hegel fly.
> Nay! single, several, or all,
> Together taken they appall.

The spelling of "appall" is perhaps intended to spur the relaxed attention; for the next couplet wants it.

> Philosophers need not agree,
> Still is philosophy to be.

The comma is a very subtle weapon! And when you discover (by and by) that his Seventh great Rule is "Never use relative pronouns!" a return to this sublime Sphinx-verse leaves you worse off than you are at the first reading.

> All knowledge is on being cast:
> The being first and knowledge last.

Quite so: you must *be* before you can know. Wait.

> But note—"The first shall be the last
> And last shall be the first" ere cast.

How's that, umpire?

Perhaps the next couplet will clear things up. No: it only serves to introduce a point—of etiquette rather than of law—which deprecates sentences containing a principal verb.

> Such knowledge only consciousness
> In case of being under stress.

White resigned.

Wm. Howell Williams, however, has now got on to his mashie. Every couplet within a foot of the hole.

> All other were mere vanity,
> Save, sadly, 'tis profanity.

And, a little later, for I cannot quote the whole twenty-three pages of this lucid introduction:

> In consciousness experience
> Is manifesting prescience.
> In prescience experience
> Establishes thought permanence.
> Nor need eventuation solve
> All prescience assume to prove.
> Beginning nor the end of time
> Eventuation need not chime.

> Time being but persistency
> Of some conditionality.

These, as Sherlock Holmes would say, are indeed deep waters, Watson.

However, Wm. gets irritated, I think, on page 13, when he says:

> Each perfectly see it is so
> And yet the fool to logic go.

But in the next verse he explains:

> He only taking in as sent
> Away will reason increment.

Still on the bullying tack! Still using words of three syllables to hide his meaning in! But the master will rise to the heights yet.

> Not faith but knowledge would lead man,
> Did he himself but see as can.

There's the true gold. Until the very last word you think it's going to mean something: and then—smash!

Very rarely, however, he tries a simpler method yet. He writes you a couplet which does mean something, though of course out of all connection with the context, and that something is the maddest nonsense.

> To give mankind a consciousness
> Lived Jesus Christ of Nazareth.

This sentence is not written merely to show off his ability as a rimester; no, the master wants you to think, "Well, Wm. means something else when he writes 'consciousness.'" Then he has you. Because never will he

give you a glimmer of his meaning. He will unsettle you
about simple terms in this way, and then leave you to
perish miserably.

Again:

> Ere was condition manifest,
> The unconditioned was at rest.

Yes, certainly. That I did know before.

> Relations of rest with unrest
> Hence did conditions manifest.

Um. Seems to skate over the difficulty a little. But go
on.

> To such relation specify
> We use the word velocity.

Do we?

> Velocity sole history
> Of uncondition's mystery.
> !..!..!

We may leave the introduction with the surmise:

> Specific trouble history
> Of introduction's mystery.

I think I have fairly caught the style!

But this is only introduction; this is all mere mashie
chips on the green: come and see what he can do with a
wooden club, this plus four Wm. Howell Williams.

On page 24 he just gives you one more flick of the
mashie, and reprints four couplets of the Introduction—
not consecutive, and of course not coherent. Then comes

the half-title "Sonnetical Notes on Philosophy" and the Magnum Opus starts. There are One Hundred and Eighty-two "Sonnets," and the master rapidly introduces some important and novel rules.

The Octet *must* end with a colon.

A sonnet should if possible contain one sentence only.

That sentence should have no subject, predicate or object. But the reader should be led to think that they are there, and gently undeceived as the sonnet unfolds.

Sonnet I exhibits these qualities in maddening perfection. I must quote it in full. Another writer might have led one up to this, might have feared a falling-off. But not so Wm. Howell Williams. Just as the Introduction went calmly on, never hesitating, never turning aside, rolling over the difficulties as if they were not there, so he begins and so he ends, never one seed of doubt in his mind.

> While man trains up the child in way men go,
> It goes without the saying that man's way
> In life convention only will display,
> As each one by himself can surely know;
> Hence may these notes that light of rush-light throw
> Where glares so-called, civilization's day,
> Without night's darkness chasing once away,
> Perchance as simple truth for some one glow.

Now I have studied Wm. as reverently as Mr Frank Harris has studied the other Wm. and I would almost swear I know what these lines mean. The secret is that line 8 belongs to line 5. The "Hence" is my real difficulty. Education leads to conventionality (lines 1–4), therefore these notes may glow as simple truth for some one.

I'm afraid

> Each perfectly see it is so
> And yet the fool to logic go

is one on me. But all speculations are futile, for the sonnet continues as follows:

> If seen the curse, if be a curse, on man
>   Is taxing self to understand, amid
>   Environment that ever keeps its place,
> What shape may take his life, if any can,
>   That haunting foolishness alone not bid
>   Him to endure, with pain, but for disgrace.

Where's your subject now? Where's your principal sentence? Where's any vestige of connection with anything? You can find a meaning of sorts if you pick out any line or two, and are allowed to supply all sorts of those cheap and nasty little words that the master has discarded: *e.g.*—

If (it be) seen (that) the curse, if (it) be a curse, on man is (that he is obliged to be) taxing (him) self to understand (the universe) amid (his) environment that ever keeps its place——

There's enough conjecture there to endear me more than ever to my dear old tutor, Dr A. W. Verrall (since I wrote this article, alas! he has joined Agamemnon)—but anyhow, there it stops. I cannot imagine in my wildest moments any nexus with the last three lines of the sestet. I cannot see the merest germ of an apodosis for that majestic protasis.

The second sonnet is not quite equal to this, in my opinion. The method is not the same—perhaps, though, this is the master's plan, to give us the same effect in a totally different fashion. But I call it sheerly meretricious to *spoil* the sonnet by a full stop after four lines.

> Man's place is truth that makes no sign, but is,
>   Which man, who seek a sign where is no sign
>   Will ever overlook till forced repine
> In dumb despair since nothingness is his.

Put "seeks" for "seek," and "to" before "repine," and it makes sense. Ah! but there's a "for" coming!

> For other than what is may not say 'tis
> But to impose on blind a fool's design
> As thorns about the brow of Christ define
> Not him, but those who mock, with emphasis:
> Less puncto see and pundit silent pass
> Mankind from truth will ever wander on—

And so on, almost intelligibly. With a single word he knocks down our castle of cards. Who or what is "puncto"?

I'm not sure about "less," it may be Wm.ese for lest. It occurs again in line 13.

> Less absolute, as absolute, be gone——

There is a fine passage in Sonnet III:

> Whence knowledge once a sensibility
> Of a present conditionality,
> Must helpless self-persistence enterprise.

These lines are rather important, as they bunch the Dramatis Personae of these sonnets. He rings the changes on Sensibility Sahib and Count Conditionality and Sir Self-Persistence all through the book. But the Principal Boy is called "propositional"; he is introduced to us in the wonderful 29th sonnet.

> A proposition: propositional
>   To imagery of presence in sense felt
>   Of actuality: is ever spelt,
> By consciousness as abstract actual,
> Persisting unperceived as well, withal,
>   As when perceived: an image nothing pelt
>   Against without itself is backward dealt
> As if by something quite perpetual:

Whence seen non-actual relation come
As mystery unveiled to simulate
In imagery that actual won't deal:
And budding thence has blossomed forth till dome
Of all creation cannot estimate
Imaginary being that existence steal.

I regard this as one of the very finest sonnets in the book. I like "pelt"; it baffles conjecture entirely. And the final "steal," which suddenly checkmates the aspiring intellect that thought the last three lines were going to mean something, is a supreme touch of Wm.'s art.

But one cannot select; the whole is so stupendous a piece of perfection. The absolute balance of phrases which mean something (if taken in watertight compartments) with those which mean nothing, and can mean nothing; the miraculous skill shown in avoiding even a suggestion of a subject, the expectation of which is so compelled by the beginning "A proposition": the admirable steam-roller obsquatulation of grammar and syntax—all these things and many more make this sonnet unique in the language. I am afraid the rest of our investigations (said I) will be anti-climax. Dear, no! Wm. Howell Williams is not so poor in pride. Whenever you stop, whenever you think he must stop, just there he begins. In Sonnet XXXV, for example:

A propositional abstractional
Remain, that proposition may include
An indisputable, as well exclude
Disputable, in sphere provisional
To stand immovable conditional,
Whence comprehension never to conclude
But ever know what thereto did intrude
Lest venturing become habitual:
As in imaginary personage
Usurp the functionality bestowed

> On creature by a providential hand,
> And rashly venturing themselves engage
> To journey through their lives without a road
> That they can see or guide they can command.

This is sublime art. To the last five lines one could put a beginning to make sense; and it seems to refer to the fear (of Providence) lest venturing should become habitual. With one single line "as in imaginary personage" the whole idea is reduced to ruin. That line is a mammoth.

Note; it is the first line of the sestet. And the first line of the octet is that dinosaur

> A propositional abstractional

with the lovely verb "remain" following it, lest any "habitual venturer" should conjecture that one or both of the adjectives was a noun.

He is evidently pleased with it himself; for XXXVI begins:

> Abstractional, as propositional.

Here is another very charming method. It consists of repeating words with different verbs and things, a sort of weaving. The only limitation of course is that of meaning. Try Sonnet LXX:

> Philosophy, as quantity, be less
>   When knowledge as a quantity be more
>   Than quantity, philosophy can score;
> Hence quantity less quality possess,
> Sensation never can put under stress;
>   Since semblance of condition cannot store
>   Shades protean as quality before
> Proportionate of quantity duress:
> Since semblance of condition unity

> Possess by holding unit under stress,
> As quantity, however, change will stay;
> While quality as mere diversity,
> Stress more or less of quality, more or less
> Enforced, with dying force will melt away.

One can only say Look! Ecce Wm.!

Another very pretty plan is to use constantly words which may be either nouns or verbs, and "that" where it may be either relative or demonstrative.

In Sonnet X, for example, he begins:

> Though aggregation form, as semblance place,
> Where mere sensation will substantial find
> Unseen relation force conditioned mind
> Form aggregation ever set to face
> Perception shall be as fixed for the case.

Remember that Wm. has suppressed prepositions. Then "form," "place," "find," "Unseen," "force," "mind," "Form," may any of them be either nouns or verbs; and of course in no case can sense be made of the sentence.

Take also the passage in Sonnet CIX:

> *Example*: Huxley nihil bonum screen;
> How:

Parse screen!

And what can it mean, this Fragment of Ozymandias? It stands there, absolutely isolated from any reference to Huxley; as an "example," but of what who can say? on all sides, boundless and bare, the lone and level sonnets stretch far away.

Did Huxley put a screen on the market called the nihil bonum?

Did he give shelter to "nothing good"? or did "nothing good" save him from exposure?

Or was Huxley's screen no good? Or it is no good to screen Huxley?

It makes me feel what he feels in No. CXIII:

> Creation absolute by absolute
>   Of absolute for absolute imply
>   What self-pride primes mere mortals to deny;
> Nor other fluting for its fluting flute,
> But idle tooting idle fancy toot
>   That never any being satisfy
>   But leaves all hungering,——

And in his last sonnet, CLXXXII, he most surely utters the supreme wish of every would-be reader:

> O Lord, arise, help and deliver us
> For Thy name's sake.

But it was time to stop: his eagle pinions droop; the last quatrain of the octet becomes sense, grammar, almost poetry.

> O Lord, arise, help and deliver us
>   From pride and foolish faith and idle fears
>   That baseless phantom Hope in man uprears
> Since Eos woke his eons dolorous.

It is his first slip; but he accepts Nature's warning, and retires into private life. This

>   henchman stout
> To blow imagination's windy flute
> That aggregrations wantoning en route
> To thin Attenuation whistles out:

returns to his propositional abstractional unconditioned absolute consciousness quality less quantity require like a mere Newton temple Rimmon "To be or not to be"

"Fools, liars, hypocrites" brigade flut, and leaves us who
have certainly "stood at the door, and knocked" long
enough to our dormant deride aggregated imagination
eradicate; until "attenuation properly, withal, Semblantic
manifestation repossess," "all sensation notes is vacancy."

Lemuel S. Innocent

THE BISMARCK OF BATTERSEA

Dante perhaps thought when he descended the fifth round of Hell that there was some consolation in the fact that he was getting near the bottom. To us, as we explore the glories of Edwardian literature, such consolation is denied. Abyss after abyss yawns beneath our feet; deep into the gloom we peer and our ears are poisoned with the fetid vapours of the ineffable slime—with the callow crapulosities of a Corelli, the slobbering senilities of a Sims, the unctuous snivellings of a Caine.

But we do not propose to descend so far—there is a limit. But stay! what is that glimmer on yonder ledge? That ledge where the Brown Dog of the Faddist fights its eternal battle with the Yellow Dog of Socialism. The ledge labelled "Battersea," supreme word of malignity in the tongue of the pit? Our laurelled guide quickly lowers us thither.

What is that bloated and beery buffoon who stands upon his head to attract attention? we ask. Bismarck, it appears, is his name. Blood and iron is his motto. 'S death! but I suspect a paradox. Maybe that by blood he means beer, by iron ink.

"Maybe this Nonconformist plum-pudding has been dipped in whale oil—and why have they stuffed it with onions?" How shall I find the key to this mystery? So portentous a sentence—and its meaning? "Christianity is only tenable through Literalism and Ritualism." Not so I read it—and my own secret interpretation sends a guffaw through the black shining sides of the prison. With that I awoke; 'twas all a dream; I must begin again—that opening will never do.

Here, therefore, beginneth the third lesson. How shall we catch the great gray water-rat "That strikes the stars (*sublimi vertice*) on Campden Hill?"

Quoth the famous consort of a famous judge, on being advised to abate the rat nuisance by plugging their holes with a mixture of tallow, arsenic, and brown paper: "Yes, but you've got to catch them first." So we, accepting her wisdom, shall not attempt to suppress the News (plain or illustrated)—we shall rather cope with the stench at its source.

This pot-bellied Publicola must be not only scotched, but killed. This megalomaniac Menenius must be put through the medicinal mangle of criticism—a thing which he has hitherto escaped, for as from the porpoise hides of the portly Monitor the round shot of the Merrimac rebounded, so has the oily evasiveness of this literary porpoise served to protect him from his foes, and now he clumsily gambols through the sea, unaware of the pursuing sword-fish. But a greater than the sword-fish (or shall I say the Sword-of-Song-fish) is here.

Just as a balloon is difficult to crush but easy to prick, so shall it be in these days.

This fellow is simply a trimmer. This seeming porpoise is only a jelly-fish; and the great black curves we saw were but the inkiness of the creature.

We draw out this leviathan with an hook, and he goes

conveniently into a beer-mug. We calculate the mass of this brilliant comet, and we find it is not to exceed that of a barrel of butter.

We are appalled by the bellowing of this Bull of Phalaris, and find that it is but an ingenious mechanism worked by the gaspings of an emasculate oyster.

Surely never in all the history of thought—and its limitations—has such a widow's cruse supplied the world with such a deluge of oil. Croton oil.

As a man who orders roast beef and gets hash, so do we look for literature and get mixed dictionary. How do we do it? We stifle the groans of our armchair by continued session and open the Encyclopedia at random. Hullo! what's this? "Schopenhauer, famous pessimist philosopher." (To the stenographer): "The splendid optimism of Schopenhauer—" (Sotto voce) "Let's see what a philosopher is!" (turns it up after a vain search through letter F) "philosopher—lover of wisdom," etc.

(To stenographer) "manifests itself in a positive loathing of all wisdom." (Another turn.)

"Reprehensible—to be condemned."

(Dictating) "and is therefore to be condemned—no! no! please, miss—*not* to be condemned." (Another turn.)

"Catamaran"—a surf-boat used in Madras, hm!—(to stenographer)—"by all Hindoo speculative mystics."

(Speculative mystics—one of our best stock lines.)

We are now fairly started on our weekly causerie, the subject being probably Home Rule.

You see, nobody can get hurt. The invertebrate cannot maul the vertebrate—so we are safe from the chance of their fury. They pay us to defend the doctrine of original sin—so we escape by defending it upon the ground that it is "Jolly." They pay us to attack Free Thought, so we label it "narrow sectarianism," and please the Hard-Shell Baptists—with the purses—without annoying the Free-thinker, who is naturally not hit.

The Romans crucified St Peter head downwards; but it was reserved for this oleaginous clown to offer that last indignity to his Master. We are paid to shore up the rotting buttresses of Christianity, and we begin our article, "A casual carpenter"—

But, let us change the subject!

There was a man—a great man—who some years ago wrote a magnificent philosophical story called the "Napoleon of Notting Hill."

More lucid and a thousand times more entertaining than Bunyan, deeper than Berkeley, as full of ecstasy of laughter as Rabelais, and of mystic ecstasy as Malory, a book of the Chymical Marriage of Christian Rosencreutz with Voltaire.

I think those summits are not unattainable by the subject of our essay—for God's sake, man, forswear sack and live cleanly, and give us something like that!

A. Quiller, Jr.

ARTHUR IN THE AREA
AGAIN

Oh, Allah be obeyed!
How infernally they played!
I remember that they called themselves the Waites.

W. S. Gilbert

Mr Waite is at the area door again! It is not altogether
unphilosophical to judge a man by the company he keeps,
and I have reluctantly decided to dismiss Mr Waite. He
must consider himself no longer my disciple. It has been
a painful step, more painful even than when I was obliged
to expel him in 1900 from the Hermetic Order of the
Golden Dawn. For he shows himself this last time in a
quite impossible avatar—that of a Satanic colporteur
eating rabbit pie in the kitchens of South Ealing.

I have before me a "Special Catalogue of Occult
Books," published by a gentleman giving the name of
Foulsham, which I hope shortly to see in *Punch* under
the heading "MORE COMMERCIAL CANDOUR."

Item No. 1 is a "talisman." "The key to unlock the
mysteries of the Universe." We hear that "charms and
talismans ensure success." "This talisman is worn to bring
Health, Happiness, and Success," a combination which I
regard as remarkably cheap at 4*s.* 3*d.* post free.

But if you haven't got 4*s.* 3*d.*, or are less ambitious, you
may still get a Parchment Talisman for wearing on the
breast, from the Great Book by Rabbi Solomon with silk

bag and cord for 1s. 3d. There are several; one for honour and riches, one for health, one for "Success in Hazard (betting—cards—games of chance)" which looks to me like cheating, one for Success in Trade, and then a set of three to which I call the particular attention of Professor von Krafft-Ebbing and Sir Charles Mathews. They are:

> For Man's Love
> For Woman's Love
> For Love of Opposite Sex

At the other end the catalogue turns from the psychopath to the servant-girl. All about the mystic meaning of moles, "love signs," and birthmarks, together with works on obstetrics (home-made), cure of Epilepsy, Worms, falling hair, and consumption, Old Moore's gazing Crystals, "Ye Witches Fortune-Telling Cards," and the rest of the rag-bag.

The ham of this exquisite sandwich is Mr Waite's *Book of Black Magic and of Pacts* as was, *Book of Ceremonial Magic* as is. But for this *clientèle* of Mr Foulsham the title is simply *The Book of Magic, including Black Magic, the rites and mysteries of Goethic* [*sic*] *Theurgy, Sorcery, and Infernal Necromancy.* Rather tempting for the people who wear talismans "for agricultural prosperity"!

I say fearlessly that this advertisement is a crude appeal to the vilest passions of the most wretched of humanity, to the people who would really love to bewitch their neighbour's cow. It is no reply to this charge to point out that the book is absolutely harmless. It is sold on the pretext that it is poison: if Locusta cheats her clients she is no less infamous: rather more.

If Mr Waite thought to escape my eagle eye by omitting his name, this note will undeceive him; I repeat that I can no longer consider him as one of my disciples; and if he continues to adopt my ideas and phrases, and to republish them as his own, I shall really be obliged to do something hardly distinguishable from taking public notice of the fact.

Aleister Crowley

A GALAHAD
IN GOMORRAH

IT is very fortunate that even in times when the greatest laxity of morals prevails, in England at least there is always found some austere and noble soul to protest against decadence; to be a witness in the midst of corruption, that there is a standard of pure and lofty thought, a City of the Soul, fortified against all evil, and whose artillery can overwhelm the savage hordes of impurity.

We do not think any one will accuse us of flattery in saying that Lord Alfred Douglas is just such a person, and this is the more striking phenomenon as it is so rare to find true moral greatness associated with poetical genius. We write thus in order to direct his attention to a little book published some years ago in Paris, but reprinted in an expurgated form in England; a book of so abominable a character that I am sure it is only necessary to direct his lordship's attention to it to raise a very considerable turmoil. We quote one or two passages:

> Their (men's) eyes for beauty are but sightless holes,
> Spurned in the dust, Uranian passion lies.
> Dull fools decree the sweet unfruitful love,

> In Hellas counted more than half divine,
> Less than half human now.

And again:

> O, food to my starved eyes,
> (That gaze unmoved on wanton charms of girls)
> Fair as the lad on Latmian hills asleep.

There is a good deal about Perkin Warbeck, a poem called "Jonquil and Fleur de Lys," of a very unhealthy character, and really very little else in the book.

Then there is a poem called "Prince Charming," incredibly sickly and sentimental; but, worse than all, the poem called "Two Loves," beginning with the celebrated quotation from Shakespeare—"My better angel is a man right fair, my worse a woman tempting me to ill." In a vision the "poet" sees two people; the first is joyous, and sings; the second walks aside:

> He is full sad and sweet, and his large eyes
> Were strange with wondrous brightness, and staring wide
> With gazing; and he sighed with many sighs
> That moved me, and his cheeks were wan and white
> Like pallid lilies, and his lips were red
> Like poppies, and his hands he clenchèd tight,
> And yet again unclenchèd, and his head
> Was wreathed with moon-flowers pale as lips of death.

This poem ends with a controversy between these two persons:

> ". . . I pray thee speak me sooth:
> What is thy name?" He said, "My name is Love."
> Then straight the first did turn himself to me
> And cried, "He lieth, for his name is Shame;
> But I am Love, and I was wont to be
> Alone in this fair garden, till he came

> Unasked by night; I am true Love, I fill
> The hearts of boy and girl with mutual flame."
> Then sighing said the other, "Have thy will,
> I am the Love that dare not speak its name."

But the great joke is a tragedy in one act entitled *When the King comes he is welcome.* There are two characters in it, Giovanni and Francisco. Francisco cannot sleep, having a presentiment that something unpleasant is about to happen. Then there is a knock, and at his private door. It cannot be Giovanni, for "that honey-bee is hived in Florence." It is Giovanni, however, and they slobber for several pages. It turns out that Giovanni had written to Francisco, but the letter had miscarried. It was an important letter. Giovanni had written to say that he was betrothed unto a noble lady. On learning this, Francisco remarked:

> "Blood of Christ—
> Betrothed!—What word is that? Curled flame of Hell!
> Thou art betrothed? Giovanni! thou, my friend!
> O! five red wounds of God, and Mary's mouth!
> How hast thou dared it?"

A mock-terrible scene follows, in which Giovanni tries to persuade his friend that it will make no real difference to their relations. Francisco pretends to be convinced, but determines to poison himself and his friend. So Francisco proposes to drink the health of Death as a kind of joke, saying:

> *Giovanni:* "I will drink to our love and Death and thee."
> *Francisco:* "Nay, nay, I favour not that toast,
>   Sweetheart,
>   What have we two to do with Death?"
> *Francisco:* "Sweet feather!
>   How soon hast thou forgot thy troth of faith.

Consider, chuck, the toast has but this weight,
That thou and I are friends, and that King Death
Is friend of both, and will not harvest us
Before the time of our ripe harvest comes."

We have surely said enough to establish clearly the abominable character of this book. We are sure that the moment it is brought to the notice of Lord Alfred Douglas he will take the proper steps to crush the perpetrator.

The title-page discloses, as might be expected, both the title of the book and the name of the author.

The former is *Poemes,* and the latter is Lord Alfred Douglas.

DEAD WEIGHT

It is with the deepest feeling that we record the passing over of our less disciple than colleague, less colleague than bosom friend, the aged saint known on earth as Arthur Edward Waite. "The disciple whom Crowley loved," they called him, and Crowley himself never gave the lie to the tender nickname by forgetting the text, "Whom the Lord loveth he chasteneth."

However, all that is over now. The beloved disciple, full of age and saintliness, is gone to his reward.

The story of his life has already been told, though, alas! inadequately, in *The Equinox* and in *Who's Who*, but no list of his achievements is given even in *What's What*, or *What Swat*, as we used affectionately to call our premier book of reference. *The Witches' Switch* has only a passing allusion.

The career of Arthur Edward Waite was largely determined by his father's fine perception.[1] "Ned, my lad," said he when the future saint was barely six years of age, "brains are not your long suit, I can see. But it doesn't matter. If you can't be wise, look wise!" These words

1. Also, of course, by Karma.—Ed.

sank deeply into the mind of the future saint, and only two days later, when his father handed him a work on the Integral Calculus, he looked through it in a steady professional manner, going backwards and forwards several times, knitting his brows, nodding his head and muttering, "H'm! ingenious," now and again. He then closed the volume with a snap, and said in a tone of infinite finality: "Inferentially inadequate data machicholated cerebro-thoracically."

"By jingo!" replied his father, "but you're it!"

In this position there was only one weak point. There are people who understand the Integral Calculus, and there are people capable of disentangling words and sentences. Or rather, at that time, that was so. The art of darkening counsel was in its infancy. The future saint was predestined to change all that.

Arthur were wise, therefore, to find, if possible, a science so abstruse and venerable that no one at all understood it, and whose most respected authors wrote in an indecipherable cryptogram. Such a science was found for little Arthur (the future saint!) in Alchemy.

To establish a reputation was the work of a moment. To be "editor" of Paracelsus, Trithemius, Flamel, Eugenius Philalethes, Ripley, Starkey, Sendivogius, Basil Valentine, and a dozen others is a splendid position in the world of humane letters. To achieve this: obtain copies of their works, and forward carriage paid to a printer, with the remark—worthy of Julius Caesar at his tersest—"Reprint!"

Would God it had stopped there! But (remember!) the future saint wasn't wise, he was only "looking wise," and he made a terrible mistake by accepting a few shillings —all too few!—to whitewash Dr Wynn Westcott (and English Freemasons generally) in the Diana Vaughan affair.

He corresponded with learned professors from Leipzig to Vladivostock; he bombarded Indian Lieutenant-Governors with long strings of questions: "Did you ever know any one called Ramaswamy[2] in Madras?" and the like; in short, he turned the world upside down to produce laboured disproof of the statements—themselves impossible in nature—of a Paris penny dreadful of the class of *Nick Carter* and *Deadwood Dick*.

Relentlessly does he demolish his adversary. If Camden is spelt Campden (which might happen to the best of French authors) he shrieks [*sic! ! !*]. Many other remarks of the future saint display a lack of any sense of proportion or humour which was deplorable, and, by his best friends, deplored.

It was also unfortunate in a way that a book purporting to deal exhaustively with the inmost cabinet secrets of high-grade Freemasonry should be written by one who was not even a craft Mason.

The result[3] was that Dr Wynn Westcott having been made to swear by all his gods that he was *not* Consulting Chemist to the British Government Underground Secret Poison Factory at Gibraltar, and that he had never received at his house a lady whom everybody but himself and the future saint (for in the whirligigs and revenges and, so to speak, *Cochons Volants* of time such was to be!) knew to be the absinthe or galette-begotten image in the mind of a French fumiste who had never in his brightest hours hoped to be taken seriously by as much as a rag-picker—people began to wonder what was the truth beneath the stories which Westcott was at such pains to deny.

However, the honour of British Professional Men was (once again) vindicated, chiefly because nobody to speak

2. Waite quotes the commonest name in all South India as if it were something too fantastic for belief.
3. Please make paragraph read clearly.—Printer's Reader. Heaven forgive you!—Ed. Can't you see that I'm trying to write like Waite?—A. Q.

of saw either attack or defence, and the future saint (for so, strangely enough, had Fate decreed!) had his reward, and was initiated in the Hermetic Order of the Golden Dawn.

The future saint (far indeed from saintship at this time—but the ways of Providence are indeed wondrous!) knew that there was an inner order, but had no idea of its name; he only noticed that he was not invited to enter it. So, to pass the time, he wrote his *Real History of the Rosicrucians,* in which he proved conclusively that there were no Rosicrucians and never had been, and that if any moderns claimed to be Rosicrucians there was "that difference between their assertion and the facts of the case in which the essence of a lie consists." No sooner had he published these remarks (amid general applause) than it was gently broken to the future saint that the liars he had been denouncing were his own occult chiefs, of whom he had been writing (elsewhere) in language which out-Mahatmaed the most eloquent-mysterious Theosophists, and left the sectaries of the Saviour high and dry. A *gaffe* of this sort would have daunted some; not so the future saint (for to this had the Moirae foreordained him!). He produced *Azoth; or the Star in the East,* a pompous rigmarole of God knows how many hundred mortal pages in folio. Like the Absolute, it had neither beginning nor end. Any sentence, if rent sufficiently by expert analysis, revealed either platitudinous banality, a puppet dressed in the rags of mediaeval diction, or refused to be interpreted at all. This was the high-water mark of the future saint's "success" in this evil path; he bought a frock-coat, and has slept in it ever since. He had wished to go down to posterity as the modern Fludd—and would have done so, only this time there were not eight persons saved.

However, this was not the worst. The future saint (as it was written that he should become!) made incursions upon

Magic, with the unhappiest results. Fundamentally incompetent to apprehend the very nature of the question, and utterly incapable of humour, the ingenious Lévi pulled his leg to the limit. The future saint[4] could see only contradictions in the profundities of the master, and in complaining that Lévi was always "stultifying himself" (when he was merely indulging the irony of which he was one of the most brilliant exponents that have ever lived), branded *stultus, stultior, stultissimus* upon his own marmorean brow.

He could not even be trusted with a text. His *Book of Black Magic and of Pacts* was not only a monument of misunderstanding, but of garbling and mutilation; nor did the future saint[4] improve matters by the dishonest trick of reissuing the volume as the *Book of Ceremonial Magic*, or *Book of Magic*, when he tried to make a market in the more benighted agricultural districts of England.

His method of throwing mud at masters naturally resulted in the gate of every occult sanctuary being slammed in his face. The future saint[4] obtained admission (it is true) to the pseudo-Rosicrucian order of Mathers, but on that order passing, as it did for a week or so, into the control of an honest man, that honest man's first act was to expel the aforesaid Waite with ignominy. Thus excluded, the future saint[4] could find no better device than to proclaim himself its head. Without warrant or charter of any kind he extracted guineas from would-be "Rosicrucians" of the servant-girl type of intellect.

True to the same policy, he next declared himself possessed of numberless degrees of Masonry, and accordingly issued two portentous volumes on the subject, volumes which betray prejudice and ignorance so nicely balanced that it is next to impossible to determine which is the inspiration in any particular passage, especially as

4. As will presently appear, he became such. *Gloria Crowleiae!*

the sentences are themselves couched in the sham mediaeval jargon with which his name has always been associated. His gradual gravitation towards Catholicism has been attributed to the receipt of a subsidy from the Society of Jesus; but this is a calumny upon the shrewdness of the fathers who, glad enough to employ a clever scoundrel like Booth—or somebody else beginning with a B—would hesitate to waste an obolus on such a literary sausage-seller.[5]

The love of obscurantism and mummery is sufficient explanation; to use Latin for English, Greek for Latin, Hebrew for Greek, was the key of his whole literary method of vain forms of observance, of meaningless archaisms and affectations. Your priest does not know why he does so and so any more than your freemason (I have yet to meet an English freemason who knows what the word freemason means, or how it should be spelt) knows why he wears an apron. It is tradition, and the Word of God is thereby made of none effect. But Waite was not content with this. He would take an intelligible living English word and metagrabolize it deliberately that he might appear pontifical. Waite would write "Placental amniotes, ultra, φονετιχω vobis, conuterinian mascules" for St Paul's "Men and brethren" even in his calmest moments. And while correcting the proofs he would put in some more hints about the Sanctuary he belonged to, the fact being that his only teacher was an ex-Cantab, named Humphreys, who had at one time been tolerated by Crowley in order to analyze the soul (if any) of the kind of man who fills his rooms with the portraits of "actresses" whom he has never seen, and boasts of their devotion to him.

His only other guide appears to have been a solicitor

5. In actual life he sold Horlick's Malted Milk, but was for all practical purposes a T—totaller.

of the kind that writes you terrible threatening letters, and on being told rudely to do what the Oldest Inhabitant of the Northumbrian Capital actually did (as we are incredibly informed) retires into the Pleroma, and confines his activities to sneaking attacks on you without mentioning your name.

Well, he reached the age of 40 years, and his very sycophants could hardly have called him a physician.

It was not many years after that, like Nicodemus, he came to Crowley secretly by night, and pleaded for initiation. Crowley was moved by his tears, and promised never to divulge the nature of the interview while Waite lived, for it was truly a pitiable thing to see one who had advertised himself as a Master clasping the feet of a man twenty years younger than himself, and begging for the very initiation of which he had boasted himself the dispenser.

It was impossible for Crowley to grant this request; the Dweller on the Threshold would have found Waite scarce a caper in her daily mayonnaise. Initiation for Waite would have meant madness, and the cold portals of the tomb, for one, to follow. It is no use "looking wise" when there is an Abramelin demon gnawing you below the belt, or burbling about the Sanctuary when the Goat of Mendes is threatening you with a 70 h.p. six cylinder, four-speed, gnarled clyster.

All night Waite stayed, and begged; it was in vain. The Master was not to be moved from a resolution both wise and kind. He, however, promised to acknowledge Waite openly as his disciple on condition of good behaviour for the future. It is with pleasure indeed that we record that Waite's lapses have been comparatively few. Waite was no Crippen, be it understood. If Crowley teasingly called him "old lag" in friendly converse round the office fire, too strict a significance, too vital an importance, may

easily be attached to the phrase. Crowley may only have
been referring to the number of his incarnations. Or some
secret meaning may lie hidden in the term. It was at least
the fact that Waite was inclined to writhe under its
application. So he did when any one said "you and
Westcott," or "you and Wilmshurst"; but this was
obviously a reference to his early errors, the reopening
of an old wound. Still more so Crowley's habitual recita-
tion from Blake—

> Steiger, Steiger, burning bright
> In the forests of the night,
> What immortal hand and eye
> Framed thy fearful syntaxy?

And he positively hated to be called "pot of basil," or
even "Columbus."

He also disliked puns on his name and allusions to his
personal appearance—his close resemblance to the excellent foreman printer at the Ballantyne Press was a
constant source of irritation—also to his style of dress,
which proved ineradicable; and he used to wince when
his familiars called him "Art," as it revived the story of
Crowley's epigram on his work, as *Art for Art's Sake.*
Again, he objected to references to the "wait-a-bit" thorn
in connection with occult style and subject, so that he
took what was really quite an unreasonable dislike to Fra.
S. P. merely because that worthiest of men had spent
some years in Africa.

However, these were small blemishes on a beautiful
character. Having given up trying to look wise, he began
to be wise; and he never forgot that the fear of Crowley
is the beginning of wisdom. To the end he combined an
intensity of holy awe with a kind of timid audacity of
reverential love for the Master, to which the latter responded with the most gracious condescension, mingled

with that peculiar affection which one feels for an old
and worthless dog belonging to somebody else. It was an
unique and altogether idyllic relation. His motto, "Fides,
spes, caritas sunt virtutes ab omnibus Christianis diligen-
dae" had to be shortened for convenience' sake to "Fides,"
or, more usually, "Fido"; and it was excessively touching
to hear the caressing austerity of the tones of the Master
when he had occasion to address him.

So, calm and even, passed the autumn of his life. It is
now a painful duty to record the passing.

Subject from youth to chronic capititis,[6] its attacks had
diminished both in frequency and severity under the wise
and patient treatment of the Master; but they still
occasionally recurred.

The shocking accident which resulted in the death of
the aged saint was due directly to an access of this malady,
whose peculiar danger is that the patient tends to seek
relief in the very things which have caused the trouble.
Poor Waite was reaching up to a bookshelf in the library
of his seat at South Ealing for a copy of his *Strange Houses
of Sleep* when his aged but saintly legs gave way. The aged
saint clutched at the bookshelf for support, and a copy of
Azoth fell, and narrowly missing the inflamed organ,
struck the nobler portions of his body, bruising both
great toes severely.

So critical did the condition of the aged saint become
that Sir Coote O. Key Coote was called in, and found
himself obliged to resort to amputation, for unluckily a
friend of the aged saint had been offered a copy of
Paracelsus for 3s. 8d., and mortification had set in.

The operation was fortunately a complete success, and
the physicians announced that their distinguished patient
might very well live for another four-and-twenty hours.

6. He had also chronic diffuse meningo-encephalitis, but only on the astral
plane.

The aged saint's one desire was of course to see Crowley, to offer the last homage, to confess his ingratitude for the benefits with which the Master had loaded him, and to receive the final benediction.

Needless to say Crowley responded to the call. To an explorer of the Himalayas the perils of a journey to South Ealing are as nothing: had they been everything, he would still have come.

It was half a day later that the writer arrived, owing to his Daimler backfiring, missing a dead-centre, and eventually trying to climb a tree on Clapham Common.

After being announced, he was ushered into the death chamber. The dying saint, his head safe in the arms of Crowley, safe on his gentle breast, whose tears mingled with his own, strove hard against the approach of the Grim Reaper. Dr Wynn Westcott was in a corner sharpening (in the worst of taste) his knives for the inevitable post-mortem on the dying saint.

Mr Wilmshurst was reading through the will in which the dying saint had left everything to Lady S——, and could find no flaw, though he had drawn it up himself. Mr Battiscombe Gunn was rapidly revising the funeral arrangements of the dying saint, which he proposed to found on some unedited documents of the Second Dynasty, which showed conclusively that the sacred lotus was in reality a corset, and the Weapon of Men Thu a button-hook.

Neuburg was improvising (for soothing of the last moments of the dying saint) a crooning lay to the tune (and the words, *mutato mutando*) of

> Jesus, lover of my soul,
> Let me to thy bosom fly,

the bass accompaniment being an obbligato by Wilfred

Merton. Mr E. S. P. Haynes (to the horror of Ada
Lakeman and Col Gormley) was reading Morrison's *Red
Triangle* to conceal his emotion. Mr Austin Harrison,
Veli Bey, Madame Strindberg, the Editor of *The Equinox*,
and some others, were avoidably absent from the death-
bed of the dying saint.

Transfusion of blood having been suggested, Crowley
readily lent himself to the operation, Neuburg thoughtfully changing to "There is a fountain."

But the physicians had made a fatal error. Blood was
altogether too strong for a circulation which even in its
most robust days had been supplied solely by Horlick's
Malted Milk; only the kind of ink they use in France
could have saved the dying saint, for no other ichor could
have mingled freely with the liquor of his veins. Throm-
bosis supervened; with one last gasp of "Rabboni, that
is to say, Master!" the dying saint clenched his moribund
grasp on Crowley's neck; the word "periphrasticalism"
burst rather than sobbed from his labia, and the thana-
togenous hagiocratist halated his ultimate.

Neuburg, as one inspired, uttered his Morte d'Arthur.

> Poor old Waite is gone to hell.
> He will soon begin to smell:
> We must meddle with him, *statim.*[7]
> Let us not incinerate him!
> Let us not be anthropophagous!
> Let us build him a sarcophagus!
> Let us bury him in state
> Worthy of our wobled[8] Waite!
> Find a weed whose tangled mazes
> May metaphorize his phrases,
> Find a bunch of camomile
> Fit to represent his style,

7. Did he mean *passim?*—Ed.
8. Cf. *Hamlet*, "mobled queen." Wobled is part mobled, part noble, and
part wobbly.

Waxen flowers to symbolize
His archaicologories,
Dandelions as a chrism
Of his dole of euphemism.
Mangroves for the intervening
Lucid intervals of meaning,
When we saw the modern Fludd
Merely a malarious mud.
Woe is me! I fear death's darticles
Close our "Quiller's" brilliant articles.
Requiescat Waite in pace,
—Gone thine occupation, A. C.!

A. Quiller, Jr.

SECTION VII

REVIEWS

PART II

REVIEWS
PART II

AN APOLOGY FOR PRINTING HONEST REVIEWS

The Editor of *The Equinox* is well aware of the tendency of modern journalism to print only favourable reviews of books, and to praise on the recommendation of the Advertisement Manager rather than that of the Literary Adviser. But he believes that this policy defeats its own end, that praise in *The Equinox* will really sell copies of the book receiving it, and that appreciation of this fact on the part of publishers will result in the enrichment of his advertising columns.

ABNORMAL PSYCHOLOGY. By ISADOR H. CORIAT, M.D.

"Stage fright is also a condition of pathological fear." To such a degree of absurdity can specialization bring an unbalanced mind. Fear is only pathological when it has no reasonable basis.

This is enough to show the worthlessness of this ill-written book.

It is amusing to find the author quoting Mrs Verrall as conclusive proof against any supernormal element in automatic writing, while Mr Hill quotes the same experiments as conclusive proof for it. But Mr Hill is a student of science; Dr Coriat a flatulent gastrologian.

ERIC TAIT

AFTER DEATH—WHAT? By CESARE LOMBROSO.

We sent this book to our undertaker for review, but he only wired back "Rot." Why are undertakers always poets?

[The late Cesare Lombroso was a mattoid and degenerate suffering from paranoiac delusions about "criminal types." He would count the hairs in your moustache, and if you had two more on one side than the other, it showed that you would commit forgery. The authorities once sent him a photograph of a murderer, and he proved that not only was he bound to murder somebody, but to do it in just that special way. By an accident, the photograph was that of a blameless grocer, an Arthur Henry Hallam of grocers.

But he went galumphing on with his monomania, until senile decay supervened, and he became a spiritualist.

Now he is dead, like Max Nordau.—Ed.]

ALCHEMY, ANCIENT AND MODERN. By H. STANLEY REDGRAVE.

A most admirable treatise on the little-understood and misunderstood science of Alchemy. More, the only treatise. Clarity and good sense mark every line. A book entirely essential to anyone who wishes to study the subject, and to understand (1) how the alchemists conceived of hierarchical monism, (2) how they preserved mysticism, (3) how they made chemistry possible.

The book is a complete refutation alike of the Pooh-Pooh and the Holy Timmie schools of critics.

LEO VIRIDIS

THE ALTAR IN THE WILDERNESS. By ETHELBERT JOHNSON.

A charming little book, a book of understanding. But this one thing he does not understand, that He who should come hath indeed come. "For we have seen His Star in the West, and are come to worship Him."

L. T.

AMBERGRIS. A Selection of Poems by ALEISTER CROWLEY.

We don't like books of selections, and you can't make a nightingale out of a crow by picking out the least jarring notes.

The book is nicely bound and printed—as if that were any excuse! Mr Crowley, however, must have been surprised to receive a bill of over Six Pounds for "author's corrections," as the book was printed from his volume of *Collected Works,* and the alterations made by him were well within the dozen!

[Yes; he was surprised; it was his first—and last— experience of these strange ways.—Ed.]

If poets are ever going to make themselves heard, they must find some means of breaking down the tradition that they are the easy dupes of every —— [Satis.—Ed.]

Just as a dishonest commercial traveller will sometimes get a job by accepting a low salary, and look for profit to falsifying the acounts of "expenses," so —— [Here; this will never do.—Ed.]

We have had fine weather recently in Mesopotamia—— [I dare say; but I'm getting suspicious; stop right here. — Ed.] All right; don't be huffy; good-bye!

S. HOLMES

THE ANCIENT CONSTITUTIONAL CHARGES OF THE GUILD FREE MASONS. By JOHN YARKER.

This is a most learned work; the author holds Solomon only knows how many exalted degrees; but besides the title-page there is much of interest to Masons in this little volume. Some of the ancient charges are quite amusing.

"That no Fellow go into town in the night time without a Fellow to bear witness that he hath been in honest company" seems, however, a bit rough on the girls.

F.

ANNIE BESANT: AN AUTOBIOGRAPHY.

It is a splendid oasis in the desert of silly memoirs, this sturdy and valiant record of a very noble life.

How surely and steadily has Mrs Besant moved, urged by the one unselfish thought, high-minded love for humanity, from her Eden through the hell of revolt to the Paradise that so few earn! And she is still fighting in the flesh, though her spirit has its peace.

Priceless and unenvied reward of suffering!

True it is, that the chosen of the Masters must leave all. The lightest breeze can stir the Feather of our Lady Maat; there must be no breath of passion or of thought, if we would live in those Halls of Hers,

> Elysian, windelss, fortunate abodes
> Beyond Heaven's constellated wilderness.

And to one who shares, however humbly, her high hope, and love exalted, and faith transcending, who is confronted by the same foes that she has beaten, assailed by the same slanders that she has lived down, her book comes as a direct message from the Masters: "Courage, child!—there lies a great reward immediately beyond. Nay! but for the work's sake, work! Though thou perish, let them be saved. And remember: there is not one single grain of dust that shall not attain to Buddhahood."

Self-doubt, and self-distrust: these find little place in Mrs Besant's story; yet surely they attack all of us alike who strive to those calm heights. Is it that they are ultimately forgotten, like all lesser ills? Is the spectre, self, laid beyond remembrance, even, of its horror — that horror which seems branded into the brain of whoso has beheld it?

Long years are they through which Mrs Besant fought with hardly a friend or a helper; must it be so for all of us? Yes, for we are all too blind to know our friends, our wardens, the Stones in the great Wall of Arhans that guards humanity.

We have been with James Thomson and watched the dreadful seeker go his unending round to the death-places of love and faith and hope; we have passed out of the doomed triangle into the infinite circle of emerald that girdles the Universe, the circle wherein stands he, the Master whose name is Octinomos.

A. C.

THE APOCALYPSE UNSEALED. BEING AN ESOTERIC INTER-PRETATION OF THE INITIATION OF IOANNES. By JAMES M. PRYSE.

It is possible to write upon this book in a freer manner, without offence, than upon any other book in the Canon of Scripture, for there is no other book which has caused so much disquiet to theologians, in all ages, as has the "Revelation of St John the Divine," and it is but in comparatively recent times that it has been generally accepted as Canonical, and this even by those who admit that they do not understand it; and to such as these *The Apocalypse Unsealed* will be a veritable "Revelation" indeed. Mr James M. Pryse accepts it unreservedly as the work of the Apostle John, but we ought to mention that there is a long string of authorities against this view. Dionysius, who was surnamed the Great, of Alexandria, was a pupil of Origen, and he of Clement of Alexandria, all catechists of the *Arcane Discipline* which taught a

Christianised version of the older Gnosis, which Clement and others had brought into the Church from the older secret, or occult, societies of which they were, or had been members. This Dionysius makes a certain John the Presbyter, as of note in Asia Minor in the 1st century, and distinct from the Apostle, to be the author of the book. Presbyter Cajus, or Gaius, of Rome, and the Alogi, attributed it to Cerinthus, a Gnostic of the independent sect of these, and Eusebius quotes both Dionysius and these Alogi; Nicephorus Callistus uses the same as saying that some who had preceded them had manipulated the book in such way, in every chapter, that the original could not be recognised. This may be an exaggeration, but amongst the eminent critics who have denied the authenticity of the book may be mentioned these, and what else can we expect when none to the present time could understand it? Against it are De Wett, Bleek, Ewald, Credner, Schott, Lücke, Neander, Michaelis, who treat the style as utterly foreign to that of John the Apostle. The first-named observes that "Revelation" is characterised by strong Hebraisms, ruggedness, and exhibits the absence of pure Greek words, whilst in the Gospel of John is to be found a calm, deep feeling, but in the Apocalypse we have great creative power of fancy;—the two minds are at variance with each other. St Jerome had an exalted opinion of the book, and says that it has much of mystery therein; possibly he saw it with the same eyes as Mr Pryse. Even both Luther and Erasmus were doubtful as to its acceptance. The *Encyclopaedia Britanica* argues that its allusions are of the 4th or 5th century. It may be mentioned here, that Dom John Chapman, D.O.S., has made an examination of the question this year, and argues, with doubtful success, that John the Presbyter and John the Apostle were the same person, and accepts both the Gospel and the Apocalypse as the works of the

Apostle John, and accounts for the difference in style as that of the amanuensis whom the Apostle John employed.

Two noticeable, but irreconcilable, attempts have in recent years been made to interpret the book, theologically and historically. The learned Dr E. V. Kenealy made sense out of it, but overdid the subject. He believed it to represent the Apocalyptic church of Adam, and found in its addresses to the "Seven Churches" the existence of a great Asian hierarchy of the seven temples of the "twenty-four Ancients," and further, in its various characters, the acts of the twelve divine incarnations, or messengers, who follow each other at periods of 600 years, as taught in regard to the manifestations of Vishnu.

Then, in 1906, we have a book of the astronomer, Nicholas Marazoff, verified by the astronomers Ramin and Lanin, who attempt an astrological view, grounded on the state of the heavens at Patmos on the 30th September, 395, at 5 o'clock at night. Jupiter—the white horse—was then in Sagittarius; whilst Saturn—the pale horse—was in Scorpio; the sun in Virgo, and the moon under her feet. John Chrysostom was then in Patmos, and immediately after 395 was called to Rome to become a presbyter; but Rome finding that the "Second Coming" did not take place, it is argued that he was deprived and banished as a "false prophet." Against this we have the fact that Chrysostom does not mention the book, but the date assigned agrees with criticisms as the book now stands.

We must defer to the superior knowledge of this modern "Unveiler," though personally I am inclined to accept the views of those early Fathers who assign the authorship to Cerinthus, and also the later German critics, who believe that the first three chapters and the last have been added by a later hand, and other portions altered to agree with the Scriptures held to be orthodox. Of course this,

if it were so, does not affect in any way the views of Mr
Pryse, but rather strengthens them, as I look upon the
imagery of the book as essentially that of the earlier and
pre-Christian Gnostics. Though we may not have absolute proof of the great antiquity of the Gnosis, such as Mr
Pryse unveils, yet it is clearly Aryan, dating from the time
of Momu—the thinker; then again the development of
the Kundalini—serpent fire—world's mother, also termed
rousing the Brahm—is said to be shown as issuing from
the foreheads of early Egyptian kings; Apollonius of
Tyana, a contemporary of our Jesus, visited the Gymnos-
ophists of the Upper Nile, but said that they were not
equal to those of India. The British Druids must have had
a knowledge of the "Serpent fire" in their secret instruction, or why exclaim, "I am a serpent." The Mythraic
Mysteries, and all the Eranoi Societies, were equally
protected by the laws of Solon seven centuries B.C., and
Mr Pryse observes that only once does the word Halle-
luiah occur in the Bible, yet we know that it formed the
close of a chant in the "Rites of Purification" in a call
to the slain god for deliverance, in pre-Christian centuries,
and further there are Mythraic traces in Revelation. We
also know from a large mass of inscriptions found in
recent times, that the early Christians made use of the
very ancient societies, and by that course spread their
doctrine. Before the issue of the "Unsealing," the same
translator published the *Magical Message of Ioannes,* a
translation of great value which receives much additional
light from the later work, and the more so as it supplies,
in a knowledge of Hermetic Greek, much meaning which
escapes us in the authorised version.

In the "Unsealing," Mr Pryse goes solid for the book,
the whole book, and nothing but the book, as the veritable
work of the Apostle John, hence the clergy may extend
a welcome hand to it. He quite believes it is a work of

the Apostle John, and defends the style; amongst these there are some doubtless who are narrow-minded, but here, and still more prominently in America, there are broad-minded clergy who will welcome the Unsealing.

The Freemasons too in their higher grades, which have more or less reached us through the Rosicrucians, have very strong allusions to the Apocalypse, and may profit by it, and this refers to several systems practised throughout the world. Thus the Order of Hérédom (Harodim) Rosy Cross, which has an unchanged Ritual from 1740, at least, draws upon Dionysius the Areopagite, a disciple of St Paul, and it has also a rhythmetical description of the New Jerusalem. Again, two entire degrees of the Scottish Rite of 33° are drawn from the Apocalypse, and certainly entered the Rite before 1758, and seem as if they were drawn bodily from the Rosicrucian Militia of the Cross: I allude to the 17° Knight of the East and West, and the 19° of Grand Pontiff, which treat upon the Heavenly Jerusalem, and the opening scene of the Revelations. It was rather a pity that when the late Albert Pike was revising the Rituals, he did not consolidate the Rite by changing the places of the 17° with the 20°, which latter treats of Zerubbabel. His predecessor Morin, in 1767, did a like thing by the Amalgamation of Prince Adept, which he had in his patent of 1762, with Knight of the Sun, and supplying the blank thus created with Patriarch Noachite. There is also the Royal Oriental Order of the Sat Bhai which was founded 1743-5, by a Brahmin Pundit at Prag, for certain Anglo-Indian officers, and which is now well established in America.

The idea that Revelation is a book of Initiation is not altogether new to Freemasons, as the late Dr Geo. Oliver elaborated that view at considerable length, but Mr Pryse's view is quite a different sort of Initiation; it is the development of the semi-miraculous powers of the Gnosis

of Clement, Origen, and the early Christian Church, the
birth of the divine three principles, the Crestos, in the
human soul. The key to this "Unsealing" is the text
itself, in which is found the Nos. 333, 444, 666, 777, 888,
999, 1000, as applied to the seven principal *chakras* of
the human body, as taught by Greek Yogis. Apart altogether from the possession of a reliable literal translation
of the book, there are seventy-five pages upon the development of the *Kundalini,* and each subject is followed in
the text by a commentary in application. Mr Pryse
expresses the view that the book is necessarily incomprehensible to the conventional theologian, yet easily comprehended by the esoteric Initiate, *i.e.,* by him who
possesses the Gnosis, and that the drama is perfect in all
its parts. I may add that most of this class of Initiative
books had a double interpretation, and hence that the
same may be equally found in the Apocalypse, but into
this Mr Pryse does not enter.

JOHN YARKER

Mr Pryse has undoubtedly found the key of the
Apocalypse, and many of his interpretations are profound
and accurate. But he is afflicted by sexual mania to an
extent positively shocking, and does not understand the
harmony of the principles. Adeptship is balanced growth,
not lopping. A rose dies if you remove the root and stalk,
Mr Pryse!

He is unfortunately a poor scholar, and has developed
the American literary sense to an incredible point. He
translates ἀκρασια, 'impotence, lack of control,' as "sensuality," ἀγγελος as "divinity," and gives us "saucers" for
'vials'!

Unfortunately, too, he has studied Eastern Mysticism
at second-hand, through Theosophical spectacles. Nor
has he kept even to Blavatsky the genius, but relied upon

her commentators, who had neither her learning nor her experience.

But he has the key, and it opens the way for a real study of "St John" by a person of greater ability.

It is a very remarkable fact, however, that Akrasia (333) and Akolasia (333) should so accurately describe Choronzon (333). No higher test of the truth of "The Vision and the Voice" could be desired.

Again, 666 is Ἡ φρην, not the Lower Mind, as Mr Pryse unhellenically says, but Tiphereth, the Lion that lieth down with the Lamb. Nor, by the way, is Iacchos a phallic God except as Ὁ Νικων himself is phallic, and has his mystic name written upon that organ, according to Mr Pryse! Iacchus = IAO = Jehovah, and concentrates I.N.R.I.

We recommend the book for its suggestion and insight; it is one of the best of the kind.

NICK LAMB

ARCANA OF NATURE. By HUDSON TUTTLE.

Faecal filth about Spiritist—nouns—in simplified "speling." Who shall cleanse the astral cesspool of these mental necrophiles?

And think of having a name like Hudson Tuttle!

THE ARCANE SCHOOLS. By JOHN YARKER.

The reader of this treatise is at first overwhelmed by the immensity of Brother Yarker's erudition. He seems to have examined and quoted every document that ever existed. It is true that he occasionally refers to people like Hargrave Jennings, A.E. Waite, and H.P. Blavatsky as if they were authorities; but whoso fishes with a net of so wide a sweep as Brother Yarker's must expect to pull in some worthless fish. This accounts for Waite's contempt of him; imagine Walford Bodie reviewing a medical book which referred to him as an authority on paralysis!

The size of the book, too, is calculated to effray: reading it has cost me many pounds in gondolas! And it is the essential impossibility of all works of this kind that artistic treatment is not to be attained.

But Brother Yarker has nobly suppressed a Spencerian tendency to ramble; he has written with insight, avoided pedantry, and made the dreary fields of archeology blossom with flowers of interest.

Accordingly, we must give him the highest praise, for he has made the best possible out of what was nearly the worst possible.

He has abundantly proved his main point, the true antiquity of some Masonic system. It is a parallel to Frazer's tracing of the history of the Slain God.

But why is there no life in any of our Slain God rituals? It is for us to restore them by the Word and the Grip.

For us, who have the inner knowledge, inherited or won, it remains to restore the true rites of Attis, Adonis, Osiris, of Set, Serapis, Mithras, and Abel.

ALEISTER CROWLEY

BEYOND LIFE. By JAMES BRANCH CABELL.

For four years I have been cast away upon a desert island, and I am seriously alarmed at beholding a footprint in the sand. As a matter of fact, the goats have acclimatized me to most things, and I take up the task of reviewing this book with all the more confidence, because the publisher begs me to abuse it. I dislike publishers intensely, and I am not going to abuse books merely because they ask me to, and even if I had wanted to abuse this book, I should have found myself in the position of Balaam.

It is an extraordinarily good book. I quite understand why the *Times* says that Mr Cabell is "one of the most pretentiously attitudinizing of American authors." The *Times* has had some. But what does the *Times* matter? It used to be the thunderer. It is now an imitation of thunder which only Martial could describe, or an ambitious Marine imitate. What in God's name is an American author to do? He has got such a dreadful milieu that it is almost impossible to discover him. I never blamed the cock who failed to notice the pearl in the dung hill. Fortunately, I had Mr Mencken to indicate Mr Cabell. Thus, I was able to read the book as if I knew nothing of its surroundings, which is of course the only way to read a book. It is admirably written. It is a defence of romance. What does it matter that it is written among a people who think that romance means Robert W. Chambers? There are extraordinary things in this book. I do not think Mr Cabell's irony so wonderful as his humour. He says, "The most prosaic of materialists proclaim that we are all descended from an insane fish, who somehow evolved the idea that it was his duty to live on land, and eventually succeeded in doing it." Insane fish is right. It is possible that the fish was not insane. It is possible that he discovered that he could not get a drink, except water, and decided to emigrate. If that is insane, I am insane. I hope that Mr Cabell is insane too, and that I shall meet him in the Solomon Islands.

ROBINSON C. CROWLEY

BHAKTI-YOGA. (Udvodhan Series.) By SWAMI VIVEK-ANANDA.

If Swami Vivekânanda was not a great Yogi he was at least a very great expounder of Yoga doctrines. It is impossible here to convey to the reader a just estimate of the extreme value of this book. But we can say that this is the best work on the Bhakti-Yoga yet written. Union through devotion is Bhakti-Yoga, and union with Isvara or the Higher Self is the highest form this union can take—"man will be seen no more as man, but only as God; the animal will be seen no more as an animal, but as God; even the tiger will no more be seen a tiger, but as a manifestation of God." . . . Love knows no bargaining . . . love knows no reward . . . love knows no fear . . . love knows no rival . . ." for "there are no men in this world but that One Man, and that is He, the Beloved."

In this excellent series can also be obtained Raja Yoga, Karma Yoga, and Jnana Yoga.

J. F. C. F.

[Yet we find Vivekânanda, at the end of his life, complaining, in a private letter to a friend, that his reputation for holiness prevented him from going "on the bust." Poor silly devil!—Ed.]

BLACK MAGIC. BY MARJORIE BOWEN.

Marjorie Bowen knows nothing of the real magic, but she has learnt the tales spread by fools about sorcerers, and fostered by them as the best possible concealments of their truth.

Of these ingredients she has brewed a magnificent hell-broth. No chapter lacks its jewelled incident, and the web that she has woven of men's passions is a flame-red tapestry stained with dark patches of murder and charred here and there with fire of hell.

Marjorie Bowen has immense skill; has she genius? How can a stranger say? So many nowadays are forced by sheer starvation into writing books that will sell—and when they have taken the devil's money, find that it is in no figure that he has their souls in pawn.

I am told that it is the ambition of W. S. Maugham to write a great play.

A. C.

THE BLUE GROTTO. ARTHUR H. STOCKWELL.

It is monstrous and iniquitous that a person, however
bearded, however resembling Bernard Shaw in name and
form, should purport to translate a Rune Stone dealing
with the Phrygian Mysteries—and scan Pandion wrong.
The masterpiece of this anonymous author is full of false
quantities, but I don't care if it is, for he has some very
beautiful lines and a sense of the musical value of words.
He writes:

> The lovers of a night appear
> In the unravell'd atmosphere.
> Phantasmagoria crisp to gold
> Under Apollo. . . .

And again:

> Caduceator for thy knees'
> Ophidian caryatides.

And again:

> And the red ibis in thy grove
> Feeds poison to the sucking dove.

And again:

> Under the brown sea-furbelow
> Anguilla slimes; . . .

He tells us:

> . . . Crassicornis seeks to grab
> The streamers of the coral-crab.

He says:

I hear the triton-music swell
Love-laden in the vulva-shell.

And speaks of:

... Corybantes o' the storm
Leaping coruscant-capriform.

I could hardly have done better myself, and Shelley
would have been put to it to do it as well.

If the ingenious though fatuous author of *The Blue
Grotto* will get a big idea and work it largely out, he
will indubitably produce a worthy contribution to the
language whose poverty he now enriches with so many
admirable new words.

A. C.

A BOOK OF MYSTERY AND VISION. By A. E. WAITE.

The Introduction. Mr Waite speaks of "a kind of secret
school, or united but incorporate fraternity, which independently of all conventional means of recognition and
communication do no less communicate and recognise one
another without hesitation or hindrance in every part of
the world. . . . Of this school the author may and does
claim that he is the intimate representative and mouth-
piece," &c.

Good.

"This mystic life at its highest is undeniably selfish."

Hullo, what's this?

"It is a striking fact that so little of any divine consequence has been uttered by poets in the English
Language."

Really?

"The inspiration of it (the sense of sacramentalism) at
certain times saturated the whole soul of Tennyson. . . .

There is scarcely a trace or tincture of this sense in Shelley."

Poor Shelley!

"In the eighteenth century there was none found to give it Voice."

Poor Blake! (William Blake, you know! Never heard of William Blake?)

"For this school it is quite impossible that Shakespeare, for example, should possess any consequence."

Poor Shakespeare!

And then—

"This book is offered by the writer to his brethren, *ut adeptis appareat me illis parem et fratrem*, as proof positive that he is numbered among them, that he is initiated into their mysteries, and exacts recognition as such in all houses, temples, and tarrying-places of the fraternity."

An adept trying to prove that he is one! An adept with thoughts of his own rank and glory! An adept exacting recognition!

What about the instant recognition all over the world of which you prated above? Mr Waite, you seem to me to be a spiritual Arthur Orton!

Mr Waite, we have opened the Pastos which you say contains the body of your Father Christian Rosencreutz— and it's only poor old Druce!

The Book. This is the strange thing; the moment that Mr Waite leaves prose for poetry, there is no more of this bunkum, bombast, and balderdash; we find a poet, and rather an illuminated poet. We have to appeal from Philip sober to Philip drunk! *In vino veritas.*

Good poetry enough all this: yet one cannot help feeling that it is essentially the work of a scholar and a gentleman. One is inclined to think of him as Pentheus in a frock-coat.

A MYSTERY-PLAY

Dionysus. I bring ye wine from above
From the vats of the storied sun—
Mr Waite. Butler, decant the claret carefully!
Dionysus. For every one of ye love—
Mr Waite. Ay, lawful marriage is a sacrament.
Dionysus. And life for everyone—
Mr Waite. And lawful marriage should result in life.
Dionysus. Ye shall dance on hill and level—
Mr Waite. But not the vulgar cancan or mattchiche.
Dionysus. Ye shall sing through hollow and height—
Mr Waite. See that ye sing with due sobriety!
Dionysus. In the festal mystical revel,
The rapturous Bacchanal rite!
Mr Waite. If Isabel de S . . . . . . should approve!
Dionysus. The rocks and trees are yours—
Mr Waite. According to the Laws of Property.
Dionysus. And the waters under the hill—
Mr Waite. Provided that you pay your water rate.
Dionysus. By the might of that which endures—
Mr Waite. Me, surely, and my fame as an adept.
Dionysus. The holy heaven of will!
Mr Waite. Will Shakespeare was not an initiate.
Dionysus. I kindle a flame like a torrent
To rush from star to star—
Mr Waite. Incendiarism! Arson! Captain Shaw!
Dionysus. Your hair as a comet's horrent,—
Mr Waite. Not for a fortune would I ruffle mine.
Dionysus. Ye shall see things as they are.
Mr Waite. Play fair, god! Do not give the show away!
[*The Maenads tear him limb from limb, and* **Madame de
S** . . . . . . *tries to brain* **Dionysus** *with a dummy writ.*]

This is a great limitation, yet Mr Waite is a really excellent poet withal. All the poems show fine and deep thought, with facility and felicity of expression. "The Lost Word" is extraordinarily fine, both dramatically and lyrically. It seems a pity that Mr Waite has no use for William Shakespeare!

The fact is (whatever George Hume Barne may say) that Mr Waite is (or has) a genius, who wishes to communicate sacred mysteries of truth and beauty; but he is too often baulked by the mental and moral equipment of Mr Waite. Even so, he only just misses. And I will bet George Hume Barne a *crème de menthe* that if Mr Waite (even now) will ride on a camel from Biskra to Timbuktu with an Ouled Nail and the dancer M'saoud, he will produce absolutely first-rate poetry within six months.

Enough. But buy the book.

A. QUILLER, JR.

A BOOK OF PREFACES. By H. L. MENCKEN.

Praise ye the Lord. Sing unto the Lord a new song, and his praise in the congregation of saints.

Believe me, I had hardly hoped to live to see this day when a book of criticism like this comes into my hand.

Let Israel rejoice in him that made him: let the children of Zion be joyful in their King.

There are plenty of brains in America, and plenty of educated brains, but it is extremely rare to find these two combined in one being.

Let them praise his name in the dance: let them sing praises unto him with the timbrel and harp.

Mr Mencken narrowly escapes the cleverness which is the Hall-mark of the silver mind, but he does escape it.

For the Lord taketh pleasure in his people: he will beautify the meek with salvation.

Mr Mencken's perception may be gauged by just one piece of navigation, the Straits of Ibsen. In 1901 I said of Ibsen, "he is the Sophocles of manners." And elsewhere spoke of him as "a purely Greek dramatist."

Mr Mencken says, "the fabulous Ibsen of the symbols (no more the real Ibsen than Christ was a prohibitionist)."

"His shining skill as a dramatic craftsman—his one authentic claim upon fame."

Let the saints be joyful in glory: let them sing aloud upon their beds.

His robust joy of castigating curs with his contempt swells a paean in my heart. "Consider one fact: the civilization that kissed Maeterlinck on both cheeks and Tagore perhaps even more intimately. . . . "

Let the high praises of God be in their mouth, and a two-edged sword in their hand;

To execute vengeance upon the heathen, and punishments upon the people;

To bind their kings with chains, and their nobles with fetters of iron;

To execute upon them the judgment written: this honour have all his saints. Praise ye the Lord.

A.C.

THE BOOK OF REVELATIONS OF JIM CROW.

The best of this book is that it reads well. I thought *à priori* (*a*) it read very well weekly; in a lump it will bore; (*b*) it only read well weekly because of its pornographic or Prudential surroundings. But, lo! it is most excellent. St James the Divine has indeed found a way to tell the truth (about most things) without frightening Respectability too much, though I think he might have spared us a thunderbolt against that feeble writer, Herbert Vivian.

Sanctus Jacobus Corvus once observed in his treatise on *Mysticism* (blue-pencilled by the common sub-editor), "Crow and Crowley—what a combination!" Not a bad one, either. If only he had stolen the holy water (as I begged him to do) and baptized our mandrakes properly —— Never mind! I advise all our readers to read his book; and if he does not advise all the readers of *John Bull* to read mine, I shall despair of human nature.

A. QUILLER, JR.

BRACKEN. By JOHN TREVENA.

This is a very fine study of west country life. Jaspar Ramridge is a schoolmaster, and can see nothing but discipline.

Cuthbert Orton is a schoolboy, and can see nothing but revolt against that discipline.

Neither grows up. So when they start to create, the boy produces a creature of naked emotion and no more; the man a creature of naked intellect and no more. The first is an animal, the second a devil.

This is our own doctrine; but never have I seen it better expressed.

It is not the province of man to create, but to beget. The father of the girl who is in turn obsessed by Orton and Ramridge is a perfect ass; but he made a very good job once in his life.

Let this admirable book be a warning to all those who seek magical power, or to teach pupils.

If you obtain magical powers, as is easy, you can only use it to destroy both yourself and your victims, unless by a greater miracle than the magic itself. If you seek to teach, your pupils are almost sure to misunderstand.

The alternative is to initiate; and this can only be done by those who are no longer men or magicians.

Let me congratulate Mr Trevena upon a most enthralling and instructive book.

O. H.

CAGLIOSTRO. By W. R. H. TROWBRIDGE.

I have a prejudice against memoirs of a century ago. They are usually pornographic tittle-tattle, absolutely pointless, the favourite reading of a Colonel Glumley.

One expects to see them in a still-life whose other ingredients are birches tied up with blue ribbons, and
imitations of the Inimitable.

What, then, was my pleasure in finding this study of
Cagliostro a well-written and profoundly interesting book!
The main problem of Cagliostro's identity is discussed
with marvellous power and fascination.

Mr Trowbridge's review of eighteenth-century occultism is strikingly sane and intelligent. Knowing nothing
of the causes *à priori*, he has judged by the effects, and
these have not betrayed him. Indeed, had Mr Trowbridge
sworn secrecy to the modern Illuminati, I am afraid that
he might have his s . . . l s . . n across, and his b . . . . s
exposed to the s . . . . g r . . s of the s . n before now!

I think Mr Trowbridge is too ready to assume that the
initiations of Egyptian Masonry were ridiculous. On what
documents does he base his description? It is always open
to a Mason to reply to an "exposure" that those who tell
don't know, and those who know don't tell. My own small
knowledge of the matter assures me that the accounts
given on pp. 111 and 112, 120 and 121 are entirely
foreign to that knowledge, and *à priori* most unlikely.
It is incredible that one to whom so many impressive
rites were accessible should found his system on tom-
foolery.

I wish Mr Trowbridge could have found time to study
intimately for a month the life of a modern master.

As it is, the most natural phenomena perturb him. The
periodical disappearances of his hero annoy the historian;
yet this is the first condition of the life of a Magus, like
the disappearance of salmon from rivers. Unless one went
back to the sea pretty often, those silver scales would
blacken.

Many other matters, too, would have suggested their
own explanation. However, the historian's native wit has

gone very far to supply him with motives for Cagliostro. What puzzles fools, whether they be Jewish, Russian, French, or naturalised Englishmen, in estimating the actions of an adept, is this; they have not the smallest notion of what he loves, or even of what he sees. Cagliostro is fortunate in finding a student with good sense and perspicacity. It is only a step from Cagliostro's vindication (successfully accomplished in this book) to his triumph. Mr Trowbridge will come one day to see that his high mission was not a failure, recognise that Dumas is the most illuminated of historians as well as the most fascinating of novelists.

ALEISTER CROWLEY

THE CANON. AN EXPOSITION OF THE PAGAN MYSTERIES PERPETUATED IN THE CABALA AS THE RULE OF ALL THE ARTS. ELKIN MATHEWS.

This is a very extraordinary book, and it should be a fair "eye-opener" to such as consider the Qabalah a fanciful concatenation of numbers, words, and names. Also it may come as rather a rude shock to some of our "fancied" knowalls, our "cocksureites," who are under the delusion that knowledge was born with their grandmothers, and has now reached perfection in themselves, for it proves conclusively enough by actual measurements of existing monuments and records that the ancients, hundreds of years ago, were perfectly well acquainted with what we are pleased in our swollenheadiness to call "the discoveries of modern science."

Every ancient temple was built on a definite symbolic design and was not a haphazard erection of brick and mortar dependent on £ s. d. On the contrary, it closely followed the measurements of the body of Christ or of a Man which it was supposed to represent.

The three great canonical numbers are 2,368 (IESOUS

CHRISTOS), 1,480 (CHRISTOS) and 888 (IESOUS). Numerous other numbers also occur but most hinge on these three. Here is an example. 888, 1,480 and 2,368 are to each other in the ratio of 3, 5 and 8. 358 is numerically equal to Messiah, and $358\frac{1}{2} \times 6 = 2,151$ which is again a symbol of the Hebrew Messiah. Alpha and Omega $= 2,152$; and a hexagon described round a circle having a circumference of 2,151 has a perimeter of 2,368. 2,151 also is the sum of 1,480 (Christos) and 671 (Thora the Bride). A vesica 358 broad is 620 long, and 620 is the value of Kether, etc. (see p. 124).

This book is a veritable model of industry and research, but in spite of an excellent index, an index in the ordinary sense is almost out of place in a work of so complicated a character as this; what is really needed is a table of the numerical correspondences, similar in type to those we have already published in our 777. Then at a glance the student can see the various numerical values and what they refer to.

J. F. C. F.

THE CASE FOR ALCOHOL. OR THE ACTIONS OF ALCOHOL ON BODY AND SOUL. By ROBERT PARK, M.D.

Dr Park is an old friend of ours; we enjoyed his masterly translation of Ch: Féré's *The Pathology of Emotions,* and his various writings in the days of the old *Free Review* and *University Review,* when J. M. Robertson was worth reading, a review (by the way) which was assassinated by the prurient pot-scourers who would put a pair of "pants" on Phoebus Apollo, and who presumably take their bath in the dark for fear of expiring in a priapic frenzy at the sight of their own nakedness.

Dr Park in this most admirable little treatise declares that Alcohol is one of "the good creatures of God"; and that Alcohol is a poison is only true relatively.

"It is not true of the stimulant dosage. It is true of it as a narcotic, in narcotic dosage. . . . So the objection to the use of Alcohol, because in overdosage it is a poison, is not only futile, but stupid."

Further, Dr Park writes:

"The burden of responsibility must lie upon the person who so misuses his means. Tea, tobacco, coffee, and beef-tea are frequently so misused, but we hear of no socio-political organisations for interfering with the liberty of individuals in regard to the use of these, or trespassing on the rights of traders and purveyors thereof."

"Alcohol," Dr Park declares, "is a food," and not only a food, but an excellent one at that. Put that in your pipes and smoke it, ye Baptist Bible-bangers—but we forget, you do not smoke, in fact you do nothing which is pleasant; you spend your whole lives in looking for the Devil in the most unlikely places, and declare that the only remedy against his craft and his cunning is total immersion in tonic-water and pine-apple syrup.

F.

A CHASTE MAN. By LOUIS UMFRAVILLE WILKINSON.

It has often been disputed as to how far a novelist is right in showing us the seamy side of life. But the answer admits of no dispute. Truth is the most precious jewel of all. The atmosphere of Mr Wilkinson's new book, despite the brightness and insouciance of the manner and the lightness of the incident, is one of the most tragic gloom. The scene opens upon the hero reminding somebody that this is the third application, etc., and unless, etc., yours faithfully, and the novel ends with his reminding somebody, probably the same person, of the same thing. Such an appalling realization of the horror of life makes one shudder and sicken. Between the two applications comes an adventure.

The hero, who is a married man, meets a charming girl of sixteen, falls in love with her—and she with him. Every conceivable circumstance conspires to bring about immoral relations, so-called, between them. The girl's father himself urges it. But the hero remains chaste. The tragedy thus brought about is absolutely nauseating. It is hard for the reviewer to think of the grim and griesly abomination which follows. The hero has to go away to Switzerland, for a month or two; and during his absence the girl marries a Canadian and goes to Canada with him. The gloom is not even lightened by any hint that she may have had some adventure previous to the marriage. No hope is held out that she may have any adventure after that. The Abomination of Desolation is set up in the holy place.

But there is reserved for us a yet more terrible contemplation. If one had said, "The girl escapes from the intrigue with her married lover, and is honorably married to a Canadian," every one would say, "What a wholesome story!" The poison of puritanism has rotted through the whole of human thought. Conventional morality is the syphilis of the soul, and it is for the God Mercury, no one less, to oppose its action. Our trouble is rendered a thousand times more grievous because most of us do not recognize how foul is our disease. The words 'marriage with a Canadian' should be expunged from human language. People should be prosecuted for printing so foul and obscene a phrase.

Yet these things happen every day. The sun turns sick in heaven to behold them. Yet we do not see his anguish. Life which involves such possibilities of infamy and horror as 'marriage with a Canadian' must surely be some atrocious species of damnation; the reward of infinite iniquity. But humanity has become so callous, so anaesthetic to any proper feeling, that many people may even fail to see the high seriousness and noble purpose of such statements as the above. The degradation of humanity has gone so far that marriage with a Canadian seems almost normal and natural.

There is no mistaking the great advance made by Mr Wilkinson upon his previous novel, *The Buffoon*. In that work, there was, indeed, power and wit. But it was on the whole a pleasant book. There was plenty of comic relief— *e.g.*, Powys' duodenum. In *A Chaste Man* the author moves stately and terrible from peak to peak of tragedy. The book reminds us a little of James Thomson, *The City of Dreadful Night*, in this respect. With infinite art the climax is set off by an adventure of the hero's sister with a man dying of consumption at St Moritz, and this single glimpse of Paradise makes the surrounding gloom more visible and shameful.

It is unfortunately the case that stories of this kind are only too true to life. Few of us, indeed, but have some experience of the classes in which such abominations are not only possible but actual. It is true that the war has done a great deal to destroy the morality of the middle classes. From all hands comes the wail of the Puritan as he is forced into a recognition that life is a savage and beautiful thing, and that his attempt to make every one behave with the decorum of a putrefying corpse is bound in the long run to fail. We find, for example, the Bishop of Worcester offering a tasteless substitute for Worcester Sauce. He complains pitifully of how he saw three women in the street trying to seduce a soldier. Apparently in consequence of the appearance of the Bishop, the soldier "saw his chance and ran away," but from what we know of Bishops it seems probable that he was trying to escape from the Episcopal rather than the feminine menace.

We hope that in Mr Wilkinson's next novel he will try to give us the brighter side of the picture. The eternal death which the bourgeoisie calls life is not the only feature of experience. St Paul has prophesied of the future of the church, "Many members in one body," and it is also written, "I know that my Redeemer liveth, and that He shall stand at the latter day upon the earth." Do not even the most pious and pig-headed agree that these are the 'last days'? Are we not come through much tribulation to the latter end of the Apocalypse, and shall we not cry with the Apostle, "The spirit and the bride say: come."? "Yea, come, Lord Jesus, come quickly."

JOHN ST JOHN

THE CHILDREN'S HOMER. By PADRAIC COLUM.

One of the points of art is adaptation of the means to the end. If the children of America are nurtured on the world's greatest story, it will be very nice for everybody in thirty years or so. It seems hopeless to get the present generation to understand that unless they read Greek, they are savages, who, if they are not cannibals, are simply so because they have no skill in cookery.

So Padraic Colum has tried to civilize young America in the right way. No more important task has ever been undertaken, for civilization, education, are fundamental. Reformers usually make the mistake of the empiric, and try to relieve the symptoms. It is quite useless to try to relieve the symptoms of America.

Willy Pogany is not Flaxman, but he is Flaxman enough for children, and now and again, as in the picture facing page 106 (and several others), he is Flaxman enough for nearly everybody. (You cannot expect an illustrator as such to be altogether Flaxman in an age where artists have to earn their living.) But it is impossible to give too much praise to the prose of Padraic Colum. It is simple enough for a child who has just learned to read. It is good enough for a book-worm-eaten hag like myself, sodden on Sterne and Swift. A book like this revives the drooping flower of hope; so long as there are people willing to try, there is still hope for humanity.

A.C.

CHRONICLES OF PHARMACY. By A. C. WOOTTON.

The title of this work justifies itself as the reader reaches the end of the second volume. To the pharmacist it is an extremely useful book, and in a great many instances furnishes information of an interesting character, which the busy man would have difficulty in finding in pharmaceutical history. To the student of the occult it ought to appeal strongly, as the author gives a long list of drugs used in religious ceremonies in different ages, and although the present century is so much in advance, we find that the incenses and sweet odours used in ceremonial magic to-day are the same as those used in Egypt, in the worship of Isis, and in the services held in the Temple of Solomon. Mention is also made of the preparations made by the ancient alchemists which were thought to have magic power. Short biographical sketches of some of the old masters of pharmacy appear, but after Liebig we have no special mention of the pharmacists of the last century.

An interesting chapter on Poisons in History, introducing the stories of poisoners and the drugs employed, furnishes material for the budding novelist, to whom in fact the whole of this excellent work may be recommended. To the occult reader the concluding chapter on names and symbols would be of considerable service, and might be useful for reference.

The book, which is published in two volumes, is profusely illustrated, and well printed and bound. Had the author not been known as the popular editor of a pharmaceutical newspaper and an authority on all matters connecting with pharmacy, *The Chronicles* would have proved an excellent monument to his memory; un-

fortunately Mr Wootton died before his book left the
publisher's hands.

E. WHINERAY, M.P.S.

THE CLAY'S REVENGE. BY HELEN GEORGE.

> . . . equal purged of Soul and Sense.
> Beneficent high-thinking, just,
> Beyond the appeal of Violence,
> Incapable of common lust,
> In "mental Marriage" still prevail
> (God in the garden hid his face)—

And well He might!

It is on these lines that Bertha and Leonard Hammersley
agree to lead their married life. The husband is a delicate,
refined, over-sensitive, under-vitalized creature, and the
arrangement suits him admirably. For a time Bertha
is content; her intellect is satisfied, her senses are
slumbering. She is not only content; when she looks
around at the married lives of her more carnally-minded
friends she feels immensely superior, and prides herself
on the purity of the relationship existing between
Leonard and herself. She wilfully closes her eyes, and if
an inner consciousness whispers to her that this vaunted
happiness is incomplete, she refuses to listen. The
whisper becomes loud—insistent. Mrs George very
cleverly shows us Bertha's slow, almost shocked,
awakening. Starved Nature revengefully, triumphantly
asserts herself. After three years of the Higher Life
Bertha changes the joys of the Intellect and Spiritual
Love for the joys of the Flesh and Human Passion.

But it is to the Man as Father, not as Lover, she at first
yields.

When, in due course, the Man returns to West Africa,
she sees him go without a pang. He has fulfilled his
purpose, and she has no further use for him.

It is only later, after the birth of the child, that she desires him as a Lover.

This change in her attitude is depicted with masterly strength and skill.

He returns after two years' absence.

Her first feeling is one of annoyance and faint fear rather than rapture.

He takes it for granted their old relationship will be renewed, and so she drifts back and changes from the passive Mother-Woman, submitting to the Man's love only as a means to her own and Nature's end—to a passionate exacting Woman, demanding Love for love's sake and love's sake alone, and putting the plan before the child.

How the child dies, and how the Lover in terror and revolt flies from his too-exacting mistress, we leave it for Mrs George to tell in her own vivid and unflinching way.

E. G. O.

THE CLEANSING OF A CITY.

"Wherefore I say unto thee, her sins, which are many, are forgiven; for she loved much: but to whom little is forgiven, the same loveth little."

JESUS CHRIST

"But this German woman, pretending to defend the cause of virtue, and to warn women against the perils of the day, produces a book (*The Diary of a Lost One*) which it is defilement to touch. . . . Before I had skimmed fifty pages I found my brain swimming; I nearly swooned."

REV. R. F. HORTON, D.D.

This book should be printed on vellum and locked up in a fire-proof safe in the British Museum, Great Russell Street, W.C.; so that future ecclesiastical historians and ethicists may learn into what a state of mental menorrhagia the adherents of the Christian Church had fallen at the commencement of the twentieth century.

The "cleansing" part of the business seems to consist in pumping filth into everything that is clean. We are not allowed to talk of leg because every leg adjoins a thigh: soon we shall not be able to put a foot into a boot without first looking to see if some nasty mess has not been deposited in it, and why? Because foot adjoins leg! Moreover, foot suggests walking, and walking, like the name of the Rev. Horton, D.D., suggests prostitution— at the thought of this we swoon.

Most of the contributors to this cesspit, like the Rev. Horton, have "D.D." after their names. Dr Bodie has informed us that "M.D." stands for "Merry Devil"; perhaps he can also enlighten us as to the true meaning of these two letters?

ANTOINETTE BOUVIGNON

THE CLOUD ON THE SANCTUARY. BY COUNCILLOR VON ECKARTSHAUSEN.

We shall be very sorry if any of our readers misses this little book, a translation from the French translation of the German original into the pretty broken English of Madame de Steiger.

It was this book which first made your reviewer aware of the existence of a secret mystical assembly of saints, and determined him to devote his whole life, without keeping back the least imaginable thing, to the purpose of making himself worthy to enter that circle. We shall be disappointed if the book has any less effect on any other reader.

The perusal of the notes may be omitted with advantage.

N.

CONTEMPORARY PSYCHOLOGY. By GUIDO VILLA. Translated by HAROLD MANACORDA.

This long and learned work is not exciting:
The good translation shames the pedant's writing.
The wise Professor reconstructs duality,
Made of mentality and animality.
His arguments are forcible and true,
But yet his propositions will not do;
For when the full circumference is run
We can resolve them gaily into one.
Nay, though he talk of monism, we feel
He does not mean it. Mind and reason reel
At this conception. Only in the soul
Can we perceive the One Unchanging Whole.
At the same time, the book is well worth study;
It summarises thought. The style is
[We regret that our space will not admit a more extended review.—Ed.]

COUNTERPARTS. Vol. XVI of THE BROTHERHOOD OF THE NEW LIFE. AN EPITOME OF THE WORK AND TEACHING OF THOMAS LAKE HARRIS. By RESPIRO.

If we are in any way to shadow forth the Ineffable, it must be by a degradation. Every symbol is a blasphemy against the Truth that it indicates. A painter to remind us of the sunlight has no better material than dull ochre.

So we need not be surprised if the Unity of Subject and Object in Consciousness which is Samadhi, the uniting of the Bride and the Lamb which is Heaven, the uniting of the Magus and the God which is Evocation, the uniting of the Man his Holy Guardian Angel which is the seal upon the work of the Adeptus Minor, is symbolized by the geometrical unity of the circle and the square, the arithmetical unity of the 5 and the 6, and (for more universality of comprehension) the uniting of the Lingam

and the Yoni, the Cross and the Rose. For as in earth-life
the sexual ecstasy is the loss of self in the Beloved, the
creation of a third consciousness transcending its parents,
which is again reflected into matter as a child; so, immeasurably higher, upon the Plane of Spirit, Subject and
Object join to disappear, leaving a transcendent unity.
This third is esctasy and death; as below, so above.

It is then with no uncleanness of mind that all races of
men have adored an ithyphallic god; to those who can
never lift their eyes above the basest plane the sacrament
seems filth.

Much, if not all, of the attacks upon Thomas Lake
Harris and his worthy successor "Respiro" is due to this
persistent misconception by prurient and degraded
minds.

When a sculptor sees a block of marble he thinks "How
beautiful a statue is hidden in this! I have only to knock
off the chips, and it will appear!"

This being achieved, the builder comes along, and says:
"I will burn this, and get lime for my mortar." There are
more builders than sculptors in England.

This is the Magic Mirror of the Soul; if you see God in
everything, it is because you are God and have made the
universe in your image; if you see Sex in everything, and
think of Sex as something unclean, it is because you are
a sexual maniac.

True, it is, of course, that the soul must not unite herself to every symbol, but only to the God which every
symbol veils.

And Lake Harris is perfectly clear on the point. The
"counterpart" is often impersonated, with the deadliest
results. But if the Aspirant be wise and favoured, he will
reject all but the true.

And I really fail to see much difference between this
doctrine and our own of attaining the Knowledge and

Conversation of the Holy Guardian Angel, or the Hindu doctrine of becoming one with God. We may easily agree that Lake Harris made the error of thinking men pure-minded, and so used language which the gross might misinterpret; but sincere study of this book will make the truth apparent to all decent men.

ALEISTER CROWLEY

[We print this review without committing ourselves to any opinion as to how these doctrines may be interpreted in practice by the avowed followers of Harris.—Ed.]

THE DANCE OF SHIVA By DR ANANDA KENT COOMARASWAMY.

The plot thickens. There is certainly no one equal to Dr Coomaraswamy for tangling up situations, perhaps not always too pleasantly. Nor can one be very sure how far Dr Coomaraswamy is himself responsible, for where-ever he is the line between *meum* and *tuum* becomes gossamer of a kind that has seen better days. Consider the first child, Narada, who is a bastard. Was the father the "worm" after all? We have nothing for it but the un-supported statement of its mother, the "worm's" second wife. This may be doubted. Even the colour tells us nothing, for there were plenty of pigmented people in London at the date of the story.

When the "worm's" first wife has divorced him, and he is married to the second wife, one might imagine that complications would be less. Not at all. The first time he leaves her alone, he sets up a harem in India, while she, travelling thither to join him under the charge of his best friend, Dr Paira Mull, immediately begins an intrigue with this fascinating Panjabi. The "worm" seems rather to have welcomed this domestic tangle, as Paira Mull is very well off.

The second child, Rohini, is the offspring of this liaison.

About this time, the "worm" is getting out a book of Indian folk songs, and he actually tries to include a number of translations made by his wife's lover as his own. However, he is forced by her (after a stormy scene) to make a very inadequate acknowledgement, and we are given to understand that he only does this because the show can be so easily given away, the "worm" not knowing ten words of the language from which he is supposed to be translating. Isn't this complex enough for anybody? Ah, no! Dr Coomaraswamy is merely flapping his wings idly. He can stage much stronger dramas. So you see the "worm" and his wife in New York—of all places! The first thing that strikes him is the High Cost Of Living, and he hastens to offer his wife to the first comer. A friendly agreement is reached in conference by which a divorce shall be obtained, and a new marriage contracted with Alice's new lover. I forget the disposition of the children, whether it was odd man out, or the first Jack, who had to look after the business.

But, three months later, the tragedy begins. The "worm" is struck by the appalling thought that perhaps Alice's new lover may not fall in so simply with the scheme. He manifests reluctance to pay the expenses of the divorce, arguing with some show of good sense that he does not see why he should pay for relieving another man of his rubbish. The situation is complicated by the fact that Alice has again become pregnant.

The "worm" resolves upon a remarkably ingenious solution of his troubles. Past experience has shown him that his wife, when in a "delicate condition of health," cannot stand a sea voyage. Previous to the birth of the second child, she had nearly miscarried and nearly died. "How then," thinks he to himself, "can I clear myself once and for all? I will make up to my wife. I will pull out the pathetic stop. I will make mischief between her and her lover. I will forge telegrams, and do anything else that may be necessary. But I will get her to go over to England. That will put an end to the child, and very likely to her too, and then perhaps Paira Mull will take at least one of the children—his own—off my hands. Narada, too, is not legally my child at all. He is just a nameless bastard." So thinks the "worm," and so he does. The only detail in which his scheme goes wrong is that his wife manages, against all odds, to survive her miscarriage.

All this time, the "worm" himself is living with a German prostitute; and, as he finds this expensive, he tries to keep the wolf from the door by getting this unfortunate woman to copy out various items from the works of his wife's lover, which are not very well known in America, and she proceeds to hawk them about New York. The man whose property they are will not be likely to hear of it, as the inexplicable conduct of Alice has more or less broken his heart, and he has become a sort of hermit.

But the wife turns up again like a bad penny. The "worm" has by this time got rather tired of the German girl, and he goes off to Chicago after another woman, leaving his wife and his mistress to share a room at the McAlpin. Instead of quarreling, they make Friends, and the wholly icily murderous plot is laid bare. Alice now makes strenuous efforts to get back her lover, but he is one of those people who learn by experience. He merely exposes the "worm's" attempt to pirate his property.

It seems to us that Dr Coomaraswamy leaves the story at what might have been its most interesting complication. It stops right there. The "worm" gets a job as curator of the Oriental Department of some Art Museum in Boston, and settles down with his wife to live happy ever after. I feel that this may be life, but it is not art.

A MOURNER CLAD IN GREEN

DEATH.   HEREWARD CARRINGTON and JOHN R. MEADER.
A most interesting and fairly able book. Mr Carrington's
hysteria is thoroughly diluted by Mr Meader, or else he
has taken a little nourishment and feels better. The
Vitality book was the scream of a schoolgirl.

The "theories" of these writers are, however, too
comic to discuss seriously. One believes in "Life," a
mystical entity flowing through one like a grease-spot
through a greenback; the other believes that Death is
caused by a man's hypnotising himself into the belief
that it must come!

Big as is the present volume, it is necessarily far from
complete. Yet I am compelled to admit much against my
will that he makes out a very strong case for the persistence
of personality after death, and its manifestation through
certain mediums. Yet I think that the "coincidence"
argument is a little better than is supposed.

The point is that the failures are unrecorded. Take
"pure chance" roulette for example. Scientifically, any
given run (say 500 on the red) is no more and no less
remarkable than any other given run, say R B B R R B
B B R R R B B B B, etc., to 500 coups. But the one is
acclaimed as a miracle, the other goes unremarked.

Now in the millions of séances of the last sixty years
the "evidential" records can be counted on the fingers of
one hand.

And it is not antecedently so very improbable that pure
chance might dictate correct answers in so small a proportion of cases.

Further, the spiritists have thrown upon science the
task of proving a universal negative.

If Sir Oliver Lodge, or Professor Munsterberg, or Lord
Cholly Cauliflower, or Mr Upthe Pole comes to me with
a tale of unicorns in Piccadilly, I merely humour him.
Munsterberg, at least, might be dangerous.

But I should not investigate his statement, and I certainly should not claim to be able to disprove it on *à priori* grounds.

Even in the evidential cases, there is so much room for a mixture of fraud, telepathy, chance, and hysteria, and humanity is so clever at stopping chinks with putty and then leaving the door open, that we must continue to suspend judgment.

An amusing case occurred some years ago at Cambridge. I offered to reproduce roughly the performance of the Zancigs (which was then puzzling the foolish in London) without preparation. A stranger to me offered to act as my "medium."

The conditions were these. The ten small cards of a suit were laid on the floor; one was to be touched in the medium's absence and in my presence. The medium was to return and say which it was. The rest of the company were to prevent us from communicating if they could.

Well, they tried everything. In a minute's interview I arranged a button-touching code with my medium, and as each new restriction was put on me I managed to invent a new code. Shifting my pipe, coughing, arranging books, winking, altering the position of my fingers, etc., all were provided against. Then I obtained a confederate. Ultimately the grand sceptic of all devised the following test just as I had passed the note to my medium, "If I can't manage any of the old ways, I'll try and write down the number and put it on the mantelpiece."

And this was the test.

The medium was to be taken from Whewell's Court (where we were) over to the Great Court of Trinity—well out of all hearing. I was to be left alone with the sceptic, who by this time suspected everybody of being a confederate. He was to touch the card in my presence and then take me away in the opposite direction. The medium was then (at a given time) to return, and tell the card. Now it happened that in the course of general argument about fairness, which I encouraged to enable myself to plot unnoticed in the confusion of talk, that I had stipulated for my sceptic to write down the number that he had touched, to avoid dispute. This he agreed to; he was allowed to hide it as he chose.

I gave up all hope but in bringing off the 9 to 1 chance of my medium's being right. The sceptic kept both eyes on me all the time; if I stirred a finger, he was up in arms. I did keep my back to the mantelpiece, but there was no way of writing down the number.

But it was just at that point that my sceptic's magnificent brain broke down. He had correctly argued everything so far; but then his brain said, "It is important that Crowley shall not know where I hide the paper with the number on it: I must hide it somewhere where he cannot see."

So instead of slipping it into one of the hundreds of books on the shelves, he hid it behind my back, *i.e.,* on the mantelpiece, where it was duly found!

I must tell just one other story to the point. It throws possibly some light on one or two of the "miracles" which Blavatsky performed in order to disgust the more foolish of her followers.

In June 1906 I was at Margate (God help me!) and asked my friend J—— to lend me his copy of Abramelin.

"Sorry!" said he. "I lent it to So-and-so, and it has not been returned."

He forgot this conversation: I remembered it.

Staying at his house six months later, I was alone one morning and found the book, which he "knew for a fact" to be in London sixty miles away. It was hidden by the panel of a glass-fronted bookcase.

I hid it in the stuffing of a music-stool, led the conversation at lunch-time to "apports," got my host to suggest my doing this very thing which he was sure I could not do, and, in the evening, did it.

If I had been a cheat, could I have produced better evidence? My host would have sworn that the book was in London in a house unknown to me, whose occupants were unknown to me. He is a man of science and of most accurate and balanced judgment. One little lapse of memory: he forgot that he had told me that the book was not in his shelves; another little lapse of memory: he forgot where the book was; and there is your miracle!

Now for my constructive policy. I suggest that a "spirit" be cultivated on the lines laid down by Eliphaz Levi, *Dogma and Ritual*, Cap. XIII, so that he may manifest more wholly. Then let him dictate to two or three segregated mediums a long passage, or a long set of meaningless figures, and get so high a degree of agreement that hardly any doubt remains.

Or if anybody wants a really high evidential proof, let him get the proof of Fermat's Last Theorem, which Fermat died without revealing, and which the united efforts of mathematicians have hitherto failed to discover.

ALEISTER CROWLEY

THE DEUCE AND ALL. By GEORGE RAFFALOVICH.

I can find no words of any known language strong and emphatic enough to express my admiration of this extraordinary volume. Twelve tales! The twelve Pointed Star of Genius! An introduction that is a Revelation! Magical knowledge thrown away! Psychology never at fault! Truly the Book to read again and again.

But, mind you, do not let it fall into the hands of elderly people. *They would never die.*

GEORGE RAFFALOVICH

THE DOCTOR'S DILEMMA, etc. BERNARD SHAW.

The preface to the first of these plays is a pointless hotchpotch of ignorant balderdash, the eavesdropping of a doctor's flunkey translated to a suburban layman. Sometimes it hits the mark; the law of chance provides for this event.

The play is even worse rubbish.

Follows a dull, dirty, stupid, prolix, foolish farrago about marriage. "By George!" cried Somerset, "three days of you have transformed me into an ancient Roman!" Bernard Shaw is the nearest approach to the redoubtable Zero that seems possible. I have had doubts about marriage, and troubles in marriage; but Shaw has made me feel partly like St Paul and partly like Queen Victoria.

But there is no need to take Shaw seriously. He has lived so long as cock-of-the-walk of his mattoid dunghill of sexless and parasexual degenerates that he has lost sight of the world altogether. Probably a sewer-rat thinks that fresh air smells nasty. Nor, one may add, is much consideration due to a person so ignorant as to write "dumbfoundered" for "dumfoundered" and "laudatores tempori acti." "Til" for "till" is doubtless only a foolish faddism intended to irritate, like the Old Philadelphia Lady in the *New York Herald,* but he has not her sense of humour.

There is some ground, though, for hoping that *The Doctor's Dilemma* and *Getting Married* merely mark the temporary eclipse of a great mind. For the remarks on the Censor are quite informed and sensible, and Blanco Posnet is really quite good. The characters are human and living—a welcome change indeed from the dogmatic dummies of the other two plays.

A. C.

THE DORIS CASE OF MULTIPLE PERSONALITY. By WALTER

F. PRINCE, Ph.D., and JAMES H. HYSLOP, Ph.D. Proceedings of the American Society of Psychical Research, Vols. IX, X, XI. 1915; 1916; 1917.

Here is a nice little piece of reading for the occult student—some two thousand pages, weighing Lord knows how many pounds! And it contains *some* stuff. Volumes I and II are by Dr Prince, and deal with the psychology of the case—its genesis and cure; Volume III is by Hyslop, and takes it up—as we might have supposed—from the "spiritualistic" point of view, and endeavours to prove that the various personalities are not such at all, in reality, but probably "spirits," who are "obsessing" the poor girl, and causing all the disturbance. Shades of witchcraft and the New Testament—here is a joyous revival, in the Twentieth Century!

We have a girl, Doris Fischer, born in 1889 (of German parents), who developed, in all, five distinct personalities, each of which received a special name. Besides the original "Doris," we find "Sick Doris," "Margaret," and "Sleeping Margaret," and "Sleeping Real Doris." These five personalities are said to have shown varied characteristics (as is invariably the case) and to be essentially different, from the psychological point-of-view. As usual, also, several of them developed as the result of emotional shock, and disappeared under hypnosis and psychological treatment; one by one they were eliminated, until only "Real Doris" survived—with traces of "Sleeping Margaret" persisting, as a sort of undercurrent of reality. These names, of course, apply to the so-called varied personalities which appeared during their shufflings back and forth; that is, their alternate appearances.

It must be admitted at once that Dr Prince has made some interesting investigations in this curious case, and if we grant the reality of the facts, they have very considerable psychological interest. Of course, it is hard to prove that the whole thing is not a clever fraud. Girls of the kind have a habit of playing such parts, because of the attention they thereby attract; but let us grant their reality, for the sake of the argument. We have, then, an abnormal individual, who needs treatment and cure; and the sooner cured the better!

Now, at this point, our friends begin messing-about with "mediums," and as the result, obtain an extraordinary amount of rubbish, wholly disconnected from the case, by which they try to prove that the alternating personalities were really "spirits"! Most of these messages were obtained through a "Mrs Chenoweth"—a medium who has figured largely in the Reports of the American Society,— though Heaven only knows why, as she gives us a constant flow of the most terrible drivel which it is possible to conceive. Looking through the so-called Reports on this medium, one is impressed with the idea that it is criminal to waste time, and the Society's money, obtaining such stuff, and criminal to keep pouring money down such a sink of Nothingness. What is the hold which this medium seems to have over the venerable Secretary of the Society? Is it more than a mere scientific interest? Are there subtler motives which cause the Head of the Psychical Movement in America to bow solemnly before the crude "Teachings" obtained through this evident fraud of a medium? Any common sense man-of-the-world, reading this stuff, would form his own opinions,—for it is plain to see that,—by merely playing upon his vanity, and flattering him to the skies,—this "medium" has managed to ingratiate herself so thoroughly with the noted Professor, that he has become blind to evidence, to facts, and to common sense.

Here are a few typical "Nuggets of Wisdom" from the sittings:

"They are not so clear about the life here as they will be when they come but they mean all right. I had faith too but the knowledge is better. I had in mind a prayer that I used to want her to say long ago for I felt it important to pray and teach her to say the little prayer." (1917, p. 327.)

If this isn't mediumistic cant, I should like to know what is!

However, on another occasion, we read: "Go to hell and there you will find the information you seek my sweet friend." (p. 622.) Here is some sound advice!

This is another little gem, which is dished-up as part of the "proof of immortality":

"Mamma gave some advice and now comes to help in the work of proving that the love and care and interest does not cease at death but all is intensified and desires become actions and have effect in friends and loved ones. No one has been able to prove the power of thought and we are not able to prove that we do some things but when we find that the things we think and wish for are taking place then we realize that our thought has had some power even though we did not speak or act. I have no interest whatever that the things said do not match with what I believed in the past. One must tell things as they find them and not as they wish they were."

O tempora, o mores! Let us admit that "immortality" has now been proved; that Hyslop's Marvellous Medium has furnished the demonstration! We are to inherit the Kingdom of Heaven, and there assist the Angels in the compilation of English Grammars (let us hope) for the use of those who communicate through Mrs Chenoweth!

When one reads through stuff like this, one is driven to ask the question: How *can* men of intelligence and learning, perhaps with skill in other lines of research, be driven to accept such nonsense as proof of anything beyond obvious fraud on the part of the "medium"? How can their sense of all that constitutes evidence be so lacking,—their judgment so at fault,—as to accept this drivel as proof of "spirits"? One can form only the opinion —one seems driven to this conclusion—that it is the "will to believe" which has influenced them in this manner— not the evidence itself, but their own warped and faulty judgment.

If one analyzes the facts, he finds that practically all those who have advertised their belief in "Immortality" are men well along in life—practically all past sixty, and some of them many years older. Evidently, they are entering their second childhood. They are so concerned with saving their own souls, with unifying "Science and Religion," with showing that they themselves are probably "Immortal," that they have lost all sense of humour, of proportion, of evidence, of all these qualities which to-gether constitute the truly scientific scholar. As they are getting along in life, and can no longer enjoy it, they are haunted by the Spectre of Annihilation; and to escape this, they grasp at any straw, accept any evidence, swallow any "facts," given through a twopenny medium, which seem to afford even the slightest "evidence" for "survival." The result is that they all accept such rubbish as that given above (which is part of the official record) and seriously claim that it affords them *proof* of survival—of Immortality! Heigh, Ho! This is a sad world, my children, but never sadder than when we see otherwise good in-tellects going to the Dogs in this fashion.

HODGSON Y. KNOTT

A DREAMER'S TALES. BY LORD DUNSANY.

Lord Dunsany's prose is like Baudelaire's. I can only criticise five of these tales; for the others I have not yet read forty times!

"Poltarnees" is the best tale ever written of the lure of

the Sea. I wish I could think that my "Anima Lunae" helped to inspire it.

"Bethmoora" and "The Hashish Man" are really one tale. Words really fail me here; if I quote one half sentence all who really understand English will know that this is the perfection of the sublime in its simplicity. "Away we went from that small, pale, *heinous* man."

"Pore Ole Bill" seems derived from "The Rime of the Ancient Mariner" and "The Yarn of the Nancy Bell." Mixed. What could be more ridiculous? Yet I read it again and again, and the oftener I read it the keener does its fascination grip me.

And what shall I say of "The Sword and the Idol"? Only this; that it is true. Lord Dunsany has really beheld the dawn of the Iron Age, and the conquest of the King by the Priest. G. W. Foote ought to publish this tale as an atheistic pamphlet; it is the best ever written. And yet to me "The Silence of Ged" (Oh bold my Lord Dunsany!) came as a voice in the wood at midnight, when the sword-holder raises his steel against Ged. Ged neither hit nor shrank—in the end the sword was laid as an offering upon his knees.

So let the adept sit smiling through all that may befall him; then those that hate him shall wonder at his strength; in the end they shall worship him. And He, an He speak, shall by speaking save; an He yet keep silence, shall by keeping silence, bless. Amen.

ALEISTER CROWLEY

THE DWELLER ON THE THRESHOLD. ROBERT HICHENS.

Mr Hichens once wrote *Flames*. This was a pretty powerful book. Today (tempted, as I suppose, by a heavy bribe, for he is an artist in his way) he gives us this book with a title borrowed, not from Lytton, whom he has obviously not read, but from some eighteenth-hand source, and contents borrowed from his own *Flames*. Hence a tedious novel,

dull novel,	unconvincing novel,
stupid novel,	futile novel,
pseudo-occult novel,	banal novel,
pot-boiling novel,	senseless novel,
tired novel,	ground-out novel,
pointless novel,	unreal novel,
fatuous novel,	sorry novel,

etc., etc., etc.

The above method of filling space I took from Rabelais. Mr Hichens' method is just as obvious.

PANURGE

THE EDUCATION OF UNCLE PAUL. By ALGERNON BLACKWOOD.

I read this book on the Express Train from Eastbourne to London (change at Polegate, Lewes, Hayward's Heath, Three Bridges, Red Hill, and East Croydon—they ought to stop to set down passengers at Earlswood) and though it's a beautiful story, and I like Nixie, I must confess to being rather bored. Rather with a capital R and a sforzando *er*. I wanted George Macdonald's *Lilith*, and Arthur Machen's *Hill of Dreams*—they have blood in them. And I was not in my library, but in a stuffy, dog-returneth-to-his-vomit-scented microbe-catcher labelled 1st Compo. Then, too, Algernon Blackwood began to remind me of Maeterlinck. There was too much bluebirdiness, and it gave me the blue devils. And then, again, though I've never read J. M. Barrie, I felt sure that he must be responsible for some of the oysters in the stew. And where was Sidney Blow?

Yes: it's a silly book; a book elaborately and deliberately silly; even laboriously silly with that silliness which cometh not forth but by prayer and fasting. . . .

And as I continued to read, it grew monotonously silly. Paul "slipped into the Crack" in several different ways, but there wasn't much difference in the result. I began to wonder if Mr Blackwood has been drinking from the wisdom-fount of Ecclesiastes and Don Juan! And oh dear! the conversations. Children don't talk bad metaphysics, nor do repatriated lumbermen. But Mr Blackwood must dree his weird, I suppose.

And then, on a sudden, the monotony breaks up into a mixture of "La Morte Amoureuse," "Thomas Lake Harris," "The Yoke" (Mr Hubert Wales' masterpiece) and "The Autobiography of a Flea told in a Hop, Skip, and a Jump."

But I prefer Mr Verbouc to Uncle Paul, and Bella to Nixie. From the point of view of pure literature, of course.

The book then slobbers off into Gentle-Darwin-meek-and-mild Theosophy.

Victoria at last, thank God! I think I'll slip into the Crack, myself!

ALEISTER CROWLEY

EVOLUTION CRITICISED. By T. B. BISHOP.

Bloody Bill is commonly supposed to have been somewhat severe with the Belgians. But only the "spurlos versenkt" suggestion of an admittedly insane agent of his approaches the maniacal savagery of I Samuel xv, 3, and by no means matches the undiscriminating imbecility of its ferocity:

> Now go and smite Amalek, and utterly destroy all that they have, and spare them not; but slay both man and woman, infant and suckling, ox and sheep, camel and ass.

Who is the author of this order? It is the father of Jesus Christ. "I and my father are one." It is therefore the God of Wilhelm von Hohenzollern, the American people (if their newspapers lie not), and a very few particularly troglodytic Englishmen of whom Mr T. B. Bishop is a striking "survival of the meanest."

Mr Bishop really believes that this tribal demon designed butterflies, and put the rainbow in the sky as a guarantee that the world would never be destroyed by water. He even thinks that it once was destroyed by water! When any student of nature discovers beauty, or design, or evidence of intelligence, Mr Bishop falls into a senile rage. He is not content with destroying his fellowman, with his wife, children, cattle, and so on; Mr Bishop is not happy unless he is sure that they will all be roasted without cessation or hope.

In the meanwhile, Mr Bishop writes a book to prove the truth of all this prehistoric nonsense. Mr Bishop's intelligence is very far beneath the human level. For example, he actually maintains that the claws and teeth of predatory animals have been given to them out of kindness towards their prey! You would think it was impossible for any one to miss the point of the argument that nature is cruel. The fact is that Mr Bishop's ideas of kindness are a little crude, like his ideas of writing a book. This is not really a book at all. It's mere scissors and paste. Its main argument is that as two men of science have differed on some minute detail of theory, there is no value in science. He does not in the least understand the subject on which he is writing. He does not understand the canon of reason. He has only one idea, which is, that the Bible (authorized translation) is literally true in every detail. His great explanation of everything that seems a little peculiar is that it is the result of sin. He claims, however, that sin was caused by the devil, who was created by God, and that God foreknew and permitted all this, in order to inflict torture upon nearly everybody except Mr Bishop.

He would however deny furiously that the God who willingly and knowingly created the devil, was in any way responsible for him. This Kaiserlich-Chautauquamericanisch-Bishopisch God is therefore an illogical impossibility and absurdity. But this doesn't detract from the unmetaphysical conception of him as a monster.

Mr Bishop is one of the best known philanthropists in England. Let us see how he acts within his family circle. Here is a quotation from a bill of costs sent in to his nephew by the family solicitor. It should be understood that the nephew in question was at the time of the transaction entitled to a considerable sum of money which was in the hands of this solicitor, and that Mr Bishop was aware of this:

"Attending Mrs Bishop when she informed us that Mr Bishop had received a letter from you that you were ill and needed money and she asked whether Mr Bishop would be safe in sending you out any and generally answering your inquiries.

"Attending Mr T. B. Bishop on his calling when he showed us the letter from you and stated that he was cabling you out £12."

A generous impulse is sometimes regretted by the impulsive one. Mr Bishop's motto seems to be, "Safety First." Many years ago, as stated in *The Equinox*, Mr Bishop worked his sister to death in order to spare himself the expense of a stenographer. Mr Bishop is a man of considerable wealth, but he never allows it to injure his moral principles. The death of his sister left him with one other sister, and for her he professed the most unbounded devotion. As she lay dead in her house, he wrote long letters to her son about One pound, three and tuppence that she owed to the grocer, sixteen and nine pence that she owed to the butcher, and so on. I suppose he had her buried by the parish, though I have no information on this point; but he was the residuary legatee of her estate, and any money expended in burying her would therefore have to come ultimately out of his own pocket, which is not very nice to think of, when you are 78 years old, rich and honoured, and your last near relative is lying dead in her house. I think possibly that he may have paid a few shillings for a cheap coffin, for the subject seems to worry him very much. Two years later he is trying to swindle this nephew aforesaid out of some property, and one of the arguments which he uses is, that if he gets this money to which he has no right, he will be able to have a stone put on the grave of his sister. I hope the readers of *The Equinox* have been ignorant hitherto that there are any people like this Mr Bishop; that they imagine the peasants in Zola's *La Terre* to be mostly imaginary: not that Zola's peasants are as disgusting as Mr Bishop. He is certainly a very strong argument against evolution, though his book is not. After wearing out his sister Ada, finding himself faced with this expense of this stenographer aforesaid, he decided that it would be cheaper to get married. So he went to Llandudno; and, rather like Abraham when he found the ram caught in the thicket by its horns, he found a cow caught in the Children's Special Service Mission by her feet, which were exceptionally large, and took her as wife in name, and secretary and general servant in function. This female, however, developed an unsuspected quality. She made him shave, and Mr Bishop, who had been going about London for forty years looking like a most venerable old gentleman, was seen to be a monkey. He looked like a monkey so much that the local zoologists used to frequent the neighbourhood of his house on Sunday afternoon. We have also seen that he thinks like a monkey, the god whom he has made in his own image being more ferocious than a gorilla, and far less intelligent. What then are the differences between Mr Bishop and a monkey? They are not obvious, and I do not think that any man of science will disagree that it is better to leave it to the monkeys to discover them. But if they insist that he is a Nuctanthropus, we must try again, and see if we cannot class him among the cockroaches. There is a great gambit in what may be called by history the olfactory argument.

H. SAPIENS

EVOLUTION FROM NEBULA TO MAN. By JOSEPH MCCABE.

Mr McCabe has written another little book on evolution: how many more of these small, small, small volumes are to appear? The subject seems a tall order for 128 pages. However, let us be thankful there are not more.

The most interesting fact that we can discover in it, or at least the only one really original, is, that Erasmus Darwin was born in 1788. This makes him only thirty years younger than his son Charles; and yet these are the good people who make such a fuss about Ahaziah being two years older than his father Jehoram!

FOUR DIMENSIONAL VISTAS. By CLAUDE BRAGDON.

It is a great pleasure to read this book, for although in some points we may find ourselves obliged to disagree with the author, the general effect is that a perusal leaves one with the feeling of having been at home; that is to say, on the planes of pure and exalted thought. We cannot say that Mr Bragdon is in any sense an original thinker, as Hinton was, but he has done something to extend and popularize Hinton's ideas. Some of the analogies in this book are very illuminating. Unfortunately, as it appears to us, Mr Bragdon is tied up with theosophical dogmas. He talks about the "new freedom," and bases his whole argument on the idea that the material world is a shadow show. Yet he seems to think that the real (that is, the ideal)

world is more easy of apprehension, if we bind ourselves
hand and foot by the senseless and cruel taboos of the
most primitive tribes. He also errs, as it seems to us, in
placing the yogi whose attainment is wholly selfish above
the man of genius. Blavatsky made no such error. She
placed the poet above the adept.

In spite of his prave 'orts, Mr Bragdon is not a clear
thinker like Hinton. He is just a little bourgeois who has
put on Hinton's hat, and it comes down very far indeed
over his eyes. He cannot see that the interpretation of
phenomena as spiritual does not destroy their reality
and the truth of their mutual relation, but rather confirms
it. Shallow thinkers always seem to be obsessed by the
stupidity that if anything is a shadow, dream, illusion,
it ceases to exist. The rules of dreams are just as rigid
as the rules of mathematics. You cannot do anything you
like with a surd merely because it is an "impossible" or
"imaginary" quantity. It is such booby traps that catch
such asses in lion's skins as Mr Bragdon.

O. M.

FROM THE WATCH TOWER. By SIDNEY T. KLEIN.

When I had the pleasure of reviewing Mr Sidney T.
Klein's *Science and the Infinite* in Number IX of the First
Volume of *The Equinox*, I remember asking him for a
second part to his book dealing with the means of attainment. Mr Klein has not exactly done this in his new
volume, but he has gone a long way on the road. He is
still somewhat handicapped by infelicity of expression,
but a more serious drawback still is the confusion of
thought caused by his early training. He is a sublime initiate, but he is trying to put his quart of Champagne into
the pint pot of the language of Christian Mysticism. He
has not seen the necessity of discarding this deuce and
trey. He stands pat on his three aces instead of trying to

catch the fourth or maybe a pair of kings in the draw. The language of Christianity, particularly Pauline Christianity, is hopelessly mired in the slough of the idea of original sin.

Mr Klein disavows this idea with noble boldness as freely as we ourselves of the A .·. A .·. would do. He has accepted the Law of Thelema. He understands that there is no law beyond "Do what thou wilt." He states it almost in so many words. And yet his congenital fetter seems to gall. He has not quite got the idea that every man and every woman is a star, and that every one's will is the will of God; at least, he does not seem settled about it. In some parts of his book he makes statements which certainly imply that this is so, but in others he appears too conscious of dividuality. He does not always make it perfectly clear that evil so-called is part of the game, which he describes as the "thought of God." We have no doubt that as he progresses, he will attain this clearer conception of the magical doctrine. He has already gone very far. His interpretation, for example, of the statement "God is Love" can hardly be distinguished from our own "Love is the law." Yet even here there is some taint of a lingering Manichaeanism. He seems to imagine "the All-Loving" as always trying to bring us to a conception of sonship. Yet this "All-Loving" is a metaphysical entity, omnipotent, omniscient, omnipresent, and so on. The result is that now and again Mr Klein's expression slips back into the language of dualism. However, it is a shame to carp.

Mr Klein's philosophical and scientific knowledge is profound. It is unified. Better still, it is dynamic and exulting. It is impossible to read a page of his book without feeling the contagion of the joy of his attainment. Too many philosophers in the past have drooled on about the Absolute with such piety of dullness, that one has wished the Absolute as the devil.

There is nothing of this in this book. We feel that Mr Klein is enjoying the Light, Life, Love and Liberty which come from the acceptance of the Law of Thelema. But I must still ask him for another volume. The greater part of his difficulty in explanation seems to arise from the fact that he has no conception of a technique of attainment. He says quite rightly that it is all a matter of thinking right instead of wrong, and certainly a study of his pages should do a great deal to clear up intellectual difficulties. But this is only a very small part of the Path. It is all very well to say that reason is full of falsity, and Mr Klein demonstrates it very much as I have myself done in many places. But how are people to use the eyes of the spirit, unless they are taught? The A ∴ A ∴ offers a technique of attainment infinitely subtle and varied, so that the need of every man is met by processes of actual practice, scientifically tested and confirmed. It is not enough merely to accept Mr Klein's explanation of the universe. That is the Giant's Robe. You must get your own clothes made to fit you. You cannot persuade yourself to think in any way contrary to your experience. Thought must be the expression of experience. For the average man to adopt Mr Klein's ideas would be as futile a formality as subscription to the Thirty-Nine Articles.

I am sure that Mr Klein knows all this perfectly well, and I hope, as I said before, that he will very soon let us have a new book, giving his ideas on the technique of attainment.

A. C.

GITANJALI AND FRUIT-GATHERING. BY RABINDRANATH TAGORE.

Knowing that whatever is good in Rabindranath Tagore is due to the style of W. B. Yeats, I expected the introduction to be by that individual, who might have been romantic if he had been willing to wash his face and put on a clean collar every month or so. The introduction begins, "A few days ago I said to a distinguished Bengali doctor of medicine, 'I know no German.'" Apart from the question as to whether Silly Willy counts his fortune in marks or not, I was much distracted by his reference.

I found myself back again in Teng-Yueh. We were sitting at dinner in the Consul's house, when the messenger broke in to tell us that the Consul—who was away among some unruly tribes—was ill, perhaps dying. We jumped up, George Forrest, the botanist, and I, and made ready. We were delayed two hours in starting by the "distinguished Bengali doctor of medicine," who needed to finish his rice. It was nine o'clock before we got off. It was a wild, windy night, the moon treacherously gleaming through blown wrack of clouds. I found it impossible to ride my pony, for his hoofs slipped on the wet flags in the darkness. Walking was almost as bad, for my ironshod mountain boots were as slippery as the shoes of the tatu. But we pushed on, gasping, up hill, down dale, all through the night. Dawn broke, chill and grey, on the crest of a great mountain. Far in the distance I saw specks. I left my pony, and ran headlong down the slopes. I had got almost to the bottom of the hill when I saw the Consul's litter. Forrest ran forward. I turned sadly back, for I saw that the Consul's legs were tied. I knew that he was dead. In that country where a thousand plagues hunt down mankind, it was most urgent that a medical man should certify the cause of death. How lucky that we had with us a distinguished Bengali doctor of medicine! There was only one slight hitch in the programme. The moment that I told him that the Consul was dead, he turned his donkey and bolted for safety. Holy Kali, it might be an infectious disease! There was no point in chasing the creature at the moment. The matter could wait our return. We brought the Consul to his house and Forrest asked me to bring the doctor round. It was necessary to make an official report of the death, and the cause of the death. I went round to the house of the "distinguished Bengali doctor of medicine." He was seated before a pyramid of rice. I attracted his attention by burying a whalebone cutting whip in the rolls of his fat. Between fifty and sixty applications of this instrument secured his presence in the room where we had the corpse. But not even the fear of the whip would induce him to touch it.

Rabindranath Tagore is the biggest bluff ever put over the unsuspecting American public. His mysticism makes even Maeterlinck's wishy-washy twaddle seem virile. I have never read such slop. The illustrations match it. The whole production of Young India is babu in the Anglo-Indian sense of the word. The spirit of India is utterly absent. Drawings and writing alike resemble the senseless flourishes of some callow student. And all this while the babu, while accepting what he imagines to be honours, such as knighthood, from England, is plotting sneakishly in the Bengali manner against her. I would to God that the British would withdraw from India for six months, so that the men of India might exterminate these fatherless fish-eaters, this spawn of female dogs that, without caste even in its own slime of bastardy, asserts itself in America as a "young nation."

KWAW LI YA

THE GRACES OF INTERIOR PRAYER. FATHER POULAIN, S.J.

It would be easy, and was tempting, to dismiss Father Poulain and his 650 pages with a jest—I have done harder things—for the mountains of his prejudice are difficult to approach across the abyss of his ignorance.

For example, he devotes just a paragraph to "Yogis." These persons he describes as "Hindu Buddhists" who are "Pantheists," and endeavour to produce "a state of stupefaction" in "their mental powers which are very low" and a "comatose condition" of their body, whose joints they dislocate. How well this describes such people as the Buddha and the author of the *Bhagavadgita!*

What a ring fence is Romanism against not merely truth but information!

We then examine Father Poulain on the scientific side. How does levitation of the Saints take place?

"The simplest explanation, and that most in conformity with the order of Providence, consists in saying: Since the angels have power to move corporeal bodies, God makes use of their ministry, so as to avoid intervening Himself without necessity."

(This is not the translator's blundering, though perhaps much more may be hoped from a lady who says that "Socrates remained for twenty-four hours lost in thought in the camp that Potidaea was besieging." It was Potidaea's way of doing her back hair that made her so generally admired.)

No; this is the real Poulain, 50 per cent above proof.

I am sorry for this hobble-skirted Atalanta. He must not study mystic facts; all he is allowed to do is to arrange, invent, delete as may suit dogma. He is obliged to accept the nymphomaniac nun Gertrude, and treat her blasphemous maunderings with reverence, or ascribe some peculiarly foul outburst to an "early temptation." He must accept every orthodox levitation, and explain it by weight-lifting competitions among the angels; he must deny every heterodox levitation, or explain it by demonic power. And as one's bitterest enemies are always one's nearest relations, so his bitterest polemics are against the Quietists who are absolutely indistinguishable from the orthodox, and in favour at Rome until the intrigues of the beasts of blood of the Society of Jesus destroyed Molinos. Father Poulain even repeats the Catholic Truths about Molinos's confession. But Father Poulain is a Jesuit.

At this stage a reviewer wants to get up and stamp such people into pulp. But the hour is not yet, though Ferrer's blood adds its cry to that of his fellow-martyrs. Rather let us consider the good points in Father Poulain's poultice.

He understands the mysticism of his own system fairly well, and his book forms a most useful document in comparative Occultism.

A. C.

THE HAND OF GOD. By GRANT ALLEN.

Grant Allen is always exciting, and this posthumous volume of essays quite keeps up his reputation of being .the G. A. Henty of Rationalism. We remember reading *The Woman who Did* a dozen and more years ago now, shortly after having closed *A Child of the Age*—both in the delightful Keynote Series. And what a difference! Rosy Howlet, a lazy rosebud, a little sweetheart and nothing else, but Herminia Barton—Lower Tooting with a dash of Clement's Inn. "As beneath so above."

HEAVENLY BRIDEGROOMS. By THEODORE SCHROEDER and IDA C——.

This book has been left entirely unedited by Mr Theodore Schroeder, with the exception of a very brief explanatory note. I may say that it is one of the most remarkable human documents ever produced, and it should certainly find a regular publisher in book form. The authoress of the MS. claims that she was the wife of an angel. She expounds at the greatest length the philosophy connected with this thesis. Her learning is enormous. She finds traces of similar beliefs in every country in the world, and (having a similar experience of her own) she can hardly be blamed for arguing that one thing confirms the other. Mr Schroeder is quite logical in calling her paper An Unintentional Contribution to the Erotogenetic Interpretation of Religion, but commits the errors of *petitio principii* and *non distributio medii* with the most exquisite nonchalance. Only a lawyer could be so shameless. He begs the question with regard to this particular case, assuming that her relation with the angel was pure hallucination, of which he has no evidence whatever. He argues that, since one person both loves and is religious, religion is nothing but a morbid manifestation of the sexual instinct. One does not have even to disagree with him to see how worthless is his reasoning. As a matter of fact, I do half agree with him in my calmer moments in a general way, but the conclusion can be carried a step further. When you have proved that God is merely a name for the sex instinct, it appears to me not far to the perception that the sex instinct is God.

This particular MS. is absolutely sane in every line. The fact that the woman committed suicide twelve or fifteen years afterwards is no more against the sanity of the MS. than the suicide of Socrates proves that the *Republic* is merely the lucubration of a lunatic. I am very far from agreeing with all that this most talented woman sets forth in her paper, but she certainly obtained initiated knowledge of extraordinary depth. She seems to have had access to certain most concealed sanctuaries. I should personally be inclined to attribute her suicide rather to the vengeance of the guardians of those palaces than to any more obvious cause. She has put down statements in plain English which are positively staggering. This book is of incalculable value to every student of occult matters. No Magick library is complete without it.

BAPHOMET

THE HISTORY OF A SOUL. By GEORGE RAFFALOVICH.

This admirable study of a modern temperament, a thoughtful and generous mind at sea in the whirl of these new forces, so difficult to understand at all, so impossible to rate at their real value is a monument of our late colleague's earlier manner.

The book is almost as abstract as Kant, more abstract than Erewhon. Mr Raffalovich when he wrote this had not that lightning flash, the concentration of infinite light into a single lucid symbol, which distinguishes his later work.

The light is calm and cool. If I had to compare this book to another, I should select one of Jane Austen's; and if it is pointed out that I have never read any of Jane Austen's, I can retort that neither have I read *The History of a Soul.*

ALEISTER CROWLEY

HISTORY OF CHEMISTRY. By SIR EDWARD THORPE, R.P.A. Vol. I.
HISTORY OF ASTRONOMY. By GEORGE FORBES, R.P.A.

Excellent! In every way excellent! After munching through all this heavy pie-crust, we are beginning to feel like little Jack Horner when he pulled out the plum. If only schools would adopt these most interesting little histories, in place of cramming a lot of ridiculous formulae and equations down children's throats, they might become places where time is not altogether wasted.

Twenty years ago I remember learning some two hundred chemical formulae, the only two which I can remember now being H_2S, because I emptied a bottle into my tutor's desk, and H_2SO_4, because I poured some on his chair to see if it would turn his trousers red, with the result that what lived beneath mine turned very pink shortly after he had discovered who the miscreant was. How I should have learnt to love Chemistry instead of hating it, if I had been taught from Sir Edward Thorpe's little book! There is more elementary education in chapter iv—The Philosopher's Stone—than ever I learnt in five years with Newth and Thompson; and after all, should not school teach us to love knowledge instead of hating it? should not school teach us the pretty little fables of great men's lives that we can use them in our conversation afterwards, rather than scores of musty dry-as-dust facts, which can only help us to pass dry-as-dust and useless examinations?

Give us more of these, Mr Watts, dozens more, and we will forgive you *From the Shades*. Best wishes to these little volumes, may you sell a million of each, but "in the sunlight," please.

A. QUILLER

HISTORY OF CHEMISTRY. By SIR EDWARD THORPE. Vol. II.

As excellent as vol. I. What is Sir Edward doing amongst this brainy goody lot?

H_2S

HISTORY OF OLD TESTAMENT CRITICISM. By ARCHIBALD DUFF, D.D.

An interesting little volume, as complete as can be expected for 146 pages. Duff, D.D., does not understand the Qabalah. We can assure him it is not a "fancied philosophy wherein everything was in reality brand new," as Zunz says. He does not understand it, but he is not alone in this. Few understand the Qabalah; and therefore few talk sense about the Pentateuch. We recommend Duff, D.D., to study "A Note on Genesis" in Vol. I, No. 2, *The Equinox*, after which if he still considers it "fancied" we shall be ready to discuss it with him.

B. Rashith

How to Sing a Song. By Yvette Guilbert.

It is commonplace that Yvette Guilbert is the greatest artist of her period. It is a tragedy that her art happens to be ephemeral. The poignancy of such a realization is like that which one feels in the eternal Greek which Synge re-awakened in the wild Western world. I am thinking of *Riders to the Sea.* Experience dulls us; words are prostituted in the brothel of life. In *Riders to the Sea,* Synge says merely, "A man was drowned." His genius sweeps away the cobwebs which time spins over the door of the cavern of our imagination. We realize the meaning of those words, "A man was drowned."

This power to make us feel is the divine thing in art. It is the creative force which answers "Yea" to the prophet's cynical, "Lord, shall these dead bones live?" Now this is exactly what Yvette Guilbert has done for song. She has not done it for one century only. She has made all time speak, give up its secret, to those who are capable to live in that divine air of the spirit which magazines, cocktails, and automobiles so easily pollute.

I see in Yvette Guilbert not only an artist in the ordinary sense of the word, but an artist like Blake. Her preface on Time might have come from a Book of Ecclesiastes written by Solomon in the period before that in which he could not do it any more. Vanity of vanities? Contemptuously Yvette Guilbert replies, "Does life ever stop?"

I am not a singer. The technique of music is to me a mournful mystery. Yet in reading this book I find a thousand splendid counsels valid for all art. This book is more than "How to sing a song." It is a philosophical treatise on How to do anything. The arts are one. There is nothing but creation. As it is written, Love is the law, love under will. It is apprehension of this fact that makes artistry of any sort possible. It explains why there are no artists in America, or at least the most we can say is, "Finger of birth-strangled babe, Ditch-delivered by a drab," the only decent ingredient in the cauldron of bourgeoisie gone mad.

It is impossible to go into details with regard to this book. In every page Yvette Guilbert unconsciously reveals her unique greatness. Her brain is great enough to comprehend the minutiae of technique without in the smallest degree forgetting the fact that technique is absolutely worthless without genius. America is full of technicians, and I suspect that a number of geniuses are born. But the genius is strangled before he can acquire technique, and the technician unfortunately is not strangled at all. But any one who wants to do something worth doing and go to prison, should sleep with this book under his pillow, if he has a pillow.

ALEISTER CROWLEY

THE HUMAN CHORD. BY ALGERNON BLACKWOOD.

If we were right in suggesting as we did in September, that Mr Edgar Jepson had stolen fire from Mr Blackwood, we must now admit that Mr Blackwood has got more than even For *The Human Chord* has a plot so like that of *No. 19* that we can hardly help thinking that Mr Blackwood must have been studying the methods of William Somerset Maugham, Esq., M.D. In both books we have a lonely place, and a strong man of the magician type, and the beautiful young lady, and the nice young gentleman, who agree after a little experience that it is much better to give up any aspiration higher than that of checking race suicide. Even the incidents in *The Human Chord* suggest *No. 19*. The horrible creature coming out of the dark is very like Mr Blackwood's personified sounds, and the final smash-up is of very much the same type. Mr Blackwood's other sources are the Qabalah, which he appears to have taken from the preface to Mathers, and if he had only added to his library a shilling handbook on sound, he would have avoided some of the more absurd blunders. The distinguishing difference between *No. 19* and *The Human Chord,* is that Edgar Jepson is a first-rate story-teller, while Algernon Blackwood is suffering from indigestion brought on by a surfeit of ill-cooked Theosophy. The theories spring up and choke the narrative, and it becometh unfruitful.

GEORGOS

INDIA AND THE FUTURE. By WILLIAM ARCHER.

Mr Archer has been through India, I should judge for as much as six weeks, with a typewriter and a provincial third-rate mind. Edmund Burke said:

"This multitude of men does not consist of an abject and barbarous population. ... (They are) a people for ages civilized and cultivated; cultivated by all the arts of polished life while we were yet in the woods."

This obvious fact is not obvious to Mr Archer. Like the clever journalist he is, he has documented himself with so many facts that he does not tell us that Indians are negroes, who throw their children to crocodiles, but on every page one can feel that he cherishes this view in his pate. His method of investigating India is the method of Count Smorltork; but Count Smorltork was a gentleman. His point of view is so ignorant and so bourgeois, that I am forced to quote passages, lest it should not be believed that any biped could print such rottenness.

"This senseless reduplication to infinity of one mincing, prancing figure produces an indescribably nightmare-like effect; and what can be said for it, from the point of view either of art or of religion, I, for my part, cannot conceive. Who the figures represent I am not sure; . . . "

"Yes, the horror—that is the only word for it. I do not mean that nowadays any particular horrors are perpetrated in the grim recesses of these giant fanes. I do not know that at any time they were the scenes of great cruelty or other abominations, though certainly they present the completest *mise-en-scène* for such excesses. What I do know is that, from the corner-stone to the coping of the highest *gopura*, they are the product of gloomy, perverted, morbidly overwrought imaginations, revelling in the most extravagant features of the most monstrous of all mythologies."

This is all that Mr Archer gets from the greatest temple, both from an artistic and religious standpoint, that is alive to-day. And in order that he may write himself down an ass for all to see, he is stupid enough to publish photographs of temples, whose beauty would, one thinks, be evident even to the bovine readers to whom he doubtless appeals.

Mr Archer's arrogance is equal to his ignorance.

"And on every hand, in its swarming courts and alcoves, you see the lowest fetishism intent in its grovelling rites."

How does this animal know what the people were doing? He could not speak a word of their language. He was seeing them for the first time, and his criticisms are just as valuable as would be those of a savage who dropped in on a telephone exchange. The wretched creature keeps on, page after page:

"Barbarian, barbarism, barbarous—I am sorry to harp so much on these words. But they express the essence of the situation."

"There never was a 'great civilization' in India . . . "

With the monuments of Indian civilization actually intact, yet the oldest of them in ruins a thousand years, two thousand years, three thousand years, who knows, before the savages of England wore clothes, it is only natural that this poor blind, globe-trotting hag should fail to understand Caste. He utterly ignores the fact that it is the caste system which has preserved Indian civilization. Constantly conquered, India absorbs her conquerors.

When the fool gets on to the spirituality, he is funnier than ever. On page 59, he gives a curiously imperfect account of the names of Hindu sacred writings, and apologizes for himself in the following note:

"I trust there is no gross error in this paragraph; but very confusing explanations are given of the nomenclature of this literature."

He then proceeds to criticise the contents of those books! It is incredible that any one can be such an ass as to write the stuff that one finds in this book. Page after page of misstatement and misunderstanding. He is even unable to see a thing like the good manners of the natives. In all the time I was in India I do not recall a single instance of bad manners, except on the part of Babus who had learned them from low-class Europeans, like William Archer.

When he comes to talk of art and culture, it gets worse, if anything.

"Remember—it is certainly not irrelevant—that India is the most tropical country that ever possessed any art of importance."

This person has never heard of Cambodia, Yucatan, Peru, Egypt, West Africa, Java. His art criticism is beneath the depth of Upper Tooting.

"Can any unprejudiced observer deny that even these exceptionally favourable specimens of Indian workmanship are marred by the gravest effects of conventionality in form, of overcrowding in composition, of excess in ornament? In a few seated female figures, viewed from behind, there is a certain natural grace, but most of the women who swarm all over the reliefs are the product of a morbid convention which gives them enormous breasts, wasp waists, and atrophied legs, and places them in attitudes suggestive of a violent dislocation of the hipjoint. Whether such figures were actually cultivated at the period, I do not know; but even if this could be proved, the sculptures could only be regarded as conventional exaggerations of an unhealthy fashion."

"Finally, and coming back to the Buddha-figures in particular, what are we to say of the marvellous spirituality of expression often attributed to them? It is to me, I own, far from apparent. The drooped eyelids, and the immobile pose do, indeed, express the idea of contemplation; but I am at a loss to find anything spiritual in the smooth, insipid faces."

Pig-mindedness can hardly go further. And yet—

"In the Indian epics, the poets are always trying to outdo themselves and each other in their search for the marvellous, whether in virtue, prowess, gorgeousness, wickedness, demoniacal fury, or mere numerical extravagance. They are constantly creating records in exaggeration, which are as constantly broken. What wonder that a people habituated from childhood to these orgies of unbridled fancy should suffer from a certain slackening of imaginative fibre, an insensitiveness to normal and wholesome stimulation? It is that insensitiveness which seems to me to account for all that is worst in Indian art. It is that insensitiveness which will have to be corrected before India can hope to make the best of her intellectual gifts in a world in which, though all may be illusory, the God-made illusion of Nature must in the end prevail over the man-made illusions of mythology and metaphysics."

I am perfectly in accord with the political conclusion of this book. He was doubtless paid to write it in this

interest. However, I had no idea that Mr William Archer
was such an unpleasant thing. The publisher says that he
was born at Perth, Scotland. Perhaps, he was one of the
famous "twin brothers of Perth, who were—ready to
exhibit a positive Wassermann—to the eyes from their
birth. Said Bill to his brother, "Well, thanks to our mother,
we're the rottenest beggars on earth.' "

THE INFERNO. By AUGUST STRINDBERG. Translated by
CLAUD FIELD.

I have already had to speak to publishers about cheap
production. In this case I must protest emphatically
against the employment of a translator who makes a
solecism nearly every time he touches Paris.

E.g. "northern railway station" for "Gare du Nord,"
"Lilas brewery" for "Closerie des Lilas," "St Martin's
Gate" for "Porte St Martin," "Rue de Fleurs" for "Rue
des Fleurs," "racecourse" for some unindicated part of
the Jardin du Luxembourg, "churchyard" of Mont-
parnasse for "cemetery," "exhibition of independent
artists" for "Salon des Independents," "Bullier's dancing
saloon" for "Bal Bullier," "Lyons Bank" for "Credit Lyon-
nais," "St Germaine des Pres" for "St Germain des
Pres," "Dr Popus" for "Dr Papus," "Rue de Madame"
for "Rue Madame," and so on.

He puts the same place-name—first in translation, then
in French, again and again; and as often as not gets both
wrong!

The constant chemical absurdities are perhaps Strindberg's own and may have been made intentionally, as the
book portrays the ravings of a melancholic with delusions
of persecution.

What sublime and septuple ass calls this Strindberg's
autobiography? Strindberg was too lazy to find his incidents in other people's lives; that is all.

And yet we find the translator note at the end: "Strindberg never actually entered the Roman Church"!

The book is a perfect clinical picture of a typical case. Chapter I describes the irritability, the fantastic dreams. He imagines himself a great author, a great chemist. He has found carbon in sulphur; he will make gold.

In Chapter II he begins to see omens in simple incidents, receives "warnings" from strangers, finds a plot against him at his hotel, notices remarkable resemblances between his neighbours and some of his "persecutors."

Chapter III develops the persecution-delusions. Roaring in the ears, electric shocks, and other physical symptoms develop. The bedstead has knobs like those of a Leyden jar, the spring mattress suggests induction coils, and so on—to the end!

For refuge he ranges from Papus to Swedenborg, and ultimately, as his mental disease increases on him, he clutches at such straws as Péladan, Annie Besant, and the Church of Rome.

In this dementia the book ends. But Strindberg did not end. He went his cheerful and polygamous way as a free-thinker. Persons who pretend otherwise are liars, probably hired liars—unless, of course, they are Englishmen, who are such natural-born fools in all matters of the soul that they not only require no bribe to lie, but can hardly be paid to see truth.

Until Strindberg's life is utterly dissociated from his art, the latter will not be truly valued.

A. C.

An Interpretation of Genesis. By Theodore Powys.

This is a most mystical interpretation of the most beautiful of the books of the Old Testament. It consists of a dialogue between the Lawgiver of Israel and Zetetes, who is not exactly the disciple, but rather the Interpreter of the Master's words. Thus it commences:

The Law-giver of Israel:

"In the beginning the Truth created the heaven and the earth."

Zetetes:

"The life that is within and the life that is without, are not these the heaven and the earth that the Truth created?"

Whether the author intends to weave into his interpretation the doctrines of the Qabalah we are not certain, but time after time we came across curious allusions. Thus on p. 3: "Within myself when the truth divided the light from the darkness wisdom arose . . . and I knew that every atom of our great Mother giveth light to other atoms. . . ." P. 4: "The truth in man is the light of the world. This we have known from the beginning, and we shall know it unto the end . . . and the Mother gave unto man her breasts. And man guided by the light within him did eat and was glad." P. 6: "The tree of Life belongeth unto the Father, it groweth in the Mother, but because darkness is still in man he may not eat thereof, but the Truth of the Father that is within man, that Truth may eat and live."

The philosophy of this little book shows that Darkness alone is not evil, and that neither is Light good. Both are beyond: but the mingling twilight begets the illusion of duality, the goodness and wickedness of things external.

It is a little volume which one who reads will grow fond of, and will carry about with him, and open at random in quiet places, in the woods, and under the stars; and it is a little book which one learns to love the more one reads it, for it is inspired by one who at least has crept into the shadow of God's Glory.

J. F. C. F.

IN THE NAME OF THE MESSIAH. BY E. A. GORDON.

The only way to read this book is to run at it, shouting

a slogan, and to stick a skean dhuibh in it somewhere and read the sentence it hits. Thus, perhaps, with perseverance and a lot of luck, one may find a coherent paragraph in the porridge of disconnected drivel, defaced with italics and capitals and inverted commas like a schoolgirl's letter.

And this is the coherent paragraph.

"There are 3 apocryphal descriptions of the man Christ Jesus. . . . All *agree* in describing Him as 'strikingly tall,' '6 ft. high,' and with curled or wavy locks.

"This, to my mind, establishes the Identity of the Daibutsu with the curl-covered head and colossal stature."

This, to my mind, establishes the Identity of Mrs Gordon with Mr J. M. Robertson.

A. C.

INTRODUCTION TO PHILOSOPHY. By OSWALD KULPE.

An excellent introduction to formal Philosophy, explaining clearly the distinctions between the various schools that at present hold the field. The author is extremely calm and impartial as a rule, but in his denunciation of materialism he shows that a passionate human heart throbs in the breast of one who seems to the harsh gaze of the sceptic to be a formalist and a schoolman.

I commend the book to all those who wish to understand the tendencies of philosophy in the universities of to-day.

A word of praise is due to Mr Titchener. He has again performed satisfactorily his difficult task of translation.

V. B. NEUBURG.

AN INTRODUCTION TO THE KABALAH. By W. WYNN WESTCOTT.

It is difficult to find words in which to praise this little book. It is most essential for the beginner. Lucid and illuminating, it is also illuminated. In particular, we are most pleased to find the correlation of the Qabalah with the philosophical doctrines of other religions; a task attempted by ourselves in *Berashith* and *777*, perhaps not so successfully from the point of view of the beginner.

There is of course much beyond this elementary study, and the neophyte will find nothing in the book which he does not know; but the book is addressed to those who know nothing. It will supply them with a fine basis for Qabalistic research.

ALEISTER CROWLEY

IS A WORLD-RELIGION POSSIBLE? By DAVID BALSILLIE, M.A.

Mr Balsillie does not seem to realise the immensity of his subject. I remember once at school, in a general knowledge paper, being asked to give "a short account of the Equator." Frankly, I funked the task, but another spirit, more bold, stated that it was nicknamed "the line" and sailors play jokes in crossing it! That is just Mr Balsillie's attitude. For my own part I would even dare to speak disrespectfully of the Equator rather than dismiss the vast subject of a World-Religion in 180 pages, a large number of which are taken up with the practical jokes of such comic mariners in deep water as Mr Myers and the Rev. R. J. Campbell.

NORMAN ROE

Balsillie for short?—A. C.

JOHN DEE. By CHARLOTTE FELL SMITH.

It is only gracious to admit that this book is as good as could possibly have been produced on the subject—the publishers are cordially invited to quote the last fourteen words, and now I can finish my sentence—by a person totally ignorant of the essence thereof.

Dee was an avowed magician; Miss Smith is an avowed intellectual prig. So she can find nothing better to do than to beg the whole question of the validity of Dee's "actions," and that although she admits that the *Book of Enoch* is unintelligible to her. Worse, she retails the wretched slanders about me current among those who envied me. I was certainly "wanted" for coining. I happened to have found the trick of making gold at a very early age, but had not the sense to exploit it properly; and when I got any sense I got more sense than to waste time in such follies. The slander that I deluded Dee is as baseless. Again and again I tried to break with him, to show him how utterly unreliable it all was. Only his more than paternal kindness for me kept me with him. God rest him; I hear he has been reincarnated as W. T. Stead.

For one thing I do most seriously take blame, that my training was too strong for my power to receive spiritual truth. For when the Holy Angels came to instruct me in the great truths, that there is no sin, that the soul passes from house to house, that Jesus was but man, that the Holy Ghost was not a person, I rejected them as false. Ah! have I not paid bitterly for the error? Still, the incarnation was not all loss; not only did I attain the Grade of Major Adept, but left enough secret knowledge (in an available form) to carry me on for a long while. I am getting it back now; with luck I'll be a Magister Templi soon, if I can only get rid of my giant personality. You may say, by the way, that this is hardly a review of a book on my old master, silly old josser! Exactly; I never cared a dump for him. He was just a text for my sermon then; and so he is now.   EDWARD KELLEY

KANT'S ETHICS AND SCHOPENHAUER'S CRITICISM. By M. KELLY.

Last year we had the pleasure of reviewing Major

Kelly's *Kant's Philosophy as Rectified by Schopenhauer,* and we hope that if in the future further volumes are to appear, and if they are as interesting as the present one, we may "continue the motion."

Kant's categories are in type similar to the Sephiroth of the Qabalah emanations from an unknown "x" sign or God, and whether this sign is called "à priori," "autonomy" or "categorical affirmative" matters no whit. Kant's ethics are futile, and to an intellect like Schopenhauer's absolutely childish. Kant never could understand "morality" because he never transcended the reason, practically, or even theoretically. If there is a moral law in the Formative World it is probably the line of least resistance. But the proof of the pudding is in the eating, and fixed laws of heteronomy and of autonomy are absurd, and if Kant had once transcended the Reason he would have had direct experience of this fact. On p. 126 Schopenhauer sets him right as follows:

"The essence of the world is will.... The only way of salvation is by negation of the will, or by self-denial and renunciation...."

And again:

"... life is the attainment of self-consciousness, in order that the will may acquire a right knowledge of its own nature...." (p. 157)

"Evil and pleasure are but different manifestations of the one will to live." (p. 177)

"The tormentor and the tormented are one.... Therefore what is good for one person may be just the opposite for another ... all suffering is nothing but unfulfilled or crossed willing." (pp. 178–182)

"When a man has so far got rid of this veil that it no longer causes an egoistical distinction between his own person and that of another, he will recognize his innermost and true self in all beings, regard their endless suffering as his own, and so appropriate to himself the pain of the whole world." (p. 184)

Here the "true-self" is the Higher Self, Atman or Augoeides, unity with which is what we have called the Great Work of the A .·. A .·..

When a soldier turns philosopher we always expect good work, and Major Kelly has not failed us; and to all such as would understand Kant as well as Schopenhauer's great work, *The World as Will and Idea*—of which an excellent English translation is published by Messrs. Paul, Trench, Trübner, we heartily recommend this masterful little volume.

F.

KANT'S PHILOSOPHY AS RECTIFIED BY SCHOPENHAUER. By M. KELLY, M.D.

This excellent little book by Major Kelly sums up in a few pages, concisely enough, the greater portion of Kant's philosophy; the only difficulty is to tell where Kant ends and where Major Kelly and Schopenhauer begin. Further, it is interesting reading, which is more than we can say of most recent works dealing with the Königsberg philosopher; except, however, two, which, as it happens, are also written by soldiers, viz., Captain William Bell McTaggart's *Absolute Relativism,* and Captain J. F C. Fuller's *Star in the West.* This work, however, more than these two, which only deal with Kant *en passant,* shows him to be, as we have always considered him, the wild Irishman of Teutonic thought, who recklessly gallops at the philosophic hurdles set up by the seventeenth-century and early eighteenth-century philosophers. Some of these he clears skilfully enough, others he crashes through and shouts *à priori,* little seeing that these innate intuitions of his are but abstractions from experience—"inherited experiences," as Herbert Spencer has since shown—without furthering the solution of the problem "What is Existence?"

In fact, in many ways Kant may be said to be the eighteenth-century Spencer, and much more so than Spencer can be said to be the nineteenth-century Kant. He succeeded Berkeley and Hume, just as Spencer succeeded Hegel and Fichte; but, like the great transfigured realist, only ultimately and unconsciously to be overthrown by the very questions he fondly imagined he had explained away. Nevertheless he answered these questions so astutely that it has taken the whole of the nineteenth century to explain what he meant! This Major Kelly indirectly, if not directly, points out by attempting to rectify the Transcendental Aesthetics Analytic and Dialectic by the critical and idealistic pantheism of Schopenhauer. Interesting as this is, it would have indeed added further to the value of this little book had Major Kelly added a chapter dealing with the philosophy of Kant from to-day's critical standpoint, instead of halting with Schopenhauer's extension of the same. Had he done so he would scarcely have asserted, as he does (or is it Kant or Schopenhauer?), that from the law of Causality results the important *à priori* corollary "that Matter can neither be created nor destroyed" (p. 35). If, however, it can be destroyed, as Gustave le Bon has attempted to prove, what becomes of the *à priority* of Causality? Nay, further, of the *à priority* of the Transcendental Aesthetic itself—of Time and of Space, the fundamental sensual perceptions of Kant's system? Must we agree with the learned author of *The Star in the West,* that Kant, after having for a hundred years lost his way in "the night of Hume's ignorance," has at length fallen victim to his own verbosity, and has indeed sadly scorched "his fundamental basis"?

THE KEY TO THE TAROT. By A. E. WAITE.

Mr Waite has written a book on fortune-telling, and we advise servant-girls to keep an eye on their half-crowns. We have little sympathy or pity for the folly of fashionable women; but housemaids need protection—hence their affection for policemen and soldiers—and we fear that Mr Waite's apologies will not prevent professional cheats from using his instructions for their frauds and levies of blackmail.

As to Mr Waite's constant pomposities, he seems to think that the obscurer his style and the vaguer his phrases, the greater initiate will he appear.

Nobody but Mr Waite knows *all* about the Tarot, it appears; and he won't tell. Reminds one of the story about God and Robert Browning, or of the student who slept, and woke when the professor thundered rhetorically, "And what *is* Electricity?" The youth jumped up and cried (from habit), "I know, sir." "Then tell us." "I *knew*, sir, but I've forgotten." "Just my luck!" complained the professor, "there was only one man in the world who knew—and he has forgotten!"

Why, Mr Waite, your method is not even original.

When Sri Mahatma Agamya Paramahansa Guru Swamiji (late of H. M. Prisons, thanks to the unselfish efforts of myself and a friend) was asked, "And what of the teaching of Confucius?"—or any one else that the boisterous old boy had never heard of—he would reply contemptuously, "Oh, him? He was my disciple." And seeing the hearer smile would add, "Get out, you dog, you a friend of that dirty fellow Crowley. I beat you with my shoe. Go away! Get intellect! Get English!" until an epileptic attack supervened.

Mr Waite, like Marie Corelli, in this as in so many other respects, brags that he cares nothing for criticism, so he won't mind my making these little remarks, and I may as well go on. He has "betrayed" (to use his own words) the attributions of some of the small cards, and Pamela Coleman Smith has done very beautiful and sympathetic designs, though our own austerer taste would have preferred the plain cards with their astrological and other attributions, and occult titles. (These are all published in the book 777, and a pack could be easily constructed by hand. Perhaps we may one day publish one at a shilling a time!) But Mr Waite has not "betrayed" the true attributions of the Trumps. They are obvious, though, the moment one has the key (see 777). Still, Pamela Coleman Smith has evidently been hampered; her designs are cramped and forced. I am infinitely sorry for any artist who tries to draw after dipping her hands in the gluey dogma of so insufferable a dolt and prig.

Mr Waite, I believe, is perfectly competent to produce indefinite quantities of Malted Milk to the satisfaction of all parties; but when it comes to getting the pure milk of the Word, Mr Waite gets hold of a wooden cow.

And do for God's sake, Arthur, drop your eternal hinting, hinting, hinting, "Oh what an exalted grade I have, if you poor dull uninitiated people would only perceive it!"

Here is your criticism, Arthur, straight from the shoulder.

Any man that knows Truth and conceals it is a traitor to humanity; any man that doesn't know, and tries to conceal his ignorance by pretending to be the guardian of a secret, is a charlatan.

Which is it?

We recommend every one to buy the pack, send Mr Waite's book to the kitchen so as to warn the maids, throw the Major Arcana out of window, and play bridge with the Minor Arcana, which alone are worth the money asked for the whole caboodle.

The worst of it all is: Mr Waite really does know a bit
in a muddled kind of way; if he would only go out of the
swelled-head business he might be some use.

But if you are not going to tell your secrets, it is down-
right schoolboy brag to strut about proclaiming that you
possess them.

Au revoir, Arthur.

ALEISTER CROWLEY

It is an awkward situation for any initiate to edit knowledge concerning which he is bound to secrecy. This is
the fundamental objection to all vows of this kind. The
only possible course for an honest man is to preserve
absolute silence.

Thus, to my own knowledge Mr Waite is an initiate
(of a low grade) and well aware of the true attribution of
the Tarot. Now, what I want to know is this: is Mr Waite
breaking his obligation and proclaiming himself (to quote
the words of his own Oath) "a vile and perjured wretch,
void of all moral worth, and unfit for the society of all
upright and just persons," and liable in addition to "the
awful and just penalty of submitting himself voluntarily
to a deadly and hostile current of will . . . by which he
should fall slain or paralysed as if blasted by the lightning
flash"—or, is he selling to the public information which
he knows to be inexact?

When this dilemma is solved, we shall feel better able
to cope with the question of the Art of Pamela Coleman
Smith.

Π.

THE LIFE OF JOHN DEE. Translated from the Latin of
DR THOMAS SMITH by WM. ALEXR. AYTON.

Wm. Alexr. Ayton's preface to this book deserves a
better subject than Dr Thomas Smith's *Life of John Dee*,
which is as dreary dull as a life crammed so full of in-

cidents could be made. In fact, if Dr Smith had collected all Dr Dee's washing bills and printed them in Hebrew, the result would scarcely have been more oppressive; anyhow it would have been as interesting to read of how many handkerchiefs the famous seer used when he had a cold as to ponder over the platitudes of this rheumy old leech.

Never since reading *Bothwell* and *Who's Who* have we read such ponderous and pedantic pedagogics. The translator in his preface informs us that Moses and Solomon were adepts; verily hast thou spoke, but thou, Wm. Alexr. Ayton, art greater than either, to have survived such a leaden task as this of putting Dr Smith's bad Latin into good English; at the completion of it you must have felt like Jacob when "he gathered up his feet into the bed, and yielded up the ghost!"

THE LOST VALLEY. BY ALGERNON BLACKWOOD.

It is the penalty of factitious success that the need of fuel increases like the dose of a drug-fiend. Instead of clothing his wit with silk from the loom of life and embroidering it with gold thread drawn from the observation of things around him, the slave of popularity wears it threadbare. Morphia won't replace bread after the first month or so!

Now we see Mr Blackwood and Nemesis. He gets a reputation by marketing his tiny scrap of knowledge of the Inner World; the public cries out for more, and the poor wage-slave, bankrupt in invention, does his best to fake—and fails.

It is the male equivalent of the harlot who has drifted from Piccadilly to Waterloo Bridge Road.

So here we see him, the shy smile changed to the open coarse appeal, the tawdry apparatus of his craft seen for what it is—rabbit-skin ermine!—and himself unmistakably the fifth-rate writer, like Baudelaire's "Old Mountebank"—surely no more pitiful—tumbling for no kindlier laugh than that of contempt. (And he might have been so fine!)

This is why success must in the nature of things spoil everybody. Make a hit with one arrow; you must never dare to do more than change the colour of the feathers— till your quiver is empty.

And how empty is Mr Blackwood's! When it comes to a father hating his twin sons because (why?) he wanted one son very badly, going mad, and after his death turning the two into one in spite of a clergyman's reading aloud of Job——

Well, hang it, Mr Blackwood, the woman has the best of it yet. It is a very foolish girl who cannot hold her own for ten years. But you who have been writing hardly half the time are only fit for the Literary Lock Hospital.

JONATHAN HUTCHINSON, Natu Minimus

THE MADMAN, HIS PARABLES AND POEMS. By KAHLIL GIBRAN.

I do not much care for the drawings in this book. They are messy, and rather conventional. But I like some of the parables very much indeed. It is not very sensible to compare Mr Gibran with Blake, because Blake was a genius whose every act was wrought from the white heat of passion. This is a smaller fish swimming in shallower and calmer waters. The spirit is more French than Irish. However, he is short enough to speak for himself. Here is one of his parables:

THE SCARECROW

Once I said to a scarecrow, "You must be tired of standing in this lonely field."

And he said, "The joy of scaring is a deep and lasting one, and I never tire of it."

Said I, after a minute of thought, "It is true; for I too have known that joy."

Said he, "Only those who are stuffed with straw can know it."

Then I left him, not knowing whether he had complimented or belittled it.

A year passed, during which the scarecrow turned philosopher.

And when I passed by him again I saw two crows building a nest under his hat.

Here is another:

THE NEW PLEASURE

Last night I invented a new pleasure, and as I was giving it the first trial an angel and a devil came rushing toward my house. They met at my door and fought with each other over my newly created pleasure; the one crying, "It is a sin!"—the other, "It is a virtue!"

Good boy!

A. C.

THE MAGNETIC MIRROR. By DR CAROLUS REX.

This little work is very skilfully written; it is intended to induce members of the higher grades of the Universal Order of B .·. F .·. to pay "Dr" "Carolus" "Rex" sums of from Two to Twenty Guineas for "Magic Mirrors," which we hope are worth as many pence.

PROFESSOR JACOBUS IMPERATOR

TO MALISE AND OTHER POEMS. By AELFRIDA TILLYARD.

A volume of sonnets, serious and not so serious—the serious portraying spiritual yearning with impelling earnestness and artistic imagery, and brimful of human sentiment. Through these poems runs the palpitating thrill of womanhood in its highest sense, refined, idealistic and restrained, as witness "A Poem to an Unborn Child."

These eighty pages of serious moods have the merit of a lightness and freshness which could never bore, even if one did not agree.

The "not so serious" mood will be welcomed by readers blessed, or cursed, with a strain of gentle flippancy in their blood. It would be a misconception to suggest one of these in particular as being indicative of the author's personality. That, for instance, beginning "Would that my songs were sausages" is not to be thought of in this connection, so we quote from the standpoint of a critic—cosmopolitan and humanitarian—namely, the "couplets" for unimaginative young men and maidens standing on the threshold of romance, longing,. but dumb. Here is a real poet ready to help them in simple yet subtle phrase. What more could one want?

A. C. Hobbs

The Maniac. A Realistic Study of Madness from the Maniac's Point of View.

Only maniacs are recommended to read this book; its dulness may bring them to their senses. For the first chapter is like the second, and the second like the third, and the third like the fourth, which almost proves the Athanasian Creed; for all chapters are but one chapter, which is infinitely dull and dismal. In fact this "realistic study" might well have been translated from Dr Thomas Smith's *Life of John Dee*, and goes a long way to prove Mr Stanley Redgrove's theory of concentric infinities.

The heroine is a lady journalist, unmarried, and on the wrong side of thirty—there's the whole tragedy in a nutshell. Stimulating work, and thirty years of an unstimulating life. Cut off the first syllable from "unmarried," and this unfortunate lady, in spite of Karezza and the Order of Melchisedec, would never have imagined that she had been seduced by a fiend, or have afflicted us with her dreary ravings.

Therefore we advise—Marry, my good woman, marry, and if nobody will have you, well then, don't be too particular, for anything is better than a second book like this!

BATHSHEBAH TINA

I found *The Maniac* both entertaining and instructive, a very valuable study of psychology. It is so far as I know the only really illuminating book on madness; and I strongly recommend its perusal to all alienists, psychologists, and members of the grade of Neophyte. It throws an admirable light on the true nature of Obsession and Black Magic.

Two things impressed me in particular. (1) The statement that the arguments held with a patient never reach his consciousness at all, despite his rational answers. This phenomenon is true of my own sane life. I sometimes chat pleasantly to bores for quite a long time without any consciousness that I am doing so. (2) The statement that medical men have no idea of the real contents of a madman's mind. I remember in the County Asylum at Inverness ("Here are the fools, and there are the knaves!" said an inmate, pointing to the city) a man rolling from side to side with an extraordinary regularity and rhythm of swing, emitting a long continuous howl like a wolf. "Last stage of G.P.I." said the doctor; "he feels absolutely nothing." "How interesting!" said I; and thought "How the deuce do you know?" I shall be very glad when it is finally proved and admitted that the consciousness is independent of the senses and the intellect. Hashish phenomena, madness phenomena, magical and mystical phenomena, all prove it; but old Dr Cundum and young Professor Cuspidor, who can neither of them cure a cold in the head, say it isn't so! The "Imbecile Theologians of the Middle Ages" are matched by the imbecile cacologians of our own. I repeat, a very valuable book; a very valuable book indeed.

FRA: O. M.

MAN—KING OF MIND, BODY, AND CIRCUMSTANCE. By JAMES ALLEN.

The important disclosures of this unpretentious volume mark a new epoch in human thought.

Good is better than evil. Bad habits should be broken. Health is more desirable than disease. Happiness gives more happiness than unhappiness does. Work is more useful than idleness. Selfishness is bad; unselfishness is good. Suffering is common. Dwelling upon one's petty troubles and ailments is a manifestation of weakness of character.

The reviewer, staggered by revelations so overwhelming, can only fall upon his knees and burst into a flood of tears.

But think of the chagrin of Lord Avebury!

M. TUPPER

THE MASTER MASON'S HANDBOOK. By BRO. FRED. J. W. CROWE, P.M. 328, 2806; Member Lodge "Quatuor Coronati" 2076, P. Prov. G. Org., Devon, etc., with an Introduction by BRO. W. J. HUGHAN, P.G.D.

A useful guide in the practical details of Freemasonry. On the subject of the serious study of the Order, however, Bro. Crowe is rather pathetic. He refers us to learned Bro. This, and illuminated Bro. That, and instructed Bro. Tother; but orthodox Freemasonry has apparently not yet any adherent who could pass the first standard in a Masonic Board School. E.g. on the apron of the 18° the Monogram of the Eternal is misspelt—blasphemously misspelt. Any Yid from Houndsditch could correct it.

And on the M.W.S. jewel, Jeheshua is usually spelt with a Resh!

> There was a fair Maid of Bombay
> Who was put in an awkward situation, the nature
>   of which it is unnecessary to discuss,
>   By the mate of a lugger,
>   An ignorant Sovereign Prince of Rose Croix
> Who always spelt Jeheshua with a Resh.

Prate not of scholarship, Bro. Crowe!

Such ignorance, when combined with the Satanic Pride to which the possession of an apron with blue silk and silver tassels, value three half-bull! naturally predisposes mankind, leads to presumption, bigotry and intolerance. So we find Bro. Crowe asserting that all other degrees than his own are "spurious and worthless." Go slow, Bro. Crowe!

The intelligence of Freemasons amy be guessed by the level at which they rate that of cowans and eavesdroppers. They print their secret rituals for any one to buy; so far, so good, why shouldn't they? But they print initials and finals of "missing words" which no single reader of *Pearson's Weekly* could miss.

"Advance a short step with your l——t f——t," would not have baffled Edgar Allan Poe!

They are even such b—— f——s—(will they decipher this?—it stands for "bright fellows")—that when by accident they do baffle you—.

"Gives him the P——e, C——w, and S——,"—they print it full in another place, but in the same connection— "The Pickaxe, Crow, and Shovel."

No, Bro. Crowe! Whoa, Bro. Crowe! (Blow Bro. Crowe!—Ed.)

But for all Masons who wish to know the mysteries of how to address a V.W. P. Pres. Brd. G. Pur., and the order of precedence of a Past Assistant Grand Director of Ceremonies, this is the Book.

K. S. I

MATTER, SPIRIT, AND THE COSMOS. By H STANLEY REDGROVE.

> Big fleas have little fleas
> Upon their backs to bite 'em;
> Little fleas have smaller fleas,
> And so *ad infinitum*.

This book consists of reprinted articles from the *Occult Review,* and some of them are quite entrancing, especially chapter i, "On the Doctrine of the Indestructibility of Matter," and chapters v and vi, "On the Infinite" and "On the Fourth Dimension."

In the first chapter Mr Redgrove tries to prove that though matter *cannot* be destroyed, its form can be so utterly changed that it can no longer be treated as such. He illustrates his theory by quoting Sir Oliver Lodge's "knot tied in a bit of string." So long as the knot is, matter is; but when once the knot is untied, though the string remains, the knot vanishes. This, however, is a most fallacious illustration, for, as Gustave le Bon has shown, the destruction of matter implies more than a mere change of "form"; it is an annihilation of gravity itself, and therefore of substance as we understand it. Matter, he shows, goes back unto Equilibrium. But what is Equilibrium? "Nothingness!" this eminent French man of Science declares: "Absolute Nothingness!"

In chapter v the author points out that as there is an infinite series of infinities, to make Space the "absolute infinite" is the merest of assumptions; he follows up this assertion by declaring that each dimension is bounded by a higher. Thus, the Second Dimension is contained in the Third, and so the Third in the Fourth, *ad infinitum*; each dimension being infinite in itself, and yet contained in a higher which is again infinite. Thus we get infinity contained within infinity, just as $\cdot\dot{7}$ is contained in $\cdot\dot{8}$, and $\cdot\dot{8}$ in $\cdot\dot{9}$; and yet $\cdot\dot{7}$ is infinite, and $\cdot\dot{8}$ is infinite and $\cdot\dot{9}$ is infinite, yet there are not three infinites but one infinite, &c.

J. F. C. F.

MAURICE MAETERLINCK. Par GÉRARD HARVEY.

I hope I shall find a Gérard Harvey at the Day of Judgment. There is none of that nasty carping spirit which spoils so many sunny natures. When the great Maurice dines alone, it is his almost monachal asceticism; when he has company, it is his genial bonhomie. He smokes—how brave of him; but of course it is denicotinised tobacco—how prudent of him! He sometimes sleeps alone—the modern Galahad; and sometimes with somebody else—"even his Heinesque moods are steeled through with a strong man's virility." In short, Dr Pangloss was indeed the greatest of philosophers—until Gérard Harvey wiped the floor with him.

A. L.

MEISTER ECKHART'S SERMONS   Translated by CLAUDE FIELD, M.A.

Too pedantic and theological to please me, though I daresay he means well.

THE MESSAGE OF PSYCHIC SCIENCE TO THE WORLD. By MARY EVEREST BOOLE.

Dull tosh.

A MODERN READING OF SAINT FRANCIS OF ASSISI. By KATHERINE COLLINS.

Not bad; might start somebody inquiring how to acquire the Cosmic Consciousness.

MY PSYCHIC RECOLLECTIONS. BY MARY DAVIES.
Just when I had given up hope, Mary Davies comes
to make a third to myself and Geo. Washington.
For on p. 2 she says, "More than forty years ago ... I
was a girl of seven years old."
This storms the citadel of confidence, and pulls out the
back teeth of the Dragon Doubt. I was therefore prepared
to believe anything she might say.
And accordingly we get a simple, charming, old-
fashioned motherly book, full of kindly thought and real
piety; that it may have no objective value for the S.P.R.
is quite unimportant for the class of readers whom it is
intended to reach.
Mrs Davies is a "professional medium"; of such I have
said things which only my incapacity for invective prevented from being severe. But though (no doubt) the
phenomena recorded in this book are "non-evidential,"
I do feel the sincerity of the writer. I am confident of her
good faith

DIOGENES

THE MYSTERY OF EXISTENCE. BY CHARLES WICKSTEED
ARMSTRONG.
Ne pedagogus ultra flagellum—for Mr Armstrong is a
schoolmaster. All he does is to rearrange other people's
prattle; and anyhow, I can't read him.
He writes "Carlisle" for "Carlyle," "future" when
he means "later," and believes in castrating anybody
who disagrees with him. Pp. 94, 123, and 114 respectively.

MYSTICISM. EVELYN UNDERHILL.
This lengthy treatise upon the simplest of subjects is
more free from pedantry and theological bias than was
perhaps to be expected. It is very complete in its way as
regards Christian mysticism; but the attempt to restrict

the term mysticism to Christian mysticism must fail. It is indeed self-destructive. To exclude the authors of the *Bhagavadgita, The Voice of the Silence, Konx Om Pax,* and the *Tao Teh King* is to exclude by implication St Teresa. To deny Crowley is to deny Christ. Similarly, the attempt to define Magic in terms contrary to its tradition, is sectarian folly. I may disagree with Huxley, but I shall not confute him by saying that he was a bigoted opponent of Evolution.

Roosevelt, in calling Thomas Paine a dirty little Atheist, when he was demonstrably a clean tall Deist, established only the record for falsehood. Mr (or Mrs or Miss?) Evelyn Underhill does the same thing when he abuses the Magi by attributing to them the doctrines and practices of sorcerers. And we think that his sense of awe misleads him in one respect. The Buddha, the Christ, and He whom some of us know as Frater Perdurabo, were all men before they became lost in the Infinity of what some call the One, others the All, others the Naught; and their documents are accessible. These documents are of immeasurably greater value than the lesser writings of the mediaeval saints. In fact, this word mediaeval is of use to us in describing Evelyn Underhill's state of mind. He, she, or it is rather narrow, vastly learned and curiously ignorant, capable of seeing far from within, utterly incapable of seeing an inch from without, a bit of a heresy-hunter and so on. It is clear that the mystic vision even is not his, or how could he remain sectarian? Had he only enough imagination to think of the earth as seen from Cor Scorpionis, all such diatribes would seem infinitely petty. We may splutter about with our little verbal fireworks, as I am doing now; but to take it seriously! "There's nothing serious in mortality;" God is All in All. The Universe is but a mote playing in that sunbeam; why bother to fill 600 dull pages? Nothing is worth writing but literature. Art is the expression of divine Truth; Mr Underhill, being no artist, expresses only human error.

CANDLESTICK

NATURE'S HELP TO HAPPINESS. By JOHN WARREN ACHORN, M.D.

This is the best book ever written on health. Go out and hold naked Nature to your breast; and you will be well.

You sleep in or you sleep out, as luck will have it; sometimes you get food, and sometimes not; it's no odds; you are one with Nature, and find that Nature is one with God.

This is my own practice; every time London can spare me I put on my climbing things and take nothing else but a supply of strong tobacco and a few pounds. Then I think of some place that sounds interesting—Madrid or Fiesole or Timbuktu—and walk there.

When I get back I am strong enough even for book-reviewing.

Go thou and do likewise!

ALEISTER CROWLEY

NEW EVIDENCES IN PSYCHICAL RESEARCH. By J. ARTHUR HILL.

A very interesting record, written fairly and conceived clearly. There is absolutely none of the sentimentality which degrades 99.9 per cent of Spiritistic "research."

I must confess that "Watson" does not impress me. He is too terribly correct in his facts. To admit the super-normal hypothesis here would be to betray all good sense. However unlikely it may appear, Watson must have known the facts.

For otherwise, if he can describe and name some fifteen

relatives of "F. K.," he ought—in the course of a lifetime —to do as much for many others. But he doesn't.

The argument is this. Suppose my aeroplane does just manage to leave the ground for a few yards, one can explain it away. But if I fly from London to New York, I show such power that it is reasonable to insist on my flying at least a few miles to order.

I challenge Watson to give me the name of one relative of a stranger that I bring him.

The cross-correspondences are more satisfactory. But the hypothesis of spirits is quite unnecessary.

If we admit, as any Pantheist would admit, that subliminal Mrs Verrall is identical with or in communication with subliminal Mrs Piper, there is no mystery left, no suggestion of Myers to pit against the blank failure of the sealed letter test. Further, I distrust "Mrs Holland." I cannot believe that any one is so imbecile as not to solve the Hodgson cipher at a single glance. But a grande hystérique forging the script might pretend to be unable to decipher it.

I have seen more fraud from the vanity of amateurs than from the cupidity of professionals. So, in the end, to this record as to all others, I enter the Scotch verdict.

A. C.

THE NEW GOD AND OTHER ESSAYS. BY RALPH SHIRLEY.

These remarkable essays have much of the depth and lucidity of Huxley, with a greater power of sustaining the interest of the casual reader. Mr Shirley has the gift of bringing life into controversies long since dead and buried, of showing their importance to us, of restating them in terms of actuality. Moreover his standpoint is most sane. He is a questioner and critic not obsessed by the microscopic accuracy of the logician, but able to see things with human eyes.

To the metaphysician professed, therefore, he may seem shallow. One may quarrel for instance with his attempted disproof of the theory that the Universe is a single phenomenon. One may assert that without experience of Samadhi it is impossible to understand what is meant by the theory. Mr Shirley cannot realize that Time and Space are accidental forms of our consciousness, no more essential to it than a harem skirt to the Venus of Milo.

Suppose a cinematograph show observed by a man on earth and a man on the sun (with a devil of a telescope!) at 10:40, and their observations compared. The solar will regard the terrestrial as a prophet, for the latter can see at 10:40 what the former sees at 10:48 or thereabouts. With space it is the same thing. Assume a fourth dimension, and Calcutta may rub streets with Buenos Ayres. The Battle of Waterloo may be merely one name for a phenomenon whose other names are John Brown, saucepan, geometry, etc.

These conceptions are hard to realize intellectually. Mr Shirley is too sane; has never tortured his mind to the point of grasping such whirlwinds and making them the breath of his nostrils. But one minute in Samadhi, and he would understand the actuality of such imaginations. Not that facts are so discovered; it is the attainment of a point of view.

And were this apex added to the broad pyramid of his common sense, we should have another St John the Divine, an incarnation of the Eagle Kerub, no longer as now merely the subtlety of the Serpent and the sharpness of the Scorpion.

LEO

[We regret that urgency forbids detailed criticism of this admirable volume. We should in particular have liked to argue the "Rite" theory of the Crucifixion. As it is, we can only refer the author to J. M. Robertson's *Pagan Christs.*—Ed.]

THE NEW SOCIAL RELIGION. BY HORACE HOLLEY.
Holley, Holley, Holley, Lord God Almighty!

K. H. A. K.

THE OCCULT ARTS: AN EXAMINATION OF THE CLAIMS MADE FOR THE EXISTENCE AND PRACTICE OF SUPERNORMAL POWERS, AND AN ATTEMPTED JUSTIFICATION OF SOME OF THEM BY THE CONCLUSIONS OF THE RESEARCHES OF MODERN SCIENCE. BY J. W. FRINGS.

This little book is very good, and might have been much better if the author had any knowledge of Science or of the Occult Arts.

A. C.

OGILVIE'S ASTROLOGICAL BIRTHDAY BOOK. BY LEO BERNART.

In the preface Mr Bernart correctly states that the exact date and hour of birth are necessary to delineate a horoscope. Yet he publishes a book which attempts such a delineation on the birthday alone. Now, the birthday tells the astrologer nothing but the position of the sun in the zodiac at the time of birth, and this position varies to a small but sufficient extent in different years. This is indeed divining Hercules not merely from his foot, but from a big toe which may not be his at all. The error is often amusingly illustrated in the book itself. For example, Wm. T. Stead and Admiral Farragut were both born on July 5th.

On July 11th, John Quincy Adams and Wanamaker. This happy combination is told, "You are a good mimic and have a singing voice. You are not as fond of literary and scientific pursuits as you should be. You prefer the

lighter side of life, which is all very well in its way, but
the serious side must have its innings also." On July 23rd,
Mr Bernart tells Cardinal Gibbons that he is religious but
not orthodox. It is also new to me that the Cardinal "likes
candy to an unusual degree."

A great many of these delineations are evidently taken
straight from the people who are mentioned as being
born. For example, October 22nd, "You are emotional
and dramatic and would make a success upon the stage
in all probability," which is Sarah Bernhardt. And on
Nansen's birthday, "You have romantic ideas in youth
which probably express themselves in seeking for lost
or buried treasures or in exploring underground passages
or little known caves." On Edward VII's, "You have a
brilliant career before you. You are fond of the world.
You have a great deal of tact and diplomacy. You are
fond of the good things of this life. You are fleeting in
your affections, and will have a good many love affairs
in your life." However, "you are eminently domesticated."

Sometimes it is rather funny. Literary ability on Conan
Doyle's and Marie Corelli's birthdays. Poetic talent on
that of Ella Wheeler Wilcox!

Enough has been said to show the absolute worthlessness of this slipshod method of dodging the trouble of
doing astrology.

COR SCORPIONIS

ON THE THRESHOLD OF THE UNSEEN. AN EXAMINATION
OF THE PHENOMENA OF SPIRITUALISM AND OF THE EVIDENCE
FOR SURVIVAL AFTER DEATH. BY SIR WILLIAM F. BARRETT.

Sir William Barrett's book is decidedly well worth
reading by those who imagine that there is nothing in
spiritualism and kindred subjects. Sir William Barrett
has marshalled his facts and fictions in a very creditable
manner. It is quite surprising how much he knows, and

how clever he is, considering the limitations imposed on him by the fact that, like most psychical researchers, he has no sort of initiation, and has therefore no organized but only haphazard material at his disposal. He exhibits quite remarkable intelligence in dealing with the problems which he discusses. It is a very marked advance upon the absolutely blithering balderdash which characterizes most writing on spiritualism, "new thought," and the like.

Sir William Barrett is critical, without being skeptical in the bad sense of the word, and his judgment is excellent for an amateur. Of course, all psychical research without initiation reminds one of art criticism by a blind man or an art critic. Apart from this, however, Sir William Barrett has written a very clever book, and I hope that these few well chosen words of approval may encourage him to further efforts, perhaps not so much in this line as in one for which he might have more original talent.

A. C.

Oscar Wilde and his Mother. A Memoir by Anna, Comtesse de Brémont.

As there are thoughts that sometimes lie too deep for tears, so there are books which it would be sacrilege to review. This is one of them. But one may say that in spite of the soul-moving pathos of the subject and the naive brilliance of treatment, the most interesting aspect of the whole is the wonderful self-revelation of La Bellissima Contessa, as all those who know her call her to distinguish her from other countesses. She is indeed the antithesis of Oscar Wilde—a "marvellous masculine soul in the feminine brain building," and in his little masterpiece it is the soul which speaks. Aum Mani Padmen Hum.

Super Sinistram

OUTLINES OF PSYCHOLOGY. By OSWALD KÜLPE.

One of the most encouraging and significant signs of the times is the new Psychology, an excellent introduction to which is provided by the present work.

Oswald Külpe's work is of an essentially Teutonic character, having nearly all the characteristics, both good and bad, that one expects to find in a German technical scientific work; eminently typical is *Outlines of Psychology* in its thoroughness.

The experimental method, in which Külpe is an adept, shows conclusively and absolutely the essential unity of body and mind.

Psychology is still in its infancy; when it attains maturity it will be the most dread enemy that Supernaturalism has to face. The subjective view of life is undoubtedly destined to be the predominant one.

Your reviewer ventures to prophesy that in the science whereof Külpe is a brilliant pioneer will be found the key to the ecstasy that is the Vision in all religions.

The translator of *Outlines* is Mr E. B. Titchener. He has succeeded admirably.

V. B. NEUBURG.

PAGANISM AND CHRISTIANITY. By J. A. FARRAR.

A good book which makes us wish we had been born before Christ.

A. Q.

PARACELSUS. Edited by A. E. WAITE. Two vols.

The only edition of the great mediaeval occultist, the discoverer of opium, hydrogen, and zinc. Mr A. E. Waite in this as in his other translations is altogether admirable, adding a delightful wit to ripe scholarship, and illuminating comment to rational criticism.

A. C.

PATIENCE WORTH. BY CASPER S. YOST.

I have so deep a debt of gratitude in my personal ledger to Mrs Emily Grant Hutchings, that I can but be prejudiced most favorably with regard to anything with which she may be connected. I consequently take especial pains to discount the obligation, and I may be relied upon to say the worst of Patience Worth. It is, I think, beyond all question the most interesting of the records purporting to be the utterance of the stiff. There is an unquestionable personality in Patience Worth with perhaps no one beyond the scope of "subliminal Mrs Curran" and the hypothesis is reasonable since Mrs Curran is always at the board when Patience manifests. To me it seems a much simpler hypothesis to suppose that Patience is Mrs Curran's subconscious memory of an Elizabethan incarnation than that Patience is wandering, unchanged for several centuries, about the astral plane, where things are so easily broken up. It is also quite feasible to imagine Patience as an elemental spirit. But undoubtedly her utterance is remarkably distinctive and coherent. It is almost entirely free from the worst of the disfigurements to which psychical researchers have acclimatized us, confound them.

The mention of psychical researchers has ruined my temper again. I am going to be nasty even to my dear Mrs Hutchings. It is very easy to spoil a case by claiming too much. Jesus preferred would stand higher in the market to-day if some would-be clever press agent had not added ridiculous Pagan stories of the Virgin Birth, and so on, to the earlier and more plausible legend. And the most serious criticism of Patience Worth is the existence of that ridiculous novel by "Mark Twain." Patience Worth is not impossible, or even improbable. She makes mistakes. She commits anachronisms. But any difficulties are fairly easy to explain away. When it comes to Mark Twain, the case is altogether different.

Anybody can sign checks, and the only question is as to whether the bank has money on deposit against that signature. But if I sign J. P. Morgan, I get a very peculiar laugh from the cashier. In all human probability they do not even trouble to arrest the "poor nut." The action of Mark Twain's heirs in trying to suppress a book whose origin was most honestly stated makes them entirely ridiculous. But this reacts terribly on poor old Patience. It makes her look like a *ballon d'essai*. I do not think that there is any question of fraud, but I do see all kinds of openings for delusion, especially in the case of people who are hardly aware that there is such a thing as magical protection. It looks to me as if a playful elemental had taken advantage of Mrs Hutchings' innocence of the Laws of Magick, and having seduced her with the honest trifle of Patience Worth had betrayed her in the deepest consequence of Samuel L. Clemens, may he rest in peace!

WILLIAM SHAKESPEARE

p.p. OUIJA BOARD

PAVANNES AND DIVISIONS.   BY EZRA POUND.

My Country, 'tis of thee.

It is by the happiest chance that Mr Ezra Pound's *Pavannes and Divisions* should have come just when Americanism is in such vogue. For Mr Pound is, if one may be pardoned so bold a phrase in a mere review, a hundred per cent American. He has all the American craving for rules, all the American belief in teaching and training, all the American itch for definition; he abounds in the curiously national characteristic that has made America the land of those Colleges and Correspondence Schools through which the earnest citizen may learn how to converse as though he had seen the world, make $125 a week, never forget any name or telephone number once heard, write a short story or a Broadway Revue, draw comic cartoons, manage his wife, never look more than thirty-five, and live to be a hundred.

Yet Mr Pound is ignored by the great American public. When all the readers and reviewers in the land should be hasting in their thousands to acclaim this "new birth of our new soil, the first American"—as indeed Mr Pound is the first Complete American high-brow, armed at all points, accoutred *cap-à-pie*—instead they persist in regarding him as an exotic, a fantastic, a new-art *poseur*. I suppose, because he lives in Europe, because he has written *vers libre*, because he has praised a man with a name like Gaudier-Brzeska. These trifling accidents do not in the least affect the essential Americanism of what he has done, and of the way in which he has done it.

He began by following rules, and now he is making them. According to precept he "copied masterwork, and proceeded to his own Composition." He has taken himself with the seriousness of Whittier and Tupper and Howells and Mr Winston Churchill. His reverence for the technique and toil of art is Bostonian. When he is not either observing the law or laying it down, he is as ill at ease as a pedagogue in a bar-room. His American Puritanism nibbles his ear all the time. His hatred of what he calls rhetoric, his mania for the "clear" and the "hard," his earnest belief that poetry must never be a "pastime," all derive from the American conscience; and so does his distaste for the Puritan poet Milton, whose extreme sensuality avenged its suppression magnificently unawares in the greater Miltonic lines.

But Mr Pound's Puritanism is too distantly inherited. Like modern American Puritanism, it is a melancholy survival, drained of creative or destructive power. It is not a fierce and terrible thing, any more than the Puritanism of the modern New Englander is fierce and terrible. It nibbles at Mr Pound, but it does not devour him; it has not strength left for that. It is not Demogorgon, but a schoolmaster, not a victim or a priest. He has all the schoolmaster's love of the chalk and the blackboard, he has the true pedagogic flair for dogma, the true pedagogic knack of rapping it out "clear and hard" on the board, with the "expert" touch under which the chalk never crumbles. No writer, you would think, could be more acceptable to the American mind, for no nation in the world believes in the schoolmaster and his methods as America believes in them, no nation venerates pedagogy so profoundly. "But what is the good of style," I was asked yesterday, "if it cannot be taught?"

Mr Pound of course would not say that a man can be taught to be a poet or a prose-writer, but he is so pathetically at the mercy of "artistic principles," he is so Puritanically conscious of artistic right and wrong, that he can never give us so much as a half-holiday from the Ethical Culture Hall of his aesthetics. Whether he is making a creative appearance, as in *Pavannes,* or a critical appearance, as in *Divisions,* he has to impose upon us the propinquity of ferule and desk. Either by example or precept he must enforce the doctrine: "Look in your note-book and write." And like all doctrinaires, Mr Pound is exposed to the besetting sin of the half-true or the maybe-true platitude. "The mastery of any art is the work of a lifetime," for example. How about the art of lyric poetry, how about Sappho and Keats and Swinburne's early work? Again, we must have "direct treatment," Mr Pound affirms, and we must "use absolutely no word that does not contribute to the presentation." Such pronouncements are either platitudes or untrue, they either mean nothing that can't be taken for granted or a good deal that can't. The last of these "principles" is that one should "compose in the sequence of the musical phrase, not in the sequence of a metronome." If this means that

> My brother John was nine in May;
> And I'll be twelve on New Year's day

is not fine poetry, let's shake hands: but if it means that

> Till the maid, knowing her mother near,
> Sobs with love, aching with sweet fear

are not poetic lines, it means nonsense. In either case, the dictum is pointless, it leads nowhere at all. We do not need an official censure of crude and jingly rime, and we need something more than the mere comparison of the regular sequence of rime to the sequence of a metronome to disparage the genius of those great poets who happened not to write free verse.

Mr Pound himself in the *Pavannes* tries rime as a "diversion." "L'homme Moyen Sensuel" once again confirms the impression of him as a serious schoolmaster, and as an American. For he relaxes consciously, he is as conscious of his diversion as the schoolmaster is of the Norfolk suit donned for a game of golf or a fishing expedition or a trip to Paris; and in his treatment of humour as a thing by itself, a thing in a separate compartment of its own, he is intensely American, American *à l'outrance*. "Stark Realism," another of the *Pavannes* pieces, proclaims this same deliberate and detached American humour, a humour that is no salt for sprinkling, but is stocked in chunks to be made a whole meal of at a time. "Stark Realism" might have got into *The Smart Set* if the manuscript had been sent there and had happened upon a hospitable editorial mood. "L'homme Moyen Sensuel" is in its way a more striking affair, because the attempt to spring is so evident that one is positively startled by its not coming off. You wonder where the author has landed; and you find, quite surprisingly, that he has not landed at all. The verse is so Byronic in its

demeanour that you feel there must be barbs in it somewhere; it is really a shock not to discover a single one.

There is a profoundly American phrase that recurs to
the reader of this book of Mr Pound's—"going through
the motions." The author "goes through the motions" not
only in "L'homme Moyen Sensuel": he is always making
you think he is about to do something, then he never does
it. Take any of the first four *Pavannes* pieces. There are
all the preliminaries, but never the achievement. The
most elaborate and painstaking preparations have been
made for Mr Pound's marriage with his Art, but alas!
the union has never been consummated.

Yet even about his sterility there is something engaging.
He is much too American for any Englishman ever to
dislike him. The Americans who rile us are the ones who
are not American enough. As it is impossible to be angry
with the authentic professor or the authentic American,
so it is impossible to be angry with Mr Pound. For one
thing, what a simple wholesome American pleasure he
culls from the use of French words and phrases! He, like
all other real Americans and real professors, disarms by
his naiveté, his earnestness, his industry, his patience.
He is untiringly patient, both with other people and with
himself. One sees clearly that he is a kind, and, I am
sure, a good man. I do not speak ironically. This American
goodness, this American patience are beautifully distinctive national qualities to which no sort of justice has yet
been done by foreign observers. They should be more
widely known: and Mr Pound's Americanism should be
more widely known.

LOUIS WILKINSON

THE PERFECT CEREMONIES OF CRAFT FREEMASONRY, WITH
NOTES AND APPENDICES BY COLONEL R. H. FORMAN,
P.G.M., A.S.F.I.

We extend the hand of brotherhood to Colonel Forman. While regretting to some extent the extreme lengths to which he has gone in making it quite clear to cowans and eavesdroppers exactly what happens in the Raising, and in publishing careful diagrams of the secret steps, etc., the only possible ambiguity, *e.g.* in the murder of H. A., being that l—— t—— might stand for left testicle, we think it is better so. Since English Freemasonry has become soulless formalism, let us at least perform the ceremonies with decorum!

Your reviewer is personally a staunch Tory, and cannot help preferring the "Emulation" working which long years have endeared to him.

But never will he consent to the foul hash of the 23rd Psalm (Milton's, I suppose) here still printed.

Colonel Forman shows a good deal of insight into the true meaning of Masonry, and a real understanding of the symbolism. He appears a suitable candidate for some more serious order, such as the M ∴ M ∴ M ∴ or even the O.T.O.

H. K. T.

THE PRIESTESS OF ISIS. By EDOUARD SCHURÉ. Translated by F. ROTHWELL, B.A.

Books I and II:

I have been trying to read this book for a week, but the rapidly recurring necessity to appear on the stage of "Pan, a comedy," in the name-part, has interfered, and I have not yet finished it. But it speaks well for the book that I have not been too bored by it.

I like both Hedonia and Alcyone, for I know them; but Memnones seems to lack cleanliness of line, and one understands Ombricius so little that one loses interest in his fortunes.

Books III and IV:

Book III did rather cheer me. But of course one knew all along that the Eruption was to be the God from the Machine. A great pity; why not another city and a less hackneyed catastrophe? But it's as well done as possible within these limits. The translation might have been better done in one or two places—Bother! here's Hedonia coming for lunch. What a wormy worm Ombricius was!

D. CARR

PSYCHICAL PHENOMENA AND THE WAR. By HEREWARD CARRINGTON.

This book is an extremely interesting and valuable contribution to the science of the future. The first part of it, which relates to normal psychology, is extremely well compiled; and offers a capital picture of the peculiar phenomena which accompany combat under modern conditions. It is a serious study of actuality, entirely free from the pathological point of view of people like Barbusse on one hand, or the average newspaper correspondent on the other.

The second and larger part of the book deals with various supernormal events connected with war. I suppose Mr Carrington's trouble is the paucity of his material. He feels that he has to fill his book, and he certainly uses a great deal of appalling rubbish. He even reaches lice of the slime like Harold Begbie. It is very unfortunate that Mr Carrington with his fine critical ability, his great experience in distinguishing between false and true, should have laid aside his weapons in his old age. It is to such persons as he is that we look for discrimination, yet in this book the most excellently authenticated narratives are cheek by jowl with "thinking horses," and the humbug of sweet Phyllis Campbell. Mr Carrington is very careless too. He tells the story of Col——'s appearance to his old regiment at great length twice over. And we have yet another complaint. He has apparently gone over almost wholly to the Spiritists, and he has allowed himself at times to take a very crude flag-waving attitude about National psychologies.

I should like to point out that every case of supernormal phenomenon is explained fully if we accept the Rosicrucian teaching with regard to elementals. There is no space for detailed exposition of these points, but those familiar with the theory will find no difficulty at all in applying it to any particular case.

This book is decidedly superior to *True Ghost Stories*; it is intended for readers of a somewhat higher type of intelligence. But Mr Carrington's way is not the way of those who become great. Herbert Spencer was contented to plug on year after year writing for readers barely mustering five score. Browning after 35 years of literary activity writes,

> Late when he who praised and read and wrote
> Was apt to find himself the self same me.

I doubt whether Barabbas was a publisher, but I think Judas was.

J. C.

PSYCHISM. By M. HUME.

Mrs Hume is a female M . . . . . . h S . . . r. She begins by a long hypothesis full of big words whose meaning she shows no sign of understanding, though the sentence "Lunatics abound" can hardly be denied. The body of the book is made up of rambling statements (unsupported by any sort of evidence) of pyschic powers that she possesses, the least of which, if substantiated, would be sufficient to overturn the entire universe; and still more Starry are the "inspirational" poems which disconnectedly impregnate the other rubbish.

Nay, take her up gently,
Dry thou her tears,
Wind thine arm round her,
Soothe thou her fears.

This seems as obviously borrowed from Hood as her great male analogue borrows from any book that he has been reading recently.

Nature's law rules supreme
Because it is God's.
He framed it,
It must be,
And men are his "lords."

At this point, as Mrs Hume observes, "the strong man reeled in his anguish."

N. W.

RAYS FROM THE REALMS OF GLORY. By Rev. SEPTIMUS HEBERT, M.A.

This book consists of theological discussions between two young men named Percy and Sidney! It must be a great help to a Master of Arts in attaining a Second Edition if he can pat his own musings on the back at psychological moments with such interpolations as "Yes," said Percy, "I like that thought!"

The clumps of quotations at the commencement of the various chapters read on occasion rather incongruously. For instance, in front of Chapter XIV:

"Jesus called a little child unto Him."—Matthew, xviii: 2.

"Uncle Tom," said Eva, "I'm going there."—*Uncle Tom's Cabin.*

NORMAN ROE

RITUAL, FAITH, AND MORALS. By F. H. PERRYCOSTE.

If you should be so depraved as to desire to become a rationalistic author, you must buy a pair of scissors, some stickphast, and a parcel of odd vols. at Hodgson's containing: Buckle, Draper, Gibbon, Lecky, an old dictionary or two of quotations and some of the Christian Fathers. The process then is easy; it consists in cutting these to pieces and in sticking them together in all possible combinations, and publishing each combination under a different name

For fifteen years Mr Perrycoste has been snipping hard, and the above work consists only of Chapters III and IV of one volume of a series of volumes. We are charitable enough to hope that Mr Perrycoste may be spared to produce the rest, so long as we are spared reviewing them.

ELIAS ASHMOLE

RUBAIYAT D'OMAR KHÁYYÁMI. Mis en Rimes francaises par JULES DE BARTHOLD.

Since the "loathsome and abominable" disclosures with regard to Edward Fitzgerald and "Posh," I suppose every decent Englishman has burnt his copy of the Quatrains. It is consequently very pleasant to find a new translation, accurately representing the original, in beautiful and lucid French. The verses flow with the sound of wine poured in a thirsty country. We can recommend this book to all lovers of whom the *Daily Telegraph* would call "the astronomer-poet of Persia," and then "the tent-maker of Naishapur."

A. L.

THE SACRED SPORTS OF SIVA.

The editor in his preface does not see the objection to Gods and especially to Siva holding sports, neither do we. But you must play square, even if you are a God; it is not cricket to slay the whole of the opposing eleven each time you are bowled. But perhaps Siva had a reputation to keep up; we'll ask Kali.

VISHNU

SALAMAN ET ABSAL, POÈME ALLÉGORIQUE PERSAN DE DJAMI. Traduit par AUGUSTE BRICTEUX, Ph.D., Litt.D., etc. etc., avec une Introduction sur le Mysticisme persan, etc. A magnificent volume without and within. This, with the single exception of the *Bagh-i-muattar*, is the greatest of Persian mystic treatises, though it is rather elementary. But we can recommend no better volume for those who know but a little. Dr Bricteux has no experience of mysticism, and so makes mistakes. This was to be expected, but I am surprised at the scholar's error of asserting that the Hindu system lacks the method of love. As ninety-five Hindus practise Bhakti-Yoga for five that practise any other kind, we advise Dr Bricteux to be more careful. But this is a small blemish on a very fine essay.

ABHAVANANDA

SANINE. By MICHAEL ARTZIBASHEF.
Sanine is not a supreme novel in the full flower of a period, like *La Cousine Bette*. It is too lyric. It is like the timid song of a young thrush in the morning of life. For this novel is much more than a great novel. It is the first novel of an epoch. It is the first attempt to depict a man who is living by the Law of Thelema, whose outlook on the world is based upon the magical formulae of the Aeon of Horus: "Every man and every woman is a star; There is no law beyond Do what thou wilt." Sanine absolutely refuses to be obfuscated by the fog of false morality. He judges actions by their real, not by their imaginary consequences.

Bernard Shaw attempted this very feebly in his portrait

of John Tanner; but Tanner, like Shaw himself, is a blustering and wordy weakling, who is entirely the slave of the morality which he condemns. Sanine actually lives up to the truth which he sees, and it makes him free, and it makes free those who follow him. This is a great book to shed light upon the greybeard slobbering of Shaw. Violet's baby is only tolerable because Violet is Mrs Malone. Shaw has not the strength of character to avow (even in a fictitious work) that a woman can assert what is evidently her first right without undergoing phantastic penalties, although there are to-day thousands of women in every country who have told morality to go to its father, the devil, as Shaw so bombastically tells it to do. The phantoms which confront the free man are really just hollow turnips in churchyards. Take poor Ambrose, for example. He occupies one of the most important positions in New York City. He lives his own life for 15 years or so. Nobody is offended. Nobody is injured. Nothing whatever happens. A pleasant time is had by all. Then, suddenly some one discovers this appalling state of circumstances, and there is Ambrose in peril of Sing-Sing and Matteawan, and all those pretty places on the Hudson. He loses his job. He is an outcast from society. He vanishes like morning mist. And there is not a single shadow of reason for all this, except an ecclesiastical nefas, based principally upon a comic Turkish superstition.

The stupidity of governments is unthinkable. People reclaim a little obvious freedom, and the authorities will not let them have it without all this cutting of throats, and robbing of churches! The Gods seem to send imbeciles like Louis XVI and Nicholas Romanoff, and certain other persons whom I will not mention, at the moment when free men decide that it is time to strike for freedom. Hear the word of the Lord: In the next few years Sanine and his like are going to hang a lot of people to a lot of lamp-posts.

666

SCIENCE AND THE INFINITE. By SYDNEY E. KLEIN. William Rider and son have moved from Aldersgate Street to Paternoster Row, but unless they are very careful they will find themselves in Carey Street. What can have come over the firm that it publishes a book written by a man who knows his subject?

For *Science and the Infinite* forms the most admirable sketch of what should surely be a great and important work. Mr Klein shows clearly and simply the nature of what we call the Infinite, and proves that the great step to be taken is for the soul to recognize its oneness with that. But in *Book 4* this conclusion is given as the result of definite experience. (See pp. 80 and 87.) Mr Klein however, seems to prefer a sacramental solution of the problem, and advocates in almost too unveiled a manner the cult of the Phallus, which he understands, evidently enough, in its best form.

We could have wished that he had given us twenty diagrams instead of one. We could have wished that his English were less latinized and his sentences shorter, and most of all—we could have wished that his book had been published in a more important form. The world is deluged with cheaply-got-up books of this kind, and it is difficult for the outsider to distinguish the cornerstone from that which should be "heaved over among the rubbish." Now a book should be a very holy thing. If it be truth, it is that which we most reverence, and it is impossible to expend too much care and lovingkindness in its worthy presentation. Considerations of the cost of production are the death of literature. Publishers are so ignorant of the value of books that they issue any quantity of worthless stuff. They have no idea of what will catch on with the public. They produce things as cheaply as possible, with the American philosophy, "It's a good bet if I lose!" Such a book as Mr Klein's loses immensely by this vulgar presentation. Rising as it does to heights of sublime poetry, it is a shock to be constantly brought back to the twentieth-century illusion, which is the very sham he is trying to expose with its rage for hurry and cheapness, by the inferior paper and inferior printing. A book of this sort should have been produced, if not quite like the Medieval Books of Hours, yet in a form which represents the highest developments of the particular art used in its production. These things do not seem to matter now. They will matter enormously in a hundred years, and it should be for that part of the Now which we stupidly call the Future that books should be produced.

This is particularly the case with a book which deals with science. It is the common idea that science is practical. It does not occur to the average man that science is holy. He does not see that the microscope is a magical instrument in the truest sense of the word, as it assuredly is when its use leads one to such results as Mr Klein has attained. Science has appeared principally practical. People say, "Look, it has given us the telephone and the motor-car!" They have not understood that science may be a religion. To most people, especially so-called religious people, God means one in their own image, the shadow of themselves thrown, enlarged and distorted, upon the background of their own ignorance—not the image of themselves as they really are, but the image of those vile insects which they think themselves to be. The evangelical Christian asserts God to be mean, revengeful, cruel, huckstering—a small tradesman in a provincial town. A single blade of grass is sufficient contradiction of the existence of such a monster. Even where the people have had no God their Great Man was fashioned in the same way. Buddha is only a magnified Buddhist. In their fierce life calm seems the only good, and so their Buddha sits eternally smiling on a lotus. Even the most elevated thinkers seem to cling to the idea of a personal God. This is because they are themselves enmeshed in the illusion of personality. It is the personal and temporary self to which they cling. They have perhaps got rid of the idea that the body is real, but the highest ideas in their mind still appeal to them. They say (in the best cases) that God is Light, Love, Life, Liberty, but they still suppose him to be a person possessing these attributes. Hardly ever, save by virtue of spiritual experience of a high order, is that conception transcended. Personality is a limitation. As long as one thing is distinguished from another there are two things; and there is only one thing. Such a conclusion Mr Klein faintly foreshadows. I am not certain whether it is his reticence or his ignorance which prevents him from adumbrating the further conception which we have set forth in *Book 4* and elsewhere.

It is very well that these conclusions, such as they are, should be restated. There is, of course, nothing new in them. They were stated by myself in almost the same language in a good deal of the poetry which I wrote when I was nineteen years old. Such perception is the birthright of the poet. But even immediate intuition of such truth is of less value than the knowledge obtained by conscious experience. The rediscovery of these truths much later in life had for me all the force of a new creation.

We wish that Mr Klein had gone deeply into the means of attainment. He seems to be of that school which holds that such attainment is the result of miracle, perhaps of accident. He does not seem to realize that there is a perfectly simple and straightforward method of arriving where he has arrived—a method which is good enough for all, and about which there is no doubt and no difficulty beyond the essential one of sticking to it. I hope that the perusal of *Book 4* will enlighten him on this point, and enable him to write a Second Part to his book which shall detail this method in language which may reach those minds to which *Book 4* does not appeal.

A. C.

THE SECRET OF EFFICIENCY. BY GRACE DAWSON.

Grace Dawson is a spiritual Grace Darling. Oh the wonderful gospel that she brings to perishing humanity! She has discovered the secret of eternal youth: like most great discoveries, it is a very simple one. "When tired, rest!" This puts Grace Dawson several streets ahead of Madame Curie, and disposes once for all of the assertion that the female brain is inferior to the male. "When tired, rest!" How grand, how simple, how sublime!

> When human souls, by passion led,
> Are overworked and underfed,
> Who tucks them in their little bed?
> > Grace Dawson.
> I yawn, I rub mine eyes, I prop
> The weary head that wants to drop—
> Who soothes me to a humming-top?
> > Grace Dawson.
> Whose smooth and soporific prose
> Lulls me to infinite repose,
> Hushes the brain and stirs the nose?
> > Grace Dawson.
> Only one shilling of your hoard!
> Even the humblest can afford
> The luxury of being bored
> > By Dawson.

MORPHEUS

THE SECRET TRADITION IN FREEMASONRY. By A. E. WAITE. 2 vols, 4to.

This is a work of over 900 pages, with twenty-eight plates, and numerous interesting head and tail pieces, sumptuously issued by the publishers. The author may be masonically justified in issuing *ex cathedra*, from his study chair, a new and mystic version of our old rites, but such, to be of value, must be grounded upon historic facts, and not upon the nonsense of garbled masonic histories. In the first volume the author shows an extraordinary lack of knowledge, and hence is unable to fix his theory of an Inner and Secret Tradition upon any solid basis, and the volume, with its inflated diction, and troubled reasoning, is very unsatisfactory. The second volume is much better, and is really an interesting study. In both however he does not seek to hide his contempt, often expressed in uncourteous language, against all who are opposed to his views, or otherwise against those degrees from which nothing could be extracted to support his theorizing, and the writer of this review comes in, with many better men, for a slating.

In September 1910 my attention was called to a review of my *Arcane Schools* in the London *Equinox,* in which I find the following: "It is true he occasionally refers to people like Hargreave Jennings, A. E. Waite, and H. P. Blavatsky as if they were authorities, but whoso fishes with a net of so wide a sweep as brother Yarker's must expect to pull in some worthless fish. This accounts for Waite's contempt of him. Imagine Walford Bodie reviewing a medical book which referred to him as an authority on paralysis!" In spite of this mild castigation he still refers to me with some contempt, and as he has so little regard for the feelings of others, generally, I may be pardoned for following suit. I fancy, to say the least, that I am quite as able to judge evidence as Bro. Waite is;

and I may say that for about sixty-five years I have made a constant study of Freemasonry, in my leisure hours, and I conceive that I have forgotten more of real Masonry than Waite ever knew, or is ever likely to know.

In the first place, he seems to be utterly ignorant of the Jacobite Ecossaisism of the Chapter of Clermont, yet it is only in their Pre-grand Lodge Harodim that he could find foundation for his theorizing. My views on this subject occupy about eighty pages, now appearing in *The American Freemason,* Salt Lake, Iowa, and to which I must refer my readers.

He cannot find what he seeks in the Hanoverian G. L. of London,—1717; or if he finds anything in the ritual of that body it will be trifling, following the religious training of the two clergymen, Anderson and Desaguliers, who founded it. On the Craft system he ought to have directed his attention to the old York ritual, and that of the Ancient Masons, which in thát of York may date from 1726 (see my "Guild Charges").

The Royal Arch degree, when it had the *Three Veils* must have been the work, even if by instruction, of a Kabalistic Jew about 1740, and from this time we may expect to find a Secret tradition, grafted upon Anderson's system; the Arch degree was, undoubtedly, developed out of the Knight of the Sword, or Red Cross, by the Harodim Templars of Clermont, and that out of the operative Harodim.

Any stupid assertion, however historically untenable, but which is supported by a large majority, is a safe stock in trade for all such writers as Bro. Waite; it pays to tickle the palate of the crowd. It would take up too much space to carry this further, but I will ask to point out, first hand, some matters of general interest.

(I, p. 4.) The A. and A.S. Rite *was not* invented in America, it was known in Geneva several years before

1802, when Charleston found out that it was of 33°, and began to trade upon it. They had, however, some years before, the *Morinite* Rite of 25° founded at Jamaica in 1767, and not 1761–2, hence anything referring to that date is false.

(P. 10.) *Heredom* is a French modification of *Harodim*; even Barruel knew this. It is a term used by the Comicini builders of London, and is still in use with operative Lodges hailing from Durham. It was known to the operative Lodges of the Co. of Durham in 1735, when two of them went under the G.L. of London, and may be ages older than that, and identical with the "Quarter Masters" of Kelwinning, etc., under the Schau Statutes of 1598 and with the "Warden Courts" of Scotland and France, existing in 1622, as Laurie points out. I can provide first-hand light as to the transliteration of the word into Heredomus, or Holy House. Many years ago, or about 1870, I was in correspondence with Mr J. W. Papworth on the subject, and he put the question to a very learned friend whom he knew at the British Museum, and who suggested to him the above derivation. As he requested that his name should not appear I sent it to the *Freemason's Magazine,* under the signature of △, and it was at once adopted by Pike; hence the term "Holy House" is about forty years old. I may mention that the Duke of Leinster's "Prince Mason" of Ireland, which is an amplified version of the London Rosecroix of 1770, but very much older than that, uses the following words in presenting the Jewel of a Pelican, "You are still a Harodim, or Master of the workmen of the Temple,"—a Clermont echo. It seems to be everywhere kept out of sight that the Pelican feeding its young with its blood was the war banner of James III when England was invaded by him in 1715.

(P. 40.) Ramsay did no more in 1737, than put his own

gloss on what he learned in the Chapter of Clermont. It is true that in 1754 a change was made in the "Illustrious Knight" (Templar and Sepulchre), and an additional degree then added by an unknown de Bonneville, which may be a Jesuit pseudonym, which in 1758 became the 25th degree, by adding the system of the Knights of the East, etc., and later the 32°, and to which some of Ramsay's views were added; he could not have been a member of the English G.L., but was a Jacobite Scotch Mason, and according to his own statement, made to his friend Gensau in 1741, was born in 1680–1681, and not in 1668 as given by Waite; such of these members as were voted Scotch rank by their Lodges, received the Harodim rank of Clermont. Thory says that these Scotch Masons in 1736 had four Lodges, and in ten years received 5,600 members. Personally, I think it likely that the Clermont claims from the Templars (Albigensian) may be just from their own operative Lodges. Fludd, rather than Ashmole, may have indoctrinated the London Masons, and I have given my reasons for this view in my American papers.

(P. 295.) Waite is mistaken in supposing that the *Order du Temple* was not established in England. There was a Convent in 1838 at Liverpool, and its members' names are preserved. The same at London, and Sussex's consent was necessary for Reception; Dr. Robert Bigsby was a member of it, as also of Burnes' revisal of Deuchar's Masonic Knight Templar, which forms the basis of our 1851 ritual, which is not that of Dunckerley who worked the Clermont Templar Kadosh. There was also a Convent under the Duke of Sussex in India.

(P. 312.) In reference to Clermont Waite is floating on his own imaginary sea. Between 1688 and 1753, Clermont had three well-known degrees of Harodim, and in 1754 a fourth was added. He quotes a garbled extract from Fratre Kristner, who is reliable, and adds a sneer against me. The Swedish Rite has knowledge that Count Scheffer was received by Derwentwater; Graf von Schmittau; Count Posse, were Received 1737, 1743, 1747. But Waite claims to be the infallible Pope, who is to judge evidence!

(P. 322.) *Prince Adept* was added to Knight of the Sun at Kingston in 1767, in order that Morin might put in its place, the Prussian *Noachite* to give countenance to his frauds.

(P. 409.) My view of Hrdm-Rsyes is that, as it now stands, it is the French Lectures of Clermont's three grades. I give my reasons for this in the *American Freemasons* papers.

(II, p. 1.) This volume, referring as it does, to more recent times, has fewer errors. It might even be extended, and earlier Hermetic details added.

(P. 36.) We here read in Waite's words of "*The thing called Co-Masonry.*" I am not a Co-Mason myself, but I occasionally send things to the independent private quarterly termed *Co-Mason.* They are usually articles unsuited to the taste of mentally deficient Masons, or things that better informed Masons desire to hide. Again the system comes in for sarcasm owing to a supposed affinity with the Count St Germain. We may not like Co-Masonry, for one thing, it affords less opportunity for the convivial Mason, who has no room for the intellectual part; but the system has come to stay, and we may as well treat it with civility.

(P. 92.) The reduced Rite of Memphis has never been so numerous as to receive respect, and Freemasons are too ignorant to understand it, and to attack it—as in Co-Masonry—may prove profitable. As a matter of fact, some mistake was made in America as to the alleged reduction, but Egypt always held to the revised system of 1862–1866; at this time the Gd. Orient and the Chief of the Rite revised the whole system, mainly on an Hermetic basis, and gave to thirty-three leading ceremonies the power to confer, at intervals, the remaining sixty-two degrees which are generally added verbally in their relative places, and recently I furnished to America the necessary changes in a MS. of 200 pages. America had the Chapter degrees, 11°–18°, carefully edited, but the higher section was somewhat chaotic, and in 1872 I did not feel justified in making any great change. Bro. Waite thrice gives plates of its 90–95° Jewel—the winged egg—but without identification.

(P. 230.) *Rite of Swedenborg.* Of this Kenneth Mackenzie was Grand Secretary from its introduction till his own death. Bro. Waite is quite mistaken in supposing that he had any hand in compiling the ritual; that and the Charter are in my hands as they came from Canada; the Charter is in the engrossment of Colonel Moore, and carries the following names: Colonel W. J. B. McLeod Moore, Gd. Master of Templars, and 33°; T. D. Harrington, Pt.G.M. of the G.L. of Canada, and 33°; George Canning Longley, 33°; the two first names were 33° Masons of the S.G.C. of Canada, then little esteemed, but founded by the Golden Square body of London; but Longley and myself were of the *Martin-Cerneau* body, though I have several 33° Patents of the *Morinite* Sect. Founded, as the Rite is, on a version of Ancient Masonry, carried back to a Feast of the Tabernacles, 5873 B.C., it is most interesting, but too lengthy for general use; under these circumstances I might feel inclined to print it for Master Masons, if Freemasonry was an intellectual body, but the needs of English Freemasonry, that in the best and most elaborate of works it is only working for the printer. The Rite was carried from London to the Americas, by Samuel Beswick, a Swedenborgian Minister, who wrote a book on the subject, and he informed me that they had rejected the matter added by Chastannier, and that what was left was the work of Swedenborg. Hence Bro. Waite's description of two secret and unnamed degrees, are of interest at this point.

(P. 368.) Knight or *Priest of Eleusis*. I have this skeleton ritual of the Early Grand; and suppose it may be the old 1838 work of Memphis, of which Dr Morison de Greenfield was an early member. As I look upon it the degree is intended to teach that early Christianity absorbed the mysteries of Eleusis, and I mention this because I hear from New York that an eminent scholar, learned in Hermetic Greek, is making a translation in which he will prove that the Gospels and Epistles are pure Greek of the Eleusinian cult, and that the Jewish references are added to give a Semitic colouring. But I must conclude: I could make a decent sized volume in criticising and contesting Bro. Waite's book.

JOHN YARKER, 33°, 90°, 97°

SEEN AND UNSEEN. By E. KATHERINE BATES.
Superstitious twaddle; aimless gup; brain-rotting bak-bak.

SELF SYNTHESIS: A MEANS TO PERPETUAL LIFE. By CORNWELL ROUND.
This is a suggestive little book by a man who revolves a matter in his mind before he writes of it, and whose common sense never quits the hub of his thoughts. Mr Round never rolls off down a side street, but always keeps to the high road between them all. He does not, so at least we read him, wobble more towards mysticism than towards materialism. He believes that a perfect equilibrium between the Subjective mind—S, and the Objective mind—O, produces the Individual mind, which he symbolises as being neither round nor square, but a simple I

or line, connecting the S and O. This I is the self-renewing link between these two, which, when it is truly balanced, renders death the most unnatural, in place of the most natural event, that we may expect once we are born.

METHUSELAH

SHELLEY'S ELOPEMENT. By ALEXANDER HARVEY.

This book is one of the most glorious blasphemies ever printed. I have long recognized in Alexander Harvey one of those extremely rare types of genius, of which, curiously enough, America seems to have a monopoly. The United States have not produced any all-round men of the first class, but they have produced quite a number of what I may call, without any intent of disparagement, monsters.

Morphy's games of chess are entirely *sui generis*. He was different not only in kind, but in degree, from all other masters, and this, owing to the peculiar nature of the game of chess, resulted in the complete over-turning of the theory of the game. In chess problems, Sam Loyd and W. A. Shinkman displayed a precisely similar quality. Their problems are not well rounded and balanced, like those of other masters of the art. They are comparable with nothing else. One feels the emotion of a naturalist familiar with all other fauna who should suddenly be introduced to Australian zoology. In art, America has George Grey Barnard, whose Lincoln is like no other type of statue ever moulded. In vaudeville, we have Eva Tanguay, of whom I have already written in terms of no little enthusiasm. While other variety artists are like different vintages of Burgundy, Claret, Port, Champagne, and other wines, she breaks the entire series by producing cocaine. In literature, there are Poe and Whitman. Neither of these great men had the broad base of education. They have shot up by the mutation of a spiritual De Vries. Alexander Harvey reminds me constantly of Poe, but he is a Poe without the element of tragedy or morbidity; while his comic spirit is more ineffably delightful than that of any other human being, past or present, with whom I am familiar. Poe's comedy was labored, clumsy, hardworking foolery. Alexander Harvey's is perfectly spontaneous, and of such exquisite delicacy and acuteness, that he reminds one of the bistoury of a crazy surgeon. In *Shelley's Elopement*, he has taken Bernard Shaw's formula for creating absurdity. It is a very simple formula. One reflects that Caesar was not a hero to his valet, and that sometimes his toga set awry. The joke consists in making the heroic figure ridiculous by making him real. Shaw's method is mere clowning. Alexander Harvey's is perfect artistic perception of the realities of life. In this book he shows you the characters concerned with the absolute fidelity of a Balzac. One understands instantly that one is actually present at these scenes of Shelley's life. The atmosphere of the first four lustres of the 19th century, with its affectations and prejudices, is the breath of our lungs as we read. Shelley is screamingly ridiculous, Principal Harlequin in a mad domestic pantomime: and here is the miracle, that Alexander Harvey can show us this insane revel of dolts, and bums, and prigs, and dowdies, and with a single touch he can "life's leaden metal into gold transmute." The sublime appears phantastically shapen out of nothing, literally without effort. And this is the secret of life. This is the sublime and sacred jest of the Gods, to take the gross, the stupid, the banal, and suddenly to manifest a flower.

For this reason I wish to put it upon record, that I think that Alexander Harvey is the greatest realist alive to-day. The dull rationalist dribbles of cause and effect, neither perceiving the one, nor understanding the other. Alexander Harvey has the mystery of Pan.

ALEXANDER TABASCO

THE SIGNS AND SYMBOLS OF PRIMORDIAL MAN. By
ALBERT CHURCHWARD.

The first thing one has to do is to compose oneself in
a comfortable position, for this book is large and weighs
I don't know how many pounds; the next to remember
that the author has an axe to grind, or at least has constituted himself leading counsel for his client Egypt, and
in a learned and most convincing argument not only
proves the undoubted antiquity of his client's claim, but
that it was from Egypt, or rather Central Africa, that the
human race originated, and that it is to Egyptian symbolism, and more particularly to the Ritual of the Dead,
that we must go if we would rightly understand the temples, rites, ceremonies, and customs of mankind past and
present. From Egypt they came and to Egypt must we go.

The book is in every sense a great book and, by the
way, it forms an excellent seventh volume to Gerald
Massey's monumental work. Brother Wynn Westcott is
very rightly condemned as displaying a peculiarly acute
ignorance of both Freemasonry and Egyptology, and
further on so is that chattering journalist, Mr Andrew
Lang—the Paul Carus of the British Isles.

Dr Churchward is a Freemason of a very high degree,
but yet not high enough to understand that secrets that
need safeguarding are no secrets at all. "L. H." for left
hand is excusable because it saves printers' ink; but
"these need no explanation to R.A.M.'s" etc., is ridiculous
because R.A.M.'s need not be told about it, and if
you are not going to divulge this frightful secret about a
"Tau" why bother to say so? Remember that "an in-
dicible arcanum is an arcanum which *cannot* be revealed,"
even by a R.A.M! The Hebrew throughout is very faulty;
either Dr Churchward knows none, or else the proofs
have been sadly neglected. But now let us turn to the
subject over which he must have spent years of labour.

Man he traces back to the Pygmies of Central Africa, these or beings very like them hundreds of thousands of years ago emigrated all over the world—they were Paleolithic man, and whether these ape-like little beings had a Mythos or not would appear to be doubtful, but the next great exodus, that of Neolithic man, carried with it the Stellar Mythos,—that of the Seven Stars and the Pole Star, and the varied quarters to which these primitive men travelled is carefully indicated on the map at the end of the book. Though it may seem strange that they crossed vast oceans, it must be borne in mind that the configurations of the globe have changed since those remote periods; besides, primitive man did get about the world in a most extraordinary way, as such islands as Madagascar and Easter Island prove. The inhabitants of the former are Polynesian and not African, of the later, seemingly Melanesian, judging by their skulls, and the Solomon Islands, the nearest Melanesian islands to Easter Island, are thousands of miles away. Ducie Island, the nearest island to Easter Island, is many hundred miles away, and the coast of South America is no less than 2,300 miles distant. And yet in this tiny island we find proofs of very high civilization, and it is curious that Dr Churchward has not mentioned the numerous hieroglyphics found there concerning which a very full account is given in the Smithsonian Reports of 1889. After these came another exodus, carrying with it the Lunar and Solar Mythos, and Horus became under varying names the supreme world-god, and his four sons, or emanations, the four quarters.

It is impossible here to enter into the numerous entrancing speculations that Dr Churchward draws, or to give any adequate idea of the vast number of proofs that he marshals to convince us—they are quite bewildering. In fact, they completely reverse our conception of poly-

theism; for it is we who are the idolators, and not our
ancestors; it is we who sacrifice to many gods, and not
those little Bushmen who felt and saw and lived with the
One Great Spirit. Let us therefore mention that the
chief points, a few out of a score, that have struck us are—
The Custom of the Mark Sacred Stone; the universality
of Horus worship; the startling identity of hieroglyphics,
all over the world, with the Egyptian; and the symbolism
of the Great Pyramid, and its use as a Temple of Initiation.

A few others, however, we do not understand. On p. 80
Dr Churchward traces the "Bull Roarer" back to Egypt.
But we can find no proofs of these ever having been used
there. In Australia, as he states, they were used, and so
also in New Zealand and New Guinea and over most of
Europe; in Sussex, country boys to this day use them
as toys. Again, the Egyptian throwing-stick (p. 67) is not
a boomerang at all; it was made of thick rounded wood
and will not return when thrown. It is as perfectly distinct
from the Australian weapon as the Australian is from the
throwing-clubs of Fiji. The double triangle symbol(?) is
so common in the Pacific Islands that it is to be found on
nearly every club and utensil; in some cases it represents
figures of men with bent knees and arms akimbo. There
are many combinations of it. In small details the author
fails, he is so keen to find proof of Egyptian antiquity in
everything. On p. 228 he quotes as an example of original
sign-language that he "watched with interest our blue-
jackets leaning over the side of a man-of-war talking to
one another" by means of their hands and fingers. Of
course what they are really doing is semaphore signalling
without flags after the official signalling with flags has
ceased.

In spite of these small over-eagernesses, this book is a
revolutionary volume, a work that should stimulate argument and comment; and we hope that it will induce others

to collect and discover the secrets of the past before they are devoured by our Minotaurean Civilization. It is a melancholy fact that though amongst the rudest of rude savages secrets have been kept and great systems maintained for hundreds of thousands of years, the "clever" children of the present with all their arts and crafts are only destroyers of the past. We defame antiquity, annihilate those who still venerate it—mentally we destroy their minds with a corrupt and idolatrous Christianity, a veritable haggis of guts and blood, and their bodies with gunpowder and loathsome diseases. In a few years all will have gone; but (say you?) all will be saved, stored in our libraries and museums. But, we answer, even these in a few centuries will be dust and ashes; the very paper of this book which we are reviewing, beautiful though it be, will, like a girl's beauty, vanish before forty years are past. Our inventions are our curse, they are our destruction. What was coagulated in the minds of barbarians for thousands and tens of thousands of years we shall have destroyed utterly, utterly, in as many days and nights. Civilization has driven her plough over Stellar and Solar mythology, wantonly, and at haphazard, and in their place she has cultivated the Unknowable and Andrew Lang!

If the Utilitarian progress in the next few years as he has in the last, soon we shall have some socialistic fellah depriving the world of its last great monuments, and building labourers' cottages out of the stones and bricks of the Pyramids, because they are so very much more useful. "Solve" is the cry to-day; the Sabbatic finger of the Goat points upwards, yet on the clouds of darkness does it scrawl a sigil of light. A new God stirs in the Womb of its Mother; we can see his form, dim and red, in the cavern of Time. Dare we pronounce his name? Yea! It is Horus, Horus the Child, reborn Amsu the Good Shepherd, who will lead us out of the sheepish stupidity of to-day. How many understand this mystery? Perhaps none save those who have seen and subscribed to the Law of Thelema.

J. F. C. F.

THE SOUL OF THE MOOR.

"Success meant life! Failure—worse than death, for there would be the everlasting self-reproach! Dare I attempt the experiment?"

This sounds familiar, but, if memory serves me right, Mr Dion Clayton Calthorpe's drama continues in this strain,—"He carefully surveyed his ashen face in the tiny glass suspended over his washhand stand, then, with hasty, trembling fingers, he dipped his leaky shaving-brush into the icy water, and proceeded, at the ghastly hour of 6 A.M., To shave!"

Perhaps the fact that "My wife was very ill" accounts for the variation.

Mr Stratford D. Jolly is much too busy a man to devote much time to the "Serious study of the occult," and it is a pity he should have spent so much time upon the forty-five chapters which comprise this work, instead of upon some other subjects with which he might be more conversant.

In short, it is a flabby, gentlemanly book, which should find a ready sale among the more "goody" portion of Suburbia, the only place where the Hero could be appreciated!

Despite the author's obvious endeavour, there is absolutely nothing immoral in this book, and I can recommend it to great-grandchildren as a suitable Christmas present for their grandmother's aunt.

My congratulations to the illustrator for so thoroughly seizing the spirit of the book.

BUNCO

Spiritism and Insanity. By Dr Marcel Viollet.
The worst type of cocksure medical dogmatising rendered into pitiably Frenchified English. This is (I am told) not the fault of the translator, but of Dr Viollet's arrogance. Good English is not good enough for him. It sounds to me like incipient G.P.I.

Tarr, M.B.

Strange Houses of Sleep. By Arthur Edward Waite.
I have always held Arthur Edward Waite for a good poet; I am not sure that he is not a great poet; but that he is a great mystic there can be no manner of doubt.

Strange Houses of Sleep, conceived in the abyss of a noble mind and brought forth in travail of Chaos that hath been stirred by the Breath, is one of the finest records of Mystical Progress that is possible to imagine.

I may be biased in my judgment by this fact, that long ago when first my young heart stirred within me at the sound of the trumpet—perchance of Israfel—and leapt to grasp with profane hands the Holy Grail, it was to Mr Waite that I wrote for instruction, it was from him that came the first words of help and comfort that I ever had from mortal man. In all these years I have met him but once, and then within a certain veil; yet still I can go to his book as a child to his father, without diffidence or doubt; and indeed he can communicate the Sacrament, the Wafer of his thought, the Wine of his music.

And if in earthly things the instructions of his Master seem contrary to those of mine, at this end it is all one. Shall we cry out if Caesar for his pleasure commandeth his servants to take one the spear and the other the net, and slay each other? Is not service service? Is not obedience a sacrament apart from its accidents?

However this may be, clear enough it is that Mr Waite

has indeed the key to certain Royal Treasuries. Unfortunately, just as to face the title-page he gives us the portrait of a man in a frock-coat, so within the book we have the Muse in a dress-improver and a Bond Street hat. Never mind; even those who dislike the poetry may love to puzzle out the meaning.

Detailed criticism is here impossible for lack of two illusions, time and space! I will only add that I was profoundly interested in the final book, *The King's Dole*. No mystic who is familiar only with Christian symbolism can afford to neglect this Ritual.

Vale, Frater!

A. C.

STRANGER THAN FICTION. By MARY L. LEWES.

Any one who likes to read rubbish can get large quantities at a reasonable price by reading this book—but it is rather amusing rubbish.

DAVID THOMAS

THE SUPERSENSUAL LIFE. By JACOB BOEHME. Translated by WILLIAM LAW.

This admirable little treatise, now so beautifully and conveniently printed, deserves a place on every bookshelf. It contains the essential knowledge of our own community in the Christian—but not too Christian—dialect. I have bought a dozen copies to give to my friends.

THE SURVIVAL OF MAN. By SIR OLIVER LODGE.

One of the most unfortunate results of the divorce between Science and Religion has been the attempt of each of the partners to set up housekeeping for itself, with the most disastrous results. I shall not run my simile to death, but I shall explain how this train of thought began in my mind.

Sir Oliver's book is mainly a defence of the Society for Psychical Research, and a plea for more scientific investigation of psychic or spiritistic phenomena; and it seems to the reviewer that a scientific society that needs a defence at all, after nearly thirty years' work, has confessed itself to be largely a failure.

Sir Oliver Lodge, and indeed Spiritualism generally, suffer enormously from their lack of knowledge, from their being devoid of theory.

Phenomena! Phenomena! Phenomena! Until the noumenon behind is obscured and disbelieved in and explained away.

This is what makes modern spiritualism so hideous and Qliphothic a thing, and "psychic researchers" such bad mystics.

There is nothing in the book under review that is fresh—nothing that was not known forty years ago—see Emma Hardinge Britten's *Modern American Spiritualism*; nothing that was not commonplace yesterday—see the current issue of *Light*.

The real Occult knowledge of Plato, of Paracelsus, of Boehme, of Levi, was based upon theories whereby all the phenomena of modern psychism had their place, and were awarded their proper value.

The pseudo-occultism and watery mysticism of the modern spiritualistic philosophers—we call them by this noble title by courtesy—is due to their complete lack of knowledge.

What serious student of religion and occultism cares for the vapourings of Ralph Waldo Trine, the philosophising of the Rev. R. J. Campbell, the poetry of Ella Wheeler Wilcox? The prototypes of these people are utterly, or almost utterly, forgotten. One recalls now with how much difficulty the names of the Rev. H. R. Haweis, of A. J. Davis, of Lizzie Doten! For there is no virtue in those who have strayed from the path to linger among the Shells of the Dead and the demons of Matter.

The line of tradition is unbroken, and the way is straight and hard; too hard for "mediums" and New Thoughtists, whose spiritual capital consists of falsehood, and sentimentality, and sham humanitarianism.

Sir Oliver Lodge is always careful and painstaking and entirely honest; he is probably as well fitted to carry on his S.P.R. work as any student in England.

And to those who are unacquainted with the phenomena of spiritualism, *The Survival of Man* is as useful a book as could be read. But to the student of religion its value is *nil*, because the occult knowledge is *nil*.

In fairness it should be added that this review is written from the point of view of a mystic; to spiritualists the book will be welcome as yet another "proof" of "spirit-return," "thought-transference," and so on.

V. B. NEUBURG

This book is a singularly lucid and complete statement of the work of many noble lives. We believe that the S.P.R. has taken up a most admirable position, and wish greater success to their work in the future. If they would only train themselves instead of exercising patience on fraudulent people, whose exploits no sane person would believe if God Himself came down from Heaven to attest them, they might get somewhere.

A. C.

THE TALES OF CHEKHOV. THE LADY WITH THE DOG and other Stories. THE DARLING and other Stories. THE WIFE and other Stories. THE DUEL and other Stories. THE WITCH and other Stories. Translated by CONSTANCE GARNETT.

I was sitting at dinner in the Brevoort with some fascinating friends when, thinking no harm, I mentioned

Chekhov. A chic adolescent at the next table introduced himself. He could not really let such an occasion pass. It was so rare to hear any one speak of Chekhov. It was he who had introduced Chekhov to the notice of English readers. He almost reminded me of what Dorian Grey used to say about Wonderful Boyhood. I thought of Keats' worst sonnet, and "Chatterton, Marvellous Boy!" But the chic adolescent, who was Mr Robert Nichols, had a bullet in his neck, which explained the whole matter immediately to my satisfaction. Mr Nichols also told me of how he was a great poet, of how he had started the war, or won it, or both. He said that his mother was called Mary, but that vulgar report erred in saying that his father was named Joseph. Chekhov cannot hope to compete with this sort of thing. I forgot all about him. But I do wish I had one of Mr Nichols' books to review.

However, here is the Macmillan Chekhov, and I maun e'en go to it.

Mr Edward Garnett, with the banality which he has trained us to expect from him, remarks that "Chekhov has been termed the Russian Maupassant, and there are indeed several vital resemblances between the outlook of the French and the Russian master." Diving deeper into the commonplace, he continues to bore us with remarks upon "the art of both these unflinching realists."

Constance Garnett, one presumes, undertook the hard work of translating Russian as a relief from the intolerable boredom of her pinchbeck husband. Thus an all-wise Providence brings good from evil, for she is an excellent translator, apt to catch the spirit of a masterpiece.

Of course, Chekhov is the Russian Maupassant, for every Russian is under the curse of being a Russian something-European. There is nothing genuinely Russian in art or literature, because the Russian is in the ape stage of evolution. No matter how great his genius may be, it has to be cast in the mould of that which has been already shaped. Have you not seen those dalmatics covered with pearls—which no one has had the taste to match—sewn by princesses? Have you not seen those Gargantuan Bibles, their covers thick with precious stones, where was no art to cut or polish, so that they look like bits of glass or half-sucked sweetmeats?

The art of Russia has always been either without art, or with art derived. Napoleon was probably in an extremely bad temper when he spoke of Saint Basil's as "that mosque," but it is a mosque. It is probably the greatest building in the world in its peculiar way, but that way is the way of the mosque, even more so than St Mark's or the cathedral at Granada. But the great Russians are not less because they have been compelled to wear civilized clothing. There is only one art purely Russian, and that is the 'Russian Ballet,' which was not invented by Russians at all. The real Russian ballet is a savage mimicry of the Italian ballet. Have you not seen those uncut emeralds, the size of a walnut, through which the Tsars bored holes to wear them on a string? In its grossest stupidities the Russian spirit is still childishly great. I suppose a Russian cook could make something tasty of Edward Garnett, as a Chinese cook makes masterpieces of puppy dogs.

Chekhov is not to be judged at all by the standard of Guy de Maupassant. He is not to have his stories split up by our Garnetts of Barnetts or Darnetts into:

      a. humorous
      b. indigenous
      c. historical—pastoral—comical
         etc.

Each story is to be judged by itself. This is of course true of every work of art, and that is why critics are such a hang-dog race of marmots. But speaking as a marmot, which is, after all, the right of marmots, Article I in the Magna Charta of marmots, I may say that Chekhov was very much better when he was not thinking of Kopecks. He has turned out a dreadful lot of bad work under the lash of the publisher. But at his best, in stories like *The Witch*, he is unsurpassed. One feels a positive anguish that one has not met that witch! Even a Gladys Belasco or a Léa de L'âme Morte—or Del Amor?—can hardly console one for her loss. *Les amours nés de l'imagination*—either one must smoke opium or hashish, or live in Russia, or allow oneself to be fooled by a Russian woman, or read Chekhov.

This is an admirable edition of Chekhov, but how is it, while I am on another subject, that a firm of the standing of Macmillan can publish Chekhov (either without fear of prosecution, or because they have squared the judges) with apparent good hope of selling a great number of copies, while a native Chekhov like Alexander Harvey finds it difficult to get a publisher, and all the other American Chekhovs can never get a story printed?

THINGS A FREEMASON SHOULD KNOW. By F. J. W. CROWE.

It is a pity that the title of this excellent manual should suggest the sexual sliminess of Sylvanus Stall, D.D., for it is a most admirable compilation, a capital handbook and *vade-mecum* which no Mason should be without. It is intensely interesting and beautifully illustrated with portraits of Masonic worthies past and present—there are no future celebrities; why the omission?—historic regalia and charitable institutions.

H. K. T

THE TRIUMPH OF PAN. By VICTOR B. NEUBURG.

Shame, Mr Neuburg! Also fie! and tut!
No dog-nosed and blue-faced baboon in rut
Feels as you feel; or if he does, God's mercies
Deny him power to tell his thoughts in verses.
This is a most regrettable collection
Of songs; they deal with unrestrained affection
Unlicensed by the Church and State; what's worse
There's no denying they are first-rate verse.
It surely cannot be that Pan's in clover
And England's days of Sunday-school are over!

PERCY FLAGE

TRUE GHOST STORIES. By HEREWARD CARRINGTON.

Mr Hereward Carrington was a very clever young man, and that was his trouble. He is still a very clever young man, and as he is older than he was, his trouble is increased. I always thought him crazy with his ideas on fasting and his weighing souls, but he always gave the impression of the greatest sincerity. He did extraordinarily good work in the case of Eusapia Palladino. He merely destroys one's confidence when he coils himself in the Flag, and issues a Bryce Report like the mysteries of Myra, lends his name to quacks like Michael Whitty (not Witty), who doesn't even deny that he is the American representative of the swindler and blackmailer Mathers, so often exposed in the columns of *The Equinox,* and helps to edit the review of an obviously fraudulent sealed letter reader like Christiansen. Nor is it particularly encouraging to those who believe in him when they find him compelled to produce a book like this. It is very cleverly compiled, most readable and amusing, but there seems to be no care to discriminate between well authenticated cases and evident inventions. The critical spirit is hopelessly undeveloped. In particular, I must protest against the publishing of Mr Machen's excellent short story about the Angels of Mons without any reference to its author, as if there were one single particle of evidence that the story were true.

Mr Carrington is a sincere and ingenious investigator of immense learning and experience. He has probably been forced into these evil courses by the abominable falsity of the publicists of America. The outrage in his case is hardly less than in Theodore Dreiser's.

The instinct of self-preservation has apparently driven him to acquire a Ph.D. degree from some so-called university in Iowa. What a tragic farce life in America is for any one with the mustard seed of intelligence! Ah! the cock crows!

HAMLET R.

THE VILLAGE. By ERNEST POOLE.

There is a dreadful wrapper by Boardman Robinson, but he probably needed the money. It is quite the right wrapper too. Ernest Poole has driven the tank of ignorance and vulgarity across the steppes of Russia. Mr Poole is not very deep, and he is exceptionally stagnant, with a thick green slime of New England prejudice on his surface. Even for a journalist he is appalling. Think of using words like "destructed"! It deserves what he calls "le peine de mort." His method is to accumulate details, none of which he understands. There is no hint of vision. There is no understanding of Russia. There is nothing but interviews with uninteresting people, whose consciousness does not in any way represent them, or, as we used to say in days of less complicated speech, who do not know what they are talking about. Has he no shame to blot the 'scutcheon of the Pooles—the other scissors-knights of Savile Row?

The book is interesting enough to any one who knows Russia even slightly, if only because there is a laugh on every page. Some old poet, I forget his name, remarked:

> Some minds improve by travel, others rather
> Resemble copper wire or brass,
> Which gets the narrower by going farther.

The days of the innocent God-help-me tourist seem to be done. The tourist of to-day has been bullied by the Y.M.C.A., in intervals between grafts, into moral responsibility and Christian earnestness, and all that sort of thing. A man can hardly go from New York to Philadelphia without writing a serious biography of George Fox. The poop-stick has given place to the prig. I have no hope whatever for the future of humanity.

S.O.S.

THE VISION. BY MRS HAMILTON SYNGE.

It was with no small degree of pleasurable anticipation that we picked up a volume by the distinguished authoress of *A Supreme Moment* and *The Coming of Sonia*. The first vision, alas! was an atrocity after Watts, R.A., but we persisted.

Chapter i is jolly good.

Chapter ii might have been better with less quotation.

Chapter iii is first rate. Mystics can only conquer the Universe when they can prove themselves better than the rest of the world even in worldly things, and that by virtue of their mystic attainment.

We cannot, however, subscribe to her doctrine of the agglutination of the Vrittis to the Atman, save only in due order and balance in the case of the adept. Yet we would not deny the possibility of her theory being correct.

In chapter iv she puts a drop of the Kerosene of Myers into her good wine.

In chapter v we begin to suspect that the authoress's brain is a mass of ill-digested and imperfectly understood pseudo-science; yet it ends finely—our task is to learn "how to love"—and we refer the reader to Mrs Synge's other books.

Chapter vi is more about James. We love our William dearly, but we hate to see dogs trotting about with his burst waistcoat-buttons in their mouths. But the clouds lift. We get Ibsen, and Browning, and Blake; and end on the right note. Oh that Mrs Synge would come and take up serious occultism seriously; leave vague theorising and loose assertion, and her "larger Whole" for our "narrow Way!"

CHRISTOBEL WHARTON

THE WAY OF THE SOUL, A LEGEND IN LINE AND VERSE. By WILLIAM T. HORTON.

A little while ago I begged the Deity to forbid that William T. Horton should become vocal. My prayer was not heard.

Again, William T. Horton begged the Deity not to let *The Equinox* review his book.

His prayer has not been heard.

Enough to shake anybody's faith!

There is a most illuminated foreword by Ralph Shirley, a thing I could wish to have written myself.

And now for the Reverse of the Medal.

The principal subject of illustration is a series of accordion-pleated cliffs made of Sunlight Soap, waters made of vermicelli, suns indicated by circles drawn with a compass surrounded by lines drawn with a very unsteady hand to represent rays—surely a ruler would have been neater?—moons cut out of cardboard probably by his little sister, trees rather well done as they are accurately copied from Morris & Co., flaming swords like fly-switches, roses and stars and the rest, all conceived and executed with inconceivable coarseness, banality, and an absolute lack of any sense of beauty on the one hand,

and technical skill on the other. Such drawing would be rejected by the vulgarest comic papers; the best examples do not reach the standard of Ally Sloper, though the feeling approximates to that journal's at its nadir.

I did not mention that there are numerous attempts to represent divine, angelic, and human forms; the subject is beyond my power of expression.

As it is, I can only beg my readers to buy this book, for these drawings must be seen to be believed. And even then? Their existence is incompatible with that of God.

The only other way to save my credit is to quote (without comment; I am only human) the "verse"; it is better than the drawings, but it will give an idea of what William T. Horton really can do.

Isis-Osiris, Lo! on Thy throne
Two-in-One, apart, alone,
Breathe on us of Thy might;
Ruler of Love and Light
Isis-Osiris on Thy golden throne
Two-in-One, apart, alone.

.   .   .   .   .   .

The Future hid,
    The Soul, in Love,
Goes where 'tis bid
    By Love above.

.   .   .   .   .   .

Within a cold and barren land,
    Whereon, at times, a moon doth shine
A tree of Life doth upright stand,
    Close by a gap, near a deep mine.

.   .   .   .   .   .

I know that over there,
    Behind the crescent moon,
There waits for me somewhere,
    One I shall meet full soon.

.   .   .   .   .   .

Thy heart shall weary
And thy Soul shall cry,
Till thou findest me,
Thy Bride from on high.

.   .   .   .   .   .

Star of my Hope to thee I call
Upon the way I stumbling fall
Shine thou upon my weary soul
Disperse the clouds that o'er me roll.

I faint for thee with dear desire
My heart with longing oft doth tire
To thee I climb—ah! shine on me
Disclose thyself, revealed be.

Why hidest thou from me thy face?
Come forth, thy hand in mine, Sweet, place;
I stand where many cross roads meet
Oh! guide and guard my faltering feet.

.   .   .   .   .   .

Within its Crystal House the Soul,
Made perfect, sits enthroned in joy,
Around it all Earth's clouds may roll,
But nought can harm it, or annoy.

.   .   .   .   .   .

Isis, Mother of all the gods,
By Thee th' aspiring Soul doth rise;
No more on Earth it blindly plods
But, Spirit-free, mounts to the skies.

The late Leonard Smithers once told me an anecdote, for whose truth I do not vouch.

William T. Horton was walking across a moor (I think it was Clapham Common) at night to be an architect, when he heard a voice,

Turn again, Hor-ton,
Ar-tist of Lon-don!

He turned. But I don't agree with Leonard Smithers' comment that William T. Horton could have made a good architect; I prefer the sober judgment of Ethel Archer that he might have been trained to be a bricklayer.

ALEISTER CROWLEY

THE WHIRLPOOL. By ETHEL ARCHER.

I can add nothing to the appreciation which I have written for preface to this volume, which all should read.

ALEISTER CROWLEY

Look at the cover, and shudder!

In this masterpiece of illustration dwells the very soul of the book,—the virgin emaciated with insatiable passion; the verminous, illicit night-bird of a prehistoric age (the only conceivable steed for such an one!); the turbid waters of imagery; the lurid sky to which tentacular arms appeal to loves too luscious for this world,—are all embodied in this simple design. The artist has seized the loathsome horror of the book,—I feared even to sign it.

Look at the cover and shudder; then read it if you dare!

E. J. WIELAND

The obscurer phases of love, the more mystic side of passion, have never been more enchantingly delineated than they are by Ethel Archer, in this delightfully vicious book.

Terrible in its naiveté, astounding in its revelations, *The Whirlpool* is the complete morbid expression of that infinite disease of the spirit spoken of in Thelema.

For my own personal opinion I refer readers to my exquisite introductory sonnet to the volume.

VICTOR

The first thing one wishes to know on completing this extraordinary volume is: What is the author's definition of Art? Some say that the definition of Art is to please; I say Art is artifice; Phil May said something which conveys nothing if translated into Latin, and is unprintable in English. If the author holds Phil May's opinion she has, of course, every right to continue printing such books; if, however, her idea of Art is to please, then Ethel Archer's idea of pleasure is as warped as her nature.

To the Philistine Public this book will have but one use—it contains just sufficient paper to set the drawing-room fire agoing in event of returning home after the domestics have retired to rest. Those, however, who appreciate good verse, will find just sufficient warmth therein to read it though the fire be out.

BUNCO

Especially after a last glance at the wonderful cover, I think that The World's Pool of Sound suggests itself as an alternative title to this thin volume. Thin but bony— nor could sweeter marrow be found elsewhere. The volume has, I am afraid, an unfortunate horoscope, owing no doubt to some affliction in Virgo, with no correspondingly strong influence from the house of Taurus. Let us leave it at that.

GEORGE RAFFALOVICH

Babes of the Abyss! behold Form without Soul! Of womanhood (philosophical Weininger-womanhood!) Ethel Archer is the supreme expression. She is passion à rebours; Là-bas in excelsis. One can imagine her writhing away from even the infamies and hysterics of Canon Docre; or, having won her broomstick, declining to go to the Sabbath. Hers is the glass fruit of Murano, with its tinkling bells; hers that obscene chastity which blasphemes love and holds the candle to vice. Hers is the prudery and respectability which can pass through all fires unscorched, unwarmed. Hers is the soul of the real succuba, as that was before man idealised it away into a vampire of voluptuousness.

Miss Archer (God help her!) is still young; her verse

halts and her technique is faulty; it is amateurish. But she only needs a little hard work and experience to produce the vilest ravings that ever foamed upon the fleshless lips of a lost soul.

Unless that work redeems her. For she is as idle as she is vicious. The book is a masterpiece of horror, in its way; every one should read it and shudder.

LAURA GRAHAME

HONI SOIT QUI MAL Y PENSE!

ETHEL ARCHER

THE WHITE SLAVE TRAFFIC.

At one time I was acquainted with many of our London demi-mondaines, and many a charming girl and good-hearted woman had I the pleasure of meeting—and clean-minded withal. To say that all end in the Lock or the river is to say that you know nothing about the subject; for many marry, as Mayhew points out; in fact, Mayhew, in his classic *London Labour and the London Poor* is the only author I know—always excepting Charles Drysdale —who in any way saw the modern London hetaira as she really is. Drysdale in his courageous work, *The Elements of Social Science,* also points out that the life of the ordinary prostitute is a very much healthier one than that of the average factory girl. The authoress of this work seems to understand this in a way, for in spite of "the awful degradation" which she harps upon, she contradicts herself by writing: "I may here remark that the girls I come in contact with, if they marry happily, make excellent wives." (p. 66)

The cure for the present degradation associated with prostitution is a common-sense one—one of not supposing that we are good and others are bad, of carting away our own manure before writing to the sanitary inspector about other people's dung, and to cease hatching mysteries between the sheets of our family four-poster. If unions were sanctioned outside the marriage bond, even if such unions were only of an ephemeral nature, there would be no necessity to procure young girls, for natural love-making would take the place of state-fostered abduction. The root of the evil lies neither in the inherent lust of man after woman, which is natural, or of woman after gold, which shows her business-like capabilities; but in the unhealthy point of view adopted by the general public. There is nothing more disgusting in the act of generation, or even in the pleasures associated with it, than there is in alimentation, with its particular enjoyments. Dessert is quite a superfluous course after a good meal, and yet it is not considered degrading to eat it; and so, as it is not considered a crime to eat for the pleasure of eating, neither should it publicly (privately of course it is not) be considered a crime if unions take place without offspring resulting. This double-faced attitude must have the bottom knocked out of it as well as the front; it must utterly perish. From the natural, that is, the common-sense point of view, there are no such things as moral or immoral unions, for all nature demands is healthy parents and healthy children, healthy pleasures and healthy pains. The Church, the Chapel, and the Registry Office must go; for, so long as they remain, prostitution will spell degradation, and marriage falsehood and hypocrisy. Chaos will not result when Virtue weds with Vice, for what is possible to the savage is possible for us, and the children will be looked after better than ever. Once teach our children the nobility of love, and the pimp, the pander, and the puir-minded presbyter will simply be starved out. Continue to foster the present unhealthy aspect with its "unfortunate," its "fallen," its "awful," its "degradation" and its "doom," and, in spite of a million Vigilance Society men on every railway platform in the Kingdom, the White Slave Traffic will continue to flourish the more it is persecuted, and become more criminal and degrading than ever.

Money is not the basis of this so-called evil, as suggested, and public indignation will not work a cure any more than public indignation against the Metropolitan Water Board will stop people drinking water. We must cease globe-polishing virtue and sand-papering vice. Away with our moral Monkey Brand and our ethical Sapolio, and back to a little genuine common-sense elbow-grease.

When a girl ceases sowing her "wild oats" and can enter any phase of life without being spat upon and "chucked out," degradation will cease. And when such women as are *born* prostitutes are utilized by the State for the benefit of men who are not monogamists by nature, procuring will vanish. But, if these women be so used, it behoves the nation to care for these talented girls, just as she cares, or should care, for her soldiers; and when the time was expired, she should pension them off, and award them a long service and good-conduct medal should they deserve it.

This is a clean-minded book so far as it goes. We have no humbugging Horton, D.D., swooning at the thought of lace, frills, and a pretty ankle. But the remedies suggested are worse than the disease. Exalt the courtesan to her proper place, bracket her name with sweetheart, wife and mother, names which are rightly dear to us, and you will find a tender heart beneath the scarlet dress, and a charming lovable woman in spite of public opprobrium. Neglect this, and all other propositions of reform spell— Muck!

A. QUILLER

I like the legislation proposed by the blackguards of "vigilance"; who, never having met a gentleman, think that everybody is an avaricious scoundrel—though sometimes in another line of business. And this attack by M.A.P. on its trade rivals in the filth-purveying business (for all journalism is filth—must we exclude this White Slave "copy" from the indictment and class it as literature?) is only what is to be expected.

Anyhow, even our Government is hardly likely to pass the suggested Act, which thoughtfully provides that you may be arrested without a warrant for offering your umbrella in a shower to a strange lady, and makes it felony to raise your hat in the street.

I once had the pleasure of meeting Mr Coote, well-groomed in ultra-respectable broadcloth, and flaunting Three Virtues in his button-hole. I looked for some others in his heart, but drew blank. If he had any others, too, I suppose he would have worn the appropriate ribbons.

The truth about Coote-Comstock crapulence is this. Manx Cats subscribe to the Society for the Suppression of Persian Cats. These funds go to support a lot of holy souteneurs in idleness—and they find it pays to foam at the mouth from time to time against the other souteneurs who live on poor prostitutes instead of wealthy virgins.

I should like, too, to ask Mr Coote a rather curious question.

We were talking about paternity. His then secretary, Mr Hewston, had given me to understand that the Vigilance Society made a practice of paying (on behalf of and at the expense of the fathers) allowances to the mothers of illegitimate children, of caring for the mothers, helping them to get work, and eventually marrying them to honest fellows of their own class.

This seemed too sensible to be true. Mr Hewston's honest heart had led him to misunderstand.

Mr Coote indignantly corrected this view of the Society's work. They never did that sort of thing, he said, *except in a few very special cases.*

Now I want to know about these very special cases. Are they by any chance those in which the fathers are reputable and pious persons, highly esteemed for their Evangelicalism and philanthropy? ...

There have been some ill-disposed persons who were not ashamed to assert that some of the methods of Vigilance Societies reminded them of blackmail.

Is there another side to the medal?

A. QUILLER, JR.

WITH THE ADEPTS. By FRANZ HARTMANN.

If you have never been to "The Shakespeare" or "The Elephant and Castle" please go; for, for the same price that you would pay for this book you will be able to obtain at either a good seat. Go there when they are playing *The Sorrows of Satan,* and you will have no need to be "With the Adepts" of Franz Hartmann. Besides, if you are not amused by the play the back of the programme will surely never fail you. There you will learn the proximity of the nearest "Rag Shop" where old bones, scrap iron, india rubber and waste paper may be sold; and should you, like us, be so unfortunate as to possess a copy of this story, may with a little persuasion induce the ragman to relieve you of it. Besides, it will also tell you where you can obtain "Sausage and mash" for two pence—and who would not prefer so occult a dish to a "bunworry" with Sisters Helen and Leila?

From page one to one hundred and eighty this is all warranted pure, like the white and pink sugar mice on a Christmas tree—quite wholesome for little children.

Not only can you meet the Adepts but the Adepts' "lady friends," you might be in Bloomsbury, but no such luck. Polite conversation takes place upon "advanced occultism," which strongly reminds us of the pink and paunchy puddings of Cadogan Court. The lady adepts are bashful

and shy, but always very proper. The Monastery might
be in Lower Tooting. The hero asks silly questions so as
to give the Adept the requisite opportunities of making
sillier answers. "I was rather reluctant to leave the presence of the ladies . . . the ladies permitted me to retire."
Outside bottles full of this sort of occult Potassium
Bromide, this novelette is eminently suited as a moral
sedative for young girls when they reach sixteen or
thereabouts and are beginning to wonder how they got
into this funny world.

The Devil: "Let us giggle."

Theodorus: "Hush, you have committed a horrible
black magical act, you have slept with" . . .

Leila [*a creamy girl*]: "Good heavens, Sir, I faint; call
a policeman."

Theodorus: "Become acquainted with the Queen of
the nymphs."

Sister Helen [*nursing expert*]: "A douche, smelling
salts, eau de Cologne, quinine . . .!"

Theodorus: "From the abode of . . . Brotherhood you
are expelled [*sobs*], to the British Museum you must go
[*snuffles*], and read [*pause*] *The Secret Symbols of the
Rosicrucians!*"

The Devil: "Tut, tut. . . . Dear Sisters, the train has
stopped, we are at Streatham Hill—let us get out."

ALICIA DE GRUYS

THE WORKSHOP OF RELIGIONS. By ARTHUR LILLIE.
Slobber.

THE WORSHIP OF SATAN IN MODERN FRANCE. By ARTHUR
LILLIE.

Arthur Lillie is as convenient as Mrs Boole from the
standpoint of the poet.

I should add that the catch-penny title is entirely mis-

leading, and has no discoverable connection with the contents, save those of a short preface, cribbed, like the title, from Mr Waite's *Devil-Worship in France.*
What a wicked place France is!

THE YELLOW WHAT-HO. A subterfuge in fugues. Not by the author of *The Blue Grotto.* No publisher. No price. No anything.

> King Crowley of Bronchitis-town
> To Bernard Smith of great renown
> To set his shaven soul at ease
> These laryngeal lymphanies.
>
> Where Digitalis roams among
> The Endotherms, and on the tongue
> Follicular papillae weave
> Their lustral locks, and rosy eve
> Sheds her soft toenails as she swings
> Her brilliant body into Spring's,
> Befell a woe—and here the bard
> His sacral plexus with the yard
> Planged, and the Ammonites of Song
> Blew their shrill spirals loud and long.
>
> On ψ Cassiopeae first
> The grave old Hippocampus curst
> Black Oxyrrhynchus! who would dare
> To camp in Berenice's Hair
> Whose vesper censers amorous
> Smoke monocotyledenous,
> What time the twisted ibex mars
> The parallax of double stars,
> And the pale hate of Vega flares,
> And swart Typhlitis next unbares
> His glaive, ere Granuloma gnashed
> His teeth, and on its shoulder gashed
> —That shoulder that had shrugged unmoved
> Though Os Innominatum loved!
>
> What happened after who can say?
> I wandered sadly by the bay,

And saw anemone's streamers wet
Like drawers of scarlet flannelette;
I watched the mermaids as they loosed
Their lids on aught might be seduced,
While earnest starfish strove to cram
The strange lore of the pentagram.

In brief, it was a busy morn.
I took the Poet's Club in scorn.
How, with the banded fountain pen
That ran me into one pound ten,
With that too finite reservoir,
How could I sing this abbatoir?
Nay! let me first imbrue mine hands
In the dun blood of Mildred Sandys!
　　　　And so on.

　　　　　　　　　　　　　　　　　A. C.

THE BUDDHIST REVIEW.　Quarterly.

Founded, as *Buddhism,* in 1902, by Allan Bennett. *Lucifer, quomodo cecidisti!*

Unwilling as I am to sap the foundations of the Buddhist religion by the introduction of Porphyry's terrible catapult, Allegory, I am yet compelled by the more fearful ballista of Aristotle, Dilemma. This is the two-handed engine spoken of by the prophet Milton![1]

This is the horn of the prophet Zeruiah, and with this am I, though no Syrian, utterly pushed, till I find myself back against the dead wall of Dogma. Only now realising how dead a wall that is, do I turn and try the effect of a hair of the dog that bit me, till the orthodox "literary"[2] school of Buddhists, as grown at Rangoon, exclaim with Lear: "How sharper than a serpent's tooth it is To have an intellect!" How is this? Listen and hear!

I find myself confronted with the crux: that, a Buddhist convinced intellectually and philosophically of the truth

1. *Lycidas,* line 130.
2. The school whose Buddhism is derived from the Canon, and who ignore the degradation of the professors of the religion, as seen in practice.

of the teaching of Gotama; a man to whom Buddhism is the equivalent of scientific methods of Thought; an expert in dialectic, whose logical faculty is bewildered, whose critical admiration is extorted by the subtle vigour of Buddhist reasoning; I am yet forced to admit that, this being so, the Five Precepts[3] are mere nonsense. If the Buddha spoke scientifically, not popularly, not rhetorically, then his precepts are not his. We must reject them or we must interpret them. We must inquire: Are they meant to be obeyed? Or—and this is my theory—are they sarcastic and biting criticisms on existence, illustrations of the First Noble Truth; *reasons,* as it were, for the apotheosis of annihilation? I shall show that this is so.

THE FIRST PRECEPT

This forbids the taking of life in any form.[4] What we have to note is the impossibility of performing this; if we can prove it to be so, either Buddha was a fool, or his command was rhetorical, like those of Yahweh to Job, or of Tannhäuser to himself:

> Go! seek the stars and count them and explore!
> Go! sift the sands beyond a starless sea!

Let us consider what the words can mean. The "Taking of Life" can only mean the reduction of living protoplasm to dead matter: or, in a truer and more psychological sense, the destruction of personality.

3. The obvious caveat which logicians will enter against these remarks is that Pansil is the Five Virtues rather than Precepts. Etymologically this is so. However, we may regard this as a clause on my side of the argument, not against it; for in my view these are virtues, and the impossibility of attaining them is the cancer of existence. Indeed, I support the etymology as against the futile bigotry of certain senile Buddhists of to-day. And, since it is the current interpretation of Buddhistic thought that I attack, I but show myself the better Buddhist in the act.
4. Fielding Hall, in *The Soul of a People,* has reluctantly to confess that he can find no trace of this idea in Buddha's own work, and calls the superstition the "echo of an older Faith."

Now, in the chemical changes involved in Buddha's speaking this command, living protoplasm was changed into dead matter. Or, on the other horn, the fact (insisted upon most strongly by the Buddha himself, the central and cardinal point of his doctrine, the shrine of that Metaphysic which isolates it absolutely from all other religious metaphysic, which allies it with Agnostic Metaphysic) that the Buddha who had spoken this command was not the same as the Buddha before he had spoken it, lies the proof that the Buddha, by speaking this command, violated it. More, not only did he slay himself; he breathed in millions of living organisms and slew them. He could nor eat nor drink nor breathe without murder implicit in each act. Huxley cites the "pitiless microscopist" who showed a drop of water to the Brahmin who boasted himself "Ahimsa"—harmless. So among the "rights" of a Bhikkhu is medicine. He who takes quinine does so with the deliberate intention of destroying innumerable living beings; whether this is done by stimulating the phagocytes, or directly, is morally indifferent.

How such a fiend incarnate, my dear brother Ananda Metteya, can call him "cruel and cowardly" who only kills a tiger, is a study in the philosophy of the mote and the beam![5]

Far be it from me to suggest that this is a defence of breathing, eating, and drinking. By no means; in all these ways we bring suffering and death to others, as to ourselves. But since these are inevitable acts, since suicide would be a still more cruel alternative (especially in case something should subsist below mere Rupa) the command is not to achieve the impossible, the already violated in the act of commanding, but a bitter commentary on the

5. The argument that "the animals are our brothers" is merely intended to mislead one who has never been in a Buddhist country. The average Buddhist would, of course, kill his brother for five rupees, or less.

foul evil of this aimless, hopeless universe, this compact of misery, meanness, and cruelty. Let us pass on.

THE SECOND PRECEPT

The Second Precept is directed against theft. Theft is the appropriation to one's own use of that to which another has a right. Let us see therefore whether or no the Buddha was a thief. The answer of course is in the affirmative. For to issue a command is to attempt to deprive another of his most precious possession—the right to do as he will; that is, unless, with the predestinarians, we hold that action is determined absolutely, in which case, of course, to command is as absurd as it is unavoidable. Excluding this folly, therefore, we may conclude that if the command be obeyed—and those of Buddha have gained a far larger share of obedience than those of any other teacher—the Enlightened One was not only a potential but an actual thief. Further, all voluntary action limits in some degree, however minute, the volition of others. If I breathe, I diminish the stock of oxygen available on the planet. In those far distant ages when Earth shall be as dead as the moon is today, my breathing now will have robbed some being then living of the dearest necessity of life.

That the theft is minute, incalculably trifling, is no answer to the moralist, to whom degree is not known; nor to the man of science, who sees the chain of nature miss no link.

If, on the other hand, the store of energy in the universe be indeed constant (whether infinite or no), if personality be indeed delusion, then theft becomes impossible, and to forbid it is absurd. We may argue that even so temporary theft may exist; and that this is so is to my mind no doubt the case. All theft is temporary, since even a millionaire must die; also it is universal, since even a Buddha must breathe.

THE THIRD PRECEPT

This precept, against adultery, I shall touch but lightly. Not that I consider the subject unpleasant—far from it! —but since the English section of my readers, having unclean minds, will otherwise find a fulcrum therein for their favourite game of slander. Let it suffice if I say that the Buddha—in spite of the ridiculous membrane legend,[6] one of those foul follies which idiot devotees invent only too freely—was a confirmed and habitual adulterer. It would be easy to argue with Hegel-Huxley that he who thinks of an act commits it (cf. Jesus also in this connection, though he only knows the creative value of desire) and that since A and not-A are mutually limiting, therefore interdependent, therefore identical, he who forbids an act commits it; but I feel that this is no place for metaphysical hair-splitting; let us prove what we have to prove in the plainest way.

I would premise in the first place that to commit adultery in the Divorce Court sense is not here in question.

It assumes too much proprietary right of a man over a woman, that root of all abomination!—the whole machinery of inheritance, property, and all the labyrinth of law.

We may more readily suppose that the Buddha was (apparently at least) condemning incontinence.

We know that Buddha had abandoned his home; true, but Nature has to be reckoned with. Volition is no necessary condition of offence. "I didn't mean to" is a poor excuse for an officer failing to obey an order.

Enough of this—in any case a minor question; since even on the lowest moral grounds—and we, I trust, soar

6. Membrum virile illius in membrana inclusum esse aiunt, ne copulare posset.

higher!—the error in question may be resolved into a mixture of murder, theft, and intoxication. (We consider the last under the Fifth Precept.)

THE FOURTH PRECEPT

Here we come to what in a way is the fundamental joke of these precepts. A command is not a lie, of course; possibly cannot be; yet surely an allegorical order is one in essence, and I have no longer a shadow of a doubt that these so-called precepts are a species of savage practical joke.

Apart from this there can hardly be much doubt, when critical exegesis has done its damnedest on the Logia of our Lord, that Buddha did at some time commit himself to some statement. "(Something called) Consciousness exists" is, said Huxley, the irreducible minimum of the pseudo-syllogism, false even for an enthymeme, "Cogito, ergo sum!" This proposition he bolsters up by stating that whoso should pretend to doubt it would thereby but confirm it. Yet might it not be said "(Something called) Consciousness appears to itself to exist," since Consciousness is itself the only witness to that confirmation? Not that even now we can deny some kind of existence to consciousness, but that it should be a more real existence than that of a reflection is doubtful, incredible, even inconceivable. If by consciousness we mean the normal consciousness, it is definitely untrue, since the Dhyanic consciousness includes it and denies it. No doubt "something called" acts as a kind of caveat to the would-be sceptic, though the phrase is bad, implying a "calling." But we can guess what Huxley means.

No doubt Buddha's scepticism does not openly go quite as far as mine—it must be remembered that "scepticism" is merely the indication of a possible attitude, not a belief, as so many good fool-folk think; but Buddha not only denies "Cogito, ergo sum"; but "Cogito, ergo non sum." (See *Sabbasava Sutta*, par. 10.)

At any rate Sakkyaditthi, the delusion of personality, is in the very forefront of his doctrines; and it is this delusion that is constantly and inevitably affirmed in all normal consciousness. That Dhyanic thought avoids it is doubtful; even so, Buddha is here represented as giving precepts to ordinary people. And if personality be delusion, a lie is involved in the command of one to another. In short, we all lie all the time; we are compelled to it by the nature of things themselves—paradoxical as that seems—and the Buddha knew it!

THE FIFTH PRECEPT

At last we arrive at the end of our weary journey—surely in this weather we may have a drink! East of Suez,[7] Trombone-Macaulay (as I may surely say, when Browning writes Banjo-Byron[8]) tells us, a man may raise a Thirst. No, shrieks the Blessed One, the Perfected One, the Enlightened One, do not drink! It is like the streets of Paris when they were placarded with rival posters:

> Ne buvez pas de l'Alcool!
> L'Alcool est un poison!

and

> Buvez de l'Alcool!
> L'Alcool est un aliment!

We know now that alcohol is a food up to a certain amount; the precept, good enough for a rough rule as it

7. "Ship me somewhere East of Suez, where a man may raise a thirst."—R. Kipling.
8. "While as for Quilp Hop o' my Thumb there,
   Banjo-Byron that twangs the strum-strum there."—Browning, *Pachiarotto* (said of A. Austin).

stands, will not bear close inspection. What Buddha really commands, with that grim humour of his, is: Avoid Intoxication.

But what is intoxication? unless it be the loss of power to use perfectly a truth-telling set of faculties. If I walk unsteadily it is owing to nervous lies—and so for all the phenomena of drunkenness. But a lie involves the assumption of some true standard, and this can nowhere be found. A doctor would tell you, moreover, that all food intoxicates: all, here as in all the universe, of every subject and in every predicate, is a matter of degree.

Our faculties never tell us true; our eyes say flat when our fingers say round; our tongue sends a set of impressions to our brain which our hearing declares non-existent —and so on.

What is this delusion of personality but a profound and centrally-seated intoxication of the consciousness? I am intoxicated as I address these words; you are drunk— beastly drunk!—as you read them; Buddha was as drunk as a voter at election time when he uttered his besotted command. There, my dear children, is the conclusion to which we are brought if you insist that he was serious!

I answer No! Alone among men then living, the Buddha was sober, and saw Truth. He, who was freed from the coils of the great serpent Theli coiled round the universe, he knew how deep the slaver of that snake had entered into us, infecting us, rotting our very bones with poisonous drunkenness. And so his cutting irony—drink no intoxicating drinks!

When I go to take Pansil,[9] it is in no spirit of servile morality; it is with keen sorrow gnawing at my heart. These five causes of sorrow are indeed the heads of the serpent of Desire. Four at least of them snap their fangs on me in and by virtue of my very act of receiving the commands,

9. To "take Pansil" is to vow obedience to these Precepts.

and of promising to obey them; if there is a little difficulty about the fifth, it is an omission easily rectified—and I think we should make a point about that; there is a great virtue in completeness.

Yes! Do not believe that the Buddha was a fool; that he asked men to perform the impossible or the unwise.[10] Do not believe that the sorrow of existence is so trivial that easy rules easily interpreted (as all Buddhists do interpret the Precepts) can avail against them; do not mop up the Ganges with a duster; or stop the revolution of the stars with a lever of lath.

Awake, awake only! let there be ever remembrance that Existence is sorrow, sorrow by the inherent necessity of the way it is made; sorrow not by volition, not by malice, not by carelessness, but by nature, by ineradicable tendency, by the incurable disease of Desire, its Creator, is it so, and the way to destroy it is by the uprooting of Desire; nor is a task so formidable accomplished by any three-penny-bit-in-the-plate-on-Sunday morality, the "deceive others and self-deception will take care of itself" uprightness, but by the severe roads of austere self-mastery, of arduous scientific research, which constitute the Noble Eightfold Path.

O. DHAMMALOYU

THE ENGLISH REVIEW was enlivened in November by a brilliant article on The Law of Divorce from the fascinating pen of Mr E. S. P. Haynes.

While sympathising to a large extent with the writer's learned views so lucidly expressed, we are of opinion that

---

10. I do not propose to dilate on the moral truth which Ibsen has so long laboured to make clear: that no hard and fast rule of life can be universally applicable. Also, as in the famous case of the lady who saved (successively) the lives of her husband, her father, and her brother, the precepts clash. To allow to die is to kill—all this is obvious to the most ordinary thinkers. These precepts are of course excellent general guides for the vulgar and ignorant, but you and I, dear reader, are wise and clever, and know better.

there is no middle course between the extreme position of the Catholic Church, that marriage is so holy a bond that nothing can break it, and to accept and even to encourage fornication rather than tamper with it, and the other extreme of allowing a marriage to determine as soon as the parties desire it, proper provision being of course made for the welfare of any offspring.

The problem is really insoluble so long as sexual relations give rise to bitter feeling of any sort. Polygamy is perhaps the most decent and dignified of the systems at present invented.

But the present degrading and stupid farce must be ended.

As things are in these islands to-day, nine-tenths of all divorces, at least in good society, are the result of cheerful agreement between the parties. Adultery on both sides is so common that a genuine grievance is as rare as a truthful witness.

In a case that recently came under my notice, for example, the nominal defendant was really the plaintiff. He had compelled his wife—for sufficient reason—to divorce him by the threat that unless she did so he would break off friendly relations with her. Next came a weary struggle to manufacture evidence, the plaintiff's lawyers keeping up the irritating wail: "Lord —— is so strict. *We must have more adultery.*" So the already overworked defendant was kept busy all the summer faking fresh evidence to satisfy the morbid appetite of a Scotch judge, while at the same time he was obliged to hold constant and clandestine intercourse with his own wife, lest she should lose her temper and withdraw proceedings!

This may have been an exceptional case—we hope so. But that any such mockery can take place anyhow and anywhere is a scandal and a reproach to the nation whose laws and customs make it possible.

We hope to hear much more from Mr Haynes, and that he will throw fearlessly the whole weight of his genius and energy into the cause of radical reform of these monstrous and silly iniquities.

ARIEL

THE LITERARY GUIDE AND RATIONALIST REVIEW, 1908-9. Monthly.

Of all the lame ducks that crow upon their middens under the impression that they are reincarnations of Sir Francis Drake, I suppose that the origin-of-religion lunatics are the silliest.

Listen to Charles Callow-Hay on Stonehenge! Here's logic for you!

Stonehenge is built in the form of a circle.

The sun appears to go round the earth in a circle.

Argal, *Stonehenge is a solar temple.*

Or, for the minor premiss:

Eggs are round.

Argal, *Stonehenge was dedicated to Eugenics.*

Listen to Johnny Bobson on Cleopatra's Needle!

The Needle is square in section.

The old Egyptians thought the earth had four corners.

Argal, *The Needle was built to commemorate the theory.*

Or, even worse!

The Needle is square in section.

It must have been built so for a religious reason.

Argal, *The Egyptians thought that the earth had four corners.*

It is impossible to commit all possible logical fallacies in a single syllogism. This must be very disappointing to the young bloods of the R.P.A.

The Rationalists have created man in their own image, as dull simpletons. They assume that the marvellous powers of applied mathematics shown in the Great

Pyramid had no worthier aim than the perpetuation of a superstitious imbecility.

Here is Leggy James translating the Chinese classics.

Passage I is of so supreme an excellence that it compels even his respect.

What does he do?

He flies in the face of the text and the tradition, asserting that "heaven" means a personal God. This shows that "God has never left himself without a witness"—even in China.

Passage II is quite foolish—*i.e.*, he, He, HE, Leggy James Himself, cannot understand it. This shows to what awful depths the unaided intellect of even the greatest heathen must necessarily sink. How fortunate are We— *et cetera.*

It is such people as these who accuse mystics of fitting the facts to their theories.

Here is Erbswurst Treacle dictating the Laws of the Universe.

It is certain (saith Erbswurst Treacle) that there is no God. And proves it by arguments drawn from advanced biology—the biology of Erbswurst Treacle.

Oh! the shameless effrontery of the Pope who asserts the contrary, and proves it by arguments unintelligible to the lay mind! How shocked is the Rationalist!

My good professor, right or wrong, I may be drunk, but I certainly see a pair of you.

So this is where we are got to after these six thousand, or six thousand billion years (as the case may be) that, asking for bread, one man gives us the stone of Homoiousios and another the half-baked brick of Amphioxus. Both are in a way rationalists. Wolff gives us idea unsupported by fact, and argues about it for year after year; Treacle does the same thing for fact unsupported by idea. Nor does the one escape the final bankruptcy of reason more than the other.

While the theologian vainly tries to shuffle the problem of evil, the Rationalist is compelled to ascribe to his perfect monad the tendency to divide into opposite forces. The οὐδέν plays leapfrog with the ἕν, as the ἕν has vaulted over the bar of the πολλα and the παν. So the whole argument breaks up into a formidably ridiculous logomachy, and we are left in doubt as to whether the universe is (after all) bound together by causal or contingent links, or whether in truth we are not gibbering lunatics in an insane chaos of hallucination.

And just as we think we are rid of the priggishness of Matthew Arnold and Edwin Arnold and all the pragmatic pedants and Priscilla-scented lavenderians, up jumps some renegade monk, proclaims himself the Spirit of the Twentieth Century, and replaces the weak tea of the past by his own stinking cabbage-water.

It seems useless nowadays to call for a draught of the right Wine of Iacchus.

The Evangelicals object to the wine, and the Rationalists to the God.

We had filed off the fetter, and while the sores yet burn, find another heavier iron yet firmer on the other foot—as Stevenson so magnificently parabled unto us.

Then how this nauseous stinkard quibbles!

This defender of truth! How he delights with apish malice to write "in England," wishing his hearers to understand "Great Britain"; and when taxed with the malignant lie against his brother which he had thus cunningly insinuated, to point out gleefully that "England" does not include "Scotland."

Indeed a triumph of the Reason!

And why all this pother? To reduce all men to their own

lumpishness. These louts of the intelligence! These clods—Clodds!

My good fellows, it is certainly necessary to plough a field sometimes. But not all the year round! We don't want the furrows; we want the grain. And (for God's sake!) if you must be ploughmen, at least let us have the furrows straight!

Do you really think you have helped us much when you have shown that a horse is really the same as a cow, only different?

Quite right; it is indeed kind of you to have pointed out that even Gadarene pigs might fly, but are very unlikely birds, and that the said horse is (after all) not a dragon. Very, very kind of you. Thank you so much. And now will you kindly go away?

MODERN ASTROLOGY. Edited by ALAN LEO. MONTHLY.

Foremost in the attempt to rehabilitate astrology on modern lines is this well-known monthly magazine. The method indicated is the sound one of accurate observation and deduction; but whether the ultimate proposition of astrology can be established is a question which your reviewer at present is disinclined to assert. It is quite easy to throw ridicule, or to demolish by inexorable logic; but such methods do not convince. At least we believe that any person with a little experience can tell almost at a glance the sign rising at a stranger's birth, and that so frequently and certainly as to put chance and coincidence out of the question. For our own part, we consider Astrology a valuable aid to concentration, and perhaps the best of the methods of determining the Sankhara-skanda of a man. In your reviewer's own experience she has found it more reliable than either Geomancy or the Tarot, in questions genethliacal, at least. A careful study of the characteristics of the signs and planets is, moreover, of the very greatest assistance in the use of the book *777*. Unable as the Editor is to find space within the restricted pages of *The Equinox* for astrological matters, we are glad to think that the subject has a specialised organ in competent hands.

ETHEL RAMSAY

THE PORCH. Vol. I, No. 1. THE OVERSOUL. By RALPH WALDO EMERSON.

The *Porch* promises to be a delightful addition to our periodical literature. Its first number gives in clear type on a nice page the magnificent essay which we all know so well, yet of which we never tire.

The one objection to Emerson is that he thinks all men know this Oversoul. They don't. It's a few holy illuminated men of God, and I hope that this includes John M. Watkins.

Vol. I, No. 2. June, 1910. A TRUE CHRISTIAN. By JACOB BOEHME.

A most exquisite treatise on the life of the soul.

Boehme is a passive mystic, or quietist, of the very first water; he really perceives the underlying realities of Christianity, a religion which is so hidden by mounds of dirt and rubbish that it needs a very great mystic to get to the bottom of things without becoming defiled.

I hope Mr Watkins is a true Christian.

V. B. N.

Vol. I, No. 3. ON THE GOOD, OR THE ONE. By PLOTINUS.

We took up this book with avidity, thinking from the title that it was about Mr Watkins. But no; at least not under that name.

Plotinus' method of mystic exercise is practically that of *Liber XVI* (A∴ A∴ publication in Class D) but it takes a deal of research to discover this in his dull pages.

He drones on in such an exalted kind of way, don't-cherknow!

There is hardly a mystic living who wouldn't be a better man for reading Gal's Gossip now and then. I wish I had a copy here!

DORIS LESLIE ("BABY")

Vol. I, No. 5. JOHN G. GICHTEL (Extracts).

Outside 21 Cecil Court I don't suppose one could find a holier man than John G. Gichtel.

He writes likes a Magister Templi, does John G.; and does indeed communicate a little that may be of use to an Adeptus of any kind. But there is nothing for naughty Neophytes, or for poor putrid Probationers. Why doesn't Mr Watkins issue easy simple straightforward instructions, like *The Equinox*?

PROBATIONER

Vol. I, No. 6. THE SEVEN VALLEYS. By FARIDUDDIN ATTAR.

A man of good repute who loved God saw Majnun sifting earth in the middle of the road, and said to him: "Oh Majnun! What art thou seeking thus?" "I seek Laylah." "Can a pearl so pure be found in that dust?" "I seek Laylah everywhere, in the hope of finding her one day somewhere."

This was my toil, and the reward is mine.

Of such gems the volume is full.

A. C.

Vol. I, No. 7. A SERMON FOR WHIT SUNDAY. By JOHN TAULER.

Awful good, but awful dull. Mr Crowley's "Pentecost" is much livelier.

H. G.

Vol. I, No. 8. THE MIRROR OF SIMPLE SOULS.

Of all this admirable series this is the best. Such prose I have rarely found in all my reading. I am beggared of wit to review it; but I implore all who seek the pure Light mirrored in flawless imagery to obtain it.

ALEISTER CROWLEY

THE QUEST. Quarterly.

We are threatened in October with the publication of a magazine of this title.

It is, we believe, to bear aloft as oriflamme not the Veil of Isis, but the stainless petticoat of Mrs Grundy. You mustn't say psychism or C.W.L.

We note, however, with satisfaction that one of the contributors, a Mr G. R. S. Mead, is a B.A. This sort of boasting is perfectly legitimate.

No. II.

This periodical is the dullest and most sodden slosh possible. No one should fail to buy a copy; a perfect bedside book.

R. N. W.

We beg to apologise for having referred in our last number to G. R. S. Mead, Esquire, B.A., M.R.A.S., as Mr G. R. S. Mead, B.A. B.A. (Baccalaureus Artium) is indeed the proud distinction awarded to our brightest and best intellects. M.R.A.S. does not mean Mr Ass; but is a mark of merit so high that dizzy imagination swoons at its contemplation. We grovel.

A. C.

PSEUDONYMS

Crowley

A. C.
Christabel Wharton
Ethel Ramsay
Ariel
A. Quiller (only in "The Open Road")
The Author of "Rosa Mundi"
N.
O. Dhammaloyu
Ananda Vigga
J. Mc. C.
Fra. O. M.
H. K. T.
Francis Bendick
A. Quiller, Junior
Doris Leslie ("Baby")
"C."
Hilda Norfolk
Elaine Carr
Martial Nay
Edward Kelley
Perdurabo
D. Carr
Caligula II
Boleskine
Jonathan Hutchinson, natu minimus
Dost Achiha Khan
Super Sinistram
Sherlock Holmes
Professor Jacobus Imperator
Percy Flage
Leo Viridis

Alice L. Foote
Probationer
H. G.
Tarr M. B.
Mohammed
M. W.
Georgos
Cantab
O. H.
Laura Graham
L. T.
Leo
Eric Tait
M. Tupper
Nick Lamb
Abhavananda
A. L.
Felix
Barbey de Rochechouart
Mary d'Este
Maréchal de Cambronne
Π
Candlestick
Panurge
John Masefield, Junior
Diogenes
David Thomas
K. S. I.
St Maurice E. Kulm
Lemuel S. Innocent
Morpheus
K. H. A. K.

Capt. Fuller

J. F. C. F.
Antoinette Bouvignon
F.
Bathshebah Tina
Methusalah
A. Quiller
Sam Hardy
Alicia de Gruys
H₂S
B. Rashith
Vishnu
Elias Ashmole
A. Q.

Norman Roe

Norman Roe

Neuburg

V. B. Neuburg
V. B. N.
Victor

R. N. Warren

R. N. W.

George Raffalovich

George Raffalovich

E. J. Wieland

E. J. Wieland
Bunco
E. le Roux

Ethel Archer
Ethel Archer

John Yarker
John Yarker, 33°, 90°, 97°

E. Whineray, M.P.S.
E. Whineray, M.P.S.

Herbert Close
Meredith Starr

Mary Bey
Mary d'Este

Elizabeth Gwendolen Otter
E. G. O.

A. C. Hobbs
A. C. Hobbs

UNSIGNED REVIEWS

A Modern Reading of St. Francis of Assisi—*Crowley*.
After Death, What?—*Crowley*.
Buddhist Review—*Crowley*.
Contemporary Psychology—*Crowley*.
Evolution from Nebula to Man—*Fuller*.
Life of John Dee—*Fuller*.
Meister Eckhart's Sermons—*Crowley*.
Seen and Unseen—*Crowley*.
The Arcana of Nature—*Crowley*.
The Hand of God—*Fuller*.

The Literary Guide and Rationalists Review—*Crowley*.
The Message of Psychic Science to the World—*Crowley*.
The Mystery of Existence—*Crowley*.
The Super-Sensual Life—*Crowley*.
The Workshop of Religion—*Crowley*.
The Worship of Satan in Modern France—*Crowley*

APPENDIX

LIBER
COLLEGII SANCTI
Sub Figurâ
CLXXXV

Being the Tasks of the Grades,
and their Oaths, proper to Liber XIII,
the publications of the A∴A∴
in Class D from A to G.

A∴A∴
Publication in Class D

This paper is to be returned to the A.˙.A.˙. by the Neophyte introducing through his Zelator.

A.˙.A.˙.   Imprimatur.
Publication in Class D.   D.D.S. Praemonstrator.

Date ....   *No.* ....

A.˙.A.˙.

THE TASK OF A PROBATIONER.

0. Let any person be received by a Neophyte, the latter being responsible to his Zelator.
1. The period of Probation shall be at least one year.
2. The aspirant to the A.˙.A.˙. shall hear the Lection (Liber LXI) and this note of his office; IF HE WILL, shall then procure the robe of a Probationer; shall choose with deep forethought and intense solemnity a motto.
3. On reception, he shall receive the robe, sign the form provided and repeat the oath as appointed, and receive the First Volume of the Book.
4. He shall commit a chapter of Liber LXV to memory; and furthermore, he shall study the Publications of the A.˙.A.˙. in Class B, and apply himself to such practices of Scientific Illuminism as seemeth him good.
5. Beside all this, he shall perform any tasks that the A.˙.A.˙. may see fit to lay upon him. Let him be mindul that the word Probationer is no idle term, but that the Brothers will in many a subtle way *prove* him, when he knoweth it not.
6. When the sun shall next enter the sign under which he hath been received, his initiation may be granted unto him. He shall keep himself free from all other engagements for one whole week from that date.
7. He may at any moment withdraw from his association with the A.˙.A.˙., simply notifying the Neophyte who introduced him.

8. He shall everywhere proclaim openly his connection with the
   A.˙.A.˙. and speak of It and Its principles (even so little as
   he understandeth) for that mystery is the enemy of Truth.
     One month before the completion of his year, he shall
   deliver a copy of the Record of his year's work to the
   Neophyte introducing, and repeat to him his chosen
   chapter of Liber LXV.
9. He shall hold himself chaste, and reverent toward his body, for
   that the ordeal of initiation is no light one. This is of
   peculiar importance in the last two months of his Probation.
10. Thus and not otherwise may he attain the great reward: YEA,
    MAY HE OBTAIN THE GREAT REWARD!

Liberty
Power
Destiny

THE OATH OF A PROBATIONER.

I, ..., being of sound mind and body, on this..........day of..
(An..........Sun in...................° ....) do hereby resolve: in the Presence of.........˙...................., a Neophyte of the A.˙.A.˙. To prosecute the Great Work: which is, to obtain a scientific knowledge of the nature and powers of my own being.

May the A.˙.A.˙. crown the work, lend me of Its wisdom in the work, enable me to understand the work!

Reverence, duty, sympathy, devotion, assiduity, trust do I bring to the A.˙.A.˙., and in one year from this date may I be admitted to the knowledge and conversation of the A.˙.A.˙.!

Witness my hand..

Motto..

This paper is to be returned to the Chancellor of the A.'.A.'. through the Zelator admitting.

A.'.A.'.
Publication in Class D.
B.

THE TASK OF A NEOPHYTE.

0. Let any Probationer who has accomplished his task to the satisfaction of the A.'.A.'. be instructed in the proper course of procedure: which is: — Let him read through this note of his office, and sign it, paying the sum of One Guinea for Liber VII which will be given him on his initiation, and One Guinea for this Portfolio of Class D publications, B-G. Let him obtain the robe of a Neophyte, and entrust the same to the care of his Neophyte.

He shall choose a new motto with deep forethought and intense solemnity, as expressing the clearer consciousness of his Aspiration which the year's Probation has given him.

Let him make an appointment with his Neophyte at the pleasure of the latter for the ceremony of Initiation.

1. The Neophyte shall not proceed to the grade of Zelator in less than eight months; but shall hold himself free for four days for advancement at the end of that period.

2. He shall pass the four tests called the Powers of the Sphinx.

3. He shall apply himself to understand the nature of his Initiation.

4. He shall commit to memory a chapter of Liber VII; and furthermore, he shall study and practise Liber O in all its branches: also he shall begin to study Liber H and some one commonly accepted method of divination. He will further be examined in his power of Journeying in the Spirit Vision.

5. Beside all this, he shall perform any tasks that his Zelator in the name of the A∴A∴ and by its authority may see fit to lay upon him. Let him be mindful that the word Neophyte is no idle term, but that in many a subtle way the new nature will stir within him, when he knoweth it not.

6. When the sun shall next enter the sign 240° to that under which he hath been received, his advancement may be granted unto him. He shall keep himself free from all other engagements for four whole days from that date.

7. He may at any moment withdraw from his association with the A∴A∴, simply notifying the Zelator who introduced him.

8. He shall everywhere proclaim openly his connection with the A∴A∴ and speak of It and Its principles (even so little as he understandeth) for that mystery is the enemy of Truth.

   Furthermore, he shall construct the magic Pentacle, according to the instruction in Liber A.

   One month before the completion of his eight months, he shall deliver a copy of his Record to his Zelator, pass the necessary tests, and repeat to him his chosen chapter of Liber VII.

9. He shall in every way fortify his body according to the advice of his Zelator, for that the ordeal of advancement is no light one.

10. Thus and not otherwise may he obtain the great reward: YEA, MAY HE OBTAIN THE GREAT REWARD!

THE OATH OF A NEOPHYTE.

I, ..., (old motto), being of sound mind and body, and prepared, on this...........day of.................... (An...........Sun in...........of...........) do hereby resolve: in the Presence of ...., a Zelator of the A.˙.A.˙. To prosecute the Great Work: which is, to obtain control of the nature and powers of my own being.

Further, I promise to observe zeal in service to the Probationers under me, and to deny myself utterly on their behalf.

May the A.˙.A.˙. crown the work, lend me of Its wisdom in the work, enable me to understand the work!

Reverence, duty, sympathy, devotion, assiduity, trust do I bring to the A.˙.A.˙. and in eight months from this date may I be admitted to the knowledge and conversation of the A.˙.A.˙.!

Witness my hand [*old motto*]..................................

New Motto ....

A.'.A.'.
Publication in Class D.
C.

THE TASK OF A ZELATOR.

0. Let any Neophyte who has accomplished his task to the
satisfaction of the A.'.A.'. be instructed in the proper
course of procedure: which is: —

Let him read through this note of his office, and sign it,
paying the sum of Three Guineas for the volume containing
Liber CCXX, Liber XXVII and Liber DCCCXIII, which will
be given him on his initiation.

Let him cause the necessary addition to be made to his
Neophyte's robe, and entrust the same to the care of his
Zelator.

Let him make an appointment with his Zelator at the
pleasure of the latter for the ceremony of initiation.

1. The Zelator shall proceed to the grade of Practicus at any time
that authority confers it.

2. He shall pass Examinations in Liber E, Posture and Breathing.
He shall have attained complete success in the former, i.e.,
the chosen posture shall be perfectly steady and easy; and
attained the second stage in the latter, i.e., automatic
rigidity.

3. He shall further show some acquaintance with and experience of
the meditations given in Liber HHH. And in this his Record
shall be his witness.

4. He shall commit to memory a chapter of Liber CCXX; he shall
pass examinations in Liber HHH.

5. Beside all this, he shall apply himself to work for the A.'.A.'. upon his own responsibility.

   Let him be mindful that the word Zelator is no idle term, but that a certain Zeal will be inflamed within him, why he knoweth not.

6. When authority confers the grade, he shall rejoice therein; but beware, for that that is his first departure from the middle pillar of the Tree of Life.

7. He may at any moment withdraw from his association with the A.'.A.'. simply notifying the Practicus who introduced him.

   Yet let him remember that being entered thus far upon the Path, he cannot escape it, and return to the world, but must ultimate either in the City of the Pyramids or the lonely towers of the Abyss.

8. He shall everywhere proclaim openly his connection with the A.'.A.'. and speak of It and Its principles (even so little as he understandeth) for that mystery is the enemy of Truth.

   Furthermore, he shall construct the magic Dagger, according to the instruction in Liber A.

   One month before the completion of his eight months, he shall deliver a copy of his Record to his Zelator, pass the necessary tests, and repeat to him his chosen chapter of Liber CCXX.

9. He shall in every way establish perfect control of his Automatic Consciousness according to the advice of his Practicus, for that the ordeal of advancement is no light one.

10. Thus and not otherwise may he obtain the great reward: YEA, MAY HE OBTAIN THE GREAT REWARD!

THE OATH OF A ZELATOR.

I, ... (motto), being of sound mind and body, and prepared, on this...........day of........... (An ....Sun in........... ° of...........) do hereby resolve: in the Presence of .... a Practicus of the A.'.A.'.: To prosecute the Great Work: which is, to obtain control of the foundations of my own being.

Further, I promise to observe zeal in service to the Neophytes under me, and to deny myself utterly on their behalf.

May the A.'.A.'. crown the work, lend me of Its wisdom in the work, enable me to understand the work!

Reverence, duty, sympathy, devotion, assiduity do I bring to the A.'.A.'. and right soon may I be admitted to the knowledge and conversation of the A.'.A.'.!

Witness my hand [*motto*].......................................

This paper is to be returned to the Chancellor of the A∴A∴. through the Philosophus admitting.

A∴.A∴.
Publication in Class D.
D.

THE TASK OF A PRACTICUS.

0. Let any Zelator be appointed by authority to proceed to the grade of Practicus.

   Let him then read through this note of his office, and sign it.

   Let him cause the necessary addition to be made to his Zelator's robe.

   Let him make an appointment with his Practicus at the pleasure of the latter for the conferring of advancement.

1. The Practicus shall proceed to the grade of Philosophus at any time that authority confers it.

2. He shall pass examinations in Liber DCCLXXVII, the Qabalah, and the Sepher Sephiroth.

   He shall attain complete success in Liber III, Cap. I.

3. He shall further show some acquaintance with and experience of his chosen method of divination. Yet he shall be his own judge in this matter.

4. He shall commit to memory Liber XXVII and pass examinations in the Ritual and meditation practice given in Liber XVI. Further, he shall pass in the meditation practice S.S.S., in Liber HHH.

5. Besides all this, he shall apply himself to a way of life wholly suited to the Path.

   Let him remember that the word Practicus is no idle term, but that Action is the equilibrium of him that is in the House of Mercury, who is the Lord of Intelligence.

6. When authority confers the grade, he shall rejoice therein; but beware, for that that is his second departure from the middle pillar of the Tree of Life.

7. Let him not venture while a member of the grade of Practicus to attempt to withdraw from his association with the A∴A∴.

8. He shall everywhere proclaim openly his connection with the A∴A∴. and speak of It and Its principles (even so little as he understandeth) for that mystery is the enemy of Truth.

   Furthermore, he shall construct the magic Cup, according to the instruction in Liber A.

   One month after his admission to the Grade he shall go to his Practicus, pass the necessary tests, and repeat to him Liber XXVII.

9. He shall in every way establish perfect control of his wit according to the advice of his Philosophus, for that the ordeal of advancement is no light one.

10. Thus and not otherwise may he obtain the great reward: YEA, MAY HE OBTAIN THE GREAT REWARD!

THE OATH OF A PRACTICUS.

I, ..., (motto), being of sound mind and body, and prepared, on this...........day of....................
(An...........Sun in........... ° of...........) do hereby resolve: in the Presence of .... a Philosophus of the A.˙.A.˙.: To prosecute the Great Work: which is, to obtain control of the vacillations of my own being.

Further, I promise to observe zeal in service to the Zelatores under me, and to deny myself utterly on their behalf.

May the A.˙.A.˙. crown the work, lend me of Its wisdom in the work, enable me to understand the work!

Reverence, duty, sympathy, devotion do I bring to the A.˙.A.˙. and right soon may I be admitted to the knowledge and conversation of the A.˙.A.˙.!

Witness my hand [*motto*]...................................

This paper is to be returned to the Chancellor of the A.'.A.'.
through the Dominus Liminis admitting.

A.'.A.'.
Publication in Class D.
E.

THE TASK OF A PHILOSOPHUS.

0. Let any Practicus be appointed by authority to proceed to the grade of Philosophus.

Let him then read through this note of his office, and sign it.

Let him cause the necessary addition to be made to his Practicus' robe.

Let him make an appointment with his Philosophus at the pleasure of the latter for the conferring of advancement.

1. The Philosophus shall receive the title of Dominus Liminis at any time that authority confers it.

2. He shall pass examinations in Liber CLXXV and in Construction and Consecration of Talismans and in Evocation. Yet in this matter he shall be his own judge.

He shall moreover attain complete success in Liber III, Cap. II.

Further, he shall apply himself to study and practise the meditations given in Liber V.

3. He shall show some acquaintance with and experience of Liber O, Caps. V, VI. Whereof his Record shall be witness.

4. He shall commit to memory a chapter of Liber DCCCXIII.

5. Besides all this, he shall make constant and profound reflections upon the Path.

Let him remember that the word Philosophus is no idle

term, but that Philosophy is the Equilibrium of him that is in the house of Venus that is the Lady of Love.

6. When the title of Dominus Liminis is conferred upon him, let him rejoice exceedingly therein; but beware, for that it is but the false veil of the moon that hangs beneath the Sun.

7. Let him not venture while a member of the grade of Philosophus to attempt to withdraw from his association with the A∴A∴.

8. He shall everywhere proclaim openly his connection with the A∴A∴. and speak of It and Its principles (even so little as he understandeth) for that mystery is the enemy of Truth.

   Furthermore, he shall construct the magic Wand, according to the instruction in Liber A.

   One month after his admission to the Grade, he shall go to his Philosophus, pass the necessary tests, and repeat to him Liber DCCCXIII.

9. He shall in every way establish perfect control of his devotion according to the advice of his Dominus Liminis, for that the ordeal of advancement is no light one.

10. Thus and not otherwise may he obtain the great reward: YEA, MAY HE OBTAIN THE GREAT REWARD!

THE OATH OF A PHILOSOPHUS.

I, ..., (motto), being of sound mind and body, and prepared on this...........day of..................... (An...........Sun in........... ° of...........) do hereby resolve: in the Presence of .... a Dominus Liminis of the A∴A∴:To prosecute the Great Work: which is, to obtain control of the attractions and repulsions of my own being.

Further, I promise to observe zeal in service to the Practici under me, and to deny myself utterly on their behalf.

May the A∴A∴ crown the work, lend me of Its wisdom in the work, enable me to understand the work!

Reverence, duty, sympathy do I bring to the A∴A∴ and right soon may I be admitted to the knowledge and conversation of the A∴A∴!

Witness my hand [*motto*].....................................

A.'.A.'.
Publication in Class D.
F.

THE TASK OF A DOMINUS LIMINIS.

0. Let any Philosophus be appointed by authority a Dominus
   Liminis.

      Let him then read through this note of his office and
   sign it.

      Let him cause the necessary addition to be made to his
   Philosophus' robe.

      Let him receive Liber Mysteriorum.

      Let him make an appointment with his Dominus Liminis
   at the pleasure of the latter for the conferring of
   advancement.

1. The Dominus Liminis shall proceed to the Grade of Adeptus
   Minor at any time that authority confers it.

2. He shall pass examination in Liber III, Cap. III.

3. He shall meditate on the diverse knowledge and Power that he
   has acquired, and harmonize it perfectly. And in this
   matter shall he be judged by the Praemonstrator of the
   A.'.A.'.

4. He shall accept an office in a Temple of Initiation, and commit to
   memory a part appointed by the Imperator of the A.'.A.'.

5. Besides all this, he shall abide upon the Threshold. Let him
   remember that the word Dominus Liminis is no idle term,
   but that his mastery will often be disputed, when he
   knoweth it not.

6. When at last he hath attained to the grade of Adeptus Minor, let him humble himself exceedingly.

7. He may at any moment withdraw from his association with the A.˙.A.˙. simply notifying the Adept who introduced him.

8. He shall everywhere proclaim openly his connection with the A.˙.A.˙. and speak of It and Its principles (even so little as he understandeth) for that mystery is the enemy of Truth.

Furthermore, he shall construct the magic Lamp, according to the instruction in Liber A.

Six months after his admission to the Grade, he shall go to his Adeptus Minor, pass the necessary tests, and repeat to him his appointed part in the Temple of Initiation.

9. He shall in every way establish perfect control of his intuition, according to the advice of his Adeptus Minor, for that the ordeal of advancement is no light one.

10. Thus and not otherwise may he obtain the great reward: YEA, MAY HE OBTAIN THE GREAT REWARD!

THE OATH OF A DOMINUS LIMINIS.

I, ..., (motto), being of sound

mind and body, and prepared, on this...........day of...................

(An...........Sun in........... ° of...........) do hereby resolve: in the

Presence of... an Adeptus Minor of

the A.'.A.'.: To prosecute the Great Work: which is, to obtain

control of the aspirations of my own being.

Further, I promise to observe zeal in service to the Philosophi

under me, and to deny myself utterly on their behalf.

May the A.'.A.'. crown the work, lend me of Its wisdom in the

work, enable me to understand the work!

Reverence, duty, sympathy do I bring to the A.'.A.'. and right

soon may I be admitted to the knowledge and conversation of the

A.'.A.'.!

Witness my hand [*motto*] ....

A.'.A.'.
Publication in Class D.
G.

THE TASK OF AN ADEPTUS MINOR.

Let the Adeptus Minor attain to the Knowledge and Conversation
of his Holy Guardian Angel.

THE OATH OF AN ADEPTUS MINOR.

I, ... (motto), being of sound mind and body, and prepared, on this...........day of.................... (An...........Sun in........... ° of...........) do hereby resolve in the Presence of... an Adeptus of the A.˙.A.˙.: To prosecute the Great Work: which is, to attain to the knowledge and conversation of the Holy Guardian Angel.

May the A.˙.A.˙. crown the work, lend me of Its wisdom in the work, enable me to understand the work!

Reverence and duty do I bring to the A.˙.A.˙. and here and now may I be admitted to the knowledge and conversation of the A.˙.A.˙.!

Witness my hand ....

TO OUR READERS

Weiser Books, an imprint of Red Wheel/Weiser, publishes books across the entire spectrum of occult and esoteric subjects. Our mission is to publish quality books that will make a difference in people's lives without advocating any one particular path or field of study. We value the integrity, originality, and depth of knowledge of our authors.

Our readers are our most important resource, and we appreciate your input, suggestions, and ideas about what you would like to see published. Please feel free to contact us, to request our latest book catalog, or to be added to our mailing list.

Red Wheel/Weiser, LLC
500 Third Street, Suite 230
San Francisco, CA 94107
www.redwheelweiser.com